Real Estate Law

OTHER BOOKS BY THESE AUTHORS

KRATOVIL AND WERNER, *Modern Mortgage Law and Practice,* Second Edition (Prentice Hall)

KRATOVIL, *Modern Real Estate Documentation* (Prentice Hall)

KRATOVIL AND KRATOVIL, *Buying, Owning, and Selling a Home in the 80s* (Prentice Hall)

KRATOVIL AND KRATOVIL, *Buying, Owning, and Selling a Condominium in the 80s* (Prentice Hall)

Professor Kratovil is also the author of over fifty published articles on various aspects of real estate law.

WERNER, *Real Estate Closings,* Second Edition (Practicing Law Institute)

Real Estate Law
NINTH EDITION

Robert Kratovil
Distinguished Professor
John Marshall Law School

Raymond J. Werner
Portes, Sharp, Herbst, and Kravets, Ltd.
of Chicago

PRENTICE HALL, Englewood Cliffs, NJ 07632

Library of Congress Cataloging-in-Publication Data

Kratovil, Robert.
    Real estate law / Robert Kratovil, Raymond J. Werner. -- 9th ed.
        p.   cm.
    Includes bibliographical references and index.
    ISBN 0-13-763343-2
    1. Real property--United States.   I. Werner, Raymond J.
    II. Title.
    KF570.K7 1988
    346.7304'3--dc19
    [347.30643]
                                                                87-24081
                                                                    CIP

Editorial/production supervision: Mary Espenschied
Interior design: Jeanne Genz
Cover designer: Edsal Enterprises
Manufacturing buyer: Barbara Kittle

© 1988 by Prentice-Hall, Inc.
A Division of Simon & Schuster
Englewood Cliffs, New Jersey 07632

Printed in the United States of America

10 9 8 7 6 5 4

ISBN   0-13-763343-2

Prentice-Hall International (UK) Limited, *London*
Prentice-Hall of Australia Pty. Limited, *Sydney*
Prentice-Hall Canada Inc., *Toronto*
Prentice-Hall Hispanoamericana, S.A., *Mexico*
Prentice-Hall of India Private Limited, *New Delhi*
Prentice-Hall of Japan, Inc., *Tokyo*
Simon & Schuster Asia Pte. Ltd., *Singapore*
Editora Prentice-Hall do Brasil, Ltda., *Rio de Janeiro*

To
Ruth, Tony, and Melanie
and
Lenore and Beth

Contents

Preface

Again, the real estate picture has changed greatly since the last edition of this treatise appeared. At this writing mortgage money seems to be in adequate supply, and as a result, creative financing has dwindled, although it has not disappeared. Estimates indicate that about 10 percent of home sales still involve some form of creative financing, mainly take-back mortgages. Take-back financing is frequently a part of large-scale real estate transactions.

A wave of fraud claims has inundated the courts with litigation. Brokers have been hard hit. Hence a new chapter on fraud has been added.

States are beginning to move away from the obligatory optional advance approach to mortgage priority. A number of states are adopting the view that the mortgage lien attaches as of the date of recording of the mortgage. At least seven states now take this route. The doctrine of economic compulsion, first advanced by these authors in an article in the *Tennessee Law Review*, has been adopted by statute in Maine, Minnesota, and Nebraska and by court decisions in other states. It is now part of several Uniform Acts. Due-on-sale litigation continues to appear in the case reports.

In response to suggestions by teachers using this text, the chapter on installment contracts has been placed before the mortgage chapters. Other chapters have been split up or moved to make teaching easier. We are grateful to the teachers who have taken their valuable time to write us and hope they will continue to do so.

Some new topics have attracted attention and litigation, such as group homes and discrimination against children. Planned unit developments are growing rapidly in popularity, and condominium governance has assumed greater importance, thereby increasing litigation relating to homeowners' associations.

Home sales are burgeoning and broker litigation is on the rise. Courts are taking a consumer protection attitude that greatly increases the risks brokers must bear.

Sales of manufactured homes continue to increase, and states are slowly increasing the pressure on the suburbs to accept them.

Incredibly, the volume of zoning litigation continues to grow.

It is going to be difficult for the instructor to select "omit" chapters. Possible omit chapters include those on land development, wetlands (many dry areas don't have this problem at all), land acquisition and assembly, and manufactured homes.

If your school offers a separate course on insurance, this chapter is a possible omit. But warn the students that most insurance courses woefully neglect the mortgagee loss clause, the legal impact of foreclosure on insurance, the rights of the parties to an installment contract where a fire loss occurs, and so on.

In short, you key the course to the area in which you teach. This means distributing local forms of deeds, brokers listings, and sale contracts. We have deliberately refrained from loading the book with forms. The local instructor can do a better job on this aspect than any author would do.

Be sure to reiterate the warning that the law changes constantly and rapidly. Your best preparation for teaching today's class is to read this morning's newspapers.

Real Estate Law

CHAPTER 1

Sources of Real Estate Law

1.01 Lack of Uniformity in Laws Governing Real Estate

In each of the United States two separate systems of law are in force: federal law and state law. With few exceptions, federal laws operate uniformly throughout the country. Each state, however, has its own constitution, laws, and court decisions. Although differences in local conditions cause laws relating to real estate to vary from state to state, the basic legal principles governing real estate are much the same throughout the country. This book will describe these basic principles, mentioning, as space permits, the more important state-to-state variations.

1.02 Sources of and Trends in Real Estate Law

The sources of real estate law include the Constitution of the United States; federal laws; regulations adopted by various federal agencies, boards, and commissions; state constitutions; state laws; regulations adopted by various state and municipal agencies; ordinances of the various local governments; and court decisions. Traditionally, the latter have been the most important source of real estate laws.

Important decisions by lower courts are often appealed to higher courts. Those courts, in announcing a decision, usually state the reasons for their decision and discuss the legal principles governing the particular case. Such a decision, with its accompanying discussion, is called an *opinion*. The opinions are bound into books called *reports* and serve as guides in the decision of similar cases in the future.

> **EXAMPLE:** Roots from poplar trees on Parcel A penetrate into the adjoining Parcel B and clog the sewer and drain pipes on Parcel B. The owner of Parcel B cuts off the roots, taking care to make the cut on his land. The trees die and

a lawsuit follows. The lower court holds that the owner of Parcel B acted rightfully, and on appeal the supreme court of the state holds likewise, stating that a landowner may in this fashion protect himself against roots of adjoining trees. This is now the law of that state for all such cases that arise in the future. Lawyers will advise their clients accordingly, citing the case, *Michalson* v. *Nutting,* 275 Mass. 232, 175 NE 490 (1931). This case may be found in Volume 275 of the Massachusetts Supreme Court Reports, p. 232, and Volume 175 of the Northeastern Reporter, p. 490. The case was decided in 1931.

Since our American real estate law stems in large part from the real estate law of England, it is not uncommon for courts today to base their decisions on similar cases that arose several hundred years ago in England. However, in dealing with present-day problems, the courts must often evolve new rules of law without much help from the past.

In recent times federal laws and regulations, together with state laws, have assumed increasing importance in the field of real estate, especially in the area of real estate finance.

Also of greatly increasing importance in modern times is the "private law" that lawyers create in the preparation of real estate documents. Those who are new to real estate may fail to understand that the "battle of the forms" is an everyday reality. Landlords' lawyers battle tenants' lawyers over lease language. Mortgage commitments are endlessly redrafted in large deals. In virtually every major transaction the word processors are kept busy with the constant reworking of the transactional documents that set the law of that particular transaction for the parties. One limitation on the rights of the parties to thus declare the "law" applicable to their situation is found in the tendency of today's courts to refuse to enforce contract terms regarded as "unconscionable," or grossly unfair. While the concept of unconscionability finds its modern roots in the Uniform Commercial Code (UCC), which applies mainly to personal property, courts choose to regard the UCC as an expression of public policy applicable to all types of transactions, including real estate transactions.

> **EXAMPLE:**   Landlord leased a filling station to Tenant. The lease gave Tenant an option to purchase. Tenant exercised the option. Due to awkward phrasing of the option, it appeared that it would take more than fifty years for full payment of the purchase price. The court said that Tenant would have to accept reasonable terms of payment or pay all cash. *Rego* v. *Decker,* 482 P2d 834 (Alaska 1971).

We long ago moved into the age of consumerism. The largest corporations are compelled to respect the needs of the consumer. The real estate arena is not excluded from this trend. For example, the federal Truth-in-Lending Act compels the disclosure of interest rates in terms that the ordinary consumer is supposed to understand. Similar state laws have also been enacted. The Interstate Land Sales Act compels disclosures that are intended to assist the unwary prospective purchaser of vacant lots in making a purchase decision. Again, similar state laws have also been enacted.

Where there is inequality of bargaining power and where the sophisticated party is pitted against the unsophisticated, the courts will intervene to protect the weaker party. Another manifestation of this tendency is found in the judicial tendency toward rewriting *contracts of adhesion*. Wherever a relatively weak consumer is confronted with a contract full of fine print, such as a lease, mortgage, or sell-and-build contract, modern courts will pull the teeth of a clause that bears oppressively on the weaker party.

All of this is merely the present manifestation of older concepts. As far back as the year 1600, English courts decided that it was unconscionable to permit a mortgagor's default to end his rights in the mortgaged land. Toward this end the courts invented the equitable right of redemption. When mortgagees, in turn, began to insert a waiver of this right in the mortgage contract, the courts struck the clause down as being unconscionable. Today the swing of the pendulum is away from enforcing contracts as written and toward resolving disputes in terms of what is fair.

1.03   Economic and Social Impact upon the Law

The law has always been shaped by economic and social forces. Recently, as the age of consumerism swept the late 1960s and early 1970s, many time-honored rules of law were changed. The law recognized the economic power and social force of consumerism. In the late 1970s and early 1980s, inflation altered so many economic relationships that the law surrounding those relationships also changed.

Nowhere was the legal impact of inflation felt more than in the area of real estate law. The changes that inflation brought to mortgage law alone were dramatic. Inflationary pressures on interest rates brought about the advent of variable rate, rollover, and shared appreciation mortgages. Prior law largely did not allow these transactions; now they are common. Federal law has preempted state usury laws covering many forms of mortgage transactions. Inflationary pressures on home prices have necessitated new forms of mortgages to facilitate home ownership. Now there is a reexamination of those forms of mortgages as inquiry is made into the question of whether they are too creative and are based on invalid assumptions with the result that the borrowers will have difficulty repaying the loans.

These changes are not limited to consumer transactions. Notably, life insurers and other large investors have shifted emphasis from mortgage financing to ownership of large projects.

The source of real estate financing has also shifted away from the thrift institutions, which were fed by depositors, to the public and private securities markets where mortgagors will have to compete for funds on an equal footing with other borrowers. Pension funds, real estate syndications, and other pools of investments are powerful forces in the real estate market.

All of these changes brought about by economic factors are causing a reshaping of the law. This is nothing new. The law has always been responsive to these types of changes and will continue to adjust the relationship of the parties as the underlying economic assumptions change.

CHAPTER 2

Land and Its Elements

2.01 Land Defined

Land, or real estate, includes not only the ground, or soil, but everything that is attached to the earth, whether by course of nature, as are trees and herbage, or by the hand of man, as are houses and other buildings. It includes not only the surface of the earth but everything under and over the surface. Thus in legal theory, the surface of the earth is just part of an inverted pyramid having its tip, or apex, at the center of the earth, extending outward through the surface of the earth at the boundary lines of the tract, and continuing on upward to the heavens.

2.02 Minerals

Since land extends to the center of the earth, it is clear that the owner of the land also ordinarily owns the minerals, which are a part of the land, and when the land is sold, the buyer ordinarily acquires such minerals, even though they are not expressly mentioned in his deed. However, a landowner may sell part or all of his land, as he chooses. Consequently, he may sell the minerals only, retaining title to the rest of the land; or he may sell the rest of the land and retain or reserve the minerals to himself.

> **EXAMPLE:** Landowner signs a deed conveying to Mineral Buyer all the coal underlying Landowner's land. Now we have two layers of ownership. Landowner continues to own the surface and may farm it or erect buildings on it. Mineral Buyer owns the coal. Landowner can sell or mortgage his layer of land, and Mineral Buyer can do the same with his. Mineral Buyer automatically has the right to sink shafts from the surface and build roads and tracks over the surface for the purpose of mining and transporting the coal. But he must not remove the coal in such a manner that the surface of the land will collapse.

4

Suppose that Farmer sells and grants the coal under his farm to *B* Coal Co. The company tunnels beneath the farm and as it mines the coal uses the tunnels for transporting coal mined from adjoining areas. May the coal company do this? All courts agree that it may, although the explanations vary from state to state. In some states the interesting theory is advanced that a sale of coal and minerals includes not only the coal and minerals but also the space they occupy, so that when the coal is mined out the coal company remains the owner of the space the coal formerly occupied. *Middleton* v. *Harlan-Wallins Coal Corp.,* 66 SW2d 30 (Ky. 1933); 83 ALR2d 665.

2.03   Oil and Gas

Contrary to popular opinion, oil does not occur in underground pools or reservoirs, but is tightly held in the tiny pores or openings of porous rocks. Natural gas is held in solution in this oil under great pressure. When a well is drilled into the rock that contains oil and gas, pressure is thereby released, and oil and gas gush forth just as a carbonated drink gushes from a warm pop bottle when the cap is removed. The oil will then flow to the low pressure area, namely, the well bore. Some states (Arkansas, Kansas, Mississippi, Ohio, Pennsylvania, Texas, and West Virginia), impressed with the fact that oil in its natural state and before drilling occurs is immovably trapped in the rocks in which it is found, say that the landowner owns the oil beneath his land in much the same way that he owns coal or other minerals. These states are called *ownership states.* Other states (California, Louisiana, and Oklahoma), impressed with the fact that oil does move from one underground location to another when wells are drilled, hold that the landowner does not own the oil until he has pumped it and thereby taken possession of it. This is called the *law of capture. Frost* v. *Ponca City,* 541 P2d 1321 (Okla. 1975). In all states, if the owner of the oil well pumps the oil and brings it to the surface, it then becomes personal property.

In ownership states, a landowner may grant ownership of the oil beneath his land to another person. As a result, there will be two vertical layers of ownership, just as when a landowner sells and conveys to another all the coal and minerals beneath his land. Oddly enough, however, all oil states, including the ownership states, follow the rule of *capture,* which holds that if a man drills on his land, he will own all of the oil and gas produced, even though some of the oil or gas has migrated to his well from his neighbor's land. His neighbor, of course, can prevent such a result by drilling his own *offset* wells on his own land and pumping the oil that would otherwise move away from his land. All oil-producing states now have laws regulating and controlling the drilling of wells and the production of oil.

The rule of capture is subject to regulation, and some states have moved away from its strict application in some instances such as where secondary recovery techniques are used. Under these methods, water or gas is injected into the well to cause the recovery of oil or gas that would not be recoverable under primary methods. This injection may affect portions of the pool that lie under other lands thereby resulting in the drainage of the pool underlying those adjacent lands. Some jurisdictions have taken the view that where these secondary recovery operations result either in drainage of valuable minerals from or damage to the adjacent lands, the adjoining landowner or mineral lessee is entitled to damages. Annot., 19 ALR4th 1182.

Landowners lack the skill, experience, capital, and gambling instinct necessary to drill for oil. Therefore, when the presence of oil is suspected, a landowner enters into an oil lease with an oil company. The basic structure of an oil and gas lease was developed by 1895. Its usual elements are: (1) a cash bonus is paid to the lessor for granting the lease; (2) a royalty is paid to the lessor if oil or gas is discovered; (3) the lease states a fixed term; and (4) the term can be extended if the lessee drills a well or pays *delay rentals* to compensate the lessor for the lessee's failure to drill. This delay rental is the price the oil company pays for the privilege of keeping the lease in force without drilling. Delay rentals will continue to fall due as long as the oil company delays drilling. The lease will come to an end if no drilling takes place unless delay rentals are paid. This is known as the *unless lease*.

In contrast to the unless lease is the *drill or pay lease*. A drill or pay provision requires the lessee to produce oil or to pay rent. In an unless lease, the lessee's rights are terminated unless production is begun. A drill or pay lease allows the lessee to pay rent as a means of keeping the lease in effect even though the primary period has expired. 2 Summers, *Oil and Gas,* §§331–351 (1959); Williams, *Oil and Gas,* §§601.5, 605 (1977).

The original *Producers 88* lease set out three rules for the payment of royalties. The lessor would receive: (1) one-eighth of the oil delivered to tanks or pipelines; (2) quarterly payments of one-eighth of the value at the well of gas produced from an oil well; and (3) monthly payments of one-eighth of the value at the well of gas produced from a well producing only gas.

Since much litigation has revolved around controversies as to whether the lessee paid the rental required to keep the lease alive, the lease may have a clause protecting the lease from termination if the lessee has made a good faith effort to make the payment. The lease will usually also require the lessee: (1) to bury pipelines below plow depth; (2) not to drill nearer than 200 feet from a house or barn; and (3) to pay for crop damages caused by the lessee's operations. These clauses appear to be for the lessor's benefit. Actually, they are inserted by the lessee to negate any contention that he has other obligations or liabilities. The lease also provides that once oil production begins, the lease will continue as long as oil is produced in paying quantities.

It is difficult to generalize about oil and gas lease terms. As is the case with most other legal relationships, there is no such thing as the "usual" form of oil and gas lease. Many years ago a lease was printed in Oklahoma that the printers christened the "Producers 88." While this form has been copied extensively, many changes have also been made as various oil lease forms have evolved over the years. Now there is considerable variation, even among the forms bearing the Producers 88 designation. Everett, *Wyoming Decisions Relative to the Law of Oil and Gas and Comments with Respect to Form "88" Leases,* 6 Wyo. L. J. 223 (1952). With domestic oil becoming a more essential part of the United States economy, we are seeing even more detail and variety in oil and gas leases.

REFERENCE: Cage, *The Modern Oil and Gas Lease—A Facelift for Old 88,* 31st Annual Institute on Oil & Gas Law 177 (1980).

Nomenclature.   The word *royalty* originated in England, when it was used to designate the share in production reserved by the king from those to whom the right to work mines and quarries was granted. In oil and gas law it is the term used to designate the rent due for the right or privilege to take oil or gas out of a designated tract of land. It is the compensation provided in the lease to the landowner for the lessee's privilege of drilling and producing oil and gas and consists of a share in the oil and gas produced. It does not include either delay rentals or a bonus.

The *working interest* is the lessee's share of oil, as distinguished from the landowner's interest, or royalty interest.

An *overriding royalty* is an interest carved out of the working interest, often by means of an assignment of the working interest that reserves to the assignor a part of the oil and gas produced by the assignee.

2.04 Air Rights

Just as a landowner may sell the minerals lying beneath the surface of the earth, so he may sell the space above the surface of the earth. A railroad company may own a tract of land, needing only enough of the space above the surface of the earth as will provide ample clearance for the tops of its trains. It does not need the space above a height of twenty-three or twenty-four feet from the surface. Yet this space is valuable for building purposes and may be sold or leased to a building corporation. *Indiana Toll Road Comm.* v. *Jankovich,* 193 NE2d 237 (Ind. 1963); 1960 Law Forum 303; Michelson, *Space Law and Air Rights from the Ground Up,* 49 Ill. B. J. 812 (1961).

In the case of the Merchandise Mart in Chicago, which was erected over the tracks of the Chicago and Northwestern Railroad, a plat or map was made and recorded, showing a subdivision in three dimensions:

1. An *air lot.* This consists of the space lying above a plane twenty-three feet above the earth's surface.
2. Quadrangular prism or *column lots* (for steel columns to support the building). These extend from the surface of the earth up to the air lot and occupy portions of the surface not occupied by railroad tracks.
3. Cylindrical or *caisson lots.* These extend from the surface of the earth down to the center of the earth. The bottom of each column lot rests within a caisson lot.

The column lots, which share the level through which the trains move, were made narrower than the caisson lots to eliminate interference with the movement of trains. The railroad thereupon sold the air lot, the column lots, and the caisson lots to the Merchandise Mart, but retained ownership of the remainder of the tract. Bell, *Air Rights,* 23 Ill. L. Rev. 250 (1928).

Another conspicuous instance of such utilization of space above the earth's surface is the Park Avenue development in New York, where fabulous sums have been invested in buildings over the New York Central and New Haven tracks.

2.05   Trespass

If without my permission you enter upon my land, this is a *trespass*. I have a legal right to sue you even though you have caused no damage, and the judge will award me *nominal damages* of $1.00.

> **EXAMPLE:**   I have no right to go upon the land of my neighbor for the purpose of putting up screens, or painting, or of effecting repairs on my house. *Taliaferro* v. *Salyer*, 328 P2d 799 (Cal. 1958).

If instead of trespassing at the surface you do so beneath the surface, this is known as *subsurface trespass* and also gives rise to an action for damages.

> **EXAMPLE:**   *A* and *B* own adjoining lands. *B* sinks an oil well near the boundary line. This well is angled so that it crosses the boundary beneath the surface and *B* is therefore pumping oil from *A's* land. This is called crooked-hole drilling. *A* can sue *B* for damages.

Trespass can also take place above the surface in the air space that forms part of the land. The old theory that one's land extends to the sky was adequate when courts were dealing with simple questions.

> **EXAMPLE:**   Thrusting one's arm across a boundary fence is a trespass. *Hannabalson* v. *Sessions,* 90 NW 93 (la. 1902). A building owner cannot maintain shutters that swing across adjoining land. *Homewood Realty Corp.* v. *Safe Deposit & Trust Co.,* 154 Atl. 58 (Md. 1931).

However, common sense revolts at the notion that the mere flight of aircraft over one's land is a trespass. Hence, it has been held that the flight of aircraft at high altitudes, causing no inconvenience to the landowner, is not a violation of the landowner's rights. It is only when the flight is low, as when a plane is taking off or landing and causing damage to the landowner, that his rights have been invaded. Such was the case in *U.S.* v. *Causby,* 328 U.S. 256 (1946), where flights at level of eighty-three feet forced landowner to give up chicken farm.

2.06   Real and Personal Property

The distinction between *real* and *personal property* is an important one. An article of personal property, such as an automobile, is called a *chattel*. It is sold by *bill of sale*. In fact, sales of chattels need not even be in writing when the sale price is under a figure fixed by law, usually $500. Ownership of real estate, on the other hand, is transferred by means of a *deed*.

It is a historical fact that rules of law come into existence when and as human beings feel a need for them. In early times when men were nomadic, driving their cattle north for the summer and south for the winter, there was no need for a law relating to real estate. Men did not aspire to the ownership of land. But there was need for a law of personal property to help men decide how cattle could be sold or who would succeed to ownership at the owner's death. And so the first crude rules of property law evolved, relating to cattle. The word *chattel* derives from cattle, the earliest subject of legal ownership. Later, when men learned to cultivate the soil, real estate law evolved to deal with questions regard-ing the ownership of land. Differences still persist between the law relating to personal property and the law relating to real estate.

2.07   Trees and Crops

All trees, plants, and other things that grow are divided into two classes:

> 1. Trees, perennial bushes, grasses, etc., which do not require annual cultivation, are called *fructus naturales* and are considered real estate or real property.
> 2. Annual crops produced by labor, such as wheat, corn, and potatoes are called *fructus industriales* and are considered personal property.

Since growing crops are personal property, they may be sold orally if the sale price is under the figure fixed by law for oral sales of personal property, *Stein* v. *Crawford,* 105 Atl. 780 (MD. 1919), or by bill of sale, as are other chattels.

CHAPTER 3

Fixtures

3.01 In General

A *fixture* is an article that was once personal property, but that has been installed in or attached to land or a building in some more or less permanent manner, so that such article is regarded in law as part of the real estate.

> **EXAMPLE:** A kitchen sink is personal property, a chattel, in a plumber's shop. It becomes a fixture and part of the real estate after it is installed in a house.

The distinction of whether an item is classified as a fixture is important for three reasons. First, does a contract and deed for the sale of realty pass ownership to these items even though they are not specifically listed in the contract? Ownership will pass to the buyer if the items are fixtures—part of the real estate. Ownership will not pass to the buyer (unless the items are expressly conveyed) if the items are chattels—personal property.

> **EXAMPLE:** Seller contracts to sell his house to Buyer. All that is described in the contract is the land. Buyer is entitled to receive the house as well as the land, because the house is a fixture and is legally part of the land. Buyer is also entitled to receive the kitchen sink, furnace, toilets, and all other articles installed in the building with a view to remaining there permanently. However, Buyer is not entitled to Seller's furniture. Articles of furniture are chattels. They do not pass with a sale of land unless specifically mentioned in the contract. Seller can take his furniture with him when he moves. He cannot remove the sink, furnace, or toilets.

Second, if a tenant installs these items in leased premises, do they become so much a part of the real estate that they cannot be removed when the tenant moves out? See §3.04. Third, the special rules that lenders must follow to obtain a security interest or mortgage lien upon these items are in part dependent upon the item's classification as realty or personalty. See Kratovil & Werner, *Modern Mortgage Law and Practice* Ch. 9 (2d ed. 1981) and §3.05, following herein.

3.02   Tests to Determine Whether an Article is a Fixture

It often becomes important to determine whether or not a particular article is a fixture.

In determining whether or not an article is a fixture, courts apply the following tests:

1. The manner in which the article is attached to the real estate.

EXPLANATION: If an article is attached to a building in such a permanent fashion that it could not be removed without substantial injury to the building, it is usually held to be a fixture. This test, in early times the only test of a fixture, has lost its preeminence in modern times. *Finley* v. *Ford,* 304 Ky. 136, 200 SW2d 138 (1947). However conservative courts continue to attach importance to the test.

EXAMPLES: Water pipes, linoleum cemented to the floor.

2. The character of the article and its adaptation to the real estate.

EXPLANATION: If an article was specially constructed or fitted with a view to its location and use in a particular building, or if the article was installed in the building in order to carry out the purpose for which the building was erected, this tends to show that it was intended that the article should become a permanent part of the building. It is usually considered a fixture.

EXAMPLES: Pews in a church; a theater sign constructed for a particular theater; screens and storm windows specially fitted to the house; electronic computing equipment installed on a floor specially constructed for it. 5 ALR3d 497.

3. The intention of the parties.

EXPLANATION: There is a pronounced tendency today to emphasize the factor of intention. *Am. Tel. & Telegraph Co.* v. *Muller,* 299 F.Supp. 157 (D.S.C. 1968). The courts will ask was the article attached with the intention of making it a permanent part of the building? Tests 1 and 2 are helpful in determining the intention of the parties, but once that intention is determined, it must govern.

EXAMPLES: Gas stoves are often installed in apartment buildings for the use of tenants. They are intended to remain there permanently, since they increase the rental value of the apartments. Therefore they are considered fixtures, even though they can be removed from the building with comparative ease. *Leisle* v. *Welfare B. and L. Assn.,* 232 Wis. 440, 287 NW 739 (1939). The same is true of electric refrigerators installed in apartment buildings. *Guardian Life Ins. Co.* v. *Swanson,* 286 Ill. App. 278, 3 NE2d 324 (1936); 7 ALR 1578. Air conditioners are necessities, not luxuries, in a modern apartment and are treated as fixtures when installed by the owner in a more or less permanent fashion. *State Mutual v. Trautwein* 414 SW2d 587 (Ky. 1967); 43 ALR2d 1378. Again, it is important to remember that conservative courts are accustomed to stress Rule 1 above and would not consider a gas stove, electric range, or refrigerator installed in an apartment building a fixture. *Elliott v. Talmadge*, 207 Ore. 428, 297 P2d 310 (1956); 52 ALR2d 1103. There is substantial agreement on the point that a gas stove or refrigerator installed in a private house is not a fixture, since the owner usually intends to take it with him when he moves.

The law of fixtures, however, is constantly developing, expanding, and changing. As customs have changed, articles once considered personal property have become fixtures. *Strain* v. *Green*, 25 Wash.2d 692, 172 P2d 216 (1946). The luxuries of one generation become the necessities of the next. Since intention is the factor that determines whether or not an article is a fixture, the same type of article may be a fixture in one kind of building and a chattel in another. For example, an old-fashioned gas stove (one not built into the wall) is a chattel in a private home and would not go automatically to the buyer with a sale of the land. In an apartment building, exactly the same kind of stove would, in many states, be considered a fixture, passing automatically with a sale of the land. Articles of furniture (tables, chairs, and so forth), whether in a home, hotel, or furnished apartment, are universally considered chattels. *State* v. *Feves*, 228 Ore. 273, 365 P2d 97 (1961). The decisions on carpeting are in hopeless confusion. 55 ALR2d 1044. Obviously, the better rule is that wall-to-wall carpeting installed by the owner is a fixture, especially where installed on a concrete slab or rough plywood floor.

The secret intention of the party installing the articles will not govern. The test for determining whether an article is a fixture measures the objective manifestations of the intent of the parties. This test requires an analysis of the nature of the article, the relation of the parties, the adaptation of the article to the property, the mode of annexation, and all other surrounding circumstances in a effort to answer the question: Would the average person consider this article a permanent fixture?

This, of course, means that you cannot determine whether a given article is or is not a fixture by sitting in a law library. You must get out there and look at it.

> **EXAMPLE:**   The question is whether an air conditioner in an apartment is a fixture. As stated, the question is absurd. Who put it there? The tenant or the landlord? Tenants usually intend to take their property with them. Permanent annexation is not in the tenant's mind. The opposite is true of the landlord. Is it an easily removable window unit? Or is it one of 100 identical air conditioners built into apertures in the masonry wall of the building? If the latter, it is almost certainly a fixture.

It will help you understand these fixture tests if you understand a little about the history of fixture law. Hundreds of years ago in agricultural England, where we find the beginnings of this law, buildings tended to be rather simple, and the annexation test worked well enough. In America some problems developed even in early times. A Virginia rail fence rests on the ground but is not attached to it. But the courts thought that, for obvious practical reasons, it ought to go with a sale of land, and they so decided. Later, when factories began to appear, it became evident that the annexation test was obsolete. If I buy a factory, obviously I am buying a going concern; yet under the old annexation test the seller would be allowed to remove the machinery, because this could be done without *injury to the building*. In response to this need, the courts invented the intention test, which enabled the buyer to claim the machinery. *Hopewell Mills* v. *Taunton Sav. Bank,* 150 Mass. 519, 23 NE 327 (1890); 109 ALR 1427. Still later, when landlords began to put gas stoves and electric refrigerators in apartments, the courts faced the same problem, and some of them decided in favor of the intention test, but some did not. Those that did not were bothered by the flimsy connection between the appliance and the building, simply plugging a refrigerator in a wall socket, for example. The current problem takes this development one step further. A professional builder equips his homes with a variety of appliances that are attractive to the housewife, who, many builders will tell you, casts the deciding vote in the purchase of a home. The problem of this "package kitchen" has not, as yet, been fully litigated. It is best to ask the builder for a bill of sale as well as a deed, the bill of sale being used to transfer ownership of the appliances. In time, quite possibly, the courts will hold that the appliances pass with the deed as fixtures without the necessity of a bill of sale.

Probably most courts will treat package kitchen items as fixtures:

> **EXAMPLE:**   Standard size dishwasher installed in a well under formica counter top next to sink and attached to electric wiring of house by flexible metal conduit through junction box; standard model garbage disposal attached to underside of sink; and standard model range hood located over drop-in counter top range were permanent fixtures although removable without damage to the building. *Builders Appliance Supply Co.* v. *A. R. John Const. Co.,* 455 P2d 615 (Ore. 1969); *State Dept.* v. *Town & Country Inc.,* 256 Md. 584, 261 A2d 168 (1970).

As you can see, in determining the intention of the party installing the fixture, the courts consider the nature of his interest in the property. It is unlikely that a tenant would wish to make permanent additions to the landlord's property. Hence the rules concerning tenant's fixtures were evolved, under which most of the tenant's installations are treated as removable chattels. But when the installations are made by the landlord, they are more likely to be thought of as true fixtures, which ought to go to a buyer landlord even though not mentioned in the deed.

3.03 Constructive Annexation

Certain objects, though in no way attached to the building, are regarded as so strongly connected with the building that they are fixtures under the doctrine of *constructive annexation.*

> **EXAMPLE:**   Ownership of the keys to a building passes when the deed is delivered to the buyer. *U.S.* v. *967.905 Acres of Land,* 305 F.Supp. 83 (D. Minn. 1969).

EXAMPLE: In the sale of a factory, spare or duplicate parts go with the land as fixtures because of their logical connection with the machinery. 109 ALR 1430.

EXAMPLE: Car unit for an electric garage door opener.

The doctrine of constructive annexation has special application in the area of the financing of large industrial complexes. Heavy machinery and computer equipment that is installed for permanent use in an industrial establishment, thereby becoming a constituent part of the factory or office building, will usually be deemed constructively annexed to the real estate under the *integrated industrial plant* rule. Parties to large commercial financings must deal with the potential application of this doctrine by carefully setting out their rights in their transactional documents. See § 3.05 *infra*.

3.04   Articles Removable by Tenants

Special rules are applicable in the landlord and tenant situation. Articles that a tenant is allowed to remove are classified into the following three classes:

1. Trade fixtures.

EXPLANATION: In order to encourage a tenant to equip himself with the tools and implements of his trade, articles installed by a tenant for the purpose of his trade or business are classed as *trade fixtures* and may be removed by the tenant at the expiration of his lease. Intention is significant here also, for it is obvious that the tenant intends to take such articles with him when he moves.

EXAMPLES: Airplane hangars; bowling alleys; greenhouses; booths, bars, and other restaurant equipment; gasoline pumps and tanks in a filling station; barber chairs; soda fountains; oil derricks.

2. Agricultural fixtures.

EXPLANATION: Articles installed by a tenant farmer for the purpose of enabling him to farm the land are called *agricultural fixtures* and may be removed by the tenant when he quits the land.

EXAMPLES: Hen houses; tool sheds; maple-sugar houses.

3. Domestic fixtures.

EXPLANATION: Articles installed in a dwelling by a tenant in order to render it more comfortable and attractive are removable by the tenant.

EXAMPLES: Bookshelves; venetian blinds.

The three classes of articles that a tenant is allowed to remove are often referred to collectively as *tenant's fixtures. Fixtures,* as described in preceding sections, are real estate. *Tenant's fixtures* are personal property. Observe, also, that *the trade fixtures rule applies only to articles installed by tenants,* not to articles installed by *the landowner. Young Elec. Sign Co.* v. *Erwin Elec. Co.,* 477 P2d 864 (Nev. 1970).

> **EXAMPLE:**   Gas pumps installed by a tenant in a rented service station are clearly trade fixtures. Pumps installed by a landowner would be true fixtures and would automatically go with a sale of the land. Machinery in a factory is a fixture if installed by the landowner. *Foote* v. *Gooch,* 96 N.C. 265, 1 SE 525 (1887).

It is important to remember that lease forms, invariably drafted for the landlord's benefit, often contain clauses forbidding removal of the tenant's installations. 30 ALR3d 998.

> **EXAMPLE:**   A lease of a filling station provided that at the termination of the lease all improvements on the premises would be the property of the landlord. The tenant was not permitted to remove gas pumps and tanks he had installed. 30 ALR3d 1034.

It is important also to remember that if the tenant moves out leaving his trade fixtures behind, they become the property of the landlord. 6 ALR2d 322. In the process they change from chattels to real estate, and ownership passes from tenant to landlord.

3.05   Secured Financing and Fixtures

When only the landowner and the real estate mortgagee are involved, the rule is that fixtures bought, paid for, and installed by the landowner *after* the execution of a mortgage on the land become subject to the lien of the mortgage and cannot thereafter be removed by the landowner. In this situation, in other words, the mortgage lien attaches to *all* fixtures, even trade fixtures, thereafter installed by the mortgagor on the mortgaged premises. Such fixtures must not be removed without the mortgagee's consent. *Bowen* v. *Wood,* 35 Ind. 268. However, trade fixtures installed by a *tenant,* whether installed before or after the mortgage, are removable by the tenant. *Standard Oil Co.* v. *La Crosse Super Auto Service,* 217 Wis. 237, 258 NW 791 99 ALR 60 (1935).

The Uniform Commercial Code (UCC) has been adopted in nearly all fifty states. Under the code, a security interest in a chattel, including a chattel that has been or will be installed as a fixture, is created by means of a *security agreement,* which replaces the old *chattel mortgage* and *conditional sale contract.* This document, however, is not recorded. Instead, a brief notice of the existence of the security agreement is filed. This notice is called a *financing statement.* Where an article has become or is to become a fixture, the financing statement must be filed in the recorder's office where mortgages on real estate are filed. When thus filed, it gives notice to all that there exists a security interest in the article. Subsequent purchasers of the real estate and subsequent mortgagees of the land are bound by this filing, and if a default occurs under the security agreement, the articles can be repossessed and removed by the security holder without liability for any incidental damage to the building occasioned by the removal. If the financing statement is not filed as required by law, a subsequent purchaser or mortgagee of the land is protected against removal of the articles and need not pay the unpaid balance due on the articles.

An important distinction must be made here. The UCC will not generally apply to the conflict between the ownership interest of a fixture lessor and a subsequent purchaser or mortgagee. In a number of jurisdictions the fixture lessor's interest will be superior to the purchaser or lender's, even if those parties have no knowledge of the fixture lessor's interest. As a practical matter, however, fixture lessors often make a fixture filing to protect themselves in the event that the fixture lease is held to be a security interest. Garfinkel, *How Objects Become Fixtures,* Vol. 1, 1#1 Pract. Real Est. Lawyer 19, 25 (Jan. 1985).

Where the article is purchased and installed on the land *after* the recording of a mortgage on real estate, the holder of the chattel security lien may remove the article from the real estate in case of default regardless of the incidental damage to the building. However, he must reimburse the real estate mortgagee for the cost of repairing any immediate physical injury to the building. Kratovil & Werner. *Modern Mortgage Law and Practice* Ch. 9 (2d ed. 1981).

3.06   Agreement of the Parties

All of the rules are statements of law that the courts have framed. These legal rules should not be interpreted to mean that the parties cannot alter the impact of the rule by their agreement, which may make personal property out of what the law would consider real property and vice versa. *Lilenquist* v. *Pitchford's, Inc.* 525 P2d 93 (Ore. 1974).

> **EXAMPLE:**   Landowner and Tenant agree that, notwithstanding the fact that the law would cause items installed in the leased premises to be tenant fixtures and removable by the tenant at the conclusion of his term, the items shall become part of the realty. This agreement will be enforced by the courts.

This agreement would not, however, be binding upon third parties unless they took with notice of its terms. 35 Am. Jur.2d *Fixtures* § 18.

3.07   Severance

If the landowner actually removes an article from the land or from the building to which it has been attached, with the intention that the removal shall be *permanent,* such article becomes personal property again and does not pass by a deed of the real estate. Thus if a landowner tears down a fence and piles the material on the land, such material does not pass by a deed of the land. The fixture has again become personal property by *severance.* If the removal is for a *temporary purpose,* as the removal of a piece of machinery for repairs, the article remains a fixture, notwithstanding its removal from the soil, and passes by a deed of the real estate.

3.08   Building Erected on Wrong Lot

A perpetual source of legal controversy concerns the rights of one who through innocent mistake erects a building on the wrong lot, usually a lot adjoining the one he actually owns. Some states allow compensation to the builder in such cases. *Voss* v. *Forgue* 84 So2d 563 (Fla. 1956); *Olin* v. *Reinecke,* 336 Ill. 530, 168 NE 676 (1929); *Hardy* v. *Burroughs,* 251 Mich. 578, 232 NW 200 (1930). Other states deny any compensation on the ground that if a man builds, it is his duty to see that he builds on the right lot. 5 De Paul L. Rev. 321 (1956); 104 ALR 577; 76 ALR 304.

The basis for the court decisions awarding compensation to the party making the innocent mistake is the law of *restitution,* which is designed to accomplish precisely that. The newer cases go strongly in this direction.

EXAMPLE: Landowner hired Builder to erect a house on Landowner's lot. Builder hired Surveyor to place the survey stakes. Surveyor, by mistake, placed the stakes on the lot next door. Landowner was entitled to a lien on this lot (which was owned by a third party) for the value his building contributed to the lot. *Duncan* v. *Akers,* 262 NE2d 402 (Ind. 1970).

NEW DIRECTIONS: The courts are taking the view that the innocent improver is entitled to compensation unless he acquires *actual* knowledge of his mistake before he begins construction. *Johnson* v. *Stull,* 303 SW2d 110 (Mo. 1957). If the true owner, without protest, watches a stranger building on his land, he is sure to be subjected to a lien for the value of the building. It is grossly unfair not to warn the stranger of his mistake. *Benedict* v. *Little,* 264 So2d 491 (Ala. 1972).

CHAPTER 4

Easements

4.01 Easement Defined

An *easement* is a right acquired by a landowner to use the land of another for a special purpose.

> **EXAMPLE:** Servient and Dominant own adjoining tracts of land. By a written instrument, signed, sealed, and recorded in the proper office, Servient grants to Dominant the right to cross Servient's tract at a particular place for the purpose of providing access to Dominant's tract from a certain highway. The right thus created is called an *easement*. Servient remains the owner of the land over which Dominant travels. Dominant has only a special and particular right in that land.

4.02 Easement Appurtenant Runs with the Land

The easement described in the preceding section is an *easement appurtenant*. An easement appurtenant is created for the benefit of a tract of land. Consequently, for such an easement to exist, there must always be two tracts of land owned by different persons, one tract, called the *dominant tenement*, having the benefit of the easement, and another tract, called the *servient tenement*, over which the easement runs. In the example given in the preceding section, Dominant's tract was the one enjoying the benefit of the easement. It was therefore the dominant tenement. Servient's tract was the servient tenement since it was the tract subject to the easement.

Although the dominant tenement need not adjoin the servient tenement, *Allendorf* v. *Dally*, 6 Ill.2d 577, 129 NE2d 673 (1955), it usually does.

An easement appurtenant is regarded as being so closely connected to the dominant tenement that, upon a sale and deed of such tenement, the easement will pass to the grantee in the deed, even though the deed does not mention it. Such an easement is therefore said to *run with the land.* In the example, if Dominant should sell his land to Purchaser, Purchaser would automatically acquire the right to cross Servient's land. Whoever owns the dominant tenement owns the easement. A separate sale of the easement is not permitted.

Usually an easement is created by a landowner over his land and is in favor of another landowner. However, an easement can run in favor of any interest in land.

> **EXAMPLE:** Landlord leases a store to Tenant and in the lease grants Tenant an easement of ingress and egress over Landlord's adjoining land. This is valid. Easements in favor of tenants are common.

4.03   Easement and License Distinguished

It is often difficult to distinguish an easement from a *license.* Ordinarily an unauthorized entry on the land of another is called a trespass and makes the trespasser liable to pay damages to the landowner. The owner may, however, grant permission to enter for a particular purpose. This permission is called a license. An example is a theater ticket which authorizes the purchaser thereof to enter the theater for the purpose of viewing the performance.

An easement is usually created by a written instrument; a license is often created verbally. An easement is a more or less permanent right; a license is of temporary character. A license is a purely personal right and cannot be sold; the ownership of an easement changes with the ownership of the land to which it belongs. An easement cannot be revoked; a license is revocable.

> **EXAMPLE:** A and B owned adjoining lots. They entered into a verbal agreement to establish a party driveway on the common boundary line between the lots. B thereafter built concrete walks and steps to the driveway. After this driveway had been in use for two years, A notified B that he intended to construct a driveway entirely upon his own lot and expected B likewise to provide for himself. When A sought to erect a fence along the common boundary, B filed a suit to prevent him from doing so. The court held that A was within his rights. Since the agreement was merely verbal, a license, not an easement, was created, and a license is revocable. *Baird* v. *Westberg,* 341 Ill. 616, 173 NE 820 (1930). With the present aversion to the unconscionable, it is doubtful the court would so hold today. *Monroe Bowling Lanes* v. *Woodfield Livestock Sales,* 244 NE2d 762 (Ohio 1969).

Also, courts today are likely to treat a license as an agreement for an easement where large sums of money are spent in reliance on it.

> **EXAMPLE:** Landowner owned Blackacre. Buyer wished to purchase the north half to erect a motel and restaurant. The parties entered into a contract of sale. Buyer explained that he would need to install drains over six inches of Landowner's land. Landowner orally agreed that he could do so. The deal was closed. Landowner later demanded that Buyer remove the drain. The court held

that this was an oral agreement for an easement that became irrevocable by *part performance* when Buyer erected his buildings. *Anastoplo* v. *Radford,* 14 Ill.2d 526, 152 NE2d 879 (1959); *Moe* v. *Cagle,* 385 P2d 56 (Wash. 1963); 11 Columb. L. Rev. 76 (1911).

EXPLANATION: In reading the *Anastoplo* case a lawyer would remind himself that the phrase *part performance* has different meanings. For example, if Seller orally agrees to sell vacant land to Buyer, and Buyer takes possession and builds a home, Buyer can compel Seller to give him a deed. Here part performance is proof that an oral contract of sale was made. 73 Am.Jur.2d *Statute of Frauds* § 427. But in the *Anastoplo* case the acts of Buyer placed him in a position where refusal to give him the right to maintain the drain would cause Buyer unjust impoverishment. 73 Am.Jur.2d *Statute of Frauds* § 408.

As can be seen, some of the strict rules which the courts formerly used yielded some harsh results. The courts responded over time, relaxing requirements to achieve more equitable results.

EXAMPLE: Landowner owned a two-story store and office building. Landowner gave ABC Advertising Co. the right to use his roof for five years for a large advertising display. The court treated this as creating an easement in gross. This achieved the fair result of preventing a revocation of the instrument. *Baseball Pub. Co.* v. *Bruton,* 302 Mass. 54, 18 NE2d 362 (1938).

Parenthetically, mortgage lenders are constantly working to clear up problems created by oral agreements between neighbors. Should a neighbor apply for a mortgage, a party driveway existing under oral agreement would instantly be detected and reported by the mortgage appraiser. The loan process would be stopped and the neighbors would be required to sign and record a written agreement.

4.04   Easement in Gross—Cable TV

An *easement in gross* resembles an easement appurtenant, but there is no dominant tenement.

EXAMPLES: Right granted to a telephone and telegraph company to maintain poles and wires over grantor's land; right granted to a city to construct, maintain, and operate a canal through grantor's land; easements for railroads, street railways, pipelines, and power lines.

A commercial easement in gross (that is, one created for profit) is alienable. It can be mortgaged or sold. Kloek, *Assignability and Divisibility of Easements in Gross,* 22 Chi.-Kent L. Rev. 239 (1944); 3 Powell, *The Law of Real Property,* ¶ 419 (1981).

The question of the apportionability of an easement in gross has assumed new and special significance since the advent of cable television. Typically, a utility company acquires from the landowner, by grant or condemnation, a broad easement in gross to install electric and telephone lines. A cable television company approaches the utility and obtains a license or easement to attach its coaxial cables to the existing utility poles. Theoretically, this adds a burden to the land-owner's land and raises a further question as to whether an easement in gross can be conveyed to a third person or its use divided in favor of a third person. There appear to be few decisions on the subject.

We must take the law step by step. As stated above, a commercial easement in gross is alienable. *Champaign Nat. Bank* v. *Ill. Power Co.*, 125 Ill. App. 3d 424, 465 NE2d 1016 (1984). Many scholarly articles have been written on the subject, pro and con, but we may now safely conclude that this is settled law. But it is equally clear that the grantee of an easement in gross cannot transfer to another grantee rights greater than such grantee was given in the easement grant. Thus, it would seem reasonably obvious that a company that has acquired an easement for one purpose only, namely, the power to cross land for the installation and operation of an electric line, could not transfer to another corporation the power to cross land with a cable TV line. This, indeed, was the precise holding in *Consolidated Cable Utilities Inc.* v. *City of Aurora,* 109 Ill. App. 3d 1035, 439 NE2d 1272 (1982).

However, it must be remembered that many existing easements in gross were created long before cable TV was invented. We therefore must expect to encounter easements that were granted for some purposes that might or might not include cable TV, depending on whether the court gives the easement grant a construction favoring the grantor or favoring the grantee.

Thus in *Hoffman* v. *Capitol Cablevision System Inc.*, 52 A.D. 2d 313, 383 NYS2d 674 (1976), the easement grant was for electricity and "messages." The court held that this included the right to hang TV cables on the poles and to assign to another the right to do so. TV programs are "messages." The court also gave us a valuable rule of construction. It held that furnishing cable TV is an important public purpose and grants should be construed to permit cable TV installation wherever possible.

In *Henley* v. *Continental Cablevision of St. Louis County Inc.*, 692 SW2d 825 (Mo. App. 1985), the court held that an easement for electric, telephone, and telegraphic service permitted the installation of cable TV. To much the same effect is *Joliff* v. *Harden Cable TV Co.*, 76 Ohio St. 2d 103, 269 NE2d 588 (1971).

In an important decision, it has been held that a cable TV company is not a public utility. *Ill. Ind. Cable TV Assn.* v. *Commerce Comm.*, 55 Ill. 2d 205, 403 NE 2d 287 (1973). This case may prove of value in construing the language of the many hundreds of subdivision documents that show an easement over the rear of the lots "for public utilities." See *Consol. Cable Utilities* v. *City of Aurora,* 108 Ill. App. 3d 1035, 439 NE2d 1272 (1982); *White* v. *Detroit Edison Co.*, 281 NW2d 283 (Mich. 1979).

A further problem must be dealt with. An appurtenant easement is normally regarded as nonexclusive. *Stevens* v. *Bird-Jex Co.*, 18 P2d 292 (Utah 1933). Thus if I grant you an easement for ingress and egress over a strip of my land, I can continue to use that strip for any purpose that does not interfere with your rights. I can even cantilever a building over the easement. *Sakansky* v. *Wein,* 86 N.H. 337, 169 A. 1 (1933). In construing an easement in gross, on the other hand, the courts are inclined to construe the easement as exclusive. *Hoffman* v. *Capitol Cablevision System Inc.*, 52 A.D. 2d 313, 383 NYS2d 674 (1976). Thus if I grant an electric company an easement to cross my land with a power line, this is usually considered to be an exclusive easement that gives the grantee the sole privilege of providing power over that right of way. I cannot give another company the right to install an electric line in that strip.

While you will not find this rule in the decisions, an examination of the decisions reveals that in interpreting *utility* easements in gross, they are commonly thought of as being exclusive because utility companies are natural monopolies. It would be pointless to run two competing electrical services over the same strip of land. But as to easements appurtenant, the rule is different. If I grant my neighbor a driveway easement over my land and he constructs a driveway, there is no reason why the driveway cannot be shared unless, of course, the grant is of an exclusive easement.

When an easement in gross is *exclusive,* only the easement owner is entitled to use it. Restatement, Property (Servitudes) §493, Comment C. Therefore there is a strong inference that the easement is *apportionable. Ibid.* This means that the easement owner may choose to share its easement with others, so long as the shared use is one permitted by the "terms" used in the creation of the easement. Restatement Property (Servitudes) § 493. The "intention of the parties" determines the true meaning of the terms used. *Ibid.* Comment B. If the easement in gross is *nonexclusive,* it is usually deemed to lack apportionability. *Ibid.* Comment D. In such case the *landowner* may grant others the right to use the easement strip. *Winslow* v. *City of Vallejo,* 148 Cal. 723, 84 P 191, 5 L.R.A. (n.s.) 851, 7 Ann. Cas. 851, 113 Am. St. Rep. 349 (1906).

The Supreme Court has held that a cable television company seeking to enter premises to service tenants must pay just compensation for this privilege. *Loretto* v. *Teleprompter,* 458 U.S. 419, 73 L.Ed. 2d 868, 102 S.Ct. 3164 (1982). Accordingly, the Illinois statutes have a provision for determining just compensation in such instances for acquiring the statutory easement. Ill. Rev. Stat., Ch. 34 ¶ 11–42–11.1, Ch. 34, ¶ 429.24.1. The statute is obscure and unique. It is unlike any condemnation statute these authors have encountered.

REFERENCES: Hamburg, *All About Cable* (1981); Stein, *Cable TV* (1985).

4.05   Creation of Easement

Easement may be created by *express grant, express reservation, agreement, mortgages, implied grant, implied reservation, necessity, prescription, condemnation, sale of land by reference to a plat,* and by *estoppel.*

4.05(a)   Express Grant

A landowner may create an easement over his land by express grant which, because it conveys an interest in land, should contain all the formal requisites of a deed. It should be in writing and should sufficiently describe the easement, the land subject thereto, the character of the easement (easement for ingress and egress, and so forth), and should be signed, sealed, witnessed, acknowledged, delivered to the grantee, and recorded in accordance with local rules governing deeds. But no particular words are necessary, and omission of the seal is not a fatal defect.

Although an instrument granting an easement is technically known as a *grant*, this is no guarantee that an instrument granting an easement will be so labeled. Very often an instrument in the form of a deed will operate as a grant of an easement by reason of the insertion of language limiting the use of the land to a particular purpose.

> **EXAMPLE:** Landowner signed a warranty deed conveying to Buyer, an adjoining landowner, a strip of land "to be used for road purposes." The quoted phrase appeared immediately following the property description in the deed. It was held that this deed did not make Buyer the owner of the strip, but only gave him an easement for road purposes. *Magnolia Petroleum Co.* v. *West,* 374 Ill. 516, 30 NE2d 24 (1940).

A grant of an easement may also be incorporated in a deed that conveys land.

> **EXAMPLE:** Landowner owns Lots 1 and 2. He sells and conveys Lot 1 to Buyer. After the property description in this deed, the following clause is inserted: "For the consideration aforesaid, the grantor grants to the grantee, his heirs and assigns, as an easement appurtenant to the premises hereby conveyed, a perpetual easement for ingress and egress over and across the south ten feet of Lot 2 in the subdivision aforesaid." The deed accomplishes two objects: (1) Transfers ownership of Lot 1 to Buyer; and (2) Gives Buyer an easement over the south ten feet of Lot 2.

The authors have enjoyed much success by suggesting the use of Professor Kratovil's Model Easement Grant, which follows on pp. 24 and 25.

4.05(b)   Express Reservation

A landowner, in selling and conveying part of his land, may reserve in the deed an easement in favor of the tract retained by such landowner.

> **EXAMPLE:** Landowner owns Lots 1 and 2. He sells and conveys Lot 2 to Buyer and, after the property description in the deed, inserts the following clause: "The grantor reserves to himself, his heirs and assigns, as an easement appurtenant to Lot 1 in the subdivision aforesaid, a perpetual easement for ingress and egress over and across the south ten feet of the premises hereby conveyed."

As in the case of grants of easements, reservations of easements, not labeled as such, are of frequent occurrence.

> **EXAMPLE:** Landowner sold and conveyed certain land to Buyer by a deed containing the following clause: "Saving and excepting therefrom a strip of land forty feet wide along the bank of the east fork of Austin Creek all the way across said land, for a road to be built at some future time." The court held that, al-

MODEL EASEMENT GRANT*

This EASEMENT GRANT is made between_____
_____(hereinafter referred to as "the grantor") and_____
(hereinafter referred to as "the grantee").

The following recitals of fact are a material part of this instrument:

A. The grantor is the owner of a tract of land described as follows and hereafter referred to as "Parcel 1":

(Here insert legal description)

B. The grantee is the owner of a tract of land described as follows and hereafter referred to as "Parcel 2":[1]

(Here insert legal description)

C. The grantor wishes to grant and the grantee wishes to receive an easement over, under and across that part of Parcel 1 described as follows and hereafter referred to as "The easement premises:"[2]

(Here describe the land to be subject to easement)

D. Parcel 1 is presently improved with a building used for_____and Parcel 2 is improved with a building used for_____.

Now, therefore, in consideration of_____ and other valuable consideration, the receipt and sufficiency of which are hereby acknowledged,[3] the following grants, agreements, and covenants and restrictions are made:

1. GRANT OF EASEMENT. The grantor hereby grants[4] to the grantee, his heirs and assigns,[5] as an easement appurtenant to Parcel 2,[6] a perpetual[7] easement for ingress and egress[8] over, under and across the easement premises.

2. USE OF EASEMENT PREMISES. Use of the easement premises is not confined to present uses of Parcel 2, the present buildings thereon, or present means of transportation.[9] The installation or maintenance by the grantee of pipes, conduits, or wires, under, upon or over the easement premises is forbidden.[10] Exclusive use of the easement premises is not hereby granted.[11] The right to use the easement premises, likewise for ingress or egress, is expressly reserved by the grantor. In addition, the grantor reserves the right to make the following uses of the easement premises:

a. The right to erect a building over the easement premises, provided all of such structure shall be located at a height of not less than_____feet above the surface of the easement premises, but construction of the improvement shall be so conducted as not to unreasonably interfere with grantee's use of the easement premises during construction.[12]

b. Any subsurface use that does not unreasonably interfere with grantee's use of the easement premises.[13]

3. USE OF PARCELS 1 AND 2. As long as this easement grant remains in effect Parcel 2 shall not be used for other than commercial or residential purposes and no building other than one suited only for commercial or residence purposes shall be constructed thereon.[14]

4. ADDITIONS TO DOMINANT TENEMENT. Said easement is also appurtenant to any land that may hereafter come into common ownership with Parcel 2 aforesaid and that is contiguous to Parcel 2.[15] An area physically separated from Parcel 2 but having access thereto by means of public ways or private easements, rights or licenses is deemed to be contiguous to Parcel 2.

5. DIVISION OF DOMINANT TENEMENT. If Parcel 2 is hereafter divided into two parts by separation of ownership or by lease, both parts shall enjoy the benefit of the easement hereby created.[16] Division of the dominant tenement into more than two parts shall be deemed an unlawful increase of burden and use of the easement may be enjoined.

6. PARKING. Both parties covenant that vehicles shall not be parked on the easement premises except so long as may be reasonably necessary to load and unload.[17]

7. PAVING OF EASEMENT. Grantee covenants to promptly improve the easement premises with a concrete surface at least_____feet in width suitable for use by delivery trucks and[18] will at all times maintain same in good repair.[19]

8. WARRANTIES OF TITLE. Grantor warrants that he has good and indefeasible fee simple title to the easement premises, subject only to the following permitted title objections:[20]

(here list encumbrances)

9. TITLE INSURANCE AND ESCROW. Should grantee so desire, he may apply forthwith for a title insurance policy insuring the easement hereby granted and grantor will make available for inspection by the title company any evidence of title in his possession.[21]

10. RELOCATION OF EASEMENT. Grantor reserves the right to relocate the easement premises as follows.[22]

1. He shall first notify the grantee of the proposed relocation by mailing notice to the grantee at his last address furnished pursuant hereto showing the proposed relocation, probable commencement and completion dates, all by mailing same, postage prepaid, at least 30 days prior to commencement of relocation.

2. The easement premises shall be moved not more than_____feet from their present location.

3. Grantor shall improve the new easement premises with a concrete driveway similar to the one replaced, to be suitable for use by delivery trucks, with connections at the termini of the driveway to be replaced, and reasonably convenient for the uses then existing on Parcel 2.

4. At the completion of the work, grantor shall record an easement grant in recordable form granting the new easement to the grantee, shall cause the same to be delivered to the grantee, and shall furnish the grantee evidence of title satisfactory to the grantee showing an unemcumbered easement in such grantee, whereupon the change in location of the easement

premises shall become effective, and appropriate releases of the prior location shall be executed in recordable form and exchanged between the parties hereto, their successors or assigns.

11. RUNNING OF BENEFITS AND BURDENS. All provisions of this instrument, including the benefits and burdens, run with the land and are binding upon and enure to the heirs, assigns, successors, tenants and personal representatives of the parties hereto.[23]

12. TERMINATION OF COVENANT LIABILITY. Whenever a transfer of ownership of either parcel takes place, liability of the transferor for breach of covenant occurring thereafter automatically terminates, except that the grantor herein remains liable for breaches of covenants of title set forth in Paragraph 8.[24]

13. ATTORNEY'S FEES. Either party may enforce this instrument by appropriate action and should he prevail in such litigation, he shall recover as part of his costs a reasonable attorney's fee.[25]

14. CONSTRUCTION. The rule of strict construction does not apply to this grant. This grant shall be given a reasonable construction so that the intention of the parties to confer a commercially usable right of enjoyment on the grantee is carried out.

15. NOTICE. Grantor's address is_____ _____and grantee's address is_____ _____. Either party may lodge written notice of change of address with the other. All notices shall be sent by U.S. mail to the addresses provided for in this paragraph and shall be deemed given when placed in the mail. The affidavit of the person depositing the notice in the U. S. Post Office receptable shall be evidence of such mailing.

16. RELEASE OF EASEMENT. The grantee herein may terminate this instrument by recording a release in recordable form with directions for delivery of same or to grantor at his last address given pursuant hereto whereupon all rights duties, and liabilities hereby created shall terminate. For convenience such instrument may run to "the owner or owners and parties interested" in Parcel 1.[26]

17. JOINDER OF SPOUSE._____ spouse of grantor joins herein for the purpose of releasing dower, homestead and all other marital rights, all of which are waived with respect to this easement.[27]

In witness whereof the grantor, his spouse and the grantee[28] have hereunto set their hands and seals this _____ day of_____A.D. 19_____.

_____(Seal)
_____(Seal)
_____(Seal)

FOOTNOTES

1. It is not necessary to describe the dominant tenement in the easement grant. The area intended to be served can be gathered from the attendant circumstances. However, as appears from the General Observations, questions often arise. Hence it is good draftsmanship to describe the dominant tenement.

2. Often enough R owning Blackacre, grants to E an easement of ingress and egress over "Blackacre." Obviously it was never the intention of the parties that E would roam over all of Blackacre. The courts have devised a means of pinning down the easement area. 110 ALR 174. But to fail to pinpoint the easement premises is wretched draftsmanship.

3. Since easements existed long before the doctrine of consideration was invented, no recital of consideration is necessary. Occasional decisions nevertheless mention the presence of consideration. It seems best to recite consideration.

4. Words of grant are necessary according to a few decisions. This corresponds to the requirement of words of conveyance in a deed. The numerous decisions holding that easements can be created by contract are obvious proof that the requirement is less formal in easement drafting.

5. There are many statutes to the effect that words of heirship are not necessary to create a fee simple by deed. Easements are rarely mentioned. But by analogy the word "heirs" is not needed to create a permanent easement. But there are some court decisions saying that an easement endures only for the life of the grantor unless words of heirship are included. Elwell v. Miner, 174 NE2d 43.

6. An easement appurtenant need not be so characterized. Normally the courts will strain to find the easement is appurtenant rather than in gross. Good draftsmanship requires that the proper label be affixed.

7. The same estates exist in easements as exist in corporeal hereditaments. Thus, you can have an easement in fee simple, for life, for years, etc. Texas Co. v. O' Meara, 377 Ill. 144, 36 NE2nd 256; 154 ALR5. It is not the practice to use the estates terminology. Instead of talking of an easement in fee simple, we talk of a perpetual easement.

8. There is no such thing as a plain "easement." It must be for ingress and egress, for light and air, or for some other specific purpose.

9. The opening sentence of paragraph 2 is a statement of existing law. 3 ALR3d 1287. However, it forces the parties to think about changes that will take place in the future. If the dominant owner tears down his store and erects an industrial plant, will the servient owner be unhappy with this turn of events? If he will be, he must provide against this.

10. This is also a statement of existing law. 3 ALR3d 1278. Again the existence of litigation indicates the need for covering this point.

11. An easement that excludes the servient owner from use of the easement premises is extremely rare. Etz v. Morrow, 72 Ariz. 228, 233 P2d 442. An exception is the railroad easement, which is exclusive by its very nature. But dominant owners always seem surprised when they hear the rule stated. Hence it belongs in the grant.

12. This is also a statement of existing law. Gahanty v. Wein, 86 N.H. 337, 169A 1. Minneapolis Athletic Club v. Cohler, 177 NW2d 786 (Minn. 1970). The presence of litigation indicates it is not generally understood. Of course, there are easements one cannot build over, such as a pipeline easement. Tide Water Pipe Co. v. Blair Holding Co., 42 N.J. 591, 202 A2d 405; 28 ALR2d 626. This would block the dominant owner's efforts to repair a break. For similar reasons the servient owner cannot put a lake over a pipeline easement. Sumrall v. United Gas Pipeline Co. 97 So2d 914.

13. Also a statement of existing law. E.M. & S.W. R.R. v Sims, 228 Ill. 9, 81 NE 782.

14. The dominant owner can change the nature of the use unless the easement grant restricts this right.

15. The dominant tenement is determined at the time the easement is created. Land acquired by the dominant owner thereafter is non-dominant land. It cannot use the easement. Weathers v. Icoa Life Ins. Co., 460 P2d 361 (Ore. 1969). This is the most common error in easement drafting and the most costly. Of course, one can easily draft around the problem. You can make the additions to the dominant tenement clause much broader, if you wish. For example:
"Said easement is appurtenant to any land in the Northwest quarter of Section 34 that may subsequently come into common ownership with said dominant tenement."
In passing, attention is drawn to the fact that by the modern rule contiguity of the dominant tenement to the easement premises is not required. Allendorf v. Daly, 6 Ill. 2d 577, 129 NE2d 673.

16. The easement runs in favor of all parts, where the dominant tenement is later divided. 10 ALR3d 960. There are some limits, however, which the courts have not clearly defined. 10 ALR3d 968. This grant sharply limits the right to divide.

17. This again is a statement of existing law. 37 ALR2d 944. Litigation over parking suggests the need to spell this out.

18. In the absence of such a clause there is no duty on the dominant owner to pave the way.

19. The dominant owner has the right, though not the duty, to repair. Kratovil, Real Estate Law (5th ed 1969) §37. But see Lynch v. Keck, 263 NE2d 176 (Ind. 1970).

20. Warranties of title exist only as expressly included in the grant.

21. Where beneficial use of his land by the dominant owner depends on dependable access via the easement, he needs title insurance on the easement as much as he needs title insurance on the land.

22. The servient owner has no right to relocate the easement unless the easement grant confers this right. An awkwardly located easement can virtually destroy the value of industrial or commercial property.

23. Covenants running with the land can be included in the easement grant. An easement grant creates the requisite privity of estate.

24. The original covenantor remains liable even after he has disposed of his land. This clause reverses the rule.

25. A litigant pays his own attorney unless the contract provides otherwise.

26. The dominant owner may wish to get rid of his covenant liability by terminating the easement when other means of ingress have been acquired. This form of clause eliminates the need for a title search of the servient tenement to get the names of the parties to whom the release is to run.

27. The authorities are divided as to the need for a spouse to join. See, e.g. Arkansas State Highway Comm. v. Marlar, 447 SW2d 329 (Ark. 1969).

28. Since covenants by the grantee are included it is appropriate for all parties to sign and acknowledge this document. Of course, it should also be recorded.

though the deed purported to except from its operation the forty-foot strip in question, nevertheless ownership of the forty-foot strip passed to the grantee in the deed, but the grantor had an easement thereover for road purposes. *Coon* v. *Sonoma Magnesite Co.,* 182 Cal. 597, 189 Pac. 271 (1920).

4.05(c)   Creation of Easement by Agreement

The law requires no technical formula of words to create an easement. The only essential is that the parties make clear their intention to establish an easement. *Scanlan* v. *Hopkins,* 270 A2d 352 (Vt. 1970).

Thus, easements may be created by contract or agreement, such contract or agreement being, in effect, a grant of an easement. A familiar illustration is the party wall agreement.

4.05(c)(1)   Party Walls

Suppose you own Lot 1 and I own adjoining Lot 2. You plan to erect a building on your lot, and I propose to erect an identical building on mine. If we can get together, we can effect an economy by means of a *party wall.* We will erect our buildings in such a way that on the common boundary line where our lots meet only one wall will be built, straddling the line, half on each side of it. Each of us will use that wall as a wall of his house. It will support my floors and roof and yours also. The economies of such an arrangement are obvious. The cost of the wall is shared. Land is conserved. Windows are eliminated, as is the expense of maintenance of one outside wall.

Legally I own the half of the wall that rests on my lot, and you own the half that rests on your lot. I have an easement of support in your half of the wall, and you have an easement of support in my half. Owners planning such an arrangement enter into a party wall agreement. Naturally a written agreement should be used, for an easement is an interest in land, and the law requires that interests in land be created in writing.

Suppose I plan to build at a time when you are not yet ready to go ahead. Here the party wall agreement gives me the right to put half of the wall on your lot and further provides that when you decide to build, you will pay me half the cost of the wall.

The duty to repair a party wall falls equally on both owners. If either owner repairs the wall, he is entitled to collect from the other owner half the expenses thus incurred.

Unless the party wall agreement provides otherwise, either owner may increase the height of the wall without the consent of the other owner. However, the entire expense must be borne by the party who heightens the wall, unless the other owner decides to use the added wall.

Additional points on party walls. (1) Each owner has the right to extend the beams of his building into the party wall, but not beyond the centerline of the wall. (2) The wall may be used for flues and fireplaces. (3) If an owner chooses not to erect a building on his side of the party wall, he may use that side of the wall for advertising signs. 2 ALR2d 1138, *69 CJS Party Walls § 15 (e)*. (4) As a rule, if one of the owners wishes to demolish his building, he may, but he must leave the wall intact for the support of the adjoining building. *Ceno Theater Co.* v. *B/G Sandwich Shops,* 24 F2d 31 (6th Cir. 1928).

4.05(d) Mortgages

When a landowner owns Lots 1 and 2 and mortgages Lot 1, he may, at the mortgagee's insistence, include in the mortgage a grant of easement over part of Lot 2. Such a clause may run somewhat as follows:

> And as further security for payment of the debt above described, the mortgagor mortgages and grants to the mortgagee, his heirs and assigns, as an easement appurtenant of Lot 1 aforesaid, a perpetual easement for ingress and egress over and across the south ten feet of Lot 2 in the subdivision aforesaid.

Likewise, the landowner may wish to reserve, for the benefit of Lot 2, an easement over part of Lot 1. In such case, an appropriate clause of reservation may be included in the mortgage.

The foregoing illustrations show how a *mortgage can create an easement.* When such a mortgage is foreclosed, ownership of the dominant and servient tenements passes into separate hands, and the real existence of the easement begins. Suppose, however, that the landowner owns a lot that enjoys the benefit of a *previously created* easement. He mortgages the lot, and in the mortgage nothing is said concerning the easement. The mortgage is foreclosed. The purchaser at the foreclosure sale enjoys the benefit of the easement, for *an appurtenant easement runs with the land even though it is not mentioned in the mortgage or in the foreclosure proceedings.* 38 Cal. L. Rev. 426.

Also, an easement acquired by a mortgagor subsequent to the giving of a mortgage automatically comes under the lien of the mortgage and passes to the purchaser at any mortgage foreclosure sale. *First Nat. Bank* v. *Smith,* 284 Mich. 579, 280 NW 57, 116 ALR 1074 (1938).

The effect of a mortgage on an easement and vice versa depends on which is *prior in time. Prior in time is prior in right.*

> **EXAMPLE:**   Owner mortgages Lot 1 to Lender in 1971. The mortgage is recorded and the mortgage funds are paid to Owner, thus creating a valid mortgage. In 1972, Owner gives his neighbor an easement of access over Lot 1. In 1973, Lender forecloses his mortgage. The mortgage being *prior in time* to the easement was *prior in right.* The foreclosure destroys the easement. *Kling* v. *Ghilarducci,* 3 Ill.2d 455, 121 NE2d 752 (1954).

> **EXAMPLE:**   Owner gives Neighbor an easement of access over Owner's Lot 1 in 1971. It is recorded. In 1972, Owner mortgages the lot to Lender. Later, the mortgage is foreclosed. The easement being *prior in time* is *prior in right* and is not affected by foreclosure of the mortgage. 46 ALR2d 1197.

Lay persons are at times disturbed by the notion that foreclosure of a mortgage can destroy an easement that was bought and paid for. It must be remembered that the law assumes that every sensible person has the title searched before he spends a penny. The title search would reveal the mortgage. One who buys an easement in the face of a prior recorded mortgage does so with his eyes wide open and deserves no sympathy. He should have received the mortgagee's subordination to the easement.

4.05(e) Implied Grant or Reservation

Often when the owner of two tracts of land sells or mortgages one of them, there is no mention at all of easements, and yet as a result of the transaction an easement is created. In such cases, the situation of the land is such that the courts feel the parties intended to create an easement even though they did not actually say so. Such easements are called *implied easements*. They are created by *implied grant* and *implied reservation*. When a landowner uses one part of his land for the benefit of another part, and this use is such that, if the parts were owned by different persons, the right to make such a use would constitute an easement, then upon a sale of either of such parts an implied easement is created. *Cheney* v. *Miller,* 485 P2d 1218 (Ore. 1971).

> **EXAMPLE:** Owner owned two adjoining lots, on each of which there was a two-story building. The buildings were separated by a partition wall. The stairway to the second floor was located entirely on one lot, and there were doors through the partition wall by which occupants of the second floor on the other lot reached their apartments. Owner sold and conveyed the lot on which the stairway was located to Buyer. There was an implied reservation of an easement for the use of the stairway, and Owner could continue to use such stairway even though the deed made no mention whatever of any easement. If Owner had instead sold Buyer the lot that had no stairway and had retained the lot on which the stairway was located, there would have been an implied grant of an easement to Buyer to use such stairway. *Powers* v. *Heffernan,* 233 Ill. 597, 84 NE 661 (1908).

4.05(e)(1) Requirements for Creation of Implied Easement

The following are the requirements for the creation of an implied easement:

> 1. The prior use of one part of the land for the benefit of the other part must have been apparent and obvious. That is, the use must have been such that it would have been disclosed on a reasonable inspection of the premises. The theory is that the parties intended to continue the obvious arrangements existing when the sale took place. *Burns Mfg. Co.* v. *Boehm,* 356 A2d 763 (Pa. 1975).

> **EXAMPLE:** Suppose a man owns Lots 1 and 2, and sewage from his house on Lot 1 drains through an underground pipe running across Lot 2. There is a catch basin on Lot 2. If *A* buys Lot 2, the presence of the catch basin with a visible

cover on the surface of the ground will give A notice and thereby create an implied easement for drainage over Lot 2. 58 ALR 824.

Note that we start with a situation where one person owns two or more adjoining tracts of land. He uses one tract for the benefit of the other. This use would be considered an easement if the lands were owned separately. For this reason, the arrangement is often said to create "quasi-easements" or "almost easements"—things that resemble easements. Remember that, at this point, *true* easements do not exist because an easement connotes rights of one person in the land of another person.

2. The prior use must have been continuous.

EXAMPLE: Where A owned two adjoining lots and constructed a driveway on the common boundary line between the lots and thereafter sold one of the lots to B, an implied easement was created for use of the driveway as a common or party driveway. *Walters v. Gadde,* 390 Ill. 518, 62 NE2d 439 (1945); *Gorman v. Overmyer,* 199 Okla. 451, 190 P2d 477 (1947). Another example would be a party wall, and still another would be a well on the boundary line serving two adjoining properties. *Frantz v. Collins,* 21 Ill.2d 446, 173 NE2d 437 (1961).

3. The easement must be "necessary." That is, the easement must be highly convenient and beneficial to the property. The test of whether or not an easement is necessary is this: Can a substitute for this easement be obtained without unreasonable expense and trouble? If it cannot, the easement is necessary.

4. The ownership of the two tracts of land must be in one person when the use commences and become separated thereafter, so that one person owns the benefited tract and someone else owns the burdened tract. 94 ALR3d 502. This is obvious, for as long as one man owns both tracts there can be no easement. By definition, an easement is a right in another's property. The manner in which the separation of ownership takes place is immaterial. Usually it takes place when the original owner sells either the benefited or the burdened tract to another person, but any other manner of separating the ownership will do. For example, if the owner of two such tracts places a mortgage on one of them, and such mortgage is later foreclosed, the ownership of the two tracts passes into different hands and an implied easement is created. *Liberty Bank v. Lux,* 378 Ill. 329, 38 NE2d 6 (1941). Or if the owner of two such tracts dies, leaving a will by which he gives one tract to A and the other to B, an implied easement will be created. *Hoepker v. Hoepker,* 309 Ill. 407, 141 NE 159 (1923). Or if a tract of land is divided by a partition suit, an implied easement may be created. *Deisenroth v. Dabe,* 7 Ill.2d 340, 131 NE2d 17 (1955).

Implied easements are an unusual feature of easement law. The circumstances outlined above that persuade the courts to hold that an easement exists suggest to the court's mind that an easement should exist whether or not the parties ever gave the matter any thought. Had they been asked, no doubt they would have replied, "Of course, we expected the situation to continue after the sale as it was before the sale." When all the requirements co-exist, this is the answer that enables the courts to say that an easement *does* exist. Why does litigation result? Most implied easement cases represent a "shakedown" effort whereby one landowner attempts to extort an unreasonable sum as compensation for the requested formal easement grant to be given to confirm the situation. Also, neighbor fights generate ill-will, and litigation results.

4.05(e)(2)   An Easement can be Implied from the Circumstances

> **EXAMPLE:**   Owner owns a lot having lake frontage and a lot landward of the beach lot. He sells the landward lot to Buyer with an easement for use of the beach. An easement will be implied to cross the beach lot to reach the beach. *Ames* v. *Prodon,* 60 Cal. Reptr 183 (1967).

4.05(e)(3)   Implied Easements—Common Scheme or Plan

It has been pointed out that where two adjoining owners erect buildings with a party wall straddling the boundary line an easement is created even though no written document exists. This idea can be carried a step further. Where two adjoining landowners engage in a scheme of common development that cannot exist without easements, easements exist.

> **EXAMPLE:**   Owner #1 owns Lot 1 and Owner #2 owns the adjoining Lot 2. By verbal agreement they erect buildings with an arcade of shops straddling the boundary line between the lots. Easements for the arcade now exist even though there is no written document. *Blakeney* v. *State,* 163 NE2d 69 (N.C. 1968).

> **EXAMPLE:**   Owner owns a large lot on which he erects row houses or town houses at right angles to the street. He sells off the town houses. Implied easements come into being for ingress, egress, sewer, water, electricity, etc. *Gilbert* v. *CT&T Co.,* 7 Ill.2d 492, 131 NE2d 1 (1956).

4.05(f)   Easement of Necessity

When the owner of land sells a part thereof that has no outlet to a highway except over his remaining land or over the land of strangers, a right of way by necessity is created by implied grant over the remaining land of the seller.

Students seem fascinated by the easement of necessity. They tend to confuse it with the implied easement. The easement by necessity rests on the philosophy that land is a valuable community asset and none of it should be rendered landlocked and useless. To allow a tract of land to go to waste because it lacks access is an intolerable waste of a valuable resource. The implied easement, on the other hand, rests on the assumption that the obvious and beneficial use was intended to continue after ownership of the parcels was severed. For this reason, the courts require only that the use be highly beneficial for this also tends to establish that it was intended to continue.

In the case of an easement by necessity, a totally *new factual situation* is created. A tract of land, previously part of a larger parcel that had access to the outside world, is suddenly converted into an island with no means of access. The courts create a *new* means of access so that the island can remain useful. Easements by necessity are rare; implied easements are common.

4.05(g)   Prescription

Prescription is the acquiring of a right by lapse of time. An easement may be acquired by prescription. Usually, the period of time required for the acquisition of an easement by prescription is the same period as that required for the acquisition of ownership of land by adverse possession. This period, called the *prescriptive period,* varies from state to state. Periods of ten, fifteen, and twenty years are common.

> **EXAMPLE:**   Owner owned a private alley and an apartment building adjoining thereto. Neighbor owned a neighboring apartment building. Without any permission from Owner, Neighbor's tenants constantly used Owner's private alley in order to enter their apartments from the rear. Whenever Owner's tenants parked their cars in the alley, Neighbor would call the police and have them put out. This continued for more than twenty years. Then Owner attempted to stop this use of the alley by Neighbor's tenants. It was held that he could not do so, since Neighbor had acquired an easement by prescription. *Rush* v. *Collins,* 366 Ill. 307, 8 NE2d 659 (1937).

> **EXAMPLE:**   Owner owned a house and lot. He constructed a garage in the rear of the lot. Because the space adjoining his house was inadequate for a driveway, he constructed one that ran partly across Neighbor's adjoining land. This was done without seeking Neighbor's permission. Owner used this driveway for over twenty years. He has a prescriptive easement to continue to use it. *Nocera* v. *De Feo,* 340 Mass. 783, 164 NE2d 136 (1959).

The following are the requirements for the creation of an easement by prescription:

> 1. The use must be *adverse.* If it is under permission or consent of the owner, the use is not adverse. There must be such an invasion of the landowner's rights as would entitle him to maintain a suit against the intruder. If the use by me of my neighbor's land is, on its face, permitted by my neighbor as a matter of neighborly accommodation, the use is not adverse or hostile.

> **EXAMPLE:**   Owner had a driveway running to his garage in the rear of his house. Neighbor often used this driveway to get his car into his backyard. He never sought Owner's permission, although they were good friends. This use will not ripen into a prescriptive easement. It is, on its face, a matter of neighborly accommodation. *Stevenson* v. *Williams,* 188 Pa. Super. 49, 145 A2d 734 (1958).

> 2. The use must be *under claim of right,* in that there must be no recognition of the right of the landowner to stop the use.
> 3. The use must be *visible, open,* and *notorious,* so that the landowner is bound to learn of it if he keeps himself well informed about his property.

EXAMPLE: The secret placing of a drainpipe in a wooded gully would not be considered notorious.

4. The use *must not be merely as a member of the public.* The use by the claimant of the easement must be sufficiently exclusive to give notice of his *individual* claim of right.

5. The use must be *continuous* and *uninterrupted* for the required period of time. That is, the easement must be exercised whenever there is any necessity therefore, and the use must be of such frequency as to apprise the landowner of the right being claimed against him.

EXAMPLE: Occasional entries upon a neighbor's land, for example, to put up screens or storm windows, to paint a wall, to trim a hedge, or to clean gutters, are not such continuous use as will ever ripen into a prescriptive easement. *Romans* v. *Nadler,* 217 Minn. 174, 14 NW2d 482 (1944).

It is not necessary that the adverse use be that of one person only.

EXAMPLE: In Illinois, the prescriptive period is twenty years. Suppose that *A* and *B* are neighbors. *A* builds a driveway over *B's* land without *B's* permission. He uses it for five years. *A* sells his land to *C,* who also uses the driveway for five years. *C* sells to *D,* who uses the driveway for ten years. Now *D* has a prescriptive easement. The prescriptive uses that *A,C,* and *D* made can be *tacked,* that is, added together to make up the required twenty years. 171 ALR 1278. Also, since the easement was used for the benefit of a tract of land, it is an easement appurtenant and will thereafter run with the land so benefited. 171 ALR 1278.

Nearly all prescriptive easements are appurtenant easements.

Where an easement is acquired by prescription or any other means, the easement owner automatically acquires as rights incidental to the easement all rights needed for the useful enjoyment of the easement.

EXAMPLE: *A* and *B* owned adjoining lots 7 and 8. *A* erected a three-story building on Lot 7. He attached a fire escape to his building on Lot 7. It extended over the space above Lot 8. As is customary, the lowest member of the fire escape extended in a horizontal direction, hinged in such a fashion that it could be lowered to the ground level of Lot 8 in case of fire. After twenty years, *B* threatened to build under this horizontal member. The court held that *A's* prescriptive easement included, as a right incidental to his right to maintain the fire escape, a right to lower his horizontal member into an unimproved area beneath. *Poulos* v. *Hill,* 401 Ill. 204, 81 NE2d 854 (1948).

4.05(g)(1)   Party Driveways

Suppose you and I own adjoining lots, each with a house on it, and pursuant to a verbal agreement we build a party driveway, straddling the boundary line between our lots and serving our garages in the rear of our lots. Each of us uses this driveway continuously for the required period of time. Most courts hold that a party driveway easement has been created by prescription. 98 ALR 1096. This is quite a legal oddity, for obviously such common use is permissive, not adverse. Yet to prevent injustice courts allow prescriptive easements to be created by such use. *Peterson* v. *Corrubia,* 21 Ill.2d 525, 173 NE2d 499 (1975); 27 ALR2d 332.

4.05(g)(2)   State Laws

State laws have been enacted, as in Illinois, that prevent the creation of an easement by prescription if the landowner posts signs forbidding use of his land. This relieves the landowner of making periodic inspections of his vacant land to see if strangers are using it.

4.05(g)(3)   Public Highways

When the public has used a privately owned strip of land for the purpose of passage for the required period of time, courts often hold that an easement for a public highway has been created by prescription.

4.05(h)   Creation of Easement by Condemnation

Although in some states laws provide that complete ownership of the land may be acquired by condemnation, the general rule is that where land is taken by condemnation for a street, highway, railroad right of way, or telephone or electric power line the taker acquires only an easement. All such easements are easements in gross.

> **EXAMPLE:**   City wishes to open a street across Owner's land, but Owner is unwilling to sell. City files a condemnation suit against Owner, and a judgment is entered fixing the full market value of the strip to be taken for the opening of the street. City pays this amount into court. Although City pays the full market value of the strip, it acquires only an easement thereover, and Owner remains the owner subject to the easement. Thus, Owner may construct subvaults beneath the street without any liability to City for payment of rent.

4.05(i)   Sale by Reference to Plat

Where a landowner subdivides his land into lots, blocks, streets, and alleys and thereafter sells lots in the subdivision, each purchaser of a lot automatically acquires an easement of passage over the streets and alleys shown on the plat or map of the subdivision, even though the deed to the lot makes no mention whatever of such right. Such a private easement becomes important where the subdivider attempts to close up a street or alley before the public has acquired the right to insist that such street or alley remain open. The lot owners are in a position to keep the street open by virtue of their easement rights, even though the street never becomes a public street. 7 ALR2d 607.

The plat also gives the city rights in the dedicated streets and public rights. In some instances the city acquires full ownership of the dedicated streets. In other cases it acquires only an easement. 11 ALR2d 549.

4.05(j)   Easement by Estoppel

There are other instances of the creation of an easement by *estoppel.*

> **EXAMPLE:**   Owner owns sewer and water pipe in a street running past his house and other vacant land he owns. Owner makes a deed of a vacant lot to Buyer but nothing is said about the sewer and water pipes. Buyer builds a house and Owner without objection watches Buyer tie into the sewer and water pipes. An easement to use the sewer and water services has been created by estoppel. *Monroe Bowling Lanes* v. *Woodfield Livestock Sales,* 244 NE2d 762 (Ohio 1969).

> **EXAMPLE:**   Corporation leased a co-op apartment in its apartment building to Tenant. Corporation had a plat in its office, showing a recreation area with swimming pool adjoining the building, and its agent always referred to this recreation area when making his sales pitch on apartments. An easement by *estoppel* has been created. Tenant can use the recreation area. *Hirlinger* v. Stelzer, 222 So2d 237 (Fla. 1969).

4.05(k)   Declaration of Easements

Easements are used so extensively in the town house, condominium, and planned unit development that they are physically separated from the deeds and mortgages and incorporated in a separate document. As a mater of convenience, this document also includes building restrictions, liens, and covenants and is called a Declaration of Restrictions, Easements, Liens, and Covenants.

4.06   Unlocated Easements and Relocation

If *R* owns a large tract of land and grants to *E* an easement thereover, manifestly it is not *R's* entire tract that comprises the servient tenement, for it is not intended that *E* shall wander aimlessly over the premises. It is, rather, the intention of the parties that some small part of the tract shall become the easement tract. The parties have simply failed to specify the precise location of the easement. In such cases, the owner of the servient tenement has, in the first instance, the right to designate the location of the easement, provided he exercises such right in a reasonable manner, having regard to the suitability and convenience of the way to the rights and interests of the owner of the dominant tenement. If the owner of the servient tenement fails or refuses to locate the way, the owner of the dominant tenement acquires the right to make his own selection of a location, having due regard to the interests, rights, and conveniences of the other party. 110 ALR

174, 24 ALR 4th 1068; 36 *id.* 769. Court action may be necessary if the parties cannot agree. Disputes and litigation can be avoided through the simple device of employing a surveyor to locate and monument the easement tract on the ground, whereupon a legal description can be prepared and included in the easement grant.

Once an easement has been placed in location or its location fixed by the easement grant, its location cannot be changed without the consent of the easement owner.

> **EXAMPLE:** Owner owns two lots. Lot 1 abuts on a highway. He sells Lot 2 to Buyer, simultaneously granting an easement of ingress and egress to the highway. The easement runs through the middle of Lot 1, rendering it unusable. Owner has no right to change the location of the easement. *Sedillo Title Gty. Inc.* v. *Wagner,* 457 P2d 361 (N.M. 1969).

But the easement can be relocated if both parties acquiesce, even without a written document.

> **EXAMPLE:** In the last example, suppose Owner and Buyer verbally agree on relocation. Owner blacktops a new driveway along the edge of Lot 1 and the old drive is torn up. The easement has been relocated by acquiescence. 80 ALR2d 743.

4.06(a)   Pipeline Easements

Most unlocated easements are pipeline easements. Pipelines extend over many miles of ground. The pipeline companies send out *right-of-way* crews to acquire the easements. Once a member of such a crew has determined the ownership of a farm, he whips out a simple form which the farmer and spouse sign. It gives the pipeline company an easement over the entire farm. This is perfectly valid. *Collins* v. *Slocum,* 284 So2d 98 (La. 1973).

A land developer who buys a farm for development cannot live with an unlocated easement. The developer should contact the pipeline company and purchase a release of the easement over all of the farm except the land through which the pipeline runs. If there is a mortgage on the pipeline, that is also released except as to the line of the pipe.

Once a pipeline has been installed in a pipeline easement, some courts hold that additional pipes or a larger pipe cannot be installed. *Winslow* v. *City of Vallejo,* 148 Cal. 723, 84 P 191 (1906). The far better rule is precisely to the contrary. *Standard Oil Co.* v. *Buchi,* 72 N.J.Eq. 492, 66 A 427 (1907), 17 Yale L. J. 200; *Weaver* v. *Natural Gas Pipeline Co.,* 27 Ill.2d 48, 188 NE2d 18 (1963). This problem should be covered in the grant.

4.07   Complex Easements

Today complex easements are employed in a number of situations.

NEW DIRECTIONS: It is almost commonplace today to find a single multi-story building divided into multiple ownerships. The lower portion, devoted, let us say, to office building use is owned by *A*. The upper portion, devoted to apartment purposes, is owned by *B*. *B* may even choose to divide his apartment area into condominium ownership so that each apartment is separately owned. Such, indeed, is the situation in the case of the John Hancock Building in Chicago. The structural members of the bottom building support the upper building. Elevator shafts serving the upper building travel through the lower building. Heating, ventilating, and air-conditioning ducts, as well as water and utilities, travel through both buildings. A very lengthy Easement and Operating Agreement is prepared. There are problems, to be sure, but they are all capable of solution.

4.08   Structure Easement—Easement through Structure

Where an easement is created in a *structure* without creating any interest in the land, ordinarily destruction of the structure destroys the easement.

EXAMPLE: Owner owned Lot 1 on which he erected a two-flat residence. When the city passed an ordinance requiring second-story apartments to have two exits, Owner acquired from Neighbor the right to make an opening into Neighbor's building, which was flush against Owner's building, and to use Neighbor's stairway as the second exit. Neighbor's building was destroyed by fire. The easement is extinguished. 154 ALR 82.

4.08(a)   Easement in Favor of Structure

If an easement is created *in favor of* a structure only, destruction of the structure terminates the easement.

EXAMPLE: *X* and *Y* were neighbors. Intending to build a stable for his riding horses, *X* purchased from *Y* *driveway rights* over *Y's* land to and from the *stable* to be erected on the rear of *X's* land. Ultimately the stable was destroyed by fire. The easement was gone. 2 Thompson, *Real Property* 764, 766 (perm. ed.).

4.09   Right to Profits of the Soil

An easement does not confer on the owner thereof any right to the profits of the soil, such as oil, hay, coal, or minerals.

EXAMPLE: County acquired a highway over Owner's land by condemnation. County has no right to drill oil wells on the land thus acquired, for it has only an easement for road purposes.

It is the landowner whose land is subject to the easement who has the right to oil, minerals, and other profits of the soil.

4.10   Use of Easement Premises—Dominant and Servient Tenements

An easement appurtenant can be used only for the benefit of the dominant tenement. It may not be used for the benefit of any other tract of land. The dominant
tenement is the land intended to be benefited *at the time the easement was created.*
Land acquired by the owner of the dominant tenement after the creation of the
easement has no right to the use of easement. It is nondominant land.

> **EXAMPLE:**   Owner owned Lot 2. There was an easement appurtenant in favor
> of Lot 2 to use a spur or switch track over Lot 1 to the west of Lot 2. Owner
> thereafter bought Lot 3, which adjoined Lot 2 to the east, and erected a power-
> house on Lot 3. It was held that the switch track could not be used to service
> the powerhouse since the switch track easement was appurtenant only to Lot
> 2. *Goodwillie Co.* v. *Commonwealth Co.,* 241 Ill. 42, 89 NE 272 (1909); *Ogle* v.
> *Trotter,* 495 SW2d 558 (Tenn. 1973); *College Inns.* v. *Cully,* 460 P2d 360 (Ore.
> 1969).

For a full discussion of this aspect of the law, see Kratovil, *Easement Law and
Service of Non-Dominant Tenements: Time for a Change,* 24 Santa Clara L. Rev. 649
(1984).

Particularly in the case of industrial easements, it is well to keep in mind at
the time easement is created that the dominant owner may later wish to acquire
other neighboring land for plant expansion. The easement grant should provide
that such subsequently acquired property shall enjoy the benefit of the easement.
For example, suppose that the dominant tenement happens to fall in Government Section 34, then let the easement grant provide as follows:

> **SUGGESTED FORM:**   Said easement is also appurtenant to any land in said
> Section 34 that may subsequently come into common ownership with said dom-
> inant tenement.

If the dominant tenement is divided, the easement runs in favor of each
part into which it is divided. 10 ALR3d 960.

> **EXAMPLE:**   Owner, owning the bed of a lake and the land surrounding the
> lake, sells Buyer a lot that does not have lake frontage. The deed includes an
> easement of access to the lake and a right to use the lake for recreation. Buyer
> sells half his lot to his brother, both parts abutting on the easement of access.
> Both Buyer and his brother can use the easements. There is some limit, not very
> clearly defined, on how far you can go with this. 10 ALR 3d 968. Suppose Buyer
> were to divide his lot into fifty lots. The courts might not permit use of the
> easements. This is an excessive *increase of burden. Crocker* v. *Advanced Sci-
> ence,* 268 A2d 844 (N.H. 1970).

Where an easement of ingress and egress is created by grant, it may be used
by the easement owner for all reasonable ingress and egress purposes, and use
is not restricted to such purposes as were reasonable at the date of the grant.

> **EXAMPLE:**   Use of the easement by automobiles will be permitted even though an easement was created when horse-drawn vehicles were in use. 3 ALR3d 1287.

With changing conditions more intensive use may be made of the easement than was contemplated at the time the easement was created.

> **EXAMPLE:**   At the time an easement of ingress and egress was created, the dominant tenement was occupied by a private dwelling. Later this dwelling was replaced by a hotel. It was held that the hotel could continue to use the easement. *White* v. *Grand Hotel* (1913) 1 Ch. 113.

However, where an easement is acquired by *prescription,* use of an easement after the prescriptive period has expired must remain pretty much the same as the use that took place during the prescriptive period.

If the width of an easement is fixed at the time of its creation, it will not grow wider even though conditions change.

> **EXAMPLE:**   In 1918 Owner granted Neighbor a ten-foot easement for ingress and egress. The fact that today's big trucks cannot use so narrow a way does not increase the size of the easement. *Feldstein* v. *Segall,* 198 Md. 285, 81 A2d 610 (1951).

On the other hand, if I grant you a ten-foot passage easement, I have no right to diminish it by placing pillars or other structures in the passageway. You have the right to use the full ten feet for passage. *Wurlitzer Co.* v. *State Bank,* 290 Ill. 72, 124 NE844 (1919).

If you have a driveway easement over my land, you can park to load and unload but cannot park overnight. 37 ALR2d 944. This does not mean, however, that the owner of an easement for ingress and egress has the *exclusive* right to use the surface of the land for that purpose. The landowner, since he remains the owner of the easement premises subject only to the prescribed rights of the easement owner, has the right to make any use of the easement tract that does not interfere with the easement. 52 ALR3d 9.

> **EXAMPLE:**   In the case of an easement of ingress and egress, the landowner may travel over the easement tract as long as he does not interfere with the easement owner's right of travel. The landowner, indeed, may even erect structures or run power lines above the easement, so long as he leaves space at the surface adequate for travel by the easement owner. *Sakansky* v. *Wein,* 86 N.H. 337, 169 Atl. 1 (1933); *Cleveland Railway Co.* v. *Public Service Co.,* 380 Ill. 130, 43 NE2d 993 (1942). Or a landowner may tunnel and mine minerals beneath an easement for ingress or egress or build over a water pipe easement.

Since an easement is a right to use another's land for a special purpose only, the easement owner must use the easement premises only for that purpose for which the easement exists.

> **EXAMPLE:**   Owner grants Neighbor an easement for ingress and egress over a part of Owner's land. Neighbor has no right to lay gas pipes in the easement premises. 3 ALR3d 1278.

4.11   Maintenance and Repair of Easement Facilities

The fact that Owner gives Neighbor an easement over Owner's property imposes no duty on Owner to pave the easement tract, keep it in repair, or do anything at all for Neighbor's benefit. 169 ALR 1152.

> **EXAMPLE:**   Owner gave Neighbor an easement to take water from a well on Owner's land. It was held that Owner was not obliged to operate the pump to furnish Neighbor's water even though that was the physical situation at the time the easement was created. *Gowing* v. *Lehmann,* 98 N.H. 414, 101 A2d 463 (1953).

Therefore if the parties agree that the owner of the burdened land is to have some affirmative duties, they must be spelled out in the easement grant.

Of course, the easement owner has the right to take all steps necessary to make this easement usable. For example, in an easement of ingress and egress the easement owner would have the right to repair or improve an existing road, to lay down a new road, to build bridges across streams, to trim encroaching trees and shrubs, to blast rocks, and otherwise to remove impediments, and so forth. 169 ALR 1147; 20 ALR3d 1026.

Also, where a private road is used by *both* the landowner and the easement owner, they must divide the cost of repairs in proportion to their use of the road, even though the easement agreement is silent on this score. *Stevens* v. *Bird-Jex Co.,* 81 Utah 355, 18 P2d 292 (1933).

If the easement tract is used only by the easement owner and falls into disrepair as a result of his neglect, he has no right to deviate from the prescribed way and travel over other land belonging to the landowner. *Dudgeon* v. *Bronson,* 159 Ind. 562, 64 NE 910 (1902). On the other hand, if the landowner obstructs the easement, the easement owner has the right to travel around the obstruction over other land belonging to the landowner.

4.12   Termination of Easement

Easements may be terminated in the following ways:

> 1. When an easement has been created for a particular purpose, it ceases when the purpose ceases.

> **EXAMPLE:**   A party wall agreement ceases when both buildings are destroyed by fire, unless the party wall agreement provides otherwise. An easement for railroad purposes ends when the railroad tears up its tracks and discontinues service. 95 ALR2d 482.

2. When the owner of an easement becomes the owner of the land that is subject to the easement, the easement is extinguished by *merger*.

3. The owner of an easement may release his right to the owner of the land that is subject to the easement.

4. The owner of an easement may terminate it by abandonment. There must be an intention to abandon the easement and acts manifesting such intention.

4.12(a)   Tax Sale

In some states a tax sale of the servient tenement extinguishes the easement. In others, it does not. 26 ALR2d 873. In many states, as in Illinois, the matter is governed by statutes that preserve the easement. See also *Arizona* R.C.I.A. *Lands Inc.,* v. *Arnsworth,* 515 P2d 335 (Ariz. App. 1973); *Fields* v. *District of Columbia,* 443 F2d 740 (D.C. Cir. 1971), citing Restatement of Property § 509 (2); 5 *Powell on Real Property* 225; Kratovil, *Tax Sales: Extinguishment of Easements, Building Restrictions and Covenants,* 19 Houst. L. Rev. 55 (1982).

4.13   Special Types of Easements

4.13(a) Streets

Easements vary, of course, as to their scope.

> **EXAMPLE:**   Owner grants Neighbor an easement for ingress and egress. This easement cannot be used for installation of water pipes or electric conduits.

However, whenever a city has an easement for street purposes, the courts give this a very broad interpretation. The adjoining owners own the land constituting the street. But the city's easement permits the use of the street for transportation of all kinds, including transportation of electricity (electric poles) or transportation of messages (telegraph poles). Kratovil, *Easement Draftsmanship and Conveyancing,* 38 Cal. L. Rev. 426. The city usually grants to utility companies the right to install these poles. This right is called a *franchise.* So far as cable television is concerned, the TV company would have to obtain a franchise from the city. But if it intends to fasten its cable to existing telegraph poles, it must also obtain a written agreement from the telegraph company.

In most, but not all, states, if a deed of land refers to an adjoining street or other way, it automatically creates an easement of access over the street or way if the grantor owns the land comprising the street or way. 46 ALR2d 461.

> **EXAMPLE:**   Owner owns Lot 1 in Block 1 in Chicago Heights and a strip of land east and adjoining known in the neighborhood as Holden Court. Holden Court is not a public street. He makes a deed to Buyer of part of Lot 1 described as "bounded on the east by Holden Court." This gives Buyer an easement right in Holden Court. This is sometimes called an *easement by estoppel.* 25 Am.Jur.2d 431. Obviously, this is a poor substitute for a properly planned easement grant.

4.13(b)   Scenic Easements

As the population continues to explode, concern grows for the preservation of open spaces, especially for scenic treasures that remain in private ownership and offer tempting sites to land developers. Under recent legislation and court decisions the state may condemn or purchase a scenic easement that, in effect, forbids the landowner to build upon his land. The Federal Highway Beautification Act offers incentives to the state to create such easements. *Markham Advertising Co.* v. *State,* 439 P2d 248 (Wash. 1968).

> **EXAMPLE:**   Owner owns a stretch of rolling farm land through which a lovely river winds, abutting a highway that commands an excellent view of the scene. The state condemns Owner's right to build upon his farm and pays him compensation for depriving him of this right. He may continue to occupy and farm the land, but it will never be built upon. This right acquired by the state is called a *scenic easement. Kamrowski* v. *State,* 31 Wis.2d 256, 142 NW2d 793 (1966). The state has acquired the farmer's "*development rights.*"

4.13(c)   Solar Easements

England has a doctrine called *ancient lights.*

> **EXAMPLE:**   Owner owns Lot 1 on which he has a house, which has been there for many years. Neighbor owns a vacant lot next door. In England, Neighbor would not be permitted to erect a high building on his lot that would cut off Owner's light.

In America, the situation is treated quite differently:

> **EXAMPLE:**   Take the facts of the previous case. In America, Neighbor can build any building that is permitted by local law even if it cuts off Owner's sunlight.

> **EXAMPLE:**   The Fountainbleu Hotel in Miami Beach added fourteen stories to its structure. This cast a shadow on the swimming pool of the nearby Eden Roc Hotel. The court held that the Eden Roc was without any legal remedy. *Fountainbleu Hotel Corp.* v. *Forty-Five Twenty-Five, Inc.,* 114 So2d 357 (Fla. 1959). See also *Blumberg* v. *Weiss,* 17 A2d 823 (N.J. 1941); 1 Am.Jur.2d *Adjoining Landowners* 753.

Of course, if an action is prompted by pure spite, the law will provide a remedy.

> **EXAMPLE:**   Owner owns a house, and Neighbor owns an adjoining vacant lot. They quarrel. Neighbor attempts to erect a wall for the sole purpose of blocking light and air from Owner's windows. The courts will stop this.

It goes without saying that the neighboring landowners are able to agree to the creation of such solar easements. See Kraemer, *Solar Law* (1978).

EXAMPLE: Owner owns a lot on which he proposes to build a solar home. He approaches Neighbor. For a money consideration Neighbor grants Owner an easement that limits the height of any building Neighbor may build so that Owner's solar energy will not be obstructed. The easement is recorded. It is binding on Neighbor and all subsequent owners of his lot.

The energy crisis of the 1970s and resultant attention that solar energy has attracted caused a legislative reaction toward the regulation of the creation of solar easements. While these laws vary from state to state, they frequently require that the description of the easement include the vertical and horizontal angles at which the solar easement extends over the servient tenement. See, for example, Cal. Civ. Code § 801.5; McKinney's N.Y. Real Prop. L. § 335.b.

Also height restrictions ordinances are valid in proper cases.

EXAMPLE: *Village* zones an area for single-family dwellings and imposes reasonable height, side-line, and front-line restrictions, such that any lot owner can safely build a house utilizing solar energy. The ordinance is valid.

Also among the laws being enacted are solar zoning ordinances. These ordinances create a zoning envelope. This is a cube of space in which a building may be erected on a lot in such a manner that the land adjoining to the south cannot be improved by a building that obstructs sunlight to the southern exposure of the building roof, where solar panels will be erected. 2 Solar Law Rep. 263 (1980).

In New Mexico a statute has been enacted that gives a solar user the right to prohibit the blockage of his solar access. Minan and Lawrence, *Legal Use of Solar Energy,* 30. Thus the first landowner to use collectors is given the right to prevent erection of others that cast shade upon them. California and Colorado both declare void any contract or covenant that prohibits the installation of a solar energy system. Minan and Lawrence, 39. Model ordinances have been drafted that protect the use of solar access. Minan and Lawrence, *supra* 51. A form of a solar access easement has been drafted. Kraemer, *Solar Law* 45. Solar zoning already exists. Kraemer, *supra,* 73.

It has been held that the owner of a solar-heated building can sue to prevent construction of a building on neighboring land that would place his solar collectors in the shade. *Prah* v. *Maretti,* 108 Wis.2d 223, 321 NW2d 182 (1982). The facts of the case suggest that the neighbor may have acted maliciously or unreasonably, in which case the rule would be like the one that bars erection of a spite fence. At all events the court held that the part creating the shade would be a nuisance. In Georgia, a statute creates an implied easement for solar access where the owner of a home and adjoining vacant lot sells the house, saying nothing about the access to sunlight. *Goddard* v. *Irby,* 255 Ga. 47, 335 SE2d 286 (1985).

4.13(d)   Conservation Easements

A number of state laws provide for the grant and donation by a landowner to some public body of a conservation easement over his land. Ill. Rev. Stat. Ch. 30, § 401. These conservation easements maintain the undeveloped state of the land to protect wildlife and natural resources. 12 Willamette L. J. 124. The landowners, after granting the easement, can continue to farm. *Ibid.* At times the statute, as in Illinois, contains a laundry list of uses that can be prohibited, e.g., dumping, removal of trees, erection of signs, etc. Or it may limit use of the land solely for nature trails or farming.

Such a donation may reduce the local tax assessment, reducing the real estate taxes.

It is evident that the conservation easement closely resembles the scenic easement. The scenic easement seems to have more frequently been acquired by purchase or condemnation. The conservation easement has often been donated, with the tax advantages in mind.

At times the two concepts are lumped together and termed "Acquisition of Development Rights," 75 Harv. L. Rev. 1635; 23 U. of Miami L. Rev. 351. Or it may be called an "Open Space Easement." 16 Santa Clara L. Rev. 359.

All these devices are means of preserving open space for public benefit.

As is also evident, the preservation of open space has become an important goal of our time. Other methods are available, for example, coastal zoning, zoning land for agricultural purposes, and large-lot zoning. Use of the planned unit development is another method. Control of wetland development is still another method.

The preparation of a conservation easement requires skill and care. 71 Ill. B. J. 430 (1983). Both state law and federal law must be complied with. The title must be searched because foreclosure of a prior mortgage will extinguish the easement. Other state law aspects, the Marketable Title Acts, for example, also must be considered.

A special type of conservation easement is a facade easement. It is a gift by the landowner to a public body or nonprofit corporation of the right to prevent any change in the outward appearance of a historic building.

REFERENCE: More than 44 states have adopted conservation easement statutes. 73 Ky. L. J. 255, 258.

CHAPTER 5

Land Descriptions

5.01 Legal Descriptions

Every deed, mortgage, or lease contains a description of the land involved. The purpose of such a description, obviously, is to fix the boundaries of the land intended to be sold, mortgaged, or leased. The description delineates a specific piece of land and cannot apply to any other. A street address is adequate for the purpose of guiding guests to your home or for mail delivery, but greater precision is needed to fix the exact point where your land ends and where your neighbor's begins. Hence, we have the legal description. Whenever you read a legal description, keep in mind that before the description had been written, some person, probably a land surveyor, went out and located the boundaries of the tract. He then put into words directions for locating the lines he had traced on the land. These written directions are called a legal description of the land. Various methods have been devised for describing tracts of land.

5.02 Surveys

In connection with any purchaser or mortgage of land it is a common practice to have the land surveyed. The survey serves a variety of purposes. It identifies on the ground the boundaries of the tract of land. This tells us, for example, whether the land has access to a street. Owners frequently build on a lot adjoining the land they own. Another disaster. It is important to determine if the building encroaches on a neighbor's land or if neighboring buildings encroach on the owner's land. We must know if the buildings encroach on adjoining streets or alleys. Basement stores and parking space often intrude into adjoining streets. This requires examination of the city permit given for this purpose. A building may violate setback lines established by city ordinances or private building restrictions. If the building is not plumb, it may extend into neighboring air space.

There may be subsurface problems with electric cables, drainage pipes, etc., unlawfully crossing the property. Neighboring doors or gates may open over the land. A telephone line may cross the land, necessitating relocation before building can begin.

Lawyers, title companies, Federal National Mortgage Association (FNMA). Federal Housing Authority (FHA). Federal Home Loan Mortgage Corporation (FHLMC), and others may have requirements concerning the survey. The survey should be prepared by a surveyor acceptable to the parties to the transaction and be accompanied by the survey reports that may be required by these institutions.

5.03   Metes and Bounds Descriptions

Metes are measures of length, such as inches, feet, yards, and rods. *Bounds* are boundaries, both natural and artificial, such as streams or streets. In a *metes and bounds description,* the surveyor takes you by the hand, as it were, and leads you over the land. He starts at a well-marked point of beginning and follows the boundaries of the land until he returns once more to the starting point. Landmarks called *monuments* often mark the several corners of the tract. A monument may be a natural monument, such as tree or river, or an artificial monument, such as a fence, stake, wall, road, or railroad.

> **EXAMPLE:**   A tract of land in Chicago, Cook County, Illinois, is described as follows, to wit: Beginning at a point in the east line of Mason Street one hundred feet north of the north line of Washington Street; running thence east on a line parallel to the north line of Washington Street 125 feet to the west line of an alley; thence north along the west line of said alley, twenty-five feet; thence west on a line parallel to the north line of Washington Street, 125 feet to the east line of Mason Street; thence south along the east line of Mason Street, twenty-five feet to the place of beginning.

The earliest descriptions in history were metes and bounds descriptions. All property in the thirteen original colonies of the United States was originally described by metes and bounds, the descriptions usually running from the mouth of a stream, or from a tree or a stump.

5.04   The Government Survey

By the treaty with England at the end of the Revolutionary War, the United States became the owner of the vast Northwest Territory, consisting of the present states of Illinois, Indiana, Ohio, Michigan, and Wisconsin. The end of the war found the United States heavily burdened with debts incurred during the war. It was decided that the new land should be sold and the proceeds used to retire the national debt. However, in selling the land to settlers, metes and bounds descriptions could not be used, for the new land was an untrodden wilderness. Hence some new system of describing land was needed. The system so devised was the rectangular system of land surveys, known as the Government Survey. Under this system, whenever a district, such as part of a state, was ready for private ownership, the government arranged for a survey of the land to be made. To begin a survey of this character, it is necessary to have some substantial landmark from which a start may be made. A place that can readily be referred to, such as the mouth of a river, is usually selected. From such a point, a line is run due north to the margin of the district to be surveyed. This first north and south line is called a *prime meridian,* or *principal meridian.* Some principal meridians have been numbered, such as the First Principal Meridian, which runs north from the mouth of the Great Miami River on the boundary between Ohio and Indiana and which governs the surveys of public lands in Ohio. Others have been named, as the Tallahassee Meridian, the Mount Diablo Meridian, the Humboldt Meridian, and the San Bernardino Meridian.

An east and west line is run intersecting the principal meridians at some prominent point. This line is called the *base line.* Both north and south of the base line, additional east and west lines are run at intervals of twenty-four miles.

Since it is the object of the survey to create a huge checkerboard of identical squares covering the entire tract to be surveyed, it is plain that many north and south lines are needed. Owing to the curvature of the earth's surface, however, all true north and south lines converge as they approach the North Pole. This is obvious, since no matter how far apart two north and south lines are at the equator, they must meet at the North Pole. Hence if continuous north and south lines were to be used in the survey, it is clear that because of the convergence of the north and south lines the tracts thus formed would grow narrower and narrower as the surveyors worked north. Although this imperfection cannot be altogether eliminated, it can be minimized in the following manner: Along the base line, both east and west of the principal meridian, and at intervals of twenty-four miles, lines running due north are run. These are called *guide meridians.* But they are run only as far north as the next *correction line,* i.e., a distance of twenty-four miles. Then new intervals of twenty-four miles are measured off along this correction line, and a new series of guide meridians based on these new intervals is run for another twenty-four miles. This process is repeated until the boundaries of the tract are reached. Similar guide meridians are run based on the correction lines lying south of the base line.

Thus the district surveyed is divided into tracts approximately twenty-four miles square. These tracts are further divided into parts six miles on each side. These smaller parts are called *townships.*

Each row, or tier, of townships running north and south is called a *range.* The first row east of the principal meridian is referred to as *Range 1 East* of that meridian. Thus the first row of townships east of the Third Principal Meridian is referred to as *Range 1 East of the Third Principal Meridian.* The row of townships next adjoining to the east is called *Range 2 East of the Third Principal Meridian,* and so on. Each row or tier of townships running east and west is identified by the number of townships intervening between it and the base line. Thus, a township in the first row north of the base line is called *Township 1 North.* The township next adjoining to the north is called *Township 2 North,* and so on. To identify a township completely, both the range number and the township number must be given, as *Township 40 North, Range 13, East of the Third Principal Meridian.* The township thus identified is in the fortieth row north of the base line and in the thirteenth row east of the Third Principal Meridian. Such a description is often abbreviated, and becomes *T. 40 N., R. 13 E. of the 3d P.M.*

Each township is divided into thirty-six tracts, each approximately one mile square. These tracts are called *sections*. The sections in a township are numbered from one to thirty-six, always commencing with the section in the northeast corner of the township. Sections are often divided into quarters, and these quarters are also often divided into quarters.

The government system of rectangular surveys has been employed in surveying the lands of the states of Alabama, Florida, Mississippi, and all of the states north of the Ohio River and west of the Mississippi River, except Texas.

Local surveys, which in some respects resemble the Government Survey, will occasionally be encountered in the other states.

5.05   Plats

Large tracts of land are often subdivided into building lots. Thereafter each building lot is conveyed by its lot number.

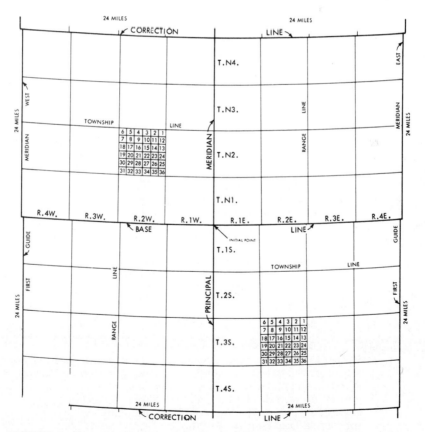

FIGURE 1. Correction Lines and Guide Meridians with Division of Townships into Sections

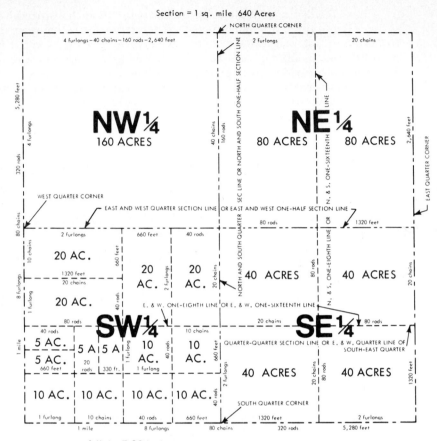

FIGURE 2. Section of Land Divided into Quarters and Showing Acreage and Distances

- 1 link—7.92 inches
- 1 rod—16½ feet
- 1 chain—4 rods or 66 feet or 100 links
- 1 furlong—660 feet or 40 rods
- 1 mile—8 furlongs or 320 rods or 80 chains or 5,280 feet
- 1 sq. rod—272¼ sq. feet or 30¼ sq. yards
- 1 acre—43,560 sq. feet or 160 sq. rods
- 1 acre is about 208¾ feet square
- 1 acre is 8 rods x 20 rods (or any two numbers of rods whose product is 160)
- 1 section—1 square mile or 640 acres

EXAMPLE: Developer believing that the tract is ripe for subdivision, buys the Northeast Quarter of the Northeast Quarter of Section 7, Township 40 North, Range 13 East of the Third Principal Meridian, in Cook County, Illinois. He hires a surveyor, who divides the tract into *blocks,* separated by streets. Each block is divided into *lots.* The lots and blocks are numbered, and the streets and the subdivision are named. For this particular subdivision, Developer selects the name ''Highwood.'' The surveyor prepares a map, called a *plat,* showing the lots and blocks, their dimensions and numbers, the width and names of the streets, the location of the quarter-section lines, and other similar information. After receiving the approval of local officials, the plat is filed or recorded in the office where deeds and mortgages are recorded. A description of a lot in this subdivision will read somewhat as follows: Lot 2 in block 5 in Highwood, a subdivision of the Northeast Quarter of the Northeast Quarter of Section 7, Township 40 North, Range 13 East of the Third Principal Meridian in Cook County, Illinois.

5.06   Description by Popular Name

Descriptions by the popular name of the tract have been held sufficient, as where a deed conveys "The Old Merchant Farm." *Hayes* v. *O'Brien*, 37 NE 73 (Ill. 1894).

5.07   General Description

A deed sometimes contains no definite description, but merely purports to convey all land owned by the grantor in a certain district, as "all the land owned by the grantor in Cook County, Illinois." Such descriptions, sometimes called *Mother Hubbard clauses,* are sufficient to pass title from the grantor to the grantee, but they may not be sufficient to impart constructive notice to third parties who do not have actual notice of the deed. *Luther* v. *Evans*, 576 P2d 1064 (Kans. 1978). To overcome this potential problem, the grantee may record an affidavit that specifically describes the property intended to be conveyed.

5.08   Street Address

A description by street address alone should never be used in a deed or mortgage. Since the proper legal description is not always available when a contract for the sale of land is being drafted, descriptions by street address will be found in contracts.

A danger sometimes present in street address descriptions is revealed by the following illustration.

> **EXAMPLE:**   Landlord leased to Tenant "certain premises known as 10 East Chicago Avenue, Chicago, Illinois." The building in question bore this address. It was a restaurant. Landlord owned a vacant lot adjoining, which patrons of the restaurant sometimes used as a parking area, although it was not a regular parking lot. It was held that a lease by street number includes only the lot on which the building is situated. *Killian* v. *Welfare Engineering Co.,* 66 NE2d 305 (Ill. 1946).

5.09   Area

Land may be described by its area, as the "North one acre of the Southeast Quarter of Section 1, Township 44 North, Range 2 East of the Third Principal Meridian, Lake County, Illinois."

5.10   Adjoining Owners

Lands are also described by reference to adjoining lands.

> **EXAMPLE:** A deed described the land as follows: "Bounded on the east by a fifty-acre tract of land owned by G. B. Turner purchased by him from N. W. Rodden; bounded on the north by the right of way of the Texas and Pacific R. R.; and on the west by a fifty-acre tract owned by the said G. B. Turner and known as the J. F. Neal tract of land; bounded on the south by the Katie Moore Boham tract of land." *Cox v. Campbell,* 143 SW2d 361 (Tex. 1940).

5.11   Foreign Grant

Portions of this country were once owned by France, Holland, Mexico, and Spain. In fact, the titles to some of the most valuable lands on Manhattan Island are based upon Dutch grants. Hence descriptions employing foreign units of land measure, such as the *vara* and the *arpent,* are often encountered.

5.12   Indefinite Description

A deed, mortgage, or other document must describe the land conveyed in a way that it can be located and identified.

> **EXAMPLE:** A deed was made of the "southeast half" of a certain section. This deed was held void for uncertainty in the description. *Pry v. Pry,* 109 Ill. 466 (1884).

It is often difficult to determine whether a description is good or bad.

> **EXAMPLE:** A deed was made to "one acre of land in the northwest corner of Block 20" in a certain subdivision. This deed was held good, because a surveyor could go to the northwest corner of the block and measure out a sufficient distance west and south to include one acre of land. *Richey v. Sinclair,* 47 NE 364 (Ill. 1897).

A deed of "my house and lot" is not considered indefinite. Oral evidence can be introduced in court to show what tract of land was intended. *Brenneman v. Dillon,* 129 NE 564 (Ill. 1920).

When a deed description is too indefinite to identify the land, but the grantee, by consent of the grantor, takes possession of premises that are within the general terms of the description and erects permanent improvements on them, the defect in the description is thereby cured.

> **EXAMPLE:** Owner made a deed to a railroad of "a strip of land one hundred feet in width over the Northeast Quarter of Section 12, Township 14 North, Range 2 East of the Third Principal Meridian." The railroad, with Owner's consent, actually occupied a strip of land one hundred feet in width and erected

railroad tracks thereon. The description, though originally too indefinite, became sufficient by occupation.

The rule that possession cures an indefinite description is also applicable to leases and to contracts of sale.

5.13 Description Containing Omissions

A deed, mortgage, or other document is valid, even though part of the description is omitted, if enough remains to identify the land conveyed.

> **EXAMPLE:** A deed to land described as being in Santa Cruz County, California, failed to name the meridian from which the township and range were numbered. This did not invalidate the deed, since all descriptions of land in that county are numbered from the Mt. Diablo Meridian. *Harrington* v. *Goldsmith*, 68 Pac. 594 (Cal. 1902).

5.14 Correction of Deed Description by Court Order

When an error occurs in the land description in a deed and the seller refuses to give a new deed to correct the error, a court order can usually be obtained correcting the erroneous description. This is known as *reformation* of an instrument. And if in the meantime the grantee has been in possession of the land, probably no great harm will result from the error. If, however, the grantee has not gone into possession, as where the land is vacant, third persons, such as judgment creditors of the grantor, may acquire rights in the land superior to those of the grantee. See 4 *American Law of Property* § 1723.

5.15 Streets or Highways as Boundaries

As previously pointed out, a city often does not own the land comprising its roads, streets, or alleys, but only has an easement thereover for street purposes. When a deed or mortgage is made of land abutting on such a road, street, or alley the land sold or mortgaged generally runs to the center of such road, street, or alley. 49 ALR2d 982.

> **EXAMPLE:** Seller gives Buyer a deed selling and conveying that part of a certain section of land "lying south of Dundee Road." By this deed, Buyer acquires all land in that particular section lying south of the *center* of Dundee Road.

The reason for this rule is obvious. The seller, having parted with ownership of his land, would have no use for the strip of road adjoining thereto. Hence it is presumed that he intended half of the adjoining road to pass to the buyer with the land sold.

When a street is used as a boundary, keep in mind that legally the street usually includes much more than the paved roadway over which cars travel. It often includes the sidewalk, the planted area known as the *parkway,* and may even include a narrow strip of land on the house side of the sidewalk. Check the recorded subdivision plat to locate the true street line.

5.16   Waters as Boundaries

If Seller owns land through which a stream flows and his ownership includes the stream bed, a deed, mortgage, or lease of land "lying south of Plum Creek" will, under a rule analogous to the highway rule, include the south half of the creek. 78 ALR3d 604.

5.17   Parts of Lots

Care should be exercised in drafting descriptions of parts of lots.

> **EXAMPLE:**   A subdivision plat indicates that Lot 2 in Block 3 is eighty feet wide. Owner gives Buyer a deed to the "east forty feet of Lot 2." When Owner sells the remainder of the lot, his description thereof should be "Lot 2, except the east forty feet thereof," and not "the west forty feet of Lot 2." The reason is obvious. Suppose Lot 2 is actually slightly more that eighty feet in width, as it well may be, for land measurements are not perfectly accurate. Deeds of the east forty feet and the west forty feet of the lot would leave a small strip of land in the middle of the lot still owned by Owner.

When the lot is not a perfect square or rectangle, use of descriptions such as the "east half" or "north half" of the lot should be avoided, since the word "half" usually is considered to mean half by area, and the boundary line will be located with an equal number of square feet on either side thereof. This may result in an unequal division of the frontage of the lot.

A deed of a part of a lot that abuts on a diagonal street should use descriptions like the "northwesterly thirty feet" rather than the "north thirty feet," since, if the diagonal street runs in a true northwesterly or northeasterly direction, it is difficult to determine which side of the lot is the "north" side. Cases will be found where two of the boundary lines may lay equal claim to being the "north" line of the lot.

5.18   Buildings

Since buildings are usually fixtures and, as such, are part of the land, a deed of the land will automatically give the buyer the buildings thereon. They need not be mentioned in the deed.

5.19 Tax Bills

Tax bills contain abbreviated, vague, and unsatisfactory descriptions of the land. They should never be used in drafting a deed, contract, or lease. Some states, however, require that the assessor's parcel number or taxpayer's identifying number be reflected on the face of the deed in addition to the legal description.

CHAPTER 6

Land Titles and Interests in Land

6.01 Estates in Land

Just as land may be divided into layers by a sale of "air rights" thereover or minerals thereunder, so the ownership of land may be divided into various types of interests. The highest type of interest, of course, is complete ownership.

> **EXAMPLE:** *A* owns a tract of land. No one else has any interest whatever in the land. He is said to be the owner in *fee simple*. This is merely a technical phrase connoting ownership of the land. When one hears it said that "*A* has title" to a particular tract of land, it is understood that *A* is the *fee owner*, he owns the land *in fee* or *in fee simple,* or has an estate *in fee simple absolute*. All these are different ways of expressing the idea that *A* owns the land, that his ownership is of unlimited duration, and that so long as he obeys the law, he may do as he chooses with the land, and, on his death, it will go to his heirs, or, if he leaves a will, to the persons named in his will. Lawyers speak of interests in land as *estates*.

Suppose, however, that *A*, being the owner in fee simple of a tract of land, executes a ten-year lease thereof to *B*. Now *A* has parted with a portion of his rights. He has for ten years given up his right to occupy the land and, in return, has received *B's* promise to pay rent for those ten years. *B* has acquired the right to occupy the land in accordance with the provisions of his lease, but has not, of course, become the owner in fee simple. He has merely acquired a *leasehold estate* or *term for years* in the land. A leasehold estate, even where the lease is for many years, is, for most purposes, legally considered to be personal property of the lessee. *Chicago* v. *University of Chicago*, 134 NE 723 (Ill. 1922) (lease for 1,000 years).

> **EXAMPLE:** Landlord makes a lease to Tenant. Tenant assigns the lease to Assignee. Tenant's wife need not join in the assignment because dower rights do not exist in personal property.

For some purposes a lease is said to be a *chattel real*. That is, it has some of the attributes of real property. Thus, a lease is entitled to be recorded in the real estates records, like a deed or mortgage of land. *Lincoln National Bank & Tr. Co.* v. *Nathan,* 19 NE2d 243 (Ind. 1939). The same would be true of a mortgage of the leasehold estate. A leasehold estate can be partitioned in the same manner as real estate. *Pierce* v. *Pierce,* 123 NE2d 511 (Ill. 1954).

The word *estate* is used to express the degree, quantity, nature, duration, or extent of an interest in land. Complete ownership is an *estate in fee simple,* but there are many other estates, such as *life estates* and *leasehold estates.* Each differs from the others with respect to the rights and duties of the owner of the estate in question.

6.02   Divisions of Land Ownership

As can be seen from this and other chapters, ownership of land can be divided according to time (as in the case of a landlord giving a ten-year lease), or divided vertically (as in the case where a railroad deeds air space to a developer), or divided according to the substance in the land (as in the case of a farmer giving a deed to a coal company of the coal beneath the farmland), or divided among co-owners (as where a husband and wife buy property as joint tenants).

6.03   Life Estates

The owner of the life estate can use and enjoy the land only during his lifetime.

> **EXAMPLE:**   Landowner dies leaving a will giving land to Widow for her life, and, at her death, to their children, C and D. Widow thus acquires a *life estate* in the land and becomes a *life tenant.* She is entitled to the reasonable and necessary use of the land for her lifetime, but she must not do anything that will in any way injure the permanent value of the property. She may collect and use the rents of the land, but must keep the property in repair and must pay the real estate taxes and the interest on the mortgage. She must not drill any new oil wells or open new mines, but may take oil or minerals from existing wells and mines. On her death, all her rights in the land will cease.

Life estates may be created by will or deed. Often, to save the expense of probating his will after his death, a father while still living will give a deed of his land to his son or daughter, and in the deed will reserve to himself a life estate.

Certain special kinds of life estates are created by law, rather than by will or deed, such as dower, curtesy, and homestead.

6.04   Trusts

A *trust* is an equitable obligation, binding a *trustee* to deal with the *trust property* or *trust estate* for the benefit of the *beneficiaries,* any of whom may enforce the trustee's obligations. There are various kinds of trusts.

EXAMPLE: Landowner dies leaving a will by which he gives all his property to Trustee, in trust, with power to sell the property and make investments, the income of the trust to be payable to Widow during her lifetime, and on her death the trust property to be distributed among Landowner's children then living. Since this trust was created by Landowner's last will and testament, it is known as a *testamentary trust.*

EXAMPLE: Landowner signs a deed conveying his land to Trustee, in trust, with power to sell the property and make investments, the income of the trust to be payable to Landowner during his lifetime, and after Landowner's death to Widow during her lifetime, and on her death the property to be distributed among Landowner's children then living. Since this trust becomes effective during Landowner's lifetime, it is known as a *living trust.*

EXAMPLE: Buyer plans to acquire a tract of land. However, he wishes to conceal his ownership of the property. He also wishes to prevent his wife and his judgment creditors from acquiring any interest in the land. On purchasing the land, Buyer directs Seller to convey the land to Trustee. The deed gives Trustee full power to sell and mortgage the land, but does not mention Buyer's name. The deed is filed for record. The deed to Trustee and also a separate unrecorded agreement signed by Buyer and Trustee recites that all title to the land is vested in Trustee and that the beneficiary's (that is, Buyer's) interest is only personal property. However, in the unrecorded agreement Trustee agrees that he will deal with the land only when directed so to do by Buyer. Buyer has accomplished his purpose. The public records do not disclose his ownership of the land. Since the trust specifically provides that Buyer's interest is only personal property, no dower rights attach, and judgments against Buyer are not liens on the land. *C.T. & T. Co.* v. *Mercantile Tr. and Sav. Bank,* 20 NE2d 992 (Ill. 1939). This is called a *land trust.*

The land trust is recognized and valid in Florida, Illinois, Indiana, North Dakota, and Virginia.

REFERENCES: Kenoe, *Land Trust Practice* (1974); Garrett, *Land Trusts,* 1955 Law Forum 655; Comment, 14 Kans. L. Rev. 97 (1965); Note, 18 U. Miami L. Rev. 699 (1964); Note, 45, N. D. L. Rev. 77 (1968).

6.05   Cemetery Lots

When a cemetery corporation sells a lot, or burial site, the purchaser does not become the absolute owner of the lot. The deed gives him merely an easement right of burial. *Steele* v. *Rosehill Cemetery Co.,* 19 NE2d 189 (Ill. 1939); 109 U. of Pa. L. Rev. 378 (1961). He also has the right to enter the cemetery to care for the graves, subject to the reasonable regulations adopted by the cemetery company as to visiting hours, monuments, grave decorations, and so on. Like any other easement, the easement of the burial may be lost by abandonment. *Trustees of First Presbyterian Church* v. *Alling,* 54 N. J. S. 141, 148 A2d 510 (N. J. 1959).

6.06   Modes of Acquiring Ownership of Land

While title to or ownership of land is most often acquired by deed, by will, or by descent, there are other modes of acquiring title to land, among them, condemnation and adverse possession.

6.06(a)   Condemnation

When land is needed for some public use, it can be acquired by the exercise of the power of eminent domain. The power of eminent domain is exercised; (1) by the United States, the state in which the land lies, cities, villages, school boards, and other public bodies; (2) by quasi-public corporations, such as railroads and public utility corporations; (3) in some states, private individuals have the right of eminent domain in limited instances as, for example, when they are land-locked. The power is subject to two conditions: The use to which the property is to be devoted must be a public one, and just compensation must be paid.

Exercise of the power of eminent domain involves a condemnation proceeding, which is usually a court proceeding initiated by the city or other public body desiring to acquire title. The just compensation to which the landowner is entitled is the fair market value of the land at the time of the taking of the land. This value is often determined by a jury.

By condemnation, the condemnor acquires either an easement or fee simple title, although federal legislation now permits the United States to acquire by condemnation the right to occupy the land for a term of years only if that is what is desired. If an easement will serve the purpose for which the land is to be acquired, the condemnor, under many laws, acquires only an easement.

> **EXAMPLE:**   As a rule, an easement only is acquired by a railroad condemning for a right of way, a city condemning for a street, a telephone company condemning for a telephone line, or a drainage district condemning for a drainage ditch. In such cases, even though the landowner receives the full market value of the land condemned, he retains the ownership of the land so condemned. The point is of importance, since if an easement for street or right of way purposes acquired by condemnation is later abandoned, the original landowner still retains his ownership free and clear of the easement. *Bell* v. *Mattoon Waterworks & Res. Co.,* 92 NE 352 (Ill. 1910).

In many cases, however, it is necessary that fee simple title be acquired, as when land is condemned for a courthouse site. Many states, therefore—Illinois, Kansas, Kentucky, Massachusetts, Michigan, Minnesota, Ohio, Pennsylvania, Texas, Virginia, and Wyoming, for example—permit the condemnor to acquire fee simple title by condemnation.

6.06(b)   Adverse Possession

Often the public records will show a complete and perfect succession of perfect deeds from the government down to John Smith. This is known as the *record title* or *paper title*. Yet the true ownership of the land may be outstanding in someone who holds possession of the land without a single document to show his ownership. The ownership here referred to is that acquired by taking possession of the land and staying in possession for a certain number of years fixed by the law. At the end of that period, which varies from state to state, the party in possession has ownership of the land even though the land was not conveyed to him, he entered the land without any right whatever to do so, and he has not placed any instrument in the public records to show his ownership.

The law providing for the acquiring of title to land by going into possession was passed for two reasons: (1) it furthers the public policy which encourages the use of land; and (2) ownership of real estate often depends on transactions that occurred so long ago that the witnesses who were familiar with the transaction are dead or have forgotten the facts.

Not every possession of land will ripen into ownership. For this to occur the possession must be legally *adverse;* that is, the possession must be *actual, hostile, notorious, exclusive, continuous,* and *under claim of right.*

For possession to be adverse, it must be actual. As the judges put it, the occupant must unfurl his flag on the land and keep it flying so that the owner may see, if he wishes, that an enemy has invaded his domain and planted the standard of conquest. In other words, the occupant must do something that will make the owner notice that a stranger has occupied his land. This does not mean, however, that the occupant must live or reside on the land.

> **EXAMPLE:**   *A* fences and farms some vacant land adjoining his farm in Illinois. This continues for twenty years. He now owns this adjoining land by reason of his adverse possession.

This rule is of importance in boundary disputes, since if a landowner erects a fence on what he claims is the boundary of his land and claims all the land to the fence, his possession will eventually ripen into ownership even though the fence is actually over on his neighbor's land. The same is true when a building encroaches over and upon adjoining land.

Usually possession is not *hostile* when the person in possession occupies a relation of trust and confidence toward the holder of the paper title.

> **EXAMPLE:**   A father's possession is not hostile to the child, the possession of a husband is not hostile to the wife, and the possession of an agent is not hostile to his employer.

The requirement that possession be *notorious* merely means that the possession of the occupant must be such that the real owner would be likely to notice it.

Adverse possession, in order to ripen into title, must be *continuous.* However, seasonal possession is often sufficient, for the possession need only be such as is usual with respect to land of similar character. For example, it is sufficient if farmland is farmed in the farming season, timberland logged in the logging season, and so on.

> **EXAMPLE:** *A* occupied *B's* hunting shack each year during the hunting season. Ultimately, *A* acquired good title by adverse possession. *Kraus* v. *Mueller*, 12 Wis.2d 430, 107 NW2d 467.

For a person to acquire title by adverse possession he must claim that he is the owner of the land, but it is enough if his acts and conduct indicate that he claims to be the owner of the land.

> **EXAMPLE:** *A* and *B* owned adjoining lots, *A* owning lot 9 and *B* owning Lot 8. *A* built a frame cottage on Lot 9, but the same extended two feet over on Lot 8. He thought the house was entirely on his own lot and never made any oral claim to this two-foot strip. He paid taxes on Lot 9 and *B* the taxes on Lot 8. After twenty years, a survey was made which disclosed the encroachment. Although *A* had made no oral claim to the two-foot strip, his acts, namely, erecting a building on this strip, showed that he claimed title to the strip. He therefore had acquired title by adverse possession. *Cassidy* v. *Lenahan*, 128 NE 544 (Ill. 1920).

As is evident, adverse possession resembles prescription in the law of easements. However, adverse occupancy often, at the *surface* of the ground, ripens into ownership by adverse possession. Adverse *use* ripens into a prescriptive easement. The utility of this distinction is reasonably obvious.

> **EXAMPLE:** *A* and *B* own adjoining lots 7 and 8. Both lots have a home on them. *A's* home is so constructed that the eaves extend over *B's* lot. When *A's* home is demolished, it would be absurd to hold that *A's* prescriptive easement runs in favor of any new home. How in the world would the air space formerly occupied by the eaves be located? A simple solution is to hold that when a prescriptive easement is created, it runs in favor of the house. When the house is gone, the easement is gone.

CHAPTER 7

Deeds

7.01 Defined

A deed is a written instrument by which a landowner transfers the ownership of his land.

7.02 Types of Deeds

The deeds commonly used in the United States are *quitclaim deeds, warranty deeds,* and *deeds of bargain and sale.*

7.02(a) Quitclaim Deed

A quitclaim deed purports to convey only the grantor's *present interest in the land,* if any, rather than the land itself. Since such a deed purports to convey whatever interest the grantor has at the time, its use excludes any implication that he has good title, or any title at all. Such a deed in no way obligates the grantor. If he has no interest, none will be conveyed. If he acquires an interest after executing the deed, he retains such interest. If, however, the grantor in such deed has complete ownership at the time of executing the deed, the deed is sufficient to pass such ownership to the grantee.

A seller who knows that his title is bad or who does not know whether his title is good or bad usually uses a quitclaim deed in conveying.

7.02(b) Warranty Deed

A warranty deed (sometimes called a *general warranty deed*) contains certain assurances or guarantees by the grantor that the deed conveys a good and unencumbered title. Such guarantees are called *covenants of title*. While these covenants differ somewhat in their scope, depending on the local practice, the covenants usually warrant:

1. That the grantor has good title to the land conveyed. This is called the *covenant of seizin.*
2. That there are no encumbrances on the land except as stated in the deed. This is called the *covenant against encumbrances.*
3. That the grantee, or his grantees, will not be evicted or disturbed by a person having a better title or lien. This is called the *covenant for quiet enjoyment.*

If the grantee suffers a loss because the title is not good as covenanted, he may sue the grantor for damages.

If any encumbrances exist that are not mentioned in the deed, the covenant against encumbrances is violated. An encumbrance, within the meaning of this covenant, includes any lien, such as a mortgage, tax lien, or judgment lien; an easement; a restriction on the use of the land; or an outstanding dower right. The grantor's liability on this covenant is not affected by the fact that the grantee knew of the encumbrance. 64 ALR 1479. If the grantor wishes to escape liability on this covenant, a "subject to" clause must be inserted to qualify the language of the deed. In this way the deed covenants will not be breached by the existence of a particularly described mortgage, restriction, or other encumbrance. Sometimes the "subject to" clause is drafted without a great degree of specificity, such as when the conveyance is subject to "restrictions of record." Obviously, grantees should be reluctant to accept such general limitations on the covenants of warranty.

It is still customary in many localities to set out in full in the warranty deed the various covenants of title. However, in many states, laws exist under which the usual covenants of title are implied from the use of certain specified words. When these particular words are used, the deed must be read as though the usual covenants of title were set out in full therein. In Alaska, Illinois, Kansas, Michigan, Minnesota, and Wisconsin, the words *convey* and *warrant* make a deed a general warranty deed. The same result is achieved in Pennsylvania, Vermont, Virginia, and West Virginia by use of the words *warrant generally,* and in Arkansas, Florida, Idaho, Missouri, and Nevada by the words *grant, bargain,* and *sell.*

The fact that the seller is willing to give a general warranty deed is little or no assurance that he has good, clear title to the land. Suppose that I were to sit down this instant and write out a warranty deed conveying the Empire State Building to you. Clearly this warranty deed would give you no title to that valuable property for the simple reason that I don't own it. 26 CJS *Deeds* § 117. You would, of course, have the right to sue me for breach of my covenants of warranty.

7.02(b)(1) Special Warranty Deed

A *special warranty deed* is one in which the grantor covenants only against the lawful claims of all persons claiming by, through, or under the grantor. This type of deed is called a *grant deed* in some states. The grantor is liable in such case if his grantee is disturbed by some claim arising through an act of the grantor himself. For example, if, prior to the execution of the deed, the grantor has himself placed a mortgage on the land that the deed fails to mention, and thereafter the grantee is compelled to pay off the mortgage, the grantor is liable for damages thus sustained by the grantee. But if the grantor has in no way encumbered the title, but later an outstanding title is asserted by some third person, the grantor is not liable. In some states, Mississippi, Pennsylvania, Vermont, Virginia, and West Virginia, for example, use of the words *warrant specially* is sufficient to create a covenant of special warranty. In California, Idaho, and North Dakota, use of the word *grant* achieves the same purpose.

7.02(c)   Deed of Bargain and Sale

There are deeds that convey the land, and not merely the grantor's *interest* therein. Therefore they are not quitclaim deeds. They do not include warranties of title. Therefore they are not warranty deeds. Such a deed is a deed of *bargain and sale,* or *deed without covenants.*

7.03   Requirements of a Valid Deed

The essential elements of a deed are a competent grantor, a grantee, recital of consideration, words of conveyance, adequate description of the land, signature of grantor and spouse, and delivery of the completed instrument to the grantee. In addition, a deed may (though it need not) contain warranties of title, recitals showing mortgages and other encumbrances, a date, witnesses, an acknowledgment, and documentary stamps. Delivery is followed by filing or recording of the deed in the proper public office.

7.03(a)   Grantor

Every deed must have a grantor. The grantor is who conveys the property. The fact that the name used by the grantor differs from his true name does not invalidate the deed.

The name of the grantor must appear in the body of the deed.

> **EXAMPLE:**   *A, B,* and *C* own certain land. A deed is made, and the names of *A* and *B* appear in the body thereof, but all three owners sign the deed. *C's* interest does not pass under the deed. *Harrison* v. *Simons,* 55 Ala. 510 (1896).

However, a deed beginning "In consideration of ten dollars, I do hereby convey" is sufficient if signed by the landowner, even though his name does not appear in the body of the deed. *Bowles* v. *Lowery,* 62 So 107 (Ala. 1913). The same is true where the deed begins with the phrase "The undersigned." *Frederick* v. *Wilcox,* 24 So 582 (Ala. 1898).

A mistake in the spelling of the grantor's name or a variance between the spelling of the name in the body of the deed and the spelling in the signature will not invalidate the deed where the identity of the person intended to be designated is obvious.

> **EXAMPLE:**   A deed is good though it names "Emmonds" as grantor, but is signed "Emmens." And a deed is good though it names "Abraham B. Kain" as grantor but is signed "A. Boudoin Kain." *Lyon* v. *Kain,* 36 Ill. 362 (1865).

7.03(a)(1)   Grantor Competency

The grantor and spouse must be of legal age and of sound mind. In many states, a deed by a person who has been declared insane by a court is void. Even if the grantor has not been declared insane, his deed may later be set aside if, as a matter of fact, he lacked the mental capacity to understand in a reasonable manner the nature of the transaction in which he was engaged and its consequences and effects on his rights and interest.

> **EXAMPLE:**   Widower has three children, Alice, Beth, and Charles. When Widower becomes too feeble to take care of himself, Alice, a married but childless daughter, moves into Widower's home with her husband. As time passes Widower becomes senile and requires constant care. Alice, feeling she should be rewarded for her care of her father, prepares a deed of the home running to herself as grantee and has Widower sign it. After Widower's death Beth and Charles learn of the deed. They file a suit to set it aside. If they can show that Widower was too senile to understand that he was parting with ownership of his home when he signed the deed, the court will set it aside. Cases of this sort occur by the thousands.

7.03(a)(1)(i)   Fraud, Coercion, and Mistake

A deed obtained by fraud, misrepresentation, or coercion may be set aside by proper court proceedings. This is particularly true when through old age, mental weakness, ignorance, illness, or some other cause, the grantor was incapable of coping with the grantee, and due to such incapacity of the grantor the grantee has obtained the property for substantially less than its value.

Mutual mistake occurs where both parties are under some misapprehension.

> **EXAMPLE:**   Seller owns Tracts 1 and 2. Believing he is buying Tract 1, Buyer receives and pays for a deed conveying Tract 2, while Seller believes Buyer wishes to buy Tract 2. The deed will be set aside and the money refunded to Buyer.

7.03(a)(2)   Grantor—Infancy

In most states, an individual achieves majority, (comes of age) at the age of eighteen. A person who is not of age is an *infant* and, after achieving majority, may sue to set aside any deed executed by him while an infant. If it is necessary that the land of an infant or an insane person be sold for his support or for some other proper purpose, court proceedings may be instituted for that purpose.

7.03(a)(3) Grantor—Corporations

A favorable vote of the directors or trustees of a corporation is usually necessary to authorize the sale of corporate real estate. Laws will often be encountered requiring a vote of the holders of two-thirds of the corporate stock to authorize any sale of substantially *all* the corporate assets. A vote of the majority of the members of a church corporation or a nonprofit corporation may be necessary for a sale of the property.

Where the property is owned by a close corporation (a corporation with few shareholders), it should have a meeting of all of its shareholders and all of its directors to adopt the resolution authorizing the sale. The secretary's certificate to the resolution should state that it was unanimously adopted at a meeting of *all* shareholders and *all* directors.

7.03(a)(4) Grantor—Partnerships

The power of a general partner to convey partnership property is addressed in the Uniform Partnership Act (UPA), the Uniform Limited Partnership Act (ULPA), and the Revised Uniform Limited Partnership Act (RULPA), which are the dominant organic partnership law in the United States. In general, the general partner of a limited partnership has all of the rights and powers of a partner in a general partnership. ULPA § 9(1). The UPA gives every partner the status of agent for the partnership for the purpose of carrying on its business, and the partner may bind the partnership by his execution in the partnership name of any instrument which apparently carries on the business of the partnership in the usual way. UPA § 9(1). The partnership is not bound by a partner's unauthorized acts if the person with whom the partner is dealing knows that the partner has no authority to do the act. UPA § 9(1). An act of the partner that is not apparently for the carrying on of the business in the usual way does not bind the partnership, unless the act is authorized by the other partners. Under the old Limited Partnership Act the general partner of a limited partnership does not have the power to do any act that would make it impossible to carry on the ordinary business of the partnership unless all of the limited partners have given their written consent or ratification of the "specific act." ULPA § 9(1)(b). Real estate lawyers expressed the fear that this provision required unanimous consent of all limited partners to a specific transaction. If that were the law, real estate syndications would be unable to efficiently deal with their assets. Unanimous consent would be very difficult to obtain. Agreeing that such a ridiculous result could not have been intended, the drafters of many limited partnership documents included a provision whereby the limited partners gave their consent in advance to a voting arrangement that did not require unanimous consent for the conveyance of partnership property.

The Revised Uniform Limited Partnership Act, as approved by the National Conference of Commissioners on Uniform State Laws in 1976, contains a section that specifically authorizes the partnership agreement to grant to all or a specified group of limited partners the right to vote on a per capita or other basis upon any matter. RULPA § 302. It gives the general partner broad powers.

REFERENCE: Kratovil & Werner, *Fixing up the Old Jalopy—The Modern Limited Partnership Under the ULPA,* 50 St. John's L. Rev. 51 (1975); See also 39 Bus. Law. 709 (new Limited Partnership Act).

7.03(a)(5)   Grantor's Spouse

Whether or not the grantor's spouse must join in the deed depends on the local law. Generally speaking, however, it is necessary for the grantor's spouse to join in the deed for one or more of the following reasons:

1. In most states, land occupied by a husband and wife as their home is known as their homestead. Any deed or mortgage of the homestead must be signed by both husband and wife, the theory being that the home should not be disposed of unless a new home satisfactory to both parties has been furnished.

2. In most states, a wife has certain rights in her husband's land, and her rights in any particular parcel of land are not defeated by any deed made by her husband unless she has joined in making the deed.

3. Depending on the local law, a husband may have *curtesy, dower,* or other rights in the land owned by his wife, and his signature on his wife's deed is required in order to relinquish these rights.

4. Some of the western states have the community property system, and in most of these states it is required that deeds of community property be signed by both husband and wife.

5. In some states (Illinois, for example) laws have been passed that seem to give some property interest in the land that is awarded to the other spouse in a divorce. This appears to make it prudent to have both spouses join in any deed of the real estate that is owned by either spouse.

It is obvious from the foregoing that the marital status of the grantor should be clearly stated in the deed, as *bachelor, widow, spinster,* or *divorced and not remarried.*

7.03(b)   Grantee

Every deed must have a grantee. If it does not, it is void.

EXAMPLE: *A* makes out a deed to *B*, who, unknown to *A*, is dead at the time. The deed is void. A dead grantee is no grantee at all. 148 ALR 252.

The grantee need not be named in the deed if he is sufficiently described.

EXAMPLE: A deed to "John Smith and wife" transfers ownership to John Smith and his wife. *Ballard* v. *Farley,* 226 SW 544 (Tenn. 1920).

A deed running directly to an unincorporated association is void for want of a grantee.

> **EXAMPLE:** A number of persons attended a particular church that was known as the "First Avenue Baptist Church." The church, however, was not incorporated. One of the members of the congregation made a deed of gift of his real estate to "First Avenue Baptist Church." The deed was void. *Heiligenstein* v. *Schlotterbeck,* 133 NE 188 (Ill. 1921).

The fact that the name inserted in the deed is not the grantee's true name does not invalidate the deed. In other words, for the purpose of any particular real estate transaction I may assume any name I wish.

> **EXAMPLE:** If I should buy land and direct the seller to insert the name "Robert Cook" as grantee in the deed, intending to hold ownership of the land by that name, the deed is perfectly valid. *Chapman* v. *Tyson,* 81 P 1066 (Wash. 1905).

This situation frequently occurs with respect to persons who pass as husband and wife although they are not legally married.

> **EXAMPLE:** A deed designated as grantees Fabrio Casini and Lucy Casini, his wife. Actually, Lucy was not the wife of Fabrio, although they passed as husband and wife. The deed was a valid deed, and the grantees became co-owners of the property. *Casini* v. *Lupone,* 72 A2d 907 (N.J. 1950); *Michael* v. *Lucas,* 137A 287 (Md. 1927).

A misspelling of the grantee's name will not invalidate the deed where the identity of the person intended to be designated is obvious. This is also true of deeds to corporations.

> **EXAMPLE:** I attend a church whose proper corporate name is First Avenue Methodist Church, and, intending to convey land to this church, I make out a deed to The Methodist Church of First Avenue. The deed is valid. *Church of Christ* v. *Christian Church,* 61 NE 1119 (Ill. 1901). This defect is technically termed a *misnomer.* Misnomer does not invalidate a deed.

In a few states, a husband cannot convey directly to his wife, or vice versa, since according to the ancient view, the husband and wife together are but one person, and it takes two persons to make a deed. However, both husband and wife may join in a deed to a third person, who may thereupon convey to the wife.

In community property states, a deed to a married person should indicate whether the grantee holds the land as community property, with the husband and wife sharing the property equally, or as "separate property," wholly free of all interest or claim of the other spouse. Since this is a choice made by the grantee, the grantee should sign the deed indicating acceptance of the conveyance in that form.

If in such a state a husband and wife wish to hold the property in joint tenancy, it is best that the deed be drafted with a place for the grantees' written express acceptance of this form of ownership.

In any event, where the grantee executes the deed to show acceptance of the form of ownership, assumption of obligations, or for any other reason, the grantee's signature should be acknowledged.

A deed to a minor or an insane person is valid.

In many states it is required that the deed show the address of the grantee, and a deed will not be accepted for recording unless this appears in the deed. However, failure to show the address does not invalidate the deed.

In the case of a deed involving a corporation, partnership, or trust, there are a number of matters to check.

1. Does the corporation exist?

EXAMPLE: A deed to *ABC Corp.* is dated December 8, 1980. The corporate charter issued by the state is dated December 15, 1980. The deed runs to a grantee that did not exist on December 8. There is a problem.

EXAMPLE: *ABC Corp.* was created by a charter dated November 1, 1975. On July 1, 1978, it was dissolved by the state for failure to pay its corporation tax. A deed to this corporation is dated December 8, 1980. A dissolution is like the death of an individual. A problem exists.

2. Is any foreign corporation in the deal duly licensed in the state?

EXAMPLE: *ABC Corp.* is formed in Delaware in 1975. It buys an office building in Illinois in 1980. But it has no license to do business in Illinois. A tenant in the building fails to pay his rent. *ABC Corp.* cannot file an eviction suit. Most states will not allow unlicensed foreign corporations to sue in their courts.

3. If a partnership is involved, how should the deed read?

EXAMPLE: *A, B,* and *C* are partners doing business as *Unity Associates.* In most states the deed to the partnership may go either way, to *A, B,* and *C* or to *Unity Associates.*

4. Does the partnership exist? A limited partnership does not exist until its certificate has been filed as required by law.
5. If a foreign limited partnership is involved, has it been licensed to do business in the state?
6. How should a deed to a trust run?

EXAMPLE: A business trust has ten beneficiaries. The trust document names *A,* as trustee, and the trust is known as *Prudence Trust.* The deed should run to *A* as trustee of *Prudence Trust.* See 88 ALR3d 704.

7.03(b)(1) Deeds in Blank

The problem of whether a deed is void for want of a grantee often arises in connection with deeds where the name of the grantee is left blank at the time the deed is signed by the grantor. Of course, if the blank space for the grantee's name is never filled in, the deed cannot be a good deed, for a deed must convey the land to someone. Where the name of the grantee is inserted by an agent of the grantor after the grantor has signed the deed, the deed is usually valid.

> **EXAMPLE:** Landowner signs a deed complete in all respects, except that the name of the grantee is left blank. He delivers this deed to Agent, with directions to sell the property for not less than a certain sum. Agent interests Buyer in the purchase of the property. Buyer is willing to pay the stipulated price. Agent fills in Buyer's name as grantee and delivers the deed to Buyer. Buyer pays the purchase price, not knowing that his name was filled in after the deed was signed. Such a deed is generally held valid, even though Agent's authority was merely verbal. *West* v. *Witschner*, 428 SW2d 538 (Mo. 1968); 175 ALR 1294. But a deed delivered with the land description left blank is held void in many states. *West* v. *Witschner*, 428 SW2d 538 (Mo. 1968).

7.03(c)   Consideration

Consideration is the value given for a conveyance of land. For many years payment of a "consideration" or price was thought to be necessary in order to create the "use" in the purchaser. Today consideration is usually recited in the deed, but actual presence of consideration is not necessary.

The deed usually recites that it was given for "$10.00 and other good and valuable consideration." In some states the actual consideration must be stated.

Deeds are usually drafted with a general statement of nominal consideration to keep the private business dealings of the parties from becoming part of the public record. These efforts are not entirely successful. People who want to know the selling price of land can usually compute that price from the transfer stamps placed on the deed.

> **EXAMPLE:** If the transfer tax is $1.00 per thousand dollars of selling price, a deed with $10 of transfer tax affixed was given for $10,000, notwithstanding the fact that the consideration clause read "$10,00 and other valuable consideration."

If the deed recites a consideration, the fact that the deed represents a gift of the land and that actually no money changed hands will not invalidate the deed. An individual may give away his land if he wishes. However, a man must be just before he is generous. If the grantor is indebted at the time of the making of the gift, his creditors may thereafter have the deed set aside as in fraud of their rights. The payment of a nominal consideration, such as $10, will not suffice to sustain the deed in such a case. A valuable consideration is needed to sustain a deed against existing creditors of the grantor.

7.03(c)(1)   Consideration—Support Deeds

Parents often convey their land to a son or daughter on the understanding that such son or daughter will support the parents for the rest of their lives. Or an elderly person without close relatives may convey his land to a stranger or to a retirement or nursing home in return for a promise of support. While ordinarily a deed cannot be set aside for *failure of consideration,* that is, for the reason that the grantee failed to receive what he bargained for, support deeds form an exception to the rule. *Bruno* v. *Bruno,* 172 A2d 863 (Pa. 1961). Where the grantee fails to keep his promise to support, the deed can usually be set aside.

> **EXAMPLE:**   A father and mother conveyed land to their son. The mother had owned the land, and it had been the home of the parents. The deed recited a consideration of $2,500. The actual consideration, however, was the son's agreement to support the parents and give them a home for the rest of their lives. Several years later the son stopped supporting them and became so abusive that they moved out and went to live with another son. The deed was set aside. *Worrell* v. *West,* 296 P2d 1092 (Kans. 1956). The grantee is not living up to his promise unless he furnishes kindness and attention, as well as physical necessaries. *Zarembski* v. *Zarembski,* 48 NE2d 394 (Ill. 1943).

7.03(d)   Words of Conveyance

Every deed must contain words of conveyance. These differ from state to state. In warranty deeds, *convey and warrant* or *grant, bargain, and sell* are often used. In quitclaim deeds the words usually are *convey and quitclaim* or *remise, release, and forever quitclaim.*

7.03(e)   Description of Land

A deed must describe the land conveyed.

7.03(f)   Waiver of Dower and Homestead

In some states, a deed must contain a clause releasing and relinquishing all homestead, dower, and curtesy rights in the premises.

7.03(g)   Date

A date is not essential to the validity of a deed, though it is the universal custom to date all deeds.

7.03(h)   Signature

The signature of the grantor is essential to the validity of the deed. A *forgery* (a deed to which some unauthorized third person has affixed the grantor's signature) is a nullity and conveys no title whatever.

The fact that the grantor's signature is misspelled will not invalidate the deed.

If the grantor is unable to write, he may sign by mark, in which case the signature line appears as follows:

His
"John X Smith (Seal)"
Mark

Everything but the "X" may be typed. The "X" must be affixed by the grantor.

Occasionally a deed is signed not by the grantor himself, but by an *attorney in fact*. An attorney in fact is simply an agent authorized by the landowner to sell and convey his real estate. In order for such deed to be valid, the following requirements exist:

1. The land owner must first sign and deliver to his attorney in fact a written instrument, called a *power of attorney*, authorizing such attorney to sell and convey the land in question. Such an instrument must be as formal as the deed itself. In states that require a deed to be sealed, the power of attorney must be sealed. In states that require a deed to be witnessed, the power of attorney must be witnessed. All the other requirements relating to deeds should be observed, including acknowledgment and recording.

2. The deed must name the landowner, not the attorney in fact, as the grantor.

3. The name signed to the deed should be that of the landowner. Under the usual method, the attorney signs the grantor's name and then places his name beneath that of the grantor, as follows:

"John Smith (Seal)"
"By Henry Brown, his Attorney in Fact"

4. The grantor must be alive on the date of the delivery of the deed, since death of the grantor automatically terminates the power of attorney. Insanity of the grantor may have the same result.

5. Since the landowner ordinarily has the power to terminate the agency at any time and thus take away the attorney's power to execute deeds on his behalf, it should be established that the agency actually had not been terminated or revoked at the date of the delivery of the deed.

NEW DIRECTIONS: Some states have enacted "durable power of attorney" laws. These statutes provide that the power continues notwithstanding the incompetency of the grantors. Mich. Stat. Ann. §27.5495.

The technical mode of executing the deed of a corporation is for the proper office to sign the corporate name, adding his own signature and official title beneath the name of the corporation. Usually, the corporate bylaws provide that deeds shall be signed by a president or vice president and attested to by a secretary or assistant secretary.

The mere fact that the grantor's name on the deed is signed by someone other than the grantor does not invalidate the deed. The execution of the deed may be ratified or otherwise authorized by the true grantor. If this is the case, the deed is as effective as though the actual grantor signed the deed.

7.03(i) Seal

In some states, principally eastern states, a seal is essential to the validity of a deed. In most states, however, a seal is unnecessary, though the custom of using a seal persists. But even in those states where a deed by an individual need not bear a seal, a deed executed by a corporation should have the official corporate seal affixed.

7.03(j) Witnesses

In many states a deed must be witnessed, two witnesses being the number commonly required. Most states require witnessing where the deed is signed by mark.

7.03(k) Taxes

Many states, counties, and municipalities have enacted laws that impose a tax upon the transfer of property. Under some of these laws, the recorder must refuse to accept a deed for recording unless proper tax stamps are affixed. See Ill. Rev. Stat. Ch. 115, §9.2a. These taxes vary from state to state and municipality to municipality. Local law and practice must be reviewed.

7.03(l) Delivery of Deeds

Delivery is essential to the validity of a deed. The word *delivery* is somewhat misleading, since it would lead one to believe that it is necessary that the deed be actually handed by the grantor to the grantee. This is not the case. Delivery is simply the final act by which the grantor, who has previously signed the deed, signifies his intention that the deed shall take effect. Whether or not a deed has been delivered depends primarily on the *intention* of the grantor. The test is: Did the grantor *do* or *say* anything to show his intention to pass ownership of the land to the grantee? A deed may be delivered by acts without words or by words without acts, though ordinarily there are both words and acts in the making of a delivery.

> **EXAMPLE:**   At the closing of a deal, Buyer hands Seller a check. Seller signs the deed and, without saying a word, hands it to Buyer. There is a delivery.

> **EXAMPLE:**   At the closing of a deal all the papers, including Seller's signed deed, are on the closing table. Having received his check, Seller tells Buyer (the grantee) to take his deed. There is a delivery.

EXAMPLE: Seller signs a deed conveying real estate to Buyer and hands it to Buyer, not with the intention of passing title, but with the understanding that Buyer will check the legal description to see if it is sufficient. There is no delivery.

EXAMPLE: Seller signs a deed conveying real estate to Buyer but leaves it in his office while he is still thinking over the deal. Buyer steals the deed from Seller's office and shows it to Third Person, who purchases from Buyer, relying on Buyer's possession of the deed. Third Person acquires no title. There is no delivery of the deed.

7.03(l)(1)   Delivery—Several Grantors

Suppose *A* and *B* own certain land, and both of them sign a deed running to *C* as grantee. *A* hands the deed to *B* for the sole purpose of having the deed checked by their lawyer. Without *A's* permission, *B* hands the deed to *C* and collects the sale price from him. This is not a good deed so far as *A* is concerned. He still owns his half interest. One joint grantor, who is not authorized by his co-tenant, cannot make a valid delivery of the deed that will be binding on the latter. 162 ALR 892.

When land is owned by several persons, all of them named as grantors in one deed, and one of the grantors signs the deed and hands it to the grantee with the statement that his consent to the sale of the land is conditioned on the other grantors also signing the deed, such deed is inoperative unless all grantors sign. *Logue* v. *Von Almen,* 40 NE2d 73 (Ill. 1941); Note, 14 Columb. L. Rev. 389 (1914).

7.03(l)(2)   Delivery—Lifetime of the Grantor

Delivery of a deed must be made in the lifetime of the grantor.

EXAMPLE: On Seller's death, an envelope with Seller's name on it is found in Seller's safe-deposit box. The envelope is opened and found to contain a deed from Seller to Buyer. The deed is void for want of delivery.

A deed is the proper instrument for transferring ownership of land from one living person to another, and, in general, this means that the deed, to be effective, must operate while both parties are alive.

However, I may legally deliver a deed to you here and now with a clause therein stating that the deed is to take effect only at my death. The deed gives you the right *now* to enjoy the property at my death. 31 ALR2d 532.

7.03(l)(3)   Delivery—Third Persons

Where the grantor hands the deed not to the grantee, but to some third person, a wholly new set of rules comes into play. A number of different situations present themselves.

EXAMPLE: Seller signs a deed running to Buyer as grantee and hands the deed to Buyer's lawyer, with the intention of giving Buyer ownership of the land here and now. This is delivery to an *agent of the grantee* and is good delivery.

EXAMPLE: Seller signs a deed running to Buyer as grantee and hands the deed to his own lawyer to check its form. There is no intention to transfer ownership and no delivery. Here the deed has been handed to the *agent of the grantor*.

EXAMPLE: Seller enters into a contract to sell land to Buyer and pursuant thereto signs a deed to Buyer. However, he hands the deed to XYZ Bank with directions to deliver the deed to Buyer when certain moneys are paid by Buyer to the bank. This is an *escrow*.

EXAMPLE: Seller signs a deed running to Son, as grantee, hands the deed to Custodian and directs Custodian to hand the deed to Son after Seller's death. This brings up the subject of *death escrows*. This is a good delivery as long as it is clear that Seller intended to part with all control over the land once he handed the deed to Custodian. Oddly enough, the courts allow Seller, in such cases, to use the land during his lifetime. They do not regard this as inconsistent with the passing of ownership to Son. It is as though Seller had conveyed outright to Son, but had reserved a life estate in the property. *Bury* v. *Young,* 33 P 338 (Cal. 1893).

7.03(l)(4) Delivery—Family Transactions

If a father executes a deed to a minor child, which deed is beneficial to the child, and the father indicates by his words and conduct that he intends the deed to operate at once, actual delivery is unnecessary. Indeed, the courts are most reluctant to upset a deed that is made as a gift by a parent to a child.

7.03(m) Acceptance

For a deed to transfer ownership of land, it is necessary that the grantor intend to transfer ownership to the grantee and that the grantee intend to accept ownership of the land. *Blankenship* v. *Meyers,* 544 P2d 314 (Idaho 1975). That is to say, delivery by the grantor must be accompanied by acceptance of the deed by the grantee. 74 ALR2d 992. Only rarely will disputes arise regarding acceptance, and the courts are not disposed to be technical about it. Indeed, the courts have gone so far as to hold that if the grantor makes and records a deed without the knowledge of the grantee, ownership will nevertheless pass if the grantee, on being informed of the deed, assents to it, even though this takes place after the death of the grantor. *Mann* v. *Jummel,* 56 NE 161 (Ill. 1891). Also, if the grantee dies before learning of the deed, his acceptance will be presumed and the deed held good. *Lessee of Mitchell* v. *Ryan,* 3 Ohio St. 377 (1854). A parent may accept for an infant. *Whitworth* v. *Whitworth,* 210 SE2d 9 (Ga. 1974).

7.04   Recording

Virtually all deeds are filed for record in some public office.

7.05   Official Conveyances

Deeds by executors, administrators, guardians of minors, conservators or guardians of insane persons, sheriffs, masters in chancery, receivers, trustees in bankruptcy, and other similar conveyances usually depend for their validity on prior court proceedings. In addition, numerous technical requirements exist that frequently expose such deeds to attack. A discussion of such requirements is not within the scope of this book.

7.06   After-acquired Title

If the grantor in a warranty deed does not have title or does not have complete title at the time of executing the deed, but thereafter acquires title, such title will automatically pass to his grantee without any additional conveyance. 44 ALR 1276; 162 ALR 566.

7.07   Title Conveyed

If the grantor owns the land in fee simple, and the deed contains no qualifying language, the deed gives the grantee good fee simple title to the land. However, deeds often contain qualifying language, which results in the grantee's acquiring something less than the fee simple title.

> **EXAMPLE:**   Seller makes a deed conveying land to Buyer "and the heirs of his body." In some states, Buyer acquires only a life estate by such deed, and his children acquire the remainder. In other states, such a deed will give Buyer the full fee simple title to the land.

> **EXAMPLE:**   Seller conveys land to Buyer by a deed that contains the following clause: "to have and to hold for and during the grantee's life." Buyer acquires only a life estate by this deed.

The law on this subject is so complex and contains so many refinements of reasoning that no one but an experienced attorney should attempt to interpret a deed containing any qualifying language whatever. In particular, words such as *heirs, heirs of the body, issue,* and *death without issue* are danger signals. Indiscriminate use of such language is an invitation to a lawsuit.

7.07(a)   Title Conveyed by Deed—Fee or Easement

If language is added to the deed indicating the purpose for which the land is to be used, this may result in giving the grantee something less than full ownership of the land. Lawyers talk about the nature of the *estate* conveyed by the deed.

> **EXAMPLE:**   By warranty deed Seller deeded to Buyer "a right of way one rod wide" over certain land. This deed gave Buyer only an easement of travel. A deed that conveys a right, especially a right of way, rather than land, gives the grantee only an easement. 136 ALR 390. As can be seen, the word "easement" is not necessary for an easement to be created. 6 ALR3d 973.

Also, if the deed conveys the land, with the words of purpose following the property description, the courts are not in agreement.

> **EXAMPLE:**   Seller made a deed to Buyer of a strip of land "to be used for road purposes." The court held that Buyer acquired only an easement for road purposes. *Magnolia Petroleum Co.* v. *West,* 40 NE2d 24 (Ill. 1940). The reason for this is that courts apply rules of interpretation. One of these is that courts cannot ignore any language in a written instrument. If any meaning is to be given the phrase "to be used for road purposes" it is that the land must be used *only* for road purposes. This makes the deed a grant of right to use the land for a specific purpose. That is what an easement is. The *estate* conveyed is not an *estate in fee simple.* Here the court interprets the language in a way that would surprise a lay person. But in other states exactly the same kind of deed will be held to give Buyer full ownership of the strip. *Biggs* v. *Wolfe,* 178 A2d 482 (Del. 1962).

> **EXAMPLE:**   Where a deed runs to a charitable corporation, frequently some reference is made in the deed to the use of the land for the charitable purposes of the corporation. Normally, this nevertheless leaves the corporation with a salable ownership in the land. Bogert, *The Laws of Trusts and Trustees* § 324 (2d ed. rev. 1977); 4 Scott, *The Law of Trusts* §348.1 (3d ed. 1967).

> **EXAMPLE:**   Seller deeds his vacant land to Hospital "for hospital purposes." The hospital finds the land not well adapted to hospital purposes. It sells the land to Third Person. This is a valid transaction. Third Person gets good title to the land.

Where a deed runs to a city, village, park district, or other public body and contains language descriptive of the use to which the land is to be put, questions may arise as to the nature of the ownership thus acquired, particularly when such use is abandoned, though in most cases the courts struggle to find that the public body acquired a good, salable title to the land. 28 Am.Jur.2d *Estates* §149; 10 McQuillin, *Municipal Corporations* §28.19 (3d ed. 1966).

> **EXAMPLE:**   Seller sold and deeded his land to City "to be used for the use and benefit of the citizens of City," this language appearing in the deed. City found the land unusable for city purposes and sold it to Third Person. This can be done. Third Person acquires good ownership of the land. *City* v. *Jones,* 122 NW2d 503 (Neb. 1963).

The fact that the deed was made because of the threat of condemnation by the public body does not alter this rule. *Mattion* v. *Trustees,* 279 NE2d 66 (Ill. 1971). *Contra: Kendrick* v. *City of St. Paul,* 6 NW2d 449 (Minn. 1942).

There is an exception to this rule in some states:

> **EXAMPLE:** Seller deeded his land to the city of Milwaukee "for highway purposes." By this deed the city acquired only an easement to use the land for highway purposes and could not sell the land. 136 ALR 399. This exception is confined to deeds for street, alley, and highway purposes, and even then, in some states, the city gets good, salable ownership of the land. 136 ALR 394.

Where a deed runs to some public body "for park purposes" there is no agreement whatever as to what such a deed conveys. 15 ALR2d 975.

7.08   Exceptions and Reservations

In conveying land, the grantor often wishes to retain some part of the land described or to reserve some right therein. This is accomplished by inserting in the deed the proper clauses of *exception* and *reservation*. An exception withholds from the operation of the deed title to a part of the land described in the deed. Thus a deed of Lot 1 *excepting the north twenty feet thereof* does not pass ownership of the north twenty feet of the lot. That portion was *excepted* from the conveyance. A *reservation* is the creation by the deed of a new right in favor of the grantor, usually an easement or life estate. Thus in a deed of Lot 1 *reserving to the grantor an easement for ingress and egress over and across the north twenty feet of Lot 1,* ownership of the north twenty feet passes to the grantee, but an easement is reserved in favor of the grantor. Sometimes the terms *excepting* and *reserving* are used inaccurately, and the courts will hold that a true reservation was created by the use of the word *excepting* or that a true exception was created by the use of the word *reserving*.

> **EXAMPLE:** Seller conveys certain land to Buyer "except the north ten feet for a right of way." Ownership of the entire tract, including the north ten feet, passes to Buyer, but the quoted clause reserves an easement for Seller over the north ten feet. 139 ALR 1348.

It is possible for the grantor in a deed to reserve a life estate in the property conveyed. Often to save the expense of probating a will after his death, a father, while still living, will give a deed of his land to his son or daughter, and in the deed will reserve to himself a life estate. The grantee becomes the owner of the land, and the grantor retains the use thereof for his lifetime.

> **WARNING:** Once such a deed is signed, the grantor cannot recall it. The psychological effect of this change in circumstances often brings about friction between the parent and child. Hence such transactions should be avoided, if possible.

7.09   Hazardous Waste

Since the use of property as a hazardous waste disposal site may forever poison the land, making it unfit for human or livestock occupancy, the public record should memorialize this fact. The U.S. Environmental Protection Agency has promulgated regulations which require that the landowner record a deed or other document that will, in perpetuity, notify any potential purchaser that the land has been used to manage hazardous waste and the land's future use is restricted. 40 CFR § 265.120.

At least one state has taken the position that a transfer of real property which is used for the generation, handling, storage, or disposal of hazardous substances or wastes will be voidable unless the seller engages in an administrative procedure requiring a written declaration that there has been no discharge of hazardous substances on the site or that any such discharge has been cleaned up in accordance with procedures prescribed by the state. If the cleanup cannot be accomplished before the sale, a cleanup plan must be approved by the state and its cost secured. N. J. Stats. Ann. § 13:K-6 *et seq.*

Irrespective of the effect of such laws on the conveyance, any party taking title to real estate should ascertain whether hazardous substances are present on the site. Liability for cleanup costs and damage to the environment may befall even an innocent landowner who acquires property without knowledge of the presence of such material. 42 U. S. C. § 9607. See also Mass. Gen. L. Ch. 21E, § 5.

7.10 Suggestions

1. *Form of deed.* If there is a contract for the sale of land, find out if the contract specifies the form of deed to be given. If the contract specifies that the seller is to give a warranty deed, then, of course, a warranty deed form must be used. If the contract does not specify the form of the deed, in most states a quitclaim deed will suffice. The seller will prefer to use this form, since it subjects him to no personal liability for defects in title. If there is no written contract for the sale of the land, the sellers will again prefer to give a quitclaim deed.

2. *Grantor.* Check the deed by which the grantor acquired ownership and see that his name is spelled the same way in the deed by which he is conveying the land. Any difference in spelling may lead to an objection when the title is examined. If a woman acquires title by her maiden name and subsequently marries, the deed should show both names; *Mary Jones, formerly Mary Smith.* Any examiner of the title will thus find a connected chain of title to the land. The grantor's marital status should be given: *bachelor, spinster, widow, widower, divorced and not remarried.* If the grantor is married, his spouse should also be named as grantor, and their marital status given: *John Smith and Mary Smith, his wife.* A married woman or widow should never be described as "Mrs. John Jones." Her legal name is "Mary Jones." Don't describe yourself as "R. John Smith." Legally your middle name or middle initial is no part of your name. Hence you should at least describe yourself as "Robert John Smith," for it is poor practice to use initials only in legal documents. If the state law requires, give the street address of the grantor and grantee. Special forms of deeds are used where the grantor is a corporation, trustee, executor, and so on. Of course all the landowners must convey if the buyer is to get good title, but different landowners may use different deeds. As a rule, it is best for a husband and wife to join in the same deed.

3. *Grantee.* Have the proposed grantee write out his name on a slip of paper—first name, middle initial, if any, and last name—and copy the name in this identical form in the proper place in the deed form. His or her marital status may, but need not, be given. State grantee's place of residence. If two or more persons are acquiring title,

the names of all must be shown in the deed. If they are taking title as joint tenants, use a joint tenancy form deed. Legal stationers usually print a special form for joint tenancy transactions. Following the names of the grantees in this form is a phrase reading somewhat like this: *as joint tenants with the right of survivorship and not as tenants in common nor as tenants by the entireties.* When husband and wife are taking title, their marital relation should be shown, as *John Smith and Mary Smith, his wife.* If a corporation is taking title, its charter should be checked and the name copied exactly and without the slightest deviation. For example, if the charter describes a corporation as The Elite Hat Shop, Inc., do not omit the *The* and do not spell out the *Inc.* A deed to a trustee should clearly identify the trust. Never draft a deed running simply to *John Smith, as trustee.* Have the deed run to *John Smith, as trustee under Trust Agreement dated June 15, 1946, and known as the Pinecrest Liquidation Trust,* or other proper designation. Have before you the trust instrument creating the trust and describe it accurately in the deed. If the deed to the trustee also creates the trust, it is serving a double purpose. (1) It is operating as a deed of the land and must contain all the necessary elements of a deed. (2) It is creating a trust and must contain all the requisite elements for the creation of a trust. Such a document should be drafted only by one thoroughly conversant with the law of trusts.

The deed should conform to the contract of sale with respect to the grantees. For example, if Seller contracts to sell to Buyer #1 and Buyer #2, Seller should not, even though Buyer #1 requests it, make a deed running to Buyer #1 only. That would violate Buyer #2's rights and make Seller liable for damages if Buyer #2 suffers a loss.

If you are creating a corporation that is to acquire real estate, be sure that the corporation's charter has been issued and that all other formalities for corporate existence are complied with *before* the deed to the corporation is made out. In other words, be sure you have an existing, legal grantee to whom to convey.

4. *Consideration.* Let the deed recite a monetary consideration, as *in consideration of the sum of $10 and other good and valuable consideration.* In a few states, it is customary or necessary to recite the true sale price of the land. In deeds by corporations, trustees, executors, and so forth, the deed should recite the true sale price.

5. *Words of grant.* Every printed form of deed contains words of grant. It is not necessary to tamper with these, since the warranty deed form will have words appropriate for a warranty deed and the quitclaim deed form will also have appropriate words.

6. *Description.* Do not attempt to draft a description unless you are sure you know what you are doing. If a title policy, abstract, or Torrens certificate has been previously issued on the land that is being sold, and the land sold is identical with the tract mentioned in the title policy, abstract, or Torrens certificate (that is, there have been no subsequent conveyances of portions of the tract, and so forth), then the description may be copied from title policy, abstract caption, or Torrens certificate, since such documents usually contain accurate descriptions. After the description has been copied into the deed form, have someone read it aloud to you while you follow the description in the title policy, abstract, or Torrens certificate, since even a microscopic error in typing may throw the whole description off.

7. *Subject clause.* If the grantor in a warranty deed wishes to avoid personal liability, he should include in the subject clause all defects in title, such as mortgages, unpaid taxes, existing leases, restrictions, and so forth. However, the contract of sale usually specifies to what objections the title will be subject when conveyed to the buyer; the seller, in preparing the deed, has no right to add items to this list. For example, if the seller agrees, by his contract, to convey the land to the buyer subject only to a certain mortgage, he cannot include in the deed *subject to mortgage recorded as document No. 10356789 and also to restrictions of record.* The buyer has the right to object to

the inclusion of the portion relating to the restrictions, since restrictions were not mentioned in the contract. In a quitclaim deed, a subject clause is unnecessary and inappropriate.

8. *Mortgages.* If the land is being sold subject to a mortgage that the grantee is to assume and agree to pay, let the deed state "Subject to a mortgage recorded in Book 100, Page 101, as Document No. 999, which the grantee herein assumes and agrees to pay."

Where the buyer is paying part cash and giving back to the seller either a mortgage or mortgage trust deed for part of the purchase money, it is better that the deed contain a recital somewhat as follows: "As part of the consideration for this transaction, the grantee herein has this day executed to _____, as trustee, a trust deed, of even date herewith, securing a promissory note in the sum of $_____, which represents part of the purchase price for said premises." This is particularly desirable where a mortgage deed of trust is involved, since if Seller sells and conveys land to Buyer and Buyer simultaneously executes a mortgage trust deed to Trustee, the public records do not clearly show that the trust deed was given as part of the purchase price unless the deed contains the suggested recital. Of course the trust deed or mortgage should also contain a recital that "this trust deed is given to secure payment of part of the purchase price of said premises."

9. *Statement of purpose of deed.* Inexperienced conveyancers tend to put in deeds various legal-sounding phrases without having any clear idea of the purpose such phrases were intended to serve. This is a very dangerous practice. Do not insert a single syllable in a deed unless you are certain what the legal effect of that insertion will be. Remember that if you add in your deed phrases like "to be used for road purposes," the result may be to create a grant of an easement out of what started to be a deed of the land. It is neither necessary nor desirable to state in the deed the purpose for which the land is to be used.

10. *Restrictions and conditions.* Restrictions and conditions must be drafted with care. Because of the drastic consequences attendant upon the enforcement of a reverter clause, the grantee should view with suspicion any attempt to insert a reverter clause in the deed. If there is a written contract for the sale of the land, the grantor has no right to insert in the deed any restrictions or conditions not provided for in the contract. If the contract provides for a building restriction, but says nothing about a condition or reverter clause, the grantor has no right to provide in the deed for a reverter of title in the event of a breach of condition. Be sure you understand the words you use in drafting restrictions, as, for example, residence purposes, dwellings purposes, business purposes. Certain words have a well-known technical meaning, and if you use such words in a deed, courts will give them their usual meaning, regardless of what special, individual meaning they may have in your own mind. You will not even be allowed to testify that such a word has a special meaning for you. On the other hand, inexperienced draftsmen often use words that have no meaning at all, such as the provision that "only houses of standard construction shall be erected on said premises." It would be difficult to get two people to agree on the definition of "standard construction." Such a phrase is so devoid of meaning that courts cannot enforce it.

11. *Easements.* A deed may contain a grant to the grantee of an easement over other lands of the seller. If there is a written contract of sale, and it makes no mention of such an easement, the seller is under no obligation to include it in the deed. A deed may reserve to the grantor an easement over the land conveyed. If there is a written contract of sale, and it makes no mention of such an easement, the grantor has no right to insert such a clause in the deed.

12. *Waiver of dower and homestead.* Almost without exception, deed forms prepared by your local stationers include the necessary waivers of dower and homestead rights. For this and other reasons, it is dangerous to use a deed form printed in your state in conveying land lying in some other state. Obtain a form printed in the state where the land lies.

13. *Date.* It is the custom to date all deeds.

14. *Signature.* Before permitting the grantor to sign, have him write his name on a piece of paper. Check the spelling with the spelling of his name in the body of the deed. Be sure that the two correspond, since even trivial variations are frequently objected to by title examiners. Type the name of the grantor beneath the signature line and direct him to sign exactly as his name is typed.

15. *Seal.* If a seal is needed on deeds of land in your state, deed forms printed in your state will show a seal on the signature line. If there are more signatures on the deed than there are printed signature lines, be sure the word *Seal* appears after each signature. The corporate seal is always necessary on deeds made by corporations.

16. *Tax stamps.* The necessary tax stamps should be attached where the state law requires.

17. *Witnesses.* Always have two or more witnesses sign the deed if any grantor has signed by mark. If all grantors are able to write, their signatures need not be witnessed unless the state law requires witnesses. Some states require that all deeds be witnessed.

18. *Acknowledgment.*

19. *Recording.* File your deed in the proper public office immediately after it has been acknowledged. Delay may prove disastrous.

20. *Statutory requirements.* Make sure to comply with all applicable state laws relating to various recitations that are required to appear on the face of the deed, i.e., compliance with local subdivision ordinances and plat acts, mailing address of the grantee, name and address of the person preparing the deed. Readiness avoids recording problems and delay.

21. *Take care in preparing the deed.* Erasures and alterations raise danger signals which proper draftsmanship and transcription should avoid. 1 *Merrill on Notice* § 81 at 106 (1952).

CHAPTER 8

Acknowledgments

8.01 In General

An acknowledgment is a formal declaration made before some public officer, usually a notary public, by a person who has signed a deed, mortgage, or other instrument, that the instrument is his voluntary act and deed. *In re McCauley's Adoption,* 131 NW2d 174 (Neb. 1964). This act of acknowledgment, memorialized by the public official, furnishes formal proof of the authenticity of the execution of the instrument.

8.02 Certificate

The officer before whom this declaration is made attaches his certificate to the instrument or fills in the printed form of certificate that appears on virtually all deed and mortgage forms. This is known as the certificate of acknowledgment. It usually recites that the grantor appeared before the officer and acknowledged that he executed the instrument as his free and voluntary act and deed. However, the form of the certificate of acknowledgment varies considerably from state to state, and from situation to situation; that is, an acknowledgement taken from an individual differs from an acknowledgment taken from a corporate officer. It is important that the proper form be followed. *In re Viking Co., Inc.,* 389 F.Supp. 1230 (1974).

An acknowledgment must not be confused with an *affidavit.* An affidavit is a statement made under oath and put in writing. At the conclusion of the affidavit the officer, usually a notary, recites that it was subscribed and sworn to. An affidavit is not acceptable as a substitute for an acknowledgment. The two serve different purposes. *Hatcher v. Hall,* 292 SW2d 619 (Mo. 1956). The acknowledgment merely makes the *prima facie* showing that the instrument was duly executed.

The affidavit or verification goes to the truth of the matters therein set forth. *D. J. Fair Lumber Co.,* v. *Karlin,* 430 P2d 222 (Kan. 1967).

8.03 Waiver of Dower and Homestead Rights

In some states the certificate of acknowledgment must specifically state that dower and homestead rights were understandingly relinquished.

8.04 Necessity

In a few states, Arizona and Ohio, for example, an unacknowledged deed is not valid. In a number of states, certain types of instruments, such as deeds of married women or deeds or mortgages of homestead land, must be acknowledged. Other deeds, however, are legally valid though not acknowledged. This statement is without significance, since, as a practical matter, every deed or mortgage should be acknowledged. In the great majority of the states an unacknowledged instrument is not entitled to be recorded (59 ALR2d 1302), and an unrecorded title is a precarious one indeed. Lack of an acknowledgment on a deed may render title unmarketable. Other technical reasons make an acknowledgment a practical necessity.

8.05 Who May Take an Acknowledgment

A deed or mortgage may be acknowledged before a notary public or some other officer designated by the local law. Such a person, it is said, *takes* the acknowledgment of the grantor. Generally, a notary who is an attorney is competent to take the acknowledgment of his client. 21 ALR3d 523. However, if the officer has any financial interest in the transaction, he is disqualified. For example, a grantee in a deed would be clearly disqualified from taking the grantor's acknowledgment. Other disqualified parties include the grantor in a deed, mortgagor and mortgagee in a mortgage, and the trustee in a trust deed. In some states, a stockholder of a corporation that is a party to the instrument is disqualified from taking the acknowledgment of the corporation. In other states the rule is the reverse.

8.06 Venue

The venue of the certificate of acknowledgment is the caption, which is usually shown as follows:

STATE OF ILLINOIS }
                     (SS)
COUNTY OF COOK }

The venue shows the place where the acknowledgment took place, that is, the place where the grantor appeared before the notary and made his formal declaration that the deed was his voluntary act.

8.07   Effect of Invalidity

It is important to keep in mind the fact that invalidity of the *acknowledgment* does not make the *deed* void. However, in most states, a valid acknowledgment is essential for proper recording; that is, if the acknowledgment is void, the deed, though recorded, is treated as an unrecorded deed. If that is the result, subsequent owners of the property are not on constructive notice of the rights of the grantee of the defectively acknowledged instrument.

8.08   Foreign

One who owns land located in a state other than that in which he resides, may sign and acknowledge a deed in the state of his residence. The acknowledgment will be valid if it conforms either to the law of the state of his residence or to the law of the state where the land lies. An acknowledgment taken outside of the state where the land lies is known as a *foreign acknowledgment*. In some states, it is required, either by custom or by law, that every acknowledgment taken outside of the state have attached thereto a certificate by a court clerk to the effect that the officer taking the acknowledgment was authorized by law to do so. This is known as a *certificate of authenticity,* or a *certificate of magistracy.* If the certificate goes on to recite that the acknowledgment is in due form, it is known as a *certificate of authenticity and conformity,* or *certificate of magistracy and conformity.*

8.09   Date

The date of the certificate of acknowledgment is unimportant. Hence omission of the date of the certificate or insertion of an incorrect date will not invalidate the acknowledgment.

8.10   Signature of Officer Taking Acknowledgment

The certificate of acknowledgment must be signed by the officer taking the acknowledgment. Otherwise it is not valid. The certificate should also show the official character of the person taking the acknowledgment, as notary public, or justice of the peace, for example.

8.11   Seal

An acknowledgment taken by a notary public is usually invalid unless his official seal is placed on the certificate. The requirements as to seals of officers other than notaries vary from state to state. If there is a trend in this area, it is toward the use of rubber stamps instead of the traditional metal seal. Rubber stamps are more readable when recorded documents are placed into the microfilm records of the county recorders and secretaries of state.

8.12   Date of Expiration of Commission

Failure of the notary public to show the date his commission expires does not invalidate the certificate.

8.13   Liability of Notary—False Acknowledgment

Both the notary public and the surety on his official bond will be liable for damages caused by the notary's willful misconduct, as where the notary falsely certifies to a forged mortgage and the mortgage is sold to an innocent purchaser. 44 ALR3d 1243. The notary and his surety will also be liable when the notary's negligence causes damage, as when the notary acknowledges the signatures on a forged mortgage without knowing the parties who appear before him and without procuring any evidence or information as to their identity. 44 ALR3d 555. See also 13 ALR3d 1039 (measure of damages).

8.14   Foreign-speaking Persons and the Handicapped

In recent years a problem has arisen relating to the relationship and business practices between notaries public and people who have immigrated to the United States from countries where the civil law prevails. In those countries the notary public is a public official of considerable importance and legal training. In this country notaries are not to give legal advice unless, of course, they are lawyers. To emphasize the importance of this point, Illinois, in the recent revision of its notary public law, expressly prohibits notaries who are not attorneys from preparing any legal instrument or filling in the blanks of an instrument other than a notary certificate. Ill. Rev. Stat. Ch. 102 par. 201–101.

To further address this problem, which is especially important in the Latin communities, Illinois notaries who are not attorneys and who advertise notarial services must include in the ad a notice that the notary is not an attorney and may not give legal advice or accept fees for legal advice.

The notary must read the instrument to a blind person before taking his acknowledgment. If the party executing the document does not speak or understand English, the notary shall not take the acknowledgment unless the nature and effect of the document are translated into a language which the person understands.

8.15   Form of Acknowledgment

The common short forms for use in taking the acknowledgment of a person signing in an individual capacity or a representative capacity follow:

Acknowledgment
(individual capacity)

State of _____

County of _____

This instrument was acknowledged before me on _____ (date) _____ by

_____ (name of person) _____ .

      (seal)   _____

                                     (signature of notary public)

Acknowledgment
(representative capacity)

State of _____

County of _____

This instrument was acknowledged before me on _____ (date) _____

by _ (name of person) _ as _ (type of authority e.g., officer, trustee, etc.) _

of _ (name of party on behalf of whom instrument was executed) _ .

      (seal)

                                     _____

                                     (signature of notary public)

CHAPTER 9

Recording and Constructive Notice

9.01   Necessity of Recording

Every state has a recording law. These laws provide, in substance, that, until recorded, a deed, mortgage, or other instrument is ineffective and void so far as subsequent purchasers or mortgagees of the same land are concerned. The policy behind these laws is that the ownership of real estate should be disclosed by the public records, and that purchasers of land should be able to rely on these records and should be protected against secret, unrecorded deeds and mortgages.

Under these laws an unrecorded deed or mortgage is good and valid *as between the parties to the instrument,* but a subsequent grantee or mortgagee may acquire superior rights in the property, if the document conferring those rights is recorded before that grantee or mortgagee has actual or constructive notice or knowledge of those prior rights. The public policy behind this concept is that persons who deal with real estate in ignorance of the unrecorded interests should be protected against those unrecorded rights.

EXAMPLE: Seller, the owner of certain vacant land, sells the same to Buyer #1 and gives Buyer #1 a deed, which Buyer #1 fails to record. Later seller dies, and his heirs, not knowing that he had previously sold the land, deed the land to Buyer #2, who records his deed. Buyer #2 purchases in ignorance of the earlier deed to Buyer #1. Buyer #2 gets good title to the real estate. He is an *innocent purchaser* or *bona fide purchaser.*

EXAMPLE: Seller owns certain land. Seller mortgages it to Lender in 1985. The mortgage, through error, is not recorded. Seller sells the land to Buyer in 1986, concealing the existence of the mortgage. Buyer owns the land free and clear of the mortgage. The innocent purchaser is protected against the unrecorded mortgage.

9.02   Constructive Notice from the Records

The recording laws have a double operation or effect. First, they protect a purchaser or mortgagee who acts in ignorance of an earlier unrecorded deed or mortgage. Second, they also provide that if a deed or mortgage is recorded, all persons who thereafter deal with the property will be deemed to have full knowledge of the recorded document. The courts will not permit a man to say that he acted in ignorance of a recorded document. Every purchaser or mortgagee of the land is said to be *charged with notice* of prior recorded documents. The courts say that the public records impart *constructive notice* of all prior recorded deeds and mortgages.

> **EXAMPLE:**   Seller conveys land to Buyer #1, who records his deed. Thereafter Seller persuades Buyer #2 to buy the same land, telling Buyer #2 that he still owns the land. Buyer #2 fails to examine the public records relating to this tract of land. Buyer #2 acquires nothing. He has constructive notice of the deed to Buyer #1.

9.02(a)   Office Where Deeds are Recorded

The name of the officer charged with the duty of keeping the public records of deeds and mortgages varies from state to state. This officer may be known as the recorder of deeds, county recorder, clerk and recorder, register of deeds, or registrar of deeds. For convenience, the officer in charge is hereinafter referred to as the *recorder,* and the public office where deeds are filed or recorded is referred to as the *recorder's office.*

9.03   What Constitutes Recording

A person wishing to record a deed or mortgage simply deposits it with the recorder. Such a deed or mortgage is said to be filed for record. It is thereupon deemed to be recorded, and all the world must take notice of its existence. The recorder copies the document in his record books, indexes it, and returns the original to the person who left it for recording. He does not pass on the validity of the document.

9.04   Persons Protected by Recording Laws

The recording laws are designed primarily to protect subsequent *bona fide purchasers* of the land. A bona fide purchaser is one who has paid the purchase price in good faith and without knowledge of the prior unrecorded deed or mortgage. A mortgagee who loans money in reliance on the public records is also considered a bona fide encumbrancer and is entitled to the protection of the recording laws.

EXAMPLE: Owner mortgages his land to Lender #1, which mortgage is not recorded. Thereafter, Owner mortgages the same land to Lender #2, and Lender #2 records his mortgage. Lender #2 does not know of the earlier mortgage to Lender #1. Lender #2 has a first mortgage on the land.

A number of states add the requirement that to be entitled to protection the subsequent purchaser or mortgagee must file his deed or mortgage for record before the recording of the earlier deed or mortgage. Under this rule, for example, it will not suffice that Purchaser has purchased a tract of land in good faith and in ignorance of an earlier unrecorded mortgage. He must also record his deed before the prior mortgage is recorded. But if he records his deed in apt time, Purchaser is protected even if the mortgagee later discovers his oversight and proceeds to record his mortgage.

In some states, a judgment creditor is also protected against prior unrecorded deeds and mortgages.

EXAMPLE: Owner makes a mortgage to Lender on November 15. The mortgage is recorded on November 20. On November 17, Creditor obtains a judgment against Owner. The judgment enjoys priority of lien over the mortgage, since it was rendered prior to the recording of the mortgage.

A substantial number of states, however, do not extend such protection to judgment creditors.

A person who has acquired land by gift is not protected by the recording laws because the donee has not given consideration for the property.

EXAMPLE: Owner mortgages his land to Lender. Lender fails to record the mortgage. Owner thereafter gives Daughter a deed to the land as a gift, and Daughter records her deed. Lender can nevertheless enforce the mortgage against her. But if, prior to the recording of the mortgage, Daughter should sell the land to Buyer, Buyer, being a purchaser, would get good title free and clear of the prior unrecorded mortgage.

Similarly, a person who acquires title by will or as an heir of the landowner is not protected.

EXAMPLE: Owner makes a mortgage to Lender, but Lender fails to record this mortgage. Thereafter Owner dies leaving a will whereby he gives this land to Son. Lender may enforce the mortgage against Son.

9.05   Effect of Actual Knowledge

Of course, one who actually knows of a prior unrecorded deed or mortgage is not protected against it. After the knowledge or notice is acquired, the party cannot be a *bona fide purchaser.*

EXAMPLE: Owner owns certain land and mortgages it to Lender in 1975. Through error, the mortgage is not recorded. Owner enters into a contract to sell the land to Buyer in 1980. The contract of sale describes the mortgage. Buyer must pay off the mortgage or take the land burdened with the mortgage. He is not protected. He is not an innocent purchaser.

Similarly, where a subsequent purchaser takes with *actual knowledge* of an instrument which was recorded, but because of some defect, does not impart *constructive notice,* no bona fide purchaser protection attaches. 3 ALR2d 589.

EXAMPLE: Purchaser obtained a title report which showed a defectively recorded deed to Stranger. This deed, though taken by the recorder, did not legally give constructive notice because it bore no acknowledgment. Purchaser will not be a bona fide purchaser and will take subject to X's right. 59 ALR2d 1318.

9.06(a)   Prerequisites to Valid Recording—Instruments Entitled to be Recorded

Deeds, mortgages, release deeds, satisfactions of mortgages, assignments of mortgages, and other instruments affecting the title to land should be recorded. However, it is only the original instrument that is entitled to be recorded. The recording of an unsigned carbon copy of an instrument is without legal effect. *Herzer* v. *Dembosz,* 167 NE2d 210 (Ill. 1960).

9.06(b)   Prerequisites to Valid Recording—Defective Instruments

In a great majority of the states, an instrument must be properly acknowledged by the grantor or mortgagor in order to be entitled to recording. In a number of states, proper witnessing is accepted as a substitute for an acknowledgment. But if the instrument is neither witnessed nor acknowledged, or the witnessing or acknowledgment is fatally defective, the instrument is not considered as a recorded instrument even though the recorder accepts it and copies it on the public records. 59 ALR2d 1299.

9.06(b)(1)   Prerequisites to Valid Recording—Defective Instruments—Legal Descriptions

Since a purchaser or mortgagee is under no obligation to examine the records affecting lands other than those that he is buying or upon which he is loaning money, the record of an instrument that was intended to convey or affect the same but which has such an erroneous description that it does not appear to affect the land in question does not bind any subsequent purchaser, mortgagee, or judgment creditor.

EXAMPLE: Owner owns the West Half of the Northwest Quarter of Section 14, Township 38 North, Range 13 East, of the Third Principal Meridian. Owner executes a mortgage to Lender that is intended as a mortgage on this same land but which, through inadvertence, describes the land as falling in Section 24 instead of Section 14. The mortgage is recorded. A person searching the records as to Owner's title has no way of knowing that this mortgage was intended for the particular land in question. Therefore this mortgage does not impart constructive notice, and subsequent purchasers, mortgagees, and judgment creditors will be protected against this mortgage. *Landis* v. *Miles Homes, Inc.* 273 NE2d 153 (Ill. 1971).

9.07   Possession as Notice

The law requires every prospective purchaser or mortgagee to examine into the possession of the real estate and to ascertain what rights are claimed by the parties in possession. Whether or not he actually does make this inspection, such purchaser or mortgagee is deemed to know the facts that such an investigation would have disclosed. In other words, possession imparts constructive notice in much the same way as the recording of a deed.

> **EXAMPLE:**   Owner sells and conveys his home to Buyer #1. Buyer #1 fails to record the deed but moves into the house. Owner offers to sell the land to Buyer #2. Buyer #2 examines the records in the recorder's office and finds title in Owner, but he fails to examine into the possession of the premises. He takes a deed from Owner. This deed passes no title. Buyer #1's possession gave Buyer #2 constructive notice of this deed.

> **EXAMPLE:**   Tenant leased the laundry rooms in a building being converted to condominiums under an arrangement which later proved to be economically unattractive to the purchasers of condominium units. Before the condominium units were sold, Tenant affixed signs and stickers to the walls of the laundry room and to the laundry machines. These signs and stickers identified Tenant as the lessee of the laundry room. The condominium purchasers brought suit to declare the lease to Tenant of no force against them. The court ruled otherwise, stating that the placement of the signs identifying an occupant different from the record owner was sufficient to place a prospective purchaser of the condominium units on inquiry notice. *Dana Point Condominium Association, Inc.,* v. *Keystone Service Company,* 491 NE2d 63 (Ill. App. 1986).

It should, however, be noted that the prospective purchaser's duty of inquiry does not necessarily exist in all situations. For example, there may be no such obligation where the tenant occupied only a part of the property or where the tenant's possession was not sufficiently visible so as to put a prospective buyer on inquiry notice. *Cohen* v. *Thomas & Son Transfer Line, Inc.,* 586 P2d 39 (Col. 1978).

It is obvious that failure to record or a defective recording of a deed is usually less dangerous than the failure to record or the defective recording of a mortgage. This follows, since the purchaser usually goes into possession of the land after receiving his deed, and this possession gives all the world notice of his rights, whereas a mortgagee rarely goes into possession before a default has been made and is therefore entirely dependent on the public records to give other persons notice of his rights.

In a few states, South Carolina and Virginia, for example, possession does not impart constructive notice.

9.08   Chain of Title

Except in a few states a title searcher tracing title by means of the public records employs an official index of names, called the Grantor-Grantee Index. Suppose, for example, that the United States Government records show that the United States sold a particular tract of land to John Jones on March 15, 1840. The title searcher will turn to the Grantor Index, which is arranged alphabetically, and, beginning with the date March 15, 1840, he will look under the letter "J" for any deeds or mortgages made since March 15, 1840, by John Jones. Naturally he would not expect to find any deeds or mortgages of that land made by Jones prior to March 15, 1840, because Jones did not become the owner until that date. Therefore the law does not require him to look for any such deeds or mortgages prior to that date. *Glen Ellyn Savings & Loan Assn.* v. *State Bank of Geneva,* 382 NE2d 1267 (Ill. App. 1978).

Suppose he finds that John Jones conveyed the land to Joseph Smith by deed dated September 10, 1860, and recorded November 1, 1860. He will now look under the letter "S" for any deeds or mortgages made by Smith on or after September 10, 1860, the date when Smith acquired title. This process is repeated until he has brought the title down to the present. This process is called *running the chain of title.*

To be considered properly recorded, a deed or mortgage must be in the *chain of title,* that is, it must be dated in the proper chronological order.

> **EXAMPLE:**   At a time when his negotiations for the purchase were virtually concluded, Joseph Smith made a mortgage on the land dated September 5, 1980, and recorded September 6, 1980. Both of these dates were prior to the date of the deed by which Smith later acquired ownership, namely, September 10, 1980. A title searcher would not find this mortgage, since he would not look under the name "Smith" for any deed or mortgage prior to September 10, 1980. Such a mortgage is not in the line or chain of title. *The legal result is the same as though the mortgage had not been recorded at all.* A person buying the land not knowing of the existence of this mortgage would get good title free and clear of the mortgage.

In other words, the records show the ownership of land passing from one person to another, and the name of each successive owner as that name appears on the public records must be searched only during the period of his ownership as such period is revealed by the public records to see what recorded deeds and mortgages he has signed.

Because of the *chain of title theory,* it is important that names be spelled correctly in deed and mortgages.

> **EXAMPLE:**   A deed runs to John O. Malley and a mortgage is thereafter made by John O'Malley. The mortgage is not in the chain of title and is treated as an unrecorded mortgage. The deed is indexed under M, the mortgage under O.

The chain of title theory is a two-edged sword. One, constructive notice is given of those instruments that are in the chain of title. Two, instruments outside of the chain of title do not impart constructive notice. *Pease* v. *Frank,* 105 NE 299 (Ill. 1914).

9.09   Tract Indexes

In a few states (Iowa, Louisiana, Nebraska, North Dakota, Oklahoma, South Dakota, Utah, Wisconsin, and Wyoming, for example), the name index (Grantor–
Grantee Index) has been supplemented by a Tract Index. This index allocates a
separate page to each piece of property in the county, and if you are interested
in a particular piece of property, you simply locate the page in the index where
you will find listed all recorded deeds and other documents relating to this piece
of property.

9.10   Record as Notice of Contents of Deed or Mortgage

An instrument duly recorded is notice to subsequent purchasers and mortgagees
not only of the instrument itself, but also of all of its contents.

> **EXAMPLE:**   A warranty deed contained a covenant that the premises were
> free and clear of all encumbrances "except a certain mortgage for $900." This
> mortgage had not been recorded. This was notice to the grantee and to all other
> persons of the existence of the mortgage.

9.11   Foreign Language

A deed or mortgage written in a foreign language, though valid as between the
parties thereto, does not impart constructive notice and must be treated as an
unrecorded document. *Moroz* v. *Ransom,* 285 N.Y.S. 846 (1936).

9.12   Liens that Need Not be Recorded

There are certain liens, such as real estate tax liens, inheritance tax liens, and
franchise tax liens, that are binding on all persons though not recorded.

9.13   Short Leases

In a number of states leases that exceed one year in duration (other states, three
years) must be recorded. Possession under a longer lease does not impart constructive notice. In consequence, a purchaser or mortgagee of an apartment
building, for example, may assume that occupants are there under short leases
where no leases have been recorded. This is a practical approach to the problem
of large buildings where checking possession is a burdensome task. In point of
fact, purchasers and mortgagees never do check all the tenants in a large building. They accept a written statement by the building manager describing the
leases and the terms of the leases.

CHAPTER 10

Real Estate Brokers

10.01 Defined

A broker is an agent employed in negotiating the sale, purchase, or exchange of land. Compensation is usually in the form of a commission.

10.02 License

In many states a person is not authorized to act as a real estate broker unless he is licensed. Real estate brokerage is a profession requiring knowledge, experience, and honesty, and in order to obtain a license, a candidate must have the qualifications that are specified by local law. In order for a real estate broker to recover commissions, he must have his license at the time he is hired to perform the services for which he claims a commission. *Schoene* v. *Hickham,* 397 SW2d 596 (1966). New York was the first state to require a written test for license applicants. Today, license officials belong to a national organization, the National Association of Real Estate License Officials. The brokers' examination is standardized to some extent. Educational and ethical standards continue to climb steadily. Many states require brokers to take continuing education courses. Other states are certain to follow. A similar trend is evident in the legal profession.

> **NEW DIRECTIONS:** In recent times real estate commissions have shown a strong tendency to hold brokers to high standards of conduct. State laws list many causes for revoking a license. Racial discrimination (steering or blockbusting) is one of them, of course. Acting in a dual capacity is another.

> **EXAMPLE:** A broker advertised to buy real estate. The ad did not disclose he was a broker. He lost his license. *Land* v. *Georgia Comm.,* 237 SE2d 243, 142 Ga. App. 860 (1977).

EXAMPLE: Commingling client's funds with personal funds is grounds for re-vocation of a license.

EXAMPLE: Acting dishonestly in transactions involving the broker individually is grounds for revoking the license. For example, in a deal where the broker was the seller he was guilty of a fraudulent misrepresentation. He was not brokering the deal. He lost his license. 22 ALR4th 136.

The system of licensing real estate brokers paralleled the growth of professionalism in the real estate business generally. The first university courses in real estate were offered in 1905. The National Association of Real Estate Boards was organized in 1908. By 1913, YMCA courses were offered throughout the country. Today, the real estate business is run by professionals.

The first treatise on real estate was Fisher's *Principles of Real Estate Practice*, published in 1923. Within three years Babcock had published a treatise on appraisals and MacChesney a treatise on real estate law.

10.03   Splitting Commission with Buyer

It has been held that the seller's broker may split his commission with the buyer where this concession is necessary to obtain the buyer's signature on the contract. This is simply a sacrifice on his part. It does not harm the seller. *Lageschult* v. *Steinbrecher*, 35 Ill. App. 3d 909, 344 NE2d 750 (1976); 63 ALR3d 121. Splitting commission in the multiple listing system is legal.

But other than as above stated, the broker must not split his commission with "finders" or other persons lacking a broker's license. Doing so will defeat a broker's claim for a commission. *Thorpe* v. *Garte*, 250 A2d 618 (Md. 1969).

10.04   Brokers' Functions in Today's Market

The old idea that the broker's task is simply one of finding a buyer has totally disappeared. Today's brokers are highly skilled professionals with a great breadth of knowledge of real estate law. Among the matters they must be familiar with are:

1. Zoning, including the ability to point out that a basement apartment in a home is illegal, that occupancy by unmarried persons who are not related may be unlawful, that an area that has numerous apartments scattered among the homes may be unable to keep out additional apartments.

2. Building codes, especially those that require replacement of plumbing and old electrical wiring where extensive rehab is contemplated.

3. Private building restriction problems, for example, those that prohibit building near lot lines and would thus bar an addition to the home.

4. Methods of financing where financing by an institution is unavailable. For example, the take-back (purchase money) mortgage, the installment contract, the wrap-around mortgage, the second mortgage, the assumable mortgage, and all the problems, draw-backs, and advantages of each method, including income tax advantages,

retention of old low-interest mortgages, high return on wraparounds, dangers of all provisions, balloon notes, and acceleration clauses, prepayment privileges, benefits to the private lender, and the deed of trust in states having no redemption laws.

5. Benefits and drawbacks of joint tenancies and tenancies by the entireties, for this arises even in preparing the contract of sale.

6. The pitfalls involved where unmarried cohabitants plan to buy a home together.

7. The dangers involved in creating lodging units in homes. A lodger whose rent has been raised unreasonably, as he contends, may be tempted to complain to the authorities.

8. The pitfalls in buying a landmark home must be explained to a buyer.

9. Buyers who are timid about entering into installment purchases must be informed about escrows and other protective devices.

10. Where informal party driveways are revealed, buyers must be advised to obtain counsel for the preparation of formal agreements.

11. In a condominium, the broker must know about restrictions on pets and renting, recreational leases, etc.

12. Brokers must know about the penalties for blockbusting and steering. Racial problems are growing more serious year by year.

13. A broker must be able to explain about assessments and special assessments in condominium and planned unit development situations, and the role of the home association.

14. Especially in industrial and commercial properties the broker must know whether the building is a nonconforming use, and if so, that it cannot be expanded.

This list is suggestive only. Of course, the broker must not usurp the lawyer's role. But the mere mention to a buyer of an older industrial plant that it is a nonconforming use may enable the buyer to make a quick decision.

10.05   Salesmen

Virtually every brokerage office maintains a staff of salesmen who do the actual leg work of showing houses and filling in sales contract forms. Salesmen are required to have a state license and pass a state examination, but it is less comprehensive than the broker's examination. In recent times the broker makes a determined effort to establish the relation between himself and a salesman as that of *independent contractor*. There is a distinction between an *employee*, who must take orders from an employer, and an independent contractor, who is hired to do a job, but does it pretty much his own way. The objective is to avoid the employer-employee relationship, so that the broker need not withhold income taxes, and so forth. Problems may arise. Salesmen often go to the "boss" on complex deals, and as soon as he starts giving directions he may become an *employer*. But the whole idea is untested. 41 Am. Jur. 2d 735. No doubt many real estate offices prefer the employer-employee relationship. This, of course, gets the employer involved in income tax withholdings. In any event, whatever the legal relationship is, courts are bound to hold the broker liable for fraudulent representations made by his salesmen.

10.06   Employment—Necessity of Contract of Employment

A real estate broker acts as an *agent*. The person who hires him is known as the *principal*. Usually the broker is hired by the landowner for the purpose of procuring a buyer. In return for finding a buyer willing to buy on the landowner's terms, the broker receives a commission from the landowner. Occasionally the broker is hired by a person wishing to buy real estate. In either case, in order to recover a commission, the broker must be able to show that he was hired by the person from whom he claims a commission. If he claims a commission from the seller, he must show that the seller hired him. If he was hired by the buyer only, he cannot claim a commission from the seller. Otherwise stated, a broker must show that the person from whom he claims a commission employed him to make the sale. However, an employment contract of agency may be *implied* from the conduct of the parties.

> **EXAMPLE:** Landowner gave Broker a description of his property and requested that Broker sell it at a designated price. This is a contract of employment, and Broker is entitled to a commission if he finds a buyer. The fact that compensation was not discussed is immaterial. Landowner must have understood that Broker would expect to be paid if he produced a buyer. *Long* v. *Herr*, 10 Colo. 380, 15 Pac. 802 (1887).

> **EXAMPLE:** Broker, without any prior request from Landowner, submitted to Landowner an offer of $3,000 for the purchase of the land. Landowner declined, stating that his price for the land was $4,000. Broker thereupon procured a buyer who was willing to buy for $4,000. Landowner refused to sell. Landowner is not liable for a commission. The mere statement by a landowner that he will take a certain sum for his land is not sufficient to authorize the person to whom the statement is made to act as agent for its sale. Landowner is entitled to assume that Broker is acting for the buyer and will look to the buyer for his compensation. *O'Donnell* v. *Carr*, 189 N.C. 77, 126 SE 112 (1925).

As is evident from the foregoing illustrations, a broker usually tries to collect from the seller. This is due to the obvious fact that it is financially easier to collect money from the seller, who is being paid the purchase price of the property, than from the buyer, who may be stretching his finances in order to buy the property. Legally, the fact remains that the broker cannot collect from the seller unless he can show that the seller hired him. If there is no formal listing contract, at the very least the seller must say or do things that make the broker believe he has been hired by the seller. *Reeve* v. *Shoemaker*, 200 Ia. 938, 205 NW 742 (1925). Or the broker must so conduct himself that it is clear to the seller that he expects to be paid a commission. *Korzendorfer Realty Inc.* v. *Hawkes*, 178 SE2d 524 (Va. 1971).

> **EXAMPLE:** Suppose in the example last given, the broker had asked, "When will my commission be paid?" Suppose the owner had replied, "At closing." This is enough to show a contract of employment.

Ordinarily a broker hired by the seller has no claim against the buyer.

EXAMPLE: Seller hired Broker, who found Purchaser. Seller and Purchaser entered into a contract of sale. However, difficulties arose and Purchaser refused to perform. Broker cannot collect anything from Purchaser. His contract of employment is with Seller only. 30 ALR3d 1399.

10.06(a)   Employment—Persons Who May Employ a Broker

A person other than the property owner may list the property for sale and become liable for a commission. 12 Am.Jur.2d *Brokers* § 163.

EXAMPLE: Wife owned certain real estate. Husband listed the property for sale with Broker, who knew that Wife owned the property. Broker found a buyer for the property, but Wife refused to sell. Husband was held liable to Broker for a full commission. Broker was entitled to assume that at the proper time Husband would procure Wife's consent to the sale. *Aler* v. *Plowman*, 190 Md. 631, 59 A2d 196 (1948); *Rose* v. *Knoblock* 194 SW2d 943 (Mo. 1946).

EXAMPLE: The land was held in community property but the husband alone signed the listing. He is liable for the full commission. *C. Forsman Real Estate Co.* v. *Hatch,* 547 P2d 1116 (Idaho).

EXAMPLE: Property was owned by Husband and Wife, in joint tenancy. Husband alone, without Wife's permission, listed the property for sale with Broker, who found a buyer for the property, but Wife refused to sign the contract of sale and the deal fell through. Husband was held liable to Broker for a full commission. 10 ALR3d 665.

10.06(b)   Employment—Necessity for Written Contract

Because of the endless litigation that has arisen concerning the existence of an employment contract, in many states the contract of employment must be in writing in order for the broker to be entitled to a commission and must state the amount of commission agreed on. 9 ALR2d 747.

10.06(c)   Employment—Form of Contract

Often the hiring of a broker is an informal, oral affair. However, written contracts, called *listing contracts,* are also used. These are usually brief documents, often in the form of printed cards. When such a form is filled in, it contains the following: (1) names of seller and broker; (2) description of property, usually by street address, 30 ALR3d 935; (3) terms of sale, including sale price, whether sale is for cash or on terms, and so forth; (4) duration of broker's employment; (5) commission to be paid; and (6) special agreements, such as the provision for an exclusive agency. Each of the countless real estate boards is likely to have its own listing form.

10.06(d) Employment—Unconscionability

Current law requires the broker to use a listing form that is fair to the party employing him. *Unconscionability and the Real Estate Broker's Employment Contract,* 5 Memphis S.U.L.Rev. 59.

10.06(e) Contract Provisions

Quite commonly a *contract of sale* will contain a provision that a commission will be paid by the seller to the broker at closing. Even if there is no proof of a *contract of employment,* this contract clause suffices to make the seller liable to the broker. *Moran* v. *Audette,* 217 A2d 663 (D.C. 1966); *B. Woodworth* v. *Vranizen,* 539 P2d 1055 (Ore. 1975). The broker is what the lawyers call a "third-party beneficiary." Of course, the broker's rights rest on the terms of the contract.

> **EXAMPLE:**   The contract of sale provided that the seller would pay the broker a commission at closing. This contract, however, was contingent on the buyer's ability to obtain financing. The buyer was unable to obtain financing. The broker collects no commission. *Shumaker* v. *Lear,* 235 Pa. Super. 509.

10.07 Code of Ethics

Many controversies involving brokers, especially those involving conflicts between two brokers, are settled by resort to the code of ethics established by the National Association of Realtors or by the local real estate board. Punishments are given according to the nature of the offense—the most severe being expulsion from the board. This cuts the broker from the multiple listing service maintained by the board and is an effective punishment indeed.

10.08 Open Listing

There are several different types of listing contracts. The *open listing* contains no provision forbidding the landowner to sell the land himself or to hire other brokers, and ordinarily an owner may hire two or more brokers unless he specifically agrees not to do so. *Kelly* v. *Beaudoin,* 298 A2d 831 (Vt. 1972). Virtually all informal verbal listing arrangements are open listings. The disadvantage of this type of contract is that it is likely to produce quarrels over the commission where several brokers produce buyers.

> **EXAMPLE:**   Landowner employed Broker to obtain a purchaser. Broker obtained a purchaser on the specified terms, but Landowner refused to pay a commission on the ground that he had already concluded an agreement to sell to a purchaser obtained by another broker. Broker sued Landowner. The court held for Landowner. The primary object to be attained in the employment of

agents to sell real estate, the court said, is the production of a single purchaser for such real estate, and that object is attained where one of several agents produces to the owner a purchaser who is ready, able, and willing to buy the real estate on the owner's terms. Where several agents are employed, the sale of the property either by the owner in person or by any of the brokers operates at once to terminate the authority of all the brokers, although they had no actual notice of the sale. This is a provision the court "reads into" every open listing.

To put this in a legal perspective, one might say that in every open listing there is an unspoken, implied precondition that to receive compensation the broker must find a willing buyer before such a buyer is procured by the owner or some other broker.

When different brokers have the property for sale, and no one of them has the exclusive right to make the sale, the broker who first finds a buyer ready, able, and willing to buy is the procuring cause of the sale and is the one entitled to the commission. Nonetheless, sellers are well advised to make the payment of commission conditioned upon the closing of the sale to the buyer procured by the broker.

Open listings are used quite often in sales of commercial property or apartments.

10.09   Exclusive Agency

Unless there is an agreement to the contrary, the landowner may hire two or more brokers to sell the same property and will be liable only to the broker who first finds a buyer. Fear that time and money spent in locating a buyer may be wasted if another broker is working on the deal has led brokers to favor a listing contract that assures the broker that as long as his employment continues no other broker will be hired. Such a listing is called an *exclusive agency*. If the owner hires a second broker who finds a buyer for the property, the owner will have to pay both brokers. *Dean Vincent Inc.*, v. *Chef Joe's Inc.*, 541 P2d 969 (Ore. 1975). However, in some states the second broker must not accept employment if he knows a prior exclusive exists. 17 ALR4th 763. The giving of an exclusive agency does not bar the landowner from selling the property through his own efforts, without the assistance of other brokers. If the property owner sells the property through his own efforts, the exclusive agency automatically comes to an end without any liability on the landowner's part for a commission and regardless of the employment period specified in the listing contract. *Martin Realty Co.* v. *Fletcher*, 103 N.J.L. 294, 136 Atl. 498 (1927); *Des Rivieres* v. *Sullivan*, 247 Mass. 443, 142 NE 111, 88 ALR2d 936. This is a provision the court "reads into" the listing. 88 ALR2d 936.

The mere fact that the listing contract refers to the broker as an *exclusive agent* is enough to create an exclusive agency. *Harris and White* v. *Stone*, 137 Ark. 23, 207 SW 443 (1918).

Again, to put this situation in a legal perspective, one might say that in every exclusive agency there is an unspoken, implied precondition that the broker must find a willing buyer before such a buyer is procured by the owner.

10.10   Exclusive Right to Sell

The *exclusive right to sell* goes one step further than the exclusive agency. It not only makes the broker the sole agent of the landowner for the sale of the property, but also provides that the named broker will receive a commission in the event the property is sold by the named broker, by the owner, *or by anyone else.* Thus even if the owner makes a sale through his own efforts, he must pay the broker. *Bourgoin* v. *Fortier,* 310 A2d 618 (Me. 1973); *Flynn* v. *La Salle Nat. Bank,* 9 Ill.2d 129, 137 NE2d 71; 88 ALR2d 941.

A broker who desires an exclusive right to sell should draft his listing contract with great care.

> **EXAMPLE:**   A form simply gave the broker "the exclusive right to sell" the property. The court felt that this did not sufficiently warn the seller that he could not sell the home through his own efforts. 88 ALR2d 948.
>
> In time brokers developed a form that states explicitly that the broker will get a commission if, during the listing period, the home is sold by the named broker, any other broker, or the owner himself. This has become the common form used almost everywhere. It is the "exclusive right to sell."

Of course, every form can be changed by the parties.

> **EXAMPLE:**   *A* has been negotiating with *B* for the purchase by *B* of *A*'s home. At times agreement was almost reached. *A* decides he can no longer wait, lists the property with *X,* a broker, but *A* insists on typing into the listing a clause stating that no commission will be paid if the home is sold to *B.* This protects *A* because of the time and effort he has already devoted to *B.*

10.11   Multiple Listing

Multiple listing is simply a means by which brokers in a given area pool their efforts to sell properties listed with any member of the pool. 45 ALR3d 190. The original, or *listing broker,* obtains from the property owner an exclusive right to sell. He then furnishes a copy thereof to all members of this pool, or this is done through a central office. If any member other than the original broker sells the property, the commission is divided between the original broker and the *selling broker* who effects the sale. In some systems the central registration office shares in the commission also. Only the original broker has the right to sue the property owner for a commission. The property owner has no contract of employment with members of the pool other than the original broker. Therefore, he can never be sued by them, *Goodwin* v. *Gleck,* 139 Cal. App.2d 936, 294 P2d 192 (1956), nor is he liable for misrepresentations made by them. 58 ALR2d 41. However, the members of the pool working on the sale owe the landowner the usual duties of a broker such as loyalty. *Frisell* v. *Newman,* 429 P2d 64 (Wash. 1967).

In some brokers' listings a paragraph is included stating that the listing will be furnished to members of the multiple listing service (MLS). Arguably the selling broker is hired, through the MLS, by the listing broker. This makes the selling broker a "subagent." *Frisell* v. *Newman,* 71 Wash.2d 520, 429 P2d 864 (1967). This may become important if the selling broker makes a misrepresentation and the buyer sues the seller. See also Vol. 1, H. Miller & M. Starr, *Current Law of California Real Estate*, § 4.8 at 18–19 (1975); 1976 B.Y.U.L. Rev. 513 (1976); 18 Wayne L. Rev. 1343, 1353 (1972).

10.11(a)   Antitrust

Since multiple listing systems may either set a commission rate or specify a recommended rate, they have come under fire as violations of the antitrust laws. Court decrees have been entered prohibiting fixing of commission rates.

   A real estate board that has operated a multiple listing system, limiting the persons who could be admitted to membership, has been held to violate the antitrust laws. *Grillo* v. *Board of Realtors*, 219 A2d 635 (1966).

   Other decisions also hold that exclusion of licensed brokers from a multiple listing service is illegal. *Marin County Board of Realtors* v. *Palsson*, 16 Cal.3d 920, 549 P2d 833, 130 Cal. Reptr. 1 (1976).

> **NEW DIRECTIONS:**   The United States Supreme Court has held that federal antitrust laws are applicable to brokers' groups that bring about a fixed rate of commission in a given area. *McLain* v. *Real Estate Board*, 100 S Ct. 502 (1980). All states have laws that forbid price fixing or restraint of trade. Under the combined pressure of federal and state laws, brokers' groups will probably liberalize their membership rules, fearing that excluded brokers may sue for damages. Persons who allege that brokers engaged in price fixing may sue for triple damages under the antitrust laws. 9 R.E.L.J. 151.

> REFERENCES: 14 Cal W. L. Rev. 298 (1978); 70 Columb. L. Rev. 1324; 60 Ill. B.J. 856; 24 U. Fla L. Rev. 266 (1974); 24 Wash. & Lee L. Rev. 67 (1967); 22 ALR 4th 103.

10.12   Performance Required of Broker

Suppose that *A* contracts with *B* to perform some act for *A*, such as building a house. *A* will pay *B* a stated sum for such performance of the contract. *B* has earned the contract price when he has completed performance of the contract. The same is true of a broker. He has earned his commission only when he has completed performance of a task he has undertaken. Generally a broker has earned his commission when he produces a buyer who is ready, able, and willing to buy on either the terms specified by the seller in the listing contract or on other terms acceptable to the seller. *Bonanza Real Estate Inc.* v. *Crouch*, 517 P2d 1371 (Wash. 1974).

> **EXAMPLE:**   Landowner hires Broker to find a buyer. Broker finds Prospect who signs a contract at less than the price asked by the seller. Landowner and Prospect negotiate until they agree on a price. Broker helps in the negotiations and therefore earns his commission.

At times, the broker may submit a contract signed by the buyer for the full contract price requested by the seller. Such a contract is a mere *offer to buy*. Until the seller signs it also, he is not bound to the contract. The broker has performed what he was hired to do, and therefore has earned a commission even if the seller changes his mind and refuses to sign the contract.

Likewise, if the seller and buyer reconsider after a contract of sale has been signed, causing the deal to be canceled, the seller remains liable to the broker. 74 ALR2d 459. Also, if the buyer has signed a contract which the seller has also signed and thereafter refuses to complete the deal, the broker has nevertheless earned his commission. 74 ALR2d 443.

The word *able* in the phrase "ready, able, and willing to buy" refers to financial ability. The buyer must be able to command the necessary funds to close the deal within the time required. *Pellaton* v. *Brunski,* 69 Cal. App. 301, 231 Pac. 583 (1924). He must have the sum of money necessary to meet any cash payment required, and be financially able to meet any further payments. *Raynor* v. *Mackrill,* 196 Ia. 1298, 164 NW 335 (1917). Otherwise stated, he must have the present ability to pay. *Boutelle* v. *Chrislaw,* 35 Wis.2d 665, 150 NW2d 486 (1967). Thus a newly organized corporation having limited funds might be considered not *able* to buy. However, it is not necessary to show that the buyer is standing outside the office door with all cash in hand. It is sufficient if the buyer is *able* to command the necessary funds on reasonable notice. *Perper* v. *Edell,* 160 Fla. 447, 35 So2d 387 (1948). Thus a buyer is *able* to buy if he has already arranged with some mortgage house to loan him the funds necessary to pay for the property. *Schaaf* v. *Iba,* 73 Ohio L.Abs. 46, 136 NE2d 727 (1955).

To *produce* a willing buyer requires that the broker must reveal his identity to the seller. 2 ALR3d 1128. A *willing* buyer is one who is willing to enter into an unconditional cash sale contract enforceable against the buyer at the time it is signed by the parties. Or, if the contract is *conditional,* the buyer becomes a *willing* buyer (willing to be personally liable to the seller) only when the condition is satisfied.

This point is of great importance because most residential contracts contain the condition that the contract is contingent on the buyer's ability to obtain financing. It is normal and expected that the broker will tender a contract signed by the buyer that differs from the contract called for by the listing contract. Once this takes place, the broker's rights rest on the terms of the contract he tendered and was accepted by the seller. If the contingency inserted by the buyer is his ability to obtain financing, the broker's right to a commission depends on the buyer's ability to obtain financing. *Schumaker* v. *Lear,* 235 Pa. Super. 509.

EXAMPLE: Owner hires Broker to sell his home for $100,000. Broker finds Purchaser, who is willing to pay the price, but needs a loan of $80,000. Owner and Purchaser sign a contract contingent on Purchaser's ability to get the loan of $80,000. Owner was not obliged to accept this condition. Legally, Purchaser was not a buyer ready, able, and willing to buy. Hence Broker has not yet earned his commission. If Purchaser fails to get his loan, Broker earns no commission. *Woodland Realty Inc.* v. *Winzenried,* 82 Wis.2d 218, 262 NW2d 106 (1978); *Cooper* v. *Liberty Nat. Bank,* 75 NE2d 769 (Ill. 1947); *Slonim Ltd.* v. *Bankers Mortgage and Realty Co.,* 42 A2d 396 (N.J. 1945).

However, since every contract by implication requires a good faith effort on each party to perform, the buyer must make a good faith effort to obtain financing. If he fails to do so, this condition drops out of the contract and the buyer is unconditionally liable to the seller. Hence the broker has earned his commission.

Buyer, to protect himself, should apply to at least two loan companies for a mortgage loan. If each gives Buyer a letter refusing to grant a loan, that is proof that he made a good faith effort and failed.

There are numerous other examples that illuminate the matter of the performance required of the broker.

> **EXAMPLE:**   No commission is payable if the buyer is willing to sign only an installment contract. 8 ALR2d 382. But, if the *seller* also is willing to sign the installment contract with the buyer, the broker earns his commission when the first installment is paid unless the contract provides otherwise. 8 ALR2d 382. The seller must act in good faith.

> **EXAMPLE:**   Seller's broker procured a buyer who signed a contract contingent on buyer's ability to procure financing within a set time. Before the time expired, the seller sold the land to third party. The broker recovers his commission because the seller acted in bad faith. *Wuadrant Corp.* v. *Spake,* 504 P2d 1162 (Wash. 1973).

> **EXAMPLE:**   Where the contract of sale is contingent on the buyer's ability to procure lender's consent to an assumption of the existing mortgage, the broker earns no commission until such consent has been obtained. *Kopf* v. *Milam,* 60 Cal.2d 600, 387 P2d 390 (1963).

> **EXAMPLE:**   Listing calls for sale on "cash or contract." Broker's buyer signs an installment contract but terms are unacceptable to seller. *White* v. *Turner,* 164 Kans. 659, 192 P2d 200 (1948). No commission.

> **EXAMPLE:**   When the broker tenders a buyer who insists on a condition in the contract making his liability contingent on some official action, the broker has not earned his commission unless and until that action has taken place. Illustrations include the requirement of city approval of buyer's plat, *Larkins* v. *Richardson,* 502 P2d 1156 (Ore. 1972), a contract of sale of a hospital or convalescent home requiring issuance to the buyer of a state license to operate the facility, *Urbanski* v. *Halperin,* 30 Conn. Super. 575, or a contract to buy a restaurant for which a state liquor license is required, *Blaine* v. *Stinger,* 79 Ariz. 376, 290 P2d 732 (1955).

The broker is entitled to no compensation or reimbursement whatever for unsuccessful efforts to sell unless the listing contract expressly so provides.

Often after a seller has listed property with a broker, and after the broker has found a buyer who is ready, able, and willing to buy at the listed price, the seller changes his mind and looks for some way to turn down the buyer without being liable to the broker for a commission. Such a seller seeks to take refuge behind the rule that if the terms offered by the broker's prospect differ from the terms specified by the seller, the broker is not entitled to a commission. 18 ALR2d 376. Keep in mind that if the broker's listing contract is silent on other terms of the transaction, the law will read various implications into it. And if the terms of sale as set forth in the contract of sale do not harmonize with the terms of sale set forth or *implied* in the listing contract, the seller may reject the broker's prospect without incurring any liability for commission.

> **EXAMPLE:** If the broker's listing is silent, the seller is required to convey only the land, building, and articles that are technically fixtures. If the contract of sale tendered by the broker requires the seller to convey furniture or other personal property, the seller may reject the contract without any liability for commission. *Sharkey* v. *Snow,* 13 Ill. App.3d 448, 300 NE2d 279 (Ill. 1973).

However, customary contract provisions, like those requiring a seller to have good title, are unobjectionable. *Adelman* v. *Caputi,* 181 SE2d 608 (Va. 1971).

But when the broker procures a purchaser ready, willing, and able to purchase on the authorized terms, and through the fault of the *owner* the sale is not consummated, the broker is entitled to a commission. A commission must be paid to the broker when:

1. The deal falls through because the owner changes his mind and refuses to sign the deed to the purchaser or a contract to sell. The rule is the same where the land has increased in value and the owner rejects the broker's buyer for this reason. If the seller refuses to sign, giving as his only reason the fact that he has changed his mind, he cannot thereafter shift his ground and claim that the buyer's offer was not in compliance with the listing. *Russell* v. *Ramm,* 200 Cal. 348, 254 P. 532 (1927).

2. The deal falls through because the owner's wife refuses to sign the contract or deed. 10 ALR3d 665. This assumes state law requires her signature.

3. The deal falls through because of defects in the owner's title. *Triplett* v. *Feasal,* 105 Kans. 179, 182 P. 551 (1919); 28 ALR 4th 1007.

4. The deal falls through because of the owner's fraud. *Hathaway* v. *Smith,* 187 Ill. App. 128.

5. The deal falls through because the owner is unable to deliver possession within a reasonable time.

6. The deal falls through because the seller insists on terms and provisions not mentioned in the listing contract, as where the seller insists on the right to remain in possession after the deal has been closed. *Brown* v. *Ogle,* 75 Ind. App. 90, 130 NE 147 (1927).

7. After the contract of sale has been signed the seller and buyer get together and cancel the contract. *Steward* v. *Brock,* 60 N.M. 216, 290 P2d 682 (1955).

8. The deal falls through because the buyer cannot procure financing and the contract is not contingent on ability to procure financing.

9. Both parties sign a contract of sale, but the buyer later defaults. 74 ALR2d 454.

> **EXAMPLE:** Seller and buyer sign an installment contract and buyer later defaults. *Engelking* v. *Boyce,* 278 Ore. 237, 563 P2d 703 (1977).

To offset the effect of this rule, a seller may wish to limit his liability to the amount of the residue of the earnest money after payment of seller's expenses.

10.12(a) Statutes

A broker must comply with laws governing brokers. If he fails to furnish the seller a copy of the listing agreement (as the local law requires), he cannot recover a commission. *Carnell* v. *Watson*, 578 P2d 308 (Mont. 1978).

10.12(b)   Performance after Expiration of Listing Period—
Withdrawal from Sale

Most listing contracts today fix an expiration date. Indeed, some state laws require this. Several rules exist.

1. If the period expires and the seller thereafter refuses to consider prospects brought in by the broker, he is within his rights. Performance must take place within the time specified.

2. Some listings specify that the broker has earned his commission if within the listing period he "introduces" a buyer to the seller, and within _____ days after expiration of the listing a contract of sale is signed with that buyer. This clause is valid. The broker has performed within the listing period by introducing a prospect to the seller before the listing has expired. 27 ALR2d 1346, 1408. Sometimes the listing speaks of a buyer "submitted by the broker" or a buyer with whom the seller has "negotiated" within the listing period. Again, the broker is entitled to a commission if such negotiations take place. 51 ALR3d 1149. Or the listing may award the broker a commission if the seller withdraws the property from sale before the listing expires. *Blank* v. *Borden*, 115 Cal. Reptr. 31, 324 P2d 127 (1974), 63 Calif. L. Rev. 102. In these cases the seller has agreed to a special kind of performance or event under which the broker need not be the procuring cause of sale. Obviously, such provisions are introduced because sellers often engage in sharp practices in order to deprive the broker of a commission.

3. To preserve the broker's rights under a clause such as that described in No. 2 above, the listing contract may include a provision permitting the broker to "register" with the seller the names of all prospects to whom the broker has shown the property. Many brokers, even in the absence of such a clause, send the seller a letter when they have shown the property to a prospect and request the seller to "protect" the broker if the property is sold to this prospect.

10.12(c)   Performance on Price or Terms Differing from Listing

In the ordinary situation in which the principal promises a broker a commission for finding a purchaser and the asking terms are stated to the broker, the usual interpretation is that the asking terms are intended merely to guide the broker in starting negotiations, and the broker will have his commission if he produces a customer ready and willing to purchase at such price or on such modified terms as the principal may accept. *Bonanza Real Estate Inc.* v. *Crouch*, 517 P2d 1371 (Wash. App.).

10.12(d)   Ellsworth Dobbs

There is some thinking that because the broker is so much better informed than the seller as to the buyer's financial ability to consummate the deal involving a home sale, if the deal falls through because the buyer cannot command the necessary financial resources, the seller should not be liable for a commission. *Ellsworth Dobbs Inc.* v. *Johnson*, 50 N.J. 528, 236 A2d 843 (1967).

> **NEW CASES:**   Cases following *Ellsworth Dobbs* are *Tristram's Landing Inc.* v. *Wait*, 327 NE2d 727 (Mass. 1975) and *Shumaker* v. *Lear*, 345 A2d 249 (Pa. 1975).

Ellsworth Dobbs comes to the rescue of the parties who have neglected to insert in the contract of a sale a clause making it contingent on the buyer's procuring financing. As stated, if the broker's purchaser insists on such a clause, as he normally should do, the broker has not procured a willing and able buyer unless and until financing is procured. But if such a clause is not inserted, technically the seller has accepted the broker's buyer as a willing and able buyer. *Ellsworth Dobbs,* as stated, comes to the rescue and bars the broker from recovering a commission if the deal falls through for lack of financing. This rescue operation affects only the broker's commission.

As between seller and buyer, the mortgage contingency clause is essential. If the contract lacks this clause and the deal falls through because financing cannot be obtained, the buyer forfeits his earnest money.

Predictably, this is the law throughout the country because it squares with the normal expectation of the parties. 5 Memphis St. U. L. Rev. 59, 71.

10.12(e)   "No Deal, No Commission" Provision

While ordinarily the broker has earned his commission as soon as he has found a buyer who is ready, able, and willing to buy, the parties may validly contract, by means of the so-called *no deal, no commission clause* inserted in the listing contract, that payment of the commission is contingent upon the closing of the deal and full payment of the purchase price to the seller. Thus if the seller cannot clear his title or if the buyer refuses to go through with the deal, the seller need not pay a commission. 74 ALR2d 437. However, if the seller's refusal to complete the sale is arbitrary and without reasonable cause or in bad faith, the broker is entitled to his commission. *Huntley* v. *Smith,* 153 Minn. 297, 190 NW 341 (1922); *Goldstein* v. *Rosenberg*, 331 Ill. App. 374, 73 NE2d 171 (1947).

In effect, the *Ellsworth Dobbs* case makes every broker's listing contingent on the procuring of financing by the buyer. Also, it is a rule of some real estate boards that no commission is to be collected unless the deal closes.

10.12(f)   Recapitulation

It seems wise at this point to recapitulate some of the rules discussed in these pages. (1) It is really not expected by either the seller or his broker that the broker will instantly produce a buyer ready, able, and willing to meet the seller's terms. Rather, it is expected that the broker will bring in a buyer's contract that offers less (in price or terms) than the seller has asked for in the listing contract. Often, the contract signed by the buyer is contingent on his obtaining financing. This is routine. If that clause is omitted, the buyer will lose his down payment if he cannot procure financing. This is disastrous for the buyer. So all three parties (seller, buyer, broker) do business on the basis of the contract produced by the broker, which is contingent on the buyer's getting financing. This means that the seller and broker have implicitly agreed that the broker's commission is contingent on the buyer's obtaining the financing. When and if this occurs, the financing condition drops out of the contract and the broker has earned his commission. The buyer is ready, willing, and able. (2) In an *Ellsworth Dobbs* case the buyer has been careless. He has omitted the provision making his liability contingent on getting financing. This case really decides nothing concerning the rights of the seller and buyer against each other. Basically, it holds that the broker cannot collect a commission from his seller if the financing cannot be obtained. Always remember that there are two contracts involved, the listing contract between the seller and broker, and the contract of sale between seller and buyer. Do not confuse these two contracts. (3) The "no deal, no commission" clause protects the seller against any liability to his broker if the deal fails to close for any reason, including the buyer's inability to procure financing.

10.13   Procuring Cause of Sale

A broker who has been hired by the landowner has earned his commission when his efforts were the primary and procuring cause of the sale. When the owner or several brokers have been active and a sale is concluded, a broker, to justify his claim to a commission, must show that he was the efficient cause of the sale. The following are typical situations in which the problem arises:

> 1. The broker finds a prospect and introduces him to the owner. Thereupon the owner and the prospect, without the broker's intervention, negotiate and conclude a sale. The broker is the procuring cause of the sale and is entitled to a commission. *Ranney v. Rock,* 135 Conn. 479, 66 A2d 111 (1949).
>
> 2. When several brokers are involved, the rule appears to be substantially this: If the first broker's efforts result in a disagreement or if negotiations are abandoned, and thereafter a second broker steps in and brings the parties together, the second broker is the procuring cause of the sale. 46 ALR2d 865. But if the first broker brings about a substantial agreement and the second broker merely works out details of the transaction, the first broker is the procuring cause of the sale. In other words, the broker whose efforts predominate in bringing about the sale gets the commission.

There are cases where the broker is entitled to damages or compensation even though he has not been the procuring cause of the sale: (1) For example, in the case of an exclusive agency, the broker will be entitled to compensation from his employer if the employer hires another broker who succeeds in selling the property, because the employer breached his contract, which obligated him to refrain from hiring other brokers. This exposes the seller to payment of two commissions. 29 ALR3d 1229. (2) Also, in the case of an exclusive right to sell, the broker may be entitled to compensation even if his employer sells the building through his own efforts. Here the employer has breached his contract not to try to sell the building through his own efforts. *Bell* v. *Demmerling*, 149 Ohio St. 165, 78 NE2d 49 (1948). (3) Or the listing contract may provide that the broker will be entitled to compensation if the property is sold to a person with whom the broker *has negotiated,* or *whose name has been furnished the seller* by the broker. Here a broker who engages in negotiations with a prospect collects even though a deal is ultimately clinched by the landowner himself or another broker. *Delbon* v. *Brazil,* 134 Cal. App.2d 461, 285 P2d 710 (1955).

> **SUGGESTION TO BROKER:**   Let the listing contract provide that broker will be entitled to a commission if within the specified time the property is sold to a person with whom the broker negotiated. 51 ALR3d 1149.

10.13(a)   Effect of Seller's Ignorance that Buyer was Procured by Broker

When a seller hires a broker to sell his property and thereafter sells the property to a buyer procured by the broker, in most states the broker is entitled to a commission despite the fact that the seller is ignorant that the buyer was procured through the broker. *Ranney* v. *Rock,* 135 Conn. 479, 66 A2d 111 (1949); 142 ALR 275. Having hired a broker, the seller should know that the appearance of a buyer may have been caused by the broker. The seller should check with his *broker* whenever a prospective buyer comes in. Inquiring of the *buyer* is rather pointless, for obviously many buyers, hoping to get a reduced price, will conceal the fact that a broker interested them in the property. Suppose, however, that *A,* a landowner, hires *B,* a broker, and *B* interests *C* in the purchase of the property. *C* procures a dummy or strawman, *D,* to make an offer for the property. *A* inquires of *B* if *B* had interested *D* in the purchase of the property. Not knowing that *D* is only a nominee for *C, B* says no, and *A* cuts his price by the amount of the commission he would have paid to *B. B* gets no commission. *A* has done all he could to protect his broker. *Zetlin* v. *Scher,* 217 A2d 266 (Md. 1966).

If the seller reduces his price to a prospect in ignorance of the fact that the prospect was procured by the seller's broker, some states, as stated above, allow the broker to collect his commission. The seller is at fault because he failed to check with the broker. Other states refuse the broker a commission. 46 ALR2d 872, 877. These latter states feel that the broker should notify the seller of each prospect he procures.

> **SUGGESTION TO BROKER:**   As soon as you find a prospect, send a postcard to the seller notifying him of the name and address of the prospect you have found.

The broker can collect damages from a buyer who attempts to cheat him out of a commission.

> **EXAMPLE:**   Owner hired Broker, and Broker interested Buyer in the purchase of the property. Buyer then contacted Owner directly and got Owner to cut his

price. He did this by representing to Owner that no broker was involved. Owner, feeling he would not be paying a commission, cut his price. Broker discovers this. He can sue Buyer for damages. 29 ALR3d 1251. Buyer was guilty of a wrongful interference with a business relationship.

10.14   Duration and Termination of Employment

Many controversies arise as to the duration and termination of the broker's employment.

10.14(a)   When no Term Limit is Specified

If the listing contract specifies no duration, the broker's authority automatically lapses after expiration of a reasonable time. 27 ALR2d 1346, 1390.

10.14(b)   Where the Listing Contract Fixes the Period of Employment

Listing contracts usually provide that they are to continue for a specified time. In such case the broker is not entitled to a commission unless within the time limit he procures a customer who is ready, able, and willing to buy.

But, in the following cases the broker will recover a commission even if he fails to find a purchaser within the period of the listing:

1. When the expiration of the listing time is attributable to the bad faith of the owner, as when the owner deliberately postpones agreement with the broker's buyer, hoping thereby to defeat the broker's claim for compensation. 27 ALR2d 1346, 1357.

2. If negotiations are begun within the time specified in the listing contract, continue without interruption, and are completed after the time has expired, the broker is entitled to his commission, particularly where the delay is due to the fault of the owner, as where it is occasioned by a defect in title. The seller is considered to have waived or extended the time limit.

3. When the listing contract contains some clause protecting the broker. For example, some listing forms, in large type, purport to run for a fixed period of time, such as thirty days, but following this will be a provision continuing the listing until a termination notice has been served on the broker.

4. Courts are unfriendly to these provisions for automatic extension of the listing period. Even if the listing contract is an exclusive agency or exclusive right to sell, it will be considered an *open listing during the extended period* if it is at all ambiguous. When a listing stated it was to be "sole and exclusive for three months and thereafter until sixty days written notice had been given," it was exclusive only for the initial three-month period. Thereafter it was only an open listing. *Boggess Realty Co.* v. *Miller*, 227 Ky. 813, 14 SW2d 140, 27 ALR2d 1420 (1929); *Wilson v. Franklin*, 282 Pa. 189, 127 Atl. 609 (1925); *Central Realty Co. v. Cutter*, 406 NE2d 515 (Ohio 1980). Other listing forms provide that the owner will protect the broker on sales made within ninety days of the expiration of the listing to prospects with whom the broker had *negotiated* or who had been *introduced* to the seller by the broker before expiration of the listing period. 27 ALR2d 1346, 1408.

In many states statutes or regulations require the listing to state an ending date.

10.14(c)   Revocation Based Upon the Nature of the Listing Agreement

Up to relatively recent times, the broker's listing agreement was what lawyers call a *unilateral contract*. Such a contract is one that contains a promise by *one* of the parties to the agreement but no promise by the other.

> **EXAMPLE OF UNILATERAL LISTING CONTRACT:**   "I, the owner of 1234 Main Street, Anytown, U.S.A., promise to pay you, John Smith (broker) a commission of 6% if you sell said house for not less than $100,000 within the next 60 days." Signed by both parties and dated. Note that the broker makes no promise to do anything. There are still many such printed forms in use.

If the listing agreement is unilateral in form, the owner may terminate it before the termination date but only if he does so before the broker has expended any money or effort. Put another way, such an agreement is revocable by the owner only up to the time the other party begins performance. *McMenamin* v. *Bishop*, 493 P2d 1016; *Stort* v. *Reinhard*, 183 SE2d 601 (1971); *Hutchison* v. *Dobson-Bainbridge Realty Co.*, 31 Tenn. App. 490, 217 SW2d 6 (1946); *Patton* v. *Wilson*, 220 SW2d 184 (Tex. Civil App. 1949); 1 Corbin, *Contracts* 154; 37 Iowa L. Rev. 370; 12 Am.Jur.2d 796; 64 ALR 404.

In these cases, any revocation after the broker has begun performance is wrongful and makes the owner liable to the broker for damages.

Most real estate boards have adopted the *bilateral listing contract*.

> **EXAMPLE OF BILATERAL LISTING CONTRACT:**   "A (the broker) hereby promises to promptly begin advertising the property for sale in one or more newspapers commonly used by realtors in this county, to show the house to prospective buyers, to conduct open-houses as time permits, to transport buyers to financial institutions that lend money on such homes," etc.

Such a listing is irrevocable from the moment it is signed. The broker has a legal obligation to do as he has promised. Any revocation by the owner before the listing period has expired will be wrongful, so long as the broker is keeping his part of the bargain.

10.14(d)   Revocation after Broker has Performed

Of course, the landowner has no right to revoke the broker's employment after the broker has brought in a buyer ready, able, and willing to buy.

10.14(e)   Revocation in Bad Faith

In all types of listings the owner will be liable to the broker for damages if he acts in bad faith in revoking the broker's employment. 27 ALR2d 1346, 1395. Even when no time of employment is specified, when the broker is concluding negotiations with a prospective purchaser, the owner cannot revoke the agency *in bad faith for the purpose of avoiding payment of commission.* In other words, when the broker has found a prospect and is concluding negotiations with him, so that the commission is virtually earned and the broker is approaching success, the owner cannot discharge the broker and thereupon step in and consummate the transaction, thus defeating the broker's right to his compensation. Restatement, Agency § 446.

> **EXAMPLE:** Landowner hired Broker to sell his land. While Broker was negotiating with a prospect, Landowner sold the land to his wife and discharged Broker. Thereupon, Landowner and his wife sold to Broker's prospect. They were liable for Broker's commission. *Alexander* v. *Smith,* 180 Ala. 541, 61 So 68 (1912); 36 Boston U.L. Rev. 302.

> **EXAMPLE:** Immediately after the listing expires, the seller sells the property to a prospect found by the broker. This is bad faith. *Feeley* v. *Mullikin,* 269 P2d 828 (Wash. 1954).

10.14(f)   Revocation by Sale

A wrongful revocation of the broker's exclusive right to sell takes place if the owner contracts to sell the land to a purchaser not procured by the broker or even if he gives the purchaser only an option to purchase. The option removes the property from the market. *Hunt* v. *Smallidge,* 321 NYS2d 825; *Coleman* v. *Mora,* 263 Cal. App.2d 137, 69 Cal. Reptr. 166; 35 U. of Colo. L. Rev. 205.

10.14(g)   Notice of Revocation of Employment

When a landowner decides to withdraw his land from sale, he must give the broker notice of the revocation of his employment before the broker has finished the job. If the broker brings in a buyer ready, able, and willing to buy, obviously no judge will allow the owner to say, "I fired you mentally five days ago." 12 CJS 152; 12 Am.Jur.2d 817.

10.14(h)   Revocation by Sale by a Person Other than Broker

A different situation is presented when the revocation of employment takes place by virtue of the fact that the land has been sold by someone else. As previously explained, in an *open listing* the employment of all brokers hired by the owner *automatically ends when a ready, able, and willing buyer is found either by the owner or by one of the brokers.* In an *exclusive agency* the broker's employment automatically ends if the owner, through his own efforts, finds a willing buyer. No duty to notify brokers rests on the owner in most states, because all brokers understand that in these situations their employment is subject to such automatic termination. *Des Rivieres* v. *Sullivan,* 247 Mass. 443, 142 NE 111; 12 Am.Jur.2d 817. These termination provisions are "read into" the listing contract by the courts.

Suppose that in an open listing a broker finds a willing buyer. However, he fails to notify the owner of this fact, and thereafter the owner signs a contract with some other buyer, procured, let us say, through another broker, the owner being still ignorant of the first broker's successful efforts. The first broker loses his commission. It is his duty to notify the owner promptly on finding a buyer. *Wilson* v. *Franklin*, 282 Pa. 189, 127 Atl. 609.

SUGGESTION TO BROKER: Notify the owner as soon as you have found a willing buyer.

10.14(i)   Damages for Wrongful Revocation of Employment

Suppose that under one of the rules discussed in this section the owner's revocation of the broker's employment is legally wrongful. How much should the courts award the broker? Some courts give the broker only the expenses incurred by him for advertising and so forth and a sum that will compensate him for the reasonable value of his services. These are restitutionary damages. *Ferguson* v. *Bovee*, 239 Iowa 775, 32 NW2d 924 (1948); *Nicholson* v. *Alderson*, 347 Ill. App. 496, 107 NE2d 39 (1952); 12 Am.Jur.2d 819. Most courts, however, on one theory or another, award the broker a full commission. 37 Iowa L. Rev. 367; 69 ALR3d 1269.

The broker will have a better chance of collecting a full commission if the listing contract has a clause covering the possibility of the seller's withdrawing the property from sale.

SUGGESTED FORM: Let the listing provide that the broker will receive a full commission "if, within the time above specified, the premises are sold by the broker, owner, or anyone else, or if, within said period, the owner withdraws the property from sale or terminates the broker's employment." *Baumgartner* v. *Meek*, 126 Cal. App.2d 505, 272 P2d 552 (1954).

10.14(j)   Statutes or Regulations Requiring Stated Expiration Date

Many states, either by law or regulation, require that the broker's listing state a specific expiration date. This is true, for example, in Illinois, Michigan, and Oklahoma.

10.15   Amount of Compensation

In a case where the broker has found a buyer, he is entitled to the commission agreed upon, and if no commission has been fixed by the parties, he is entitled to the usual and customary commission for such services. He is usually not entitled to extra compensation for incidental services.

The compensation is computed on the gross sale price.

EXAMPLE: Owner owns property on which there is a $120,000 mortgage. He lists it with a broker at $150,000, and the broker finds a buyer. Although Owner will obtain a net of only $30,000 ($150,000 less the $120,000 required to pay the mortgage) he must pay a commission based on a price of $150,000.

10.15(a)   Lien for Commission

A broker hired by the seller has no lien on the seller's land for the payment of his commission unless the listing contract so provides. 125 ALR 921. In other words, even though the broker has earned his commission, his only remedy, if the seller fails to pay, is to sue the seller and obtain a judgment against him. The broker cannot do anything to block sale of the land by the seller to the broker's customer or anyone else.

10.16   Earnest Money

The seller's broker ordinarily has no authority to accept an earnest money deposit. 30 ALR2d 805, 810. Quite commonly, however, the broker is permitted to hold the earnest money with no written agreement regarding disposition of such money. If the sale is completed, the money must be returned to the seller. *Mader* v. *James,* 546 P2d 190 (Wyo. 1976). If the sale is not completed and the buyer is not at fault, the broker must return the money to the buyer. *Mader* v. *James,* 546 P2d 190 (Wyo. 1976); 12 Am.Jur.2d 852; 38 ALR2d 1382. But if the seller is not at fault, the broker is liable to the seller if he returns the earnest money to the buyer. *Lake Co.* v. *Molan,* 131 NW2d 734 (Minn. 1965). A seller's broker who returns the earnest money to a defaulting purchaser also loses his commission. 69 ALR2d 1244. Most cases hold that where the seller's title proves defective, or the deal falls through for some other fault of the seller, the broker must return the earnest money to the buyer. 38 ALR2d 1382. But the better rule is that when a deal falls through, the broker should return the earnest money to his seller-employer, leaving it to the buyer to collect from the seller. *Schultz* v. *Clements,* 7 Ill. App.2d 510, 130 NE2d 1 (1955); 12 Am.Jur.2d 852. The broker should not be asked to assume the role of judge and thus determine, as between seller and buyer, who is entitled to return of the deposit. Of course, either the listing contract or the contract of sale can give the broker specific directions on this score, and he should follow them.

Many sale contracts name the broker as the party who holds the earnest money. Many listing contracts contain a paragraph telling what the broker is to do with the earnest money when trouble arises, as where seller or buyer refuses to close the deal. Often the contract requires the broker to determine who is at "fault." As is obvious, even judges experience difficulty in determining who is at fault. Is it wise for brokers to undertake this task?

10.16(a)   Risk of Loss Caused by Broker's Embezzlement

Where the earnest money is in the hands of the seller's broker, the rule is a simple one. If the broker is not authorized *by the seller* to accept a deposit, the money is the buyer's money entrusted to the broker, and he must bear the loss resulting from the embezzlement. 30 ALR2d 808. If the listing contract authorizes the broker to accept a deposit, risk of loss in on the seller.

Even when a seller accepts a *down payment* taken by the broker from the buyer, it does not constitute authority by the seller to the broker to accept the balance of the purchase price. The seller is entitled to assume that the broker was acting as the *buyer's agent* in transmitting the down payment. Suppose that the listing contract authorizes the broker to sign a contract of sale on behalf of the seller. Here the broker necessarily has implied authority to accept the down payment, for a down payment is made when the contract is signed. 30 ALR2d 816. The broker holds the money as agent of the seller, and if the broker embezzles the money, the loss falls on the seller. If the listing contract authorizes the broker to *sell and convey* the property, or if the seller entrusts the deed to the broker for delivery to the buyer, then the broker has implied authority to receive all of the purchase price. This must be so, for the seller's agent, not the seller, will be present at the closing of the deal, and the buyer must pay someone.

A number of states have adopted statutes under which brokers are required to contribute to a fund that is used to compensate victims of a broker's defalcations. *Ariz. R.E. Dept.* v. *Arizona Land Title Co.*, 9 Ariz. App. 9, 449 P2d 71 (1968).

10.17   Splitting Commission—Multiple-broker Deals

Agreements to divide commissions are common and are usually enforced.

EXAMPLE: Broker A (who has no office) uses the office of Broker B. A stated to B, "If I ever get a deal in your office, I'm going to split my commission with you." This event in fact occurred. B was entitled to half the commission. 71 ALR3d 601.

In general, the participating broker will collect his share of the commission if and when the commission is collected.

EXAMPLE: Broker A was hired to sell some parcels of land. He contacted Broker B offering to split his commission in any parcel B sold. B is entitled to his share as and when A collects the commission on sales engineered by B. 71 ALR3d 606.

A broker may become liable to another broker for wrongful deprival of a commission.

EXAMPLE: Owner listed land for sale with Broker #1. Broker #2 contacted Owner and was told to obtain Owner's terms from Broker #1, which Broker #2 did. Broker #2 found Buyer #1, ready, able, and willing to buy, and Owner accepted him. Broker #1 and Broker #2 agreed that they would share the commission equally. Then Broker #1 persuaded Owner to sell the land to Buyer #2 in a deal with Broker #1 obtaining all of the commission. Broker #1 is liable to Broker #2 for the commission of which Broker #2 was deprived by Broker #1's wrongful conduct. It is wrongful to interfere with a contract right. 34 ALR 3d 730.

And if the broker hired by the seller asks a second broker to help him sell it and the second broker finds a buyer and collects a commission, he must divide the commission with the first broker. *Wheeler* v. *Waller*, 197 NW2d 585 (Iowa 1972). The brokers have engaged in a joint venture, and each party in a joint venture owes a duty of good faith to the other.

If Seller hires Broker and Broker finds Buyer, but Buyer offers less than Seller is willing to accept, Broker may legally share his commission with Buyer. This is often done. 63 ALR3d 1219.

10.18   Duties of the Broker—Loyalty and Double Agency

In general, the duties of a broker are the same as those of any other agent. They arise because the broker is an agent. They need not be spelled out in the listing contract. An agent must be loyal to his principal. If, without the knowledge and consent of his principal, he is also acting for the other party to the transaction, the principal may, when he discovers this fact, declare the contract void. This is true even though the transaction is a good one for the principal and the other party acts in good faith and was unaware of the double agency. *Gordon* v. *Beck,* 196 Cal. 768, 239 P. 309 (1925). It is to the interest of the seller to obtain the highest possible price and of the buyer to pay the least. Clearly, no one agent can serve both these interests. *Duffy* v. *Setchell*, 38 Ill. App.3d 146, 347 NE2d 218 (1976). Such a broker also loses his commission.

> **EXAMPLE:**   Owner hired Broker #1 to sell his land, and Buyer hired Broker #2 to find land of this character for Buyer to purchase. Broker #1 and Broker #2 conferred and agreed to split their commissions down the middle. Neither broker can collect any commission. 63 ALR3d 1211, 1219.

Suppose a broker is hired by the buyer to find land or a building in a certain area, the buyer to pay a commission. Suppose that thereafter a property owner lists land of this description for sale with this broker. The broker reveals this fact *to the buyer only*, and a deal is closed between the seller and buyer, without, however, any knowledge on the seller's part that the broker was originally hired by the buyer. The broker collects his commission from the seller and now sues the buyer. To the brokers' surprise, the buyer claims that the broker cannot collect any commission whatever in a double agency situation. This is correct. The fact that the buyer knew of the double agency makes no difference. A fraud was perpetrated on the *seller,* and the law will not help a party to the fraud, the broker, to collect from the other party to the fraud, the buyer. *McConnell* v. *Cowan,* 44 Cal.2d 805, 285 P2d 261 (1955); 80 ALR 1077, 1087. The fact that the broker felt he was acting for the best interests of both parties is immaterial.

A *middleman,* who merely brings the parties together, leaving them to negotiate, may serve both parties. Here the double agency rule does not apply. 14 ALR

472; 58 ALR2d 42, 58. But if the broker assists either party or in some degree influences the parties, he is not a middleman. It is obvious that very few agencies fall in the middleman category.

The rule against double agency is often applied with great strictness.

> **EXAMPLE:**   Buyer requested that Broker find him a home. Broker contacted Homeowner, and a contract of sale was signed. Both Buyer and Broker expected that Broker would receive his commission from Homeowner. Buyer did not expect to pay a commission to Broker. This was also Broker's understanding. Nevertheless, Broker was working for both parties and should have revealed this to Homeowner. *Duffy* v. *Setchell,* 347 NE2d 218 (Ill. App. 1976).

> REFERENCES ON DOUBLE AGENCY: *Timmerman* v. *Ankron,* 487 SW2d 567 (cites authorities); 34 Columb. L. Rev. 552; 20 Marq. L. Rev. 163; 35 Yale L. J. 503; 63 ALR3d 1211.

10.19   Duties of the Broker—Conflict of Interest Problems

An agent must not have any individual interest in the transaction without the knowledge and consent of his principal.

> **EXAMPLE:**   Owner placed his property with Broker. Negotiations resulted in a sale by Owner to Buyer for $3,200, the Brokers receiving a commission of $160. After the deed was given, Owner discovered that Buyer was one of Broker's employees. Owner was entitled to have the conveyance set aside. *Johnson* v. *Bernard,* 323 Ill. 527, 154 NE 444 (1926). Owner also gets the commission back.

The rule even precludes a sale by the broker to his wife unless the seller is informed of the relation. If, however, the broker fully discloses the facts to the landowner, he may buy for himself, for a relative, or for himself and others.

10.20   Duties of the Broker—Disclosure and Nondisclosure

An agent must make full disclosure to his principal of all matters that may come to his knowledge pertaining to the subject of the agency. 2 ALR3d 1123.

> **EXAMPLE:**   Owner placed his property with Broker. Broker wrote Owner, stating that he and several other parties would buy the land at $400 per acre. The contract was signed, and Broker received a commission. Later Owner discovered that, prior to making this offer, Broker had received an offer for this property of $600 per acre. Owner was entitled to have the contract canceled. *Rieger* v. *Brandt,* 329 Ill. 21, 160 NE 130 (1928); 7 ALR3d 693.

> **EXAMPLE:**   The broker is liable if he transmits an offer to the principal but conceals a more favorable offer. 7 ALR3d 696.

EXAMPLE: While the property is listed with the broker, it increases in value. The owner is ignorant of this fact, but the broker knows of it. He fails to disclose this circumstance to the owner. He has violated his duty of full disclosure. *Eastburn* v. *Jos. Espalla, Jr. & Co.,* 112 So 232 (Ala. 1927); 33 ALR4th 944.

EXAMPLE: The buyer procured by the broker has a poor financial status. The broker knows this but fails to reveal it to the seller. A contract is signed, but the deal fails to go through because the buyer cannot raise the necessary funds. The broker has violated his duty of full disclosure. *McGarry* v. *McCrone,* 97 Ohio App. 543, 118 NE2d 195 (1954); *Nugent* v. *Scharff,* 476 SW2d 414 (1972); *Mason* v. *Bulleri,* 543 P2d 478 (Ariz. 1975); 34 ALR4th 191.

EXAMPLE: The buyer procured by the broker is a distant relative of the broker. He must reveal this fact to the seller. 26 ALR2d 1308. The broker must disclose the true identify of the purchaser. 2 ALR3d 1119.

In other words, the broker's duty is not discharged simply by his handing a contract to the seller for signing. He must notify the seller of all facts that might influence the seller in accepting or rejecting the offer, or else he is liable for damages. He must give his opinion as to the price that can be obtained, the likelihood of a higher price being offered in the future, the possibility of making a favorable trade or other use of the property, etc. *Moehling* v. *O'Neil Construction Co.,* 20 Ill.2d 255, 170 NE2d 100 (1960).

The converse of the broker's duty of disclosure is his duty not to reveal secret information to prospective buyers. Thus the seller's broker violates his duties if he reveals to a prospective buyer that the seller will take less than the listed price for the property, for obviously no buyer will pay the listed price if he knows that the seller will take less. *Haynes* v. *Rogers,* 70 Ariz. 257, 219 P2d 339 (1950).

10.21 Duties of the Broker—Misrepresentations

A broker hired by the seller will be held liable to the buyer in damages if the broker, acting on his own, makes a willful misrepresentation that induces the buyer to enter into the contract of sale. 58 ALR2d 10, 27; 8 ALR3d 553.

EXAMPLE: The broker falsely represented that the house was stucco-covered brick, whereas it was not brick. *Perkins* v. *Green,* 26 Ariz. 219, 224 P 620 (1924). He was liable to the buyer.

Of course, if the buyer chooses to rescind (cancel the deal and obtain return of his down payment) because of a misrepresentation made by the broker, the broker loses all rights to a commission from the seller. 9 ALR2d 504.

10.22 Duties of the Broker—Skill and Care

Like other agents, a broker must exercise skill and care in the service of his employer. 94 ALR2d 468.

EXAMPLE: A broker hired to sell land found a buyer and drew a contract of sale which the parties signed. Thereafter the buyer refused to go through with the deal. The court held that the contract was so poorly drawn that the buyer was not legally bound. The broker thereby forfeited his commission. *Dingman* v. *Boyle,* 285 Ill. 144, 120 NE 487 (1918). Moreover, he is liable to the seller for any damages the seller has suffered. *Mattieliegh* v. *Poe,* 57 Wash.2d 203, 356 P2d 328, 94 ALR2d 464 (1960).

EXAMPLE: A broker hired to buy or trade has a duty to determine the value of the real estate he acquires for his employer. If he fails in this respect and the property turns out to be a poor buy, he is liable and forfeits his commission. *Smith* v. *Carroll Realty Co.,* 8 Utah2d 356, 335 P2d 67 (1959).

EXAMPLE: A broker employed to find a property for a buyer must exercise skill and care if he undertakes to close the deal for the buyer without an attorney. Thus if the broker fails to procure a clear title for the buyer, he is liable to buyer for damages. *Lester* v. *Marshall,* 143 Colo. 189, 352 P2d 786 (1960).

EXAMPLE: A broker can be held liable for loss caused by his ignorance of zoning. *Burien Motors Inc.* v. *Balch,* 513 P2d 582 (Wash. 1973).

EXAMPLE: A broker can be held liable for careless title search. *Mayflower Mtg. Co.* v. *Brown,* 530 P2d 1298 (Colo. 1975).

10.23   Duties of the Broker—Liabilities and Penalties for Breach of Duty

Where the broker breaches his duties toward his employer, one or more of several penalties may follow:

1. In almost every case the broker will lose his commission. If he has already been paid, he must refund it. 2 ALR3d 1126.
2. If he has made a profit, as where the broker has bought the property from his employer through a nominee and resold it at a profit, he must pay such profit over to his employer.
3. If his employer has suffered any damages as a consequence of the broker's breach of duty, the broker will be liable for such damages.
4. Where the broker's misconduct is deliberate, as where he secretly buys the property from his employer, the court may see fit to punish the broker by compelling him to pay exemplary damages, that is, damages greater than the damage the employer has actually suffered. *Ward* v. *Taggart,* 51 Cal.2d 736, 336 P2d 534 (1959).
5. For a serious offense, such as secretly buying his employer's property, failing to disclose material facts to his employer, embezzling his employer's funds, etc., the broker may have his license suspended or revoked altogether. 56 ALR2d 573. Fraud in his own land transactions will also result in the loss of his license. *Holland Realty Inv. Co.* v. *State,* 436 P2d 422 (Nev. 1968).

As is true with respect to lawyers, doctors, architects, and others, the courts are holding brokers to higher and higher standards of professional ethics and competence. This is a desirable trend and is likely to continue.

10.24   Duties to Purchaser

It will be remembered that a broker is normally hired by the seller. One would think that he therefore has no duties to the purchaser. This is not so.

> **NEW DIRECTIONS:**   The newer decisions take the position that the broker is a special type of agent. He is licensed by the state after passing a comprehensive examination. He enjoys a monopoly in that unlicensed persons are barred from the profession. In effect, the state holds the broker out as being a responsible and capable person. He therefore has duties to the purchaser as well as to the seller. *Ward* v. *Taggart,* 325 P2d 502 (Cal. 1958); *Ocala Mfg. Co.* v. *Canal Authy,* 301 So2d 495 (Fla. 1974); *Sawyer Realty Group* v. *Jarvis,* 89 Ill.2d 379, 432 NE2d 849 (1982); *Dugan* v. *Jones,* 615 P2d 1239 (Utah 1980); 12 CJ5 *Brokers* § 104 p. 296.

> **EXAMPLE:**   Seller's broker misrepresented zoning to buyer. Broker held liable. *Barnes* v. *Lopez,* 544 P2d 694 (Ariz. 1976).

> **EXAMPLE:**   If the listing broker furnishes false information to his listing service and a member of the service transmits this false information to a buyer, the listing broker is liable to the buyer, just as if he himself had made the misrepresentation directly to the buyer. *Grandberg* v. *Turnham,* 333 P2d 423 (Cal. 1959), *First Church* v. *Cline S. Dunton Realty Inc.,* 19 Wash. App. 275, 574 P2d 1211 (1978).

> **EXAMPLE:**   If the broker arranges "creative financing," such as balloon note financing, he is liable if the buyer suffers damage. Zumpano & Marsh, *Creative Financing Arrangements: Risks and Liabilities,* 12 R.E.L.J. 115 (1983).

> REFERENCE: 18 Wayne L. Rev. 1343.

Just as a broker must not have an individual interest that conflicts with the interest of the seller, the broker must not have an individual interest that conflicts with the interest of the purchaser.

> **EXAMPLE:**   Seller's broker, after receiving an inquiry from a buyer, rechecked the property and secretly had a partner buy the property. Broker is liable to buyer. *George* v. *Bolen-Williams,* 580 P2d 1357 (Kan. 1980).

It may strike the reader as curious to find the courts are holding the seller's agent liable to the buyer, who is, in fact, the seller's adversary. This is explained in *Walter* v. *Moore,* 700 P2d 1219 (Wyo. 1985). There the court points out that the salesperson spends weeks or months in a close relationship with the buyer, driving side-by-side in the salesman's car, going through homes together, probably getting on a first-name basis. This confidential relationship places on the salesperson the burden of dealing fairly with the purchaser.

10.25   Unauthorized Practice of Law

The law appears to differ from state to state with respect to the propriety of a broker's filling in a form contract of sale where this is merely incidental to the earning of his commission for procuring a buyer. 53 ALR2d 796. However, if the broker makes a separate charge for filling in a form, he is guilty of unauthorized practice of law. 53 ALR2d 804. Likewise, if a broker prepares a will or deeds to put land in joint tenancy, he is guilty of the unauthorized practice of law. 53 ALR2d 807.

10.26   Authority of Broker to Sign Contract

Ordinarily a broker does not have authority to sign a contract on behalf of his employer. 43 ALR2d 1014.

10.27   Racial Discrimination

The law places a heavy burden on the broker and salesman with respect to racial discrimination.

10.28   Franchising

A development in brokerage law is the advent of franchising. The real estate broker retains his independent status. However, the franchiser furnishes advertising, training, procedure manuals, forms, and so forth. Each franchiser is furnished a list of other franchisees, which enables each franchiser to furnish a national referral service, for example, in employee-transfer situations. If the franchising agreement gives the franchiser the right to allocate territory, that portion of the agreement is likely to draw fire from the federal government. The laws against monopolies forbid territory allocation. Dowling & Hines, *Here Comes the Real Estate Franchise,* 7 Real Estate Rev. 48 (Summer 1977).

10.29   Integrated Financial Organizations

Large national corporations have embarked upon the business plan of furnishing the consumer with total financial services. The theory goes that the consumer can have "one-stop" service from these organizations. By shopping in one place, the consumer can obtain banking, stock brokerage, insurance, and real estate brokerage services. Some such organizations even have retail stores where these services can be obtained. From the business point of view, one customer base feeds the other. From the consumer's point of view, there is comfort in dealing with a business concern that the consumer has come to know and trust. In some instances the customer can obtain a discount on a bundle of goods and services provided by the same entity. This packaging of services has been upheld. *Coldwell Banker Residential Real Estate Services of Ill.* v. *Clayton,* 475 NE2d 536 (Ill. 1985).

CHAPTER 11

Contracts for the Sale of Land

11.01   Why a Contract for Sale of Land is Needed

Where *A*, a landowner, agrees to sell his land to *B* for $10,000 in cash, one may ask why it is necessary that a contract be signed. Why does not *A* then and there give a deed to *B* and *B* pay *A* the agreed price? The chief reason is that at the time the agreement is reached, *B* has no assurance, other than *A*'s statement, that *A* is in fact the owner of the land and that there are no defects in his title. Ordinarily, therefore, *B* will insist that a contract be signed and that it provide for an examination of *A*'s title, such examination to show that *A* has good title, before *B* pays the purchase price. In other words, the prudent purchaser is unwilling to buy a pig in a poke. The cash sale contract defines the type of title the seller will deliver; how, when, and where proof is to be made that title is good; and what is to be done if defects in title are revealed. In the meantime, the parties are bound to their bargain by the contract. The seller cannot sell to someone else who offers a higher price, and the buyer is bound to go through with the deal on the agreed terms set forth in the contract. There are other matters that must be attended to. Insurance policies bought, canceled, or transferred, leases assigned, financing arranged, inspections conducted. These take time. Some device must hold the buyer and seller together while this is done. The contract does just that.

The cash sale contract contemplates that the deal will be promptly closed. There is also a type of contract called the *installment contract, contract for deed,* or *land contract.* An installment contract provides for a down payment, with balance of purchase price payable in installments. The buyer receives his deed when all the installments have been paid or when the unpaid balance of the purchase price has been reduced to a certain agreed figure, whereupon the buyer is to receive a deed and give the seller a purchase money mortgage for the balance of the purchase price.

11.01(a)   Necessity for Written Contract

It is necessary that the fundamentals of a contract for the sale of land be in writing. Oral contracts to sell land cannot be enforced. The law that so provides is known as the *Statute of Frauds.* To satisfy the Statute of Frauds the *memorandum* of the contract must contain the names of seller and buyer, a sufficient description of the land, the contract price, the terms of sale if other than cash, and the signature of "the party to be charged," that is, the signature of the party against whom suit is brought on the contract. A few states require both parties to sign the contract, and there appears to be a trend in this direction. As a rule, oral testimony cannot be introduced in court for the purpose of supplying omissions in the written document. The fact that a sale is intended should also appear in the writing.

The Statute of Frauds may leave the parties in an uncertain situation.

Suppose that I enter an oral contract with you to buy your land, and I give you a down payment. Thereafter, I change my mind. Although you cannot sue me for the balance of the contract price, neither can I get my down payment back from you as long as you are willing to go through with the deal. 169 ALR 187.

Where the only memorandum is one that contains only the bare bones of the contract, the courts will read into the contract some of the missing terms.

EXAMPLE: If the contract is silent on these matters, the courts will assume a *cash sale* was intended with closing to take place in a *reasonable time;* that the sale price and deed will change hands *simultaneously;* that the deed will be a *quitclaim deed;* that the *buyer* will be entitled to *marketable title free from all encumbrances;* that any defects in marketability must be raised *before the deal is closed;* that the buyer will determine marketability *at his own expense,* and so on.

No particular form is required, so that a binding contract may be in the form of one or more letters, escrow instructions, receipt, a check, a promissory note, and so on.

EXAMPLE: A contract was as follows:

Chicago, January 8, 1904
Received of Anton Ullsperger $100 on said purchase of property No. 1031 Milwaukee Avenue, Chicago, Illinois at a price of $14,000.

C. Meyer

Meyer refused to perform, and Ullsperger sued him. The court compelled Meyer to give Ullsperger a deed. *Ullsperger* v. Meyer, 217 Ill. 262, 75 NE 482 (1905).

It will be observed in the last example that Ullsperger, who had *not* signed the contract, was allowed to enforce the contract against Meyer, who *had* signed it. However, Meyer could not have enforced the contract against Ullsperger. This is in accord with the general rule that in a land contract a seller may legally compel performance if he can produce a contract signed by the buyer, and the buyer can demand performance if he can produce a contract signed by the seller. Signature by both parties is not necessary.

Such a contract, although it meets the minimum requirements of the law, is altogether unsatisfactory, as will become apparent from the subsequent discussion. Obviously, it is best to have both seller and buyer sign the contract, and this is the usual practice.

Many documents that are legally sufficient as contracts for the sale of land are quite short, as the foregoing discussion reveals. Moreover, such documents are often given misleading names, such as *sales deposit receipt* or *offer to purchase*. People sign such documents without realizing that they have obligated themselves to buy or sell real estate. Sometimes such brief documents state that the parties will later sign a "regular" real estate contract. The court decisions are conflicting as to the effect of the inclusion of this phrase. As long as the main terms of the sale are stated in the document, most courts hold that the failure to sign a formal, detailed contract is unimportant, especially where the parties proceed with the details of the transaction as though a binding contract existed. *Sewel* v. *Dalby*, 171 Kans. 640, 237 P2d 366 (1951). Other states feel that the parties did not intend to be bound until a formal, detailed contract was executed, as called for in the short form, and therefore hold that the short document is not binding. *Brunette* v. *Vulcan Materials Co.*, 119 Ill. App.2d 390, 256 NE2d 44 (1970); *Lippman* v. *Featherston*, 247 Mich. 153, 225 NW 489 (1929); 17 Am.Jur.2d *Contracts* §26.

11.02   Questions the Parties Intending to Enter into a Contract Should Ask

Before *listing* the property with a broker for sale, the *seller* should ask himself:

1. Do I really want to sell?

COMMENT: If I list my property and the broker finds a buyer ready, able, and willing to buy at my price, I must pay a commission even if I then decide that I really don't want to sell.

2. Does my spouse want to sell?

COMMENT: If the broker finds a buyer and I am willing to sign the contract of sale, but my wife refuses to do so, in most states the buyer will refuse to go through with the deal because, unless she signs the contract, she is not legally obligated to sign the deed, and this will leave her dower or other legal rights outstanding. The deal fails, but the broker gets his commission.

3. Am I really in a position to sell?

COMMENT: Suppose my broker finds a willing buyer, but it develops that my title is defective, or I cannot pay off the existing mortgage, or my new house will not be ready for occupancy for a long time. Again the deal falls through, but I must nevertheless pay a commission.

Before *signing a contract of sale*, the *buyer* should ask himself these questions and attend to the following matters:

1. If I am buying vacant land, are there any zoning or environmental laws or ordinances that forbid or hamper the use I wish to make of the land?

COMMENT: Suppose I sign a contract to buy a vacant lot and intend to erect a filling station thereon, and thereafter I discover that the lot is zoned for residences only. I must nevertheless go through with the deal. Suppose my *building* complies with the ordinance. Do my plans provide adequate off-street parking to comply with the ordinance? Or does an environmental ordinance forbid any building on wetlands?

2. Under local ordinances, how far from the front, side, and rear lines must buildings be erected? Does this leave room for the type of building that I have in mind?

3. If I plan to use septic tank construction, is the lot big enough to qualify for septic tank construction under local ordinances?

4. If there is an airport in the vicinity, are there any regulations prohibiting the erection of electric poles or other structures that might prove a hazard to aircraft?

5. If there is a building on the land but I expect to remodel it, are there any ordinances that require new wiring or plumbing?

6. Does the building on the property violate existing zoning or building ordinances?

COMMENT: If it does, I may be compelled to remodel the building to conform to the ordinances, or even to tear it down.

7. Is the building a nonconforming use?

COMMENT: If it is, I cannot enlarge or alter it or rebuild it if it is substantially damaged by fire. If it was legally abandoned, the city can forbid its use.

8. Especially if the building is new, has a certificate of occupancy been issued?

9. Does the seller have a permit for any structure that requires a city permit, such as a swimming pool, a water tank on a roof, or a sign that extends over a sidewalk? Where a cocktail lounge is involved, am I, as the buyer, certain that I can procure an assignment of the liquor license?

10. If the contract of sale states that title will be subject to building restrictions, easements, mineral rights, and so on, how will these affect my building plans?

11. Are there sewers and water pipes in adjoining streets, and if there are, will I have the legal right to connect my proposed building to them? What is the connection charge?

12. Are there any utility lines, including underground lines, drainage ditches, draintiles, and so on, that will interfere with my building program?

13. Are existing streets, walks, sewers, or water pipes fully paid for and if not, will they be paid for by the seller, buyer, or by future special assessments? What does the contract say regarding this matter?

14. Will my building program interfere with my neighbor's drainage?

15. Keeping in mind that the law often says, "let the buyer beware," are there any defects in the building, for example, termites, defective heating plant, basement that floods, inadequate well, or septic tank?

16. Is the soil adequate for my building program, and should soil tests be made?

17. Is the building I'm buying so close to adjoining vacant land that, if my neighbor excavates, there is danger that my building will fall into the excavation?

18. Is my neighbor's building so close to the boundary line that, if I build on the vacant land I'm buying, my excavation will involve possible collapse of his building and possible litigation?

19. Keeping in mind that I will become personally liable for personal injuries as soon as the deal is closed, are the elevators, boilers, gas, water, and sewer in the building in safe condition?

20. Since risk of loss in many states falls on the buyer as soon as the contract is signed, is the existing insurance policy for an adequate amount? Suppose, for example, that the building burns to the ground before the deal is closed.

21. Is the property being used for a purpose that invalidates existing insurance policies?

SUGGESTION: Have the insurance policies checked by a reliable insurance broker. Have a rider *(contract-of-sale clause)* attached immediately to the policies so that you, as well as the seller, are covered. Only the seller is covered until this is done.

22. Are any public projects scheduled for this area that may result in the taking of this property by the public? It is discouraging for a businessman to build up neighborhood goodwill over a period of time and then find his property taken for a public improvement.

23. Are any zoning or building code changes likely to take place that will interfere with my building program?

24. Are there any judgments against me? Once I sign a contract to buy land, the seller will be obligated to deed the land to me, and then my creditors may take it away from me.

25. Where the contract calls for the buyer to accept the property subject to "existing leases," what do the leases provide? If the leases contain clauses that are very burdensome to the landlord, the buyer may wish to reconsider the desirability of entering into the deal.

26. If the contract requires the buyer to accept the property subject to the existing mortgage, the contract should require the seller to furnish, at closing, a statement signed by the mortgagee showing the balance due on the mortgage. The buyer should check the mortgage to make sure it does not give the mortgagee the right to declare the mortgage debt due in case the mortgagor sells the property without the mortgagee's permission.

27. Has the building been designated as a landmark or historical site? Is it in a flood plain?

28. Inquire about proposed new construction in the area that might make the neighborhood undesirable.

29. Confirm operating costs and taxes and determine whether special property assessments are planned. They could impose a financial burden on the buyer.

30. Various certificates are required to show that the building complies with energy laws, ordinances, and regulations.

31. Parking should be checked. Is street parking permitted? Is parking of boat trailers forbidden?

32. The area should be checked for mud slides, floods, earthquakes. Flood insurance is usually available under a federal program. If earthquake insurance is available, probably an additional premium is required.

33. Questions should be asked about need for new school construction. This would result in tax increases.

34. There are many sites where toxic chemicals have been stored. Inquiry must be made to determine if the land in question contains such chemicals. If it does, avoid the property like the plague. Suits by emloyees who become ill can total astronomic sums. As an owner, the buyer could become liable for the cost of cleaning the property. This cost could exceed the value of the property.

35. In addition, inspect the neighborhood carefully to determine if a zoning change is imminent.

EXAMPLE: The neighborhood includes both homes and apartments. This suggests that the owners of vacant lots may press for zoning changes that will enable them to build condominium apartments.

36. If you plan to rehab an older building, check with an architect before you sign the contract. The city may have a "grandfather clause" that insulates older buildings from enforcement of the building code. But when major rehab occurs, the ordinance may require that you bring the entire building "up to code." This means new wiring, new plumbing, the works. The expense may be great.

In any case, you should get an architect's estimate of the probable cost of rehab before you sign. Also check with a lender to see if you can obtain a loan that covers your refinancing needs on the purchase, and also the cost of rehab.

37. A buyer of an office building must check it carefully. For example, even recently constructed buildings may have inadequate electrical systems that will not accommodate tenant computer requirements.

38. If you do not plan to pay off the existing mortgage, does it contain a due-on-sale clause?

39. Some cities have mapped future streets. They do not appear in the recorder's office. Check the building codes office. If you build over mapped streets, you may later be compelled to demolish the building.

40. If the building is new, there may be warranties or guarantees of the roof, heating plant, etc. These should be assigned to the buyer; the contract should so state.

41. If the buyer intends to occupy a leased building, the cancellation clause must be analyzed for its validity and applicability, and the contract should specify how the parties plan to cancel the lease. Under some lease cancellation clauses a safe cancellation requires the seller and buyer to join in notice of cancellation and to attach it to the contract of sale. If the building is a free-standing building (warehouse), the buyer may want the right to cancel unless the tenant agrees to vacate by a date certain.

42. Liability for toxic waste has become something of a nightmare. The federal law is the Comprehensive Environmental Response Compensation and Liability Act (CERCLA) 42 USCA Sec. 9601 *et seq.* It imposes personal liability for the cost of cleanup of toxic waste. The total innocence of the landowner is no defense.

Since a mortgagee may become a landowner by foreclosure, he is concerned as well. The liabilities are very great. *US* v. *Maryland Bank & Tr. Co.* (D. Md. April 9, 1986) (foreclosing mortgagee is liable).

Making an ordinary soil test is probably a waste of money. Toxic waste may occur at varying depths. A soil test that goes down 20 feet may miss buried tanks or drums that are 50 feet below the surface.

Even a careful engineer's test may not help. Waste buried on adjoining land may later migrate to the property. Even the presence of toxic waste in the vicinity of the property may devalue it.

In its multifamily loan operation, FNMA requires a history of the title transactions to determine if a manufacturer ever owned the site. It may insist on a letter from the local environmental agency that no toxic waste has been encountered in the vicinity of the property. FHLMC is preparing similar requirements. FNMA also checks on asbestos pipe covering and formaldehyde insulation.

A number of states have enacted laws creating liens for waste removal. These liens may have priority over all mortgages.

If land is being purchased with a view to demolishing or rehabilitating the building thereon, the buyer must inquire into the risk of liberating asbestos in the process of demolition or liberating toxic waste buried in the ground. The latter problem exists also in the purchase of vacant land.

REFERENCES: Stensvaag, *Hazardous Waste Law and Practice* (1986); 42 Bus. Law 215; PLI, *Hazardous Waste, Toxic Tort and Products Liability Insurance* (Commercial Law #378 [1986]).

Before signing the contract, the seller should ask:

1. Is my title to the property a good, clear title? If not, I may be liable for damages if I cannot clear the title.

2. What problems will I have with my existing mortgage in the property? If I, as seller, must get my existing mortgage released, I should check to see that it has a prepayment clause, and, if not, determine that the mortgagee is willing to accept prepayment. I should also get the mortgagee to agree either to accept payment at the closing of the deal or to deposit his mortgage papers and release or satisfaction thereof in escrow since I will have no funds to pay the mortgage debt before then.

3. Can I accept the buyer's word that I will not have to pay my broker a commission? The buyer may be seeking a reduction in the seller's asking price on the ground that no broker's commission is involved. Check with the broker as to the truth of the buyer's claim that the broker was not instrumental in interesting this buyer in the property. The contract itself should contain representations and warranties as to the obligations of the parties to pay brokerage commissions and identify any brokers with whom the parties have dealt.

4. Can I comply with all ordinances applicable to my property? A number of laws and ordinances have been enacted that require the seller to have his home inspected immediately prior to sale. The inspector is sent by the Building Department. If he finds there are no violations of the building code, he issues a current certificate of occupancy. If he finds violations of the building code, they must be corrected before the deal is closed.

11.03   The Seller

Just as a deed must have a grantor, a contract must have a seller.

> **EXAMPLE:**   A hotel known as the Glen House, together with its furniture, was sold at auction to Joseph Grafton for $90,000. He refused to go through with the deal. The only document signed by Grafton was the following:
>
> I, the subscriber, do hereby acknowledge myself to be the purchaser of the estate known as the Glen House, with furniture belonging to it, in Green's Grant, New Hampshire, and sold at auction, Tuesday, May 16, 1871, at 11 o'clock a.m., and for the sum of $90,000, the said property being more particularly described in the advertisement hereunto affixed; and I hereby bind myself, my heirs, and assigns to comply with the terms and conditions of the sale, as declared by the auctioneer at the time and place of sale.
>
> Joseph Grafton
>
> The court held that this was not an enforceable contract of sale, since the seller was not named therein. *Grafton* v. *Cummings,* 99 U.S. 100 (1878).

The following are the chief requirements as to the seller: (1) If the title is held by co-owners, all should be named as seller. (2) The seller should be an adult of sound mind. (3) If the seller is a corporation, the sale must be authorized by its directors and sometimes by its stockholders. (4) Where the seller is a trustee or executor, a check should be made to determine that he had the power to sell the land, since neither an executor nor trustee has power to sell land unless the will or trust instrument expressly gives him that power.

A contract by a shareholder in a corporation to cause the corporation to sell and convey corporate land is valid. *Borg* v. *Warner,* 16 Ill.2d 234, 156 NE2d 513 (1958).

Subpurchase.   Not uncommonly a seller in a contract is himself merely the buyer under another contract relating to the same land. This is unobjectionable.

> **EXAMPLE:**   Seller contracts to sell to Buyer #1 and Buyer #1 contracts to sell to Buyer #2. They can hold a double closing, preferably in escrow, and Seller and Buyer #1 will get their money, and Buyer #2 will get ownership of the land. *Waggoner* v. *Saether,* 207 Ill. 32, 107 NE 859 (1915).

11.03(a)   Signature of Seller's Spouse

In some states, the spouse of a landowner has certain rights, dower, and curtesy in the land and these rights cannot be extinguished without the spouse's signature. When the seller's spouse, in such a state, has not signed the contract of sale and refuses to sign a deed to the property, courts differ as to the courses open to the buyer. In general, the buyer may decline to go through with the deal and may obtain return of his down payment on the ground that the seller is unable to deliver clear title.

In those community property states that require the wife's or husband's consent to a disposition of the community property, the wife's consent is needed for a valid contract to convey community real estate.

Where land is occupied by a family as their home, then regardless of whether the land is owned by the husband or the wife, both must join in any deed of the land. Laws relating to homestead require the double signature. Both must join in the contract to sell.

In states that have abolished dower and curtesy, and that also permit either spouse to convey his or her own land without the signature of the other spouse, the spouse's signature is not necessary either on the contract of sale or on the deed, unless, of course, the land to be sold is a homestead.

In states that have abolished dower, but have substituted some statutory interest that the wife retains if she fails to sign the husband's deed, the courts show the same conflict of opinion as prevails in the states that still have dower. Some allow a deduction from the purchase price to compensate the buyer when the seller's spouse refuses to sign the deed and some do not. *Free* v. *Little,* 31 Utah 449, 88 P. 407 (1907).

The failure of the spouse to join in the contract is a harmless mistake if she is willing to join in the deed. *Davis* v. *Dean Vincent, Inc.,* 465 P2d 702 (Ore. 1970).

11.04   The Buyer

Just as a deed must have a grantee, so a contract must have a buyer. The buyer should be named in the contract. If there are two or more buyers and they wish to acquire title as joint tenants, it is necessary that they be so described in the contract. Otherwise serious difficulties may develop if one of the buyers dies before the deed is executed.

In any event the contract should specify the nature of the estate to be created by the deed. If the buyers are husband and wife and state law permits, the contract should state that the deed is to run to them as tenants by the entireties. If they wish to acquire ownership as joint tenants, the contract should so specify. Special language is needed in many states to accomplish this result, so that in some states the deed will describe the grantees "as joint tenants with the right of survivorship and not as tenants by the entireties." In community property states the contract may call for a deed to " _____a married man, as his sole and separate property." Or if, in a community property state the husband and wife wish to own as tenants in common (as may well be the case if each has children by a prior marriage), the contract and deed both will need a clause stating that the buyers have agreed that each will hold a half interest as tenant in common with the other. In such event the deed will be signed by the grantees to reflect this agreement, and the contract should indicate that the buyers will sign the deed.

If the buyer is a partnership, there should be a written partnership agreement. The title company will require this. If a limited partnership is involved, there should be a detailed Articles of Partnership and a recorded Certificate of Partnership.

If a foreign limited partnership (one created outside the state where the land is located) is involved, the advice of a competent partnership attorney is needed.

If the buyer is a corporation, the charter should be examined for its special requirements, if any, for acquiring this land. A foreign corporation needs a certificate of good standing from the state of its incorporation and a license to do business in the state where the land lies.

A real estate investment trust presents complex problems, and a specialist is needed to advise the parties.

11.05 Sale Price—Payment Provisions

The contract of sale must state the sale price. A common fault in contracts is the failure to state precisely how the purchase price will be paid.

The parties should consider stating what part of the sale price is allocated to realty and what part is allocated to chattel. Real estate taxes, for example, are based on value of real estate. Personal property will have a shorter depreciable life for income tax purposes.

11.06 FIRPTA Withholding

The tax law that became effective in 1985 generally requires that buyers of property withhold a tax equal to ten percent of the sales price if the seller is a person from another country. 11 U.S.C. Sec. 1445. While the act only requires that the transferee withhold only in the case of a disposition of United States Real Property Interest by a foreign person, the only safe way for the transferee to protect itself is to withhold or fall within the exemptions of the act as documented in the transactional documents.

For this reason the contract should allow the buyer to withhold the appropriate amount from the closing proceeds and, in turn, bind the buyer to make the appropriate payments to the Internal Revenue Service. The seller will probably want this payment to be made under some form of controlled situation, such as through escrow or by the closing agent. If the seller believes that he falls within an exemption from the act's withholding requirements, the seller will want to have the contract drafted in such a manner so as to allow the seller to document the exemption as an alternative to withholding.

11.07 Property Sold

Disputes over a deficiency in the quantity of land sold are common, especially in the case of farmland. The usual rule is that a deficiency in quantity is immaterial if the sale is *in gross*. A sale in gross is a sale of a specific tract of land by name or description. 1 ALR2d 18.

> **EXAMPLE:** Seller contracts to sell to Buyer "the Evergreen Ranch in Coles County, Colorado, containing 640 acres, more or less, at a price of $500,000."

A survey shows the ranch contains only 620 acres. No deduction will be allowed from the sale price. The sale was of the ranch, not of 640 acres. The fact that the price was a gross price, not a *per acre* price, helps establish this. 1 ALR2d 28. This rule will be applied unless the deficiency is very great. *Maxwell* v. *Reid,* 496 P2d 1320 (Kans. 1972). Deficiencies as high as 20 percent have been disregarded.

Where the sale is on a price-per-acre basis the buyer is sometimes given some sort of relief if there is a deficiency in quantity. 94 ALR3d 1091.

EXAMPLE: Seller contracted to sell to Buyer "the North seven acres of the Hawkins Tract at a price of $5,000 per acre." The deal was closed and $35,000 paid to Seller. Thereafter, it was discovered the tract conveyed was short three-fourths of an acre. Buyer can sue Seller for the deficiency. 153 ALR 37.

In an acreage sale it is best to insert a *usable acreage* clause.

CLAUSE: At a price of $_____per usable acre, but if survey reveals acreage of less than_____usable acres, buyer shall have the right to rescind within_____days after delivery of copy of survey to seller. Areas falling in (1) open or dedicated public streets or ways, (2) recorded private easements of ingress, or (3) areas fenced by adjoiners are not deemed usable acres. All other acres are deemed usable.

The land sold necessarily includes all fixtures comprising part of the land. However, in the case of apartment buildings, hotels, and so on, there may be items of personal property used in connection with the land sold that might not be considered fixtures, such as furniture. If these items are also to go to the buyer, the contract should contain a provision to the effect that such personal property shall be transferred to the buyer at the time of the giving of the deed. In the absence of such provision, the buyer is not entitled to any items that are not fixtures.

11.07(a)   Description of the Land Sold

The contract must contain a reasonably certain description of the land sold. While the description need not be as formal as that contained in a deed, it must be sufficiently definite to identify the land sold with reasonable certainty. 23 ALR2d 6.

There are two views as to the sufficiency of a contract that contains some description of the property but that requires resort to oral testimony to identify the particular property intended to be sold. In states that take a strict view, such contracts are not enforceable.

EXAMPLE: A contract described the land as "real estate situated in the County of Cook and State of Illinois, to wit: One five-room flat and two six-room flats at 3517 Palmer Street." The city in which the land was located was not mentioned. It was held that this description was too indefinite. *Herous* v. *Roma-*

nowski, 336 Ill. 297, 168 NE 305 (1929). Since verbal evidence would be needed to establish the city and state in which the land is located, the contract is not sufficient. This is the rule followed in most states.

On the other hand, liberal courts enforce such contracts.

EXAMPLE: A contract identified land as ''305 S. Negley Avenue.'' Oral testimony was admitted to prove that the seller owned property of this address in Pittsburgh, Pa. *Sawert* v. *Lunt,* 360 Pa. 521, 62 A2d 34 (1948).

If the city and state are given, a description by street address is sufficient. 23 ALR2d 39. But it is preferable, of course, to use a correct legal description of the land sold.

Where a contract contains a defective street address description but also states that the legal description may be inserted later, the court decisions are conflicting. One line of cases states that the buyer can insert the proper legal description. *Schmalzer v. Jamnik,* 407 Ill. 236, 95 NE2d 347 (1950). Other courts hold the contract void. *Murphy* v. *Morse,* 96 Ga. App. 623, 100 SE2d 623 (1957).

Where the seller owns a house a vacant lot adjoining, great care must be exercised in preparing the description. Likewise, care should be taken where the building has several addresses. *Goebel* v. *Benefit Tr. Life Insurance Co.,* 88 Ill. App.2d 19, 232 NE2d 211 (1967).

At times a contract for the sale of land refers to a building that it is expected seller will construct on the land, but the description of the building is totally inadequate. The contract cannot be enforced. *Landgraver* v. *De Shager,* 398 P2d 193 (Ore. 1965).

11.08   Completeness

In order to be enforceable, a contract must be complete in all its parts. All the terms of the contract must be settled, and none must be left to be determined by future negotiation. 68 ALR2d 1222.

EXAMPLE: A contract called for a sale price of $75,000, $5,000 cash, ''time of possession and balance of payment to be arranged at a later date.'' This contract is not enforceable even if the buyer wishes to pay cash. *Murphy* v. *Koll Grocery Co.,* 311 Ky. 771, 225 SW2d 466. Note that if the contract had simply stated a price of $75,000 and had said nothing regarding terms, the contract would have been good. The court would have read into the contract that a cash deal was intended, deal to be closed in a reasonable time. But since the parties intended something other than a cash deal, but left the exact terms unsettled, the contract was incomplete. A similar holding followed where a contract stated that balance of price was payable ''by future agreement on or before January 1, 19___.'' *Bentzen* v. *H.N. Ranch,* 78 Wyo. 158, 320 P2d 440 (1958); 68 ALR2d 1221 (1958). The court held likewise where the contract stated that a price of $85,000 was payable ''as per terms agreed on.'' *Roberts* v. *Adams,* 164 Cal. App.2d 312, 330 P2d 900 (1958). The same was held where the contract stated ''balance in monthly payments.'' *Cefalu* v. *Breznik,* 15 Ill.2d 168, 154 NE2d 237

(1958). The court also held likewise where the contract said that the balance of $50,000 was payable "as lots are released at purchaser's convenience." *Edward H. Snow Co.* v. *Oxsheer,* 62 N.M. 113, 305 P2d 727 (1957).

In other words, where the written memorandum indicates on its face that parties intended additional terms that were to be negotiated at some future time, the contract is incomplete. The courts explain that they can enforce a contract that the parties have made but cannot make or complete a contract that the parties have failed to complete by leaving some provisions for future bargaining. Quite commonly this rule is applied when it appears that some sort of credit sale was contemplated, but the terms were not agreed upon. Today's courts will supply minor terms that the parties have omitted. Corbin, *Contracts* § 1137; 11 Williston, *Contracts* (Jaeger ed.) § 1424.

If the contract calls for a purchase money mortgage but fails to specify the due date thereof, it is incomplete and cannot be enforced. *Sweeting* v. *Campbell,* 8 Ill.2d 54, 132 NE2d 523 (1956); 60 ALR2d 251. And where a contract provided that the seller would give the buyer a deed that would reserve a vendor's lien for the balance of the purchase price, and the contract further provided that "the rate [of interest] will be agreed upon later," it was too incomplete and indefinite to be enforced. *Hume* v. *Boyle,* 204 SW 673 (Tex. Civ. App. 1918).

11.08(a) Certainty

In addition to being complete, the contract must be definite and certain. If the court cannot tell what the parties agreed upon, it cannot force them to carry out their agreement.

> **EXAMPLE:** Seller agreed to sell certain land to Buyer for $5,000, "one-half cash, balance one to four years, with interest at 7 percent." This contract is too vague and indefinite to be enforced. No one can be certain what the quoted portion means. *Crawford* v. *Williford,* 145 Ga. 550, 89 SE 488.

11.09 Type of Title, Deed, and Evidence of Title

There are three separate ideas that are sometimes confused.

> **EXAMPLE:** A contract of sale is silent as to the *type of title* the buyer is to receive. In such case the buyer is entitled to a marketable title, free of all encumbrances. This will be explained later.

> **EXAMPLE:** The contract is silent as to the *type of deed* the buyer is to receive. In most states the buyer must be content with a quitclaim deed.

> **EXAMPLE:** The contract is silent as to the *type of evidence of title* (abstract, title policy) the buyer is to receive. In such case the buyer must procure his own evidence of title at his own expense.

11.09(a)   Type of Deed

A contract is enforceable even though it does not specify the type of deed to be given. Nevertheless, since there is a vast difference between a quitclaim deed and a warranty deed, the contract should specify the type agreed upon.

If the contract is silent regarding the type of deed to be given, in some states the seller need only give a quitclaim deed or a deed of bargain and sale without covenants. *Morris* v. *Goldthorp,* 390 Ill. 186, 60 NE2d 857 (1945); *Boekelheide* v. *Snyder,* 71 S.D. 470, 26 NW2d 74 (1947); *Vitra Seal Co.* v. *Jaycox,* 1 N.J.S. 560, 62 A2d 431 (1948); *Tymon* v. *Linoki,* 16 NY2d 293, 213 NE2d 661 (1965); 16 ALR3d 1430. This does not excuse the seller from giving a marketable title. It simply means that once the title has been shown to be marketable, the seller may deliver a quitclaim deed and be rid of any possibility of future worry regarding presently unknown title defects. Other states imply that a warranty deed was intended.

It is best for the buyer to insist on a warranty deed. In some states, the mere fact that the buyer is content to take a quitclaim deed is enough to keep him from being a bona fide purchaser, and he will take the land subject to unrecorded deeds, mortgages, liens, and so forth.

> **EXAMPLE:**   Pursuant to a contract of sale Seller gave Buyer a quitclaim deed. Buyer then discovered that Seller had placed an unrecorded mortgage on the property. In some states a grantee in a quitclaim deed is not considered a bona fide purchaser and the unrecorded mortgage would be good against Buyer.

The deed should comply with the contract in all respects.

> **EXAMPLE:**   Seller contracts to sell to Husband and Wife in joint tenancy. He made the deed to Husband only. Wife is entitled to have the deed reformed to run to Husband and Wife as joint tenants. *Wahl* v. *Fairbanks,* 405 Ill. 290, 90 NE2d 735 (1950).

> **EXAMPLE:**   Seller contracts to sell to Buyer. The deed calls for a warranty deed. Nothing is said about encroachments. A survey shows the building encroaches 3 inches into the street. Seller wants to make his warranty deed subject to the encroachment. He cannot do so. The deed must follow the contract.

> **EXAMPLE:**   Seller contracts to sell to Buyer and to give Buyer a warranty deed. Actually Seller has the property in the name of Nominee, and offers Buyer a warranty deed signed by Nominee. Buyer need not accept it. 57 ALR 1507.

> **WARNING:**   One must not attach too much importance to the giving of a warranty deed. After all, I could sit down at this moment, write out, sign, and deliver to you a warranty deed purporting to convey to you the Merchandise Mart, the Tower of London, Westminster Abbey, and all the motels in the Holiday Inn chain. As a result of this activity you would own absolutely nothing. I cannot convey what I do not own. A warranty deed is like the frosting on a cake. It's nice to have if the grantor really owns the land. But if you really want to know that I own what I am trying to convey, you must insist on receiving evidence of title, written proof that I really own the land I am attempting to

convey. If the land is really owned by the grantor in the warranty deed, but the title search fails to show some unpaid real estate tax, unpaid mechanic's lien, and so forth, the warranty deed might help the grantee collect from the grantor the tax he is compelled to pay to protect his title. This, however, is about all the warranty deed is useful for.

11.09(b)   Marketable Title

Unless the contract provides otherwise, the seller must convey a marketable title. Such a title is also described as a *merchantable title*. This means that the seller must have a good title, free from liens, encumbrances, or defects other than those specified in the contract. As a general rule, every buyer of land has a right to demand a title that shall put him in all reasonable security against loss or annoyance by litigation. He should have a title that is free from doubt, one that will enable him not only to hold his land, but also to hold it in peace and free from the hazard of litigation. If he wishes to sell the land, he should be reasonably sure that no flaw will come up to disturb its market value. *Firebaugh* v. *Wittenberg*, 309 Ill. 536, 141 NE 379 (1923).

> **SUGGESTION:** The contract should contain a *subject clause* specifying the permitted objections. These are the objections the seller knows are against his title, usually those that were in existence when he bought the land, and usually of a character such that they cannot be removed, such as building restrictions, and usually such that the buyer finds unobjectionable. As long as they are listed in the subject clause, they do not render title unmarketable.

In point of fact, the marketable title problem has two separate aspects. First, the earlier history of the title may contain defective deeds and other such matters. Second, the title must not be subject to easements, liens, or other "encumbrances" except those specified in the contract.

In every state, and even in different localities within a state, lawyers have struggled to evolve lists of permitted objections appropriate to the locality. Such lists often find their way into printed contract forms prepared by bar associations, real estate boards, and title companies. Several dangers are present: (1) Since new laws are enacted constantly, there is always danger that a given form is outdated. (2) A form appropriate to one locality must not be used elsewhere. (3) A form suitable for a home may be totally inapplicable to a purchase of vacant land or an office building.

Law students are puzzled at times by an apparent conflict between two situations. They know that *recording imparts constructive notice*. All persons are deemed to know what the public records reveal. Why, then, is it customary to set forth in the contract of sale the encumbrances which the buyer must accept *(permitted objections)* in general form, such as building restrictions of record? The answer is, of course, that at this point practice and law differ. In point of fact, the parties cannot be certain what encumbrances exist *until the title search has been completed.* This search is made *after* a bargain has been struck and a contract signed. Meanwhile, the parties must agree on a list of *permitted objections* that neither party considers objectionable.

As can readily be seen, the rules of law that operate on a point that the parties have failed to cover in their contract are often hopelessly impractical. It is for this reason that lawyers and form writers constantly "draft around" these rules. And, of course, even the forms are often imperfect and require modification. This is usually the task of the lawyer. Real estate brokers or salesmen are, in many states, forbidden to change forms to fit the situation. This is considered the unauthorized practice of law.

One of the important functions of contracts, then, is to spell out the rights and duties of the parties so as to reach a result different from that offered by the rules of law. This is perfectly legal and is done constantly.

EXAMPLE: The contract of sale should list the encumbrances the seller is powerless to remove and which the buyer agrees to accept. Building restrictions contained in the plat of subdivision would provide an instance of this sort if they are not violated by present uses of the property.

EXAMPLE: The contract of sale may provide that within___days seller will deliver to buyer an updated abstract of title.

The question of marketability of title must be disposed of before the deal is closed. In other words, if the buyer wishes to avail himself of his right to insist upon a marketable title, he must point out such defects as he discovers and must do this before he pays his money and receives his deed. Once the deal is closed, the money paid, and the deed delivered, the buyer cannot demand his money back if the title proves defective. 57 ALR 1261; 84 ALR 1025, 1027, 1032; 92 CJS 15; 92 CJS 559. However, if the buyer has received a warranty deed from the seller, he may sue the seller for damages should the title prove defective.

11.09(b)(1)   Marketable Title—Mortgages and Other Liens

Unless the contract provides otherwise, the buyer has the right to demand a title free and clear of all mortgages, tax liens, judgment liens, mechanics' liens, and all other liens. It is not sufficient for the seller to offer to deduct the amount of such liens from the purchase price. The buyer may reject the title unless it is actually cleared of such liens. Suppose, however, that there is a mortgage or other lien on the property, and the seller can arrange to have the mortgage paid in full out of the purchase money due the seller and the mortgagee deliver a release of the mortgage to the buyer. Must the buyer go through with the deal in this manner if the contract does not require him to do so? In most states, the answer is in the affirmative. The seller's title is not considered unmarketable if he can arrange to have the owner of the mortgage, judgment, or other lien present at the closing of the deal ready to turn over proper releases to the buyer on receiving payment of the amount due from the buyer. *Kaiser* v. *Wright,* 629 P2d 581 (Colo. 1981); 53 ALR3d 678.

CLAUSE FOR SELLER'S BENEFIT: If at the date of closing there is any mortgage encumbrance which the vendor is obligated to pay and discharge, the vendor may use any portion of the balance of the purchase price to satisfy the same, provided the vendor shall at closing of deal either (1) deliver to the purchaser an instrument in recordable form sufficient, in the judgment of purchaser's title company, to satisfy such encumbrance of record, or (2) deposit with the purchaser's title insurance company sufficient money required by it to insure the recording of such satisfaction and the issuance of title insurance to the purchaser free of any such encumbrance, together with the mortgagee's payoff letter indicating its willingness to accept such payment.

11.09(b)(2) Marketable Title—Easements

Easements render the title unmarketable, unless, of course, the contract requires the buyer to take title subject to easements.

In recent decisions the title is not rendered unmarketable by the existence of *visible* and *beneficial* easements.

> **EXAMPLE:**   The contract is silent regarding easements. A utility company has an easement over the rear five feet of the land for an electric power line, and such a power line is, in fact, located on the rear five feet. The power line services the property in question. In many states the title would be considered marketable. 57 ALR 1426.

> **SUGGESTION TO SELLER:**   Check your title insurance policy or other evidence of title. If it shows your title to be subject to an easement, state in the contract that title will be subject "to easement recorded as Document No. 1234567."

> **SUGGESTION TO BUYER:**   Do not sign a contract stating that seller will deliver title subject "to easements of record." This would obligate you to take title subject to a recorded easement for a one-hundred-foot highway running right through the middle of the house. Insist that the contract specifically describe the easements to which the title is subject and read them over before you sign the contract.

11.09(b)(3) Marketable Title—Building Restrictions

Often the use to which a tract of land may be devoted is restricted by building restrictions contained in recorded deeds or subdivision plats. Unless the contract provides otherwise, the buyer is not required to accept a title encumbered with restrictions as to the character of the buildings that may be erected, the use to which the property may be put, and so on, even though such restrictions actually enhance the value of the property.

> **EXAMPLE:**   Seller contracts to sell Buyer a vacant lot in a high-class residential subdivision. The contract does not mention restrictions. In the recorded plat of the subdivision, there is a restriction providing that only single-family dwellings may be erected in the subdivision. Buyer may reject the title. 57 ALR 1414.

Suppose the contract requires the buyer to accept title subject to "building lines and building restrictions," but it appears that the building on the property violates existing restrictions. The buyer may decline to go through with the deal, for a *violation of a restriction* is a defect or encumbrance separate and distinct from the restriction itself.

> **EXAMPLE:** A contract required the buyer to accept title subject to building and use restrictions. There was a building restriction prohibiting the erection of buildings within five feet of any side line. The buildings actually extended into the prohibited area. It was held that the buyer could refuse to go through with the deal. *Herb* v. *Severson,* 32 Wash.2d 159, 201 P2d 156 (1948); *Lohmeyer* v. *Bower,* 170 Kans. 442, 227 P2d 102 (1951).

> **SUGGESTION TO BUYER:** Never sign a contract which states that title will be subject to "restrictions of record." This obligates you to take title subject to any restriction, no matter how absurd, even a restriction that the only building permitted on the land is a chicken coop. If the seller's title insurance policy is available, look at it. If it shows a restriction, go to the title company or the recorder's office and read the restriction. If you have no objection to it, let the contract read that title will be "subject to restriction recorded as Document No. 123456." Where the contract must be signed at a time when information as to existing building restrictions is not available, and the land is improved with a building that is the principal subject matter of the sale, you might employ the following clause: "Subject to covenants and restrictions of record, provided same are not violated by the existing improvements and the use thereof." When you are buying *vacant* land you *must* insist on reading the restrictions in full before signing the contract.

11.09(b)(4)   MarketableTitle—Zoning and Building Code Violations

Building restrictions imposed by deeds or plats must be distinguished from zoning and building ordinances. Such ordinances, though they may greatly restrict the use that may be made of the land, do not render title unmarketable. Generally, the attitude of the courts is that zoning and building ordinances are part of the law of the land, and all persons are supposed to take notice of them. 39 ALR3d 370. Ignorance of the law excuses no one. Suppose that the premises contain actual, existing *violations* of zoning or building ordinances. Here the rule is different. In most of the more recent decisions, courts have held that substantial existing violations of *zoning ordinances* render title unmarketable. 5 *American Law of Property* § 11.49; *Lohmeyer* v. *Bower,* 170 Kans. 442, 227 P2d 102 (1951); *Mayer* v. *De Vincentis,* 107 Pa. Super. 588, 164 Atl. 111 (1933); *Hartman* v. *Rizzuto,* 123 Cal. App.2d 186, 266 P2d 539 (1954); 39 ALR3d 375.

> **EXAMPLE:** A building containing three apartments was erected in an area where the ordinance prohibited construction of a building containing more than two apartments. The court held that the buyer could terminate the contract and obtain return of his down payment. *Oates* v. *Delcuze,* 226 La. 751, 77 So2d 28 (1954).

In many cities, violations of building ordinances (like those forbidding basement apartments, requiring certain minimum sanitary arrangements, requiring separate exits for each apartment, requiring fireproof material, etc.) now entail drastic punishment. Cities have come to recognize that the fight against the slum is a fight for survival. Building ordinance violations, like zoning ordinance violations, are being recognized as flaws in the marketability of title, for they impose on a purchaser the same hazards of litigation that the rule of marketability of title was designed to avoid. *Brunko* v. *Pharo.* 3 Wis.2d 628, 89 NW2d 221 (1958) noted, 1958 *Wis. L. Rev.* 641; *Bronen* v. *Marmer,* 206 NYS2d 909 (1960). *Contra: Stone* v. *Sexsmith,* 28 Wash.2d 947, 184 P2d 567 (1947); *Ableman* v. *Slader,* 80 Ill. App.2d 94, 224 NE2d 569 (1967).

The prudent buyer will insist that the contract of sale provide that the seller will deliver the property "free from all violations of zoning and building ordinances," and a check with city officials for such violations should be made before the deal is closed. The seller will not be allowed to avoid by trickery or subterfuge his responsibility for ordinance violations.

> **EXAMPLE:**   The sale involved a house with an illegal basement apartment. The seller could not bring the building into compliance by tearing out the illegal apartment, for what the contract really contemplates is that the seller will get a permit from the city legalizing the condition as it was when the contract was signed. As it stands, the title is unmarketable. *Hammer* v. *Michael,* 243 N.Y. 445, 154 NE 305 (1926). See 39 ALR3d 362.

Advertising for sale a building that contains ordinance violations may constitute a fraud upon the buyer.

> **SUGGESTION TO LAWYERS:**   A comparable problem arises when a warranty deed is given that makes no mention of zoning or building code violations. Some courts say that the grantor is not liable. *Domer* v. *Sleeper,* 533 P2d 9 (Alaska 1975); *Marathon Builders Inc.* v. *Polenger,* 263 Md. 410, 283 A2d 617 (1971). Other courts hold the grantor liable. *Wilcox* v. *Pioneer Homes, Inc.* 41NCA 140, 254 SE2d 214 (1979).

> REFERENCES ON ZONING AND BUILDING CODE VIOLATIONS: 24 Albany L. Rev. 167; 27 Rocky Mt. L. Rev. 255; 1957 Wis. L. Rev. 204 (nonconforming use).

11.09(b)(5)   Marketable Title—Leases and Tenancies

Unless the contract so provides, the buyer need not accept a title subject to existing leases or even to existing tenancies without leases. *Haiss* v. *Schmukler,* 201 N.Y.S. 332. If such leases or tenancies exist, the contract should provide that the title is subject to such leases or tenancies.

> **SUGGESTION TO BUYER:**   Do not sign a contract to accept title subject to *existing leases and tenancies.* The existing leases may be very favorable to the tenant and disadvantageous to the property owner. The seller should therefore

be required to include a schedule, either in the contract or in a separate document, listing the expiration date, tenants, and rentals on all existing leases and
tenancies, together with a statement as to whether the leases include an option
to renew or to purchase the property.

11.09(b)(6)   Marketable Title—Encroachments

Encroachments are of three kinds: (1) The building on the land sold encroaches
onto neighboring land. (2) The building on the land sold encroaches onto adjoining streets or alleys. (3) Buildings on adjoining land encroach upon the land sold.
47 ALR2d 331.

When the seller's buildings extend over and upon neighboring land, the
factor that renders title unmarketable is the danger that the neighbor may obtain
a court order directing removal of the offending portion of the structure, a task
that may involve great expense; or the neighbor may institute litigation in an
effort to obtain such an order, and the buyer will be put to the expense of defending the litigation. This is in harmony with the principle that a title is not marketable if there is an appreciable risk of litigation. *Very slight* encroachments will not
render the title unmarketable, as where a wall of the building on the premises
sold extends three-fourths of an inch on neighboring land. *Traxler* v. *McLeran,* 116
Cal. App. 226, 2 P2d 553 (1931). The reason such property remains marketable is
that, when (1) the encroachment of my building on your land is slight, (2) the
cost of removal is great, and (3) the benefit to you from removal of the building
is slight, courts will not compel removal of the encroachment. *Nitterauer* v. *Pulley,*
401 Ill. 494, 82 NE2d 643 (1948). Also, when the building that encroaches on
neighboring land is old or dilapidated, or a temporary structure of small value, or
a structure that is removable at only slight effort or expense, the title is deemed
marketable. With respect to permanent structures, it is hard to draw the line
between objectionable and unobjectionable encroachments. The encroachment
of a house one and one-half inches on neighboring land has been held to render
title unmarketable. *Stokes* v. *Johnson,* 57 N.Y. 673.

When buildings on neighboring land encroach on the premises being sold,
courts are more liberal. At the worst, the buyer will be deprived of some portion
of the land that the seller has agreed to sell. If the area occupied by the encroaching building is insignificant when compared with the total area of the land being
sold, the title is marketable. *Merges* v. *Ringler,* 54 N.Y.S. 280.

When buildings on the land sold extend over adjoining streets or alleys, as
in the case of buildings extending over and upon neighboring privately owned
land, there is danger that a suit will be instituted to compel removal of the encroachment. Title is unmarketable. Still, if the encroachment is trivial, so that
action by the city authorities is highly improbable and it is unlikely that a court
would order the encroachment removed, the title is marketable.

> **EXAMPLE:**   A building encroached two inches on an adjoining street. The title
> was held to be marketable. *Mertens* v. *Berendsen,* 213 Cal. 111, 1 P2d 440
> (1931).

Suppose the contract provides that the seller agree to deliver a title "subject to questions of survey" or "subject to such a state of facts as an accurate survey would show." Such clauses are inserted to relieve the seller of all responsibility with respect to encroachments. If the existence of encroachments is revealed, the buyer must nevertheless go through with the deal. *McCarter* v. *Crawford*, 245 N.Y. 43, 156 NE 90 (1927).

Suppose the contract requires the seller to deliver title "free from all encumbrances and encroachments." Here the existence of trivial encroachments, such as would ordinarily not render title unmarketable, will nevertheless justify the buyer's rejection of the title.

11.09(b)(7)   Marketable Title—Chattels

Many sales of land specifically include valuable chattels, as, for example, when a hotel is being sold. The buyer is entitled to marketable title to the chattels. *Peters* v. *Spielvozel*, 163 So2d 59 (Fla. 1964).

11.09(b)(8)   Marketable Title—Miscellaneous Defects

There are many other defects or encumbrances that may render a title unmarketable. For example, a deed signed by some prior landowner may be defective in that the property is not properly described therein, or a signature may be lacking, or the grantor's wife may have failed to sign the deed. Court proceedings on which the title depends, such as mortgage foreclosures, sales by guardians, and the like, may have been defectively conducted. Estates of deceased landowners may have been improperly probated. It is impossible to enumerate within the allotted space the many defects that may render a title unmarketable. Marketability of title plays an important part in those situations where the buyer, after having signed a contract to purchase the land, regrets his bargain and wishes to get out of the deal. His attorney will then subject the title to a minute scrutiny, hoping to find some defect that renders the title unmarketable, so that his client may declare the contract at an end and obtain a return on his down payment.

11.09(b)(9)   Marketable Title—Title Insurance

The fact that a title company is willing to insure the seller's title does not make it marketable.

> **EXAMPLE:**   Seller entered into a contract to sell real estate to Buyer. The contract required Seller to furnish a clear policy of title insurance. The title search revealed a recorded easement. The title company was willing to issue a clear policy. Buyer was permitted to back out of the deal. Buyer is entitled to a marketable title and title insurance. *New York Investors, Inc.* v. *Manhattan Beach Bathing Parks Corp.*, 243 N.Y.S. 548, 30 Columb. L. Rev. 1215.

> **SUGGESTION TO SELLER:**   Let the contract provide that the title policy is conclusive evidence that the title is good as therein stated but it shall not be evidence of any matters not insured by said policy. This relieves the seller of the obligation to deliver a marketable title. This gets rid of the flyspecking present in marketable title law.

11.09(b)(10)   Marketable Title Laws

With each passing year it has grown increasingly difficult to prove that any given title to land is marketable. Year by year the chain of deeds, mortgages, wills, and other recorded matters relating to the title, beginning with the original grant from the government, grows longer and more complex. In consequence, abstracts of title and title searches grow longer, more difficult, and more complex. Many more opportunities present themselves for technical errors that impair the marketability of title. For these difficulties a solution had to be found. It has, indeed, been found in a number of states. In many states laws have been passed to promote the marketability of title. In general, laws such as this select a particular period of time. In Illinois, for example, the period is forty years. If an examination of the public records shows that for the last forty years title to a particular tract of land has passed from one person to another in a connected fashion, that this connected chain of title culminates in a deed to X, and that X is in peaceable possession of the land in question, X will be deemed to have good and marketable title to that tract of land free and clear from any adverse claims to the title that antedate the forty-year period. This does not mean that all claims that are forty years old or more are automatically wiped out. Each of these marketability laws provides a period of time during which a person claiming an interest that is more than forty years old (or whatever the statutory period may be) may record an affadavit or other claim stating the nature of his interest in a particular piece of land. In this fashion, any claim to the title of land must appear on the records within the last forty years, or it is automatically outlawed. Consequently, a person searching the title to the land need only search the title during the past forty years, and if he finds a connected chain, he need not concern himself with recorded matters that antedate the forty-year period. Each of these marketability laws lists certain interests that are not affected or outlawed by the legislation.

> **EXAMPLE:**   A common provision is to the effect that a person claiming an easement need not record his claim of easement if the existence of such an easement is revealed by a physical examination of the land itself. Thus if a neighbor claims party wall rights or an easement for a driveway extending over the premises, it is fairly clear that a mere glance at the property will reveal the existence of such easement claims. Therefore they need not be rerecorded.

Another common exception relates to claims of the United States government. No state has the power or right to pass laws that extinguish the rights of the United States government. But whatever the claim may be, if it does not fall within the list of claims not affected by the legislation, it is outlawed unless a document in proper form showing the existence of such claim is recorded within the forty-year period. 31 ALR4th 11; 16 *id.* 967.

REFERENCES: 53 Cornell L. Rev. 45; 2 Drake L. Rev. 79; 47 Iowa L. Rev. 413; 46 Ky. L. J. 605; 56 Mich. L. Rev. 225; 51 Minn. L. Rev. 356; 50 Marq. L. Rev. 15; 29 N. D. L. Rev. 265; 44 N. C. L. Rev. 99; 34 Okla. B. J. 2357; 1957 U. Ill. L. F. 491; 13 U. Miami L. Rev. 51; 4 Washburn L. J. 240; 1942 Wis. L. Rev. 258; 11 Wyo. L. J. 19; Basye, *Clearing Land Titles* §§ 171–189 (2d ed. 1970); 31 ALR4th 11; 16 *id*. 967.

11.09(c)   Time of Existence of Good Title

Ordinarily the seller need not have good title on the date of the contract. It is sufficient if he has good title at the time fixed for delivery of the deed, or even later, for example, at the time the court, in a specific performance suit, orders the contract to be enforced. *Gibson* v. *Brown*, 214 Ill. 330, 73 NE 578 (1905).

If the contract provides that time is of the essence and also provides that the seller will furnish the buyer an abstract of title or other evidence of title within a specified period of time, the seller must meet this deadline, or the buyer will have the right to declare the contract at an end.

11.09(d)   Evidence of Title

It is important to distinguish between the seller's duty to deliver good title and his duty to furnish evidence that his title is good. As above stated, unless the contract provides otherwise, the seller must furnish the buyer a *marketable title*. But if the contract does not require him to do so, the seller is under no obligation to furnish the buyer *any evidence that the title is good*. The buyer makes his own title search unless the contract specifies otherwise.

11.09(d)(1)   Time for Furnishing Evidence of Title and Curing Defects in Title

If the contract requires the seller to furnish evidence of title, but does not fix a time limit for the furnishing and examination of the abstract or other evidence of title, it is assumed that a reasonable time was intended. In such case:

1. The seller has a reasonable time to furnish the buyer the abstract or other evidence of title.
2. The buyer has a reasonable time to examine the abstract and point out defects in title.
3. The seller has a reasonable time to eliminate or cure defects in title disclosed by the abstract or other evidence of title.

To eliminate uncertainties and speculation by either party on the rise or fall of the value of the property before choosing to perform his part of the contract, the contract should:

1. Fix the time allowed the seller to furnish the buyer evidence of title.

EXPLANATION: When the contract requires the seller to furnish evidence of title by a day named and provides that time is of the essence, and the title evidence is not furnished by the day named, the buyer may rescind, i.e., declare the contract terminated, and may recover his deposit. *Johnson* v. *Riedler,* 395 Ill. 412, 70 NE2d 570 (1941). Most forms of contracts fix a specific time for furnishing the evidence of title and provide that time is of the essence.

2. Fix the time allowed the buyer to examine the abstract and require him to point out any defects in title within the time limited, failure to do so to constitute an acceptance of the title as good.
3. Fix the time allowed the seller to cure defects in title.
4. Fix a time within which the buyer must choose to accept or reject a defective title that the seller cannot cure within the time allowed him.

11.10   Earnest Money

Earnest money is a deposit or down payment made by the buyer as a guaranty that the contract will be performed on his part. If he does perform, it applies as a part payment of the purchase price. If he defaults, it is retained by the seller. Usually, the contract specifically permits the seller to retain the earnest money where the buyer defaults. But even in the absence of such a provision, a buyer who is in default cannot recover his earnest money from the seller. *Zersky* v. *Sheehan,* 413 F2d 481 (1969); 31 ALR2d 8. Courts have allowed the seller to retain rather substantial down payments; for example, $300,000 on a sale price of $3,000,000, and $35,000 on a sale price of $140,000. Corbin, *The Right of a Defaulting Vendee to the Restitution of Installment Unpaid,* 40 Yale L. J. 1013 (1931). But retention of an earnest money deposit of $30,000 on a sale for $95,000 is unconscionable. *Hook* v. *Lomar,* 320 F2d 536 (5th Cir. 1968).

SUGGESTION TO SELLER: The seller should, for his protection, require a deposit large enough to cover the broker's commission, the expense of the title search, and the compensation to the seller for the loss of his bargain should the buyer default.

SUGGESTION TO BUYER: Provide that the earnest money shall be held in escrow by some third person pending the closing of the deal to insure that the buyer will experience no difficulty in obtaining a return of his deposit should it prove impossible for the seller to deliver clear title. *Gauss* v. *Kirk,* 77 A2d 323 (D.C. 1950).

SUGGESTION TO BUYER: If you put up a check as earnest money, be sure there is money in your bank account to cover it. If the seller attempts to have the check certified, and the bank refuses because funds are lacking, the seller then has an excuse that gives him the right to refuse to carry out the deal. *Gallinero* v. *Fitzpatrick,* 267 NE2d 649 (Mass. 1971).

SUGGESTION TO BUYER: If the seller insists that his broker hold the earnest money, let the contract provide that if the broker fails to return the money to the buyer when the buyer is entitled to it, the seller will pay the amount of the earnest money to the buyer. This will force the seller to think twice about entrusting a large amount of money to an individual. Banks, title companies, and trust companies charge a very small fee for holding earnest money deposits.

With respect to earnest money there is a common misconception shared by the seller and his broker. They tend to view the earnest money as belonging to the seller. This is not the case.

EXAMPLE: Buyer pays Seller earnest money but Seller's title proves unmarketable. Obviously, Seller must refund Buyer's earnest money. This suffices to show that the money is held by Seller for the benefit of both parties at least until Seller shows that he is able to perform. 40 Yale L. J. 1030. Until then Seller's right to the earnest money is inchoate, that is, it has not yet ripened. 35 ALR2d 1384, 1379, 1380.

11.11   Mortgages and Financing in Real Estate Sales

In the financing of real estate sales several possibilities are present:

1. The land may have no mortgage on it, and the buyer may be ready to pay cash. No mortgage figures in the sale of the land.
2. The land may have no mortgage on it, but the seller may be willing to accept part cash and to take back a purchase money mortgage for the balance of the purchase price. For example, an insurance company owns a building that it has acquired by foreclosure of a mortgage. It will wish to sell the land, since it is not in the real estate business, but since it also wishes to keep its money in good investments, a purchase money mortgage may be the ideal situation for both seller and buyer.
3. The land is clear of mortgages, but the buyer will need to mortgage the property in order to raise the full purchase price.
4. The land is subject to an existing mortgage, and the buyer is willing to buy the property subject to such existing mortgage.
5. The land is subject to an existing mortgage, but it is too small, or the payments are not convenient for the buyer, so that it will be necessary for the buyer to put a new mortgage on the property for an amount and payable on such terms as will meet his needs. This means that the sale involves paying the existing mortgage and simultaneously placing a new mortgage on the property.
6. The sale may be by an installment contract with clause reserving right to seller to mortgage the land, buyer to take title subject to the mortgage.
7. The sale may be by an installment contract with provision that buyer will receive deed when specified amount is paid in, buyer then to give seller mortgage for balance of purchase price.
8. The sale may be by an installment contract with no mortgage provisions.
Special laws. In Maryland, a law provides that when the purchaser in an installment contract has paid 40 percent of the purchase price, he is entitled to demand a deed

upon executing a purchase money mortgage to the seller for the balance. 13 Rutgers L. Rev. 625.

Unless the contract provides otherwise, the buyer need not accept title subject to a mortgage. If there is a mortgage on the land and the buyer is to accept the land with the mortgage remaining unpaid, the contract should specify: (1) that the land is being sold subject to such mortgage; (2) the amount remaining unpaid thereon; (3) whether or not the buyer *assumes and agrees* to pay the mortgage, since if he does, he becomes personally liable to the mortgagee for the mortgage debt. If he does not *assume and agree* to pay the mortgage, he may lose the land by foreclosure should he default in his mortgage payments, but no personal judgment can be rendered against him. If the contract calls for the buyer to take the land subject to a mortgage but misdescribes the mortgage, the buyer can back out of the deal. *Crooke* v. *Nelson,* 195 Iowa 681, 191 NW 122 (1922).

11.12   Contingent Contracts

Often a clause will be inserted in a contract making it subject to some contingency, so that if the specified event does not occur, the deal is off and the buyer gets back his down payment. Usually such clauses are inserted at the buyer's request. One example would be a clause making the contract contingent on the buyer's ability to procure a mortgage loan of a specified sum. Or the contract may be contingent on the buyer's ability to procure a transfer to himself of the seller's liquor license. Or the contract may be contingent on the rezoning of the premises within a specified time. 39 ALR3d 385. For example, if a buyer needs the property for an industrial plant but it is presently zoned for residential purposes, he will insist that the contract have a provision rendering it void unless rezoning is obtained within a certain number of days.

At times these contingency clauses tend to be rather vague. Nevertheless some courts will enforce them.

EXAMPLE: Where the contract called for a soil compaction report satisfactory to the buyer, the court held that this meant a report satisfactory to a reasonable person. *Collins* v. *Vickter Manor,* 47 Cal.2d 875, 306 P2d 783 (1957).

Some, but not all, modern decisions seem to sanction a good bit of indefiniteness in the contingent clause.

EXAMPLE: The contract stated it was contingent on the buyer's procuring a mortgage loan of a stated sum "with interest at current prevailing rate." This was held to be sufficiently definite. *Barto* v. *Hacks,* 124 Ga. App. 472, 184 SE2d 188 (1971).

EXAMPLE: A contract of sale for $28,000 stated it was contingent on the buyer obtaining a mortgage of $_____. The court held that a mortgage for a "reasonable amount" was intended, and where the buyer tried to get a mortgage of $21,000 and failed, the contract was at an end. *Grayson* v. *LaBranche,* 225 A2d 922 (1967).

11.12(a)   Contingent Contracts—Financing

The buyer must make a reasonable effort to procure financing. *Fry* v. *George Elkins Co.,* 327 P2d 905 (Cal. 1958). What defines a reasonable effort is not always clear. A buyer who fails to make a reasonable effort is guilty of *bad faith.* As a result the contingency clause becomes void and the buyer will lose his earnest money.

If the contract is contingent upon the buyer's procuring a mortgage of a specified amount, and he makes *no effort* to procure one (as is likely to occur when the buyer has changed his mind about buying the property), the clause is waived, and the seller is entitled to forfeit the buyer's earnest money. *Huckleberry* v. *Wilson,* 284 SW2d 205 (Tex. 1955). The buyer must act in good faith.

It is best that the contract give details of the mortgage such as interest rate, time of payment, and so forth. Often the contract gives the buyer 10 days to procure financing, and if he fails the seller is then given ten additional days to procure financing for the buyer. A seller may procure a mortgage loan of the desired amount for the buyer and the buyer reject it in horror because the interest rate is too high. Obviously, all such details should be covered in the clause. If, however, the details are omitted, the courts are likely to insist that the terms of the offered mortgage be "reasonable"; otherwise the buyer is not required to accept it. *Lach* v. *Cahill,* 138 Conn. 418, 85 A2d 481 (1951). *Chambers* v. *Jordan,* 262 A2d 505 (Md. 1970). Minds differ so much as to what is reasonable that controversy and litigation easily develop in such a situation.

> **SUGGESTION TO SELLER:**   Also tie the contingent clause into the printed clause of the contract form. The contract may give the buyer *thirty* days in which to procure a mortgage of a specified amount. Yet the printed portion of the contract may state that the seller must deliver to the buyer evidence of seller's good title within *twenty* days of the date of the contract. Why should the seller have his title examined when he does not even know that he has a deal with the buyer?

If the contract is contingent on the buyer's obtaining a mortgage and if the buyer acting in good faith cannot procure the mortgage, he is entitled to a return of his earnest money deposit. *Levicki* v. *Chrachol,* 56 Ill.App.2d 54, 205 NE2d 491 (1965).

All contract clauses contingent on obtaining financing are being revised at present. If the contract is contingent on obtaining an adjustable rate mortgage (ARM) type of mortgage, the advice of an experienced real estate lawyer is needed. Aiken, *"Subject to Financing" Clauses in Interim Contracts for the Sale of Realty,* 43 Marq. L. Rev. 265 (1960); 62 *id.* 123; 78 ALR3d 880.

To show that he is acting in good faith, the buyer should make a written application to a mortgage company for the type of loan described in the contract. If the lender rejects the buyer, the buyer should insist upon receiving a written, signed rejection that can be used in court if litigation develops. 9 Am.Jur. *Proof of Facts* 2d 120; 78 ALR3d 880.

One application is not enough to show good faith in some states. The buyer should make application to a second lender and procure a second letter of rejection. 78 ALR3d 880.

Nearly all contingency clauses require the buyer to notify the *seller* in writing within a specified time of the inability to obtain the financing. This must be done, else the seller will keep the earnest money. Phoning the broker is totally inadequate. Written notice to the seller is needed.

Some older decisions indicate that stating the terms of the desired mortgage in detail is not necessary. *Smith* v. *Vernon,* 6 Ill. App.3d 434, 286 NE2d 99. Reasonable terms, they say, will be implied. These decisions should be ignored. There are many mortgage plans available today, and they vary greatly. What is reasonable to me may be totally unreasonable to you. *Neiss* v. *Franze,* 422 NYS2d 345 (1979); see 34 Kan. L. Rev. 43.

11.12(b)   Contingent Contracts—Subject to Resale

A new type of contingency clause has made its appearance in this period of difficult financing.

> **EXAMPLE:**   Broker finds Purchaser, who has $15,000 cash to apply on a sale price of $100,000. Purchaser, of course, insists on a clause making the contract contingent on his ability to get a loan of $85,000. Seller is unwilling to take his home off the market while Purchaser hunts down financing of this amount. He therefore is willing to sign the contract only if the contract is subject to sale to a third party who firms up his financing prior to Purchaser's obtaining his commitment. Purchaser desperately needs a place to live. He will agree to such a clause. Obviously any loan application he signs should permit Purchaser to recover his application fee if the deal falls through because another buyer (who has a larger down payment) can obtain a loan commitment more rapidly.

Frequently clauses of this type have a "kickout" provision which saves the contract for the buyer if he waives the contingency.

> **EXAMPLE:**   Buyer and Seller enter into a real estate contract for the purchase of Seller's house. This contract is contingent upon Buyer selling his existing home. Seller will go along with this as long as a firmer deal does not come along. If it does, Seller may notify Buyer that he has an offer from another buyer. Buyer then has a stated period of time (usually one or two days) to decide whether to waive the contingency. If the contingency is waived, Buyer must go through with the deal or lose the earnest money, whether Buyer sells his existing home or not. If Buyer elects not to waive the contingency, the seller is allowed to accept the offer of the new buyer and the contract between Buyer and Seller becomes void. Buyer gets his earnest money back at that point.

11.12(c)   Contingent Contracts—Approvals

Many contracts for the purchase of homes are signed on Sunday, when advice of legal counsel is not available. It seems advisable for the parties to insert some clause making the terms of the contract, other than price, subject to the approval or amendment by a lawyer. Also, the buyer often recognizes that he is unable to determine the physical condition of the property. He needs the help of an expert. All of this simply reflects the fact that a buyer needs expert advice. *Indoe* v. *Dwyer,* 424 A2d 456 (N.J. 1981); 15 ALR4th 752.

If the parties agree to make the contract contingent on approval by the buyer's inspector, and the contract requires the inspector to list specific defects he discovers, the question remains whether the seller should be given the right to cure the defects and, if so, how much time he should be allowed. This whole matter presents thorny problems.

11.13   Possession and Rents

The general rule of law is that the right to possession of land follows the legal title. Since the purchaser does not acquire the legal title to the land until he receives his deed, as a rule he is not entitled to possession until that time. 56 ALR2d 1272. The contract, however, may expressly authorize the buyer to take possession before he receives his deed. Such a provision should normally be included in an installment contract, for in such a contract a purchaser usually expects to take possession long before he is ready to receive his deed. Also, the contract may by implication confer the right of possession on the buyer, as where it contains a provision requiring the buyer to keep the buildings in repair or to give up possession in case of default.

The party who is entitled to possession is entitled to the rents of the land. Ordinarily, therefore, rents falling due before the seller gives the buyer a deed belong to the seller; rents due after the delivery of the deed are payable to the buyer.

11.14   Taxes

Unless the contract provides otherwise, the seller must give the buyer good title free and clear of taxes that were a lien at the time the contract was made. In fact, if the seller remains in possession after the contract is made, and taxes become a lien while the seller is in possession, the seller must pay these taxes. However, if the buyer goes into possession and taxes thereafter become a lien, the buyer must pay these taxes. To eliminate questions, the contract usually specifies the taxes to which the land will be subject when the deed is made.

11.15   Insurance and Risk of Loss

It sometimes happens that before the deal is closed the building is destroyed or damaged by fire or other casualty. In some states the loss so caused falls on the buyer. In other words, the buyer must go through with the deal and pay the full contract price, even though the building has been destroyed. 27 ALR2d 466; 27 ALR3d 572; 51 Ill. B.J. 124; 52 *id.* 464. This risk is not limited to fire. It includes damage from flood, windstorm, vandalism, boiler destruction, hurricane, erosion, subsidence, collapse of retaining wall, and freezing of an orange grove. Most states give the buyer the benefit of the seller's insurance.

In an increasing number of states, including California, Connecticut, Illinois, Kentucky, Maine, Massachusetts, Michigan, New Hampshire, New York, Oregon, Rhode Island, South Carolina, South Dakota, and Wisconsin, laws or court decisions put the risk of loss on the seller, so that if a substantial loss by fire or other casualty occurs before the buyer has been given a deed to the property, the buyer may cancel the deal and obtain return of his down payment. *Dixon* v. *Salvation Army,* 191 Cal. Reptr. 11 (1983). An important factor in some of these states is the fact of possession. The one in possession is in a better position to prevent fires. *Skelly Oil Co.* v. *Ashmore,* 365 SW2d 582 (Mo. 1963). Hence, in these states, if the buyer is put in possession before the deal is closed, the courts or the laws will assign this as a reason for putting the risk of loss back on the buyer.

In all states the risk of loss falls on the seller where: (1) The contract specifically provides that risk of loss pending closing of the deal rests on the seller; (2) the seller does not have a good marketable title at the time of the loss, the reason being that it is unfair to put the risk of loss on a buyer when the seller is in no position to perform his obligations under the contract, *Eppstein* v. *Kuhn,* 225 Ill. 115, 80 NE 80 (1906); (3) the seller is at fault in causing the delay in closing the deal, and during this delayed period of loss occurs; (4) the loss is due to the carelessness of the seller, as when he leaves the house during a cold spell without draining the heating system and all the radiators are cracked by ice formation. 3 Corbin, *Contracts* 661.

11.16   Prorating or Apportionment

Provision is frequently made for prorating, adjustment, or apportionment of rents, taxes, insurance premiums, water taxes, interest accrued on mortgage indebtedness, personal property taxes on personal property transferred to the buyer, gas and electric bills, janitor's salary, management fees on current rent collections, and charges on service contracts, such as exterminator or scavenger service. It is also customary to provide that fuel on hand shall be purchased by the buyer at current prices as of the proration date. Although it is usual to prorate certain items not mentioned in the contract, it must be remembered that, in the event of controversy, the party contending that an item should be prorated will be unable legally to compel proration in the absence of provision in the contract therefor. *Lathers* v. *Keogh,* 109 N.Y. 583, 17 NE 131 (1888); *Antietan-Sharpsburg Mus.* v. *William H. Marsh, Inc.,* 249 A2d 221 (Md. 1969); *Wilson* v. *Campbell,* 425 SW2d 518 (Ark. 1968).

11.17   Date

The contract need not be, but usually is, dated.

11.18 Signature

As heretofore pointed out, the contract must be signed by the party against whom enforcement of the contract is sought. Of course, in practice the contract is almost invariably signed by both seller and buyer.

Suppose land is owned jointly by A and B. C negotiates with A for the purchase of the property and agrees with A that the land will be sold for the sum of $10,000. A contract is prepared, designating A and B as sellers and C as buyer. A and C sign the contract; B refuses to sign. Is the contract binding on A? No, for the contract shows on its face that a sale was intended only if both landowners agreed. *Madia* v. *Collins,* 408 Ill. 358, 97 NE2d 313 (1951); 154 ALR 778; 92 CJS 547.

11.19 Contracts Signed by Agents

A person may authorize an agent to enter into contracts on his behalf for the purchase or sale of real estate. In many states this authorization must be in writing, and in all states it is customary to employ a written authorization. Such an agent is called an *attorney in fact,* and the document granting this authority is called a *power of attorney.*

11.20 Seal

A seal is not necessary to the validity of a contract.

11.21 Delivery

Suppose you list your land with a broker for sale and he finds a buyer interested in its purchase but who does not wish to pay the price you are asking. The buyer prepares and signs a contract of sale stipulating a lower price. This is an *offer.* He hands the contract to the broker, who hands it to you. You sign the contract and return it to the buyer. This is an *acceptance.* The contract is now in force. Suppose, however, that you simply hold on to the contract, hoping that a higher offer will appear, and refuse to answer the buyer's telephone calls. This last situation poses the questions: (1) Must the buyer be *notified* that his offer has been accepted? In other words, can he legally withdraw his offer at any time before he is *notified* that the offer has been accepted? (2) Is delivery necessary to the validity of a contract? The buyer, you will notice, is in an awkward spot. He cannot risk signing a contract to buy some other house, for if he does, he may find himself obligated to buy two houses. Some courts protect the buyer and allow him to revoke his offer in this last situation, stating either that the acceptance is ineffective until the buyer is notified thereof or that delivery is necessary for a written contract to be binding. *Hollingshead* v. *Morris,* 172 Mich. 126, 137 NW 527 (1912); 8 Wm. Mitch. L. Rev. 991 (1982).

> **SUGGESTION TO BUYER:**   Let the contract be prepared in duplicate. The buyer signs both duplicates. Each duplicate contains a provision that the buyer's liability, if any, is terminated and his down payment returned, unless a duplicate signed by the seller is delivered to the buyer within three days after the date of the contract. The buyer hands both duplicates to the seller but retains a carbon copy, so that he can always prove his nonliability if he fails to receive a signed duplicate within the specified time.

11.22   Acknowledgments

An acknowledgment is not necessary, although it is desirable since it simplifies proof of the contract in any suit brought thereon. If the contract is to be recorded, acknowledgment is necessary in nearly all states.

11.23   Witnesses

If the contract is not acknowledged, it should, as a practical matter, be witnessed, although this is not necessary as a matter of law. The fact that the signatures are witnessed simplifies use of the contract in any litigation that may develop.

11.24   Recording

Some contracts will go so far as to include a clause providing that the contract is void if the buyer records it. A buyer who is hopelessly in default will sometimes record the contract, hoping thereby to cloud the seller's title and to obtain a return of part of the purchase price paid. In view of the public policy behind recording law, such provisions are of doubtful validity. 12 Wayne L. Rev. 402.

11.25   Effect of Contract—Interest of Purchaser

The signing of a contract for the sale of land does not give the buyer legal title to the land. Ownership can be transferred to the buyer only by a deed. However, the buyer does acquire an interest in the land. This interest is known as equitable title.

The equitable title of the buyer results from the doctrine of equitable conversion. *Shay* v. *Penrose,* 25 Ill.2d 447, 185 NE2d 218 (1962); 91 CJS *Vendor and Purchaser* §106. In most states this equitable title arises the moment the contract is entered into.

> **EXAMPLE:**   Seller enters into an installment contract with Buyer. Buyer dies without a will, leaving Heir as his only heir. Administrator is appointed adminis-

trator of Buyer's estate. The equitable interest of Buyer passes to Heir, as real estate. 33 CJS *Executors and Administrators* §112. Suppose Seller dies and *ABC Co.* is appointed his administrator. ABC Co. will be entitled to collect the contract payments. 33 CJS *Executors and Administrators* §112. Since Buyer was the equitable owner of the land, the courts will, for most purposes, treat Seller's interest under the contract as personal property, going to his administrator.

As a result of this rule, a contract purchaser can mortgage his contract interest by means of a real estate mortgage. 73 ALR2d 1400.

11.26   Effect of Deed

When the deal is closed and the seller's deed delivered to the buyer, the deal is regarded as consummated. The contract of sale has served its purpose. It is *merged* in the deed. 38 ALR2d 1310. The contract no longer exists. For this reason, if matters remain to be attended to after closing of the deal, it is best that they be set forth in the deed. This is particularly important as to title matters, for the buyer waives his right to cancel the contract because of defects in title if he accepts and pays for a deed while the title is defective or encumbered. 84 ALR 1001, 1031. However, there are some exceptions to the merger rule. In particular, when the contract calls for something to be done after the deal is closed, delivery of the deed does not extinguish that aspect of the contract.

> **EXAMPLE:**   The contract required the seller to lay water mains and sewers after closing of the deal. The deal was closed, and the deed delivered to buyer. Thereafter, the seller failed to lay the water mains and sewers. The buyer filed a damage suit against the seller, and the seller was held liable. *McMillan* v. *American Suburban Corp.,* 136 Tenn. 53, 188 SW 615. The same would be true where the contract requires the seller to build a house on the land sold. 84 ALR 1023. If the contract warrants that the building is in sound condition, this warranty survives the closing of the deal, for that obviously was what the parties intended. *Levin* v. *Cook,* 186 Md. 535, 47 A2d 505 (1946). Contract provisions as to the date on which possession will be turned over to the buyer are not merged in the deed. In all these cases the buyer's only remedy, if the seller fails to perform, is to sue the seller for damages. He cannot sue to get his money back. *De Bisschop* v. *Crump,* 24 F2d 807 (1928).

Also when the deal is closed and the deed accepted by the buyer-grantee, all questions of *marketability of title* are at an end. 66 C.J. 847, 1480; 84 ALR 1025, 1027, 1032; 57 ALR 1261. Of course, a grantee who receives a warranty deed can sue the grantor for damages if a title defect shows up; but he cannot get his money back. The buyer's right to sue the seller for the seller's misrepresentations is not affected by the closing of the deal. Normally the buyer does not discover these misrepresentations until after he has taken possession.

> **RECAPITULATION:**   Thus it can be said with respect to merger that:
>
> 1. The obligations of the seller to furnish a title of a particular character, or evidence of such title, ends with the closing of the deal.

2. The obligations of the seller to perform acts after closing (such as landscaping) do not end with closing.

3. The buyer's rights with respect to the seller's misrepresentations or nondisclosure do not end with closing, since normally they are not discovered until after the buyer takes possession.

11.27   Assignment of the Contract

The buyer may assign his interest in the contract. By virtue of the contract, the buyer has the right to demand a deed to the property on performing his part of the contract. He may sell and transfer his right to a third party, which is accomplished by means of a brief instrument called an *assignment*. Such third party is called the *assignee*. The assignee has the right to make the payments required by the contract and to demand a deed from the seller. In other words, the assignee steps into the shoes of the buyer and may compel the seller to perform his part of the contract.

However, the assignee does not become personally liable to the seller for payment of the purchase price, unless the assignment provides that the assignee *assumes and agrees to pay* the purchase price. *Lisenby* v. *Newton,* 120 Cal. 571, 52 P. 813 (1898).

Of course, the buyer cannot escape personal liability for payment of the purchase price by assigning the contract. He remains liable to the seller notwithstanding the assignment. If the rule were otherwise, a buyer could always rid himself of a burdensome contract by assigning it to a pauper.

The contract may forbid assignment.

11.28   Deed by Seller to Stranger

When the seller, after entering into the contract, sells and conveys the land to some third party, the question arises as to whether the buyer under the contract can compel such third party to give him a deed to the land on payment of the contract price. The buyer can compel such third party to give him a deed on payment of the contract price in the following cases:

1. When the contract was recorded prior to the making of the deed to the third party.

2. When, though the contract was not recorded, the buyer took possession of the land prior to the making of the deed to the third party.

3. When, even though the contract was not recorded and the buyer did not take possession of the land, the third party actually knew of the earlier contract at the time he received his deed.

If the case does not fall within these three rules, the buyer cannot compel the third party to give him a deed. In other words, he has lost all his rights in the land. However, the buyer may then sue his seller and recover from him any amounts paid on the purchase price.

If the contract requires the seller to give a warranty deed, the buyer need not accept a warranty deed signed only by the seller's grantee. The seller must also join in the deed. *Crabtree* v. *Levings,* 53 Ill. 526 (1870).

11.29   Time for Performance

The contract should specify the date on which the deal is to be closed. If the contract does not specifically fix the time when it is to be performed, it will be implied that it is to be performed within a reasonable time, and the purchase price must be paid at that time. Most contracts fix a specific time for the performance of all acts thereunder. If the contract provides that *time is of the essence,* each act required by the contract must be done promptly at the time specified. In a cash sale where time is of the essence, if either party fails to perform promptly he will be unable to obtain specific performance.

> **EXAMPLE:**   Contract called for earnest money down payment, balance to be paid within five days after seller's title was shown to be good, and time to be of the essence. Seller delivered evidence of good title on August 5. Buyer did nothing. On August 19, seller served notice on buyer to close deal within five days. Buyer again did nothing. On September 10, buyer tendered balance of purchase price. Seller refused to accept. Buyer now filed suit for specific performance and the court refused to grant it. Buyer was in default and time was of the essence. *Johnson* v. *Riedler,* 395 Ill. 412, 70 NE2d 570 (1946).

11.30   Remedies of the Seller—Remedies Other than Forfeiture or Foreclosure

If the buyer fails or refuses to perform, the seller, in lieu of declaring a forfeiture, may pursue one of the following courses:

> 1. The seller may *rescind* the contract. *Rescission* is not the same as *forfeiture. Coe* v. *Bennett,* 46 Idaho 62, 266 P. 413 (1928). By rescinding, the seller declares the contract at an end and surrenders all rights thereunder. Both seller and buyer must be restored, as far as possible, to the situation existing before the contract was made. In an installment contract, the seller, on rescinding, must give back to the buyer the payments he has made, less a fair rent for the time the buyer has been in possession. *Hillman* v. *Busselle,* 66 Ariz. 139, 185 P2d 311 (1947). The right to rescind does not depend upon any provision in he contract. However, most installment contracts give the seller the right to declare the contract forfeited if the buyer defaults. Forfeiture is a right expressly reserved in the contract itself. *Realty Securities Corp.* v. *Johnson,* 93 Fla. 46, 111 So 532 (1927). By declaring a forfeiture, the seller terminates the contract but retains all payments previously made by the buyer, since this right is expressly conferred by the contract. The seller may thereupon file a suit to clear his title of the cloud created by the forfeited contract. *Ibid.*
>
> Some states allow the seller to rescind, apply the earnest money in reduction of his damages, and sue the buyer for any other damages he has sustained. Dobbs, *Remedies* 855 (1974). This is a sensible rule. *Anderson* v. *Long Grove Country Club Estates,* 111 Ill. App.2d 127, 249 NE2d 343 (1969).

2. In some states, the seller may tender a deed to the buyer and then sue the buyer for the purchase price.

3. The seller may sue the buyer for damages.

4. The seller may sue the buyer for specific performance of the contract.

5. The seller may simply retain the earnest money.

11.30(a)   Remedies of the Buyer

In case of the seller's refusal or failure to perform, the buyer may pursue one of the following courses:

1. He may *rescind,* that is, declare the contract terminated, and recover his deposit. To rescind is the buyer's normal remedy when the land has decreased in value. One difficulty here is that the seller usually is reluctant to give back the buyer's deposit. The buyer, of course, has the right to file a suit against the seller and obtain a judgment, which can be enforced in the usual ways, by levy on property, by garnishment, and so forth. However, while the suit is pending, the seller may very well decide to sell the particular land to someone else and then spend or secrete the money.

2. The buyer has a lien on the land as security for repayment of purchase money paid in and may enforce such lien if the seller is unable or unwilling to convey good title. 33 ALR2d 1384. A buyer who wishes to obtain return of his down payment from a defaulting seller would be well advised to file a suit to enforce his purchaser's lien, for this ties up the seller's property and prevents him from selling the land to others. This is not true if the buyer merely sues the seller for a money judgment.

3. The buyer may sue the seller to compel *specific performance* of the contract, that is, to compel the seller to give him a deed on receiving payment of the purchase price. The buyer will resort to this remedy when he wants the land for some particular purpose, for example, to keep out a competitor, or when he anticipates that the land will appreciate in value. In general, specific performance is a more effective remedy than a suit for money damages, since damages are always hard to prove and judgments for money are hard to collect.

4. The seller, of course, cannot compel the buyer to accept a bad title. But sometimes the buyer wants to go through with the contract and the seller refuses. The seller's title may be clouded with some unpaid tax, unpaid mortgage, or easement. To make things more difficult for the buyer, the seller refuses to make any effort to eliminate these defects. Here the buyer may wish to file a suit for specific performance and ask the court to make deduction from the purchase price because of the defects in title.

EXAMPLE: The contract price is $10,000. An examination of title reveals the existence of $1,000 in unpaid taxes. The court will order specific performance on the buyer's depositing $9,000 in court for the seller if the seller refuses to pay the taxes. This remedy of the buyer is called *specific performance with an abatement from the purchase price.*

5. Where the seller will not or cannot go through with the deal, the buyer may sue the seller for *damages.* In such an action, the buyer ultimately will receive a judgment for money damages. In the meantime, however, while the suit is pending, the seller is at liberty to sell the land to others, and any buyer who gets a deed before the buyer obtains his judgment takes the land free of the buyer's claims.

11.30(b)   Remedies—Restitutionary Damages—Promissory Estoppel

On occasion, *even where a contract has not been signed,* there will be a liability for damages.

> **EXAMPLE:**   Hoffman and his wife owned a small store. Red Owl, a national franchiser, advised Hoffman to sell his store, promising to find a party to buy some land, build a bigger building and lease it to the Hoffmans with an option to purchase. The Hoffmans would receive a Red Owl franchise. All this was arranged orally. The Hoffmans sold their store in reliance on Red Owl's promises. Red Owl refused to go through with the deal. Red Owl was held liable for all the damages the Hoffmans suffered. Red Owl made a promise knowing the Hoffmans would rely on it. Under modern ethical concepts of the law (promissory estoppel) the promisor is liable for the damages his promisee incurs. Although the promises were made to Hoffman only, Red Owl could foresee that his wife would also rely on Red Owl's promise. Hence they are liable to her as well. *Hoffman v. Red Owl Stores Inc.,* 26 Wis.2d 683, 133 NW 267 (1965). Lawyers often speak of this as *detrimental reliance.*

> REFERENCES: 77 Harv. L. Rev. 401; 97 *id.* 678; 51 Cornell L. Q. 351; 35 Rutgers L. Rev. 472. 56 ALR3d 1037 (enforcement of oral promise).

11.30(c)   Remedies—Election of Remedies

Some remedies are so inherently inconsistent that if a party chooses one he cannot resort to remedies he would otherwise have.

> **EXAMPLE:**   A seller in an installment contract elects to exercise his forfeiture clause. He cannot thereafter sue the buyer for payment of the purchase price. 91 C.J.S. §376.

> **EXAMPLE:**   In some states an installment seller has a *statutory right* to cancel the contract by giving the buyer notice of his default and forfeiture. Thereafter he cannot sue the buyer for damages. *Zirinsky v. Sheehan,* 413 F2d 481 (1969).

11.30(d)   Remedies of the Seller and Buyer—Exclusiveness of the Remedies Spelled Out in Contract—Choice of Inconsistent Remedies

In the case of a cash sale, even though the contract is silent on the point, the seller may, in the event of default by the buyer, retain the buyer's earnest money deposit. This is a form of forfeiture that is universally permitted. Often the contract specifically provides that in the case of the buyer's default the seller may declare the contract ended and keep the earnest money. This is not an *exclusive remedy.* 81 CJS 531; 32 ALR 584, 98 ALR 887. In other words, the seller, *in lieu of retaining the earnest money, has the right to sue the buyer for specific performance or for damages.*

But the contract often provides that, in the event the seller's title proves defective, the buyer must either take the title *as is* or be content with a return of his earnest money deposit. This is then the buyer's exclusive remedy if the seller is *in good faith unable* to clear his title. *Old Colony Trust Co.* v. *Chauncey,* 214 Mass. 271, 101 NE 423 (1913); *Nostdal* v. *Morehart,* 132 Minn. 351, 157 NW 584 (1916). If the buyer wishes to accept title *as is,* he must notify the seller of his decision within the time allowed by the contract. *Miller* v. *Shea,* 300 Ill. 180, 133 NE 183 (1921). However, if the seller's title examination reveals defects that the seller could easily clear, but he refuses to do so because of his reluctance to go through with the transaction or if the seller knew his title was defective when he signed the contract of sale, then the clause is not deemed to provide an exclusive remedy, and the buyer may file for specific performance with an abatement from the purchase price or for damages. *Mokar Properties Corp.* v. *Hall,* 179 NYS2d 814 (1958). This clause protects the seller only where he is truly unable to deliver a clear title and was unaware of the defects in his title. *Blau* v. *Friedman,* 140 A2d 193 (N.J. 1958).

If a seller has a right to declare a *forfeiture* of the contract because of the buyer's default, and he does so, he cannot thereafter sue the buyer for damages or for the balance due on the purchase price. *Morey* v. *Huston,* 85 Ill. App.2d 195, 28 NE2d 44 (1967). 92 CJS 311. He must choose to forfeit *or* sue for damages or recovery of the purchase price. And if the seller files a suit to foreclose the contract, this automatically sets aside any forfeiture that the seller has previously declared because of the buyer's defaults. *Zumstein* v. *Stockton,* 199 Ore. 633, 264 P2d 455 (1953).

11.31 Abandonment

Through abandonment, either buyer or seller may lose his rights under the contract. If either party clearly shows by his acts that he does not intend to go through with the contract, the other party may assume that he has abandoned the contract. 68 ALR2d 581.

> **EXAMPLE:** The buyer, under an installment contract, took possession of the premises. Later he fell far behind in his payments and eventually accepted a lease from the seller. When oil was discovered, he attempted to enforce the contract. The court held that his rights had been lost by abandonment. *Dundas* v. *Foster,* 281 Mich. 117, 274 NW 731.

11.32 Hardship

On occasion a court will refuse to enforce a contract where enforcement would cause undue hardship.

11.33 Fairness and Inadequacy of Consideration

If the price is far below the real value of the land, and the parties are not on equal terms, as when the buyer is an experienced businessman and the seller is ignorant, mentally feeble, or inexperienced, the court will refuse to compel the seller to give a deed.

> **EXAMPLE:** Shortly after the Chicago fire, the owner of certain lots in Chicago, a weak-minded man who was ignorant of the value of the land and of business generally and who was unable to understand English well, was persuaded by a shrewd man to sell the lots for $21,000. The lots were worth much more, and their value was rapidly rising. Owners of adjoining lots had just made arrangements to build on these adjoining lots. These facts were known to the buyer but not to the seller. The court refused to compel the seller to give a deed. *Fish v. Leser*, 69 Ill. 394 (1873).

11.34 Mistake

The very word *contract* implies that there must be a meeting of the minds. Occasionally both parties to the contract are mistaken as to some matter. This is called a *mutual mistake*. When there is a mutual mistake, either party may cancel or rescind the contract.

> **EXAMPLE:** The owner of certain land verbally offered to sell the land for $6,000. The buyer misunderstood the price to be $3,000 and agreed. Under such misunderstanding the deed was executed and delivered. There was no meeting of the minds here, and the owner was entitled to a reconveyance. *Neel v. Lang*, 236 Mass. 61, 127 NE 512 (1920).

11.35 Misrepresentation and Fraud

So many statements are made by each party in the course of a sale of land that almost always some untrue statement, called a *misrepresentation,* is made. If the misrepresentation is of some unimportant or trivial matter, generally speaking, it will not affect the contract. Such a misrepresentation is said to be immaterial. Suppose, however, that a misrepresentation is made as to some important matter. It is clear, first of all, that such a misrepresentation does not make the contract null and void. After the misrepresentation has been discovered, the party who was deceived may nevertheless wish to enforce the contract. He may do so. If the contract has not yet been performed—that is, the seller has not yet given a deed—and the buyer who was guilty of the fraud files a suit to enforce the contract, the other party may use the fraud as a defense to such a suit. He will bring to the court's attention the fact that the party who is bringing the suit made a misrepresentation as to an important matter, and the court will refuse to enforce the contract.

If the contract *has* been performed—that is, the seller has given the deed and the buyer paid the purchase price—and one party then discovers that an important misrepresentation has been made, he may file a suit to get his land back (rescission), if he was the seller, or get his money, if he was the buyer.

Remember that the buyer is seldom in a position to discover the seller's misrepresentation until he has taken possession of the property. And the buyer may rescind (get his money back) even if the misrepresentation was not intentional, which is rare.

The topic of fraud and misrepresentation on the part of the seller, the selling broker, and the listing broker has given birth to a vast amount of litigation in recent times. Therefore an entire chapter is hereafter devoted to this topic.

11.36 Hardship

At times, if circumstances change after the contract is signed, and as a result it would be a substantial hardship to compel performance of the contract, the courts have refused to enforce it. 11 ALR2d 390.

> **EXAMPLE:** After the contract was signed the city rezoned the land for residence purposes. The buyer, as was known to seller, planned to erect a factory. The court refused to enforce the contract. *Clay v. Landreth,* 187 Va. 169, 45 SE2d 875 (1948). To some considerable extent, the concept of hardship is being replaced by the concept of unconscionability.

11.37 Liability for Injuries

The matter of implied warranties of the building is one that deals with (1) new buildings erected by a merchant-builder and (2) damages suffered by the buyer because of defects in the building which the buyer must expend funds to repair. A different question is presented when the buyer (or a member of his family) or a member of the public suffers injuries because of a defect in the building or land sold.

The seller may be liable because he knew of a hidden defect that created a danger to occupants.

> **EXAMPLE:** Seller knows that there is a dangerous break in the flooring of a dark closet. Seller also knows that it is unlikely that Buyer will discover the danger. Seller fails to warn Buyer. Buyer's wife is injured while hanging clothes in the closet. Seller is liable. *O'Connor v. Altus,* 123 N.J. Super. 379, 303 A2d 329 (1973), citing Restatement *Torts* 2d §353.

> **EXAMPLE:** There is an unused well on the property which Seller has covered with sod. Wife of Buyer steps on the sod and the rotten boards break, plunging her into the well. Seller is liable for failure to warn Buyer. *Cooper v. Cordova Sand Co., Inc.,* 485 SW2d 261 (Tenn. 1972).

> **EXAMPLE:** The building in question has a cornice that has been weakened by water freezing in the spaces between lengths of the cornice. There is an obvious danger to members of the public on adjoining sidewalks. Seller sells the property to Buyer. The cornice falls, injuring a pedestrian. Seller is liable because he sold a nuisance. Buyer is liable because he knowingly maintained a nuisance. *O'Connor v. Altus,* 123 N.J. Super. 379, 303 A2d 329 (1973), citing Restatement *Torts* 2d §373; 58 Am.Jur.2d *Nuisances* §§ 50, 51.

It is evident that these rules greatly resemble those involved in landlord and tenant situations.

Except as above, an ordinary seller is not liable for defects or injuries occurring after the sale. *Kimberlin* v. *Lear,* 500 P2d 1022 (Nev. 1972).

REFERENCE: 48 ALR3d 1027.

11.38   Liability of Vendor—Installment Contracts

Because installment contracts figure prominently in today's creative financing, they deserve a special glance.

> **EXAMPLE:**   Seller entered into an installment contract to sell to Buyer on May 1, 1963. Buyer moved in. On May 7, 1963, Buyer's daughter fell through a stair rail from which several slats were missing. The court held that Seller was not liable. No nuisance was involved. The defect was not hidden. *Anderson* v. *Cosmopolitan State Bank,* 54 Ill.2d 504, 301 NE2d 296 (1973), criticized in 5 Loyola U.L. J. (Chicago) 669. An unspoken consideration here is that normally the seller cancels out his liability insurance when the deal is closed.

11.39   Suggestions on Contract Draftsmanship

Preliminary observations. The goal to be achieved in drafting a contract of sale is two-fold: (1) to draft a contract that the courts will enforce, since many contracts are so poorly drafted that courts cannot and will not enforce them; (2) after the seller and buyer have explored all aspects of the deal and reached an agreement as to all their rights and duties, to specify all the terms that the parties have agreed on and to state them so clearly that there can be no controversy as to their meaning.

Parties. In general, the suggestions made regarding parties to deeds are applicable to contracts to parties.

Purchase price. State the purchase price and terms of payment.

Earnest money. For the seller's protection, the deposit should be adequate. Insist on a certified or cashier's check. Buyer should insist that money be held in escrow by a bank or trust company.

Purpose for which buyer is purchasing the property. Careful thought must be given to the purpose for which the buyer is purchasing the property. For example, it may be that the buyer intends to use the property for a purpose forbidden by the zoning ordinance. If so, the contract must contain a clause for the buyer's protection requiring an amendment to the zoning ordinance to be procured within a limited time, and in default thereof, the buyer to be entitled to cancel the contract and obtain a return of his money. Seller should convenant to join in the rezoning petition. If the contract is prepared and signed at a time when information concerning the provisions of recorded building restrictions or applicable zoning and building ordinances is unavailable, but the seller feels that neither restrictions nor ordinances will prevent use for the buyer's intended purpose, a clause may be added giving the buyer the right to terminate the contract within a specified time if it shall appear from recorded covenants, conditions, or restrictions, or from zoning or building ordinances, official maps or plans, or applicable statues that the premises cannot legally be used for the intended purposes.

Description of the land. In considering the adequacy of the land description of the contract, the parties should consult also the specific suggestions hereinafter set forth.

Streets and alleys. The seller will usually have some right, title, or interest in and to the streets or alleys adjoining the premises sold, including private streets and vacated streets, and it is desirable that the contract of sale call for the seller to convey, without warranty, all such right, title, and interest.

Items to be conveyed to buyer or retained by seller. A contract for the sale of land obligates the seller to deliver title to the land and all fixtures, including the building, for it, of course, is a fixture, and fixtures are part of the land. Chattels, however, such as furniture, are not included, unless the contract expressly so provides. Any items that are clearly personal property might give rise to controversy.

Chattel clause. Together with the following chattels for which a bill of sale will be given at closing:

Air conditioning equipment, awnings, bar and bar stools, bookcases, cabinets, carpets (particularly stair carpets), chandeliers and lighting fixtures, clothes washer and dryer, crops, curtains, curtain rods, draperies, and other interior decorations, dryers, electric fans, electrical equipment, fireplace grates and andirons, dishwasher, doorbells and chimes, fuel, furniture, garage door openers and car units, garbage cans, garbage disposal, garden statuary, gas logs, high fidelity or stereo equipment that has been built in, ironing boards, lamps, lawn mowers, and garden equipment, linoleum, mirrors, perennial plants, refrigerators, rugs, screen doors, security systems, shelves, space heaters, sprinkling equipment, stokers, storm doors and windows, shrubbery, stoves, supplies, TV antennas and masts, tools and equipment (particularly janitor's tools), water softener, trade fixtures, venetian blinds, ventilators, wash tubs, water heaters, towel racks and bars, water meter, window shades, and window screens.

As a minimum, the contract should require the seller to warrant his title to any easement premises.

Assignments. Are there leases to tenants? Are there other types of insurance policies? Let the contract call for the assignment and delivery thereof to the purchaser. The contract should also require seller to assign to buyer any other items that buyer wishes to receive, e.g., service contracts (contracts with exterminators, scavengers, and so on), roof guaranties, or tenant's deposits.

Fixtures. What does the seller expect to retain after the deal is closed? Once the contract is signed, the seller is obligated to deliver to the buyer all fixtures, for they are legally part of the land. If the seller expects to retain attached machinery or other items that might be considered fixtures, provision to this effect should be included in the contract.

Encumbrances to which the title is to be subject and to which the buyer agrees. The seller should see that he has listed in the contract all the encumbrances or other defects in title that he does not propose to clear before the deal is closed. Most contract forms contain a printed list of common encumbrances, such as leases or building restrictions, but it is intended that the seller will add to this list as necessary. Suppose, for example, that the seller's title is subject to an easement. Is it mentioned in the contract? If not, and the buyer changes his mind and decides to back out of the deal, he may be able to do so because the title, as finally examined before the deal is closed, must reveal no encumbrances other than those listed either in general or in specific language in the contract.

The buyer should carefully analyze every encumbrance listed by the seller. For example, if in the contract he agrees to take subject to "existing leases," he must accept the property subject to any lease, no matter how ridiculously low the rent may be. If the contract says that the buyer will accept title subject to "building the other restrictions of record," "easements of record," and "mineral rights," as many printed forms provide, will any of these restrictions, easements, or mineral rights interfere with his building program, assuming that he is buying land to build on? Moreover, will some easement documents to which the land is subject obligate the buyer in some way as owner of this land? For example, an easement for road purposes may obligate me to keep my neighbor's road in repair. Similar personal liability provisions may be contained in restriction documents.

Mortgage provisions. These should be detailed and complete. For example, if the contract calls for a purchase money mortgage, are the amount, interest rate, maturity date, and form of mortgage clearly set forth? Similar details should be included in a clause giving the buyer the right to cancel if he cannot procure the mortgage of a specified amount, and in this clause also specify the time allowed to procure the mortgage. If land is being sold subject to a mortgage, specify the amount and whether or not the buyer assumes personal liability, and that no defaults exist. If the seller has a mortgage on his land that must be released, the contract should provide that the seller will have the right to pay it off at the closing of the deal, using the buyer's sale price for this purpose.

Evidence of title. The contract should provide: (1) What type of title evidence is to be furnished, title insurance, abstract, and so forth. (2) Who is to furnish and pay for same. (3) Time allowed: (a) for furnishing evidence of title, (b) for buyer to point out defects in title not permitted by the contract, (c) for seller's clearance of objections, and (d) for buyer to decide whether to accept title *as is* if objections cannot be cured (4) If abstract of title is specified, for the seller's protection a clause should be included giving the seller the right to cure any of the buyer's objections to the title by delivery of a clear policy of title insurance. This may save the seller the time and expense of a quiet title suit when the buyer's attorney raises numerous unimportant objections to the title. (5) The seller should not sign a form of contract that calls for title insurance if his land is registered under the Torrens system, for this will subject him to a double expense if the buyer insists on his contract rights.

Clearing title by escrow deposits. For the protection of the seller, the contract should contain a provision allowing the seller to leave money in escrow with some bank or title company if his title is not clear on the day that he must deliver clear title. Otherwise, a deal may fall through simply because a seller is not in a position to remove some trivial defect, such as a small mechanic's lien, within the time allowed for clearing title.

Chattel lien search. Specify if the seller is to furnish search for financing statements or other liens on personal property being sold, and if so, time allowed for same.

Building ordinance violations. If the seller is to furnish a formal, official report as to building code violations, cover this, including the time allowed for this purpose. The buyer should endeavor to have the contract provide that the seller "warrants the building on said premises is now and at the date of closing will be free and clear of all violations of laws and ordinances, and for breach of this warranty buyer may rescind this contract, before or after closing, or, at his election, may sue for damages."

Survey. If the seller is to furnish a survey, specify the time allowed for this and that it is to be satisfactory to the buyer's attorney. The time allowed for the buyer to raise objections based on the survey should tie into the time allowed the buyer for raising objections to the title. If the seller objects to paying for a survey, the buyer may decide to get one at his own expense. Is a survey necessary? Business judgment should be used in answering this question. For example, if A is buying a forty-year-old dwelling where the fences have also been up for that length of time, it is unlikely that any encroachment trouble will develop. Age has set the matter at rest. If, on the other hand, *A* is buying a recently erected commercial building that apparently extends to the property lines, a survey is definitely advisable, for the building may actually extend over property lines. Again, how can the buyer be sure that the legal description in the contract covers the property that the buyer has inspected and wants to buy? The only really satisfactory proof of this is a land survey. A survey is always advisable if new construction is contemplated, so that the building is set within the lot lines and within lines established by ordinances and private restrictions.

Building and other restrictions. If the seller wishes to place building restrictions on the land sold, he must make provision for this in the contract.

Risk of loss. Suppose the building is destroyed or damaged by fire or other casualty before the deal is closed. The right of the buyer to cancel the deal and his right to insurance money if he does not back out should be covered.

Miscellaneous documents to be furnished to the buyer. If a new building requires a certificate of occupancy or an approval by the underwriters of electrical installations, or if it is customary to obtain similar certificates with respect to plumbing and the like, the contract should provide that the seller will deliver these at the closing. In case of a new building, guaranties by the subcontractors are customary. There is usually a roof guaranty and a guaranty of the plumbing and heating equipment and electrical installations. The contract should provide that the seller will transfer and deliver these to the purchaser at the closing. The buyer should obtain the "as built" architect's plans and specifications for the building. Also, the buyer should obtain appropriate evidence that the building is free from infestation.

Possession. Cover the date on which possession is to be given.

Leases. Provide for assignment to buyer of all seller's leases, including leases for advertising signs.

Concessionaire contracts. Provide for assignment of all such contracts.

Tenant's security deposits. Assignment of tenant's security deposits to buyer must be covered specifically.

Advance payments of rent. The contract should allow the buyer a credit against the purchase price where a tenant has already paid the seller the rent for the last several months of the term.

Prorated items. These should be covered in great detail to avoid arguments at closing over who pays for janitor's vacation pay, water bills, and so forth.

Documents. All miscellaneous documents that the buyer will need should be provided for in the contract. The seller is under no legal obligation to furnish any document that the contract does not call for.

Signatures, acknowledgment, witnessing. All the parties must sign, being careful to sign as their names appear on the contract. Witnessing and acknowledgment are desirable, so that the buyer may record the contract, for without witnessing and acknowledgment, the contract is not recordable in many states.

Unions. If the sale is of a substantial property it is quite possible that the seller employs union members and that a collective bargaining agreement. In such case a labor lawyer should be consulted, since the buyer must change, recognize or renegotiate the existing collective bargaining agreement, or to terminate it. Or the buyer as a "successor employer" may become liable if unemployment contributions have not been paid by the seller.

Utilities, etc. If vacant land is being sold, the contract should warrant that utilities, water, sewer, and so on, are available at the property lines and are connectible.

Access. As to vacant land, seller warrants that the land has access to abutting streets by buyer's trucks.

Easements. With the help of a surveyor, buyer should determine if property is serviced by an easement over adjoining land. If it is, the contract must require the seller to convey the easement and to furnish title insurance or other evidence of title (such as abstract) to show that the seller owns an unemcumbered easement. The land is useless to the buyer if he has no legal access.

If the sale involves granting the buyer an easement over the seller's adjoining land, this must be carefully planned. A title search of that land is needed, and the easement must be in a form a title company will insure.

Purchase money mortgage. If the seller is taking back a purchase money mortgage, details of the mortgage and of the transaction (who pays for title insurance, etc.) must be covered.

Contiguity of parcels. If the land is vacant and consists of several parcels, the buyer should insist that the title company certify that the parcels do indeed adjoin each other. Alternatively, the surveyor should draft a new perimeter description that embraces the entire tract. His survey will then reveal if there are strips between the parcels.

Merger. If there are matters (landscaping, paving driveways) that the seller should attend to after closing, add a sentence that these covenants do not merge in the deed.

Inspection before closing. The buyer is always given the right to inspect the day before closing a home deal to determine if the seller has removed valuable fixtures (chandeliers, etc.)

Zoning and building code violations. In some areas of the country the building must be inspected by the city before closing, since local law does not permit recording the deed unless it has the building inspector's approval. In larger deals (hotels, office buildings) the seller makes a careful inspection before he signs the contract, always remembering that in some states violations of these codes are not considered as affecting the marketability of title. In home deals the private inspector who inspects for the buyer is able to detect violations and should cover this in his report. It is unwise to omit any mention of this in the contract. This becomes a battleground because the seller argues that every building has some violations (which is true) and that the buyer will simply use this as an argument to lower the price. At a minimum the contract should require the building to be free of officially posted ordinance violations. All title companies will insure against zoning violations (for a fee). Few will give insurance against building or housing code violations.

Warranties of the condition of the building. Many home sales require the building to pass a private inspector's inspection. This clause appears so frequently in contracts because if the buyer simply holds off signing until he has his inspection made, another buyer may "steal the deal." If the seller refuses to permit this clause, the buyer may ask him to represent and warrant that the heating, electrical, plumbing, etc., are in working order. Some sellers will agree to this. If the buyer wants the seller to warrant that the appliances are in "good working order," the seller may not agree. What is "good" working order? The seller will argue for a clause that *all* buyer's rights in this regard terminate at closing.

Brokers. Some sellers want protection by the buyer against claims of a broker other than the broker paid by the seller.

Service contracts. In larger deals the seller may be liable on a variety of service contracts, elevator inspection, termite inspection, waste removal, burglar alarm service, and so on. He will want copies attached to the contract and an agreement by the buyer to assume them.

Unrented space. If it is anticipated that large rental space may become vacant before closing, the parties should agree on who rents the space, who approves, who pays the rental broker, etc.

Water stock. In some localities mutual water companies are formed to service the community. Each property owner holds a stock certificate signifying the number of shares in his name. Provision should be made for transfer of this stock.

Subdivisions. If the contract involves vacant subdivided land, the seller will have complied with the local laws that regulate subdivisions.

Lease schedule. The lease schedule should be complete and should state that leases will be subject to the buyer's approval unless the buyer has approved them in advance. Many office leases have rent concessions (free rent for part of a year.) These are granted in periods of high vacancy. The lease schedule should warrant that there are no concessions, no options to renew, etc. The impact of rent control ordinances should be considered. Determine what lease brokerage commissions are payable on existing leases and who pays them. The seller covenants to assign his interest in all leases at closing and to deliver the leases to the buyer, together with notices to tenants to pay rent to the buyer.

REFERENCE: Holtzchue, *Real Estate Contracts* (1985).

CHAPTER 12

Installment Contracts

12.01 In General

In general, the cash sale contract contemplates that the deal will be closed as soon as the seller's title is examined and found to be good. There is also a type of contract called the *installment contract, contract for deed,* or *land contract.* An installment contract provides for a down payment, with the balance of the purchase price payable in monthly installments. The buyer receives his deed when all the installments have been paid or when the unpaid balance of the purchase price has been reduced to a certain agreed figure, whereupon the buyer is to receive a deed and give the seller a purchase money mortgage for the balance of the purchase price.

Before signing an installment contract, the seller should remember that he is going into the credit business. For this reason, the seller should do the same evaluation of the buyer as a lender does in the loan underwriting process. Is the buyer creditworthy? A credit check must be made. Does the buyer have the income to make the periodic payments as they come due? Check the buyer's annual income by inquiry of his employer or a review of his income tax returns. A good real estate broker can be of great help to the buyer in attending to these details and in evaluating the information.

12.02 Broker's Commission

Where the broker's listing contract permits an installment contract (as distinguished from a cash sale) or the seller decides to accept an installment purchaser, the broker's commission is earned once the contract is signed.

SUGGESTION TO THE SELLER: In the listing contract provide for the commission to be payable in installments. The seller doesn't want to pay a full commission if the buyer defaults in the early months of the sale.

12.03 Spouse's Signature

Both seller and spouse should join in the contract of sale because of marital and homestead rights.

12.04 Purchasers as Joint Tenants

Where a husband and wife are buying it is probably wise to have them purchase as joint tenants or as tenants by the entireties. Over the relatively long life of the contract, one of the buyers may die.

12.05 Title Search and Closing

The installment sale contract is usually used because the buyer does not have enough cash to qualify for a regular mortgage or because mortgage financing is not available. Still, the buyer usually must make a substantial down payment. Hence the buyer will want proof of the seller's condition of title before the payment of any of the down payment. A common method of handling this situation is for the contract to provide that the buyer is to make a down payment (for example, $1,000) to be held in escrow by the seller's broker or some other third party. A title search is then made and a survey obtained, just as in a cash sale. The buyer's lawyer then examines the title evidence and survey to determine the acceptability of the state of title. If the title is acceptable or, more exactly, in conformity with the contract, an initial closing is held at which prorations are made as in a cash sale, and the balance of the down payment is paid. The buyer then takes possession of the property.

In some areas this is handled more formally. A preliminary contract is signed. When the title is shown to be in conformity with the preliminary contract and the prorations are agreed upon, the parties sign an installment contract, the balance of the earnest money is paid, and the buyer takes possession. Some lawyers prefer this approach. After all, during the years the installment payments are being made, the preliminaries such as prorations are no longer of interest, and the remaining rights and duties of the parties are set forth in a shorter, simpler installment payment document.

In larger deals this document may require the seller to prepare and sign a deed running to the buyer. This deed is delivered "in escrow" to a bank or title company, which holds the deed under a formal escrow agreement that may call for the installment payments to be made to the escrowee.

The final payment is a "balloon," that is, a large payment. When it is due, a second title search is made. If that search verifies clear title at that time, the last payment is made and the escrowee delivers the deed to the buyer. Thus even if the seller has died during the life of the contract, his deed is available and is quite valid.

In many areas the buyer's lawyer will insist that the buyer receive a "contract purchaser's" title policy when the down payment is made. This policy is issued in duplicate, one to each party, and shows the buyer's interest under the recorded contract. It insures the validity of the contract and insures the buyer against future matters involving the seller, such as bankruptcies. Under this method the buyer is virtually certain that if payments are made regularly, a clear title policy will be issued.

Where the contract is substantial, the original contract is acknowledged before a notary and recorded in the Recorder's Office. Title companies usually insist on this. Where abstracts are used the buyer will want his contract to appear in the abstract.

In small transactions, usually involving old homes sold with a nominal down payment, the unsophisticated buyer signs the contract with no title search to be made until payment has been completed. Such transactions expose the purchaser to an incredible risk of loss of title. Nevertheless they occur. There are instances where a purchaser has occupied and paid on a home for many years and in the end has been unable to obtain clear title.

12.06   Recording

Some printed forms forbid the recording of the contract. There is some doubt as to the validity of such a clause. Illinois forbids this clause in residential contracts.

12.07   Assignment by Buyer

In order to control the occupancy of the property, the seller may wish to include a clause forbidding assignment of the contract by the buyer without the seller's consent. Such a clause is valid. *Immel* v. *Travelers Ins. Co.,* 373 Ill. 256, 26 NE2d 114 (1940).

Where an assignment is made, thought should be given to the liability of the assignee. By the weight of authority, a mere assignment does not create a personal liability of the assignee to the seller. *Quest* v. *Robinson,* 71 Ill. App.3d 678, 318 NE2d 1335 (1980). In a few states, the assignee does become so liable. *Rose* v. *Vulcan Materials Co.,* 194 SE2d 521 (N.C.) (citing authorities pro and con). Of course, if the seller's consent is needed, he may insist that the assignee sign an instrument assuming personal liability in consideration of receiving the seller's consent.

Clauses forbidding assignment of the contract by the buyer do not prevent the buyer's signing an installment contract to sell his interest. Such a contract is called a *subpurchase. Covington* v. *Clark,* 346 P2d 225 (Cal. 1959); *Lake Shore Club* v. *Lake Front,* 398 NE2d 893 (Ill. App. 1979). *See also* 4 Stanf. L. Rev. 443; 100 U. Pa. L. Rev. 1073; 27 Univ. N.Y.L. Rev. 174; 3 Utah L. Rev. 257 (all dealing with subpurchase contracts).

In point of fact, the restriction on assignment can take one of three forms, namely: (1) The contract contains a covenant not to assign. Presumably, for a breach of this covenant the remedy would be a suit for damages. (2) The contract may state that the making of an assignment without the required consent makes the *assignment* void, or (3) makes the *contract* void at the option of the injured party. Murray, *Contracts* § 305, p. 623 (1974). It is therefore important to frame the clause carefully, selecting the particular choice with care. Again, in states where forfeitures are frowned upon, and this is a long list of states, one wonders if option (3) is a realistic option.

Actually, a fourth option exists, namely, inclusion of a due-on-sale clause that is triggered either by an assignment or subpurchase contract.

12.08   Prepayment Privilege

The buyer will insist that the contract give him the right to prepay the installment balance of the purchase price. If the contract does not expressly give this privilege, the contract balance cannot be prepaid. *Burns* v. *Epstein,* 413 Ill. 476, 109 NE2d 774 (1952). Sellers are concerned about the income tax impact of prepayment and may require deferred payments. Sellers may even exact a stiff prepayment penalty. Courts will uphold it if it is reasonably related to the seller's risk of incurring increased income tax liability. *Williams* v. *Fassler,* 167 Cal. Reptr. 545 (1980).

12.09   Impounds

Many installment contracts in home sales require the buyer to make monthly payments that include one-twelfth of the yearly real estate tax and fire insurance premium. This, of course, is a common provision in home mortgages. In such case, failure of the buyer to include these *impound payments* in his monthly remittance would be a default under the contract and might eventually lead to a forfeiture.

12.10   Acceleration Clause

From the seller's point of view, it is desirable that an installment contract authorize the seller to declare the entire purchase price due in case of default. Otherwise, a chronically delinquent buyer can drive a seller to distraction by curing his defaults each time the seller serves notice on him of the seller's intent to declare a forfeiture.

> **EXAMPLE:**   Owner contracts to sell real estate to Buyer at a purchase price of $20,000 payable in monthly installments. Buyer is constantly late in making payments. The contract contains an acceleration clause. Owner sends Buyer notice to cure all his defaults within thirty days, otherwise Owner will declare the entire purchase price due. This is permitted under the acceleration clause. After acceleration has taken place, Owner is in a position to forfeit unless Buyer can pay the entire purchase price. This is helpful in getting rid of the chronic delinquent. But, as in the case of mortgage law today, the seller must not exercise his rights unfairly.

The acceleration clause is commonly regarded as valid. *Benincash* v. *Mihailovich,* 188 NW2d 136 (Mich. 1971). However, it is probably necessary for the seller to give the purchaser notice and an opportunity to cure his defaults within a reasonable time. *Brannock* v. *Fletcher,* 155 SE2d 532 (N.C. 1967). If the seller accelerates unfairly, courts will set the acceleration aside.

> **EXAMPLE:**   The seller cannot declare an acceleration where there is an honest dispute as to the amount due. *Moore* v. *Bunch,* 185 NW2d 565 (Mich. 1971).

12.11   Insurance

It seems wise for the contract to spell out all the appropriate insurance requirements and to require the buyer to furnish evidence periodically that the insurance is in force. Both seller and buyer should have liability coverage. To be sure, the brunt of liability will fall on the buyer—occupant, but the seller may be named a defendant in personal injury suits, and an insured seller will be entitled to have the insurer defend the lawsuit without charge. The hazard insurance should have a "manuscript" rider covering both seller and buyer.

> **SUGGESTION TO THE SELLER:**   Draft a paragraph for the insurance endorsement stating that acts of the buyer (arson, for example) will not invalidate seller's coverage. Existing forms of this rider are inadequate.

12.12   Judgments Against Seller—Equitable Conversion

In many states the buyer is regarded as the equitable owner of the property. In these states commonly the interest of the seller is a bare, naked legal title. Judgment liens against the seller do not attach to such a title. *Bank of Sante Fe* v. *Garcia,* 102 NM 588, 698 P2d 458 (1985), 87 ALR 1505, 1512. The state law must be checked. Some contract forms contain a provision that the purchaser acquires no title, legal or equitable, until the sale price is paid in full. The validity of these clauses has been sustained. *Cox* v. *Supreme S. & L. Assn.,* 126 Ill. App.2d 74 (1970) (holding valid clause that buyer acquires no interest in land until contract price is paid in full).

This clause is objectionable to the purchaser and should be deleted. It negates the equitable conversion that would result from the signing of the contract and deprives the purchaser of the protection this doctrine provides against judgments against the seller.

At times, during the life of the contract, the buyer will learn that a judgment or other lien has, in fact, been filed against the seller. This raises a problem of great difficulty. The seller may, in good faith, be appealing or otherwise contesting the lien. But the buyer is put to the hazard of continuing his payments on a title that may be clouded when it is conveyed to him. Some relief is obtained by a clause providing that in such cases the buyer may elect to make his payments to a bank in escrow for both parties until assurances have been given, satisfactory to buyer's attorney, that these liens will not affect the buyer's title. However, there is no device that is really satisfactory to both parties. A long-term escrow may help if accompanied by a title policy protecting the buyer against future liens. Or the title may be placed in a trust at the time the contract is signed with directions to the trustee to give a deed to the buyer when the last payment is made.

Again, a title company may be persuaded to give the buyer a clear policy on the theory that, in states where equitable conversion exists, the seller holds a naked legal title in trust for the buyer and such a title is not subject to judgment liens. *Reuss* v. *Nixon*, 272 Ill. App. 219; *Lynch* v. *Eifler*, 191 Ill. App. 344; 87 ALR 1505, 1515.

12.13 Mortgages

Both seller and buyer have interests that may be mortgaged. *Tanglewood Land Co.* v. *Boyd*, 256 SE2d 270 (N.C. 1979).

As to the seller's interest, the contract should provide that the buyer's interest is subordinate to any mortgage that does not exceed the balance due on the contract or the interest rate or monthly payments stated therein; likewise, that in case of any default in the mortgage, the buyer may make the payments on the mortgage and such payments shall reduce the contract balance.

As to the buyer, a clause is needed under which the seller joins in the mortgage or subordinates his interest thereto. Some rehab contractors accept a mortgage on the buyer's interest only. This is legally valid, but unsound. If the buyer's interest is terminated for default, this wipes out the mortgage.

> REFERENCES: *Nelson* v. *Bailey,* 54 Wash.2d 161, 338 P2d 757, 73 ALR2d 1400 (1959); *Simonson* v. *Wenzel,* 27 N.D. 638; 147 NW 804, LRA 1918C 780 (1914); *Eade* v. *Brownlee,* 29 Ill.2d 214, 193 NE2d 786 (1963) (all holding that contract purchaser has interest that may be mortgaged).
>
> *Norlin* v. *Montgomery,* 367 P2d 621 (Wash. 1962) (seller's interest is not subject to mortgages executed by buyer).
>
> *Eade* v. *Brownlee,* 29 Ill.2d 214, 193 NE2d 786 (1963); and *Miles Homes* v. *Grant,* 134 NW2d 569 (Iowa 1965) (both holding buyer's mortgagee not entitled to notice of forfeiture). *Contra: Kendrick* v. *Davis,* 452 P2d 222 (Wash. 1969). As to notice to lien creditors of buyer generally, see *Hayes* v. *Carey,* 287 Ill. 774, 122 NE 524 (1919); *MGIC Mtg. Corp.* v. *Bowen,* 572 P2d 547 (N.M. 1977).
>
> *Knauss* v. *Miles Homes Inc.,* 173 NW2d 896 (N.D. 1970) (holding that purchaser's mortgage is necessary party to seller's suit to quiet title).
>
> 87 ALR 1505, 1515; 43 Mo. L. Rev. 371; and 45 Wash. L. Rev. 645, all dealing with situation where after installment contract is recorded the seller mortgages his interest, and issue is whether buyer can claim priority over mortgage for payments made after he learns of the mortgage.

12.14 Bankruptcy of Seller

The new Bankruptcy Act protects a buyer in possession against the bankruptcy of the seller. The former Bankruptcy Act did not. The buyer should insist that the title policy issued when the contract is signed contain affirmative protection against the seller's bankruptcy. Then if the bankruptcy court attempts to reach the asset, the title company will defend the buyer. The buyer must be in possession to receive this protection.

12.15   Building Code Regulations

Laws will be encountered that require an installment seller, prior to signing of the contract, to furnish information as to reported building code violations. Ill. Rev. Stat. Ch. 29, §§8.31, 8.32. A question remains as to the liability of the seller for building code violations that develop later. The buyer, of course, is liable, since he has possession and control of the building. *Cox* v. *Supreme S. & L. Assn.,* 126 Ill. App.2d 293, 262 NE2d 74 (1970). However, the code language may be broad enough to impose liability on the seller as well. *Cocanig* v. *City of Chicago,* 21 Ill.2d 464, 173 NE2d 482 (1961); *City of Chicago* v. *Porler,* 26 Ill. App.2d 323, 168 NE2d 468 (1960). Of course, the seller will be liable to the city for building code violations existing when the contract was signed. *Cox* v. *Supreme S. & L. Assn.,* 126 Ill. App.2d 293, 262 NE2d 74.

In some states the fines for building code violations are substantial. Obviously, the seller should require the buyer to keep the building free from building code violations and make violation of this agreement grounds for forfeiture. He should retain the right to make reasonable inspections of the building and exercise this right. If substantial code violations appear, he should declare the contract forfeited.

12.16   The Forfeiture Process

Every installment contract contains a forfeiture clause. If the buyer fails to meet his payments, this clause gives the buyer the right to terminate the contract and to retain the payments the buyer has made. This is what lawyers call an *agreed remedy.* It exists only if the forfeiture clause is found in the contract. *Realty Securities Corp.* v. *Johnson,* 93 Fla. 46, 111 So 532 (1927). In this respect *forfeiture* differs from *rescission.* Rescission is a right the courts give the seller even where the contract is silent. The seller may terminate the contract if the buyer fails to met his payments, but should "restore the status quo." This means he should return to the buyer the payments made by the buyer less a fair rent for the time the buyer has been in possession. *Hillman* v. *Busselle,* 66 Ariz. 139, 185 P2d 311 (1947). Obviously, the seller wishes to keep those payments. Hence the importance of the forfeiture clause. By declaring the contract forfeited, the seller terminates the contract and retains all payments previously made by the buyer. 77 Am.Jur.2d *Vendor and Purchase* § 500.

Just as we so often find that tenants do not pay their monthly rent exactly on the day it is due, so we often find that purchasers under installment contracts do not pay their payments exactly on the day they are due, or they may from time to time make payments of less than the amount due. The overwhelming majority of installment sellers go along with the buyer, hoping that he will be able to straighten out his finances. Ultimately, the seller may decide that he can no longer be indulgent. Then he faces a problem that his own indulgence has created.

> **EXAMPLE:** An installment contract provided that time was of the essence, but the seller often accepted payments after the dates fixed for payment. This constituted a waiver of the provision that time was of the essence. The reason

is that the seller, by accepting payments after the dates fixed, had led the buyer to believe that he would not insist on the provision that payments must be made strictly on the specified dates. It would therefore be highly unjust to permit the seller suddenly to declare a forfeiture of the contract for the buyer's failure to pay one of the installments promptly. *Fox v. Grange,* 261 Ill. 116, 103 NE 576 (1913); 31 ALR2d 55, 85.

The seller may *revive* the provision that time is of the essence. He may serve a *warning notice* on the buyer that in the future he will insist on strict performance of the contract according to its terms, and thereafter the buyer must make his payments promptly or the seller may declare a forfeiture. This warning notice must be followed by a declaration of forfeiture if the buyer fails to cure his defaults within the allotted time. Such a warning notice must not be a mere dun. It must state unequivocally that the contract will be forfeited if the defaults are not cured within the specified time. *Monson v. Bragdon,* 159 Ill. 61, 42 NE 383 (1895). Many printed contract forms contain a provision that acceptance of late payments shall not constitute a waiver of the provision that time is of the essence. Some courts refuse to give this provision effect. *Morrey v. Bartlett,* 288 Ill. App. 620; *Scott v. Cal. Farming Co.,* 4 Cal. App.2d 232, 40 P2d 850 (1940). In many states, a warning notice must *always* be given before an installment contract is forfeited. *County of Lincoln v. Fischer,* 216 Oreg. 421, 339 P2d 1084 (1954); 31 ALR2d 14.

It is obvious that forfeiture involves a number of steps. The first step is the giving of notice to the purchaser, as has been stated. Where there are two or more purchasers, each is entitled to separate notice. In short, the seller should never send a notice addressed to "Mr. and Mrs. John Smith."

Sending a notice to the wrong address is a fatal defect if the seller knows the correct address. *Kingsley v. Roeder,* 2 Ill.2d 131, 117 NE2d 82 (1954).

If the purchaser has assigned his interest to a third party or placed a mortgage on his interest, obviously the better practice is to serve all notices on all such parties. Whether failure to so notify these parties will invalidate the forfeiture is a difficult question to answer. *Eade v. Brownlee,* 29 Ill.2d 214, 93 NE2d 786 (1963) (purchaser's mortgagee not served). *Holiver v. Dept. of Public Works,* 127 NE2d 790 (Mass. 1955); *Miles Homes Inc., v. Grant,* 134 NW2d 569 (Iowa 1965) (purchaser's mortgagee not entitled to notice). *Kendrick v. Davis,* 452 P2d 222 (Wash. 1969) (purchaser's mortgagee is entitled to notice).

12.16(a)   Trifling Defaults

At times the buyer will argue that forfeiture ought not be permitted where the default is trifling in amount.

> **EXAMPLE:**   A buyer in a $30,000 contract deliberately defaulted in a payment of $10.48. The court sustained the forfeiture. Where a default is deliberate, the buyer is, in effect, demanding a reduction in the sale price. He cannot force this decision on the seller. *Miller v. American Wonderlands,* 275 NW2d 399 (Iowa 1979).

But where there are minor defaults not due to stubborn defiance, the courts often set aside or refuse forfeiture. *Fisel v. Yoder,* 320 NE2d 783 (Ind.).

12.16(b)   Forfeiture Procedure—Acceleration Improper

For some unexplained reason, many installment contracts lack an acceleration clause. In such case, a seller seeking to declare a forfeiture may demand payment of only those installments that are delinquent. However, on occasion a seller will, quite improperly in such cases, declare an acceleration in his notice of his intention to declare a forfeiture. By the better view this is a fatal defect. The forfeiture must be set aside. *Rader* v. *Taylor*, 333 P2d 480 (Mont. 1959). A buyer facing a demand for the entire balance due when he is having a hard time making the regular monthly payments will throw up his hands in despair. It is unfair to give him the impression that he can save his interest only by paying the entire balance due.

12.16(c)   Forfeiture Procedure—Declaration of Forfeiture

Of course, following the seller's notice to the buyer to cure defaults or suffer a forfeiture, the seller must declare the forfeiture. A forfeiture cannot be made in the seller's mind. It must be communicated to the buyer. *Lovins* v. *Kelly*, 19 Ill.2d 25, 166 NE2d 69 (1960). If, and only if, the contract requires it, the declaration of forfeiture must be recorded. *Tobin* v. *Alexander*, 380 NE2d 45 (Ill. 1978).

12.16(d)   Forfeiture Procedure—Recovery of Money Paid by Buyer

Even where a forfeiture has been declared, the buyer's rights may be revived. This occurs where the seller waives the forfeiture by conduct indicating that he considers the contract still in force, as by negotiating with the buyer concerning the title of the property, possible repurchase by the seller, extension of time of payment, and the like. 107 ALR 345. All owners of the land must join in the notice of forfeiture. 66 CJ *Vendor and Purchaser* §62 p. 762.

Where a recorded contract has been properly forfeited, the seller can obtain a court decree declaring the buyer's rights terminated.

Where the buyer is in military service, the contract cannot be forfeited without a court order. The court may either postpone the forfeiture or order the repayment of prior installments before permitting forfeiture of the contract.

In California, Georgia, Montana, South Dakota, Wisconsin, and Utah, a purchaser whose contract has been forfeited is allowed to get back the amount he has paid, less a reasonable compensation to the seller for the use of his land. Illinois, Iowa, and Minnesota allow the purchaser to cure his defaults within a specified grace period and thus preserve this contract. Arizona also provides a grace period that increases in proportion to the amount paid on the contract. 13 Rutgers L. Rev. 624; 24 Mo. L. Rev. 244. In Florida, Indiana, and Maryland, the contract must be foreclosed like a mortgage. *Mid-State Inv. Corp.* v. *O'Steen* (Fla.) 133 So2d 455; *Stendzel* v. *Marshall*, 301 NE2d 641 (Ind. 1973). However, in most states, the forfeiture provisions in the contract will be enforced. *Coe* v. *Bennett*, 46 Idaho 62, 266 P. 413 (1928); 31 ALR2d 38, 71.

Perhaps the most important clause in an installment contract, from the seller's point of view, is the forfeiture clause.

In various circumstances, courts will allow the buyer to recover a portion of the purchase price he has paid. 4 ALR4th 993.

12.16(e)   Relief Against Forfeiture—Forfeiture and Damages

Courts will on occasion set aside a forfeiture of an installment contract. 55 ALR3d 10; Restatement, *Contracts,* §§ 275, 276. The more money the buyer has paid in, the more likely the court is to do this. Where the buyer has made substantial improvements, he is quite likely to obtain this sort of relief. *Krentz* v. *Johnson,* 36 Ill. App.3d 142, 343 NE2d 165 (1976). The more lenient the seller has been in accepting short payments or delayed payments, the greater the likelihood that the forfeiture will be set aside. *Krentz* v. *Johnson, supra.* Where the buyer's breach consists of failing to make repairs, the seller's notice must give him a reasonable time to make repairs. Otherwise the forfeiture cannot stand. *Reeploeg* v. *Jensen,* 490 P2d 445 (Wash. 1971). Where the forfeiture notices were sent to the wrong address, the forfeiture cannot stand. *Kingsley* v. *Roeder,* 2 Ill.2d 131, 117 NE2d 82 (1954). Whenever it would be unreasonable to let the seller keep the buyer's payments and oust him from the land, the forfeiture is set aside. *McWilliams* v. *Urban Land Co.,* 194 NW2d 920 (Mich.). In such cases the court may order foreclosure by sale, which gives the buyer a right to redeem. *Ruhl* v. *Johnson,* 159 Neb. 810, 49 NW2d 687 (1951). Where the buyer's payments amount to little more than the rental value of the land he has occupied, his case for relief is poor. But where the seller is himself in default, any forfeiture he declares will be set aside.

Some states that normally allow the remedy of forfeiture, nevertheless insist on foreclosure where the buyer has paid in substantial amounts.

> **EXAMPLE:**   Court refused forfeiture and ordered foreclosure where buyer had paid in 30 percent of sale price. *Morris* v. *Weigle,* 383 NE2d 341 (Ind. 1978).

Some courts put this on the ground that a forfeiture in such case is *unconscionable. Williams* v. *Havens,* 444 P2d 132 (Idaho 1968). Other courts state that forfeiture in such cases "shocks the conscience of the court." *Kay* v. *Wood,* 549 P2d 709 (Utah 1976); *Jenkins* v. *Wise,* 574 P2d 1337 (Hawaii 1978). Of course, some courts are more liberal with purchasers than others. It is not possible to state a definite rule as to what investment will protect a buyer against forfeiture. *Clements* v. *Castle Mtg. Service Co.,* 382 A2d 1367 (Del. 1977).

> REFERENCES: The question of a defaulting buyer's right to recover his earnest money or other purchase money paid has been the subject of many articles: 24 Mo. L. Rev. 244; 47 So. Cal. L. Rev. 201; 25 Southern L. Rev. 387; 1950 U. of Ill. L. Forum 249; 12 U. of Detroit L. J. 59; 19 U. of Miami L. Rev. 552; 20 *id.* 1. The great leading article is Corbin, *The Right of a Defaulting Vendee to the Restitution of Installment Unpaid,* 40 Yale L. J. 1013 (1913).

12.16(f)   Remedies of Seller—Foreclosure

A seller may file a foreclosure suit if the buyer defaults. The foreclosure may be a *strict foreclosure. Walker* v. *Runnenkamp,* 373 P2d 559 (Idaho 1962); 77 ALR 282.

In such a foreclosure, the purchaser will be given a period of time to pay up, and if he fails to do so, his rights are extinguished. Or the court may order a foreclosure sale of the land. 77 ALR 276. If foreclosure is by sale, some states allow some sort of redemption period. 51 ALR2d 672. Other states allow no redemption period.

As in the case of forfeitures, the court may hold in foreclosure cases that the seller has waived the contract provision that time is of the essence.

EXAMPLE: Seller entered into an installment contract with Buyer. It contained an acceleration clause. From time to time Buyer was delinquent in his payments and Seller wrote him dunning letters. Finally, Seller, in exasperation, declared all the contract price due and filed a suit to foreclosure. Buyer tendered all his back payments into court. The court dismissed the foreclosure. *Stinemeyer* v. *Wesco,* 487 P2d 65 (Oreg. 1971).

NEW DIRECTIONS: This last example is new law but is likely to become the law in many states. In this age of consumerism, the courts, in their desire to ameliorate hardships, are quite likely to set aside accelerations.

12.16(g)   Remedies of Seller—Statutory

In some states, Minnesota for example, the seller uses a statutory remedy to terminate a defaulting buyer. 77 Am.Jur.2d *Vendor & Purchaser* §585.

CHAPTER 13

Fraud and Misrepresentation in Real Estate Transactions

13.01 The Beginnings

Suits for fraud or misrepresentation have been in our courts for many years. Of course, virtually all such suits were filed by disappointed purchasers who discovered that the seller had made a false statement (misrepresentation) concerning some important (material) aspect of the real estate sold. In the usual situation the falsity of the statement was discovered after the deal was closed and the buyer had occupied the property. It was then that the buyer would discover the misrepresentation. The buyer had a choice. He could file a suit against the seller in either of two courts. He could file a suit for money damages in a *law court*. If he did this, he kept the property he had purchased and was compensated for the damages caused by the seller. Or he could file a suit in a *chancery court* (today called an *equity court*) and seek to have the transaction set aside (rescinded). If the buyer succeeded in the rescission suit, he would get his money back and return the land to the seller.

> **EXAMPLE:** Seller represents to Buyer that the home being sold is free from termite infestation. Seller knows that infestation is present. Buyer believes Seller, buys the house, moves in, and finds heavy termite infestation.
>
> 1. Buyer can sue Seller in a chancery court and have the deal rescinded (set aside). Buyer gets his money back. Seller gets the land back.
> 2. Buyer can sue Seller in a law court for money damages. He keeps the house and repairs the termite damage.

This distinction between the remedies afforded by the two branches of the court exists today.

If Buyer chooses to sue Seller for damages, the earliest rule required Buyer to prove that Seller *knew* his statements were false and intended to deceive Buyer. In effect, the law courts would only punish a deliberate lie.

The chancery court, however, did not insist on proof of a deliberate lie. If the misrepresentation was as to some material fact (such as termite infestation), the chancery court would set the transaction aside, even though seller was ignorant of the defect. This court does not require proof of an *intention to deceive.* The seller may be innocent, yet chancery sets the deal aside. *Norton* v. *Poplos,* 443 A2d 1 (Del. 1981). Of course, chancery would also rescind if Seller had deliberately lied. Dobbs, *Remedies,* Ch. 4.

Today we no longer have two separate courts. The same court can either award damages or set the transaction aside. But the requirements remain. To recover damages Buyer must prove that Seller knew he was lying.

13.02 Fraud by Conduct

Most fraud consists of spoken or written words. Conduct can also constitute fraud.

> **EXAMPLE:** Seller owns a home. The basement floods whenever it rains heavily and there are marks along the entire basement wall showing the level which flood water reaches. Seller decides to sell his home. He paints the basement, obliterating the flood line or mark. Seller does not mention this topic. Buyer inspects the basement. Believing the home to be watertight, Buyer buys the home. The first rain reveals the problem. Buyer can sue Seller for damages or to set the deal aside. *Russow* v. *Bobola,* 2 Ill. App.3d 837, 277 NE2d 769 (1972).

> **EXAMPLE:** Seller used deodorant to conceal the fact that carpets were soaked with dog urine. He is liable for damages. *Campbell* v. *Booth,* 526 SW2d 167 (Tex. Civ. App. 1975).

> **EXAMPLE:** Running an ad that misstates the facts is fraud. *Horton* v. *Poplos,* 443 A2d 1 (Del. 1985).

> **EXAMPLE:** The seller showed the property to the buyer as a multiple-family dwelling and commented on the rents he collected. This was a *tacit representation* that the premises were legally usable as an apartment building, which was false, for such use violated the city ordinances. It was held that the buyer could rescind (declare contract void) on discovering the imposition. *Gamble* v. *Beahm,* 198 Ore. 537, 257 P2d 882 (1953). This would be true also if there is any statement on the contract or advertisement for sale that can be construed as representing that the existing use of the building is a *legal one,* as when the contract describes the building as a "store and dwelling" when such use is actually illegal. 27 Rocky Mt. L. Rev. 258; 1958 Wis. L. Rev. 641.

13.03 Nondisclosure

Failure of the Seller to disclose some basic fact or flaw known to the seller that would not be evident on any ordinary inspection of the premises furnishes grounds for a suit for damages or a rescission.

EXAMPLE: Seller (a builder) builds a home on filled ground. Building on land-fill usually results in serious settling and cracks in the house. Seller says nothing to Buyer. The house looks fine. Buyer buys it and later cracks begin to develop. Buyer can sue for damages or rescission. 80 ALR2d 1453.

EXAMPLE: Seller owns a home that he knows is termite infested. Seller sells the home to Buyer saying nothing. Again, most courts today say that Buyer can sue for damages or rescission. 22 ALR3d 972.

EXAMPLE: Seller failed to disclose to Buyer that a woman and her four children had been murdered in the home. This is fraud. No one wants to be a landlord to ghosts. *Reed* v. *King,* 193 Cal. Reptr. 130 (1983) (citing many cases.)

This is an example of the ever-changing nature of the law. Seller says or does nothing to deceive Buyer. In former times Buyer would have no remedy. The law said, "Let the buyer beware." This attitude is rapidly disappearing. *Passive concealment* is as morally reprehensible as a deliberate lie. *Holcomb* v. *Zinke,* 365 NW2d 507 (N.D. 1985). See also 90 ALR3d 569 (flooding) and 90 *id.* 592 (roof leaks.)

In a recent decision a sale of a home was involved. The sellers failed to disclose that the roof leaked badly. The deal was closed and the buyers occupied the home. It was then they discovered the defect. The court held that they were entitled to rescind the deal. *Johnson* v. *Davis,* 480 So2d 625 (Fla. 1986). The eloquent language of this court should put an end for all time to the notion that caveat emptor still governs the sales of homes (pp. 628–629):

" . . . The courts in some jurisdictions, including Florida, hold that where the parties are dealing at arms's length and the facts lie equally open to both parties, with equal opportunity of examination, mere nondisclosure does not constitute a fraudulent concealment. *See Ramel* v. *Chasebrook Construction Co.,* 135 So2d 876 (Fla. 2d DCA 1961). The Fourth District affirmed that rule of law in *Banks* v. *Salina,* 413 So2d 851 (Fla. 4th DCA 1982), and found that although the sellers had sold a home without disclosing the presence of a defective roof and swimming pool of which the sellers had knowledge, '[i]n Florida, there is no duty to disclose when parties are dealing at arms length. *Id.*' at 852.

"These unappetizing cases are not in tune with the times and do not conform with current notions of justice, equity and fair dealing. One should not be able to stand behind the impervious shield of caveat emptor and take advantage of another's ignorance."

13.04   Broker's Liability

Seller's broker is his agent. Seller is liable for his agent's fraud, misrepresentation, or fraudulent concealment of facts.

EXAMPLE: Seller's broker knew that several earth movements and slides had damaged the building. This was not disclosed to Buyer. The broker was held liable to Buyer. *Easton* v. *Strassburger,* 199 Cal. Reptr. 383 (Cal. App. 1984).

Thus the seller's broker is under a duty to disclose to the buyer material defects known to the broker but unknown to the buyer and not observable on ordinary inspection. The court went on to say that the broker is liable for negligence, that is, for failure to inspect and discover defects and reveal them to the purchaser. This last liability of the broker is a relatively new development in the law. Negligence is very different from fraud.

If we get into the *multiple listing system* (MLS) and the liability it creates, again we are in new legal territory. There are some decisions.

EXAMPLE: Seller listed his home with Weagley, a broker-member of the MLS. Weagley prepared the listing sheet which stated, "All In Top Shape." The listing sheet was furnished to Graham, a member of the MLS. He showed it to Buyer. The house turned out to have severe defects. Buyer sued Graham and was awarded damages. *Gouveis* v. *Citicorp Person-to-Person Fin. Center, Inc.*, 686 P2d 262 (N.M. 1984).

EXAMPLE: The listing broker put an incorrect area statement in the listing sheet, and this false information was transmitted by the MLS to the selling broker. The selling broker gave this false information to the buyer. The buyer sued *both* brokers and *both* were held liable. *First Church etc.* v. *Cline J. Duntom Realty*, 574 P2d 1211 (Wash. 1978). This court held that a listing broker (agent of the seller) has authority to hire another broker to help him sell the property. This is done through the MLS and the selling broker becomes the subagent of the seller. This so-called "subagency" makes the selling broker liable to the buyer.

In addition to state laws, state *regulations* may impose a liability on the broker.

EXAMPLE: In Illinois the state regulations concerning brokers provide that the broker must reveal to the buyer all knowledge he has concerning the property offered for sale. Such regulations have all the force and effect of laws. This is why every broker must have in his office an up-to-date copy of all state regulations regarding brokers.

NEW DIRECTIONS: The broker has a potential liability under various laws enacted to protect consumers.

EXAMPLE: Seller wished to sell his home, but needed the proceeds of sale to buy another home. He explained this to his broker. He asked the broker what price he could expect to receive from his home sale. The broker stated a sale price of $162,000. The seller bought a new home but could not sell his old home even at a reduced price of $137,000. The broker was totally innocent. He believed the old home could be sold for much more. Nevertheless, under the Consumer Fraud Act (which many states have enacted) the broker is liable for damages. *Duhl* v. *Nash Reality Inc.*, 102 Ill. App.3d 474, 429 NE2d 1267 (1982).

EXAMPLE: Seller's broker represented to Buyer that the existing mortgage (which Buyer intended to assume) bore an interest rate of 9%. It later turned out the interest rate was 12%. The broker was held liable to Buyer under the Consumer Fraud Act. *Beard* v. *Gress,* 90 Ill. App.3d 622, 413 NE2d 448 (1980).

As is evident, new and terrifying liabilities are being thrust upon the broker. It is a Catch-22 situation. If the broker reveals the facts and defects, he kills the deal. If he does not, he will be stuck with a liability for damages.

These state consumer fraud acts can be traced back to federal legislation. Deceptive acts and practices are declared unlawful by Sec. 5(a) of the Federal Trade Commission Act 15 U.S.C. Sec. 45. The state laws are modeled after this federal law. They usually provide for public or private enforcement.

The Illinois Consumer Fraud Act was amended in 1982 to protect a broker or his salesperson from liability for the communication of any false, misleading, or deceptive information provided by the seller of real estate located in Illinois unless the salesperson or broker *knows* of the false, misleading, or deceptive character of such information.

NEW DIRECTIONS: Some courts are beginning to hold the broker liable for *innocent misrepresentation.*

EXAMPLE: Broker innocently stated to buyer that hotel was on five acres of land. Buyer later found land was only half that size. Broker was held liable. *Bauarke* v. *Rozza,* 332 NW2d 804 (Wis. 1983).

EXAMPLE: Broker innocently represented that a well supplied an adequate amount of water. The supply was found to be inadequate. Broker was held liable. *Bevins* v. *Ballard,* 665 P2d 757 (Alaska, 1982).

EXAMPLE: Seller's broker represents to Buyer that the land is zoned commercial when in fact part of it is zoned residential. Broker is liable to Buyer. *Barnes* v. *Topaz,* 25 Ariz. App. 477, 544 P2d 694 (1976).

A broker must have general knowledge of the building code and zoning ordinances applicable to the property he is selling. *Amato* v. *Rathbun Realty Inc.,* 647 P2d 433 (N.M. 1982).

The philosophy here seems to be that since a broker holds himself out as an expert, and his business consists of supplying information to others, he must accept this added liability. In other words, he must *carefully* analyze the property offered for sale. Whether a trend is developing is an open question.

13.05   Recent Decisions

In a recent decision a purchaser of a home sued the seller and his broker for fraud. *Munjal* v. *Baird & Warner, Inc.,* 485 NE2d 855 (Ill. App. 1985). The defect complained of was extensive flooding of the basement, of which the seller was aware. He failed to disclose this fact to the buyer. The broker was unaware of the flooding, but when the buyer drew his attention to a leak, he urged the seller to consult his attorney. The court held the seller liable, stating that his failure to disclose the problem constituted fraud. This, of course, is the modern rule.

As to the broker, the court held that no liability had been shown. The broker was unaware of the problem, and the court was unwilling to impose on the broker a duty to make an exhaustive inspection to ascertain the presence of the defect.

This strikes one as being a sensible decision. It is the practice of realtors to examine a home before accepting a listing. This is done to determine the probable market value, to fix a suggested listing price, and to point out matters that might make the home more attractive and salable, such as repairing leaking faucets, washing or painting walls, etc. The broker, after all, will represent the seller. It is his duty to help the seller.

However, the buyer should not expect the broker to make the kind of inspection that a professional inspector will make for a buyer. Professional inspectors will inspect the home for the buyer and assume the negligence liability this entails. Many of them give written warranties.

13.06   Conclusion

Clearly the courts are imposing stricter standards of liability on sellers of real estate and their brokers. Predictably, the development of this trend will be spotty. Some states will move faster and farther than others. Brokers in particular will be faced with some serious problems.

REFERENCE: Peterson, *Tort Claims by Real Estate Purchasers,* 1983 So. Ill. U. L. J. 161.

CHAPTER 14

Closing Real Estate Transactions: Loan Closings: Escrows

14.01 Sale Closing Defined

After the contract of sale has been signed, a number of details must be addressed. For example, the title must be examined to determine if the seller really owns the property and what mortgages, liens, and restrictions encumber it. A survey must be ordered. The premises must be inspected to ascertain the presence of encroachments, unrecorded easements, and unrecorded rights of parties in possession. At the end of this process the seller gives the buyer a deed, and the seller is paid the balance of the purchase price. All of this is the process of "closing the deal." Often much the same process is taking place with respect to the buyer's mortgage, and there will be a contemporaneous "mortgage closing."

Although the two closings, sale and mortgage, involve simultaneous processing and may culminate in a single meeting when both transactions are finalized, each process will be discussed separately. This is in recognition of the two distinct sets of relationships, which, although they involve the same subject matter, give rise to different rights and obligations.

14.02 The Lawyer's Role

The need for counsel in a real estate transaction is best demonstrated by example.

EXAMPLE: Buyer signed a contract of sale to buy a vacant corner lot upon which the buyer intended to erect a service station. He had no lawyer. After the deal closed, he discovered that the lot was zoned for single-family dwellings and that service stations were a prohibited use of the property. A lawyer would have inquired into the zoning of the property before the contract was signed or would have called for the production of adequate evidence that the intended use could be had of the property.

> **EXAMPLE:**   Without counsel, Buyer entered into a contract for the purchase of a vacant lot upon which Buyer intended to construct a veterinary hospital. The preprinted form contract called for Buyer to accept title subject to "building restrictions of record." When the title search was produced, it showed that the title was subject to a building restriction which permitted only residential uses. Buyer was faced with either going through with a transaction that he no longer wanted or forfeiting his earnest money. This predicament could have been avoided if Buyer had retained counsel before signing the contract.

Obviously, examples such as these take place each year. They need not occur. The attorney is needed from the precontract stage through the closing. Many people fail to recognize this need until it is too late. This is particularly true in residential transactions, perhaps the largest single transaction many people ever have in their lifetimes. Rather than rely upon the advice of counsel, many consumers eagerly execute the purchase contract and rely on sheer luck to pull them through. Inflation has caused many "average" homes to have selling prices of six figures, but these buyers and sellers only rarely have representation when the blueprint for this transaction, the real estate sales contract, is executed. What is more incredible is the number of people who carry the transaction through to closing without counsel only to find to their chagrin that they were pennywise and dollar foolish.

14.02(a)   Conflict of Interest

It has long been a rule of legal ethics that a lawyer is forbidden from representing conflicting interests in a transaction without full disclosure and consent by all of the parties. This disclosure must not only be of the multiple representation, but also of the effect of this representation upon the exercise of the lawyer's professional judgment on behalf of each party. Disciplinary Rule 5-105. The real estate sales transaction is a somewhat frequent scene for this practice, as in the case of a developer's attorney who is automatically denominated as buyer's counsel as a form of repayment for services rendered to the developer. See *In re Kamp*, 194 A2d 236 (N.J. 1963). This activity may lead to professional sanctions being taken against the lawyer. *The Florida Bar* v. *Tietelman*, 261 So2d 140 (Fla. 1972). It may also have repercussions for the clients.

> **EXAMPLE:**   A purchaser was entitled to rescind a real estate sales contract when he was represented by seller's counsel who failed to disclose to the purchasers the existence of a lien on the property. The court found this to be a material fraud on the part of the seller. *Holley* v. *Jackson*, 158 A2d 803 (Del. 1959).

Some lawyers are also real estate brokers and insurance brokers. They should maintain separate offices for each line of endeavor. The real estate brokerage, the insurance business, and the law practice must be operated completely separately. 48 Fordham L. Rev. 38 (1980). See also Ill. St. Bar Assn. Ethics Opinion No. 84-14.

REFERENCES: 68 ALR3d 967; Werner, *Real Estate Closings,* 5 (2d ed. 1987).

14.03   Matters to be Considered before Closing

14.03(a)   Evidence of Title

If the contract requires the seller to furnish an abstract or other evidence of title, he should do so *within the time allowed by the contract,* for if he fails to do so, a reluctant buyer may seize the opportunity to cancel the deal. If the seller is furnishing a title commitment, it must be a signed, original commitment. The buyer, in turn, should *within the time allowed by the contract,* draw attention to any defects in title not permitted by the contract. Otherwise he will be regarded as waiving such defects. The seller should then, *within the permitted time,* cure any defects pointed out by the buyer. When the contract specifies that the seller shall furnish an abstract of title showing clear title, the buyer has a right to insist that quitclaim deeds needed to clear the buyer's title objections be recorded in the recorder's office and included in the abstract of title. *Kincaid* v. *Dobrinsky,* 225 Ill. App. 85 (1922). When the contract calls for a title insurance policy showing clear title in the seller, the buyer has the right to insist that all unauthorized objections be cleared from the title policy by the seller.

The buyer should consider whether special coverage endorsements, i.e., zoning coverage or an encroachment endorsement, should be ordered from the title insurance company. Even though the contract does not require the seller to provide these special endorsements or the transaction may not be contingent upon the title company's willingness to issue such coverage, the buyer may be well advised to order the special endorsements that are appropriate for the transaction.

REFERENCE: Werner, *Real Estate Closings,* Ch. 2 (2d ed. 1987).

14.03(b)   Closing Documents

Closing document preparation takes a great deal of time and care. In larger deals it is usual for the closing documents to be identified in, or even made exhibits to, the real estate sale contract. In other transactions the exact nature and form of the closing documents must be worked out as the closing approaches. Typical closing documents are:

1. Sellers' affidavit. (If the transaction is going to be insured by a title insurance company, an ALTA Loan and Extended Coverage Owner's Policy Statement may be substituted.) A misrepresentation in the affidavit will support an action for damages. *Somerset County* v. *Durling*, 415 A2d 371 (N.J. 1980).

2. Bill of sale for personal property.

3. Evidence of compliance with fire, health, building, and zoning laws and ordinances.

4. Bulk sales affidavit.

5. Chattel lien search.

6. Closing statement.

7. Condominium association's waiver of the right of first refusal.

8. Corporate resolutions.

9. Declaration of homestead.

10. Deed.

11. Foreign Investment in Real Property Tax Act documentation needed to establish an exemption or to meet withholding requirements.

12. Indemnity agreements called for by the contract or agreed upon during the closing to take care of contingencies and further performance which the parties agree can be performed after the closing.

13. Insurance policies, if they are to be assigned, together with evidence of premium payment and the insurer's consent to the assignment.

14. Minutes of the closing meeting.

15. Mortgages to be assumed by buyer. A buyer who is taking subject to existing financing should obtain a copy of the outstanding mortgage and note. The existing mortgagee should also give an estoppel statement showing the amount due on the existing mortgage so that it cannot later assert that a larger amount is due. If the buyer is taking title subject to an existing mortgage, the contract should be contingent upon, and the closing documents include, the lender's written consent to the sale if the mortgage has a due-on-sale clause.

16. Opinions of counsel regarding the validity of corporate documents, usury, zoning, etc.

17. Memorandum of closing, stating that all contract requirements have been fulfilled, is sometimes signed by the buyer and seller to preclude bickering over what should have been done prior to the closing.

18. Payoff statements on encumbrances to be paid off and released at the closing and which can be relied on by the parties. *Mid-State Homes, Inc.* v. *Startley*, 366 So2d 734 (Ala. 1979). A special problem is presented when the existing mortgage is a revolving credit or credit line mortgage. The outstanding balance on these loans fluctuates as the borrower, often unilaterally, obtains an additional advance. This can be done by going to the lender to obtain additional funds to be secured by the mortgage, or, in some consumer loan settings, by simply writing a check or using a charge card. Lenders are unwilling to give binding payoff statements in this setting unless the borrower is deprived of the ability to increase the loan balance. Obviously, these payoffs must be carefully worked out on a case-by-case basis. Most importantly, the underlying loan must first be identified as a revolving credit or credit line mortgage to enable the problem to even be addressed. If the existing lender is consenting to the sale subject to the existing mortgage, on the condition that the interest rate be increased, loan term altered, or the like, the documents recasting the loan must be drawn and executed. Here, too, the lender should give a statement of the current status of the

loan, stating the date through which payments have been made; the loan balance, including both principal, interest, late charges; and the balance in the real estate tax and insurance escrow accounts.

19. Permits for curb cuts, awnings, etc.

20. Pest control report.

21. Plans and specifications. On big buildings, the buyer wants to get the plans that depict the building "as built." No building is ever built 100 percent according to the original plans. Pipes and conduits are often relocated when construction reveals that the planned locations are impractical.

22. Power of attorney.

23. Real estate tax bill upon which the tax proration will be based.

24. Real estate transfer tax declaration or return.

25. Receipt for broker's commission.

26. Contracts for scavenger service, janitorial service, exterminator service, and the like and their assignment.

27. Soil test report.

28. Survey.

29. Tenant roster, rent roll, outstanding leases, assignment of leases, letter to tenants. Where a building is managed by a responsible management firm, buyers and lenders customarily accept a manager's letter as to apartment leases. On commercial properties, space leases are usually checked unless they are short-term office leases. The manager's letter always covers renewal options, purchase options, advance payments of rent, and security deposits.

30. Title evidence.

31. Warranties from the builder, roofer, appliance manufacturers, etc. A full discussion of these and other closing documents can be found in Werner, *Real Estate Closings*, Ch. 3 (2d ed. 1987).

14.03(c)   Prior Approvals

Since closings are apt to be fairly hectic, it is a good idea for the parties to submit to each other, in advance of closing, all the documents that will then be exchanged, such as the deed, mortgage note, survey, leases, and assignments. The documents are then checked in the quietude of one's office and pencil initials are placed in a corner of the document. Further scrutiny of the form at the time of closing is then omitted although a check of signatures and acknowledgments will still be needed at that time. If the documents are at all unusual, it is best to have them approved by the title officer before they are executed.

14.03(d)   Income Tax Withholding—FIRPTA

In 1980, Congress enacted the Foreign Investment in Real Property Tax Act (FIRPTA), which required foreign investors in United States real estate to make certain disclosures or filings. FIRPTA was difficult to implement and was met with a storm of criticism. The Deficit Reduction Act of 1984 largely repealed FIRPTA's reporting requirements, substituting the requirement that the buyer deduct and withhold 10 percent of the purchase price on the sale of a United States Real Property Interest. If the buyer fails to deduct and withhold this amount and the transaction is not otherwise exempt, the buyer will be exposed to liability to the I.R.S. 26 U.S.C. Sec. 1445; 26 C.F.R. Sec. 1.1445-1T, *et seq.*, 49 Fed. Reg. 50667 *et seq.* (12/31/84).

The parties should have their real estate sales contract drawn to accommodate the handling of this withholding requirement. When the deal works its way to the closing stage, the buyer must insure that the transaction either falls within an exemption to the act or that a withholding is made. Either of these approaches will typically involve the preparation and execution of additional closing documentation. If FIRPTA is to be accommodated by withholding, the transferee is to report and pay the withholding to the I.R.S. within ten days after the transfer date. I.R.S. forms 8288 and 8288A are used for this purpose.

FIRPTA does allow exemptions to its withholding requirement. If exempt, all but the most sophisticated real estate transactions will fall within one of three categories. Perhaps the most common exemption applies in situations where the property is acquired by the buyer for use as a residence and the purchase price is $300,000 or less. For this exemption to apply, the buyer must plan to live in the property for at least 50 percent of the days that the property is in use during the first two twelve-month periods after the sale. The danger in relying upon this exemption lies in the fact that the buyer's change of plans could make the buyer liable for the tax if the seller does not pay it.

If the buyer relies upon this residential exemption, no special documentation is required, but, of course, the possible need to prove to the I.R.S. that withholding was not required on the transaction is one more reason for the buyer to retain the transactional documents such as the contract, closing statement, deed, and title policy.

Another exemption applies if the seller is not a foreign person. While the buyer may use any, or no, means to determine whether the seller is a foreign person, FIRPTA establishes a means by which the buyer can be protected from tax liability if it is later determined that the seller is a foreign person. This is accomplished by the buyer simply obtaining a Certificate of Non-foreign Status, wherein the seller, under penalty of perjury, states that he is not a foreign person and gives his name, address, and taxpayer identifying number. The buyer may rely upon this certificate, and make no withholding, even if the certificate is false, unless the buyer knows that the certificate is false or receives notice of its falsity. The buyer must retain this certificate for five years after the year of transfer and make it available to the I.R.S upon request.

Another exemption applies when the parties rely upon a Withholding Certificate, which is issued by the I.R.S. and which states either that no withholding or a reduced withholding is appropriate.

Whatever device is used, the contract must set out a blueprint for handling this withholding requirement, and the transactional documents either must evidence the applicability of an exemption or a withholding must be made. If not, the buyer is exposed to tax liability for the foreign seller's failure to pay the tax relating to a gain realized upon the disposition of the property.

14.03(e)   Income Tax Reporting

Provisions of the Internal Revenue Code in effect before the passage of the Tax Reform Act of 1986 required brokers to file returns showing the gross sales proceeds of transactions in which they were involved. I.R.C. Sec. 6045(a). The broker was also required to furnish customers with a statement reflecting the information shown on the return. I.R.C. Sec. 6045(b). The term "broker" was broadly defined to include any person who in the ordinary course of trade or business stands ready to effect sales to be made by others. Treas. Reg. Sec. 1.6045-1. Although these provisions had required the reporting only on the proceeds of sales of securities, commodities, regulated futures contracts, and precious metals, new I.R.C. Sec. 6045(e) requires that "real estate brokers" must file both the information return and statement for real estate transactions in which they are involved. This return is to be made on Form 1099-B promulgated by the IRS under its Announcement 86-115.

This reporting requirement has direct impact upon attorneys, title companies, mortgage lenders, and real estate brokers. This is because the term "real estate broker" is defined in such a way so as to place the responsibility for this reporting upon a hierarchy of participants in the closing in the following order.

1. The person (including any attorney or title company) responsible for closing the transaction.
2. The mortgage lender.
3. The seller's broker.
4. The buyer's broker.
5. Such other person designated in the regulations.

These reporting requirements may well cause increasing use of the settlement services of escrowees to thereby shift the responsibility and the cost of providing these returns and statements to that closing agent. Real estate purchase and sale contracts should be drafted with that possibility in mind. They should at least contain the standard provision that either party may require that the transaction be closed in escrow with both parties bearing one half of the escrow fee.

Further, revisions should be made to standard real estate contract forms to require that the identification of the seller include the seller's social security number or taxpayer identification number to facilitate the filing of these returns.

In the event that the payor fails to properly furnish his taxpayer identifying number, and in certain other instances, the "broker" may have to deduct and withhold 20 percent of the amount which would otherwise be paid to the taxpayer. The Tax Reform Act imposes this backup withholding requirement on real estate brokers. I.R.C. Sec. 3047(B)(3)(C).

In the event that the real estate broker fails to file the return, a penalty of $50 for each failure shall be imposed. I.R.C. Sec. 6652 (a)(1)(B). In the event that the failure to file amounts to an intentional disregard of the filing requirement, the penalty shall be 5 percent of the gross proceeds required to be reported. I.R.C. Sec. 6652(a)(3).

14.03(f)   The Survey

Check the date on the survey. A survey made ten years ago, for example, obviously will not cover buildings erected since then. Does the survey locate the property with reference to known monuments, such as government section corners? Does it show the location of all outbuildings? All neighboring buildings? Are all buildings, walks, and so on well within the lines of the lot on which they belong? Do any structures extend over the setback lines established by city ordinances or building restrictions? Does the survey show whether upper portions of the building (bay windows or eaves) extend over the lot lines? Are there possible subsurface encroachments, such as footings on the building, extending into adjoining land?

The certificate of the survey should also be checked for an express declaration that it is intended to be relied upon, and, if erroneous, can be sued upon by the buyer, his mortgagee, and their title companies. *Rozny* v. *Marnul,* 250 NE2d 659 (Ill. 1969); Note, 64 N.W.U.L. Rev. 903 (1961). See Kratovil, *Modern Real Estate and Documentation,* Ch. 7 (1975).

14.03(g)   Chattel Lien Search

If valuable chattels are included in the sale, a search of the Uniform Commercial Code records should be made for financing statements affecting such chattels. This search requires care. Code filings relating to fixtures, crops, and consumer goods (stoves, refrigerators, and other appliances found in the ordinary home) are found in some local office, often the recorder's office, but in some states in a department separate from the department where ordinary deeds are filed. Filings covering furniture and other chattels in a hotel or furnished apartment or raw materials in an industrial plant are likely to be found in some central office, usually that of the secretary of state in the state capitol.

14.03(h)   Ordinance Violations Search

If in the particular community it is possible to procure a title company or other search of city records as to building ordinance violations, this should be done. In lieu thereof, an architect or engineer should check the building carefully for violations, probably also examining the office of the local building department.

14.03(i)   Inspection of the Property

Before closing the deal the buyer should make a careful physical inspection of the property. Possession imparts constructive notice, and the buyer will take the property subject to the rights of the grantee in an unrecorded contract, or others whose interest is disclosed by their possession. If the premises are occupied by tenants, their occupancy is notice of their rights. Therefore tenants' leases should be checked for options to renew or purchase. The buyer must not accept the seller's assurance that the tenants are on month-to-month tenancies. He should check with the tenants to determine such things as the term of their tenancy, what furniture, appliances, and so on, they claim, what security deposit they have made, and the status of their rental obligation.

The buyer checks for the existence of unrecorded easements, for the buyer takes subject to unrecorded easements if their existence would be revealed by an inspection of the premises. Check to see whether this particular sale will result in the creation of any implied easements. Check to see whether rear or side exits run over adjoining property, thus making an easement necessary, and whether shutters open over adjoining premises. Check to see if heat is furnished by an adjoining building, thus making a written agreement necessary. Check for vaults, marquees, and so forth extending into public streets, which would make permits necessary. If you defer inspection until after the abstract or other evidence of title has been furnished, you can check to see whether the building violates any recorded building restrictions. It should be remembered that, even if the contract requires the buyer to take subject to "building restrictions," he is not required to take subject to violations of restrictions. Such violations constitute a separate and distinct defect in title. Check also for violations of zoning or building ordinances and for recent repairs or construction that might ripen into a mechanic's lien.

It is also customary to have an inspection shortly prior to the closing so that mechanical systems (heating, air conditioning, and so forth) can be checked to determine whether they are in operating condition and how they function. Sometimes the buyer may want an inspection by a qualified home inspection company. An appropriate contingency clause is often inserted in the contract, stating that the sale will close only if the inspection shows all systems in working order. Where other than single-family property is involved, it is customary for the buyer's engineer to make an inspection of the building. This is also a good time for the seller to set out the drawings, blueprints, plans and specifications, warranties, instruction manuals, and so forth for the buyer and his staff. If the seller is reluctant to actually surrender these items until the sale closes, at least the buyer will know where to find these things when possession is obtained. Recent local laws call for the inspection of the premises by local officials prior to the closing. This results in some official determination that the property is in compliance with the current building code, that is, that it has the required number of smoke alarms, and so on. Other recent ordinances require the seller to disclose recent heating and cooling costs.

Certainly, where the buyer is purchasing a newly constructed property, the buyer will want a certificate of occupancy issued by the local building department.

14.03(j) Maintenance of Property from Date of Contract to Date of Closing

It is the seller's responsibility to maintain the property in a reasonable manner between the date of contract and the date of closing. If he permits it to deteriorate, the buyer may sue him for damages even after the deal is closed. Goldberg,

Sales of Real Property 442; 92 CJS *Vendor & Purchaser* § 286a; Note, 48 Harv. L. Rev. 82 (1935).

14.04   Closing Practices

Closing practices vary from locality to locality, and even within the same county or city. In various areas, closings are conducted by lending institutions, title insurance companies, escrow companies, real estate brokers, and attorneys for the buyer or seller.

The "New York" style of closing is spreading to many parts of the country, especially in large transactions. A title company representative is present at this style of closing to "mark up" a copy of the most recent title commitment, waiving matters which are cleared at the closing. He also accepts the deed and other documents for recording.

14.05   Bulk Sales Affidavits and Notices

A sale of real estate may incidentally involve the sale of the entire stock of goods, wares, or merchandise of some retail establishment operated by the seller on the premises. It is necessary that such a sale comply with the local Bulk Sales Act, which usually involves giving notice of the pending sale to the creditors of the business so that they can protect their rights. UCC § 6-101 *et seq.*

14.06   Closing Date

The contract of sale should fix a closing date, the time the deed is to be delivered, and the balance of the purchase price paid. If no closing date is fixed in the contract, it is presumed that the deal is to be closed within a reasonable time, and either buyer or seller may select a reasonable date and notify the other that he will be prepared to close at such time. Often one of the parties is not prepared to close on the date specified in the contract and requests an adjournment of closing. In such case, the other party, in granting the request for adjournment, specifies that the prorating or apportionment will be computed as of the original date or the adjourned date, whichever is more favorable to him. For example, if the adjournment is made at the request of the seller and the income of the building is greater than the carrying charges, the buyer will insist that the apportionment or prorating be computed as of the original date. The buyer will receive the rents from the date originally fixed for closing, and the seller will be entitled to interest on the unpaid balance of the purchase price and the purchase money mortgage from the original closing date. Of course, if the contract fixes a closing date and provides that time is of the essence, the party who is ready to close on the date fixed need not grant a request for an adjournment.

Some contracts fix a date that is to govern the prorating or apportionment, regardless of the date of the delivery of the deed. Other contracts provide that prorating or apportionment shall be computed as of the date of the delivery of the deed.

The buyer should not rely on any extension of time granted by the seller's lawyer or broker. Normally, neither of them has the power to grant extensions.

14.07   Matters to be Attended to at Closing

14.07(a)   Title

The buyer should make a final check to see that the title is clear and subject only to the encumbrances permitted by the contract of sale. If the deal is not closed in escrow, an informal check should be made of the records to cover the period between the date of the abstract or title search and the date of the closing of the deal. Judgments or other liens may attach during the interval, and will, of course, be good against the buyer. The buyer should at least insist that the seller's attorney give him a written statement that he will not turn the buyer's check over to the seller until after the deed to the buyer has been recorded and the title searched to cover that date. Of course if the deal is closed in escrow, all danger from this source is obviated. If, by agreement, the seller is to clear certain objections after closing, the buyer should retain part of the purchase price, usually double the amount of the lien involved, to insure performance on the part of the seller.

14.07(b)   Form and Contents of Documents Involved

The documents should all be checked to see if they are in proper form and comply with the contract. For example, if the deed to be given is a warranty deed, the subject clause of the deed should be checked to make certain that it does not include any items that were not included in the subject clause of the contract. The deed should also be checked to see if the recorder of deeds will accept it for recording. For example, in many states, laws forbid "metes and bounds" subdivisions, that is, the division of a tract of land into plots for sale without the formality of recording a subdivision plat. The recorder will often reject such a deed, and the buyer is left with a deed that he has paid for but cannot record.

If, as is so often the case, the major portion of the purchase price is being furnished by the buyer's mortgage lender, the attorneys will make a final check of the mortgage and note to see that the principal amount, interest rate, and monthly payments are in accordance with the loan commitment. If this has not previously been attended to, a similar check should be made of the other loan documents, such as the assignment of rents or waiver of defenses.

14.07(c)   Water and Other Utility Bills

The buyer should call for the production of paid water and other utility bills. If these bills have not been paid, service to the building may be cut off.

14.07(d)   Production of Seller's Deed

The buyer should require the seller to produce the deed by which he acquired title. This affords some measure of protection against forgery and impersonation.

14.07(e)   Prorations or Adjustments

Prorations or adjustments should be computed and a closing statement prepared.

14.07(f)   Payment of Purchase Price and Delivery of Documents

The balance due according to the closing statement should be paid and the documents to which each party is entitled delivered.

14.08   Closing Statement—Prorations

The contract of sale usually provides that various items shall be adjusted or prorated. Items not mentioned in the contract are nevertheless often prorated because of the prevailing local custom. *O'Donnell* v. *Lutter,* 156 P2d 958 (Cal. 1945); *Valley Garage, Inc.* v. *Nyseth,* 481 P2d 17 (Wash. 1971). This prorating or adjustment results in credits and debits against each party. These are usually shown on a closing statement, which is also called a settlement sheet. Forms of closing statements vary and may be imposed by a regulatory agency, i.e., HUD's RESPA mortgage closing statement. A form commonly used lists in one column all credits due the seller and in a separate column all credits due the buyer. The completed statement is approved by buyer and seller. An extended discussion of the closing statement and its elements can be found in Werner, *Real Estate Closings,* Ch. 4 (2d ed. 1987).

While these calculations traditionally have been made by the use of the proration table on page 196, prorations today are often made by using pocket calculators or computers specially programmed to produce closing documents, including the closing statement and prorations.

14.08(a)   Closing Statement—Credits Due Seller

The usual credits due the seller are:

1. Full purchase price.
2. Taxes and insurance reserves in existing lender's impound account if buyer is taking subject to existing mortgage.
3. Unearned insurance premiums if insurance policy is to be assigned to buyer.
4. Fuel on hand and building supplies.
5. Any charges paid by the seller in advance, such as water tax, prepayments on exterminator or other service contracts, real estate taxes paid in advance.

Prorating Table for Rents, Taxes, and Insurance

Number of years, months and days	RENTS One Month		TAXES & INS. One Year		INSURANCE						Number of years, months, and days
	Days to Month					Three Years			Five Years		
	30	31	Months	Days	Years	Months	Days	Years	Months	Days	
1	.0333	.0323	.0833	.0028	.3333	.0278	.0009	.2000	.0167	.0006	1
2	.0667	.0645	.1667	.0056	.6667	.0556	.0019	.4000	.0333	.0011	2
3	.1000	.0968	.2500	.0083	1.0000	.0833	.0028	.6000	.0500	.0017	3
4	.1333	.1290	.3333	.0111		.1111	.0037	.8000	.0667	.0022	4
5	.1667	.1613	.4167	.0139		.1389	.0046	1.0000	.0833	.0028	5
6	.2000	.1935	.5000	.0167		.1667	.0056		.1000	.0033	6
7	.2333	.2258	.5833	.0194		.1944	.0065		.1167	.0039	7
8	.2667	.2581	.6667	.0222		.2222	.0074		.1333	.0044	8
9	.3000	.2903	.7500	.0250		.2500	.0083		.1500	.0050	9
10	.3333	.3226	.8333	.0278		.2778	.0093		.1667	.0056	10
11	.3667	.3548	.9167	.0306		.3056	.0102		.1833	.0061	11
12	.4000	.3871	1.0000	.0333		.3333	.0111		.2000	.0067	12
13	.4333	.4194		.0361			.0120			.0072	13
14	.4667	.4516		.0389			.0130			.0078	14
15	.5000	.4839		.0417			.0139			.0083	15
16	.5333	.5161		.0444			.0148			.0089	16
17	.5667	.5484		.0472			.0157			.0094	17
18	.6000	.5806		.0500			.0167			.0100	18
19	.6333	.6129		.0528			.0176			.0106	19
20	.6667	.6452		.0556			.0185			.0111	20
21	.7000	.6774		.0583			.0194			.0117	21
22	.7333	.7097		.0611			.0204			.0122	22
23	.7667	.7419		.0639			.0213			.0128	23
24	.8000	.7742		.0667			.0222			.0133	24
25	.8333	.8065		.0694			.0231			.0139	25
26	.8667	.8387		.0722			.0241			.0144	26
27	.9000	.8710		.0750			.0250			.0150	27
28	.9333	.9032		.0778			.0259			.0156	28
29	.9667	.9355		.0806			.0269			.0161	29
30	1.0000	.9677		.0833			.0278			.0167	30
		1.0000									31

Example:

Rent $135.00 per mo.
To find value of 23
days of a 31 day mo.
From Table:—
23 days =   .7419
.7419 × 135.00 =
$100.16

Example:

Taxes =   1215.12.
To find value of 7
mos. and 19 days
From Table:—
7 mos. =   .5833
19 days =   <u>.0528</u>
7 mos. 19
days =   .6361
.6361 × 1215.12
= 772.95

Example:

3 Year Policy Premium
= 58.75
To find the value of 1
yr. 3 mos. 11 days
From Table:—
1 yr. =   .3333
3 mos. =   .0833
11 days =   <u>.0102</u>
1 yr. 3 mo. 11
days =   .4268
.4268 × 58.75
= 25.07

Example:

5 Yr. Policy Premium
312.82
To find value of 3
yrs. 4 mos. 13 days
From Table:—
3 yrs. =   .6000
4 mos. =   .0667
13 days =   <u>.0072</u>
3 yrs. 4 mos. 13
days =   .6739
.6739 × 312.82
= 210.81

14.08(b)   Closing Statement—Credits Due Buyer

The usual credits due the buyer are:

1. Earnest money.

2. Existing mortgages if the sale is for part cash and the balance to be paid by the assumption of those existing mortgages.

3. Interest accrued and unpaid on existing mortgages that are to be assumed by the buyer.

4. Amount of the purchase money mortgage that the seller has agreed to take back as part of the purchase price.

5. Unearned rents that have already been collected. Since rents are usually collected on the first day of the month, the buyer, under most contracts, will be entitled to his proportionate share of the current month's rent collections together with any other rent prepayments. This includes unearned rent on all leases, including such unusual leases as advertising space and signs.

6. Security deposits made by tenants.

7. Taxes. Since the seller has had the rents of the property for prior years and for part of the current year, it is only fair that he pay all taxes for those prior years and his proportionate share of the current year. Often tax prorations are based on "the most recent ascertainable tax bill." Tax bills are based upon many factors such as the assessed value, equalization factors, and the tax rate. A change in any of the factors will not yield an "ascertainable tax bill" until the other factors are set. Until those other factors are determined, a change in any one of the factors will not justify a change in the basis of the proration from the most recent tax bill. *Lenzi* v. *Morkin,* 469 NE2d 178 (Ill. 1984). If the seller has not already paid those taxes and the contract so provides, the taxes should be apportioned with the buyer getting the appropriate credit. In some localities, however, it is not customary to apportion current taxes. In periods of rising taxes, a clause in the contract may call for proration of taxes at a base in excess of the latest tax bill, for example, "107 percent of the latest available tax bill." As an alternative, the contract may call for reproration of taxes, if the actual bill, when received, substantially exceeds the latest available tax bill, say by 10 percent or more. Without such a provision, neither party can seek adjustment, even if the variation is costly. *3700 S. Kedzie Bldg. Corp.* v. *Chicago Steel Foundry Co.,* 156 NE2d 618 (Ill. 1959). Do not confuse taxes with special assessments. While the former may be proratable, the latter are not, unless the contract so provides. *Alder* v. *R. W. Lotto, Inc.,* 517 P2d 227 (Wash. 1973). Note also that proration of taxes does not transfer the personal liability from the owner on the date of assessment or levy to the buyer. The seller may retain this liability under local real estate tax law.

8. Items based on meter readings, such as water tax, electricity, and gas, if not paid in advance.

9. Wages and other charges accrued and unpaid, such as janitor's salary, scavenger service, and so on.

10. Release fee and recording charge incurred by the buyer in obtaining and recording a release of the seller's mortgage.

14.08(c)   Closing Statement—Other Items

Some charges are allocated to either the buyer or seller, depending upon the terms of the contract and local custom. Those charges include:

1. Condominium and PUD assessments must be prorated with appropriate credits given to buyer and seller, depending upon whether the assessments are paid in advance or in arrears.

2. In the Midwest, the contract often requires the title charges to be borne by the seller. These are therefore a debit against the seller. In New York the buyer bears this cost.

3. Who pays for the survey? This is a matter of negotiation. Most often the contract allocates this cost to the seller.

4. The chattel lien search fee and termite inspection cost are usually paid by the seller.

5. Real estate transfer taxes imposed by states, counties, and cities are subject to varying practices.

6. The buyer pays the recording fee for the deed, and the contract usually requires the buyer to pay for the recording of any purchase money mortgage and the cost of title evidence covering that mortgage.

7. Escrow fees are often divided between the buyer and the seller.

8. The broker's commission is usually paid out of the proceeds of sale and charged against the seller.

14.09   Matters to Attend to After Closing

After closing, the buyer, the escrowee, or title company should immediately record the deed and any release of mortgage obtained at the closing. The title evidence should be brought down to cover the recordation of the closing documents. The seller should record and obtain title insurance for any purchase money mortgage. If the contract documents did not obligate the seller to notify the janitor, building manager, scavenger service, exterminator, and so forth of the termination of their employment, the buyer should give those termination notices. The buyer should also: (1) have the water, gas, and electric accounts changed to his name; (2) have the name of the assessee changed on the local real estate tax collector's books; (3) arrange for janitor, scavenger, building manager, and other services; (4) once again check to see that appropriate insurance is issued to protect the buyer's interest and that the mortgagee loss clause is included in the insurance package; (5) obtain workman's compensation and employer's liability insurance, if necessary; and (6) make sure that tenants are notified of the transaction and that future rental payments should be made to the buyer.

14.09(a)   The Closing Letter

After the deal has been closed, the buyer's lawyer usually writes a closing letter to the buyer. This letter encloses and describes the documents that the buyer is receiving and describes the documents that are still to come. For example, it often takes some time for the recorder of deeds to complete the recording process and send the recorded deed to the buyer's attorney, who will send it on to the buyer.

The letter should suggest to the buyer what he is to do in the future. For example, the letter should suggest: the date on which tax bills should be received;

that the buyer retain the contract and closing statement for income tax records; and that the deed and title policy be placed in a safe-deposit box.

14.10   Mortgage Closing

Just as a sale is closed by delivery of the deed to the buyer and the purchase price to the seller, a mortgage transaction is closed by delivery of the mortgage and note to the lender and the disbursement of the mortgage funds to the mortgagor or pursuant to the mortgagor's direction.

14.10(a)   Borrower's Concerns

In shopping for a lender, the borrower should have numerous areas of concern. This is especially so in light of the wide range of mortgage programs available today. Beyond the obvious questions of interest rate, loan charges or points, loan-to-value ratio, and loan term, the borrower should also ask the lender the following questions:

1. Is the borrower required to carry life or disability insurance? Must he obtain it from a particular company? He may prefer no insurance or may wish to obtain it at a better premium rate elsewhere.

2. Is there a late payment charge? How much? How late may the payment be before the charge is imposed? The borrower should be aware that late payments may harm his credit rating.

3. If the borrower wishes to pay off the loan in advance of maturity (for example, if he moves and sells the house), must he pay a prepayment penalty? How much? If so, for how long a period will it apply?

4. If the borrower is dealing with the lender who holds the existing mortgage, he might be able to take over the prior loan in a transaction called an "assumption." This form of transaction usually saves the borrower some settlement costs and benefits the buyer if the interest rate on the prior loan is lower than current market rates. Since the assumption transaction will typically involve a higher down payment than the transaction wherein the buyer obtains institutional financing, the buyer may want to ask the seller to take back a second mortgage to finance all or part of the difference between the sales price and the balance on the existing mortgage.

5. The borrower may want this flexibility when he becomes the seller and should inquire whether the loan will be assumable at the time. If so, will the lender have the right to charge an assumption fee or raise the rate of interest and will the lender release the borrower from personal liability?

6. If the borrower has a financial emergency, will the terms of the loan include a future advance clause, permitting him to borrow additional money on the mortgage after he has paid off part of the original loan?

7. Will the borrower be required to pay monies into a special reserve (escrow or impound) account to cover taxes or insurance? If so, how large a deposit will be required at the closing of the sale? May a savings account be posted in lieu of monthly impound payments? How large an account is needed? How long must it remain posted?

8. In looking for the best mortgage to fit the borrower's particular financial needs, the borrower may wish to check the terms and requirements of a private conventional loan versus a loan insured through the Federal Housing Administration or Farmers Home Administration or guaranteed by the Veterans Administration. The FHA, VA, and Farmers Home Administration loans involve federal ceilings on permissible charges for some settlement services, which may be of interest to the borrower. Ask lenders about these programs.

14.10(b)   RESPA

The Real Estate Settlement Procedures Act, 12 USC § 2601, has an impact upon lenders, brokers and real estate attorneys.

The Act's primary impact upon the closing process is directed toward lenders of "federally related mortgage loans." These are loans that are both secured by a first lien on residential (one to four family) real properties and meet any one of the following four criteria: (1) the loan is made by a lender which has its deposits insured by or which is regulated by the federal government; or (2) the loan is insured, guaranteed, supplemented, or assisted under a federal housing or urban development program; or (3) the loan is intended to be sold to FNMA, GNMA, or FHLMC; or (4) the loan is made by any creditor who makes or invests in residential loans aggregating more than $1,000,000 per year. 12 USC § 2602. As you can see, the coverage of the Act is very broad, with most lenders being made subject to its strictures.

The Act now requires: that most residential loans be closed through the use of the HUD settlement sheet, 24 CFR § 3500.8(d), which must be available to the borrower before the closing, 12 USC § 2603(b); that within three days of the application, the lender make a good faith estimate of likely settlement service charges, 12 USC § 2604(c) & (d), 24 CFR § § 3500.6 & 3500.7(a); and that the HUD booklet, *Settlement Costs and You,* be given to the borrower with the estimate. 12 USC § 2604. The buyer should ask for an explanation of all settlement charges.

The Act also limits impound or escrow accounts for the payment of real estate taxes and insurance. 12 USC § 2609.

REFERENCES: Barron, *Federal Regulation of Real Estate* (Rev. ed. 1983 with Cum. Supp. No. 1); Kratovil & Werner, *Modern Mortgage Law and Practice* § § 27.06 *et seq.* (2d ed. 1981).

14.10(c)   Title Defects

It is, of course, important to the mortgagee to be sure that his mortgage is a first lien on the land and that no title defects exist. Among the precautions he should take in this regard are the following:

1. Check the mortgage for errors in filling in the blanks, signatures, witnesses, acknowledgment, etc. Before disbursing the mortgage proceeds, have the mortgage filed or recorded and obtain title evidence covering the date of recording. This will disclose

liens that have appeared of record prior to the recording of the mortgage. Any such liens should be paid and released or subordinated to the mortgage. The prudent lender will weigh the true worth of the various means of evidencing title. Sophisticated lenders tend to insist on the ALTA form of lender's title insurance policy. Among other advantages, it insures that the mortgage is valid and enforceable. It also insures against unfiled mechanic's liens, unrecorded leases, unrecorded easements, encroachments, and other questions of survey, and lack of legal access to the mortgaged property. If the lender is forwarding funds to a title company's agent or approved attorney, the lender should insist upon receiving the title company's *insured closing letter* or *statement of settlement service responsibility,* which insures the mortgagee against embezzlement of loan funds or the agent's failure to follow the mortgagee's directions. If the mortgage is being assigned, the assignee should obtain a mortgage assignment endorsement insuring the validity of the assignment and substituting the name of the assignee as the insured.

2. Analyze all objections to the mortgagor's title disclosed by the examination of title. All defects in title should be cleared. If the title search reveals building restrictions or conditions, ascertain whether existing buildings violate such restrictions. Of course, copies of the instruments creating restrictions, easements, and so forth should be obtained and analyzed.

3. The mortgagee should inquire into the rights of parties in possession for the purpose of discovering unrecorded leases with options to purchase, unrecorded deeds and contracts, unrecorded easements, and so on. He must keep in mind the fact that the mortgagee, in nearly all states, takes his mortgage subject to the interests of all parties in possession of the premises.

4. The mortgagee should: (a) inspect the building carefully for signs of recent work, and if any appears, demand to see paid bills and mechanic's lien waivers for any substantial work; (b) get an affidavit from mortgagor that all work or materials furnished to premises have been paid in full, which, if false, will subject him to criminal prosecution; (c) if the building is occupied by persons other than the mortgagor (tenant, contract purchaser, and so on), see that notice of nonliability for mechanic's liens is posted on the property in the states where such notice is effective.

5. A survey should be obtained to determine whether any encroachments or other survey defects exist.

6. The mortgagee should obtain the usual mortgagor's affidavit to the effect that there are no judgments, bankruptcies, and so on against such mortgagor.

7. Within the time limits specified by the law and regulations, the lender must disclose to the borrower all matters required by the federal Truth-in-Lending Act (15 USCA §§1601–1665). See Kratovil and Werner, *Modern Mortgage Law and Practice,* §4.13 *et seq.* (2d ed. 1981).

14.10(d)   The Loan Closing Statement

Seldom does the borrower receive the full amount of the mortgage loan. Various deductions are made for title searches, surveys, recording fees, and other items. Therefore, on disbursement of the loan, the mortgagee will prepare a loan settlement statement similar to that prepared for the buyer and seller. This form should be used for three reasons: (1) it furnishes the borrower with a complete record of all disbursements made by the mortgagee from the proceeds of the loan; (2) it provides the mortgagee signed authorization by the borrower for all such disbursements and thus eliminates all possibility of any legal action that might be taken if the mortgagor claims improper charges were made against his loan; and (3) in those cases where there is no binding loan commitment, it fixes the date on which the mortgage becomes a lien on the land, since where there is no binding commitment, the mortgage does not become a lien on the land in some states until the date on which the loan is paid out to the mortgagor. In general, this settlement statement shows the full amount of the loan and all deductions from it and their amount. It also shows the net amount available to the mortgagor and contains an acknowledgment by him that he has received that amount. The statement should be dated and signed by both mortgagor and mortgagee when the loan is closed. The HUD form is used on residential deals.

Many miscellaneous items are debited against the borrower upon the closing of the mortgage loan. It is important that each debit be provided for in the loan contract documents, that is, the application, commitment, and acceptance. Among the items often debited against the borrower are:

1. Lenders usually require that borrowers pay at settlement the interest accruing on the mortgage loan from the date of settlement to the beginning of the period covered by the first mortgage payment.

EXAMPLE: Suppose settlement takes place on April 16 and the buyer's first regular monthly payment is due on June 1. At settlement, the lender will collect interest for the period from April 16 to May 1. The June 1 mortgage payment will pick up the interest that accrued during May.

2. The fee for the lender's title protection.
3. On some mortgage loans, the mortgagee insists on *private mortgage insurance* to insure the mortgagee against loss in the event of default and foreclosure. The premium for this insurance is debited against the borrower.
4. Most homebuyers take out a new *Homeowners' Policy* to cover fire loss, liability coverage, etc. The first year's premium is usually a debit against the borrower.
5. Most lenders insist that the monthly payment include one-twelfth of the estimated real estate taxes and hazard insurance premiums for the current year. These are called impounds. In these cases there is an initial payment called the *impound reserve* that is debited against the borrower.
6. There may be miscellaneous fees that are debits against the borrower.

EXAMPLE: Lender's attorney's fee, mortgage tax, fees for recording mortgage and accompanying documents.

7. Lenders may charge both points and miscellaneous loan origination fees, which may be debits against the borrower on the loan closing statement.

14.10(e) Zoning and Building Code Violations

A check should be made for violations of local zoning and building ordinances which the mortgagee might be compelled to remedy at his own expense were he to acquire title by foreclosure.

14.10(f)   Insurance

Existing fire insurance policies should be checked to determine that the amounts thereof are adequate and that the policies are properly written with mortgage clause attached.

14.10(g)   Documents of the Loan File

The mortgagee's loan file should include the following papers:

1. Application for the loan, signed by the borrower, and a copy of the mortgagee's letter of commitment.
2. Plat of survey.
3. If the loan is made to finance the purchase of property, the mortgagee should have a copy of the contract of sale in his files. This will prove helpful in making an appraisal of the property.
4. Appraisal.
5. Mortgagee, mortgage note, chattel lien on personal property in building, and assignment of rents and leases.
6. Assignment of mortgage and waiver of defenses if loan was purchased from original lender.
7. Credit reports on the borrower.
8. Insurance policies, with mortgagee loss clauses attached.
9. Abstract and opinion, mortgage title policy, Torrens certificate, or other evidence of title.
10. Mortgagor's affidavit as to judgments, divorces, recent improvements, and other pertinent facts.
11. Copy of escrow agreement, if the loan was closed in escrow.
12. Loan closing statement, including receipt for loan proceeds signed by borrowers.
13. If loan was a refinancing loan, the canceled mortgage and note that were replaced by the new loan.
14. If the loan is part of any federal program—that is, VA guaranteed, FHA insured, or sold in the secondary market to FHLMC or some other similar purchaser—the special documents that make up such loan package and are required by those entities must be a part of the loan file.
15. The requirements of any loan servicing contract relating to document retention must also be followed. Many of these servicing contracts require that the loan file be retained for a stated period after the loan is repaid.
16. Subordination of reverter if one was obtained. If any other prior mortgage or other lien was subordinated to the current mortgage, the subordination agreement, of course, should also be in the loan files.
17. Certified copy of corporate resolutions if the mortgage was made by a corporation. If the property mortgage is all, or substantially all, of the assets of the corporation, resolutions by both directors and stockholders may be necessary.
18. Will, trust indenture, or other trust instrument, or a copy of these, if mortgagor is a trustee.
19. Full copy of building restrictions affecting the mortgaged premises, particularly if the loan is a construction loan.

20. Leases to key tenants and assignments thereof to mortgagee.

21. Necessary statements, waivers, and so forth necessary to document compliance with federal and state disclosure laws, the Real Estate Settlement Procedures Act (12 USCA § 2601 *et seq.*) and similar local laws. A discussion of these disclosure laws may be found in Barron, *Federal Regulation of Real Estate.*

14.11   Nature of Escrow

A deed is delivered *in escrow* when it is deposited with a third person with directions to deliver the deed to the grantee only upon the performance of some condition set forth in the escrow instructions but not in the deed. The third person, to whom the deed is delivered, is called the *escrow holder, escrow agent,* or *escrowee.* The instructions defining the conditions to be performed prior to delivery of the deed to the grantee are called the *escrow agreement* or *escrow instructions.*

14.11(a)   Operation and Purpose of Escrows

A contract for the sale of land usually requires the seller to furnish title evidence showing the condition of the seller's title. Suppose that on May 10, Seller agrees to sell a parcel of land to Buyer for $50,000. The contract is not recorded, and Seller remains in possession of the property. Seller orders the title evidence, which is received on May 20, and shows the condition of title sometime between May 10 and May 20, say May 15. The title evidence shows that as of May 15, Seller held clear title and Buyer paid his money and received a deed. It then develops that on May 16, the I.R.S. filed a tax lien against Seller. Other liens and encumbrances such as judgments, suits attacking title, or mortgages may also arise during this interval or gap between the effective date of the title evidence and the recording of the deed to Buyer. The seller may even die, leaving minor heirs, who obviously would be incapable of signing any deed.

In order to avoid these and other similar risks, sales may be closed in escrow. In an escrow transaction, both the deed and mortgage are delivered to some disinterested third party, often a title insurance company, with written instructions to record the deed and mortgage, order an examination of title, and, if the title shows clear *in the buyer,* pay over the purchase price to the seller. The escrow agreement also provides that, if it shall appear that the seller's title is defective and the defects are not cured within a certain specified time, the buyer shall be entitled to the return of his money upon reconveying the title to the seller. In those cases where the seller has not recently had his title examined, the procedure is often divided into two steps. First, before the deed is recorded, the escrow holder is instructed to cause the seller's title to be examined down to a current date. This first step may even be taken before the escrow agreement is signed. Then if title shows clear in the seller, the instructions provide that the deed be recorded and the examination of title brought down to cover the recording of the deed.

When the transaction follows the procedure above outlined, it is common for the grantee to deposit with the escrowee a quitclaim deed conveying the land back to the grantor. Then if the title proves defective, the quitclaim deed can be recorded by the escrowee so that the records will once more show title in the grantor.

A question is always asked: How can the title company insure clear title in the seller after the transaction is unwound because of a judgment against the buyer which was shown by a title search after the deed to the buyer was recorded? The answer is that the buyer acquired only a conditional title. This title, by the very words of the escrow, will be defeated if the deal cannot close. Hence, when the buyer's title vanishes, the judgment lien against the buyer's interest vanishes.

The question is also asked: If the title shows clear in the buyer except for the seller's old mortgage, on what theory can the escrowee use the buyer's funds to pay the old mortgage? The answer is that as soon as the title shows clear in the buyer, subject only to the old mortgage, the seller's proceeds in the escrow belong to the seller. The escrow also contains an instruction to the escrowee to use enough of those proceeds to pay the old mortgage.

In counties where it is possible to examine titles very quickly, the procedure may follow these lines: The seller will have his title examined down to a current date. If title shows clear, the seller deposits his deed with a title company as escrowee. The escrowee orders a second examination of title to cover the period intervening between the date of the last examination and the close of recording hours on the day the deed is deposited. This examination can be made quickly, for it covers a period of only a few days. If title shows clear, the seller's deed is recorded the next morning the moment the recorder's office opens.

Under either system, the buyer's money is not paid to the seller until the buyer is assured of receiving clear title.

Escrow practices and the frequency of their use differ quite a bit from state to state. In many communities, escrows are virtually unknown. This is particularly true of small communities where seller and buyer know and trust each other. The danger here that the seller will make a deed or mortgage to some third person is not so great as in large communities, where relationships are apt to be more impersonal.

Another benefit of the escrow is that if objections to the title that can be removed by use of the purchase money appear, such as judgments against the seller or unpaid taxes, the buyer may with absolute safety, after title is recorded in his name, allow the escrow holder to use part of the purchase money for the purpose of removing such objections.

Escrows are also used in land assemblies. In this context, the seller who has given an option is required to put a deed in escrow to be given to the buyer upon the buyer's timely performance of the conditions of the option. Through this device the seller who learns that his deal is part of a large assembly is powerless to hold up the larger transaction having already given the deed to a neutral third party.

Even where a sale transaction is not closed in escrow, some of the closing proceeds are often put into an escrow to take care of some element of the seller's performance that remains incomplete, i.e., new construction that is not finished, damage to the property that occurred between the contract date and the closing date that is the seller's responsibility to repair.

14.11(b) Requirements of an Escrow

Good escrow practice requires that:

1. There be a valid and enforceable contract for the sale of the land. *Johnson* v. *Wallden,* 173 NE 790 (Ill. 1930). The escrow agreement may in itself contain all the essential requirements of a contract of sale. *Wood Bldg. Corp.* v. *Griffitts,* 330 P2d 847 (Cal. 1958). The existence of a valid contract of sale, either in the escrow instructions or in a separate instrument, is, however, indispensable for a binding escrow. If this were not true, it would be possible to have what is in effect a contract for the sale of land without the written agreement that the law requires for land sales. *Campbell* v. *Thomas,* 42 Wis. 437.

EXAMPLE: Two landowners executed deeds to each other pursuant to an oral exchange agreement and delivered such deeds to an attorney with verbal directions to deliver each deed to the grantee named therein when each landowner had presented a receipt showing payment of back interest on existing mortgages. Before these receipts were delivered, one of the landowners demanded return of his deed. The court held that he was entitled to the return of his deed. The contract of exchange was only oral and therefore unenforceable. *Jozefowicz* v. *Leickem,* 182 NW 729 (Wis. 1921).

2. The escrow agreement contain a *condition,* something that must be done before the buyer's money is paid to the seller. The usual condition, of course, is the showing of clear title of record in the buyer, subject only to those objections listed in the contract of sale and escrow instructions.

3. The deed be a good and valid deed.

4. The escrow holder be some third person. Neither the buyer nor seller may act as escrow holder.

14.11(c) Contents of Escrow Agreement

The escrow agreement usually covers the following matters:

1. The names and signatures of the buyer and seller with the written acceptance of the escrow by the escrowee.

2. A list of the deposits into escrow to be made by the seller. These deposits will typically include: the deed, bill of sale, leases, assignments of leases, notices to tenants to pay the rent to the buyer, paid tax bills, service contracts, insurance policies, assignments of insurance policies with consents to the assignments by the insurer, warranty contracts, and a pest report.

3. A list of deposits to be made by the buyer. These deposits will include: the purchase price and purchase money mortgage, if one is to be given, or the proceeds of the mortgage obtained by the buyer. These mortgage proceeds often come from a separate money lender's escrow established with the same escrowee, with the funds "poured over" into the buyer-seller escrow when the conditions for the closing of the money lender's escrow are met. Often this occurs simultaneously with the close of the buyer-seller escrow.

4. An instruction on when the deed is to be recorded—immediately, upon the proper title evidence being produced, or when the buyer's check clears.

5. The type of title evidence to be produced.

6. A list of permitted title exceptions which the buyer agrees to accept as a condition of title to the conveyed property.

7. The time allowed for the seller to clear the title of unpermitted title exceptions.

8. How and when the purchase price is to be disbursed, with directions as to which items are to be prorated or apportioned.

9. Directions for the delivery of the escrow deposits upon the close of escrow.

10. Directions for the return of deposits to the respective parties if the conditions for closing the escrow are not met within the allotted time periods.

11. Directions for the payment of escrow, title and recording charges, broker's commissions, and attorneys' fees.

12. A notice procedure for the parties to use in the event of a default and a mechanism for adjusting the default.

While an escrow often takes the form of instructions by the buyer and seller to the escrowee, the legal fact remains that the escrow is an agreement of contract among its parties.

14.11(d)   Escrow is Irrevocable

When a valid escrow agreement has been executed and the instruments provided for are delivered to the escrow holder, neither party can revoke the escrow and obtain the return of his deposit. At times one party to a sale of land changes his mind and makes a demand on the escrowee for return of his deposit. The escrowee is justified in refusing to comply with an unwarranted demand. If the situation is legally doubtful, the escrowee may insist on a court adjudication of the rights of the parties. *Franks* v. *North Shore Farms, Inc.,* 253 NE2d 45 (Ill. 1969); *Cocke* v. *Transamerica Title Ins. Co.,* 494 P2d 756 (Ariz. 1972).

14.11(e)   Conflict between Contract of Sale and Escrow Agreement

Since the escrow is a means of carrying out the terms of the contract of sale, there should be no conflict between the two agreements. In the event of conflict, however, disposition of the deed and money deposited in escrow must be governed by the escrow instructions. *Widess* v. *Doane,* 112 Cal. App. 343, 296 Pac. 899 (1931).

14.11(f)   When Title Passes

Prior to the performance of the condition specified in the escrow, title to the land remains in the seller even though his deed to the buyer is recorded. This is a technical, but important concept. Since ownership of the land remains in the seller until the conditions specified in the escrow instructions have been met and performed, even though a deed from seller to buyer has been recorded, the seller remains in possession, collects the rents, and pays taxes, until the escrow conditions have been performed.

Even an innocent purchaser or mortgagee from the grantee is not protected in such cases. *Osby* v. *Reynolds*, 103 NE 556 (Ill. 1913); *Clevenger* v. *Moore*, 259 Pac. 219 (Okla. 1927).

> **EXAMPLE:** An escrow agreement required the buyer to deposit the purchase price in escrow. Before this was done, the buyer persuaded the escrow holder to give him the deed, which the buyer thereupon recorded. He thereafter placed a mortgage on the property. When the seller discovered this mortgage, he filed suit, and the court canceled the mortgage as a cloud on his title, even though the mortgagee had acted in entire good faith. *Blakney* v. *Home Owners' Loan Corp.*, 135 P2d 339 (Okla. 1943).

However, if the grantor allows his deed to be recorded, an innocent purchaser from the grantee will usually be protected if the grantor has also allowed the grantee to take possession of the land, for in such case *both the records and the possession show the grantee as the apparent owner,* and an innocent purchaser from such grantee should be protected, for there is nothing to apprise him of the grantor's rights. *Mays* v. *Shields*, 45 SE 68 (Ga. 1903).

Immediately upon the performance of the conditions specified in the escrow agreement, ownership of the land passes to the buyer and ownership of the purchase price passes to the seller. Thereupon the escrow holder becomes the agent of the buyer as to the deed and of the seller as to the money. *Shreeves* v. *Pearson*, 230 Pac. 448 (Cal. 1924). At that moment the escrow holder holds the deed for the grantee, it is as though the grantee himself held the deed. Thus delivery of the deed has been completed, and actual manual delivery of the deed by the escrow holder to the grantee adds nothing to the grantee's title. *Shirley* v. *Ayers*, 14 Ohio 307. However, it is the practice to provide for a delivery of the deed by the escrow holder to the grantee. This is the so-called *second delivery.*

14.11(g) Relation Back

Where the grantor delivers a deed in escrow, then dies, and thereafter the condition of the escrow is performed, the deed is considered as passing title as of the date of the delivery of the deed to the escrow holder. It is said that the title *relates back* to such time.

> **EXAMPLE:** Seller entered into a written contract to sell a parcel of property to Buyer. Seller signed the deed and delivered it to the escrowee. Buyer deposited the purchase price with the escrowee. The escrowee recorded the deed as permitted by the escrow instructions, which also provided that the purchase

price was to be delivered to Seller when the title evidence showed the title to be clear of unpermitted objections. Before the examination was completed, Seller died leaving minor children as heirs. Thereafter, the title evidence was produced showing acceptable title in Seller. The deed was good since the transfer of title related back to the time when Seller was alive.

So too, if the grantee dies after the deed has been delivered in escrow, and the condition of the escrow is thereafter performed, the deed will be treated as relating back to the delivery in escrow and may be delivered for the benefit of the grantee's heirs. *Prewitt* v. *Ashford,* 7 So 831 (Ala. 1890).

The same theory follows when the seller marries or becomes insane after the delivery of the deed into escrow.

The rule that title relates back to the time of the original delivery of the deed to the escrowee is confined to the examples given above. In other situations, *transfer of ownership of the land takes place as of the time when the terms and conditions of the escrow are performed.* For example, if the escrowee absconds with the buyer's purchase money before the terms and conditions of the escrow have been performed, the loss must fall on the buyer, because *at the time of the defalcation the purchase money still belonged to the buyer. Hildebrand* v. *Beck,* 236 P. 301 (Cal. 1925); 39 ALR 1080. On the other hand, if the terms of the escrow have been performed and thereafter the escrowee absconds with the money, the loss falls on the seller, because *after the escrow terms have been met and performed, the money on deposit belonged to the seller. Lechner* v. *Halling,* 216 P2d 179 (Wash. 1950); *Lawyers Title Ins. Co.* v. *Edmar Const. Co.,* 294 A2d 865 (D.C. 1972).

Thus if a lender is a party to an escrow and the escrowee embezzles the mortgage money before the title has been cleared as required by the escrow instructions, the mortgage funds still belong to the mortgagee who must suffer the loss of his funds and cannot collect from the mortgagor even though he holds the mortgagor's promissory note. *Ward Cooke, Inc.* v. *Davenport,* 413 P2d 387 (Ore. 1966).

14.11(h)   Mortgages

Since, as against third parties, a mortgage, in some states, does not become a lien until a debt which the mortgage secures exists, mere recording of a mortgage does not create a lien. Liens attaching to the land *prior to the time that the mortgage money is disbursed to the mortgagor* may obtain priority of lien over the mortgage. But if the mortgagee deposits his mortgage money in escrow, with directions to pay the money over to the mortgagor if an examination of title shows the mortgage as a first lien on the date of its recording, then immediately upon the recording of the mortgage its position as a first lien is established. Payment into escrow is treated as payment by the mortgagee to or for the benefit of the mortgagor.

Again, there are cases where a buyer is borrowing money to complete his purchase. The mortgagee does not want his money paid out until title shows clear in the buyer, who is the mortgagor. The seller will not want to give a deed until and unless he is assured of receiving the purchase price. This difficult situation is easily taken care of through an escrow. The deed, mortgage, and mortgage money are deposited with an escrowee under written instructions to record the deed and mortgage and pay the mortgage money to the seller if the title examination shows the mortgage as a first lien. The interests of all parties are protected.

> **EXAMPLE:**   The contention has been advanced by the creditors of the mortgagor that they can garnishee such funds. The courts have rejected this contention. Kratovil & Werner, *Modern Mortgage Law and Practice*, §25.34 (2d ed. 1981). The same result occurs where creditors attempt to garnishee construction money held by the mortgagee. The funds cannot be garnisheed.

14.11(i)   Long-term Escrows

The long-term escrow is used in the sale and financing of real estate as an alternative or supplement to the installment contract. This device operates somewhat as follows: The seller enters into a contract for the sale of real estate with a buyer who is unable or unwilling to pay the entire purchase price at the time of closing. The seller desires to retain a security interest in the property to secure the deferred payment of the purchase price and to swiftly terminate the buyer's interest upon the buyer's default. To accomplish these objectives the property is conveyed to a bank or title company, as trustee. The trust agreement incorporates the installment contract. The trustee is authorized to collect the payments due under the contract, remitting them to the seller. When the final payment is made, the trustee conveys the property to the buyer. If the buyer defaults, the property is conveyed to the seller. In some states this conveyance to the seller occurs after a statutory forfeiture procedure is conducted. In other areas the seller conducts the forfeiture of the buyer's interest after the return conveyance from the trustee.

Bogert, *Trusts and Escrows in Credit Conveyancing*, 21 *Ill. L. Rev.* 655 (1927). The disadvantages of this arrangement are:

> 1. Until completion of the payments, the public records show title in the Seller. This gives the Seller the opportunity to defraud the Buyer by making a deed or mortgage to some third person who is unaware of the contract's existence. *Waldock* v. *Frisco Lumber Co.*, 176 P. 218 (Okla. 1918). This would not be true if the contract were recorded or if the buyer went into possession of the land.
>
> 2. The depositary may deliver the deed to the buyer notwithstanding the fact that he has not completed his payments, and recording of this deed will cloud the seller's title.
>
> 3. Default on the buyer's part after he has made substantial payments may result in a lawsuit against the depositary. *Phoenix Title & Trust Co.* v. *Horwath*, 19 P2d 82 (Ariz. 1933). To avoid becoming involved in forfeiture proceedings, the escrowee often insists that after a lapse of time without payments by the buyer, the escrowee may return the seller's deed to him. The seller then proceeds to declare the forfeiture.
>
> 4. In some states a buyer in an escrow deal takes subject to judgments rendered against the seller while the deal is in escrow but before the purchase price is fully paid and the deed recorded. *May* v. *Emerson*, 96 Pac. 454 (Ore. 1908); 117 ALR 69, 85–88. The danger from this risk is increased when the escrow extends over a long period

of time. In addition to the danger of judgments, there is the danger that, while the escrow is running, federal income tax liens may be filed against the seller or the seller may go into bankruptcy. Kratovil and Werner, *Modern Mortgage Law and Practice* §39.11 (2d ed. 1981).

The use of the long-term escrow is spreading to all parts of the country. To avoid becoming involved in forfeiture proceedings, the escrowee often insists that after a lapse of 6 days without any payments by the buyer, the escrowee may return the seller's deed to him. The seller then proceeds to declare the forfeiture.

14.11(j)   Closer's Liability

Whether the closing is conducted by an escrowee, lending institution, or lawyer, the closer may incur liability for improper or mistaken performance of its closing duties.

> **EXAMPLE:**   Where an escrowee breaches the escrow instructions, the escrowee will be liable for damages proximately caused by the breach.

> **EXAMPLE:**   Where a lender fails to obtain the proper insurance coverage for a buyer who has instructed the lender to obtain the insurance, the lender will be liable if a loss occurs. *Parnell* v. *First Fed. Sav. & Loan Assn.,* 336 So2d 764 (Miss. 1976); *Taylor* v. *Colonial Sav. Assn.,* 533 SW2d 61 (Tex. 1976).

> **EXAMPLE:**   A savings and loan association which closed a real estate transaction was held liable to the buyer for failing to disclose the results of a termite inspection. *Miles* v. *Perpetual Savings & Loan Assn.,* 388 NE2d 1364 (Ohio, 1979).

14.11(k)   Today's Escrow Practices—Residential Sales

Back before interest rates began to rise and wiggle about, most home sales were closed in the lender's office. In part, the lender's wish to do this stemmed from the lender's desire to pressure the seller to deposit the proceeds of sale in a savings account. These deposits are pretty much of a vanishing species. The seller is in the stock market, money markets, and so forth. Thus the residential lenders have lost interest in providing space and employee time for closings. In Illinois, for example, most residential lenders have closed their loan closing departments. Each lender has a form agreement with each title company stating, in essence, that the lender will be sending loan documents and money to the title company, and when the title company is prepared to issue its mortgage policy, clear of objections, to the lender, it may use the lender's money. The title company personnel examine the title, call in the sellers and buyers, get all necessary documents signed, do the prorating, record the deed and mortgages, and pay the seller. As a rule, the parties have their lawyers present to make sure the closing is being handled correctly and to check into problems that arise, but the mechanics are handled by title company personnel.
The buyer's lawyer has a copy of the title search. When the title company

tells him all objections have been cleared, he can safely advise the buyer that his money can safely be used. This does not minimize the lawyer's role. He reads the easements, the building restrictions, the survey, and leases, if any. But he is relieved of the burden of paying state and city document taxes, prorating rents on a four-flat, and so on.

14.11(l)   Large Transactions

Where a sale escrow is set up on a large transaction, between seller, buyer, and a title company, the lender that is financing the purchase of the property may seek to protect itself by giving a written instruction to the title company that it will wire funds to the title company's escrow bank account when the conditions to its willingness to fund the loan have been met. These conditions are derived from the lender's loan commitment. They include such matters as: (1) the willingness of the title company to insure the mortgage as a first lien, subject only to taxes not yet due and other permitted exceptions; (2) confirmation of the validity of the leases that provide cash flow for payment of the mortgage; (3) confirmation of the validity and priority of the lender's chattel lien documentation; and (4) the existence of adequate hazard insurance, etc.

CHAPTER 15

Evidence of Title: Title Insurance: Abstracts

15.01 Historical Background

It is obvious that a purchaser of land cannot merely rely upon the fact that he receives a warranty deed as conclusive evidence that he is receiving good title. For example, anyone could give a deed to the Merchandise Mart in Chicago. That deed would give no title whatsoever. It would merely give the grantee the right to sue the grantor, a right that may be quite empty.

So there has arisen the practice of furnishing evidence of title to the buyer. The form of this evidence of title is agreed upon in the contract of sale. Since the nature of title evidence varies from area to area, it may be necessary for the buyer and seller to conform their needs to the customs of the area where the land lies. Generally speaking, in large-scale transactions, the mortgage lender dictates the nature of the evidence of title because it has the largest stake in the transaction. Often the lender requires title insurance.

In all events, the history of the development of title evidence is interesting and useful. In the early days of this country, the nation was predominantly agricultural. Transfers of ownership were infrequent. Indeed, farmers tended to hold the land in the family, passing it from generation to generation. Hence the land record books in the county courthouse were not numerous, and it was easy for a lawyer to go to them to examine the title to a particular tract of land.

Also, going back to the old days, when villages were relatively small, business was done largely on a first-name basis. The lawyer for the buyer in a real estate transaction would go to the courthouse to examine the land records. He would have a friendly conversation with the recorder of deeds who was thoroughly familiar with everything that had happened in the courthouse in recent memory. The recorder could probably tell the lawyer what transactions there were relating to the land in question. The lawyer would make a formal check of the land records. He would then go to the tax office and again have an informal talk with the tax collector followed by a quick search of the tax records. The lawyer would then return to his office and prepare an opinion of title which would reflect the result of his searches. The whole process was quite informal.

However, as time went on, other factors caused this friendly format to become more formalized. One of these factors was the opening of the Erie Canal in 1825. When that occurred, it became possible for ships to move from the Atlantic seaboard through the Great Lakes to Chicago. It was also no longer necessary for people traveling westward to use the ancient Indian trail roads that were at times impassable. This in turn created a flow of commerce that sharply increased land values and a good deal of land speculation resulted. As a result, land transactions became numerous and the land record books in the courthouse multiplied. The number of recordings increased again when railroads began to enter the picture. The speculation became feverish. It was no longer easy for a lawyer to check the growing number of land records. It was no coincidence that abstract offices began to open at this time.

As recorders would leave their elected office, they would often open an abstract office near the courthouse. A courthouse man would be hired to make trips to the recorder's office to note all documents filed in the public record on a particular day. He would also check the tax records to determine what tax sales or payments were made. He would then return to the nearby abstract office and enter those transactions in the abstract company's books. These entries were made in a far more convenient form than existed in the courthouse. For example, suppose that we are involved in a sale of Lot 1 in Block 1 in Sheffield's Addition to Chicago. The abstractor would open a page in his book with that particular description at the top of the page, and every transaction involving that particular lot would be entered in chronological order on that page. This was done in anticipation of future title examination orders that might be placed with this abstractor.

When the lot was being sold, the contract of sale would call for the seller to furnish the buyer an abstract of title. At that time, the abstractor would look at his books and make a list of all the transactions appearing on that particular page. This list is sometimes referred to as a "chain." The chain would be taken to the courthouse and very brief copies of each instrument appearing in the chain would be made. The abstractor would then prepare a brief history of the title beginning with the first grant from the United States. Each transaction would appear in chronological order but in a highly abbreviated form. Today, many abstractors prepare their abstracts by photocopying each document in the chain of title. This is the *abstract* that is referred to in this chapter. The abstract would be handed to the buyer's attorney for examination and the preparation of an *opinion of title*. This was a very important step forward in the process of examining and evidencing title. The lawyer was liberated. He could examine the title to the property in the comfort and convenience of his office by merely using the abstract.

For many years the abstract system worked very well. Indeed, it is still used in the agricultural parts of the Midwest. However, from time to time, defects in the abstract system came to light.

EXAMPLE: Owner is selling an apartment building that is encumbered with a $200,000 mortgage. Owner could, of course, clear the mortgage by paying it

off. But, for a much lesser cost, Owner could merely forge the lender's execution of a mortgage release and record the document. While this apparently rids
the record title of the mortgage, the release is really a nullity. Buyer would actually be acquiring the property subject to the $200,000 mortgage.

Many other such defects came to light. These are the "hidden risks" that are
referred to in this chapter. Abstracts did not protect against these hidden risks.

Beginning around 1880, the abstractors took on an additional chore. They
would prepare their abstract as usual. An in-house attorney would examine the
abstract and render his title opinion. Then the abstractor would issue an insurance policy insuring the purchaser of the property that he was acquiring good
title to the property. In this fashion, the insurer took the risk of forgeries, misrepresentation of marital status, and so on, the so-called hidden risks.

In the early days of title insurance, the abstractor was unwilling to inspect
the property. Nonetheless, there are certain defects in title that do not appear
on the public records but appear only from an examination of the property itself.
For example, if the property is occupied by a purchaser under an unrecorded
contract, the contract will be valid and binding on any other purchasers because
possession imparts constructive notice of the possessor's rights. Also, if there is
an unrecorded easement crossing the property, it will be valid and binding
against a purchaser. Also, if there are any encroachments, such as the encroachment of my building onto the adjoining property, the encroachment will not
appear from the public records, but may be revealed only by a survey. Because
of this, the title insurance policies set up certain exclusions for those facts that
could be found only upon an examination of the property, such as the unrecorded rights of parties in possession. The title insurer refused to insure against
title defects that could not be seen from a review of the public records because
the title insurer did not visit the premises to look for such defects.

However, as time went on, purchasers of title policies came to demand more
protection. As a result, the title insurance companies, which had replaced the
abstractor-insurer, began to inspect the property to determine if the exceptions
relating to parties in possession, encroachments, unrecorded easements, and
mechanic's liens could be removed.

As the title insurance companies began this practice, they also discovered
the need for other special coverages. For example, if a building violates a building restriction, a special endorsement could be given insuring the purchaser
against loss arising by reason of this violation.

Finally, title insurers formed the American Land Title Association (ALTA),
a national trade association, and a degree of uniformity in title policies and endorsements made its appearance.

15.02   Abstract

As discussed, an abstract is a history of the title to a particular tract of land. It
consists of a summary of the material parts of every recorded instrument affecting the title. It begins with a description of the land covered by the abstract,
which description is called the *caption*, or *head*, of the abstract, and then proceeds

to show, usually in chronological order, the original government grant and all subsequent deeds, mortgages, release deeds, wills, judgments, mechanics' liens, foreclosure proceedings, tax sales, and other matters affecting the title.

Of course all these items are shown in a highly abbreviated form. In fact, usually a bare outline of the deed, mortgage, or other instrument is shown. "Fine print" provisions are omitted altogether or summarized in a few words. The manner in which the instrument was signed is not shown unless there is some irregularity in this respect. If the acknowledgment is in due form, the abstractor merely indicates that the instrument was acknowledged. A purchaser or mortgagee may rely on the abstractor to draw attention to these irregularities, since where an abstract purports to state the substance of a deed, mortgage, or other instrument, and there is nothing on the face of the abstract to indicate an error, the customer is justified in assuming that no irregularity exists in those portions of the document that the abstractor has omitted from his abstract. *Equitable B. & L. Assn.* v. *Bank of Commerce & Trust Co.*, 102 SW 901 (Tenn. 1907).

The abstract concludes with the *abstractor's certificate*. This discloses what records the abstractor has examined and, what is more important, what records he has *not examined*. For example, some abstractors will not examine records located outside of the county seat, and their certificates reflect that fact. In such case, it is necessary to supplement the abstract by obtaining the necessary searches. If an abstractor certifies that he has made no search of federal court proceedings affecting the property, it will be necessary to write to the clerk of the district court, who will supply the search for a small charge. The certificate also shows the date covered by the abstractor's search of the records. Because of the unavoidable delay intervening between the filing in the recorder's office of a particular day's deeds and mortgages and the entry of the same on the abstractor's books, the abstractor is not in a position to certify on any particular day as to the status of the record title on that day. His certificate will certify today as to the status of the record title on some previous day.

15.02(a)   The Abstractor

Abstracts are prepared by public officials, lawyers, and abstract companies. In some states, an abstractor is required to post a bond to protect all those who rely on his abstracts against any loss resulting from a lack of care or skill on his part. Many abstractors keep their own books. They take great pride in their "abstract plant," and in many communities the abstractor's records are more accurate than the public records. Other abstractors prepare their abstracts from the public records.

Since abstracting is a profession requiring much legal knowledge and careful research, a prudent purchaser or mortgagee will rely only on abstracts furnished by abstractors possessing the requisite skill, care, and experience. The financial responsibility of the abstractor and the existence and limits of his *errors and omissions insurance* are likewise important, since if an error is made in preparing the abstract of the title to a valuable tract of land, there should be no doubt as to the ability of the abstractor to respond in damages.

15.02(a)(1) Abstractor's Liability

The abstractor is in no sense a guarantor of title. He merely undertakes to exercise due care in the preparation of his abstract. He renders no opinion as to the title. If he includes in his abstract all recorded instruments affecting the title, and, as a consequence, the abstract discloses a fatally defective title, the abstractor has fully discharged his responsibilities. But, if an intending purchaser orders an abstract prepared and the abstractor negligently omits therefrom a mortgage, judgment, or other lien that the purchaser is thereafter compelled to pay, the purchaser can obtain reimbursement from the abstractor. 28 ALR 2d 891. The abstractor's liability may also extend to third persons not parties to the contract for abstracting services. 34 ALR3d 1122.

> **EXAMPLE:**   Purchasers relied upon an abstract prepared for sellers by abstract company. The court held that the purchasers could recover even though the abstract was prepared before the contract of purchase. *Williams* v. *Polgar,* 204 NW2d 57 (Mich. 1972).

To be safe, it is best for anyone who relies upon the abstract to have it certified by the abstractors to that person, and to the purchaser's mortgagee.

15.03 Examination of Title

The mere fact that a purchaser or mortgagee has received an abstract of title affords him no protection. In fact, examination of the abstract may disclose that the title is hopelessly clouded. Hence, after an abstract has been prepared by a reliable abstractor and certified so that the buyer or mortgagee can rely thereon, it should be delivered to a competent attorney for examination. This attorney will thereupon examine the abstract and prepare his *opinion* as to the title, which will show the name of the titleholder and all defects and encumbrances disclosed by the abstract.

15.04 Certificate of Title

In some localities the making of an abstract is dispensed with. The attorney merely examines the public records and issues his certificate, which is his opinion of title based on the public records that he has examined. Like an abstractor, such an attorney is liable only for damages occasioned by his negligence. 59 ALR3d 1176. The same is true when a certificate of title is issued by a title company. *Lattin* v. *Gillette,* 30 P 545 (Cal. 1892); *Bridgeport Airport Inc.* v. *Title Guaranty & Trust Co.,* 150 A 509 (Conn. 1930).

15.05   Risks Involved in Relying on Record Title

There are certain defects in title that even a perfect abstract or certificate of title will not disclose because these hidden defects or hidden risks cannot be discovered by an examination of the public records. These hidden risks include:

1. *Forgery.* A deed in the chain of title may seem entirely regular but may nevertheless be a forgery. Such a deed is totally void and a purchaser or mortgagee of such title is not protected. Likewise, a forged release of mortgage does not discharge the mortgage lien.

2. *Insanity and minority.* A deed or release of mortgage executed by a minor or insane person may be subject to cancellation by subsequent court proceedings.

3. *Marital status incorrectly given.* A deed or mortgage may recite that the grantor or mortgagor is single, whereas in fact he may be married. This may later result in a dower or other claim by his spouse.

EXAMPLE: *H* owns an apartment building and is married to *W*, but is separated from her. *H* has an opportunity to sell the building to you at a good price, and does so. *H* signs *W*'s name to the deed. Spouse's right in the property remains outstanding, and if *W* survives *H*, she will be able to force a sale of the building and her rights will be paid her out of the sale price.

4. *Defective deeds.* A recorded deed may never have been properly delivered. For example, it may have been found by the grantee among the grantor's effects after the grantor's death and then placed on record. Such deeds, of course, pass no title.

EXAMPLE: *A* owns an apartment building. He is a bachelor. He shares a safe-deposit box with his nephew, *X*. *A* dies. *X* opens the box and finds a deed from *A* to *X* to the apartment building, with a note pinned to it stating that *A* wants *X* to have the building. *X* records the deed. The deed is void. The mere fact that the deed was recorded after *A*'s death discloses that there is something wrong with the deed.

There are many other defects in title that the public records do not disclose. There are also certain other risks not of a legal character that are encountered when a deal is closed in reliance on a certificate of title or abstract and opinion. One of these risks is the risk of unwarranted litigation attacking the title. A landowner's title may be good as a matter of law, but if some other person entertains the notion that he has some title to, or interest in, the land, he may institute litigation asserting his supposed rights, and such litigation, even though successfully defended, may prove costly. Again, a competent attorney examining an abstract for a purchaser may reach an entirely correct opinion that the title is good. But when the purchaser, in turn, is selling or mortgaging the land, the attorney for the subsequent buyer or mortgagee may arrive at a different conclusion. This may necessitate the institution of litigation to clear the title. It is this fear of objections to the title by some subsequent examiner that prompts attorneys to scrutinize abstracts closely and raise every technical objection apparent therefrom. This practice is known as *fly-specking.*

15.06   Title Insurance

It is the function of title insurance to shift or transfer to a responsible insurer risks such as those mentioned in the preceding section. Title insurance is a contract to make good a loss arising through defects in title to real estate or liens or encumbrances thereon. As a rule, a title company will not insure a bad title any more than a fire insurance company would issue a policy on a burning building. However, title companies disregard many of the technical objections that would be raised by an attorney examining an abstract. If an examination of the title discloses that good title is vested in a particular person, the company will issue its policy whereby it agrees, subject to the terms of its policy, to indemnify such person against any loss he may sustain by reason of any defects in title not enumerated in the policy and to defend at its own expense any lawsuit attacking the title where such lawsuit is based on a defect in title against which the policy insured.

15.06(a)   The Title Insurance Policy

Title companies issue both *owner's policies* and *loan policies*. The owner's policy is usually issued to the landowner himself or to his buyer. Mortgage or loan policies, of course, are issued to mortgagees. Unlike other types of insurance policies, which insure for limited periods of time and are kept in force by the periodic payment of renewal premiums, an owner's title insurance policy is bought and paid for only once, and then continues in force without any further payment until a sale of the property is made. At that time, the title is examined to cover the period of time since the issuance of the policy, and a new policy is issued to the purchaser. A charge is then made for the issuance of this new policy.

It may help you understand title insurance if you compare it with fire insurance.

> **EXAMPLE:**   *X* buys a home and the deed to *X* is received on April 1, 1986. He receives a title insurance policy insuring his title as of April 1, 1986. On the same day he takes out a one-year fire insurance policy. The title insurance policy insures *X* against any defects in title not shown in the policy where such defects occurred *on or prior to April 1, 1986.* No annual premium need be paid. As to fire insurance, that policy insures against any fire damage *occurring after April 1, 1986.* Annual premiums must be paid to keep the fire policy in force.

The mortgage policy terminates when the mortgage debt is paid. However, if the mortgage is foreclosed, then the protection of the mortgage policy continues in force, protecting against any defects of title that existed on, or prior to, the date of the policy. In both policies, the company usually undertakes, subject to the terms of its policy, to defend at its own expense any lawsuit attacking the title where such lawsuit is based on a defect in title against which the policy insures. This is one of the attractive features of title insurance to property owners, since "nuisance" litigation affecting real estate is quite common and is expensive to defend, even though not well founded. A policy of title insurance usually shows the name of the party insured and the character of his title, which is usually fee simple title, although title policies are also issued on other interests, such as leaseholds or easements. It also contains a description of the land and, if the policy is a mortgage policy, a description of the mortgage. The policy lists those matters which affect that particular tract of land, such as any mortgage, easement, lien, or restriction thereon. Like other insurance policies, it contains printed conditions and stipulations.

Common printed exceptions found in owner's policies relate to the rights of parties in possession and questions of survey. Often real property is in the possession of those whose rights are not disclosed by the records. Common instances are tenancies under oral or unrecorded leases and rights of those in possession under unrecorded contracts of purchase. When no survey has been furnished the company, it has no means of knowing what encroachments exist, if any. The policy will therefore be subject to encroachments and other matters that a survey would reveal, also the rights of persons in possession claiming under some unrecorded document.

15.06(b)   Title Insurance—Residential Policy

In 1980, a new residential form of owner's title insurance was introduced. This policy, issued only to consumers for residential transactions, is a dramatic innovation for two reasons. First, it is written in "plain language" in response to laws in some states that require insurance policies to be written in clear and understandable language. Second, the new policy offers expanded coverage to the homebuyer. This additional coverage includes:

1. Protection against unrecorded matters such as survey problems, unrecorded easements, and unrecorded mechanic's liens.

2. As a protection against the effects of inflation, the policy amount will automatically increase by 10 percent per year for the first five years of coverage.

3. Insurance for actual loss incurred as a result of the forced removal of the existing structure because it extends onto adjoining land or onto any easement or because it violates a restriction shown in the policy or because it violates the zoning law.

4. Insurance against actual loss incurred if the insured cannot use the land for a single-family residence because such a use violates a restriction shown in the policy or an existing zoning law.

5. In the event that the insured cannot use any of the land because of a claim against the title, the insurer will repay the insured for rent paid until the cause of the claim is removed.

15.06(c)   Title Insurance—Endorsements

Where the evidence of title reveals defects not permitted by the sale contract (or permitted by the contract only where title insurance thereover is available), the parties may choose to avail themselves of title insurance coverage afforded against the potential loss or damage which could be incurred by the existence of such defects. Also, the insured may desire greater coverage than that given by the standard form of policy. Title companies offer such endorsements to cover encroachments, restrictions, foundations, zoning, and the like.

15.06(d)   Title Insurance—Leasehold Policies

Suppose a tenant is about to take a lease on a store, theater, restaurant, or other commercial location in which he plans to make a substantial investment for re-modeling. Just as a buyer of land needs to know that his seller has a good, clear title, this tenant needs to know that his landlord has a good, clear title to the leased premises and that the tenant will not be dispossessed in the middle of his lease by foreclosure of mortgages or other liens on the landlord's title. Contracts for such leases are drawn along the lines of a contract for the sale of land. They require the landlord to have his title examined and to furnish the tenant a *leasehold policy* issued by a title company insuring the validity of the tenant's lease free from mortgages or other encumbrances. Also, when the leasehold is the security for a mortgage, the lender will require a leasehold loan policy.

ALTA has also promulgated standard forms of leasehold owners and loan policies. Prior to that time various title companies insured leaseholds by "doctoring up" regular owner's and loan policies. The new policies define the insured leasehold estate to include the right of possession for the term of the lease subject to the conditions of the lease. The policies also describe a method of evaluating the leasehold estate and lists the items of incidental damage which will be paid if the insured is forced to surrender occupancy of the premises due to matters insured against.

15.06(e)   Title Insurance—Easement Policies

Suppose you are selling me a tract of industrial property that has access to a railroad by means of an easement for a spur track over adjoining land. The validity of the easement is just as important to me as the fact that you have good title to the land I am buying. I will therefore insist that the policy you furnish me insures the validity of the easement.

15.06(f)   Title Commitments

Suppose that *A* had purchased some land in 1940 and had received a title policy at that time. He is now selling this same land to *B*. Naturally, *B* would not want to rely on such an outdated document. Therefore, the contract of sale will call upon *A* to have the title company bring its title search down to the present date, which they will do. The title company will issue a *commitment* obligating the company to issue its policy to *B* subject only to the matters shown in the commitment. If any defects appear on the commitment that the seller must clear up—unpaid back taxes, for example—the seller pays off the item, receives paid tax bills or other documents, and exhibits them to the title company, which thereupon stamps the item "waived." When the title is clear, the land is conveyed by the seller to the buyer, the deed recorded, and a title policy issued in the name of the buyer.

15.07   The Torrens System

In a few counties in the United States, there is, in additon to the system of transferring title under the Recording Acts, a system known as the *Torrens system.* Under the Recording Acts, when a deed is made conveying land, the grantee in the deed usually takes it to the recorder's office and leaves it there for recording. The recorder makes a copy of the deed, places this copy in record books, which are available to the public, and returns the original deed to the grantee. The recorder does not pass upon the validity of the deed. If the grantee wishes to satisfy himself that he has received a good title, he may obtain title insurance, an abstract and opinion of title, or a title certificate.

The Torrens system operates quite differently. A landowner who wishes to register his land under the Torrens system first obtains a complete abstract of title to the land. He then files in the proper public office an application for the registration of title. This application lists the names of all persons who appear to have any interest in the land. These names are obtained from the abstract and from an investigation of the possession of the premises. The application constitutes the filing of a lawsuit against all persons named therein, and any person wishing to contest the applicant's claim of title may do so on receiving notice of the filing of the application. If the applicant is successful in proving that he is the owner of the land, the court enters an order so finding and also stating the mortgages, liens, restrictions, and so on to which said title is subject. The court also orders an official known as the *Registrar of Titles* to *register* such title. The registrar then makes out a *certificate of title,* showing the title as found by the court. These certificates are bound up in books and are public records. At the same time that the registrar makes out the original certificate, he makes out a *duplicate certificate of title,* which he delivers to the owner.

When a tract of land has been registered under the Torrens system, no subsequent transaction binds the land until such transaction has also been registered. When the land is sold, the deed itself does not pass ownership of the land. The deed must be taken to the registrar's office, and if the registrar is satisfied that the deed is valid, he cancels the old certificate of title and issues a new one to the grantee. It is this *registration* that puts ownership in the grantee. The deed is not returned to the grantee but remains in the registrar's office. In other words, the registrar of titles, unlike the recorder of deeds, investigates to determine the validity of the transfer, and only after he is satisfied that the transfer of title is valid will he issue a new certificate in the grantee's name. Thus, as to Torrens land it is said that "title passes by registration, not by deed." Likewise, a mortgage is not effective against the property until the registrar has checked it as to form and signature and entered it on the certificate of title. However, the registrar does not check on or guarantee the essential validity of the mortgage, for example, to see whether or not the mortgage money has been paid out or whether the interest is usurious. No judgment or other lien is valid against Torrens property until a copy has been filed in the registrar's office and the lien noted on the certificate of title.

Use of the Torrens system is largely confined to a few metropolitan areas, such as Boston, Chicago, Duluth, Minneapolis–St. Paul, and New York City.

The Torrens certificate purports to be conclusive proof that the title is as therein stated. As in the case of other evidences of title, there are exceptions and objections that the Torrens certificate does not cover. These vary somewhat from state to state. Unlike a policy of title insurance, the Torrens certificate does not require the registrar to assume the defense of litigation attacking the title of the registered owner. The property owner must defend the litigation at his own expense, and if he is successful, he cannot obtain reimbursements from the registrar for the expenses of the litigation.

REFERENCE: *Title Insurance: The Lawyer's Expanding Role,* A.B.A. (1985).

CHAPTER 16

Insurance

16.01 In General

In the past, insurance was purchased in pieces. A fire policy with extended coverage was bought from one carrier, a liability policy from another, and so on. Today, coverage on homes is offered in a package best exemplified by the homeowners' policy. Nonetheless, a historical perspective is in order.

16.02 Development of Standard Fire Policy

The need for fire insurance first became apparent after the Great Fire of London in 1666. However, the policies that came into use in England following that catastrophe contained numerous and varied fine-print exceptions that led to much litigation and disappointment on the part of the policyholders. These conditions also prevailed in America, and, in 1873, agitation for a standard policy led to the adoption of a standard policy form in Massachusetts. In 1886, New York adopted a standard policy form, which was revised by a law effective in 1918. This policy still strongly favored the insurer, and in 1943, New York adopted a form more favorable to the insured. This old form was widely adopted everywhere and used for many years. It is still used on properties other than homes. The old policy covered loss by fire only. Loss from other hazards are covered by a rider known as the extended coverage endorsement. The following are other hazards not coverd by the fire policy unless it has an endorsement extending its coverage:

1. Explosion damage. If an explosion not caused by fire occurs on the premises and no fire results, none of the damage is covered. If a fire starts *first* and the fire causes an explosion, all loss is covered whether due to fire or explosion, for the fire is the cause of the loss. 82 ALR2d 1128. If an explosion occurs first and fire results, the policy covers the damage caused by the fire but not the damage caused by the explosion.

2. Water damage not resulting from a fire, as damage from water seepage in a basement or from a leaking sprinkler system.

3. Windstorm damage. As in the case of explosions, if a fire results from windstorm damage, the fire loss is covered by the policy.

4. Loss from hail, riot, civil commotion, aircraft, and many other hazards.

Breakage, water damage, and damage from chemicals caused through efforts to extinguish the fire are considered to be caused by fire and are therefore covered by the policy.

16.03(a)   Extended Coverage Endorsement

A rider attached to the fire policy on payment of an extra premium is known as an *extended coverage endorsement.* Its content varies according to locality, but it often covers loss from windstorm, hail, explosion, riot, civil commotion, aircraft, vehicles, and smoke from friendly fires, except those in fireplaces. The windstorm damage coverage of the extended coverage endorsement does not cover rain, snow, or other water damage as such, except where caused by or resulting from windstorm or another peril specified in the extended coverage endorsement.

EXAMPLE: In a heavy rain, the sewer backs up and floods the basement. The damage is not covered by the extended coverage endorsement.

EXAMPLE: A tornado tears off a roof and the debris breaks water pipes. The water rushes out of the pipes, causing damage. All the damage is covered by the insurance, for the basic cause of the entire loss is the windstorm.

EXAMPLE: A hailstorm breaks windows, and the rain and wind sweep in, causing damage. All the damage is covered, because the original cause is a hailstorm, which is a peril specified in the extended coverage endorsement.

Damage caused by explosion of a steam boiler on the premises is not covered. Damage caused by vehicles driven *by the landowner* is not covered, but if, for example, a delivery truck entering a drive runs into the building, this damage is covered.

16.03(b)   Hazards Covered—Homeowners Policies

For many years after the adoption of the New York 1943 form, the traditional fire insurance policy was offered as a basic form of coverage, which together with a rider or endorsement covered loss by windstorm and other perils. In recent times, however, this policy has been largely replaced for homeowners' insurance by the package of coverage offered in the homeowners policy. The current forms of homeowners policies do away with fine print, long sentences, and lawyers' language opting for a booklet type of presentation with readable type, simple sentences, and the absence of hypertechnical language.

There are two basic types of homeowners' policies. One is the old-fashioned *"named peril"* policy. This form names the risks or perils insured against. There are presently two forms of this policy, the HO-1 and the HO-2. The HO-1 covers losses caused by the following perils:

Fire or lightning
Windstorm or hail
Explosion
Riot or civil commotion
Vehicles
Smoke
Vandalism and malicious mischief
Theft
Breakage of glass

The HO-2 form expands the coverage of the HO-1 form, also insuring against losses caused by:

Falling objects
Weight of ice, snow, or sleet
Collapse of a building or any part of a building (71 ALR3d 1072)
Accidental discharge or overflow of water or steam
Sudden and accidental tearing apart or bulging of a heating, air conditioning, or hot water system
Freezing of plumbing, heating, air conditioning system, or household appliance
Sudden and accidental damage from artificially generated electrical current

The HO-3 is an "all-risk" policy. In this format, instead of enumerating the perils insured against, it insures against all perils except those listed as uninsured risks. 88 ALR2d 112.

The HO-6 condominium owner's policy covers the condominium unit and personal property in the same basic fashion as the HO-2 coverage. All-risk coverage is also available for the condominium owner.

Consistent with the concept of providing homeowners with a package of insurance, the HO policies provide other coverages that are a natural part of a full package of protection for homeowners. Be warned that the specifics of coverage vary from company to company.

16.03(b)(1)   Personal Property Coverage

Personal property coverage extends to the homeowner's personal effects, that is, furniture; stereo equipment, color TV, clothes, and so forth. The policy coverage on valuables such as jewelry, furs, silverware, and so forth is very low. The insurance agent should be consulted for a special policy or floater covering valuables. Sophisticated homeowners have inventoried and photographed these items for use in claiming loss and to help the insurer recover the stolen articles. An appraisal is a requirement to recovery of insurance on valuables such as furs, jewelry, antiques, fine paintings, etc. An appraisal will also help the insured make his claim if the property is stolen.

Scheduling of personal property removes the restrictions caused by the formula coverage built into the policy for personal property. Typically, unscheduled personal property is covered to the extent of 50 percent of the coverage on the building. The face of the policy so states. Therefore a policy with $50,000 in coverage on the building would provide $25,000 of coverage for unscheduled personal property. Those formulas are inapplicable to scheduled personal property, which has its own value statement unrelated to the amount of coverage on the building.

16.03(b)(2)   Liability Coverage

In addition to providing coverage for the building and its contents, the home-owners' policies provide liability coverage for bodily injury and property damage to others arising out of the insured's negligence. This coverage applies to accidents occurring both on and off the insured premises and extends to damages caused by members of the insured's family who live with the insured and the insured's pets. Typically, the coverage is for a low amount. It can be increased by endorsement.

16.03(b)(3)   Medical Payments

The liability insurance protects the insured for damages which he causes to someone else. Medical payment coverage defrays the cost of injuries that occur through no one's fault, events that are purely accidental. This coverage, usually $5,000 per person and $25,000 per accident, is available for injuries occurring to anyone other than the insured and the insured's family.

16.04   Other Insurance

The popularity of certain forms of coverage varies from region to region. For example, in the Midwest, earthquake coverage is cheap but practically never purchased. In California it is popular, and its price varies depending upon the type of structure and locale.

In making the decision as to which coverage is appropriate, it is good to note that the disparity in price between the premiums for the least comprehensive and most comprehensive homeowner's policies is relatively minor. The extra coverage is usually well worth the few extra dollars spent. Be watchful also to increase coverage as you increase value to your property. For example, if there is a room addition, the policy should be appropriately endorsed.

Some property is in slum or riot-prone areas where insurance is not ordinarily available. A federal program, the FAIR plan, exists to provide coverage for these properties. Flood insurance is available in flood-prone areas. FNMA and federal lenders in general require flood insurance in such areas. 42 USCA Sec. 400.

16.05   Rent Loss and Business Interruption

Since the policy covers fire damage to the *building*, it does not cover loss of rents when a rental building is rendered untenantable by fire, nor does it cover loss of *profits* when operation of a business is interrupted by fire. Both items can be covered by riders attached to the policy or by separate insurance such as rent insurance and business interruption insurance.

16.06   When Protection Attaches

It often takes some time for a formal policy of insurance to be prepared and forwarded to the insurer. Hence oral coverage is perfectly valid, pending the issuance of the policy. This gives the insured the coverage of the standard policy subject to its terms and conditions. *Bersani* v. *General Accident, Fire & Life Assur. Corp.*, 330 NE2d 68 (N.Y. 1975). Oral coverage is usually confirmed by letter. Certificates of insurance or binders are available to provide evidence that protection has attached even though the policy is not yet issued.

16.07   Description of the Property Insured

The property insured should be accurately described in the policy, and all policies applying to the same property should contain identical descriptions.

The street address of the property is often used in insurance policies. There has been a tendency in recent times, however, to insist on the insertion of a full legal description so that there will be no dispute as to the property covered. This is particularly true with respect to houses recently constructed which often do not have a street address at the time the policy is written.

16.08   Insurable Interest

The insured must have some insurable interest in the property. Otherwise the policy is void. Persons having an insurable interest include both buyer and seller in a contract for the sale of land, mortgagor, mortgagee, part owner, trustee, receiver, and life tenant.

16.09   Interest Covered by Policy

The present form of policy is an *interest policy*. It protects only the party insured and covers only the financial loss suffered by the insured, which can never be more than the value of his interest in the property and which may be less than the actual damage to the building.

> **EXAMPLE:**   A bachelor buys a home and takes out a policy in his name. He then marries and has the home placed in joint tenancy. He now owns only a half interest in the home and could collect no more than half of any loss. Suppose further that a loss occurs after the husband's death. Here his entire interest in the property has passed to his wife, but she has no insurance whatever.

Some homeowners' policies cover the named insured "and relatives living on the premises."

16.10   Acts of the Party Insured

Naturally, where the party insured causes the loss, as when the building is set on fire to collect the insurance, the insurance company is not liable. The problem arises most frequently where real estate is owned by a husband and wife and they are jointly insured. They quarrel bitterly, separate, and the party leaving sets fire to the house.

Some courts hold that this is an "act of the assured," which invalidates the entire policy. *Lovall* v. *Rowan Mutual Fire Ins. Co.,* 302 N.C. 150, 274 SE2d 170 (1981); *Klemens* v. *Badger Mut. Ins. Co.,* 99 NW2d 865 (Wis. 1960); 10A Couch, Insurance Sec. 42.680.

Other courts allow the occupant to recover for half interest. *Morgan* v. *Cincinnati Ins. Co.,* 411 Mich. 267, 307 NW2d 55 (1981); *Fuston* v. *National Mut. Ins. Co.,* 440 NE2d 751 (Ind. 1982).

16.11   Unoccupancy Clause

The policy provides that the insurer shall not be liable while the building is vacant or unoccupied beyond a period of thirty consecutive days. The words *vacant* and *unoccupied* are not synonymous. *Vacant* means without inanimate objects; *unoccupied* means without animate occupants. A dwelling is unoccupied when it has ceased to be a customary place of habitation or abode and no one is living in it. Thus if furniture remains in the building, it is not vacant, but if the owner has left the dwelling with the intention of permanently residing elsewhere, the building is unoccupied, and the insurance may become void. *Vandalism coverage* usually ceases if the building is unoccupied for thirty days.

Because the danger of vandalism has greatly increased in recent times, insurance companies are enforcing this clause. This requires that the owner obtain an endorsement waiving the clause or provide an occupant if a lengthy absence is planned.

16.12   Increase of Hazard

The policy provides that the company shall not be liable for any loss occurring while the hazard is increased by any means within the control or knowledge of the insured. The operation of this clause is restricted to physical changes in the building or in the use or occupancy of the premises. Any alteration or change in the building or in the use of the property that will increase the risk of loss violates this clause if it is of a more or less permanent nature. 28 ALR2d 762.

> **EXAMPLE:**   The following operations increase the hazard and invalidate the insurance: (1) Tenant began operating a still. (2) Owner turned off a sprinkler system. (3) Owner brought fireworks on the premises. (4) Owner began use of a room as a tinshop.

But doing something that involves risk, that is a more or less normal and expected routine operation, is not considered an increase of hazard that invalidates the policy, for example, using a torch to burn off old paint preparatory to repainting. 28 ALR2d 771 Also, the increase of the hazard must contribute to or cause the loss. *Northern Assurance Co.* v. *Spencer,* 246 F.Supp. 730 (1965).

16.13   Double Insurance

Unless a policy endorsement provides otherwise, the insured may procure additional insurance. However, the liability of each company is limited to the proportion of the loss that its insurance bears to the total insurance covering the property. If the same property is insured in two companies through two policies of $5,000 each, and if a loss of $2,000 occurs, the maximum liability of each company would be $1,000.

The insured should check to see that all portions of all policies covering the same property read exactly alike.

16.14   Amount Recoverable

When insurance is bought, the insured is concerned with two things. First, what hazards or risks are covered? Second, what amount will the insurance company pay if a loss occurs? The premium is based upon many factors, but it is primarily determined by the combination of these factors. Obviously, it is the amount of coverage that sets the maximum limit on a claim.

Aside from the amount of coverage purchased, the amount that the insurance company will pay is determined by whether the policy calls for the loss to be measured by the *actual cash value method* or the *replacement cost method.*

Under the still-used 1943 New York Standard Policy, the measure of loss is the "actual cash value of the property at the time of loss," but not more than the cost to replace or repair the damaged property. Thus if the actual cash value of the loss was $1,000, but the cost to replace was $700, the insurance company would pay $700, not $1,000.

While the term "actual cash value" is easy to say, its meaning is not always easy to determine. Indeed, the courts have found three different ways to apply this term as a measure of loss. Some courts hold that actual cash value is determined by subtracting the fair market value of the property after the loss from the fair market value of the property before the loss. Other courts have adopted the cost of repair or replacement less depreciation formula. Yet other courts use the broad evidence rule that takes all factors into consideration, i.e., obsolescence, utility of buildings, depreciation, market value, etc. Cozen, *Measure and Proof of Loss to Buildings and Structures Under Standard Fire Insurance Policies—the Alternatives and Practical Approaches,* 12 Forum 647 (1976); Dykes, *"Actual Cash Value"; the Magic Words—What Do They Mean?,* 16 Forum 391 (1981); 8 ALR4th 533.

Replacement cost insurance can be obtained by adding an endorsement or rider to the standard fire policy. Under this coverage, the insured is paid the actual cost of replacing or restoring the building. 66 ALR3d 885. This method eliminates the guesswork and argument involved in agreeing upon the application of the actual cash value standard. FNMA now requires replacement cost coverage.

The modern homeowners' form of policy provides replacement coverage for the buildings but not the personal property. Chattels are covered on an actual cash value basis unless a personal property replacement cost endorsement is purchased. This endorsement will not cover fine paintings, antiques, jewels, computers, and so on. They must be insured under a special schedule or floater.

The replacement cost coverage of the homeowners' policy is conditioned upon the property being insured for 80 percent of its replacement cost. This provision and the coinsurance clause require the insured to be watchful of the amount of insurance purchased so as always to have the required percentage of coverage.

The amount of coverage purchased is also important because other coverages, i.e., liability, personal property, and medical payments, are set at percentages of the building coverage. The insured should compare his needs for these coverages to the amounts set by the application of these formulas. Most notably, an inventory of personal property should be made and compared to the amount of personal property insurance to determine whether the amount of insurance is sufficient.

16.15   Coinsurance Clause

Very few fires or other casualties cause a total destruction of the property. Insureds are aware of this fact. If it were not for the coinsurance clause the insured might be inclined to take part of the risk of total loss while passing the first layer of loss, where most losses will fall, to the insurer. To prevent this ploy and to encourage insurance to the full value of the property, insurance companies have added the coinsurance clause. This provision requires the owner to keep the property insured to a prescribed level, often 80 percent of the replacement value, if insurance benefits are to be paid in full. The customary use of the 80 percent coinsurance factor stems from the fact that generally only 80 percent of a building's value is destructible. The masonry, foundation, underground utilities, and the like will remain even after a catastrophe. If the owner insures for less than the stated percentage, the coinsurance clause operates to reduce the amount of loss payable to the insured.

> **EXAMPLE:** Assume an 80 percent coinsurance clause, a building worth $10,000, and insurance in the amount of $4,000. The most the insurance company will pay is 50 percent of any loss. The same formula applies to rent loss coverage.

Typically, the insurance value of new buildings is easily determined. The older the building gets, however, the easier it is to inadvertently fall into a coinsurance problem. To avoid this, some insurance companies have adopted the use of *automatic increase endorsements* or the *agreed amount clause.* Through the latter device, the insurer agrees that the amount of insurance coverage satisfies the coinsurance requirement. Without these provisions, the owner should obtain a replacement cost appraisal from a real estate appraiser or from the insurance company, to be sure that the coverage meets the 80 percent requirement.

16.16   Mortgage Interests

Both the mortgagor and the mortgagee have an insurable interest. Both interests may be, and usually are, covered in one policy. But each may take out a separate policy. This right is of value to the mortgagee when the mortgagor has defaulted in his mortgage payments and declines to take out insurance since he feels that he will lose the property anyway. If the mortgagee obtains his own insurance with his own money and a loss occurs, the mortgagor is not entitled to the insurance money. If the insurer pays off the mortgage in such case, he is entitled to an assignment thereof and may foreclose. Of course the mortgagee's recovery is limited to the balance due on the debt, for that is the measure of his interest in the property.

On the other hand, in the absence of any clause in the mortgage requiring the mortgagor to insure for the mortgagee's benefit, the mortgagee is not entitled to insurance money paid under a policy obtained by the mortgagor in his own name and at his own expense. 9 ALR2d 299. However, most mortgage forms require the mortgagor to keep the buildings insured for the benefit of the mortgagee, and if a loss occurs in such case, the mortgagee is entitled to have insurance money applied in reduction or payment of the mortgage debt. *Sureck* v. *U.S. Fidelity & Guaranty Co.,* 353 F.Supp. 807 (1973). Where a mortgage containing a covenant to insure is assigned, a right to the insurance proceeds is created in the assignee. *Kintzel* v. *Wheatland Mutual Ins. Assn.,* 203 NW2d 799 (Iowa 1973).

16.16(a)   The Mortgage Clause

Formerly it was customary for the mortgagor to take out insurance in his own name and, with the insurer's consent, to assign the policy to the mortgagee. This did not adequately protect the mortgagee. He simply stood in the mortgagor's shoes, and if the mortgagor violated the conditions of the policy so that it became void, the mortgagee was unable to collect the insurance. For example, if the mortgagor committed arson, the policy became void. The same result followed where the *open mortgage clause* was used. This clause simply stated that loss, if any, was payable to the mortgagee *as his interest shall appear,* which still left the mortgagee's insurance subject to be destroyed by the ignorance, carelessness, or fraud of the mortgagor. *Central National Insurance Co.* v. *Manufacturer's Acceptance Corp.,* 544 SW2d 362 (Tenn. 1976). Hence the *mortgagee loss clause,* also known as the *New York, standard,* or *union loss clause,* was developed. *Syndicate Ins. Co.* v. *Bohn,* 65 Fed. 165 (1894). This clause, now in general use, provides that the insurance shall not be invalidated by acts of the mortgagor. Under this clause, if the mortgagor does any act that would ordinarily make the policy void, for example, commits arson or brings dynamite on the premises, *such act merely makes the policy void as to the mortgagor, but the insurance remains in force for the benefit of the mortgagee. City-Wide Knitwear* v. *Safeco Ins. Co.,* 366 NYS2d 81 (1973). When such a clause is used, there are really two separate contracts, one between the insurer and the mortgagor and the other between the insurer and the mortgagee, and most matters that would invalidate the first of these contracts leave the second intact and in full force.

Since the standard mortgage clause is a separate contract between the mortgagee and the insurer giving the lender coverage that is separate from the homeowner's, it follows that many acts that invalidate the homeowner's coverage do not affect the lender's coverage. Thus, the mortgagee's protection continues even where:

1. The policy is canceled without the mortgagee's consent. *Mutual Creamery Ins. Co.* v. *Iowa Nat. Ins. Co.,* 294 F.Supp. 337 (1969). Do not confuse cancellation with expiration. If the policy expires, the mortgagee is not entitled to any special notice and the mortgagee's protection ends. 60 ALR3d 164.
2. The mortgagor increases the hazard in the use of the property without the mortgagee's knowledge, for example, by storing flammable substances.
3. The mortgagor is negligent or intentionally damages the insured property. This is very important to the lending industry at a time when arson is a national problem.

EXAMPLE: *John Smith* takes out fire insurance with *ABC Co.* on a home he occupies. He mortgages the home to *XYZ Mortgage Co.* and the standard mortgage clause is attached to the fire policy. Needing money desperately, *John Smith* sets fire to his home. It is destroyed. This act of *John Smith* precludes him from collecting on the insurance if the arson can be proved. But *XYZ Mortgage Co.* will collect insurance up to the amount remaining due on the mortgage. Its separate contract (the mortgagee loss clause) is not affected by *Smith's* acts.

There are limits on the protection afforded by the mortgagee loss clause. The mortgagee must notify the insurer of any change in ownership of the property that comes to the knowledge of the mortgagee. The mortgagee is also bound by the coinsurance clause and any limitation periods in the policy upon the time in which a suit on the policy may be brought. *Greater Providence Trust Co.* v. *Nationwide Ins. Co.,* 355 A2d 718 (R.I. 1976).

Since the mortgage clause is a separate and independent contract of insurance, the name of the mortgagee as party insured must be stated in the mortgage clause. *Pacific Ins. Co.* v. *R. L. Kirmsey Cotton Co.,* 151 SE2d 541 (Ga. 1966). And if the mortgage is released and a new mortgage placed on the property, then a new mortgagee clause must be issued even though the mortgage runs to the same mortgagee who was covered by the previous mortgage clause. *Attleborough Sav. Bank* v. *Security Ins. Co.,* 46 SE 390 (Mass. 1897).

The homeowners' policy forms now include the mortgage loss clause in the body of the policy. It runs in favor of the mortgagee "named in this policy." On the cover page of the policy is a place for the insertion of the name of the mortgagee. I0A Couch, Insurance, Sec. 42.682, 42.716. It is important that this blank be filled in. Unless this is done, the mortgagee has no independent coverage. *Pac. Ins. Co.* v. *R. L. Kimsey Co.,* 151 SE2d 341 (Ga. 1966). This could be fatal, for example, if the landowner commits arson. The insurance policy becomes void and a mortgagee not named has no coverage. This point must be stressed because people do change insurance agents from time to time. The new agent may fail to fill in the blank because he has not been told about the mortgage.

16.16(a)(1)   The Mortgage Clause—Foreclosure

The mortgagee loss clause continues to protect the lender after foreclosure. *Northwestern Nat. Ins. Co.* v. *Mildenberger,* 359 SW2d 380 (Mo. 1962). But see *Consolidated Mortgage Corp.* v. *American Sec. Ins. Co.,* 244 NW2d 434 (Mich. 1976), which requires notice to the insurer of the foreclosure. The mortgagee that takes a deed in lieu of foreclosure also has continued protection. *Union Central Life Ins. Co.* v. *Franklin County Farmers Mutual Ins. Assn.,* 270 NW 398 (Iowa 1936). But see *Insurance Co.* v. *State Savings & L. Assn.,* 425 F2d 1180 (7th Cir. 1970). These statements must be taken with a grain of salt, as the following points out.

A serious problem exists as to the rights of the mortgagee after the foreclosure sale. In most cases the mortgagee is the highest bidder at the foreclosure sale, and he usually bids an amount close to the amount of his mortgage debt. In a number of cases the courts have stated that this amounts to a satisfaction or payment of the mortgage debt in the amount of the sale price. The thinking here is that if a third party had been the successful bidder, his cash money would have gone to the mortgagee in reduction of the mortgage debt, and the result should be the same where the mortgagee "bids his mortgage" at the foreclosure sale. The consequence is that if a fire occurs after the foreclosure sale, the mortgagee recovers at a maximum the difference between the foreclosure sale price and the amount due on the mortgage debt, which difference is usually a trifling amount. *Northwestern Nat. Ins. Co.* v. *Mildenberger,* 359 SW2d 380 (Mo. 1962). *Whitestone S. & L. Assn.* v. *Allstate Ins. Co.,* 270 NE2d 694 (N.Y. 1971). Other courts say that the mortgagee should be allowed full recovery where a mortgagee loss clause exists. *Trustees of Schools* v. *St. Paul Fire & Marine Ins. Co.,* 129 NE 567 (Ill. 1921); *City* v. *Magnur,* 329 NE2d 312 (Ill. 1975).

> **SUGGESTION:**   The mortgagee should procure a new policy or a rider to the existing policy the moment he has made his successful bid at the foreclosure sale.

16.17   Contracts for the Sale of Land

When a landowner takes out insurance and thereafter contracts to sell the land to a purchaser, the sensible course is to have the insurance endorsed to cover both parties as their interests may appear. Then, in case of serious loss, the company will pay the seller the balance due on the contract, and the balance will be paid to the buyer.

When a policy taken out by the buyer is payable to the seller, and a fire occurs and the company pays the unpaid balance of the purchase price to the seller in satisfaction of the insurance claim, all rights of the seller in the property are extinguished, and the company is not entitled to any assignment of the contract. *Fields* v. *Western Millers Mutual Fire Ins. Co.,* 37 NYS2d 757 (1942). The buyer is entitled to a deed to the land since the insurance money has paid the purchase price. *Dysart* v. *Colonial Fire Underwriters,* 254 Pac. 240 (Wash. 1927).

When the buyer takes out a policy with loss payable to the buyer and seller as their interests may appear, and thereafter the seller declares the contract forfeited because of the buyer's default in his payments, the seller is still covered by such insurance. *Aetna Ins. Co.* v. *Robinson,* 10 NE2d 601 (Ind. 1937). And mere default in his payments does not terminate the buyer's insurance. He remains covered until the seller declares a forfeiture of the contract.

Suppose the contract of sale (as is customary in installment contracts) requires the buyer to take out insurance for the benefit of seller and buyer, but the buyer takes out insurance in his own name only. If a loss occurs, the courts will require the buyer to carry out his contract by forcing him to apply his insurance money in payment of the contract price due to the seller. *American Equitable Assurance Co.* v. *Newman,* 313 P2d 1023 (Mont. 1957); 64 ALR2d 1416.

It now seems clear that where a landowner has entered into a contract of sale and a fire occurs after the buyer has substantially reduced the balance due, the seller may nevertheless collect for the full amount of the loss.

> **EXAMPLE:**   A took out a fire insurance policy and thereafter contracted to sell the land to B. When the contract had been paid down to $16,000, a fire loss occurred. A was allowed to collect $46,750 in fire insurance. *First National Bank* v. *Boston Ins. Co.,* 160 NE2d 802 (Ill. 1959); *Edlin* v. *Security Ins. Co.,* 269 F2d 159 (1959).

Although a contract-of-sale endorsement can be obtained to add the purchaser as an insured, no satisfactory standard form endorsement for the homeowners' policy exists to protect the installment contract seller.

> **EXAMPLE:**   Seller enters into an installment contract to sell a home to Buyer. The existing homeowners' policy was written to insure Seller. A new policy is written to insure the Buyer, but with an endorsement making loss payable to Buyer and Seller, as their interests may appear. Buyer commits arson and the building is totally destroyed. Seller may be unable to collect on the insurance. *Langhorne* v. *Capitol Fire Ins. Co.,* 44 F.Supp. 739 (D. Minn. 1942).

For proper protection, a *manuscript endorsement* should be used. This is a tailor-made endorsement used when no adequate printed form is available. It should state that no acts done or suffered by the buyer will in any way affect or impair the coverage to the seller.

16.18   Assignment

Assignment of the policy does not render the policy void, but the assignment itself is not valid except with the written consent of the company. For this reason, when the policy is assigned in connection with a sale and deed by the seller of all his title to the property, the seller could not collect on the policy for a subsequent loss since after sale he has no insurable interest in the property. Nor could the buyer collect if the assignment had not been consented to by the company. In other words, hazard insurance does not "run with the land." It must be assigned to the buyer for the buyer's protection. *Eastway Const.* v. *New York Property Underwriting Assn.,* 382 NYS2d 949 (1976). The prudent buyer will procure oral coverage and/or a binder giving protection until the assignment is consented to.

The right to the insurance proceeds is assignable *after loss. Travelers Indemnity Co.* v. *Isseal,* 354 F2d 488 (1965).

As a practical matter the problem of assignment has become less significant in recent years. Frequently, the seller's policy is canceled upon closing. Similarly, the buyer must tailor his protection and seek his own coverage, possibly written by the family insurance agent. Oral coverage and/or a binder should be obtained to procure coverage until the new policy is issued.

16.19   Liability Insurance

A building owner and lessee must carry liability insurance to protect them against loss caused to someone as a result of their involvement with the real estate.

> **EXAMPLE:**   A customer who slips on the threshold and breaks a leg will sue the building owner and the tenant who runs the store.

The homeowners' policy includes liability insurance.

Obviously, an injured party will sue everyone involved with the property. It is best to have coverage if for nothing more than protection against the costs of defending a case of this type.

16.19(a)   Liability Insurance for Contractors

A liability policy issued to a general contractor is likely to contain exclusions colloquially referred to as "x," "c," and "u." The "x" exclusion excludes liability for blasting. An endorsement can be obtained deleting this exclusion. The "c" exclusion excludes liability for collapse of building, and coverage for this liability should be purchased. The "u" exclusion excludes liability for damage to under-ground facilities such as conduits and sewers. Coverage should be obtained.

Completed operations insurance covers liability for a completed job.

EXAMPLE: A contractor completes a bridge and later it collapses, causing bodily injury and property damage.

In general, a mortgage lender wants to see that all proper insurance is obtained.

EXAMPLE: Lender is lending money on a large construction loan, with Contractor acting as general contractor. A bridge built by Contractor in another state collapses. With no insurance coverage, Contractor goes broke. A new contractor must be found and costs go up astronomically.

16.19(b)   Builder's Risk Insurance

Builder's risk insurance is fire and extended coverage insurance for a building under construction. In its natural state, the amount of coverage under this form of policy increases as the building is completed. Today, a completed value form is available from the very outset of construction. This form eliminates the need to report construction progress. Also, in its natural state, builder's risk insurance will not cover an occupied project. An endorsement can be obtained, either at the outset of the job or at completion to give this coverage.

16.19(c)   Business Interruption Insurance

The ordinary fire policy covers damage to the building caused by fire. It does not cover loss of business profit. Business interruption insurance is required to protect from loss of income and continuing expenses when a business property is destroyed or damaged. There are two kinds of business interruption insurance. The "gross earnings" form pays an amount roughly equal to the gross earnings lost while business was interrupted. This coverage puts the insured business in the place it would have been if the business continued. It pays lost profits only to the extent that profits would have been earned. If losses would have been sustained, no payment is made under the insurance policy. Proving the amount of loss under this form is fairly complicated. Another form of business interruption insurance is the *valued* form under which the insurer and the insured agree at the time the policy is issued on the duration and amount of coverage.

EXAMPLE: You take out a policy that pays $1,000 per week for a period of not more than six months while your plant is shut down by fire damage. There is a fair amount of guesswork in this type of coverage.

REFERENCE: Miller, *Business Interruption Insurance: A Legal Primer*, 24 Drake L. Rev. 799 (1975).

16.20 Public Insurance Adjuster

Some insureds who have suffered a loss immediately turn to a public insurance adjuster for expert help in gathering the evidence of the extent of loss. For a fee of usually 10 percent of the recovery from the insurance company, the adjuster will prepare inventories of damaged property, determine the extent of seen and unseen damage, calculate the cost of repair and replacement, and the like. Adjusters also have access to a group of support personnel, expert engineers, architects, appraisers, and others who aid in determining the loss.

Public adjusters also offer other valuable services where a fire occurs. The policy requires the owner to board up windows and take other steps to minimize loss. The homeowner is in a state of shock. He has no idea as to how to go about these things. The public adjuster is an expert in this area. The insurance company has its own adjuster. His job is to minimize the amount the company pays. Use the public adjuster.

CHAPTER 17

Land Acquisition and Assembly

17.01 In General

One intending to build upon or develop vacant land must acquire it. The suggestions made in the chapters on contracts of sale and land development are, of course, applicable to the process of land acquisition. The mechanics of land acquisition and assembly call for special expertise.

17.02 Precautions Prior to Undertaking Assembly

Before undertaking a land assembly, the developer routinely visits with the title company and gets an idea of the ownerships involved. Obviously, it is easier to assemble three or four ownerships than thirty or forty ownerships. He also can get some idea as to the existence of building restrictions or easements that might thwart his building plans.

17.03 Gaps and Gores

It is often necessary to acquire and assemble the lands of several adjoining land-owners, for example, for a subdivision, or a factory site. Here the danger is that the descriptions used may leave small gaps between the parcels.

> **EXAMPLE:** Buyer proposes to acquire the Northwest Quarter of Section 10 in a government township. He assumes that it contains exactly 160 acres, which it theoretically should contain. Actually, of course, owing to inaccuracies in surveying there is no such thing as a perfect quarter section, and it happens that his quarter section contains 161 acres. Suppose, then, that Buyer acquires from Seller #1 the "east eighty acres" of the quarter section and gets a deed from

Seller # 2 to the "west eighty acres" of the quarter section. This leaves a one-acre strip between the two eighty-acre tracts. Buyer thus does not acquire title to this strip.

These small strips between parcels are called *gores*.

This suggests the need for a *boundary survey* to be made by a surveyor before the contract is signed, so that the buyer's earnest money is not tied up until it can be seen that there are no gaps or gores.

Where one seller owns all the parcels being acquired, the surveyor can be asked to furnish a *perimeter description*. This is a description that describes the entire tract being acquired by metes and bounds. Then the survey will be made while the title is being examined, and if gaps or gores are revealed, the buyer can report the title as unmarketable. Alternatively, the buyer can insist that the title company insuring the title furnish a special endorsement insuring *contiguity* of all the several parcels, in which case the buyer again can back out of the deal if the title company refuses to insure contiguity.

17.04   Nominees

Land is often acquired in the name of a nominee, often a skilled negotiator from a local real estate firm. This is done because asking prices soar when it becomes known that some well-known company is acquiring land in the area. The nominee need not disclose that he is acting for an undisclosed principal. 32 Iowa L. Rev. 790 (1947). But if the seller inquires, the nominee must not misrepresent the identity of the purchaser, for if he does, the seller has the right to terminate the contract because a material misrepresentation has been made. Friedman, *Contracts and Conveyances of Real Property* § 2.2 (3d ed. 1975); 121 ALR 1162; 35 ALR3d 1374. Indeed, if such misrepresentation is made, the seller can have his deed set aside even after the deal has been closed, so long as he acts promptly on learning of the misrepresentation. The nominee must refrain from misrepresenting the use to which the property will be put. 35 ALR3d 1369.

> **EXAMPLE:**   Nominee went to Seller and persuaded Seller to sell a vacant lot adjoining Seller's home. He stated that he planned to build a house. When it later developed that Nominee was buying on behalf of a church, the deed was set aside. *Keyerleber* v. *Euclid Congregation,* 143 NE2d 313 (Ohio 1957); 6 ALR2d 812.

This rule has special force where the seller retains some land and the buyer intends to devote the land to some offensive use, such as a junkyard, cemetery, or bar. 35 ALR3d 1370.

If bad blood or previous dealings lead a buyer to believe that the seller will not sell to him, it is useless to hire a nominee. The seller can have the deal set aside. 6 ALR2d 814; 35 ALR2d 1374.

There seems to be some advantage in having the developer form a straw corporation with some bland name to acquire the land. This would be a wholly-owned subsidiary of the developer. The subsidiary could then hire the nominee, who if asked, or even if not asked, could truthfully state: "I'm working for *Real Estate Associates, Inc.*"

Where it is decided to attempt a secret assembly, some developers use a different nominee, lawyer, and real estate broker for each acquisition.

Obviously, a nominee who has no judgments or other liens against him should be used. Often a bachelor is employed, for then no spouse's rights questions arise.

At times the nominee will request that his employer sign an indemnity agreement protecting the nominee against liability by reason of his ownership of the land.

17.04(a)   Written Authority

Because an agent's authority to buy land must be in writing in some states, there should be a written contract of employment.

17.04(b)   Trust Declaration by Nominees

The nominee routinely signs a brief trust agreement reciting that he is acquiring the land and will hold it in trust for _____ (the developer). This is acknowledged, just as a deed is acknowledged, but it is not recorded. This is an indispensable document, for example, if the nominee dies while the ownership of the land stands in his name. It is especially important in land assemblies that may take a long period of time. Some developers also require the nominee to sign an unrecorded quitclaim deed as soon as he acquires ownership of a parcel.

17.05   Escrows

A seller who senses that he is not dealing with the real purchaser may become uneasy. To quiet his fears the deal should be closed in escrow.

> **EXAMPLE:**   Nominee tenders a contract of sale to Seller, with a provision that the entire purchase price will be held by *ABC Bank* under an escrow agreement providing that Seller gets the entire purchase price or gets ownership of his land back just as it was before the contract was signed.

17.06   Subdivision Trusts

In Arizona extensive use is made of the *subdivision* trust.

> **EXAMPLE:**   Seller enters into a contract to sell vacant land to Buyer for $100,000. Buyer pays $20,000 down. Seller now makes a deed of the land to *ABC Title Co.* in trust. Seller is the first beneficiary of the trust and Buyer is the

second beneficiary. The trustee files a plat of subdivision. Buyer engages in sales of lots. Lot buyers make their payments to *ABC Title Co.* which remits to Seller and Buyer according to a schedule with a minimum amount due periodically. The lot buyers receive their deeds from *ABC Title Co.* Ultimately Seller is paid the balance of the purchase price. If sales collapse and Buyer cannot meet the schedule of payments, Seller can declare a forfeiture of Purchaser's interest. Thereupon *ABC Title Co.* deeds the unsold lots to Seller. Carlock, *The Subdivision Trust—A Useful Device,* 5 Ariz. L. Rev. 2 (1963).

17.07   Land Trusts

The land trust is an ideal vehicle for land assemblies. It enables the developer to acquire the individual parcels in the name of a trust company.

17.08   Holding Agreements

In California and Nevada a device somewhat similar to the land trust is used, called a *holding agreement.*

17.09   Purchase Money Mortgage

Often the developer who is purchasing a development parcel will arrange the purchase with the seller taking back a purchase money mortgage. Any such transaction must have special provisions for the developer's benefit. First, the purchase money mortgage must have a clause that requires the seller/mortgagee to join in the plat of subdivision and execute necessary consents and governmental documentation for the platting and sale of the property. Platting statutes require that mortgagees join in the execution of the subdivision plat. Otherwise, foreclosure of the prior mortgage will extinguish the streets and other public areas dedicated on the plat.

Another necessary clause requires the mortgagee to give partial releases as lots or parcels are sold. This is necessary to clear title for the buyer and mortgagee.

If the developer plans to put a construction mortgage on the property, the purchase money mortgage must contain a clause whereby the seller/mortgagee subordinates the purchase money mortgage to the construction mortgage. This is done in anticipation that the construction lender will insist upon a first mortgage to secure the construction loan. A great deal of caution must be used in drafting this clause. If it is not complete and precise in its terms, it may be unenforceable. See Kratovil & Werner, *Modern Mortgage Law and Practice,* Ch. 30 (2d ed. 1981).

Of course, standards should be included in all of these clauses. The seller/mortgagee should not obligate himself to execute just any document that the purchaser/mortgagor tenders. Rather, the documents tendered by the purchaser/mortgagor should conform to standards that had been previously agreed upon between the parties. The subdivision plat must be for a particular type of development in which the seller/mortgagee has confidence. The partial release clause should set out partial release prices or a formula for the giving of such releases. The seller should also guard against the release of noncontiguous parcels lest the seller/mortgagee be left with an unsalable checkerboard of land as security for the mortgage.

If there are barns or other buildings on the land being sold, the contract and mortgage should give the developer the right to demolish them. A mortgagee can block demolition of buildings on mortgaged land unless the mortgage provides to the contrary.

17.10 Options

Options are often used in land acquisitions.

> **EXAMPLE:** Buyer plans a site that requires assembly of ten separately owned tracts of land. Buyer hires agents who procure options on all ten tracts of land. If Buyer is unable to obtain options on all ten tracts, Buyer allows all options to lapse. If all ten options are procured, Buyer exercises all options.

17.11 Taxes

Assessors usually assess farmland considerably lower than subdivided land. This suggests that the development proceed in stages, if this is possible. Leave as much as you can in farmland until you are ready to go forward with subdivision and sale. And if you plan a commercial area, postpone platting this until you are ready to build, for the tax assessor will assess commercial land higher than residential land or farmland.

17.12 Leasehold Acquisitions

Obviously, acquisition of a leasehold presents problems different from those involved in acquisition of outright ownership.

> **EXAMPLE:** Condominium Developer acquires a leasehold. He then discovers that local law does not permit condominium developments on leaseholds.

> **EXAMPLE:** Co-op Developer acquires a leasehold and erects a high-class apartment building. He encounters sales resistance. Prospective tenants point out that as the mortgage on the leasehold is reduced by payment, the equity of the apartment owner becomes so substantial that it becomes difficult to sell the apartment for cash and mortgage financing on a co-op is virtually unobtainable. This makes it almost necessary for the ground lease to contain some provision for the landlord joining in the ground lessee's financing. Obviously, there is a problem here.

CHAPTER 18

Co-Ownership—Community Property

18.01   In General

Once people decide to own property jointly, they must decide upon the form of their co-ownership. Should they form an artificial entity—i.e., a corporation, partnership, or trust—or should they hold their property in their own names? If they choose the latter approach, should they own the property as joint tenants or tenants in common? If they are married, what of the impact of tenancy by the entireties, community property, or other laws dealing with marital rights? In determining what form of ownership to use, the parties must consider, among other things, the income tax and estate planning consequences of the various forms of ownership. These decisions are not easily made and are not entirely legal in nature. The law tells the parties the consequences of their actions; the parties must then choose which consequences they want.

As indicated, a person can be the sole owner of a tract of land or may own the land with others. Where there are two or more co-owners they are known as *co-tenants*. There are different kinds of co-ownerships, or co-tenancies, as they are called. Persons may own the land as *joint tenants*, as *tenants by the entireties*, or *as tenants in common*, or *in community property*.

18.02   Joint Tenancy—Tenancy in Common Distinguished

When a deed is made to two or more persons who are not husband and wife and nothing is said in the deed concerning the character of the tenancy created by the deed, the grantees acquire title as tenants in common. That is, on the death of either party, his interest in the real estate will go to his heirs if he dies without leaving a will, or, if he leaves a will, to the persons named therein.

244

> **EXAMPLE:**   Seller conveys land to Brother #1 and Brother #2. Since the deed is not in joint tenancy form, Brother #1 and Brother #2 are tenants in common. Brother #1, a widower, dies without a will, leaving Child #1 and Child #2 as his only children. Brother #2, and Child #1, and Child #2 own the land as tenants in common, Brother #2 owning a half and Child #1 and Child #2 each a fourth.

If, however, the deed runs to two or more persons as joint tenants, a different rule applies. While both joint tenants are alive, they are co-owners of the land, but as soon as one dies, his title passes automatically to the surviving joint tenant.

> **EXAMPLE:**   In the above example, if Brother #1 and Brother #2 held the property in joint tenancy, Brother #2 would have become the sole owner of the property upon the death of Brother #1. Child #1 and Child #2 would have no interest in the property.

Any number of persons may hold real estate in joint tenancy.

> **EXAMPLE:**   Seller makes a deed to *A, B, C,* and *D,* as joint tenants. *D* dies. *A, B,* and *C* now own the land as joint tenants. *A* dies. *B* and *C* own the land as joint tenants. *B* dies. *C* is now the sole owner.

For the impact of community property law on these rules, *see* §18.12 *et seq.*

18.02(a)   Abolition of Survivorship

Some states have enacted laws that purport to abolish the joint tenant's right of survivorship, so that on the death of a joint tenant, his share goes to his heirs or to the persons named in his will, just as if a tenancy in common had been created. See Ariz. Rev. Stat. §33–431; Fla. Stat. Ann. §689.15. However, even in these states, the right of survivorship is not absolutely prohibited. If the deed to the joint owners expressly states that upon the death of one owner, the property shall go to the surviving grantee, the right of survivorship will be enforced. *Chandler* v. *Kountze,* 130 SW2d 327 (Tex. 1939); 69 ALR2d 1058.

18.02(b)   Joint Tenancy—Creation

To create a joint tenancy, a deed must state that the grantees are acquiring title as joint tenants. The actual language used varies somewhat from state to state, but it is best to use comprehensive language in creating a joint tenancy. 46 ALR2d 523.

> **SUGGESTED FORM:**   To *A* and *B* as joint tenants with the right of survivorship, and not as tenants in common or as tenants by the entirety, or as community property.

A deed to persons who are husband and wife poses special problems. It may create a tenancy by the entireties. 32 ALR3d 570. It may create community property. But if it does neither of these things and is not a joint tenancy deed, the husband and wife are tenants in common.

> **EXCEPTION:**   In Wisconsin and New York, a deed to husband and wife creates a joint tenancy unless the deed states otherwise.

A joint tenancy may also be created when the parties have ineffectively attempted to create a tenancy by the entireties.

Rather frequently today we find a husband and wife helping a newly married son or daughter to buy a house. Often the two couples buy a two-apartment dwelling for their joint occupancy, each couple acquiring a one-half interest in the property. The old couple wants their half interest held in joint tenancy, but does not want the young couple to have any interest in the old couple's half. The young people feel the same about their half. Each couple wants its half to be in joint tenancy, so that when one dies the surviving wife or husband will own the entire half interest, but they want a tenancy in common as between the two half interests. To accomplish this, it is best to use two separate joint tenancy form deeds, one going to each couple. Before the land description in each deed, insert, "An undivided one-half interest in . . . " Thus, each couple will have its own deed. If one of the owners dies, the surviving spouse will own a one-half interest in the property as the surviving joint tenant. The others continue to own their half as joint tenants. The two halves are as separate for this purpose as if they were separate tracts of land.

A similar problem results when friendly couples purchase property together.

> **EXAMPLE:**   John Jones and Mary Jones, his wife, and Henry Brown and Susan Brown, his wife, are friends. They decide to invest in real estate and buy a twelve-unit apartment building together. They take title as "John Jones and Mary Jones, as joint tenants as to an undivided one-half interest, and Henry Brown and Susan Brown, as joint tenants as to an undivided one-half interest."

Of course, the parties should have a written agreement spelling out their respective rights and duties. This agreement should address: upkeep and maintenance obligations, occupancy rights of the parties, rights to rents and profits of the property, debt service obligations, buy-out obligations, right of first refusal, and the like.

In states that have abolished survivorship rights in joint tenancies, some special problems exist.

> **EXAMPLE:**   In a state where the law states that the right of survivorship in joint tenancies is abolished, Seller makes a deed to Husband and Wife "as joint tenants with the right of survivorship and not as tenants in common." Husband dies. Wife takes all as the survivor. However, the cases are not in agreement as to the nature of the interest created by the deed. One line of cases says that a joint tenancy was created by agreement of the parties. It becomes an ordinary joint tenancy. In other states it creates an estate for lives with the right of sur-

vivorship. Neither party can sever it by deed as can be done in an ordinary joint tenancy. It is an indestructible right of survivorship. *Anson* v. *Murphy,* 32 NW2d 271 (Neb. 1948); *Bernhard* v. *Bernhard,* 177 So2d 565 (Ala. 1965). Statutes of the type discussed will likely disappear in time. They cause difficulties with common, necessary joint tenancies, such as those in bank accounts.

18.02(b)(1)   The Four Unities

Not every deed that describes the grantees as joint tenants is sufficient to create a joint tenancy. In the creation of a joint tenancy, the four unities of time, title, interest, and possession must be present. That is, the joint tenants must have one and the same interest, acquired by one and the same deed, commencing at one and the same time; and they must hold by one and the same undivided possession.

> **EXAMPLE:**   Owner owned a tract of land. Thereafter, he married and executed a deed to himself and his wife "as joint tenants." No joint tenancy was created by this deed. Owner and his wife did not acquire title at the same time or by the same conveyance, since Owner had owned the land long prior to the making of the deed. The unities of time and title were not present. The deed actually created a tenancy in common. Owner and his wife should have conveyed title to a third person, and this third person should have thereupon reconveyed the title to Owner and his wife as joint tenants. *Deslauriers* v. *Senesac,* 163 NE 327 (Ill. 1928).

Pointless technicalities like these are going out of fashion. Hence, in many states, laws have been passed under which a deed by a landowner to himself and another as joint tenants creates a good joint tenancy. See, e.g., Cal. Civ. Code §683; Ill. Rev. Stat. Ch. 76, §lb.

For reasons relating to community property, dower, and homestead, the landowner's spouse should join in the deed. One often sees a landowner and his wife conveying to themselves as joint tenants, and the whole thing, though odd, is quite legal in most states. 44 ALR2d 605.

When a deed reveals an intention to create a joint tenancy, but fails to for some technical reason, some modern courts tend to show little patience with the old technicalities and give the property to the survivor, even though a true joint tenancy has not been created.

> **EXAMPLE:**   A husband who owned some land in his own individual name signed a deed conveying a half interest in this land to his wife, the deed stating that they were to hold the land as joint tenants. In some states this does not create a valid joint tenancy, for the four unities are lacking. Nevertheless, on the death of the husband the court awarded the entire property to the surviving wife. *Runions* v. *Runions,* 207 SW2d 1016 (Tenn. 1948). There can be a right of survivorship even though the land is not owned in joint tenancy, which is something of a subtle distinction but has the happy result of achieving what the parties wanted.

It is impossible to make a deed to *A* of a one-fourth interest in the land and to *B* of a three-fourths interest to hold as joint tenants. A deed creating joint tenancies must give the joint tenants equal shares as to the property conveyed in joint tenancy. This does not prevent a joint tenant from owning a different and distinct interest in the land.

EXAMPLE: *X* conveys a half interest to *A* and a half interest to *A* and *B* as joint tenants. This is perfectly valid. *In re Galletto's Estate,* 171 P2d 152 (Cal. 1946).

18.02(c)   Severance of Joint Tenancy

There is nothing sacred about a joint tenancy. Either joint tenant has the right to break the joint tenancy as he wishes. 64 ALR2d 918. Certain actions will break the joint tenancy and convert it into a tenancy in common even against the wishes or without the knowledge of the other parties.

1. A conveyance by a joint tenant to a third party destroys the joint tenancy.

EXAMPLE: *A* conveys to *B* and *C* in joint tenancy. *C* conveys his half of title to *D. D* thereafter conveys this interest back to *C. C* dies. His title passes to his heirs, not to *B.* The conveyance from *C* to *D* severed or terminated the joint tenancy. The joint tenancy was not revived by the reconveyance. At *C's* death, *B* and *C* were holding title as tenants in common. *Szymczak v. Szymczak,* 138 NE 218 (Ill. 1923). It is not necessary that *B* be informed of the fact that *C* is breaking the joint tenancy. *Burke v. Stevens,* 70 Cal. Reptr. 87 (1968).

In some states, where a deed runs to *A* and *B* as joint tenants with the right of survivorship, neither joint tenant alone is permitted to sever the joint tenancy.

Where there are three or more joint tenants, and only one makes a deed to a third party or to one of the other joint tenants, some highly technical problems are encountered.

EXAMPLE: *A, B,* and *C* own land as joint tenants. *C* conveys his third to *D. A* and *B* continue to hold their two-thirds as joint tenants. *Morgan v. Catherwood,* 167 NE 618 (Ind. 1929); *Hammond v. McArthur,* 183 P2d 1 (Cal. 1947).

EXAMPLE: *A, B,* and *C* own land in joint tenancy. *A* conveys to *B* by quit-claim deed. *B* and *C* continue to own a two-third interest in the land in joint tenancy, and *B* owns a one-third interest as tenant in common. *Shelton v. Vance,* 234 P2d 1012 (Cal. 1951); *Jackson v. O'Connell,* 177 NE2d 194 (Ill. 1961).

EXAMPLE: *A, B,* and *C* own land in joint tenancy. *C* conveys one-twentieth of his interest to *X. A* and *B* continue to own their two thirds in joint tenancy. *C* and *X* are tenants in common. *Giles v. Sheridan,* 137 NW2d 828 (Neb. 1968); Swenson & Degnan, *Severance of Joint Tenancies,* 38 Minn. L. Rev. 466, 472 (1954). This severance occurs notwithstanding the fact that the deed was not recorded. *Carmack v. Place,* 535 P2d 197 (Colo. 1975).

2. An involuntary transfer of title will sever a joint tenancy.

EXAMPLE: *A* and *B* hold title as joint tenants. *A* goes into bankruptcy. Under the old bankruptcy law, title to all of *A's* property was automatically transferred to the bankruptcy trustee. This transfer severed the joint tenancy. *In re Victor,* 218 F.Supp. 218 (S.D. 111. 1963). Whether the same result will follow under the new bankruptcy law is not entirely clear. Rather than transferring the debtor's property to the bankruptcy trustee, the new law creates a bankruptcy estate when the bankruptcy case has begun. 11 USC §541.

The actions of creditors of one of the joint tenants can also sever the tenancy.

EXAMPLE: *A* and *B* hold title as joint tenants. Creditor obtains a judgment against *A,* and a sheriff's sale is held to obtain money to pay the judgment. Buyer purchases the property at the sheriff's sale and obtains a sheriff's deed. This severs the joint tenancy. Buyer and *B* now hold as tenants in common. However, the rendition of a judgment against one joint tenant and the making of a levy on his interest will not sever a joint tenancy. *Van Antwerp* v. *Horan,* 61 NE2d 358 (Ill. 1945); *Hammond* v. *McArthur,* 183 P2d 1 (Cal. 1947); *Eder* v. *Rothamel,* 85 A2d 860 (Md. 1953). It has even been held that a sheriff's sale under such a judgment does not sever the joint tenancy and that the joint tenancy is not severed until a sheriff's deed issues. If the joint tenant against whom the judgment was rendered dies before the sheriff's deed issues, the other joint tenant takes all the property free and clear of the judgment creditor's rights. *Jackson* v. *Lacey,* 97 NE2d 839 (Ill. 1951)

3. In title and intermediate states, a mortgage executed by one of the joint tenants severs the joint tenancy, notwithstanding the fact that the mortgage is subsequently paid and released by the mortgagee. 64 ALR2d 918. *But see Harms* v. *Sprague,* 473 *NE2d 930 (Ill. 1984).*

REFERENCE: Mattis, *Severance of Joint Tenancies by Mortgages: A Contextual Approach,* 1 So Ill. U. L. J. 27 (1977).

EXAMPLE: *A* and *B* hold title as joint tenants. *A* executes a mortgage on his half of the title and thereafter pays off the mortgage, which is released. Thereafter, *B* dies. *B's* half of the title passes to his heirs, not to *A. A's* mortgage severed the joint tenancy.

But a mortgage executed by both joint tenants does not sever the joint tenancy.

EXAMPLE: *A* and *B* hold title as joint tenants. They both join in a mortgage. Thereafter, *A* dies. *B* takes title as the surviving joint tenant. 64 ALR2d 918, 935. In a lien state, a mortgage signed by one joint tenant is extinguished as a lien against joint tenancy property upon the death of the joint tenant. *D.A.D. Inc.,* v. *Moring,* 218 So2d 451 (Fla. 1969); *Harms* v. *Sprague,* 473 NE2d 930 (Ill. 1984).

4. A contract by one joint tenant to sell or convey his interest in the land to a third person will operate as a severance of the joint tenancy. *Naiburg* v. *Hendricksen,* 19 NE2d 348 (Ill. 1939); 39 ALR 4th 1068.
5. If one joint tenant files a partition suit against the other, and a partition decree is

entered, the joint tenancy is severed. *Schuck* v. *Schuck,* 108 NE2d 905 (Ill. 1952); *Hammond* v. *McArthur,* 183 P2d 1 (Cal. 1947).

6. A husband and wife own land in joint tenancy. One files a divorce suit against the other. A divorce decree is entered. It orders the land sold and the proceeds of sale divided between them. The joint tenancy is severed. *Baade* v. *Ratner,* 359 P2d 877 (Kans. 1961). Indeed, if a husband and wife own land in joint tenancy and they enter into a separation agreement providing that the land will be sold when the divorce decree is entered and the proceeds of sale divided between them, this agreement will sever the joint tenancy. *Carson* v. *Ellis,* 348 P2d 807 (Kans. 1960).

7. A simple, written, signed, and recorded declaration by one joint tenant that the tenancy has been severed has been held sufficient to terminate the joint tenancy, thereby converting it into a tenancy in common. *Hendrickson* v. *Minneapolis Fed. S. & L. Assn., 161 NW2d 688 (Minn. 1968).*

8. Any agreement between the joint tenants that shows an intention to treat the land as a tenancy in common will cause a severance. 64 ALR2d 941.

9. In one or two states the making of a lease by one joint tenant severs the joint tenancy. *Alexander* v. *Boyer,* 253 A2d 359 (Md. 1969).

There are other events that do *not* break the joint tenancy:

1. A will by the deceased joint tenants.

EXAMPLE: *A* and *B* own land as joint tenants. *A* makes a will giving all his property to *C. A* dies. *B* takes all the joint tenancy property, and *C* gets no part of it. *A's* will does not break a joint tenancy. *Eckardt* v. *Osborne,* 170 NE 774 (Ill. 1930).

2. A lien created against one of the joint tenants.

EXAMPLE: *A* and *B* own land as joint tenants. *A* judgment lien, internal revenue lien, or other lien is filed against *A* only. *A* dies before he has lost his title through enforcement of the lien. *B* takes the entire title free and clear of the lien. In other words, if *A* is a joint tenant, a lien against him attaches not to the land but to *A's interest in the land,* which is an interest that will be totally extinguished if *A* dies before *B* does, so long as the parties are joint tenants when *A* dies. One who has a lien on *A's* interest ordinarily can have no greater rights than *A* has, and if *A's* rights will be extinguished by his breach, so will the lien. 134 ALR 957.

3. A contract to sell the property which is executed by both joint tenants. *But see In re Baker's Estate,* 78 NW 2d 863 (Iowa, 1956), criticized in Kratovil, *Joint Tenancies and "Creative Financing"—the Land Contract,* 5 U. Ark. Little Rock L. J. 475 (1982). See 39 ALR 4th 1068. Law here is unclear.

4. An easement created by one joint tenant only.

EXAMPLE: *A* and *B* own land as joint tenants. *A* alone signs an easement grant to *C,* and *A* dies before *B* does. *B* then owns the entire title free and clear of the easement.

5. Dower and curtesy of a spouse of a deceased joint tenant.

EXAMPLE: If *A* and *B,* both married men, own land as joint tenants, and *A* dies first, his wife has no dower in the land because at *A's* death all his title to the land is extinguished, leaving nothing to which dower can attach.

6. Divorce. State laws differ on the subject of divorce.

EXAMPLE: In some states, a divorce does not break a joint tenancy. Where no specific law exists, if *H* and *W* own land as joint tenants, are divorced, and if nothing is said in the divorce decree about the property, the joint tenancy is unbroken. Suppose that *H* thereafter marries another person, *X. H* dies before *W* does. *W,* the former wife of *H,* takes the entire property, and *X* takes nothing. *H* could have prevented this by breaking the joint tenancy by deed. On the other hand, in some states the entry of a divorce decree automatically converts the joint tenancy into a tenancy in common. This is by virtue of special laws.

7. The making of a lease by one of two joint tenants does not sever the joint tenancy. *Tindall* v. *Yeats,* 64 NE2d 903 (Ill. 1946). See Note 7 Baylor L. Rev. 97 (1955); Comment 25 Cal. L. Rev. 203 (1937).

8. One joint tenant files a partition suit against the other, but one of them dies before a partition decree is entered. The survivor takes all as surviving joint tenant. 129 ALR 813.

9. A deed by one joint tenant to himself does not sever the joint tenancy because it is nothing but an empty ceremony. *Clark* v. *Carter,* 70 Cal. Reptr. 923 (1968), and the contrary has also been held. *Minonk State Bank* v. *Grassman,* 432 NE2d 386 (Ill. 1982). See 7 ALR4th 1268.

10. Where one of two joint tenants grants a life estate to another this does not sever the joint tenancy. *Hammond* v. *McArthur,* 183 P2d 1 (Cal. 1947).

11. The mere granting of an option to purchase one joint tenant does not sever the joint tenancy. *Alexander* v. *Boyer,* 253 A2d 359 (Md. 1969).

REFERENCE: *Severing Joint Property Interests,* 16 Real Prop., Prob. & Tr. J. 435 (1981).

18.02(d)   Disadvantages of a Joint Tenancy

Rather frequently, when title is held in joint tenancy by a husband and wife and one of them dies, the survivor, impressed with the simplicity of transfer of ownership on the death of a joint tenant, ponders the advisability of creating a new joint tenancy in which the surviving spouse will be joint tenant with one of the spouse's children. This has certain disadvantages. Such a deed cannot be unmade without the consent of both parties. Suppose that the surviving spouse and the child named as joint tenant quarrel, which is not uncommon. Indeed, the mere fact that the parties share ownership of the real estate seems to trigger quarrels. The child may file a partition suit and put property up for sale. Thus the surviving spouse may find himself or herself without a place to live. Perhaps judgments may be rendered against the child, and creditors will force the property to a sale. Many lawyers counsel the surviving joint tenant to avoid setting up a joint tenancy such as this. Where a will is made, it can always be changed. It gives no one any right in the property until the landowner dies. Perhaps this may strike a cynical note, but the fact remains that when there is a will rather than a deed, there is much less likelihood of family quarrels.

18.02(e)   Joint Tenancy—Creditors' Rights

A judgment or other lien creditor against one joint tenant's interest is in a somewhat fragile position. If the lien is not transformed into ownership, as for example by an execution sale, before the death of the debtor joint tenant, the interest of the lienor is cut off. The deceased joint tenant's interest vests in the surviving joint tenant free of the lien. To an opposite effect, if the other joint tenants die before the debtor joint tenant, the lien will spread to the entire fee interest that vests in the surviving debtor joint tenant upon the death of the other joint tenants.

> **EXAMPLE:**   *A* and *B* own Blackacre as joint tenants. Creditor obtains a judgment lien against *A*. The following results are possible: (1) if *A* dies before levy and execution sale, Creditor's lien is extinguished and *B* acquires Blackacre free of Creditor's lien; (2) if *B* dies before levy and execution sale, *A* owns a 100 percent interest in Blackacre which is entirely subject to Creditor's lien; (3) if Creditor levies, executes, and purchases at the execution sale, the joint tenancy is severed and Creditor and *B* own undivided one-half interests in Blackacre.

18.03   Tenancy by the Entireties—In General

In many states a form of joint tenancy, known as tenancy by the entireties, exists. This tenancy exists only where the co-owners are husband and wife, and is based upon the common law notion that they are one person, and each are holders of the entire estate. Unlike a joint tenancy, no words are necessary to create such a tenancy.

> **EXAMPLE:**   In a tenancy by the entireties state, *X* makes a deed to *H* and *W*, husband and wife. Nothing is said as to the character of their co-ownership. They are tenants by the entireties.

> **EXCEPTION:**   In some tenancy by the entireties states, laws have been passed stating that the deed must expressly show an intention to create a tenancy by the entireties.

Tenancy by the entireties resembles joint tenancy in that upon the death of either husband or wife the survivor automatically acquires title to the share of the deceased spouse.

Tenancy by the entireties differs from joint tenancy in that neither spouse has the power to defeat or sever the tenancy by any deed or mortgage to a stranger made without the signature of the other spouse. *Hoffman* v. *Newell,* 60 SW2d 607 (Ky. 1932).

> **EXAMPLE:** A deed is made to a husband and wife, nothing being said as to the character of their tenancy. Thereafter, the husband makes a deed that purports to convey his interest in the land to X. The wife does not join in this deed. Thereafter, the husband dies. The wife now has full title to all the land. X has nothing.

However, a deed by both husband and wife will, of course, give the grantee good title.

As long as the marriage exists neither spouse may have a partition of the estate by the entireties. *Lawrence* v. *Lawrence,* 190 A2d 206 (N.J. 1963).

> **EXAMPLE:** A and B hold property as *tenants in common.* If they disagree upon the disposition of the property, they can ask the court either to physically divide the property between them (this is called partition in kind) or sell the property and divide the proceeds. This relief is not available to *tenants by the entireties.*

> **EXAMPLE:** Where H and W hold property as *tenants by the entireties* and W sues H for divorce, H can ask that the court, but only if a divorce is allowed, to divide the property or sell it and divide the proceeds. *Bastians v. Bastians,* 321 NYS2d 480 (1971).

Tenancy by the entireties is not recognized in community property states.

18.03(a)   Creation of Tenancy by the Entireties

In the states where tenancies by the entireties are recognized, there is much difference of opinion as to the legal effect of a deed to a husband and wife that describes the grantees as joint tenants. In some states such a deed creates a joint tenancy rather than a tenancy by the entireties. *Witzel* v. *Witzel,* 386 P2d 103 (Wyo. 1963). But in most of the states that recognize tenancies, such deeds are held to create a tenancy by the entireties. *Hoag* v. *Hoag,* 99 NE 521 (Mass. 1912); 161 ALR 470. If a joint tenancy is desired, the deed should always state that the grantees are "joint tenants and not tenants in common or by the entireties." This should avoid litigation over the issue.

However, when a deed to a husband and wife describes them "as tenants in common," such a deed is almost universally regarded as creating a good tenancy in common rather than a tenancy by the entireties.

For the creation of a tenancy by the entireties, it is necessary that the grantees be husband and wife. If they are not husband and wife, even express language in the deed declaring an intention to create a tenancy by the entireties will not create such a tenancy.

In many states a landowner who marries is permitted to give a deed to himself and his spouse as tenants by the entireties. The more traditional format used to accomplish this end is for the landowner and spouse to deed the property to a nominee who in turn deeds the property back to the landowner and his new spouse.

18.03(b)   Defective Tenancy by the Entireties as Creating a Joint Tenancy

Tenancy by the entireties exists only as between husband and wife. A deed to parties who are not husband and wife creates some other kind of tenancy even though a tenancy by the entireties is specified. 9 ALR 4th 1189.

> **EXAMPLE:**   A deed to *A* and *B,* who claimed to be, but were not, husband and wife, recited that it was made to them as tenants by the entireties and not as tenants in common. Since this revealed a general intention to create survivorship rights, but could not create a tenancy by the entireties, the parties not being husband and wife, the court held that a joint tenancy was created. Kepner, *The Effect of an Attempted Creation of An Estate by the Entirety in Un-married Persons,* 6 Rutgers L. Rev. 550 (1952); Note 37 Notre D. Law 441 (1962); Note 37 Cornell L. Q. 316 (1952).

> **EXAMPLE:**   In New Hampshire and Wisconsin, which do not recognize tenancy by the entireties, a deed to husband and wife "as tenants by the entireties" creates a joint tenancy. *In re Ray's Will,* 205 NW 917 (Wis. 1925); 1 ALR2d 247.

> **EXAMPLE:**   A deed to two sisters "as tenants by the entireties" has been held to create a joint tenancy. *In re Richardson's Estate,* 282 NW 585 (Wis. 1938). Likewise this was true where the deed was to two brothers. *Penn. Bank & Tr. Co.* v. *Thompson,* 247 A2d 771 (Pa. 1968).

However, in most states a deed to *H* and *W,* describing them as tenants by the entireties or as husband and wife, creates only a tenancy in common if they are, in fact, not married. *Pierce* v. *Hall,* 355 P2d 259 (Oreg. 1960); 9 ALR4th 1189.

> **EXAMPLE:**   A deed was made to Charles Smith and Julia Smith, *husband and wife.* Actually they were not married. Julia died. Charles, describing himself as a "surviving spouse," made a deed to a purchaser. Then three sisters of Julia appeared and claimed her half of the property as her heirs. They succeeded. Only a tenancy in common existed and Charles was not even an heir. *Thurmond* v. *McGrath,* 334 NYS2d 917 (1972).

18.03(c)   Tenancy by the Entireties—Deeds Between Spouses

Suppose a husband or wife owns land in his or her own name, or they own land as tenants in common. They wish to put the land in their names as tenants by entireties. The traditional way of accomplishing this is to have the husband and wife join in a deed to a nominee, and such nominee then deeds the land back to the husband and wife as tenants by the entireties. Just as in the case of joint tenancies, the old rule is: In order to have good tenancy by the entireties, the husband and wife must acquire title by the same deed, and the dummy convey-ance satisfies this requirement.

Just as in the case of joint tenancies, recent laws and court decisions allow a husband or wife to create a tenancy by the entireties without deeding out to a dummy. In these states, if the husband owns land and wishes to create a tenancy by the entireties with his wife, he makes out a deed running to himself and his wife "as tenants by the entireties, and not as joint tenants or as tenants in common." Phipps, *Tenancy by Entireties,* 25 Temple L. Q. 24, 43 (1952); 44 ALR2d 598. For reasons relating to dower and homestead, the wife should join in this deed as co-grantor.

However, in a few other states it has been held that it is still necessary, if a good tenancy by the entireties is to be created, that the husband landowner and his wife join in a deed to a third person, who thereupon conveys to the husband and wife. This practice should be followed unless it is clear that your state has abolished the need for a third-party conveyance.

When land is held in tenancy by the entireties, a deed by the husband to the wife gives her good title even though she does not join in the deed to herself. The same is true of a deed by the wife to the husband. 8 ALR2d 634.

18.03(d)   Tenancy by the Entireties—Deeds, Mortgages, Leases, Rents, and Brokers' Listings

As a rule, a deed or mortgage of property owned in tenancy by the entireties must be signed by both husband and wife.

In most states, when a tenancy by the entirety exists, a deed to a stranger signed by the husband or wife alone is void. Phipps. *Tenancy by Entireties,* 25 Temple L. Q. 24, 46 (1952). In a few states the deed is given some effect, but the effect varies from state to state. It may grant a share of the rents or may be operative if the grantor survives the other spouse. In any event, in all states the deed becomes void if the spouse who did not join in the deed survives the spouse who conveyed.

Both parties should sign any lease. In many tenancy by the entirety states, husband and wife have equal rights to rents and possession, and any lease must be signed by both. Phipps, *Tenancy by Entireties,* 25 Temple L. Q. 26,46, (1952); 141 ALR 202.

Certainly this is the impact of new laws designed to equalize the rights of the wife and those of the husband. Mich. Stat. Ann. §26.210(1).

If the husband alone lists property with a real estate broker for sale, he will be liable for a commission if the broker finds a buyer. It is no defense that the wife failed to sign. *Taub* v. *Shampanier,* 112 Atl 322 (N.J. 1921).

REFERENCE: Phipps, *Tenancy by Entireties,* 25 Temple L. Q. 24 (1952); *Koster* v. *Boudreaux,* 463 NE2d 39 (Ohio App. 1982) reviews this law nationwide.

18.03(e)   Tenancy by the Entireties—Creditor's Rights

In most tenancy by the entireties states, a judgment creditor of either husband or wife alone can acquire no rights by a sheriff's sale of the land. Since neither husband nor wife alone can make a voluntary sale of his or her interest in the land, an involuntary or forced sale of the interest of either husband or wife alone cannot be valid. 75 ALR2d 1175. In a few states, a husband's interest can be sold by the sheriff under a judgment against the husband alone, but the sheriff's deed will automatically become void if the wife survives the husband. The wife then remains the sole owner, free of the judgment. Phipps, *Tenancy by Entireties*, 25 Temple L. Q. 24, 39 (1952); 75 ALR2d 1183.

Of course, if the judgment is against both husband and wife, the land may be sold by the sheriff, provided it is not their homestead.

As above stated, in most of the tenancy by entirety states, the rents of the land belong to the husband and wife jointly. Therefore a creditor of either the husband or wife alone cannot reach the rents, income, or crops of the land.

> **EXCEPTIONS:**   In some states, creditors of either the husband or wife are allowed to reach the debtor's share of the rents, income, or crops of the land. In other states, creditors of the husband, but not those of the wife, may reach all the income of the land held in tenancy by the entireties while the tenancy continues. Phipps, *Tenancy by Entireties,* 25 Temple L. Q. 24, 39 (1952). See 8 Rutgers Camden L. J. 707, 714; 1 Wayne L. Rev. 105.

18.03(f)   Tenancy by the Entireties—Divorce

A divorce converts a tenancy by the entireties into a tenancy in common. Some states, however, have an opposite rule, which holds that divorce changes a tenancy by the entireties to a joint tenancy with the right of survivorship. *Shepherd* v. *Shepherd,* 336 So2d 497 (Miss. 1976).

18.04   Murder—Joint Tenancies and Tenancies by the Entireties

When one joint tenant or tenant by the entireties murders his co-tenant and later is convicted of such murder in a court trial, one of three results is possible.

> 1. The murderer will, despites his crime, take the entire property by virtue of his right of survivorship. This is a bad rule that is certainly doomed to disappear.
> 2. The murderer, because of his crime, loses all his interest in the property, and the heirs of the murdered co-owner take the entire property. *Vesey* v. *Vesey,* 54 NW2d 385 (Minn. 1952); *In re King's Estate*, 52 NW2d 885 (Wis. 1952).
> 3. The murder is regarded, in legal effect, as converting the tenancy into a tenancy in common, so that the murderer retains his half interest, and the heirs of the murdered co-tenant take the other half. This rule is followed in most states. *Abbey* v. *Lord,* 336 P2d 226 (Cal. 1959); *Bradley* v. *Fox,* 129 NE2d 699 (Ill. 1955); Note, 5 DePaul L. Rev. 316 (1956).

Of course, if in the murder trial the killer is acquitted—on the ground of self-defense, for example—the killing is not murder but justifiable homicide, and the survivor will take the entire property even though he caused the death of his co-tenant.

18.05   Contracts of Sale—Joint Tenancies and Tenancies by the Entireties

A contract to sell property owned in tenancy by the entireties obviously should be signed by both husband and wife. If it is not, the buyer will be unable to obtain specific performance, though the seller who signed might be liable for damages. *Cartwright* v. *Giacosa,* 390 SW2d 204 (Tenn. 1965).

In tenancy by the entireties states, when a landowner signs a contract to sell his land to a husband and wife, the buyers hold the contract interest as tenant by the entireties, so that if either dies the deal is closed, the seller's deed should be made to the survivor. *Comfort* v. *Robinson,* 118 NW 943 (Mich. 1908).

If the state does not recognize tenancy by the entireties or community property, a contract to sell land to *H* and *W,* who are husband and wife, creates a tenancy in common in the contract interest. If *H* dies, his contract interest passes to his heirs or devisees, and the seller must not make the deed to *W* alone. Obviously when an installment contract is involved, it may take years to pay up, and the death of one of the buyers is a distinct possibility.

> **SUGGESTED FORM:** To avoid the endless complications of tenancy in common or necessity of probate, suggest to buyers that they agree to buy the land "as joint tenants with the right of survivorship, and not as tenants in common nor by the entireties nor as community property."

Of course if land is owned in joint tenancy, all owners must join as sellers in any contract to sell the land.

Where a husband and wife enter into a contract to sell their land, and one of them dies before the purchase price is fully paid, questions arise as to who gets the balance of the purchase price, the surviving spouse or the estate of the decedent. Where the sellers held the land in joint tenancy or tenancy by the entireties some courts hold that the right to the money goes to the survivor just as though there were a right of survivorship as to the contract price. *Watson* v. *Watson,* 126 NE2d 220 (Ill. 1955); *Hewitt* v. *Biege,* 327 P2d 872 (Kans. 1958); *DeYoung* v. *Mesler,* 130 NW2d 38 (Mich. 1964). *In re Maguire's Estate,* 296 NYS 528 (1937); Kratovil, *Joint Tenancies & Creative Financing,* 5 U. of Ark. Little Rock L. Rev. 475 (1982).

> **EXAMPLE:** *H* and *W,* joint tenants, enter into a contract to sell their land to *X.* After a few payments are made on the contract, *H* dies leaving a will giving all his property to children by a former marriage. *W* will get the entire remainder of the purchase price.

There are cases taking a contrary view.

> **EXAMPLE:** *H* and *W,* joint tenants, entered into a contract to sell land. *H* dies. His heirs got his share of the sale price. In a few states sale proceeds are treated as though held in tenancy in common. *Register of Wills* v. *Madine,* 219 A2d 245 (Md. 1966). *In re Baker's Estate,* 78 NW2d 863 (Iowa 1956); *Buford* v. *Dahlke,* 62 NW2d 252 (Neb. 1954).

EXAMPLE: *H* and *W*, tenants by the entireties, entered into a contract to sell land. *H* died. His heirs got his share of the purchase price. *Panushka* v. *Panushka,* 349 P2d 450 (Oreg. 1960); Note, 14 Vand. L. Rev. 687 (1961). This result is dictated by the rule in some tenancy by the entireties states which do not recognize this type of tenancy in money or *personal property.*

Once again, the sellers can take the uncertainty out of this eventuality by agreeing in advance as to the disposition of these proceeds.

Of course once the money has been paid by the buyer to the sellers, the cash money, even if held intact by the sellers in a joint safe-deposit box, is owned by them in tenancy in common. *Ill. Public Aid Commission.* v. *Stille,* 153 NE2d 59 (Ill. 1958).

Suppose that the sellers are tenants by the entireties. They give a deed to the buyer and take back a purchase money mortgage. Some states hold that the mortgage is owned as tenants by the entireties. *Ciconte* v. *Barba,* 161 Atl. 925 (Del. 1932). Others hold that the mortgage is owned in tenancy in common. 64 ALR2d 8; 22 ALR4th 459.

The problem extends even to condemnation awards.

EXAMPLE: *H* and *W* owned land in tenancy by the entireties. The city condemned the land and deposited $100,000 as a condemnation award. *H* died. *W* takes the entire award as the surviving tenant by the entireties. *H's* other heirs take nothing. *Smith* v. *Tipping,* 211 NE2d 231 (Mass. 1965); *In re Idlewild Airport,* 85 NYS2d 617 (1948).

Community property states present special problems.

EXAMPLE: In a community property state, *H* and *W*, joint tenants, entered into a contract to sell land. The proceeds of sale are community property. *Smith* v. *Tang,* 412 P2d 697 (Ariz. 1966).

The problem also exists with respect to the proceeds of fire insurance policies.

The better rule is that the money goes to the survivor. Had the parties been asked about this when they received their deed, virtually all would have been astonished to hear any question raised as to the right of the survivor to get the money. This intention ought to be controlling.

SUGGESTION: Let the contract read that the price is payable to the sellers *as joint tenants with the right of survivorship and not as tenants in common* nor *as tenants by the entireties nor as community property.*

Suppose that a contract of sale names the buyers as joint tenants. Their rights *as between themselves* are established as soon as the contract is signed.

EXAMPLE: Seller contracts to sell a home to Husband and Wife, as joint tenants. Husband persuades Seller to make the deed run to Husband only. Wife discovers this. She is entitled to a court order reforming the deed to run to

Husband and Wife as joint tenants. *Remus* v. *Schwass,* 406 Ill. 63, 92 NE2d 127 (1950).

18.06   Tenancy in Common

Co-owners who are not joint tenants, tenants by the entireties, or owners of community property are tenants in common. Their shares need not be equal. For example, one co-owner may have an undivided one-tenth interest and the other the remaining undivided nine-tenths interest. They need not have acquired their titles at the same time or by the same instrument.

Tenants in common are entitled to share the possession and rents of the property according to their shares in the property. Except for their sharing of possession and rents, however, the situation is almost as if each tenant in common owned a separate piece of real estate. Each tenant in common may convey or mortgage his share, and the share of each tenant in common is subject to the lien of judgments against him.

Upon the death of a tenant in common, his share goes to his heirs or the parties named in his will. Also, only the decedent's share of the property is included in his estate.

18.07   Partition

If tenants in common, or joint tenants, for that matter, wish to terminate their joint possession of the land, any of the co-tenants may file a suit to partition the real estate. The court will appoint commissioners to divide the land into separate tracts according to the shares of the co-tenants, so that each will become the sole owner of the tract set aside for him. If the land cannot be divided in this manner, the court will order the land sold and will divide the proceeds of the sale among the co-tenants according to their respective interest.

> **EXAMPLE:**   *A* dies owning a tract of land improved with a single-family dwelling and leaving no widow and no will, but leaving as his heirs a son, *B,* and two grandchildren, *C* and *D,* who are children of a deceased son, *E. B* owns one-half of the title, and *C* and *D* own one-fourth each. *B* files a partition suit against *C* and *D*. The court finds, as it obviously must, that the land cannot be divided among the three tenants in common. It orders the land sold at public auction, whereupon the same is sold to *F,* the highest bidder, for $6,000. *B* receives $3,000 from the proceeds of the sale, and *C* and *D* each receive $1,500.

Partition can, of course, be accomplished by the voluntary action of all co-owners without the necessity of court proceedings. Frequently this is impossible, since many co-ownerships involve minor heirs, who cannot participate in voluntary partition.

As a rule, community property and land held in tenancy by the entireties are not subject to partition during the continuance of the marriage. *Stanley* v. *Mueller,* 350 P2d 880 (Oreg. 1960); *Lawrence* v. *Lawrence,* 190 A2d 206 (N.J. 1963).

18.08 Rights and Obligations of Co-owners

Co-owners must, as a rule, contribute ratably toward payment of taxes, special assessments, mortgages, and repairs of the property. 48 ALR2d 1305. If one co-owner, through refusal of the other co-owners to contribute, is compelled to pay more than his share of the necessary expenses, he thereby acquires a lien analogous to a mortgage lien on the shares of the other co-owners, and he may foreclose such lien if they persist in their refusal to contribute. *Calcagni* v. *Cirino,* 14 A2d 803 (R.I. 1940). But one co-owner cannot purchase the property at a mortgage foreclosure sale or tax sale of the land and thus acquire a title that would enable him to oust the other co-owners. The title thus acquired is acquired for the benefit of all co-owners if they seasonably contribute their respective proportions of the expense incurred by the tenant who purchased the outstanding title. *Laura* v. *Christian,* 537 P2d 1389 (N.M. 1976).

If one co-owner collects all the rents but does not himself occupy the land, he must account to the other co-owners for their share of the rents. *Thompson* v. *Flynn,* 58 P2d 769 (Mont. 1936). A few states have laws making a co-owner liable to the other co-owners for rent where he alone occupies the land, collecting no rent therefrom. *Hazard* v. *Albro,* 20 Atl. 834 (R.I. 1890). But in many states, a co-owner who personally occupies the premises and does not rent them out is not liable to the other co-owners for the rental value of the premises unless he has agreed to pay them rent or has forcibly kept them out of possession. *Burk* v. *Burk,* 22 So2d 609 (Ala. 1945). But a co-owner who exclusively possesses the premises must bear the entire burden of taxes, repairs, and mortgage interest payments. *Clute* v. *Clute,* 90 NE 988 (N.Y. 1910).

18.09 Grants by One Co-tenant

Obviously, a mortgage signed by only one of the co-owners does not bind the others. It creates a lien only on the interest of the one who signs. *Rostan* v. *Huggins,* 5 SE2d 162 (N.C. 1939). Likewise, a judgment, federal lien, or other lien against one of the co-owners creates no lien on the shares of the others. The lessee of one co-tenant becomes, for the term of the lease, a co-tenant of the nonjoining owners. *Garland* v. *Holston Oil Co.,* 386 SW2d 914 (Tenn. 1965). The actions of the nonjoining co-tenants may amount to a ratification, thereby estopping them from denying the validity of the lease even as against their interest.

> **EXAMPLE:**   *H* and *W* owned recreational property. *H* leased the property to *T. W* knew of lease renewals and received some rent payments. The court held that *W* acquiesced in *H's* leasing of the property and was estopped from denying the validity of the lease. *Gleason* v. *Tompkins,* 375 NYS2d 247 (1976).

18.10 Bankruptcy of Co-tenant

Where land is owned by two or more persons in any kind of co-tenancy, and one of the co-tenants goes bankrupt, the bankruptcy court has the power to sell all of the property. 11 USC § 363(h). The obvious reason is that it is almost impossible to sell a fractional interest in property. Because of this eventuality, great care must be used in selecting co-owners.

18.11   Federal Tax Liens

Where two or more persons own land as co-tenants, and a federal lien (for unpaid income tax, for example) is filed against one co-tenant, the federal government may force a sale of the entire property. *United States* v. *Rodgers,* 76 L.Ed.2d 236 (1983). The nondelinquent spouse is entitled to so much of the sale proceeds as represents complete compensation for the loss of its interest, the government will receive the amount of the tax delinquency, and the balance, if any, will be distributed to the delinquent taxpayer and others having an interest in the property. Again, this is evidence that one must use care in choosing investment partners. However, in most states where tenancy by the entireties is recognized, and a creditor of one spouse cannot reach any share of the property, the federal lien does not attach at all if it is against only one spouse. Plumb, *Federal Tax Liens* 37 (3d ed. 1972).

18.12   Community Property—In General

The community property system is of Spanish origin and obtains in states that were subject to Spanish influence, namely, Arizona, California, Idaho, Louisiana, Nevada, New Mexico, Texas, and Washington. The law of these states recognizes two kinds of property that may belong to the spouses in case of marriage—the *separate property* and the *community property.* The separate property of either husband or wife is what he or she owned at the time of marriage and what he or she acquired during marriage by inheritance, will, or gift. The separate property of each spouse is wholly free from all interest or claim on the part of the other and is entirely under the management and control, whether by deed, mortgage, will, or otherwise, of the spouse to whom it belongs. All other property is community property.

18.12(a)   Theory of Community Property

It is the theory in these states that the husband and wife should share equally in property acquired by their joint efforts during marriage. Thus the husband is as much entitled to share equally in acquisitions by the wife through her industry as she is entitled to share equally in acquisitions by the husband, and each spouse owns one-half of all that is earned or gained, even though one earned or gained more than the other or actually earned or gained nothing. *See* Cal. Civ. Code § 5105.

18.12(b) Property Acquired During the Marriage

Property *purchased* with separate funds is the separate property of the purchaser, whereas property purchased with community funds is community property.

Property acquired by *purchase* during the marriage is ordinarily presumed to vest in the husband and wife as community property, regardless of whether the deed is made to the husband, wife, or both. Under the community property system, the ownership of property does not depend upon the question of who happens to be named as grantee in the deed.

In California prior to January 1, 1975, and in New Mexico prior to July 1, 1973, it was provided that real estate conveyed to a married woman in her separate name was presumed to be her separate property. So far as the husband and wife are concerned, this presumption can be destroyed by proof that the property was purchased with community funds and that the placing of title in the wife's name was not made with the intention of making a gift to her. Such property is community property. But the presumption that the property is the separate property of the wife and can be sold or mortgaged without the husband's signature is conclusive in favor of purchasers and mortgagees dealing with the wife in good faith and for a valuable consideration. *Fulkerson* v. *Stiles,* 105 Pac. 966 (Cal. 1909).

In most community property states a husband and wife may by agreement change the status of property from separate to community property or from community to separate property. Income tax returns are often received as evidence of such agreements.

A deed by the husband to the wife raises a presumption that this was intended to convert the land into her separate property. But this presumption can be rebutted. 41 CJS *Husband & Wife* §491(c).

In some states a deed to husband and wife as joint tenants makes the property the separate property of each, which property they hold in ordinary joint tenancy. *Collier* v. *Collier,* 242 P2d 537 (Ariz. 1952); *Siberell* v. *Siberell,* 7 P2d 1003 (Cal. 1932). However, oral evidence can be admitted in court to show that the husband and wife really intended this to be community property, and such intention will prevail. *Gudelj* v. *Gudelj,* 259 P2d 656 (Cal. 1953). Rather than leaving the matter of the vaguries of proof of oral statements, the deed should state the mode of ownership which was intended. In Nevada the grantor can deed the land to husband and wife "as community property with the right of survivorship."

REFERENCE: Mennell, *Survivorship Rights in Community Property,* 11 Comm. Prop. J. 5 (1984).

It is difficult, however, to present briefly an accurate picture of the law in community property states relative to joint tenancies. The law is complex and some standard treatise should be consulted. Baxter, *Marital Property* § 18.5 (1973); 21 Natural Resources J. 593. Only one thing seems clear, namely, the fact that the deed runs to the husband and wife as joint tenants will not prevent a court from holding that the land is held as community property. In states other than California, the claim of community ownership seems to be favored despite the joint tenancy form of the deed.

A husband may transfer his interest in community property to his wife and it will become her separate property. A like result occurs where the land is purchased with community property and the husband directs that the land be conveyed to the wife.

A gift made to both spouses is community property.

18.12(c)   Deeds and Mortgages of Community Property

In all community property states both husband and wife must sign if the property constitutes their home.

In any event, it is desirable and customary in most states for the husband and wife to join in any deed of any kind of land. And their joining is legally necessary where the land conveyed is occupied by the parties as their home. In most community property states that require the wife's consent to a deed of community property, the wife's signature is also needed for a valid contract to convey community property. *Rundle* v. *Winters,* 298 Pac. 929 (Ariz. 1931); *Chapman* v. *Hill,* 137 Pac. 1041 (Wash. 1914); *Elliott* v. *Craig,* 260 Pac. 433 (Idaho 1927); *Adams* v. *Blumenshine,* 204 P 66 (N.M. 1922). The wife should also join in all but short-term leases of community property. *Bowman* v. *Hardgrove,* 93 P2d 303 (Wash. 1939).

The aspects of the community property system that give sole control to the husband are invalid on constitutional grounds. The battle is being fought both in the state legislature and the courthouse. See *Kirchberg* v. *Feenstra,* 101 S.Ct. 1195 (1981); *Powell on Real Property* § 626(2); 15A Am.Jur.2d *Community Prop.* § 78.

18.12(d)   Wills and Descent of Community Property

The descent of community property when there is no will varies from state to state. It must be remembered in this connection that, regardless of the legal title, each spouse owns one-half of the community property.

In some community property states, in the absence of a will that specifies another disposition of the property, the surviving spouse succeeds to the decedent's share of the community property. In other states the decedent's share goes in whole or in part to his or her descendants. All community property states recognize the right to make a will by the first spouse to die.

CHAPTER 19

Rights of Spouses and Unmarried Cohabitants: Dower, Curtesy, Homestead

19.01   Dower—In General

Dower is the interest in the real estate of the husband which the law in some states gives to the widow to provide her with a means of support after her husband's death. It is a life estate in one third of the lands that the husband owned during the continuance of the marriage relation. *Dickson* v. *Ind. Bank,* 348 A2d 26 (R.I.). The requirements for dower are: (1) a valid marriage; (2) that the husband own the land during the continuance of the marriage relation; and (3) that the husband die prior to the death of the wife.

The right of dower originated in early times when a man's wealth consisted largely of real estate. Many states have recognized the widow's need for more than a life estate in the husband's realty and have passed laws that give the widow a share in her husband's estate. See *Powell on Real Property* § 213. These laws vary from state to state.

In all states laws have been enacted that alter the old rules concerning the rights of one spouse in land owned by the other. These laws must be consulted.

19.01(a)   Inchoate and Consummate Dower

During her husband's lifetime, the wife's rights consist merely of the possibility that she may become entitled to her dower. Until his death, the wife' dower is said to be *inchoate.* It is not such an interest that the wife can convey to a stranger, nor can it be sold at a forced sale to pay the wife's debts. The right can be released, however, as where the wife joins in her husband's deed of the property to a third party.

Should the wife predecease her husband, even this incipient right is automatically extinguished. Thus if her husband has previously conveyed his land without obtaining her signature on the deed, the grantee's title becomes perfect upon the wife's death before her husband's. It is as though her dower had never existed.

On the husband's death, her dower becomes *consummate*. It has ripened into something that she is certain to enjoy.

If the husband conveys his land without his wife joining in the deed, and the wife survives her husband, she then becomes entitled to her dower.

If the husband is indebted at the time of his death, the widow's dower rights are superior to any claims of his creditors in and to the land. This is one of the important characteristics of dower.

19.01(b)   Joint Tenancy and Dower

Although a widow has dower in lands owned by her husband in tenancy in common with others, there is no dower in a joint tenancy.

> **EXAMPLE:**   Two men, A and B, hold title in joint tenancy. A is married to C, and B is married to D. A conveys to X. A's wife, C, does not join in the deed. Ordinarily when a wife does not join in her husband's deed, her dower remains outstanding, but here no dower remains outstanding in C because A held title as a joint tenant. However, A's conveyance breaks the joint tenancy, and B and X now hold title as tenants in common, and their wives have dower in the real estate. *Johnston* v. *Muntz,* 4 NE2d 826 (Ill. 1936).

19.01(c)   Mortgages and Other Liens

When a wife fails to join with her husband in the execution of a mortgage on the husband's land, any title acquired through foreclosure of such mortgage will be subject to the wife's dower in states where dower is recognized. *Thomas* v. *Thomas,* 18 S2d 544 (Ala. 1944). An opposite result occurs where the mortgage provides the purchase money for the property mortgaged. *Frederick* v. *Emig.* 57 NE 883 (Ill. 1900). The same results follow in some states that have substituted some ownership share for dower but requires the wife to join in any deed in order to release her ownership share. And the same result follows in many states where the husband has curtesy, dower, or an ownership share in the wife's real estate and fails to join in her mortgage. Obviously where land is owned by either husband or wife, it will usually be necessary for the spouse to join in any mortgage on the land.

Dower is subject to any liens or encumbrances to which the land was subject at the time of the marriage or at the time the husband acquired title.

> **EXAMPLE:**   A buys a tract of land on which there is a mortgage. On foreclosure of this mortgage, the dower of A's wife will be extinguished.

19.01(d)   Leaseholds

The leasehold interest of a tenant under his lease is personal property, and since dower is a right that attaches to real estate only, a tenant's wife has no dower in the leasehold. 173 ALR 1260. Ordinarily a tenant may assign his leasehold with-out the wife's signature when no homestead rights are involved.

19.01(e)   Contract for Sale of Land

If a husband signs a contract for the sale of land, but his wife does not, she cannot be compelled to join in the deed to the buyer and her dower will remain outstanding. Obviously, any prudent buyer will insist that the wife sign the contract.

19.01(f)   Release of Dower

The widow is entitled to have dower assigned out of any land conveyed, mort-gaged, or leased by her husband during the marriage without her signature. Hence it is important that the landowner's wife release her dower by joining with him in any deed, mortgage, or lease of his land.

19.01(g)   Dower—Election

Many states give the widow, at her husband's death, a right to elect between her dower or some ownership (fee simple) share of the land.

19.01(h)   Dower—Fee Title Given in Lieu of Dower

In a number of states a widow is given a share in fee simple of her deceased husband's land in lieu of dower. Instead of acquiring merely a life estate, she may become the outright owner of one-third, or some other fraction, of her husband's land on his death.

The law of some of these states gives the widow's share only in lands that the husband owned *at his death.* Thus the widow has no claim whatever upon land conveyed by the husband during his lifetime and without the wife's signature. In other states that give the widow an ownership share in lieu of dower, the widow is entitled to her share in any land conveyed by the husband in his lifetime without her signature. Obviously, in these last states, the wife's signature is necessary on any deed, mortgage, or contract of sale given by the husband.

19.01(i)   Curtesy

In some states, a widower has a life estate known as *curtesy,* in the lands owned by his wife during their marriage. 100 U. Pa. L. Rev. 196. It is somewhat analogous to the widow's dower, but there are these points of difference:

1. In some curtesy states, a child must be born to the couple for this interest in land to arise. Most states have abolished this requirement.

2. The widower's curtesy, according to the old English law, was a life estate in all the land owned by the wife during the marriage, as contrasted with the one-third allowed the widow as her dower. In most of the curtesy states, however, the husband's share has been reduced by modern laws to some fraction, such as one-third.

In a number of states the husband is given dower instead of curtesy.

Whenever a husband has dower or curtesy, obviously he should join in the wife's deed, mortgage, or contract of sale of her property. However, in some states, a deed given by the wife conveying her own land bars the husband's curtesy even if he does not join in the deed.

In a number of states a surviving husband is given a share in fee simple of the wife's lands in lieu of curtesy. In some of these states, for example, the widower's share is limited to the land that the wife owned at her death. He has no claim whatever upon land conveyed by her in her lifetime without his signature.

In still other states that give the widower an ownership share in lieu of curtesy, the widower is entitled to his ownership share in any land conveyed by the wife in her lifetime without his signature.

Many states that give a widower curtesy or dower allow him, at the wife's death, to choose an ownership share instead.

19.01(j)   Divorce

Divorce terminates dower, curtesy, and their statutory substitutes. Some state laws provide, however, that a divorce bars only the dower or curtesy of the spouse for whose fault the divorce was obtained.

> **TIPS FOR LAWYERS:** The Uniform Marriage and Divorce Act has been adopted in a number of states. It provides for an equitable division of property on divorce without regard to marital fault. This eliminates the false adultery and cruelty charges that formerly characterized divorce. *Kujawinski* v. *Kujawinski,* 71 Ill.2d 563, 376 NE2d 1382 (1978). As to real estate owned separately by one of the spouses, such as land owned by the spouse before marriage, that spouse may sell and convey the land before divorce without obtaining the signature of the other spouse. *Ibid.* This rule applies as soon as divorce proceedings have been filed. *Cady* v. *Cady,* 581 P2d 358 (Kan. 1978). Of course, this does not apply to the marital home. In all states having homestead laws, such a deed requires both signatures. See 68 Ill. B. J. 320, 698.

19.02   Marital Property Rights

The trend today is for dower and curtesy laws to be replaced with statutes that give the surviving spouse a statutory share of all of the assets of the deceased spouse. An even more far-reaching trend is embodied in the Uniform Marital Property Act (UMPA). This act gives each spouse an immediate ownership interest in marital property similar in kind to a community property interest. Wisconsin is the first and only state to enact a marital property law modeled after UMPA.

REFERENCE: 21 Houston L. Rev. 595.

19.03   Homestead

When a family owns and occupies a tract of land as its home, in many states that portion of the tract that does not exceed in area or value the limit fixed by law for homesteads is the family homestead, and certain rights, called homestead rights, are created therein. These homestead rights may, of course, extend to the entire tract if it is within the area and value limits fixed by law.

There are three principal motives behind the various state homestead laws. One is the protection of the family against being evicted from their home by enforcement of the claims of creditors. The homestead portion of the tract of land is protected against sheriff's sales on a judgment against the landowner.

The second object of the homestead laws is to protect the wife against the husband. The lawmakers thought it would be a good idea if the husband were not allowed to sell his own home if the wife was opposed to the idea. Evidently, the theory was that the old home should not be disposed of until a new home suitable for the family had been provided. To accomplish this result, the lawmakers provided that the husband could not convey good title to his own home unless his wife signed the deed. It is therefore necessary that both husband and wife join in any deed or mortgage of homestead property, except, of course, a purchase money mortgage.

As a final protection of the wife against the husband and his creditors, the homestead laws provided some protection for the widow after the death of her husband. This was necessary because dower did not afford the widow adequate protection. Dower does not give the widow any right to the occupation of any real estate until a particular tract of land has been set apart or assigned to her as dower. Immediately upon the husband's death, the widow might be subject to eviction from the home. Protection was afforded by the laws providing for the widow's homestead. Even a husband who has quarreled bitterly with his wife cannot legally deprive her of this protection. A final development in this direction was the *probate homestead,* which created a home for the widow in land that the husband had never occupied as his home. In this regard, the widow's rights are superior to the rights of any creditor of the deceased husband. Land so occupied by the widow cannot be sold to pay the deceased husband's debts.

For a valid deed or mortgage of the homestead, it is necessary that both husband and wife join in the same deed or mortgage. The wife is thus protected against the improvidence of the husband. In some states it is necessary that the deed or mortgage of the homestead contain a clause expressly releasing or waiving all homestead rights, and in many states a deed or mortgage of the homestead land must be acknowledged in order to be valid.

19.04   Unmarried Cohabitants

Recent years have seen an increase in the number of instances where individuals have established housekeeping units without the benefit of formal marriage. This may cause problems.

> **EXAMPLE:** *A,* a bachelor, and *B,* a spinster, buy a house. The deed simply runs to them as *A* and *B.* Both sign the mortgage required for part of the pur-

chase price. Both contribute to the cash payment, since both have jobs. There is no contract between them. *A* dies. *B* is a stranger and inherits nothing from *A*. Still *B* must continue making payments on the mortgage to prevent foreclosure.

Of course, the parties can quite simply solve this problem.

EXAMPLE: In states where joint tenancy is recognized, *A* and *B* can have the deed run to them as joint tenants.

And in states that recognize tenancy by the entireties and joint tenancy, some courts come to the rescue.

EXAMPLE: *A* and *B*, unmarried persons, buy a home and the deed runs to them "as tenants by the entireties." Some states will treat this as a joint tenancy.

Except in those jurisdictions which still recognize common law marriage, dower, curtesy, spouse's rights statutes, and the law relating to distribution of property upon divorce are inapplicable to unmarried cohabitants. *Hewitt* v. *Hewitt*, 394 NE2d 1204 (Ill. 1979). But see 81 ALR3d 6; 81 ALR3d 110; Comment, 1978 So. Ill. U. L. J. 423, relating to the rights of a putative spouse. 3 ALR4d 13.

Various reasons have been given by courts in the various states in refusing to recognize property rights in unmarrieds. The most extreme of these is the courts' refusal to enforce contracts relating to property rights of unmarried persons who live together. Courts in other states will honor the contract if it is properly drawn.

Some courts make a distinction between cases involving parties who honestly thought they were married and those who know full well that they were not married. Evans, *Property Interests Arising from Quasi-Marital Relations,* 9 Cornell L. Q. 246 (1924).

EXAMPLE: *M,* thinking his divorce from *F* is final, engages in a marriage ceremony with *W*. Both *M* and *W* intend to marry and have otherwise complied with all formal requirements. The failure of *M* to be finally divorced from *F*, however, rendered the marriage of *M* to *W* a nullity. This is a *putative* marriage and *M* and *W* are *putative husband and wife.* The courts will treat their property as if they were husband and wife.

EXAMPLE: *M* and *W* decide to live together and engage in sexual relations without the benefit of any formal marriage. The older decisions refer to this as *concubinage.* Some courts refuse to recognize property rights by either in the property of the other.

There are various grounds for awarding property rights to the parties of a nonmarital relationship. Primary among them is the *express agreement.* The parties may expressly agree to pool their assets and share in their accumulations, enter into a partnership or joint venture agreement, or exchange property for services. An express agreement is certainly the preferable course of action, since they are almost always enforced by the courts if sexual conduct is not mentioned in the contract. Unfortunately, most cohabitants do not have the foresight to enter into such agreements. This is folly especially where substantial assets are involved.

It is preferable that such agreements be in writing. The intent of the parties and the terms of the agreement are more easily proved. Oral agreements are nonetheless enforceable. While these agreements are sometimes subject to the defense of illegality as encouraging immorality, they will only be declared invalid where sexual services are the principal consideration. Courts frequently hold, however, that if the woman makes a financial contribution, she will be protected.

> **EXAMPLE:**   M and W lived together for seven years. All property acquired during this period was taken in M's name. At the outset of the relationship, M and W orally agreed that while the parties lived together they would combine their efforts and earnings and would share equally in all accumulations as a result of their individual or combined efforts. W also agreed to render services as companion and homemaker. M agreed to provide for W's financial support and needs for the rest of her life. W gave up a lucrative singing career to devote her time to her household responsibilities. During the period of cohabitation, and as a result of their efforts and earnings, M and W acquired substantial property in M's name. The relationship then came to an end. The court allowed the enforcement of this oral contract even though sexual relations may have been involved. *Marvin* v. *Marvin*, 557 P2d 106 (Cal. 1976).

There are other grounds for awarding property to the parties to a nonmarital relationship. The courts may struggle to find some sort of partnership, trust, or gift as grounds for allocating property rights between the parties. These courts try to allow the bargain of the parties to be enforced rather than allow one of the parties to be deprived of what was jointly accumulated. *Latham* v. *Latham*, 547 P2d 144 (Oreg. 1976). Modern courts will try to enforce the reasonable expectations of the parties. *Carlson* v. *Olson*, 256 NW2d 249 (Minn. 1977). The decisions go so far as to order specific performance of an oral promise to convey real estate. *Tyranski* v. *Piggins*, 205 NW2d 595 (Mich. 1973).

Older decisions that deny protection to the unmarried woman no longer appear to be valid. The courts should be free to inquire into the conduct of the parties to determine whether their conduct demonstrates an implied contract or implied agreement of partnership or some sort of trust. Also, the older barrier against recovery for the reasonable value of services rendered may well be removed. *Marvin* v. *Marvin*, 557 P2d 106 (1976).

Unmarried cohabitants are vulnerable where a zoning ordinance forbids occupancy of homes by unrelated persons. Granting that these ordinances were aimed at communes, they have been used against unmarried cohabitants.

19.05   Homosexual Cohabitants

No dependable statement can be made regarding the property rights of cohabiting homosexuals. Arguably, express agreements between them relating to their property rights should be enforced. Public policy, however, may stand in the way. *Jones* v. *Daly*, 176 Cal. Reptr. 130 (1981); Baxter, *Marital Property* § 35.15 (pocket part 1980).

> REFERENCES: The authorities on the rights of unmarried cohabitants are many. Baxter, *Marital Property* § 35.15 (1980 pocket part); Burch, *Property Rights of De*

Facto Spouses Including Thoughts on the Value of Homemaker's Services, 10 Fam. L. Q. 101 (1976); Evans, *Property Interests Arising from Quasi-Marital Relations,* 9 Cornell L. Q. 246 (1924); Kaminski, *Joint Tenancy and a Residential Mortgage: An Unmarried Couple's Estate Tax Problem,* 69 Ill. B. J. 706 (1981); 50 Ind. L. J. 389 (1975); 3 ALR4th 13. Numerous articles deal with the leading case involving movie star Lee Marvin. 90 Harv. L. Rev. 1708; 16 J. Family L. 331; 8 New Mexico L. Rev. 81; 30 Okla L. Rev. 494; 17 Santa Clara L. Rev. 947; 11 Suffolk L. Rev. 1327; 10 S.W.U. L. Rev. 699; 52 Tul. L. Rev. 188; 46 U. Cinn. L. Rev. 924; 53 Wash. L. Rev. 145; 23 Wayne L. Rev. 1305; 65 Cal. L. Rev. 937.

CHAPTER 20

Real Estate Finance—Mortgages

20.01 Mortgage Defined

A mortgage may be defined as a conveyance of land given to secure the payment of a debt. On analysis, this definition discloses the existence of two elements: (1) Like a deed, a mortgage is a conveyance of land. (2) However, the intention is not, as in the case of a deed, to effect a sale of land, but to provide security for the payment of a debt.

20.02 History of Mortgage Law

The history of mortgage law is the history of hundreds of years of ceaseless struggle for advantage between borrowers and lenders. The lawbooks reflect the constantly shifting fortunes of this war. Occasionally, the battle has gone in favor of the lenders. More recently, however, the consumerism wave has resulted in court decisions and new laws favorable to the borrowers. The tide of battle, as it has many times in the past, has shifted in the borrowers' favor. To understand how the modern mortgage developed out of these centuries of struggle is to take a long step toward understanding modern mortgage law. Much of our mortgage law comes to us from England. In that country mortgage arrangements of various kinds existed even in the Anglo-Saxon times before the conquest of England by William the Conqueror in 1066. However, it will suffice for our purposes to begin with the mortgage of the fourteenth century. This document was a simple deed of the land, running from the borrower (mortgagor) to the lender (mortgagee). All the ceremonies needed for a full transfer of ownership took place when the mortgage was made. The mortgagee became the owner of the land just as if a sale had taken place. However, this ownership was subject to two qualifications:

1. The mortgagee, as owner, could oust the mortgagor, take immediate possession of the property, and collect the rents. However, the rents so collected had to be applied on the mortgage debt. For this reason, the mortgagee often permitted the mortgagor to remain in possession.

2. The mortgage described the debt it secured and stated a date of payment, known as the *law day*. The mortgage gave the mortgagor the right to pay the debt on the law day. If he did, the mortgage provided that it thereby became void. This provision was known as the *defeasance clause,* for payment of the debt on the law day defeated the mortgage and put ownership back in the mortgagor.

In early times, the courts enforced the mortgage as it was written. Foreclosure proceedings did not exist. Failure to pay the mortgage debt when due, a *default,* automatically extinguished all the mortgagor's interest in the land.

20.03   The Equity of Redemption

For many years no one dreamed of questioning this scheme of things. Then, slowly at first, and later in greater numbers, borrowers who had lost their property through default began to seek the assistance of the king. A typical petition by such a borrower would set forth the borrowing of the money, the making of the mortgage, the default in payment, and the resulting loss of the land. The petition would continue with the statement that the borrower now had funds and offered to pay the mortgage debt in full, with interest. The petition would then ask that the king order the mortgagee, who now owned the land, to accept the proffered money and convey the land back to the borrower. The king had little time or inclination to tend to these petitions personally, and so he habitually referred them to a high official, the lord chancellor. Since the king was the fountain of all justice, it was the chancellor's duty to dispose of these petitions justly and equitably, according to good conscience. This he did. In cases of hardship or accident, for example, where the mortgagor had been robbed while on his way to pay the debt, the chancellor would order the mortgagee to accept payment of the debt from the borrower and to convey the land back to the borrower. A mortgagee who refused to do as he was told was sent to jail. In time, by about the year 1625, what had begun as a matter of grace on the part of the king had developed into the purest routine. Borrowers filed their petitions directly with the chancellor, who was now functioning as the judge of a court, and with regularity his order was issued commanding the mortgagee to reconvey. Thus a new and very important right was born, the right of the mortgagor to pay his debt even after default and in this manner to recover his property. This right came to be known as the *equitable right of redemption,* or the *equity of redemption.* Later the courts held that the mortgagor could sell this equitable right of redemption, that he could dispose of it by his will, and that if he died leaving no will, the right could be exercised by his heirs. You will perceive that as a result of these developments, the mortgagor, even after default, retained very important rights in the land. Technically, the mortgagee became full owner of the land upon default, but, practically, the mortgagor could now be regarded as the owner even after default, since he could reacquire ownership by exercising his equitable right of redemption.

20.03(a)   Waiver of Right of Redemption

The mortgagees reacted to the development of the equitable right of redemption by inserting clauses reciting that the mortgagor waived and surrendered all of his equitable rights of redemption. The courts, however, nipped this idea in the bud by holding that all such clauses were void. This result was based upon the courts' feeling that it was their duty to protect the needy borrower who would sign anything. This rule flourished and exists in full vigor today. Any provision in the mortgage purporting to terminate the mortgagor's ownership in case of failure to make payments when due is against public policy and is void. *Once a mortgage, always a mortgage.* It cannot be converted into an outright deed by the mere default of the mortgagor. No matter how the mortgage seeks to disguise an attempted waiver of the equitable right of redemption, the courts will strike it down.

> **EXAMPLE:**   At the time the mortgage was made, the mortgagor signed a deed conveying the property to the mortgagee. He then delivered the deed to a third person in escrow with directions to deliver the deed to the mortgagee in case of default in the mortgage payments. This deed and escrow were held invalid as an attempted waiver of the equitable right of redemption. *Plummer v. Ilse,* 82 P. 1009 (Wash. 1905); *Hamud v. Hawthorne,* 338 P2d 387 (Cal. 1959).

20.03(b)   Clogging the Equity

Other means were invented to hamper the exercise of the equitable right of redemption. Rather than waiving the right, mortgagors executed documents that limited the manner of exercise of the right of redemption. Courts would not allow arrangements where the right of redemption could be exercised only for a certain period after law day or only by the mortgagor himself. Osborne, *Handbook on the Law of Mortgages* §§ 96 and 97 (2d ed. 1970). The courts will also use their powers to invalidate any agreement whereby the mortgagee oppresses or takes unconscionable advantage of the mortgagor. 55 Am.Jur.2d *Mortgages* § 514; 59CJS *Mortgages* § 113.

> **EXAMPLE:**   Owner mortgaged his Lot 1 to Lender. Lender demanded and received from Owner an option to buy Owner's Lot 2. When Lender sought to exercise this option, Owner resisted and litigation ensued. The court held the option void. *Humble Oil & Refining Co.v. Doerr,* 303 A2d 898 (N.J. 1973). A mortgagee is entitled to payment of the mortgage debt. He cannot take advantage of the mortgagor by compelling him to grant "collateral advantages."

20.04   Development of Foreclosure

The efforts of the courts to rescue the mortgagor in turn placed the mortgagee at a disadvantage. The mortgagee, it is true, became the owner of the land when the mortgagor defaulted, but he could not be certain he would remain the owner, for the mortgagor might choose to redeem. To remedy this situation a new practice sprang up. Immediately upon default in payment of the mortgage debt, the mortgagee would file a petition in court, and the judge would enter an order, called a decree, allowing the mortgagor additional time to pay the debt. If he failed to pay within this time, usually six months or a year, the decree provided that his equitable right of redemption was thereby barred and foreclosed. Thereafter he could not redeem his property. Thus developed the *foreclosure suit,* a suit to bar or terminate the equitable right of redemption.

The method of foreclosure just described is known today as *strict foreclosure.* It is still used in Connecticut and Vermont and occasionally elsewhere.

The next development was foreclosure through public sale. The idea emerged that in mortgage foreclosures, justice would best be served by offering the land for sale at public auction, for if at such sale the property sold for more than the mortgage debt, the mortgagee would be paid his debt in full and the surplus proceeds of the sale would be salvaged for the mortgagor. This method of *foreclosure by sale* is the most common method of foreclosure in the United States today. This development constituted another major victory for the mortgagor. More important still, it led to another and even greater victory for the borrowers. As the practice of foreclosure by sale grew more common, the view began to emerge that the mortgage, despite its superficial similarity to a deed, was really not a deed of conveyance but only a *lien* on the land—that is, merely a means of bringing about a public sale to raise money for the payment of the mortgage debt.

20.05   The Institutionalization of Mortgage Law

Mortgage lending has also progressed from pre–World War I days, when the majority of mortgage lenders were individuals, to a time when lenders are primarily institutions. Mortgage lending today also takes place against the backdrop of the secondary mortgage market and mortgage-backed securities that give virtual anonymity to the ultimate investor and isolation between it and the borrower. This evolution has taken mortgage processing from an individual-to-individual context to a context where the borrower deals with a skilled professional lender. Kratovil, *Mortgage Law Today,* 13 John Marsh. L. Rev. 251 (1980).

While first mortgage lending has become institutionalized and federalized, creative financing has given rise to second mortgage lending by individuals.

20.06   Federalization of Mortgage Law

The federalization of mortgage law has been accomplished by direct federal legislation such as the Real Estate Settlement Procedures Act, the Equal Credit Opportunity Act, and so forth, and by the involvement of the U.S. Department of Housing and Urban Development (HUD) largely through the Federal Housing Administration (FHA). HUD attempts to help people purchase homes on a sound basis. Under the HUD system, a homebuyer makes a small down payment and obtains a mortgage loan for the balance of the purchase price. The loan is made by a bank, savings and loan association, mortgage banker, or other HUD-approved lender and is insured by HUD. This insurance protects the lender against loss on the loan, which in turn allows the lender to be more liberal in granting the loan—thereby extending home ownership opportunities to families that would otherwise be unable to buy a home.

Through a similar program, the Veterans Administration (VA) guarantees loans made to veterans.

The Federal Home Loan Bank Board (FHLBB), regulating federal savings and loan associations, and the Comptroller of the Currency, regulating national banks, have also had an impact on lending practices of those lenders as do the federally regulated instrumentalities of the secondary market.

All of these programs have their own sets of standards and regulations, which have played a large role in shaping underwriting requirements, the terms of loan documents and foreclosure practices to align mortgage practices with federally sponsored social goals.

REFERENCE: Weimer, Hoyt, & Bloom, *Real Estate,* Ch. 16 (7th ed. 1978).

20.07   Secondary Mortgage Market

The mortgage industry today is divided into two markets, the primary market of loan originators and the secondary market of investors that purchase the loans from the originators, holding them in a loan portfolio for a long-term investment. This secondary market has several benefits, both for the investors and the housing industry. First, it provides liquidity in that an investor in a mortgage security has a ready market for the sale of that asset. Second, it tends to moderate dips in the flow of mortgage capital, allowing lenders to sell portfolios of loans to replenish their supply of funds. Third, it moves capital from one area of the country to another. And fourth, it permits investor portfolio diversification. Dennis, *Fundamentals of Mortgage Lending* 108 (1978).

One of the principal participants in the secondary mortgage market is the Federal National Mortgage Company (FNMA), sometimes called "Fannie Mae." FNMA was begun in 1938 as a corporation wholly owned by the federal government. In 1968, FNMA was split into two separate corporations. One, the Government National Mortgage Association (GNMA), sometimes called "Ginnie Mae," continues to be wholly owned by the federal government. The other, FNMA, became a privately owned, federally chartered corporation subject to federal regulation. FNMA is the largest supplier of mortgage funds for homes and apartments, purchasing these loans from the originator thereby giving the lender funds to lend again. FNMA has long specialized in buying FHA-insured or VA-guaranteed loans, but it also buys large quantities of conventional loans that are not backed by the government. FNMA either holds the mortgages in its own portfolio or sells them to investors. All the while, the loan is typically being serviced by the originating lender or some other local entity.

GNMA is organized a bit differently. It is still a government agency, but it buys pools of mortgages and holds them as security for certificates that are issued to investors.

EXAMPLE: Mortgage Banker has originated a volume of mortgages that are sold to GNMA. GNMA gets the funds to make this purchase by selling certificates, *mortgage-backed securities,* that may be purchased by investors with as little as a $25,000 minimum investment.

The pools are made up of FHA and VA mortgages, and the investors' security lies both in the mortgages backing the pool and the full faith and credit of the United States Treasury that also guarantees payment. Every month the investors receive a check that represents one month's interest on the remaining balance plus repaid and prepaid principal. These securities are held primarily by large investors such as banks, savings and loan associations, credit unions, and pension funds. Billions of dollars of such securities have been issued.

The Federal Home Loan Mortgage Corporation (FHLMC), sometimes called "Freddie Mac," buys conventional, nongovernment-insured mortgages in the secondary market. These mortgages are also placed in pools, and certificates backed by these pools are sold to investors who ultimately receive the payments made by the mortgagors.

Investors in the secondary market are not all government-related entities. Pension funds, insurance companies, and others also play a role as mortgage loan buyers. Some lenders have attempted to make their own mortgage pools selling shares in that pool, or using the pool as collateral for mortgage backed bonds. See, generally, Kratovil & Werner, *Modern Mortgage Law and Practice,* §§29.04 *et seq.* (2d ed. 1981).

REFERENCE: FNMA, *A Guide to Fannie Mae* (1979).

20.08   Title and Lien Theories

The relatively recent view that the mortgage is not really a conveyance of land but only a lien, has reached its fullest development in the agricultural and Western states. Certain states, called *title theory states,* still take the older view that a mortgage gives the mortgagee some sort of legal title to the land. *Conference Center Ltd.* v. *TRC,* 455 A2d 857 (Conn. 1983). In other states, called *lien theory states,* the view that the mortgagee has the legal title is entirely superseded by the view that he has merely a lien to secure his debt. Some states take a position midway between these two views. These are called *intermediate states.*

It is not possible, however, to draw any hard and fast line between these groups of states, since vestiges of title theory will be found in lien theory states, and many title theory states have adopted rules developed by lien theory courts. The differences in point of view are of importance in determining the mortgagee's rights with respect to possession and rents of the mortgaged property.

20.09   Types of Mortgages

There are several different types of mortgage instruments. Those commonly encountered are regular mortgages, deeds of trust, equitable mortgages, and deeds absolute given as security for debts.

20.09(a)   Regular Mortgages

The ordinary printed form of mortgage encountered in most states today is referred to herein as the regular mortgagee. It is, in form, a deed or conveyance of the land by the borrower to the lender, followed or preceded by a description of the debt and including a provision to the effect that such mortgage shall be void on full payment of such debt.

20.09(b)   Deeds of Trust

The regular mortgage involves only two parties, the borrower and the lender. In the trust deed, also known as the deed of trust, the borrower conveys the land, not to the lender, but to a third party, a *trustee,* in trust for the benefit of the holder of the note or notes that represent the mortgage debt.

The deed of trust form of mortgage has certain advantages: the chief one is that in a number of states it can be foreclosed by trustee's sale under the power-of-sale clause without any court proceedings. The power-of-sale trust deed is used in Alabama, Alaska, California, Colorado, District of Columbia, Mississippi, Missouri, Montana, Nebraska, Nevada, New Mexico, North Carolina, Oregon, South Carolina, Tennessee, Texas, Virginia, Washington, and West Virginia.

20.09(c)   Equitable Mortgages

As a general rule, any instrument in writing by which the parties show their intention that real estate be held as security for the payment of a debt will constitute an equitable mortgage, capable of being foreclosed in a court of equity.

> **EXAMPLE:**   A landowner borrowed money from a mortgagee giving a promissory note to evidence the debt. On this note the borrower placed the following recital: "This note is secured by a real estate mortgage on . . . '' (here followed a description of the land). No separate mortgage was executed. The court held that the note itself, with the quoted endorsement, constituted an equitable mortgage on the land, for it clearly expressed an intention that the land should stand as security for the debt. *Trustees of Zion Methodist Church* v. *Smith,* 81 NE2d 649 (Ill. 1948).

An instrument intended as a regular mortgage, but which contains some defect, may also operate as an equitable mortgage.

> **EXAMPLE:**   When, through inadvertence, a trust deed altogether omitted the name of a trustee, it was obviously ineffective to transfer title or create a power of sale in any one since it lacked a grantee. However, it was sustained as an equitable mortgage, which could be foreclosed by means of a foreclosure suit. *Dulany* v. *Willis,* 29 SE 324 (Va. 1898).

20.09(d)   Deeds Absolute Given as a Security

Often when a landowner borrows money he gives as security an absolute deed to the land. By "absolute deed" is meant a quitclaim or warranty deed such as is used in an ordinary land sale. On its face, the transaction looks like a sale of the land. Nevertheless, the courts treat such a deed as a mortgage where the evidence shows that the deed was really intended only as a security for a debt.

> **EXAMPLE:**   Owner owns a home, which is already mortgaged to a bank. He needs money for medical expenses and goes to his brother, Lender, for a loan of $1,000. Lender loans Owner the money but insists that Owner sign a simple promissory note and give a quitclaim deed to his home. It is agreed orally that if the debt is paid when due, Lender will quitclaim the property back to Owner. Owner fails to pay the debt. Lender is not the owner of the land. He merely holds a mortgage on it, which he must foreclose. And remember that all the world has notice of the true nature of his deed, for undoubtedly Owner will remain in possession, and possession imparts constructive notice.

A deed such as that described in the above example is regarded by the courts as an attempt to "waive the equitable right of redemption." The courts often use the maxim, "Once a mortgage, always a mortgage." It cannot be converted into a conveyance of absolute ownership by mere default. Hence it becomes necessary for the courts to go back to the very beginning of the transaction. The task is a simple one. Either the deed was then intended as an absolute *transfer of ownership* (as in a land sale), or it was then intended merely to provide *security to a lender.* So the court listens to all the testimony regarding the beginnings of the transaction. Oral testimony is received as to what was said and done. And the court hears testimony as to what occurred thereafter. Usually it is child's play to distinguish between a deed intended to transfer absolute ownership and one that was merely intended to provide a lender with security.

The following circumstances are usually considered:

1. *Adequacy of consideration.* If owner conveys land worth $10,000 and receives only $5,000, the indication is that the transaction is a mortgage. Normally land will sell for its full value.

2. *Prior negotiations between the parties.* When Owner applies to Lender for a loan and the transaction is consummated by Owner giving Lender a deed to the land, this tends to show that the transaction is a mortgage. It is as if Lender had said: "I will lend you the money, but give me a deed as security." Of course, if it appears that Lender rejected the application for a loan, this tends to show that the transaction is a sale. It is as if Lender had said: "I will not loan you any money, but I am willing to buy your land."

3. *Subsequent conduct of the parties.* If Owner receives money from Lender and gives Lender a deed to Owner's land, but Owner thereafter remains in possession, paying taxes, insurance premiums, and so on, this tends to show that the transaction is a mortgage, for in a normal land sale the buyer takes possession.

4. *Possession.* If the transaction is merely a security transaction, almost invariably the borrower retains possession of the land, and his possession gives the whole world

notice of the fact that the deed was merely a security deed and that foreclosure must take place.

If the court construes the transaction to be a deed given as security for a debt, the mask of the sale transaction is stripped away and the mortgage aspects of the transaction are exposed. This means that the grantor/borrower has redemption rights according to state law. He may repay the debt and demand reconveyance of the property just as in the case of an ordinary mortgage. If the debt is not paid, the grantee/lender must foreclose just as if a regular mortgage had been made.

The return going to the lender/grantee is also measured against the usury laws to determine whether the charges assessed against the borrower resulted in a greater return than authorized by law. *Schulte* v. *Franklin,* 633 P2d 1151 (Kans. 1981). A return greater than the usury laws permit tends to stamp the transaction as a disguised loan.

Another result of a deed being held to be a security device lies in the fact that truth-in-lending requirements may be applicable. If the proper disclosures were not made, the truth-in-lending penalty provisions may be invoked against the lender. *Long* v. *Storms,* 622 P2d 731 (Ore. App. 1981).

REFERENCE: Cunningham & Tischler, *Disguised Real Estate Security Transactions as Mortgages in Substance,* 26 Rutgers L. Rev. 1 (1972).

20.10   Sale and Leaseback

This form of transaction typically involves a landowner in need of funds to use in its business. While the landowner cannot give up use of its business property, the landowner can give up ownership of the property. An investor is found to buy the property at its full value and lease the property back to the seller. Hence the term *sale and leaseback.* There are other frequently found characteristics of this form of transaction. The seller–lessee is usually a retailer or industrial concern of high credit standing. The lease is usually for a term of twenty to thirty years and the seller–lessee is usually given options to renew the lease and to purchase the property. The rental on the original term pays the buyer an amount equal to the purchase price plus a return higher than could be obtained on a conventional mortgage. The lessee is required to pay all real estate taxes, fire insurance, repairs, and so forth in a "net" rental arrangement. There are some variations on the sale and leaseback pattern.

EXAMPLE: *XYZ Hamburgers,* a chain, spots a good location. *ABC Realty Investment Trust* buys the land, finances construction through an affiliate, and leases the location to *XYZ Hamburgers.*

The attraction of this type of transaction to the seller–lessee lies in the fact that he gets the full value of the property instead of the smaller amount that he could obtain on a mortgage, and he is under no obligation to repay this amount if he is willing to forego his repurchase of the land. In other words, he is not saddled with a debt, as he would be if he had made a mortgage on his land. Note, of course, the seller–lessee may have a continuing rental payment obligation. The advantage to the buyer is that foreclosure is not necessary if default is made in the rent payments, since the transaction is a sale and lease, not a mortgage.

Use of this device in a modified form is common today. An industrial corporation wants money to use in its business. It sells its plant to an investor, receiving the full cash value. The investor then leases the land back to the industrial corporation. Hence the term *sale and leaseback.*

Among the advantages to the lessee of such an arrangement are the following:

1. A tax advantage. In computing its income for income tax purposes, the lessee deducts its rent payments under the lease. Were the transaction a mortgage, the only permitted deductions would be interest and depreciation. Also, if the building is not newly constructed, it may be that the current value and sale price are substantially less than the price paid when the seller–lessee bought the building, and the sale to the investor represents an income tax loss to the seller-lessee.

2. By selling the property for its full value to the lessor, the lessee obtains much more cash money than it could raise on a mortgage, for no mortgagee will loan up to 100 percent of the value of the property.

3. Existing mortgages, corporate charters, debenture agreements, or other documents binding on the lessee may place restrictions on its right to borrow money. Since a lease is not a loan, the leaseback arrangement provides a method of getting around these restrictions.

The chief disadvantages to the lessee are:

1. If the building goes up in value, the investor, not the lessee, will reap the benefit of this increase once the lease expires.

2. The lessee has all the burdens of ownership, for the lease requires the lessee to pay taxes, insurance, and so on. But the lessee lacks the freedom of action that an owner enjoys. Under the terms of the lease, the lessee cannot sell the leasehold without the consent of the investor. Even if the investor consents, there are many prospective purchasers who are reluctant to buy leaseholds. Moreover, the lessee cannot tear down or remodel buildings as business needs dictate unless the investor consents. Likewise, to erect new buildings would be foolish, for they would belong to the landlord at the end of the lease period.

20.10(a)   Sale and Leaseback—Consequences of Transaction Being Set Aside

The sale and leaseback transaction is indeed very complex and is a financing vehicle. It must be distinguished from a deed absolute to secure a debt. *Matter of Kassuba,* 562 F2d 511 (7 Cir. 1977). Merely labeling a transaction a sale and leaseback will not make it immune from attack, and when the transaction is attacked, the courts will carefully analyze the relationship between the seller–lessee and the buyer–lessor to determine whether a sale really occurred or whether the transaction is really a mortgage. *Burton* v. *Smith,* 357 So.2d 324 (Ala. 1978). If the transaction is found to be a mortgage, consequences befall both the seller-lessee and the buyer–lessor. The relationship of mortgagor–mortgagee with its requirement of foreclosure and redemption rights replaces the relationship of landlord and tenant with its quick possessory remedy of forcible entry and detainer. Usury law may come into play as a standard for evaluating the fairness of the return to the buyer–lessor who has unexpectedly found itself in the role of lender. The income tax treatment that both parties had used and anticipated will not be available, and, indeed, past years' tax returns will have to be amended.

As can be seen, the transaction is quite complex and should only be entered into after careful consultation with an experienced counsel and tax advisor. The consequences of a mistake can be awesome.

20.10(b)   Sale and Leaseback—Recent Developments

In the case of a sale and leaseback where the rent provision contained an escalator clause tied in some way to the inflationary spiral, rentals have increased at times to a point where the transaction is no longer favorable to the tenant. Deals that looked bad for the investor in the late 1960s are now looking better. In some cases the investor is selling the shopping center or other property back to the tenant at a profit and deferring the capital gains tax by exchanging a "like kind" property of comparable value.

> REFERENCE: Kratovil and Werner, *Modern Mortgage Law and Practice,* Ch. 23 (2d ed. 1981). See § 23.03(a) of that text, discussing *Frank Lyon* v. *U.S.,* 435 U.S. 561, commented on in 49 J. Taxation 42 (1978); 56 Taxes 618; 6 R.E.L.J. 199 (1978).

20.11   Vendor's Lien Reserved by Deed

In some states, a seller, in lieu of taking back a mortgage from the buyer, expressly reserves in his deed to the buyer a lien on the land to secure payment of the balance of the purchase price. Such a lien is called a *vendor's lien.* It is really a mortgage.

> **EXAMPLE:**   *A,* a landowner, conveyed to *B* by a warranty deed that warranted that title was free from all encumbrances excepting three certain notes executed by *B,* for which a vendor's lien was retained until said notes and the interest thereon should be fully paid. The court held that this clause created a lien on the land. Such a lien is regarded as partaking of the nature of an equitable mortgage. This device is governed by the same rules as a mortgage and may be foreclosed as such. *Crabtree* v. *Davis,* 186 So 734 (Ala. 1939); *Lusk* v. *Mintz,* 625 SW2d 774 (Tex. 1981).

Such a lien enjoys priority over subsequent liens and encumbrances and, like a purchase money mortgage, has priority over prior judgments against the purchaser. The grantee under such deed does not become personally liable for the purchase money unless he has signed a promissory note, as in the above example, or otherwise obligated himself personally to pay the debt. And a purchaser from such grantee does not become personally liable to the holder of the vendor's lien unless by his deed he assumes and agrees to pay the unpaid balance of the debt. The debt may be assigned, and the assignee will have the right to foreclose the lien.

20.12   Purchase Money Mortgages

Purchase money mortgages taken back by sellers provide a major form of real property financing in periods of tight credit. In such times, this form of financing vehicle provides the basis of most forms of creative financing that allows property to be sold.

20.13   Application and Commitment

A mortgage transaction usually begins with an application for a loan. The application serves a double purpose: (1) it is a source of information on which the lender will base his decision as to making the loan; and (2) it defines the terms of the loan contract. The application is usually made on the mortgagee's preprinted form and signed by the prospective borrower. After investigating the prospective borrower's financial circumstances and appraising the real estate, the lender may write the applicant a letter stating that the loan application has been accepted. This letter is sometimes referred to as a *commitment*. This will usually result in a contract for the making of a mortgage loan.

Technically, the application is an *offer* by the mortgagor to give a mortgage and note on the terms specified in the application. Vance, *Insurance* §35 (3d ed. 1951).The commitment is an *acceptance* of the offer, *Burns* v. *Washington Savings*, 171 So2d 322 (Miss. 1965), which, under basic contract law, creates a contract. If the letter of commitment makes any changes in the terms, it is technically a *counteroffer*. There is no contract in this instance unless the applicant agrees to the new terms, which he may do by writing the word "accepted" and his signature on the mortgagee's letter of commitment. To the lawyer this is the typical "offer and acceptance" problem.

Since the application and commitment define the terms on which the loan is to be made and constitute a contract that neither party can change or add to without the other's consent, the application should state the terms in detail. Indeed, a failure to include essential terms will lead a court to hold that no binding contract came into existence. *Calosso* v. *First National Bank,* 143 So2d 343 (Fla. 1962). All contracts must be complete and certain. The mortgagee will, of course, want to see to it that the offer and acceptance contain various other clauses which may or may not be essential to the formation of a contract. Included among these other terms is the agreement of the borrower to sign a note and mortgage in a certain specified form; the borrower's agreement to furnish evidence of title and survey at his expense; the borrower's agreement to sign chattel security documents and to sign an assignment of leases and rents; provisions for deducting title and other charges from the proceeds of the loan; provisions that the lender

Residential Loan Application

MORTGAGE APPLIED FOR ☑	☐ Conventional ☐ VA	☐ FHA	Amount $	Interest Rate %	No. of Months	Monthly Payment Principal & Interest $	Escrow/Impounds (to be collected monthly) ☐ Taxes ☐ Hazard Ins. ☐ Mtg. Ins. ☐

Prepayment Option

Subject Property

Property Street Address	City	County	State	Zip	No. Units

Legal Description (Attach description if necessary)	Year Built

Purpose of Loan: ☐ Purchase   ☐ Construction-Permanent   ☐ Construction   ☐ Refinance   ☐ Other (Explain)

Complete this line if Construction-Permanent or Construction Loan ☑	Lot Value Data	Original Cost	Present Value (a)	Cost of Imps. (b)	Total (a + b)	ENTER TOTAL AS PURCHASE PRICE IN DETAILS OF PURCHASE.
	Year Acquired	$	$	$	$	

Complete this line if a Refinance Loan	Purpose of Refinance	Describe Improvements [ ] made [ ] to be made
Year Acquired	Original Cost	Amt. Existing Liens		
$	$			Cost: $

Title Will Be Held In What Name(s)	Manner In Which Title Will Be Held

Source of Down Payment and Settlement Charges

This application is designed to be completed by the borrower(s) with the lender's assistance. The Co-Borrower Section and all other Co-Borrower questions must be completed and the appropriate box(es) checked if ☐ another person will be jointly obligated with the Borrower on the loan, or ☐ the Borrower is relying on income from alimony, child support or separate maintenance or on the income or assets of another person as a basis for repayment of the loan, or ☐ the Borrower is married and resides, or the property is located, in a community property state.

Borrower			**Co-Borrower**		
Name	Age	School Yrs	Name	Age	School Yrs
Present Address No. Years ___ ☐ Own ☐ Rent			Present Address No. Years ___ ☐ Own ☐ Rent		
Street			Street		
City/State/Zip			City/State/Zip		
Former address if less than 2 years at present address			Former address if less than 2 years at present address		
Street			Street		
City/State/Zip			City/State/Zip		
Years at former address ☐ Own ☐ Rent			Years at former address ☐ Own ☐ Rent		
Marital Status ☐ Married ☐ Separated ☐ Unmarried (incl. single, divorced, widowed)	DEPENDENTS OTHER THAN LISTED BY CO BORROWER NO. AGES		Marital Status ☐ Married ☐ Separated ☐ Unmarried (incl. single, divorced, widowed)	DEPENDENTS OTHER THAN LISTED BY BORROWER NO. AGES	
Name and Address of Employer	Years employed in this line of work or profession? ___ years Years on this job ___ ☐ Self Employed*		Name and Address of Employer	Years employed in this line of work or profession? ___ years Years on this job ___ ☐ Self Employed*	
Position/Title	Type of Business		Position/Title	Type of Business	
Social Security Number ***	Home Phone	Business Phone	Social Security Number ***	Home Phone	Business Phone

Gross Monthly Income				**Monthly Housing Expense****			**Details of Purchase**	
Item	Borrower	Co-Borrower	Total	Rent	PRESENT	PROPOSED	Do Not Complete If Refinance	
Base Empl. Income	$	$	$	First Mortgage (P&I)	$	$	a. Purchase Price	$
Overtime				Other Financing (P&I)			b. Total Closing Costs (Est.)	
Bonuses				Hazard Insurance			c. Prepaid Escrows (Est.)	
Commissions				Real Estate Taxes			d. Total (a + b + c)	$
Dividends/Interest				Mortgage Insurance			e. Amount This Mortgage	( )
Net Rental Income				Homeowner Assn. Dues			f. Other Financing	( )
Other† (Before completing, see notice under Describe Other Income below.)				Other:			g. Other Equity	( )
				Total Monthly Pmt.	$	$	h. Amount of Cash Deposit	( )
				Utilities			i. Closing Costs Paid by Seller	( )
Total	$	$	$	Total	$	$	j. Cash Reqd. For Closing (Est.)	$

Describe Other Income

NOTICE: † Alimony, child support, or separate maintenance income need not be revealed if the Borrower or Co-Borrower does not choose to have it considered as a basis for repaying this loan.

⇨ B–Borrower C–Co-Borrower	Monthly Amount
	$

If Employed In Current Position For Less Than Two Years, Complete the Following

B/C	Previous Employer/School	City/State	Type of Business	Position/Title	Dates From/To	Monthly Income
						$

These Questions Apply To Both Borrower and Co-Borrower

If a "yes" answer is given to a question in this column, please explain on an attached sheet.	Borrower Yes or No	Co-Borrower Yes or No
Are there any outstanding judgments against you?		
Have you been declared bankrupt within the past 7 years?		
Have you had property foreclosed upon or given title or deed in lieu thereof in the last 7 years?		
Are you a party to a law suit?		
Are you obligated to pay alimony, child support, or separate maintenance?		
Is any part of the down payment borrowed?		
Are you a co-maker or endorser on a note?		

	Borrower Yes or No	Co-Borrower Yes or No
Are you a U.S. citizen?		
If "no," are you a resident alien?		
If "no," are you a non-resident alien?		
Explain Other Financing or Other Equity (if any).		

*FHLMC/FNMA require business credit report, signed Federal Income Tax returns for last two years; and, if available, audited Profit and Loss Statement plus balance sheet for same period.
**All Present Monthly Housing Expenses of Borrower and Co-Borrower should be listed on a combined basis.
***Optional for FHLMC

FHLMC 65 Rev. 10/86

Fannie Mae Form 1003 Rev. 10/86

This Statement and any applicable supporting schedules may be completed jointly by both married and unmarried co-borrowers if their assets and liabilities are sufficiently joined so that the Statement can be meaningfully and fairly presented on a combined basis; otherwise separate Statements and Schedules are required (FHLMC 65A/FNMA 1003A). If the co-borrower section was completed about a spouse, this statement and supporting schedules must be completed about that spouse also.   ☐ Completed Jointly   ☐ Not Completed Jointly

Assets		Liabilities and Pledged Assets				

Indicate by (*) those liabilities or pledged assets which will be satisfied upon sale of real estate owned or upon refinancing of subject property.

Description	Cash or Market Value	Creditors' Name, Address and Account Number		Acct. Name if Not Borrower's	Mo. Pmt. and Mos. Left to Pay	Unpaid Balance
Cash Deposit Toward Purchase Held By	$	Installment Debts (Include "revolving" charge accounts)			$ Pmt /Mos.	$
		Co.	Acct. No.			
Checking and Savings Accounts (Show Names of Institutions (Account Numbers) Bank, S & L or Credit Union		Addr.				
		City				
		Co.	Acct. No.		/	
Addr.		Addr.				
City		City				
Acct. No.		Co.	Acct. No.			
Bank, S & L or Credit Union		Addr.				
		City			/	
Addr.		Co.	Acct. No.			
City		Addr.				
Acct. No.		City				
Bank, S & L or Credit Union		Co.	Acct. No.			
		Addr.			/	
Addr.		City				
City		Other Debts including Stock Pledges				
Acct. No.						
Stocks and Bonds (No. Description)		Real Estate Loans Co.	Acct. No.			
		Addr.				
		City				
Life Insurance Net Cash Value Face Amount $		Co.	Acct. No.			
		Addr.				
Subtotal Liquid Assets		City				
Real Estate Owned (Enter Market Value from Schedule of Real Estate Owned)		Automobile Loans Co.	Acct. No.			
Vested Interest in Retirement Fund		Addr.				
Net worth of Business Owned (ATTACH FINANCIAL STATEMENT)		City				
		Co.	Acct. No.			
Automobiles Owned (Make and Year)		City				
Furniture and Personal Property		Alimony, Child Support, Separate Maintenance Payments Owed to				
Other Assets (Itemize)						
		Total Monthly Payments			$	
Total Assets	A $	Net Worth (A minus B) $			Total Liabilities	B $

SCHEDULE OF REAL ESTATE OWNED (If Additional Properties Owned Attach Separate Schedule)

Address of Property (Indicate S if Sold, PS if Pending Sale or R if Rental being held for income)	Type of Property	Present Market Value	Amount of Mortgages & Liens	Gross Rental Income	Mortgage Payments	Taxes, Ins. Maintenance and Misc.	Net Rental Income
		$	$	$	$	$	$
TOTALS →		$	$	$	$	$	$

List Previous Credit References

B - Borrower C - Co-Borrower	Creditor's Name and Address	Account Number	Purpose	Highest Balance	Date Paid
				$	

List any additional names under which credit has previously been received _____

AGREEMENT   The undersigned applies for the loan indicated in this application to be secured by a first mortgage or deed of trust on the property described herein, and represents that the property will not be used for any illegal or restricted purpose, and that all statements made in this application are true and are made for the purpose of obtaining the loan. Verification may be obtained from any source named in this application. The original or a copy of this application will be retained by the lender, even if the loan is not granted. The undersigned   ☐ intend or   ☐ do not intend to occupy the property as their primary residence.

I/we fully understand that it is a federal crime punishable by fine or imprisonment, or both, to knowingly make any false statements concerning any of the above facts as applicable under the provisions of Title 18, United States Code, Section 1014.

_____ Date _____   _____ Date _____
Borrower's Signature   Co-Borrower's Signature

Information for Government Monitoring Purposes

The following information is requested by the Federal Government for certain types of loans related to a dwelling, in order to monitor the lender's compliance with equal credit opportunity and fair housing laws. You are not required to furnish this information, but are encouraged to do so. The law provides that a lender may neither discriminate on the basis of this information, nor on whether you choose to furnish it. However, if you choose not to furnish it, under Federal regulations this lender is required to note race and sex on the basis of visual observation or surname. If you do not wish to furnish the above information, please check the box below. Lender must review the above material to assure that the disclosures satisfy all requirements to which the lender is subject under applicable state law for the particular type of loan applied for.

Borrower ☐ I do not wish to furnish this information.   Co-Borrower ☐ I do not wish to furnish this information.
Race National Origin   Race National Origin
American Indian Alaskan Native   Asian Pacific Islander   American Indian Alaskan Native   Asian Pacific Islander
Black   Hispanic   White   Black   Hispanic   White
Other (specify)   Other (specify)
Sex   Female   Male   Sex   Female   Male

To Be Completed by Interviewer

This application was taken by:
face to face interview
by mail
by telephone

Interviewer _____   Name of Interviewer's Employer _____

Interviewer's Phone Number _____   Address of Interviewer's Employer _____

FHLMC Form 65 Rev. 10/86   **REVERSE**   Fannie Mae Form 1003 Rev. 10/86 shall have possession of the fire insurance policies and shall have the power to determine the quality and quantity of coverage afforded by those policies.

The foregoing description of the residential application and commitment procedure has been modified in recent times. The great diversity in loan terms offered by residential lenders has made it almost impossible for the applicant to do anything but furnish personal information and say, "I want a loan." A discussion ensues or a computer prints out a variety of available mortgage plans. Some plan is agreed upon, and the lender prepares a commitment outlining the plan and listing the various deductions from the loan amount that will be required to defray loan expenses, such as appraisal fees. About this time, the lender will furnish the prospective borrower a Truth-in-Lending statement and a Federal Reserve Bank pamphlet describing the new forms of mortgages. If the borrower is satisfied, he signs the acceptance of the commitment, and a loan contract is created. The commitment, of course, is conditioned on satisfactory appraisal, satisfactory title, and so on.

The commitment sets forth the loan terms the lender is willing to give. The residential commitment will either tie the mortgagee to the rate stated in the mortgage or to the "market rate" at the time of closing. All commitments have time limits. If the time expires before the deal is closed, the process goes back to square one. A higher interest rate may be in force. If the borrower is willing to proceed, he signs a statement accepting these terms. The application form itself often is one designed by the Federal Reserve Board. It conforms to Reg. B 12 CFR Sec. 202.5e (see the accompanying form).

Reg. B requires the lender to notify the applicant of the action taken on the application and, if refused, why credit was refused him.

The requirements of a residential loan commitment should look ahead to the possibility or probability that the loan will be sold in the secondary market. It should require, for example, those things that FNMA will require.

Application and commitment procedures vary depending upon whether the loan is a residential or commercial loan. In the commercial transaction the developer's loan application on a construction loan is often merely a sales pitch describing the proposed project. It is too skimpy to be regarded as a legal document. If the bank is interested in the project, its loan committee will set out the terms on which it is prepared to make the loan in the form of a "commitment." See Kratovil and Werner, *Modern Mortgage Law and Practice* § 25.05 (2d ed. 1981). There is some bargaining before a commitment acceptable to both parties is agreed upon. Then the developer accepts the commitment, and a loan contract comes into existence. This acceptance ought to contain a promise by the borrower to perform his part of the bargain.

This entire aspect of the mortgage business is not well understood, even by sophisticated lawyers. A good, binding loan contract is needed if the mortgage lien is to maintain its priority as an "obligatory advance" mortgage. As illustrative of the lack of understanding of this procedure in the mortgage business, not too many years ago residential lenders were giving *oral commitments*. Indeed, this still happens. A mortgage loan comes under the Statute of Frauds. Everything must be in writing.

As to the provisions of the commitment the borrower is particularly interested in the duration of the commitment and the interest rate. As of this writing, interest rates have been volatile. If borrower gets a 45 day commitment at 10%

interest, the time may run by without completion of the required steps. Slow production of the appraisal is a constant complaint. The lender then may quote a new market interest rate, 11%, to the borrower. The result may be to increase the monthly payments beyond the borrowing power of a marginal borrower. A borrower may wish to insist on a 60-day commitment. When she pays her application fee, she has this option. She also may choose a fixed or floating rate.

> **NEW DIRECTIONS:** A number of states are considering legislation on this subject. Probably the new laws will call for locked in rates or a bold face warning on floating rates. Jumps from 8½% to 10½% in sixty days are simply intolerable.

On a commercial loan the commitment will describe the leases and lender will check them before closing. The commitment will call for an assignment of leases and rents, survey, requirements as to guarantees by third-parties, survey and chattel lien search, etc. On a construction loan the commitment contains a wealth of detail regarding disbursement of the loan proceeds.

20.13(a)   Commitment Fees

Quite commonly, in larger loans, the borrower pays a commitment fee which is refundable only if he performs his part of the bargain.

> **EXAMPLE:** R procured a commitment from E for a mortgage loan on a shopping center. The commitment was contingent upon R's procuring eight leases with major tenants. R paid E a commitment fee. R was able to procure only six leases. E could keep the fee. *Boston Road Shopping Center* v. *Teachers Ins. & Annuity Assn.*, 11 NYS2d 831 (1962). *Accord, White Lakes Shopping Center, Inc.* v. *Jefferson Standard Life Ins. Co.*, 490 P2d 609 (Kans. 1971); 93 ALR3d 1156.

20.13(b)   Damages

A lender will be liable to the borrower for damages if the lender does not live up to the commitment. *St. Paul at Chase Corp.* v. *Manufacturer's Life Ins. Co.*, 278 A2d 12 (Md. 1971); *Liben* v. *Nassau S. & L. Assn.*, 337 NY2d 310 (1972); 36 ALR 1408; 4 ALR4th 682.

> **EXAMPLE:** Lender commits to loan Borrower $1,000,000 at 12 percent interest. Lender refuses to make the loan when the time for funding arrives. Borrower obtains a loan from Banker at 14 percent interest. Lender is liable to Borrower for the 2 percent interest differential. *Pipkin* v. *Thomas & Hill, Inc.*, 258 SE2d 778 (N.C. 1979).

Some further examples may help to illustrate how this problem is being handled by the courts today.

> **EXAMPLE:** Buyer applied to Lender for a mortgage and was given a commitment at an interest rate of 6 percent. At closing Buyer was told by Lender that interest rates had risen and he would have to pay 7.25 percent. Buyer had no

place to live so he closed the deal at 7.25%. He filed suit and the court ordered Lender to reduce the rate to 6 percent. *Leben* v. *Nassau S. & L. Assn., 337 NYS2d 310 (1972).*

If the lender wishes to protect itself against rising interest rates, the commitment should so provide.

EXAMPLE: Borrower signed a note containing a variable interest rate clause. Borrower asked Lender's officer about a variable interest rate and was told that Lender "probably" would not raise its rates. In less than a year Lender raised the interest rate. The court refused to permit Lender to foreclose and awarded damages to Borrower. *Peoples Bank* v. *Humphrey, 451 NE2d 1104 (Ind. 1983).*

EXAMPLE: Seller obtained a commitment from Lender to Buyer before the contract of sale was signed. Relying on the commitment, Seller signed the contract and also contracted to buy a new house. Lender backed out of the commitment. Seller could sue Lender for damages. *Morrison* v. *Home S. & L. Assn., 346 P2d 917 (1960).*

20.13(c)   Specific Performance

As an alternative to damages, especially in large loans, the borrower may sue the lender for specific performance. *Vanderventer* v. *Dale Const. Co., 334 P2d 183 (Ore. 1975); 82 ALR3d 1116.*

EXAMPLE: Owner gives Lender #1 a mortgage, which is a construction loan to build an office building. Lender #1 makes the loan in reliance on Lender #2's commitment to make a new mortgage when the building is completed, the funds to be used to pay Lender #1's mortgage. When the building is completed, the mortgage market and office building market are dead. Funds are simply unobtainable elsewhere. Specific performance can be used to force Lender #2 to go through with his commitment.

20.13(d)   Credit Information

The most important information the residential lender requires concerning the borrower is his credit rating. This information must be provided and obtained in accordance with the terms of the Fair Credit Reporting Act, 15 USCA Sec. 1681. This law protects the borrower against inaccurate credit reports. The FHLBB Fair Lending Regulations and Guidelines are in 12 C.F.R. Sec. 528 and Sec. 531. Basically, they are designed to protect borrowers against unfair practices, such as a refusal to lend on a home simply because of its age.

By enacting the Equal Credit Opportunity Act, 15 USCS §§ 1691 *et seq.*, Congress has acted to make credit available with fairness, impartiality, and without discrimination on the basis of race, color, religion, national origin, sex, marital status, or age. While marital status inquiries are not absolutely prohibited to the mortgage lender, 12 CFR §202.4(c)(l), only the terms "married," "unmarried," or "separated" may be used. 12 CFR §202.4(c)(2). The thought is that other inquiry is not directed toward an applicant's creditworthiness. The creditor cannot discount the income of an applicant or an applicant's spouse solely because it is derived from part-time employment, but the probable continuity of such income may be considered. 12 CFR §202.5(e). Inquiries into the birth control practices and child-bearing intentions of the applicant are forbidden. 12 CFR §202.4(h); 13 J. of L. Reform 102 (1979). A lender may be fined for violating this law and a wrongfully rejected applicant may sue for damages.

The Act does not prohibit a lender from establishing valid credit criteria. The lender may for example inquire into the fact that the applicant has taken bankruptcy or lacks U.S. citizenship. *Nguyen* v. *Montgomery Ward & Co.,* 513 F.Supp. 1039 (1981).

20.13(e)   Denial of Loan Application

A lender must advise a loan applicant of the denial of the application and give the applicant a statement of the reasons for the denial. 15 USC §1691.

20.13(f)   False Applications

In today's world of tight money and high interest rates, many borrowers are tempted to falsify their loan applications in order to get a loan or to get the loan at more favorable terms.

> **EXAMPLE:**   A borrower states that he is paying a 20 percent downpayment when really the seller is receiving 10 percent in cash and taking back a second mortgage for 10 percent of the purchase price. Some buyers and sellers go so far as to have two sets of documents, one stating the form of the transaction as the lender wants to see it and the other stating the form that the transaction really takes.

> **EXAMPLE:**   A borrower will state his intent to occupy the property when he has no real intent of living there.

These kinds of false statements are violations of state law and, if a federal instrumentality is involved, federal law. See, for example, 18 USC §§1010–1014; Ill. Rev. Stat. Ch. 38, §17–1(c).

20.13(g)   Truth-in-Lending

The Federal Truth-in-Lending Act, 15 USC §§1601 *et seq.,* was enacted to give the consumer a disclosure of various credit terms to enable him to shop several lenders to obtain the best deal possible. The required disclosures include: the annual percentage rate; the number, amount, and due dates of scheduled payments; the amount of any balloon payments; the conditions of refinancing; the amount of the late payment charge; a description of any security interest; whether after-acquired property will be subject to the security interest; a description of any prepayment penalty; and the amount of any escrow account required for the payment of taxes, insurance, and the like. 12 CFR § 226.8. Special disclosures are also needed of the provisions of a variable rate or graduated payment mortgage.

20.13(h)   Flood Insurance

The lender must disclose to the borrower if the property is located in an area designated by the federal government as flood prone. If the community participates in the federal government flood program, flood controls on development (state and federal) will be in force and flood insurance will be available. Ordinary insurance does not cover flooding. It is rash to build or buy in such areas without obtaining flood insurance.

Most municipalities and counties base their flood plain development plans on the state's model ordinance for cities. The ordinance defines minimum state and federal guidelines for land-use planning and development in designated flood hazard areas.

Here are some of the model ordinance's highlights:

   1. Buildings may be constructed on permanent landfill in layers no greater than one foot deep before compaction.
   2. The lowest floor (including basement) must be at or above the flood protection elevation (the elevation of the base floodplain plus one foot at any given location in a flood hazard area.)
   3. Landfill must be protected against erosion during flooding by vegetative cover and other erosion-protection implements.
   4. Landfill must not adversely affect the flow of surface drainage from or onto neighboring properties.
   5. Buildings may be elevated on crawl space, walls, stilts, piles, or other foundations.
   6. Structural walls must have permanent openings (windows, doors) no more than one foot above the level of the lot.
   7. Foundation and supports must be anchored and aligned in relation to flood flows and adjoining structures so as to minimize exposure to known hydrodynamic forces such as current, waves, ice, and floating debris.
   8. Areas below the flood protection elevation must be constructed of materials resistant to flood damage.
   9. Electrical, heating, ventilation, plumbing, air-conditioning systems, and utility meters must be placed at flood protection elevation.
   10. Water and sewer pipes, electrical and telephone lines, and submersible pumps also must be placed at flood protection elevation.

20.14   Mortgage Forms and Practice

In the field of residential mortgage, both homes and apartments, mortgage forms follow the forms and practice set forth by FNMA, FHLMC, FHA, and VA. The old diversity of forms has vanished. Moreover, the details of mortgage practice are set forth in the detailed Servicer's Guides—for example, those of FHLMC and FNMA. The capable legal and lending personnel of these agencies have set forth in detail requirements that offer a mortgage practice guide of the very highest quality.

To a very great extent, lenders today choose to use the FNMA form of mortgage and note, either because they intend to sell the loan immediately in the secondary market or may have need to do so in the future. For this reason, sample forms are included on pp. 292–297. As is obvious, these forms consist in large part of uniform provisions that are the same country-wide. A small section of the mortgage is devoted to provisions required by the local law.

20.14(a)   Deviations from the FNMA/FHLMC Form

A lender who does not plan to immediately assign the mortgage in the secondary market can attach a rider including provisions the secondary market would not accept. It should contain a clause stating, for example, that such rider will become void immediately upon transfer to FNMA. Thus the document is brought into compliance with the secondary market requirement that its forms be used without modification.

20.15   The Mortgage Note

After the mortgagee has given his commitment to make the loan, the mortgagor signs a promissory note and mortgage. The mortgage stands as security for payment of the note. *The chief function of the note is to make the mortgagor personally liable for payment of the mortgage debt.* If the mortgagor signs such a note and then decides that he does not want the building, he cannot simply abandon the property and move elsewhere. Wherever he goes he takes his personal liability with him, and if the mortgage is foreclosed, the mortgagee can obtain a personal judgment against him for any deficiency between the foreclosure sale price and the amount of the mortgage debt. Armed with such a judgment, the mortgagee can garnishee the mortgagor's wages or have his other property sold to pay the balance due.

The mortgage note in common use today is the FNMA form.

20.15(a)   The Mortgage Note—Negotiability

If a note is drawn to meet certain technical requirements, it can obtain the legal status of *negotiability*. This means that it can pass from the original creditor to a holder in due course. While the debtor may have had some defenses against the original creditor, that is, the full debt was not disbursed, those defenses will not work against the holder in due course.

A problem is posed by the new mortgages where interest rates vary from time to time as selected indexes move up and down. It seems doubtful that those mortgage notes are negotiable. A. *Alport & Son Inc.*, v. *Hotel Evans, Inc.*, 317 NYS2d 937 (1970). The importance of negotiability appears to be diminishing.

Text continued on p. 298.

NOTE

...., 19.........   ...., ...
                                                            [City]   [State]

....
[Property Address]

1. BORROWER'S PROMISE TO PAY

In return for a loan that I have received, I promise to pay U.S. $... (this amount is called "principal"), plus interest, to the order of the Lender. The Lender is .... I understand that the Lender may transfer this Note. The Lender or anyone who takes this Note by transfer and who is entitled to receive payments under this Note is called the "Note Holder."

2. INTEREST

Interest will be charged on unpaid principal until the full amount of principal has been paid. I will pay interest at a yearly rate of ....%.

The interest rate required by this Section 2 is the rate I will pay both before and after any default described in Section 6(B) of this Note.

3. PAYMENTS

(A) Time and Place of Payments

I will pay principal and interest by making payments every month.

I will make my monthly payments on the .... day of each month beginning on ...., 19......... I will make these payments every month until I have paid all of the principal and interest and any other charges described below that I may owe under this Note. My monthly payments will be applied to interest before principal. If, on ...., ..., I still owe amounts under this Note, I will pay those amounts in full on that date, which is called the "maturity date."

I will make my monthly payments at ....
.... or at a different place if required by the Note Holder.

(B) Amount of Monthly Payments

My monthly payment will be in the amount of U.S. $..

4. BORROWER'S RIGHT TO PREPAY

I have the right to make payments of principal at any time before they are due. A payment of principal only is known as a "prepayment." When I make a prepayment, I will tell the Note Holder in writing that I am doing so.

I may make a full prepayment or partial prepayments without paying any prepayment charge. The Note Holder will use all of my prepayments to reduce the amount of principal that I owe under this Note. If I make a partial prepayment, there will be no changes in the due date or in the amount of my monthly payment unless the Note Holder agrees in writing to those changes.

5. LOAN CHARGES

If a law, which applies to this loan and which sets maximum loan charges, is finally interpreted so that the interest or other loan charges collected or to be collected in connection with this loan exceed the permitted limits, then: (i) any such loan charge shall be reduced by the amount necessary to reduce the charge to the permitted limit; and (ii) any sums already collected from me which exceeded permitted limits will be refunded to me. The Note Holder may choose to make this refund by reducing the principal I owe under this Note or by making a direct payment to me. If a refund reduces principal, the reduction will be treated as a partial prepayment.

6. BORROWER'S FAILURE TO PAY AS REQUIRED

(A) Late Charge for Overdue Payments

If the Note Holder has not received the full amount of any monthly payment by the end of .... calendar days after the date it is due, I will pay a late charge to the Note Holder. The amount of the charge will be ....% of my overdue payment of principal and interest. I will pay this late charge promptly but only once on each late payment.

(B) Default

If I do not pay the full amount of each monthly payment on the date it is due, I will be in default.

(C) Notice of Default

If I am in default, the Note Holder may send me a written notice telling me that if I do not pay the overdue amount by a certain date, the Note Holder may require me to pay immediately the full amount of principal which has not been paid and all the interest that I owe on that amount. That date must be at least 30 days after the date on which the notice is delivered or mailed to me.

(D) No Waiver By Note Holder

Even if, at a time when I am in default, the Note Holder does not require me to pay immediately in full as described above, the Note Holder will still have the right to do so if I am in default at a later time.

(E) Payment of Note Holder's Costs and Expenses

If the Note Holder has required me to pay immediately in full as described above, the Note Holder will have the right to be paid back by me for all of its costs and expenses in enforcing this Note to the extent not prohibited by applicable law. Those expenses include, for example, reasonable attorneys' fees.

7. GIVING OF NOTICES

Unless applicable law requires a different method, any notice that must be given to me under this Note will be given by delivering it or by mailing it by first class mail to me at the Property Address above or at a different address if I give the Note Holder a notice of my different address.

Any notice that must be given to the Note Holder under this Note will be given by mailing it by first class mail to the Note Holder at the address stated in Section 3(A) above or at a different address if I am given a notice of that different address.

MULTISTATE FIXED RATE NOTE—Single Family—FNMA/FHLMC UNIFORM INSTRUMENT   Form 3200 12/83
BFSL 4323-1

8. OBLIGATIONS OF PERSONS UNDER THIS NOTE

If more than one person signs this Note, each person is fully and personally obligated to keep all of the promises made in this Note, including the promise to pay the full amount owed. Any person who is a guarantor, surety or endorser of this Note is also obligated to do these things. Any person who takes over these obligations, including the obligations of a guarantor, surety or endorser of this Note, is also obligated to keep all of the promises made in this Note. The Note Holder may enforce its rights under this Note against each person individually or against all of us together. This means that any one of us may be required to pay all of the amounts owed under this Note.

9. WAIVERS

I and any other person who has obligations under this Note waive the rights of presentment and notice of dishonor. "Presentment" means the right to require the Note Holder to demand payment of amounts due. "Notice of dishonor" means the right to require the Note Holder to give notice to other persons that amounts due have not been paid.

10. UNIFORM SECURED NOTE

This Note is a uniform instrument with limited variations in some jurisdictions. In addition to the protections given to the Note Holder under this Note, a Mortgage, Deed of Trust or Security Deed (the "Security Instrument"), dated the same date as this Note, protects the Note Holder from possible losses which might result if I do not keep the promises which I make in this Note. That Security Instrument describes how and under what conditions I may be required to make immediate payment in full of all amounts I owe under this Note. Some of those conditions are described as follows:

Transfer of the Property or a Beneficial Interest in Borrower. If all or any part of the Property or any interest in it is sold or transferred (or if a beneficial interest in Borrower is sold or transferred and Borrower is not a natural person) without Lender's prior written consent, Lender may, at its option, require immediate payment in full of all sums secured by this Security Instrument. However, this option shall not be exercised by Lender if exercise is prohibited by federal law as of the date of this Security Instrument.

If Lender exercises this option, Lender shall give Borrower notice of acceleration. The notice shall provide a period of not less than 30 days from the date the notice is delivered or mailed within which Borrower must pay all sums secured by this Security Instrument. If Borrower fails to pay these sums prior to the expiration of this period, Lender may invoke any remedies permitted by this Security Instrument without further notice or demand on Borrower.

WITNESS THE HAND(S) AND SEAL(S) OF THE UNDERSIGNED.

....(Seal)
                                                                                          -Borrower

....(Seal)
                                                                                          -Borrower

....(Seal)
                                                                                          -Borrower

[Sign Original Only]

—————————————————— [Space Above This Line For Recording Data] ——————————————————

MORTGAGE

THIS MORTGAGE ("Security Instrument") is given on ....,
19.......... The mortgagor is ....
.... ("Borrower"). This Security Instrument is given to ....
...., which is organized and existing
under the laws of ...., and whose address is ....
.... ("Lender").
Borrower owes Lender the principal sum of ....
.... Dollars (U.S. $................................). This debt is evidenced by Borrower's note
dated the same date as this Security Instrument ("Note"), which provides for monthly payments, with the full debt, if not
paid earlier, due and payable on .... This Security Instrument
secures to Lender: (a) the repayment of the debt evidenced by the Note, with interest, and all renewals, extensions and
modifications; (b) the payment of all other sums, with interest, advanced under paragraph 7 to protect the security of this
Security Instrument; and (c) the performance of Borrower's covenants and agreements under this Security Instrument and
the Note. For this purpose, Borrower does hereby mortgage, grant and convey to Lender the following described property
located in .... County, Illinois:

which has the address of ...., ...
                                 [Street]   [City]
Illinois .... ("Property Address");
         [Zip Code]

TOGETHER WITH all the improvements now or hereafter erected on the property, and all easements, rights,
appurtenances, rents, royalties, mineral, oil and gas rights and profits, water rights and stock and all fixtures now or
hereafter a part of the property. All replacements and additions shall also be covered by this Security Instrument. All of the
foregoing is referred to in this Security Instrument as the "Property."

BORROWER COVENANTS that Borrower is lawfully seised of the estate hereby conveyed and has the right to
mortgage, grant and convey the Property and that the Property is unencumbered, except for encumbrances of record.
Borrower warrants and will defend generally the title to the Property against all claims and demands, subject to any
encumbrances of record.

THIS SECURITY INSTRUMENT combines uniform covenants for national use and non-uniform covenants with
limited variations by jurisdiction to constitute a uniform security instrument covering real property.

ILLINOIS—Single Family—FNMA/FHLMC UNIFORM INSTRUMENT

UNIFORM COVENANTS Borrower and Lender covenant and agree as follows:

1. Payment of Principal and Interest; Prepayment and Late Charges. Borrower shall promptly pay when due the principal of and interest on the debt evidenced by the Note and any prepayment and late charges due under the Note.

2. Funds for Taxes and Insurance. Subject to applicable law or to a written waiver by Lender, Borrower shall pay to Lender on the day monthly payments are due under the Note, until the Note is paid in full, a sum ("Funds") equal to one-twelfth of: (a) yearly taxes and assessments which may attain priority over this Security Instrument; (b) yearly leasehold payments or ground rents on the Property, if any; (c) yearly hazard insurance premiums; and (d) yearly mortgage insurance premiums, if any. These items are called "escrow items." Lender may estimate the Funds due on the basis of current data and reasonable estimates of future escrow items.

The Funds shall be held in an institution the deposits or accounts of which are insured or guaranteed by a federal or state agency (including Lender if Lender is such an institution). Lender shall apply the Funds to pay the escrow items. Lender may not charge for holding and applying the Funds, analyzing the account or verifying the escrow items, unless Lender pays Borrower interest on the Funds and applicable law permits Lender to make such a charge. Borrower and Lender may agree in writing that interest shall be paid on the Funds. Unless an agreement is made or applicable law requires interest to be paid, Lender shall not be required to pay Borrower any interest or earnings on the Funds. Lender shall give to Borrower, without charge, an annual accounting of the Funds showing credits and debits to the Funds and the purpose for which each debit to the Funds was made. The Funds are pledged as additional security for the sums secured by this Security Instrument.

If the amount of the Funds held by Lender, together with the future monthly payments of Funds payable prior to the due dates of the escrow items, shall exceed the amount required to pay the escrow items when due, the excess shall be, at Borrower's option, either promptly repaid to Borrower or credited to Borrower on monthly payments of Funds. If the amount of the Funds held by Lender is not sufficient to pay the escrow items when due, Borrower shall pay to Lender any amount necessary to make up the deficiency in one or more payments as required by Lender.

Upon payment in full of all sums secured by this Security Instrument, Lender shall promptly refund to Borrower any Funds held by Lender. If under paragraph 19 the Property is sold or acquired by Lender, Lender shall apply, no later than immediately prior to the sale of the Property or its acquisition by Lender, any Funds held by Lender at the time of application as a credit against the sums secured by this Security Instrument.

3. Application of Payments. Unless applicable law provides otherwise, all payments received by Lender under paragraphs 1 and 2 shall be applied: first, to late charges due under the Note; second, to prepayment charges due under the Note; third, to amounts payable under paragraph 2; fourth, to interest due; and last, to principal due.

4. Charges; Liens. Borrower shall pay all taxes, assessments, charges, fines and impositions attributable to the Property which may attain priority over this Security Instrument, and leasehold payments or ground rents, if any. Borrower shall pay these obligations in the manner provided in paragraph 2, or if not paid in that manner, Borrower shall pay them on time directly to the person owed payment. Borrower shall promptly furnish to Lender all notices of amounts to be paid under this paragraph. If Borrower makes these payments directly, Borrower shall promptly furnish to Lender receipts evidencing the payments.

Borrower shall promptly discharge any lien which has priority over this Security Instrument unless Borrower: (a) agrees in writing to the payment of the obligation secured by the lien in a manner acceptable to Lender; (b) contests in good faith the lien by, or defends against enforcement of the lien in, legal proceedings which in the Lender's opinion operate to prevent the enforcement of the lien or forfeiture of any part of the Property; or (c) secures from the holder of the lien an agreement satisfactory to Lender subordinating the lien to this Security Instrument. If Lender determines that any part of the Property is subject to a lien which may attain priority over this Security Instrument, Lender may give Borrower a notice identifying the lien. Borrower shall satisfy the lien or take one or more of the actions set forth above within 10 days of the giving of notice.

5. Hazard Insurance. Borrower shall keep the improvements now existing or hereafter erected on the Property insured against loss by fire, hazards included within the term "extended coverage" and any other hazards for which Lender requires insurance. This insurance shall be maintained in the amounts and for the periods that Lender requires. The insurance carrier providing the insurance shall be chosen by Borrower subject to Lender's approval which shall not be unreasonably withheld.

All insurance policies and renewals shall be acceptable to Lender and shall include a standard mortgage clause. Lender shall have the right to hold the policies and renewals. If Lender requires, Borrower shall promptly give to Lender all receipts of paid premiums and renewal notices. In the event of loss, Borrower shall give prompt notice to the insurance carrier and Lender. Lender may make proof of loss if not made promptly by Borrower.

Unless Lender and Borrower otherwise agree in writing, insurance proceeds shall be applied to restoration or repair of the Property damaged, if the restoration or repair is economically feasible and Lender's security is not lessened. If the restoration or repair is not economically feasible or Lender's security would be lessened, the insurance proceeds shall be applied to the sums secured by this Security Instrument, whether or not then due, with any excess paid to Borrower. If Borrower abandons the Property, or does not answer within 30 days a notice from Lender that the insurance carrier has offered to settle a claim, then Lender may collect the insurance proceeds. Lender may use the proceeds to repair or restore the Property or to pay sums secured by this Security Instrument, whether or not then due. The 30-day period will begin when the notice is given.

Unless Lender and Borrower otherwise agree in writing, any application of proceeds to principal shall not extend or postpone the due date of the monthly payments referred to in paragraphs 1 and 2 or change the amount of the payments. If under paragraph 19 the Property is acquired by Lender, Borrower's right to any insurance policies and proceeds resulting from damage to the Property prior to the acquisition shall pass to Lender to the extent of the sums secured by this Security Instrument immediately prior to the acquisition.

6. Preservation and Maintenance of Property; Leaseholds. Borrower shall not destroy, damage or substantially change the Property, allow the Property to deteriorate or commit waste. If this Security Instrument is on a leasehold, Borrower shall comply with the provisions of the lease, and if Borrower acquires fee title to the Property, the leasehold and fee title shall not merge unless Lender agrees to the merger in writing.

7. Protection of Lender's Rights in the Property; Mortgage Insurance. If Borrower fails to perform the covenants and agreements contained in this Security Instrument, or there is a legal proceeding that may significantly affect Lender's rights in the Property (such as a proceeding in bankruptcy, probate, for condemnation or to enforce laws or regulations), then Lender may do and pay for whatever is necessary to protect the value of the Property and Lender's rights in the Property. Lender's actions may include paying any sums secured by a lien which has priority over this Security Instrument, appearing in court, paying reasonable attorneys' fees and entering on the Property to make repairs. Although Lender may take action under this paragraph 7, Lender does not have to do so.

Any amounts disbursed by Lender under this paragraph 7 shall become additional debt of Borrower secured by this Security Instrument. Unless Borrower and Lender agree to other terms of payment, these amounts shall bear interest from the date of disbursement at the Note rate and shall be payable, with interest, upon notice from Lender to Borrower requesting payment.

If Lender required mortgage insurance as a condition of making the loan secured by this Security Instrument, Borrower shall pay the premiums required to maintain the insurance in effect until such time as the requirement for the insurance terminates in accordance with Borrower's and Lender's written agreement or applicable law.

8. Inspection. Lender or its agent may make reasonable entries upon and inspections of the Property. Lender shall give Borrower notice at the time of or prior to an inspection specifying reasonable cause for the inspection.

9. Condemnation. The proceeds of any award or claim for damages, direct or consequential, in connection with any condemnation or other taking of any part of the Property, or for conveyance in lieu of condemnation, are hereby assigned and shall be paid to Lender.

In the event of a total taking of the Property, the proceeds shall be applied to the sums secured by this Security Instrument, whether or not then due, with any excess paid to Borrower. In the event of a partial taking of the Property, unless Borrower and Lender otherwise agree in writing, the sums secured by this Security Instrument shall be reduced by the amount of the proceeds multiplied by the following fraction: (a) the total amount of the sums secured immediately before the taking, divided by (b) the fair market value of the Property immediately before the taking. Any balance shall be paid to Borrower.

If the Property is abandoned by Borrower, or if, after notice by Lender to Borrower that the condemnor offers to make an award or settle a claim for damages, Borrower fails to respond to Lender within 30 days after the date the notice is given, Lender is authorized to collect and apply the proceeds, at its option, either to restoration or repair of the Property or to the sums secured by this Security Instrument, whether or not then due.

Unless Lender and Borrower otherwise agree in writing, any application of proceeds to principal shall not extend or postpone the due date of the monthly payments referred to in paragraphs 1 and 2 or change the amount of such payments

10. Borrower Not Released; Forbearance By Lender Not a Waiver. Extension of the time for payment or modification of amortization of the sums secured by this Security Instrument granted by Lender to any successor in interest of Borrower shall not operate to release the liability of the original Borrower or Borrower's successors in interest. Lender shall not be required to commence proceedings against any successor in interest or refuse to extend time for payment or otherwise modify amortization of the sums secured by this Security Instrument by reason of any demand made by the original Borrower or Borrower's successors in interest. Any forbearance by Lender in exercising any right or remedy shall not be a waiver of or preclude the exercise of any right or remedy.

11. Successors and Assigns Bound; Joint and Several Liability; Co-signers. The covenants and agreements of this Security Instrument shall bind and benefit the successors and assigns of Lender and Borrower, subject to the provisions of paragraph 17. Borrower's covenants and agreements shall be joint and several. Any Borrower who co-signs this Security Instrument but does not execute the Note: (a) is co-signing this Security Instrument only to mortgage, grant and convey that Borrower's interest in the Property under the terms of this Security Instrument; (b) is not personally obligated to pay the sums secured by this Security Instrument; and (c) agrees that Lender and any other Borrower may agree to extend, modify, forbear or make any accommodations with regard to the terms of this Security Instrument or the Note without that Borrower's consent.

12. Loan Charges. If the loan secured by this Security Instrument is subject to a law which sets maximum loan charges, and that law is finally interpreted so that the interest or other loan charges collected or to be collected in connection with the loan exceed the permitted limits, then: (a) any such loan charge shall be reduced by the amount necessary to reduce the charge to the permitted limit; and (b) any sums already collected from Borrower which exceeded permitted limits will be refunded to Borrower. Lender may choose to make this refund by reducing the principal owed under the Note or by making a direct payment to Borrower. If a refund reduces principal, the reduction will be treated as a partial prepayment without any prepayment charge under the Note.

13. Legislation Affecting Lender's Rights. If enactment or expiration of applicable laws has the effect of rendering any provision of the Note or this Security Instrument unenforceable according to its terms, Lender, at its option, may require immediate payment in full of all sums secured by this Security Instrument and may invoke any remedies permitted by paragraph 19. If Lender exercises this option, Lender shall take the steps specified in the second paragraph of paragraph 17.

14. Notices. Any notice to Borrower provided for in this Security Instrument shall be given by delivering it or by mailing it by first class mail unless applicable law requires use of another method. The notice shall be directed to the Property Address or any other address Borrower designates by notice to Lender. Any notice to Lender shall be given by first class mail to Lender's address stated herein or any other address Lender designates by notice to Borrower. Any notice provided for in this Security Instrument shall be deemed to have been given to Borrower or Lender when given as provided in this paragraph.

15. Governing Law; Severability. This Security Instrument shall be governed by federal law and the law of the jurisdiction in which the Property is located. In the event that any provision or clause of this Security Instrument or the Note conflicts with applicable law, such conflict shall not affect other provisions of this Security Instrument or the Note which can be given effect without the conflicting provision. To this end the provisions of this Security Instrument and the Note are declared to be severable.

16. Borrower's Copy. Borrower shall be given one conformed copy of the Note and of this Security Instrument.

17. Transfer of the Property or a Beneficial Interest in Borrower. If all or any part of the Property or any interest in it is sold or transferred (or if a beneficial interest in Borrower is sold or transferred and Borrower is not a natural person) without Lender's prior written consent, Lender may, at its option, require immediate payment in full of all sums secured by this Security Instrument. However, this option shall not be exercised by Lender if exercise is prohibited by federal law as of the date of this Security Instrument. *Due on Sale Clause*

If Lender exercises this option, Lender shall give Borrower notice of acceleration. The notice shall provide a period of not less than 30 days from the date the notice is delivered or mailed within which Borrower must pay all sums secured by this Security Instrument. If Borrower fails to pay these sums prior to the expiration of this period, Lender may invoke any remedies permitted by this Security Instrument without further notice or demand on Borrower.

18. Borrower's Right to Reinstate. If Borrower meets certain conditions, Borrower shall have the right to have enforcement of this Security Instrument discontinued at any time prior to the earlier of: (a) 5 days (or such other period as applicable law may specify for reinstatement) before sale of the Property pursuant to any power of sale contained in this Security Instrument; or (b) entry of a judgment enforcing this Security Instrument. Those conditions are that Borrower: (a) pays Lender all sums which then would be due under this Security Instrument and the Note had no acceleration occurred; (b) cures any default of any other covenants or agreements; (c) pays all expenses incurred in enforcing this Security Instrument, including, but not limited to, reasonable attorneys' fees; and (d) takes such action as Lender may reasonably require to assure that the lien of this Security Instrument, Lender's rights in the Property and Borrower's obligation to pay the sums secured by this Security Instrument shall continue unchanged. Upon reinstatement by Borrower, this Security Instrument and the obligations secured hereby shall remain fully effective as if no acceleration had occurred. However, this right to reinstate shall not apply in the case of acceleration under paragraphs 13 or 17.

NON-UNIFORM COVENANTS Borrower and Lender further covenant and agree as follows:

19. Acceleration; Remedies. Lender shall give notice to Borrower prior to acceleration following Borrower's breach of any covenant or agreement in this Security Instrument (but not prior to acceleration under paragraphs 13 and 17 unless applicable law provides otherwise). The notice shall specify: (a) the default; (b) the action required to cure the default; (c) a date, not less than 30 days from the date the notice is given to Borrower, by which the default must be cured; and (d) that failure to cure the default on or before the date specified in the notice may result in acceleration of the sums secured by this Security Instrument, foreclosure by judicial proceeding and sale of the Property. The notice shall further inform Borrower of the right to reinstate after acceleration and the right to assert in the foreclosure proceeding the non-existence of a default or any other defense of Borrower to acceleration and foreclosure. If the default is not cured on or before the date specified in the notice, Lender at its option may require immediate payment in full of all sums secured by this Security Instrument without further demand and may foreclose this Security Instrument by judicial proceeding. Lender shall be entitled to collect all expenses incurred in pursuing the remedies provided in this paragraph 19, including, but not limited to, reasonable attorneys' fees and costs of title evidence.

20. Lender in Possession. Upon acceleration under paragraph 19 or abandonment of the Property and at any time prior to the expiration of any period of redemption following judicial sale, Lender (in person, by agent or by judicially appointed receiver) shall be entitled to enter upon, take possession of and manage the Property and to collect the rents of the Property including those past due. Any rents collected by Lender or the receiver shall be applied first to payment of the costs of management of the Property and collection of rents, including, but not limited to, receiver's fees, premiums on receiver's bonds and reasonable attorneys' fees, and then to the sums secured by this Security Instrument.

21. Release. Upon payment of all sums secured by this Security Instrument, Lender shall release this Security Instrument without charge to Borrower. Borrower shall pay any recordation costs.

22. Waiver of Homestead. Borrower waives all right of homestead exemption in the Property.

23. Riders to this Security Instrument. If one or more riders are executed by Borrower and recorded together with this Security Instrument, the covenants and agreements of each such rider shall be incorporated into and shall amend and supplement the covenants and agreements of this Security Instrument as if the rider(s) were a part of this Security Instrument. [Check applicable box(es)]

☐ Adjustable Rate Rider   ☐ Condominium Rider   ☐ 2–4 Family Rider

☐ Graduated Payment Rider   ☐ Planned Unit Development Rider

☐ Other(s) [specify]

BY SIGNING BELOW, Borrower accepts and agrees to the terms and covenants contained in this Security Instrument and in any rider(s) executed by Borrower and recorded with it.

....(Seal)
—Borrower

....(Seal)
—Borrower

———————————— [Space Below This Line For Acknowledgment] ————————————

STATE OF ....
                             } SS:

COUNTY OF ....

I,..., a Notary Public in and for said county and state, do hereby certify that ...., personally appeared before me and is (are) known or proved to me to be the person(s) who, being informed of the contents of the foregoing instrument, have executed same, and acknowledged said instrument to be .... free and voluntary act and deed and that
                                                    (his, her, their)
.... executed said instrument for the purposes and uses therein set forth.
   (he, she, they)

Witness my hand and official seal this.............................. day of ...., 19......

My Commission Expires:

....(SEAL)
Notary Public

297

This instrument was prepared by...
44771

20.16   Parties to the Mortgage

The borrower, who corresponds to the grantor in a deed, is known as the *mortgagor.* The lender, who corresponds to the grantee in a deed, is known as the *mortgagee.* It is important that the names of the parties be given accurately and fully in the mortgage. The marital status of the mortgagor, as *bachelor, spinster,* or *widower,* should be recited. The same considerations that require the grantor's spouse to join in a deed require the mortgagor's spouse to join in a mortgage. A mortgage by a minor or an insane person is subject to the same objections that exist in the case of deeds. A mortgage by a corporation must be authorized by proper corporate resolutions, which should show that the money is being borrowed for proper corporate purposes. In general, the requirements relative to the grantor and grantee in a deed are applicable to the mortgagor and mortgagee in a mortgage.

20.17   Private Mortgage Insurance

FHA and VA were slow to process insurance applications. As a result, private insurance companies have sprung up that furnish mortgage insurance for a premium (PMI) paid by the borrower. The secondary market (FNMA and FHLMC) has introduced requirements of such insurance in their lending guides.

> **EXAMPLE:**   On some loans premium mortgage insurance is required if the loan exceeds 80 percent of the property value. This happens to correspond with a requirement of the FHLBB. 12 CFR Sec. 545.32(d).

All PMI requirements vary as the economic scene changes. When foreclosures are numerous, the requirements for PMI grow stricter.

In general, regulatory requirement for PMI tends to end when the loan is paid down to 80 percent of property value.

20.18   Foreclosure Provisions and Power of Sale

Provisions are usually included in the mortgage for the foreclosure thereof, and in states permitting foreclosure by exercise of power of sale, the power of sale is fully set forth in the mortgage.

20.19   Waiver of Homestead and Dower

In some states a mortgage on homestead land must include a clause releasing and waiving homestead rights. Again, in some states, a mortgage signed by the spouse of the mortgagor should contain a clause stating that such spouse thereby waives all dower as against the mortgagee.

20.20   Execution

The mortgagor and spouse should sign the mortgage. Some states require that the word "SEAL" appear after their signatures. A corporation should always affix its corporate seal. In some states witnesses are required. The mortgage should also be acknowledged and delivered to the mortgagee.

20.21   Recording

As a practical matter, a mortgage must be recorded, since an unrecorded mortgage is void as to subsequent purchaser, mortgagees, or, in some states, judgment creditors who are ignorant of the existence of such mortgage. It is important that the mortgage be filed or recorded as soon after its execution as possible.

As a general rule, the priority of successive liens often is determined by priority of recording, the first mortgage recorded being a first lien on the land, the second mortgage recorded being a second lien, and so on. The importance of early recording thus becomes obvious, since foreclosure of a first mortgage will extinguish all junior liens, such as second mortgages.

In states that have mortgage taxes, the recorder will want proof that the tax was paid.

20.21(a)   Master Mortgage

To save recording expenses, mortgagees have turned to the *master mortgage*. A mortgage lender records his usual mortgage form with none of the blanks filled in. This is the *master mortgage*. Thereafter each mortgage recorded by the mortgage company simply refers to the book and page of the master mortgage for the fine-print provisions, enabling the mortgagee to get all the necessary recordable data of each mortgage in a one-page document. Laws permitting this have been enacted in many states.

20.22   Debt—in General

In order for a mortgage to exist there must be a debt for the mortgage to secure. Without the debt there is nothing to secure, and the mortgage has no effect. Ordinarily, the debt takes the form of an obligation to pay money, such as a promissory note or a bond, which may or may not be negotiable. This is not necessarily so, however, and the debt may be in the form of any contractual relation.

The requirement of a debt is not a requirement that there be *personal liability* for the payment of the debt. It is competent for the parties to make any bargain on this subject as they please. They may agree that the mortgagee will look only to the real estate as security for repayment of the loan. *Gagne* v. *Hoban,* 159 NW2d 896 (Minn. 1968). In such case the mortgagee cannot obtain a personal judgment or deficiency decree against the mortgagor should the mortgaged land prove insufficient to satisfy the mortgage debt.

The mortgage lien is measured by the amount of the mortgage debt. Thus if a mortgage recites a debt of $10,000, but actually only $5,000 is loaned, the mortgage stands as security for only $5,000. Likewise, the mortgage lien diminishes as the mortgage debt is reduced by payment. Thus if a mortgage of $10,000 is paid down to $5,000, the mortgage lien is reduced accordingly, and if the mortgagee thereafter loans the mortgagor additional funds, these additional funds are not secured by the mortgage unless the mortgage contains a clause covering *future advances*.

20.22(a)   Debt—History of Debt Payment Structure of Home Loans

Prior to the Great Depression first mortgages on homes were usually payable in five years, with one principal note and ten interest coupons due semiannually. When the maturity date arrived, quite commonly the mortgagor made a nominal payment on principal, and the balance was extended. The extension agreement was recorded. Evidently, no one was greatly concerned about ultimate repayment of the principal. Second mortgages were common. They were used where the purchaser of the home lacked funds to make the required down payment. Many second mortgages were sold to individuals, who purchased them because of the higher return they provided.

Following the crash of 1929, many mortgages went into foreclosure. Banks closed. Mortgage funds dried up.

The Roosevelt administration put the FHA insurance program in place. Mortgage lenders could loan money safely once more on homes, since the loan was insured by a federal agency. But FHA insisted that the mortgage be amortized. Monthly payments were made, so that a constant reduction of the portion devoted to interest assured ultimate repayment of the principal. To be sure, few mortgages ran their full course, since homes are sold at intervals, perhaps seven years, and at each sale, the existing mortgage is commonly repaid through funds obtained by the purchaser on a new mortgage.

While this amortization mortgage served the country well and is still in use, other forms of mortgage adapted to an inflationary economy have been created. These are discussed elsewhere.

20.22(b)   Debt—Personal Liability

Of course, the parties are at liberty to make any agreement they wish concerning personal liability.

> **EXAMPLE:**   The borrower's personal liability may be limited to rents collected, the theory being that this prevents the borrower from milking the property. Kratovil & Werner, *Modern Mortgage Law and Practice* §10.04(b) (2d ed. 1981). Or liability may be limited to defaults occurring during the first three years.

20.22(c)   Debt—Priority of Lien

Any discussion of mortgage debt inevitably involves questions of priority of lien. Often there will be two or more liens against the same property.

> **EXAMPLE:**   Owner mortgages his property to Lender #1 in 1981 and then mortgages the same property to Lender #2 in 1982. If both mortgages are valid and both are properly recorded, Lender #1's mortgage is a first lien, and if he is compelled to enforce it by foreclosure, he will extinguish Lender #2's mortgage, which is a subordinate or inferior lien. Of course, Lender #2 has the right to pay Lender #1's mortgage to prevent this extinguishment and to foreclose for the amounts due on both mortgages. It is said, in such circumstances, that Lender #1 enjoys priority of lien. Lender #2's lien is subject to Lender #1's.

The same situation exists when the liens are of different kinds.

> **EXAMPLE:**   Lender acquires a mortgage lien on the property in 1981. Creditor acquires a judgment lien on the same property in 1982. Mechanic acquires a mechanic's lien on the property in 1983. Normally, these liens have priority according to the time they attach to the land. First in time is first in right. There are, however, many exceptions to the rule.

20.22(d)   Debt—Description of Debt

A mortgage must in some way describe and identify the debt that it is intended to secure. 145 ALR 369; 89 ALR3d 937, 938, 939. The character and amount of the debt must be defined with reasonable certainty in order to preclude the parties from substituting debts other than those described. *Bowen* v. *Ratcliff*, 39 NE 860 (Ind. 1895). Otherwise, in some states, subsequent mortgagees, purchasers, or judgment creditors will acquire rights superior to those of the mortgage. 2 *Merrill on Notice* § 1090 (1952); 5 *Tiffany on Real Property* § 1407 (1939).

> **EXAMPLE:**   Owner borrows $10,000 from Lender and gives Lender his note therefor. To secure the loan, Owner gives Lender a mortgage, but the mortgage does not recite the amount of the loan. The mortgage is recorded. Thereafter, Creditor obtains a judgment against Owner. Creditor's judgment is a prior lien, coming in ahead of Lender's mortgage. *Bullock* v. *Battenhousen*, 108 Ill. 28 (Ill 1883). See also *Flexter* v. *Woomer*, 197 NE2d 161 (Ill. 1964).

The mortgage need not state the maturity date of the debt. 1 *Jones on Mortgages* 549, 559 (8th ed. 1928). *Contra: Sullivan* v. *Ladden*, 125 A. 250 (Conn. 1924). However, it is advisable that it do so. Similarly, the mortgage need not state the interest rate. *Metropolitan Life Ins. Co.* v. *Kobbeman*, 260 Ill. App. 508 (1931).

Where the note provides for future advances, the mortgage should state the maximum amount of future advances that the mortgage will secure. *Northridge Bank* v. *Lakeshore Commercial Finance Corp.*, 365 NE2d 382 (Ill. 1977).

20.22(e)   Debts—Terms of Repayment

Most mortgage financing of homes is governed today by some form of federal regulation that supersedes state regulation. See, for example, 12 CFR Part 595.33. The loan term must not exceed forty years. *Ibid.* National bank loans are limited to thirty years. The secondary market imposes its own regulations on debt terms. FNMA, for example, wants the monthly payment to be payable on the first day of each month. In short, the old pre-Depression mortgages, drafted to suit the needs of particular institutions, have all but disappeared in the home loan field.

20.22(f)   Debt—Future Advances—Obligatory Advances

A mortgage debt is rarely created at the same instant that the mortgage is signed. Normally, the mortgagor will receive his money sometime after the signing and recording of the mortgage. The question that arises is whether the mortgage has priority over junior mortgages, judgments, and other liens that may attach to the land before the money is paid out. The problem usually arises in three situations:

> **EXAMPLE:**   An ordinary mortgage loan is applied for. The mortgage is executed and recorded. Payment of the mortgage money to the mortgagor is delayed pending the completion of a title search. A judgment or other lien attaches to the land after the recording of the mortgage. Thereafter, the mortgagee's title search is completed, but since the search covers only the date of the recording of the mortgage, the mortgagee is unaware of the judgment. Thereafter, the mortgagee pays out the mortgage money to the mortgagor.

> **EXAMPLE:**   An ordinary mortgage loan is made and the mortgage money is properly paid out to the mortgagor. The mortgage contains a provision to the effect that it also secures future advances to the mortgagor not in excess of $2,000, or some other sum. This is called an *open-end mortgage.* A year or so after the mortgage has been made, the mortgagor applies to the mortgagee for additional funds and receives an additional loan of $2,000. Before he receives his money, a judgment or other lien attaches to the land. The mortgagee pays out the $2,000 in ignorance of the existence of the judgment lien.

> **EXAMPLE:**   A construction loan is involved. The mortgage disburses the mortgage money as the building goes up, and before construction is completed other liens attach to the land.

Where a mortgagee is obligated by contract with the mortgagor to advance funds to be secured by the mortgage, such mortgage will be a valid lien from the time of its recording, as against all subsequent encumbrances, even though the mortgage money is paid to the mortgagor after such subsequent encumbrances have attached to the mortgaged land. This holds true even though the mortgagee is actually aware of the existence of the subsequent encumbrances at the time he pays out the mortgage money. 80 ALR2d 191, 196, 199, 217, 219. Such advances are called *obligatory advances.* Because of the mortgagee's obligation to pay out the money, the mortgage debt is regarded as being in existence from the time of the contract. The obligation is usually created in one of two ways: (1) where the mortgagor has made written application for a mortgage loan and the mortgagee is contractually obligated to go through with the transaction; (2) where a construction loan is involved, the obligation is usually created by a construction loan agreement, which is an agreement entered into between mortgagor and mortgagee when the purpose of the loan is to provide funds for the construction of a building. This agreement authorizes the mortgagee to disburse the mortgage funds as the building goes up and seems to obligate disbursement. See Kratovil & Werner, *Mortgages for Construction and the Lien Priorities Problem—The "Unobligatory" Advance*, 41 Tenn. L. Rev. 311 (1974). It also binds the mortgagor to complete the erection of the building and to turn over to the mortgagee for disbursement such money as the mortgagor is furnishing from his own funds toward the erection of the building. The agreement also authorizes the mortgagee to act as the mortgagor's agent in dealing with the contractor and subcontractors. This agreement should dovetail into the construction contract between the mortgagor and his builder, so that the builder will not be clamoring for money at a time when the mortgage is not yet required to pay out funds.

Let us return to consideration of the application and commitment. It is not always easy for mortgage personnel to think of these documents as creating a contract for a loan so that the money subsequently advanced is an obligatory advance, and yet a simple illustration will prove that is the case.

> **EXAMPLE:**   *A* applies to *ABC Corp.* for a $1,000,000 mortgage loan at 13 percent interest on his hotel building. The corporation gives a commitment to make this loan. Thereafter, *ABC Corp.* refuses to honor its commitment. *A* goes to *XYZ Corp.,* which gives him a loan on the same property at 14 percent interest. Without the slightest doubt, *ABC Corporation* is liable to *A* for the difference between 13 percent and 14 percent interest over the life of the loan. This is so because *ABC Corp.* broke its obligation to loan the funds to *A* at 13 percent.

Of course, in all states expenditures made by the mortgagee to preserve the lien of his mortgage, such as payments made by the mortgagee on delinquent real estate taxes that the mortgagor has failed to pay, are considered obligatory expenses, and the mortgagee has the same lien for such advances as he has for his original debt.

20.22(g)   Debt—Future Advances—Optional Advances

Suppose that the mortgage does not absolutely bind the mortgagee to fund the mortgage debt. Advances under such a mortgage are called *optional advances.* Despite the fact that such mortgage is duly recorded, it is by no means certain that it will operate as a lien from the date of its recording as against all other liens attaching after that date. The argument that can be made against the mortgage is that a mortgage is a conveyance to secure a debt and that without a debt there is no mortgage. It must therefore follow that *until* the money has actually been advanced to the mortgagor no legal mortgage exists, for until that time the mortgagor owes no money to the mortgagee, and therefore no debt exists. In the case of obligatory advances, the courts dispose of the argument by saying that since the mortgagee must at all events loan the money, as he has contracted to do, for all practical purposes the debt exists as soon as the obligation to make the loan is created. Since this obligation is normally created, either by application and commitment or by a construction loan agreement, an obligatory advance mortgage is good against the whole world, including subsequent lienors, from the date the mortgage is recorded. As to mortgages where the mortgagee has not entered into a binding contract to advance the funds, the problem is far more complex, as the ensuing discussion of the open-end mortgage reveals.

Note that the same debtor and creditor may have both secured and unsecured relationships.

> **EXAMPLE:**   Lender gave Owner a loan secured by a mortgage. This defines the extent of the secured relationship between Lender and Owner. Lender may later extend other credit to Owner that is completely unrelated to the mortgage. Unless the mortgage has an anaconda or dragnet clause the other advance would be unsecured.

20.22(h)   Debt—Future Advances—Open-end Mortgages

The open-end mortgage provides that the mortgage secures not only the original note and debt, but also any additional advance that the mortgagee may choose to make to the mortgagor in the future. This means that if in the future, the mortgagor wishes to borrow additional funds for the improvement of the property or for some other purpose, he can borrow this money from the mortgagee if the latter sees fit to lend it. The advantages are obvious. The expense of executing a new mortgage is obviated. The mortgagee's security is enhanced by the additions or repairs. Recourse to short-term high-rate consumer financing is eliminated.

Clearly, the open-end mortgage is an optional advance mortgage. That is, the mortgagee is under no legal obligation to loan the additional funds. The problem here is one of intervening liens.

> **EXAMPLE:**   Owner borrows $10,000 from Lender #1 on January 31 and gives Lender #1 a future advance type (open-end) mortgage. The mortgage is duly recorded. On July 1, Owner borrows $1,000 from Lender #2 and gives him a junior mortgage on the land, which he records. On December 1, Owner comes to Lender #1 and borrows an additional $1,000 under the future advance clause of the mortgage. Will this new advance, with the original first mortgage amount, enjoy priority over the junior mortgage of July 1, or will the July 1 mortgage enjoy priority over the new advance so that it is in effect a third mortgage on the property? In a majority of the states, the additional advance will enjoy priority over the intervening lien, the junior mortgage of July 1, unless Lender #1 has actual knowledge of the second mortgage when he gave Owner the advance. In Illinois, Michigan, Ohio, and Pennsylvania, a mortgagee must, before making an optional future advance, search the records for intervening liens. Record notice of intervening liens is enough to give the intervening lien priority over the additional advance. 138 ALR 566. In these states title companies make special,

inexpensive title searches to cover mortgages that propose making additional advances.

A mortgage secures only the debt described therein. Hence, a mortgage designed to secure optional future advances should draw attention to that fact. The older decisions are somewhat liberal in this regard. 5 DePaul L. Rev. 76, 80 (1955); 81 ALR 631. However, since the open-end mortgage has become popular, the notion that such mortgages should describe such future advances seems to be winning acceptance. At a minimum today, for safety's sake, the mortgage should specify the upper limit of the future advances to be made.

NEW LAWS: A great many states have enacted laws governing open-end mortgages. In Rhode Island, for example, an open-end advance that does not exceed $3,000 has the same priority as the original mortgage.

It is necessary also, that the future advances fall within the description thereof given in the mortgage.

EXAMPLE: If the mortgage, by its terms, secures future advances made to the mortgagors, an advance made to one of the mortgagors probably is not secured by the mortgage. *Capocasa* v. *First Nat. Bank,* 154 NW2d 271 (Wis. 1967). Likewise, an advance made to a grantee of the mortgagors might not be secured by the mortgage unless the mortgage so provides. *Walker* v. *Whitemore,* 262 SW 678 (Ark. 1924).

Finally, the documents evidencing the future advance should refer to the mortgage, so that it is evident that such advances were meant to be advances secured by the mortgage.

WARNING: If the mortgage makes no reference to future advances, any later document securing future advances must be executed and acknowledged like an original mortgage, recorded, and the title searches brought down to cover recording, for it is, in legal effect, a new mortgage on the property.

To sum up, most states make one or more of three requirements on an optional future advance, namely: (1) the mortgage must in some way describe its future advance; (2) the maximum amount of the future advance may be limited; (3) there may be a limit on the time for making a future advance. Barnett and McKenzie, *Alternative Mortgage Instruments,* pp. 4–29 (1984).

NEW DEVELOPMENTS: Many mortgage experts have criticized the distinction between optional and obligatory advances. The law is beginning to change. In a number of states, subject to specified requirements, the priority of a mortgage dates from its *recording* regardless of when the loan is disbursed. A common requirement is that the mortgage state the maximum amount to be advanced. Kansas, Maine, Massachusetts, Minnesota, Nebraska, Nevada, New Hampshire, and other states have laws of this kind. See, for example, *Fidelity Svgs. Assn.* v. *Witt,* 665 P2d 1108 (Kan. 1983).

Clearly construction loan advances needed to complete a half-built structure fall in this category. *See* Maine 9-B Sec. 430, Minn. Sec. 51A 38 Sub.6, Neb. 76–23801. This seems to derive from Sec. 302 Uniform Land Security Interest Act.

20.22(i) Debt—Revolving Funds

In recent years the revolving fund junior mortgage has become popular. Many married couples have seen their homes appreciate in value while their monthly payments have greatly reduced the amount remaining due on the first mortgage. Thus a substantial equity has been created. Lenders have been urging landowners to borrow money on the security of this equity. Many people are using this type of debt instead of their credit cards to take advantage of interest deductions for income tax purposes that were otherwise eliminated by the Tax Reform Act of 1986. Generally, a statute is needed to validate such liens, for example, Ill. Rev. Stat. Ch. 17 par. 6405. The mortgage must be for a minimum amount ($5,000 in Illinois), and usually must state an upper limit, $100,000 being customary in Illinois. The interest rate floats, often at two points over prime. Ten years is a common maturity date. As the borrower draws on the line of credit, the debt increases and the line of credit is reduced. As payments are made on the mortgage, the opposite occurs. The borrower draws on the credit line by writing checks. The statute must deal specifically with the priority this type of mortgage enjoys, since obviously the mortgage secures a number of liens accruing at the times that draws are made on the line of credit.

Title companies issue policies insuring these mortgages. In Illinois the title insurance does not protect against mechanic's liens. In other states insurance does not protect against federal liens. Real estate taxes always enjoy a superior lien.

This is a new type of mortgage. There is little law on the subject.

REFERENCE: 66 Chicago Bar Record 158 (1984).

20.22(i)(1) Debt—Revolving Funds—Federal Savings and Loans

Federal thrift institutions may make revolving fund loans that are junior liens. 12 CFR Sec. 545.32, 545.33. There are detailed federal regulations. *Ibid.* 41 Bus. Law 1081 (1986).

20.22(i)(2) Debt—Revolving Funds—State Institutions

Every state has either laws or court decisions that govern revolving fund loans. Since this type of loan is a future advance type of loan, it may be governed by some state law applying generally to future advance loans. In other states there are specific statutes dealing with the priority of lien accorded future advances. 41 Bus. Law 1084 (listing the statutes in roughly half of the states).

20.22(i)(3) Debt—Revolving Funds—National Banks

National banks can make revolving fund mortgage loans. 41 Bus. Law 1079. The Comptroller of the Currency has interpreted the law to preempt various state restrictions, including those on repayment of principal balances, balloon payments, and maximum limits on the total loan term. It is important to note that state law provisions not preempted include state-imposed *usury ceilings*, certain restrictions on second mortgages, and non–purchase money adjustable-rate mortgages, homestead laws, and *lien-priority,* recording, and tax provisions. Further, the regulation provides that other applicable federal laws and regulations, including disclosure statutes and, presumably consumer protection statutes, continue to apply to national banks making real estate loans. 42 Bus. Law 1080 (1986).

20.22(i)(4) Debts—Revolving Funds—Title Insurance

The revolving fund mortgage in the form of a junior mortgage on a home is a new type of legal document in most states. There is practically no case law on the subject. The big unanswered question relates to the priority of the lien of the advances made.

To protect itself, Lender should procure a lender's policy with an endorsement that insures Lender that all its advances will have priority over liens that attach after the mortgage is recorded.

20.22(j) Debt—Anaconda Clause

One type of future advance clause is called the *anaconda clause.*

> **EXAMPLE:** A mortgage from Owner to Lender secures a promissory note of Owner for $10,000 and all other obligations of Owner owned by Lender. Here Lender can buy up Owner's other obligations, perhaps at a steep discount, and enforce the mortgage for the face amount of all such debts in addition to the $10,000. 172 ALR 1079. The clause is also called a *dragnet clause.*

The courts are hostile to these mortgages and construe them strictly.

> **EXAMPLE:** Husband and Wife give Lender a mortgage securing a note and all other obligations of Husband and Wife acquired by Lender. Lender bought a note signed by Husband only. The court held that this note was not secured by the mortgage. It was not an obligation of Husband and Wife. 172 ALR 1101.

In order for this type of clause to include other indebtedness, the second indebtedness must have been reasonably within the contemplation of the mortgagor and mortgagee at the time of the mortgage transaction. *Airline Commerce Bank* v. *Commercial Credit Corp.,* 531 SW2d 171 (Tex. 1975); 3 ALR4th 690. This clause in a normal mortgage transaction will not be allowed to embrace a claim for damages for breach of contract.

In all mortgages securing future advances, the lender's title insurance policy must be analyzed to make certain it insures the priority of such advances. Urban, *Future Advances & Title Insurance,* 15 Wake Forest L. Rev. 329 (1979).

20.22(k)   Debt—Guarantees

Many mortgages are signed by corporations having little capital. It is advisable to have the debt guaranteed personally by the principal shareholders. Prior to making the loan, the lender should obtain dependable financial statements and should analyze these statements carefully. And the guarantee should be prepared by a competent lawyer.

> **EXAMPLE:** *ABC Corp.* mortgages its land to Lender and signs the customary mortgage note. Guarantor, a shareholder, signs a guarantee. Later, the loan gets into trouble and the borrower and Lender recast the loan, reducing the monthly payments and extending the date of final maturity. This discharges Guarantor's liability unless he consents to the recasting. Hence the guarantee must contain an agreement by Guarantor that recasting of the loan will not affect his liability.

The practical question relates to the efficacy of the guarantee. Experience shows that it is effective. The guarantee, being a personal liability, appears on Guarantor's financial statements. If the loan goes into default, this is a black mark that will seriously affect Guarantor's ability to obtain credit. He will struggle to prevent this. And if there is a loan workout, he will come up with a financial contribution in order to procure a release of his guarantee.

20.23   Participations

The mortgagee may sell a share of his mortgage to a third party. This is called a participation.

> **EXAMPLE:**   Owner gives a mortgage to Lender for $100,000. Lender, the *lead,* sells a 50 percent interest in the mortgage to Participant. Nothing is recorded as to this participation and no notice is given to Owner. There is a participation agreement between Lender and Participant, outlining Lender's rights and duties. But as to the rest of the world, it is as if Lender remained the full owner of the mortgage.

> **EXAMPLE:**   In the foregoing example, Owner and Lender conspire to defraud Participant. Lender records a release of the mortgage, and Owner sells the land to Bona Fide Purchaser. The mortgage is extinguished. All Participant can do is sue Owner and Lender.

20.23(a)   Participation Problems

Some sellers of loan participations have submitted fraudulent appraisals or otherwise defrauded purchasers of participations. Various precautions have been suggested. Most are useless if the seller becomes insolvent. But it might help to insert in the participation agreement clauses stating that the buyer is relying on the completeness and accuracy of the appraisals and other representations of the seller and clauses warranting that the loan documents are accurate and fully disclose all facts relevant to the loan. The agreement should give the buyer the right to compel the seller to repurchase the participation if he changes the terms of the loan, violates laws or regulations, or is guilty of misrepresentation.

If the buyer wants extra protection, the agreement with the seller will provide that the seller's share of the mortgage is subordinated to the buyer's share. A legend to that effect can be placed on the mortgage near the recorder's stamp and a photostat mailed to the buyer. This will also prevent the seller from selling the same mortgage to others.

20.24   Description of the Mortgaged Property

An accurate description of the mortgaged land is of great importance. Even greater care must be exercised in this regard than is necessary in the case of deeds, since a purchaser usually goes into the possession of the land under the deed and thereby gives all the world notice of his rights, whereas a mortgagee rarely goes into possession and therefore depends entirely on the recording of the mortgage to give subsequent purchasers and mortgagees notice of rights.

When a mortgage is foreclosed, the mortgagee should be in a position to take over the mortgaged building as a functioning and operating unit. This is something to be considered at the time the mortgage is made. For example, if the building contains personal property necessary for its proper functioning, such as furniture in a furnished apartment building, some arrangement must be made to enable the mortgagee to take over these items in the event the mortgage is foreclosed. To accomplish this, it may be necessary to have the mortgagor sign a financing statement and security agreement under the Uniform Commercial Code on such personal property; for a real estate mortgage, although it covers fixtures, does not cover personal property.

In the *package mortgage* method of financing, the home loan also finances the purchases of equipment such as stoves, refrigerators, dishwashers, or washing machines, which are essential to the livability of the property. Following the legal description in the mortgage is a clause containing a general catchall enumeration of the common items and a provision reciting that all such items are fixtures and therefore part of the real estate. The package mortgage attempts to make specific articles fixtures by means of an agreement between the mortgagor and mortgagee, even though, in the absence of such agreement, the articles would be chattels. The practical advantages of this course are obvious. Installation of such equipment by the builder makes the house more salable. Moreover, it enables the prospective homebuyer to finance the initial purchase of such equipment at a lower interest rate and over a longer term than if the purchases were made separately from a department store. Kratovil, *Fixtures and the Real Estate Mortgage,* 97 U. Penn. L. Rev. 180, 210 (1948); 6 Kans. L. Rev. 66 (1957).

When the article is actually removed from the mortgaged premises and then sold to a bona fide purchaser, it is then to all appearances a chattel, and in some states such a purchaser will acquire good title to the article. If this were not the law, any purchaser of chattels would incur the risk of losing them if it should later develop that they were wrongfully removed from mortgaged land. In other states the real estate mortgagee is permitted to reclaim such articles, even when he finds them in the possession of an innocent purchaser. And generally a purchaser of such articles who buys them while they are still installed on the mortgaged land will not be protected. *First Mortgage Bond Co.* v. *London,* 244 NW 203 (Mich. 1932); *Dorr* v. *Dudderar,* 88 Ill. 107 (1878). To prevent such articles from passing into the hands of a bona fide purchaser, mortgagees have initiated the practice of pasting a notice directly on the equipment stating that the article is covered by the real estate mortgage. Purchasers of articles so marked would not be protected if they saw the notice, since they would not be bona fide purchasers.

Since it is by no means certain that, even with elaborate fine-print clauses, the real estate mortgage alone will afford the mortgagee protection against the removal of readily removable articles, many mortgagees insist upon a separate security agreement and financing statement under the Uniform Commercial Code. In other words, where chattels form a substantial part of the mortgage security, the mortgagor will give the mortgagee a security agreement, and both will sign a financing statement that will be filed with the appropriate chattel filings under the Uniform Commercial Code.

20.25   Interest

The mortgage should state the rate and time of payment of interest, though failure to do so will not invalidate the mortgage.

20.25(a)   Interest—Usury

At one time, most states had laws fixing the maximum rate of interest that may be charged. These laws, which find their origins in Old Testament times, were designed to protect the needy unsophisticated borrower from crafty and knowledgeable lenders. Time and upward pressure of interest rates brought exceptions to these laws.

There is no reason to protect knowledgeable and sophisticated borrowers, so exceptions were made for loans to corporations and businesses. There is likewise no need to protect the public from well-regulated, responsible financial institutions, so loans made by such lenders, such as savings and loan associations, were exempted from the usury laws of some states. As market interest rates pushed upward against antiquated usury ceilings, state legislatures reacted by legislating higher interest rate limits or floating maximum rates that are set periodically by reference to various economic indicators.

The national mortgage market was a confusing hodgepodge of usury laws and exemptions. Mortgage funds in states with below-market levels of interest flowed to other states where higher yields were available. This artificial disruption of the availability of funds was harmful to potential homebuyers in states with low interest rate ceilings and frustrated national housing programs and policies.

Finally, in 1980, the federal government reacted by preempting state usury laws to the extent that they apply to most first mortgages on residential real property. 12 USC §1735F-7; 12 CFR §590.

The institutions so preempted include all federally regulated institutions that lend on residential properties, so that virtually all home loans are preempted. There is no usury limit on these loans. The preemption on business and agricultural loans has expired; these are back under state law. 12 USCS Sec. 86a.

The federal law gave the states the right to choose to remain under state law. States that rejected the federal law, in whole or in part, are Colorado, Hawaii, Iowa, Kansas, Maine, Massachusetts, Minnesota, Nebraska, Nevada, South Carolina, South Dakota, and Wisconsin. Even today a state may limit certain charges ("points," for example) on residential loans.

A loan is a residential loan even if there are stores in the building. However, the building must be partly residential.

In states where the federal preemption of usury laws is inapplicable, some mortgage loans will have their interest rates, loan charges, disclosure, etc. governed by the Uniform Commercial Credit Code.

REFERENCE ON USURY LAW: Kratovil and Werner, Modern Mortgage Law and Practice, Ch. 13 (2d ed., 1981).

20.25(b)   Exceptions to the Federal Preemption

The federal statute that preempts state usury laws has no application to some state aspects of finance charges, such as late charges, prepayment charges, and attorneys' fees. It also applies only to first mortgages, not second mortgages.

It does, however, specifically sanction floating interest rates in loans made by institutions.

It does apply to first liens on co-op stock and to first liens on mobile homes.

The law does preempt state laws prohibiting a lender from charging points.

A simple assumption of an old mortgage is not affected by the federal law.

Since the law covers federally insured lenders, it affects nearly all state banks and state chartered thrift institutions.

20.26   Escrows

A subject of much litigation, legislation, and writing is the so-called *mortgage escrow* or *impound* that lenders establish to insure payment of taxes and insurance premiums. For many years this device was an effective and virtually unchallenged tool which lenders used to insure that necessary payments were made. Of late, however, consumer groups have taken to the courtroom and statehouse to correct some alleged abuses that may have crept into the use of this form of escrow. The attack has been primarily aimed at attempting to force the lender to limit the size of or pay interest on the impounded amount. The judicial response has been almost universally that the lender does not have to pay interest absent a statute, regulation, or mortgage provision to the contrary. *Sears* v. *First Federal S. & L. Assn.*, 275 NE2d 300 (Ill. 1971); *Tierney* v. *Whitestone S. & L. Assn.*, 83 Misc.2d 855 (N.Y.

1974). *Contra, Derenco, Inc.* v. *Benjamin Franklin Federal S. & L. Assn.,* 577 P2d 477 (Oreg. 1978). Borrowers then addressed their pleas to legislatures and found that the response was more favorable to the borrowers' situation. Perhaps the most significant factor in the ability of the legislature to respond was the fact that, as opposed to the courts which were called upon to act in the face of the contract binding upon the mortgagor and mortgagee, the legislation enacted takes prospective effect only, operating on transactions entered into after its effective date.

> **NEW LAWS:** The states enacted various types of laws relating to such escrow accounts. Some laws require that lenders pay interest on the funds. See Cal. Civ. Code §2943. Others limit the size of the impound, Neb. Leg. Bill 502, Laws of 1976, or provide that the borrower be allowed the option of pledging an interest-bearing savings account in lieu of the monthly escrow payment. Ill. Rev. Stat. 1975 Ch. 95, §101 *et seq.* The Real Estate Settlement Procedures Act falls into the category of those laws that limit the size of accounts held by lenders in connection with federally related mortgage loans. 12 USCS §2609.

Some creditors of borrowers have attempted without success to garnishee monies paid into these funds by borrowers. Kratovil and Werner, *Modern Mortgage Law and Practice,* §25.34 (2d ed., 1981).

> REFERENCES: The subject of interest in these escrows or impounds has attracted considerable comment. 54 Boston U. L. Rev. 516 (1974); 25 Catholic U. L. Rev. 102; 12 Creighton L. Rev. 697 (1978); 25 Me. L. Rev. 315; 41 Mo. L. Rev. 133; 23 Syracuse L. Q. 352 (1974); 7 Urb. Law 702; 50 ALR3d 697.

20.27 Real Estate Taxes

Especially in connection with parcels having an irregular shape, some question may arise as to whether the mortgaged land is identical with the land on which the real estate tax bill issues. This is due to the fact that tax authorities attempt to shorten the description. Some competent person must determine that the two descriptions cover the identical tract of land. Federal lenders want such proof.

Most mortgage companies contract with a tax service company. This company receives the tax bills and arranges for their payment. The contract for this service should make the service liable for any errors and fix a time limit for reimbursement. Many complaints have been made about errors by tax servicers. In this connection, it should be noted that many statutes allow the tax bill to be sent to the lenders rather than the landowner. Ill. Rev. Stat. Ch. 120. pars. 578, 584, and 671.

20.28 Leases Antedating Mortgage

It is important to distinguish between the rights of a tenant under a lease made prior to the mortgage and those of a tenant under a lease made subsequent to the mortgage. When the lease is made subsequent to the mortgage, the mortgagee can, by foreclosing his mortgage, extinguish the rights of the tenant under his lease. When the lease antedates the mortgage, the mortgagee must respect the tenant's rights, and regardless of foreclosure, the tenant cannot be evicted prior to the expiration of the lease, unless, of course, he fails to pay his rent. Here again we have an application of the rule that "prior in time is prior in right."

Again, *in title or intermediate theory states,* if the lease antedates the mortgage, then immediately upon the mortgagor's default, the mortgagee may serve a demand upon the tenant that he pay all rents to the mortgagee. Thereafter, the tenant must pay all rents to the mortgagee. *King* v. *Housatonic R. R. Co.,* 45 Conn. 226; L.R.A. (1915C) 200. Of course, the tenant may continue to pay rents to the mortgagor until such demand has been served upon him.

In *lien theory states* the mortgagee ordinarily is not entitled to make such a demand on the tenant. L.R.A. (1915C) 200.

20.29 Leases Subsequent to Mortgage

Obviously, a mortgagor cannot make any leases that will give the tenant greater rights than he, the mortgagor, possesses. Most important, where the lease is subsequent to the mortgage, it is inferior to the mortgage, and the mortgagee can extinguish the lease if and when he forecloses his mortgage. Likewise, in *title* and *intermediate states,* the mortgagor has no right to retain possession after default. Tenants who occupy by virtue of leases made after the making of the mortgage also have no right to retain possession of the premises after the mortgagor's default, and the mortgagee may evict such tenants. To avoid eviction, the tenant, upon the mortgagee's making demand for possession, may agree to pay rent to the mortgagee, and the mortgagor will have no right to collect further rent from such tenant. *West Side Trust & Savings Bank* v. *Lopoten,* 358 Ill. 631, 193 NE 462; *Del-New Co.* v. *James, III* N.J.L. 157, 167 Atl. 747; *Anderson* v. *Robbins,* 82 Maine 422, 19 Atl. 910. One disadvantage of this course is that such action automatically terminates the lease, and the tenant becomes a tenant either from month to month or from year to year. *N.Y. Life Ins. Co.* v. *Simplex Products Corp.,* 135 Ohio St. 501, 21 NE2d 585; *Gartside* v. *Outley,* 58 Ill. 210. If the lease is one favorable to the landlord, the mortgagee will prefer to have a receiver appointed, since in many states the receiver can hold the tenant to his lease.

In *lien theory states,* in the absence of some provision in the mortgage, the mortgagee is not entitled to collect rents even under leases made after the making of the mortgage.

When the lease is favorable to the landlord, a mortgagee will attempt to preserve the lease even though he wishes to consummate foreclosure of the mortgage. In some states, Florida, New Jersey, and New York, for example, a mortgagee may, if he so wishes, leave unaffected by his foreclosure a lease that was executed subsequent to the mortgage, and the mortgagee, on acquiring title by foreclosure, may hold the tenant on such lease. 109 ALR 457. In other states completion of the foreclosure automatically wipes out any lease made after the mortgage and thus relieves the tenant of further liability. 109 ALR 455. In these states, there is nothing that the mortgagee can do to keep the lease alive after foreclosure.

Many lawyers feel that an express provision in the lease that it will survive foreclosure if the mortgagee desires will be valid, even as to a junior lease. Alternatively, the tenant and mortgagee might enter into a separate agreement that they will sign a new lease on the old terms if the old lease is extinguished by foreclosure. Or as a further alternative the mortgagee and lessee may sign a subordination, under which the lease is made prior and superior to the mortgage. Bear in mind that many mortgage loans today are made in reliance on the financial strength and pulling power of the tenant, and loss of that tenant could be disastrous.

20.30   Possession and Rents

The difference in viewpoint between title theory and lien theory states is of greatest importance with respect to the mortgagee's right to the possession and rents of the mortgaged property. To illustrate the significance of this statement, let us list, in chronological order, some important dates in a defaulted mortgage transaction: (1) the date when the mortgage is signed by the mortgagor; (2) the date when the mortgagor first defaults; (3) the date when the mortgagee files his foreclosure suit; (4) the date of the foreclosure sale; and (5) the date when the statutory redemption period expires and the mortgagee receives the deed under which he becomes the owner of the mortgaged property.

Let us first make our broad generalizations and thereafter list the particular points of difference that exist. In general, the title theory states regard the mortgage as retaining some of its early character; that is, they view it as a conveyance of the land, so that immediately on the signing of the mortgage, the mortgagee has the right to take possession of the property and collect the rents thereof. On the other hand, the lien theory states regard the mortgage as merely creating the right to acquire the land through foreclosure of the mortgage so that the mortgagor remains the full owner of the land with the right to possession and rents until the statutory redemption period has expired and the foreclosure deed has issued to the mortgagee. In other words, at its most extreme, this difference in point of view represents to the mortgagee the difference between dates (1) and (5) in the above list so far as the right to possession and rents is concerned. In title states, therefore, rents are an important part of the mortgagee's security. In lien states, this is not so. *Grether* v. *Nick*, 213 NW 304, 215 NW 571 (Wis. 1927).

Now let us analyze the situation in somewhat greater detail, from the point of view just expressed:

1. In a number of title theory states, Alabama, Maryland, and Tennessee, for example, the mortgagee, immediately upon execution of the mortgage, has the right to take possession and collect the rents of the mortgaged property. *Darling Shop Inc.* v. *Nelson Realty Co.*, 79 So2d 793 (Ala. 1953). The right exists even though the mortgage is silent on this point. There are two exceptions: (1) in recent times laws have been passed in some title states giving the mortgagor the right of possession until default occurs — in effect, these laws convert such states into intermediate states; (2) many mortgage forms used in title states give the mortgagor the right of possession until default.

2. In intermediate theory states, Illinois, New Jersey, North Carolina, and Ohio, for example, the mortgagor has the right of possession until his first default, but after default the mortgagee has the right to take possession.

3. In lien theory states, in the absence of a contrary provision in the mortgage, the mortgagor is entitled to possession and rents at least until the foreclosure sale.

4. In some lien theory states, either by express provision in the mortgage or by a separate assignment of rents signed at the time that the mortgage is signed, the mortgagor may give the mortgagee the right to take possession and collect rents as soon as a default occurs, and such provisions are valid. *Penn Mutual Life Ins. Co. v. Katz,* 297 NW 899 (Neb. 1941); *Kinnison v. Guaranty Liquidating Corp.,* 115 P2d 450 (Cal. 1941); *Dick & Reuteman Co. v. Jem Realty Co.,* 274 NW 416 (Wis. 1937). However, some of these lien theory states make special rules as to owner-occupied homes. In New York, for example, a homeowner cannot be compelled to pay rent pending foreclosure. *Holmes v. Gravenhorst,* 188 NE 285 (N.Y. 1933).

5. In other lien theory states, the provisions described in No. 4 are considered void as against public policy. *Rives v. Mincks Hotel Co.,* 30 P2d 911 (Okla. 1934); *Hart v. Bingham,* 43 P2d 447 (Okla. 1932). In some states that formerly took this view (for example, Minnesota, Washington, Oregon), statutes have been enacted validating the assignment of rents.

6. In all states, if the mortgagor, after defaulting in his mortgage payments, voluntarily turns over possession to the mortgagee, the mortgagee has the legal right to remain in possession. Notice that in No. 5 it is the provision binding the mortgagor to give up possession *at some future time* when default occurs that is held void. The same agreement made *after default* is valid. The mortgagee is then called a *mortgagee in possession.*

7. Whenever a mortgagee takes possession before he has acquired ownership of the property by foreclosure, the rents he collects must be applied in reduction of the mortgage debt. A mortgage does not become the owner of the property by taking possession. Foreclosure is still necessary.

8. Whenever a mortgagee has the right to possession and fails to exercise that right, allowing the mortgagor to remain in possession and to collect rents, the rents so collected belong to the mortgagor.

9. In many states, there is a statutory period of redemption. No general rule can be laid down as to the right of possession during this period, for each state has its own rule.

20.30(a)   Practical Aspects of the Problem

A mortgage lender seeks a regular return on a safe investment and does not wish to assume the responsibilities of management. A lender is most unlikely to make a loan that will require him to go into immediate possession of the land, and this right is, therefore, seldom exercised. On the mortgagor's default, however, it is imperative that prompt action be taken to seize the rents so that they will not be diverted to the mortgagor's own personal use. An eviction suit to enforce the mortgagee's right to possession is often a long, drawn-out affair, especially when the mortgagor is interposing all the legal obstacles available to him. However, if the mortgagee files a foreclosure suit, he might be able to have a receiver appointed, and this is the course usually preferred. Other technical reasons exist for preferring the remedy of receivership.

Courts differ as to the grounds for appointment of a receiver. Some say it is enough that the property be inadequate security for the mortgage debt. Other courts require a showing that the security is inadequate and that the mortgagor is insolvent. Still others appoint a receiver only when the property is in danger of destruction. 26 ALR 33.

It is important to distinguish between possession problems related to a home and rent problems relating to commercial developments such as office buildings and shopping centers. The lender who lends on a shopping center makes his loan in reliance on the cash flow coming from rentals paid by high-credit tenants. If the project runs into trouble, the lender wants to step in at the earliest possible time to collect the rents and manage the property. To give the lender these powers, the mortgagor, at the time the mortgage is signed, also signs an assignment of leases and rents. Notice of this assignment is given to existing tenants. The assignment is recorded, thus giving notice to subsequent tenants.

The assignment does not give the lender the right to begin collecting rents the moment the assignment is signed. Indeed, the courts will not permit the lender to start collecting rents until a default occurs. This suits the lender just fine. He does not wish to step into the picture while things are going smoothly. He wants the right to step in when the project runs into trouble. Thus the lender's right to collect rents ripens when the assignment is "activated." The mechanics of activation need not be discussed here. See Kratovil and Werner, *Modern Mortgage Law and Practice* 276 (2d ed. 1981).

Let us look, for example, at a typical commercial lease, say a ten-year lease of space in a shopping center. Certainly, this lease gives the landowner important rights, such as the right to collect rents for the duration of the lease. These rights can be transferred to others. Suppose the landowner makes a mortgage on his shopping center to a lender. Simultaneously he assigns his rights under the said lease to the lender. Now the lender has two sets of rights, the right to foreclose the mortgage and acquire the shopping center if default occurs and meanwhile to collect the rents that have been assigned by the assignment aforesaid. In a regional shopping center the rents accruing on the numerous leases amount to a huge sum of money.

Let us look, then, at the way in which such an assignment affects the lender's right to rents:

1. In most lien theory states, an assignment of rents enables the mortgagee to reach the rents accruing prior to foreclosure sale and to treat them as part of the security for his debt. This gives the mortgagee in a lien theory state virtually as favorable a position with regard to rents as the mortgagee has in title and intermediate states.

2. Since the assignment does not contemplate that the mortgagee will begin collecting rents immediately upon the signing of the assignment, but only after a default occurs, the assignment is inoperative until it is activated by some action of the mortgagee. *Ivor B. Clark Co.* v. *Hogan,* 296 F.Supp. 398 (1968); 2 Glenn, *Mortgages,* 940 (1943); 59 CJS *Mortgages* §317. Rents collected by the mortgagor before the assignment is activated belong to the mortgagor. *Sullivan* v. *Rosson,* 223 NY 217, 119 NE 405 (1918).

3. Everywhere the assignment is properly activated if, after default and pursuant to the assignment, the mortgagor consents to collection of the rent and the tenants begin paying rent to the mortgagee.

4. In title and intermediate theory states, the assignment is activated on default by the mortgagee's serving notice on the tenants to pay rent to the mortgagee. The mortgagor's consent is unnecessary. *Randal* v. *Jersey Mortgage Inv. Co.,* 306 Pa.1, 158 A

865 (1932); *Grannis-Blair Audit Co.* v. *Maddux,* 167 Tenn. 297, 69 SW2d 238 (1934). Frequently, however, the mortgagor and mortgagee make conflicting demands upon the tenants, and the issue must be resolved by a court which may prefer to appoint a receiver. Lifton, *Real Estate in Trouble; Lender's Remedies Need an Overhaul,* 31 Bus. Lawyer 1927, 1932 (1976). Where the mortgagee is a substantial financial institution, it can usually overcome the tenant's fears about being liable for rent to his landlord by offering the tenant an indemnity agreement.

5. In some lien theory states, the assignment can be activated in the same manner as in title theory states. *Kinnison* v. *Guaranty Liquidating Corp.,* 115 P2d 450 (Cal 1941).

6. In other lien theory states, as has been stated, the assignment can be activated only by the mortgagee's filing a foreclosure suit and applying for the appointment of a receiver, *Dick & Reuteman Co.* v. *Jem Realty Co.,* 14 P2d 659 (Kan. 1932); *Hall* v. *Goldsworthy,* 274 NW 416 (Wisc. 1937); *State C. & Hall* v. *Goldsworthy,* 14 P2d 659 (Kan. 1932), or obtaining possession of the property. *Lincoln Crest Realty, Inc.* v. *Standard Apartment Development,* 211 NW2d 501 (Wisc. 1973). Of course, these same steps will serve to activate an assignment in a title or intermediate state.

7. Rents collected by the mortgagee under an activated assignment may be applied to taxes, repairs, insurance, and, in most states, the mortgage debt.

8. Whenever a mortgagee acts under an activated assignment, he does not destroy existing leases, as sometimes occurs when a mortgagee takes possession under his mortgage. An assignment preserves valuable leases.

9 A mortgagee acting under an assignment is accountable to the mortgagor only for rents actually collected.

10. When a mortgagee who holds an assignment of rents sells and assigns his mortgage, he should also assign the assignment of rents to the assignee of the mortgage.

With respect to the language of the assignment, some suggestions might be pertinent:

1. It should be a document separate from the mortgage. *Harris* v. *Lester,* 54 NYS 864 (1898); *Franzen* v. *G. R. Kinney Co.,* 259 NW 850 (Wisc. 1935); Note, 50 Harv. L. Rev. 1322 (1937). After all, foreclosure of the mortgage extinguishes the mortgage. And there are decisions holding that the assignment of rents clause in the mortgage is meaningless. *Myers* v. *Brown,* 92 N.J.Eq. 348, 112 A2d 844, aff'd 115 A 926 (1921). It should assign the mortgagor's interest in all existing leases and the interest of the mortgagor, or his assignee, in leases that may be executed in the future by the mortgagor or his assignees. Leases of any importance should be specifically set forth in the assignment. The assignment should merely give the mortgagor the privilege of collecting rent until default. Careful draftsmanship is very important. The courts make the distinction between a pledge of the rents as additional security and an absolute assignment effective in operation upon default. *In re Ventura-Louise Properties,* 490 F2d 1141 (1974).

SUGGESTED CLAUSE: Notwithstanding that this instrument is a present assignment of said rents, it is understood and agreed that the undersigned has permission to collect the same and manage said real estate and improvements the same as if this assignment had not been given, if and only so long as the undersigned shall not be in any default whatever with respect to the payments of principal and/or interest due on said loan, or in the performance of any other obligation to be performed thereunder, but this permission terminates automatically on the occurrence of default or breach of covenant.

WARNING: In some states the courts have held, quite erroneously, that such an assignment is not entitled to be recorded. 75 ALR 261. In these states the mortgage should make specific reference to the accompanying assignment of rents and, for greater safety, state that all of the terms thereof are incorporated in the mortgage.

2. The mortgage should refer to the assignment of rents and the assignment of rents to the mortgage, so that the mortgagee can resort to one or the other as convenience dictates, and should permit entry under mortgage as to part of the premises and under assignment as to other parts of the premises.

EXAMPLE: As to one store in the building, a lease junior to the mortgage is so unfavorable that it should be terminated and the tenant ousted. Enter under the mortgage in title and intermediate states.

EXAMPLE: As to another store, a lease junior to the mortgage is very favorable. Enter under the assignment.

3. The right to cancel or alter leases should be included.

4. The assignment should include the right to use and possession of furniture, appliances, and so forth. While such a provision will be helpful, neither a rent assignment nor the appointment of a receiver is a substitute for a security agreement and financing statement under the Uniform Commercial Code. In other words, if there is valuable personal property on the mortgaged premises, for example, a hotel, the mortgagee may not have the legal right to the possession of such personal property unless he has legal chattel security. Note, 44 *Yale L. J.* 701 (1935).

5. The assignment should include the right to operate the business and to take possession of books and records, stationery, promotional material, and so forth.

6. The assignment should confer the right to apply rents to the payments on furniture bought on credit, to insurance premiums on personal property, and so forth.

7. The assignee should be given the right to apply rents to the mortgage debt. Otherwise some states limit application of rents collected to taxes and maintenance. *Western Loan & Bldg. Co.* v. *Mifflin,* 297 P. 743 (Wash. 1931).

8. The document should provide that the assignee shall not be accountable for more monies than he actually receives from the mortgaged premises, nor shall he be liable for failure to collect rents.

9. The document should forbid any cancellation or modification of leases by the landowner and should also forbid any prepayment of rent except the normal prepayment of monthly rent on the first of the month.

10. Authority should be given the assignee to sign the name of the mortgagor on all papers and documents in connection with the operation and management of the premises.

11. The assignment should provide that any assignee of the assignment shall have all the powers of the original assignee.

12. It should contain a recital that (a) all rents due to date have been collected and no concessions granted and that (b) no rents have been collected in advance.

13. It should provide that the assignee may execute new leases, including leases that extend beyond the redemption period.

14. Compliance with the U.C.C. filing requirements is not necessary. *In re Bristol Associates Inc.*, 505 F2d 1056 (3rd Cir. 1974).

Of course neither an assignment of rents nor any other device can make a good lease out of a bad one.

EXAMPLE: A shopping center lease to a department store provides that if 5% or more of the parking lot is condemned, the tenant may terminate the lease. This is a key lease, providing revenue for retirement of the mortgage. It must be amended, because if 5% or more of the parking lot is condemned, for example, for a street widening, and the tenant terminates the lease, the mortgage will go into default.

If the lease provides for a security deposit by the tenant with the landlord, an assignment of leases and rents standing alone gives the mortgagee no right to the security deposit. *Anuzis* v. *Gotowtt*, 248 Ill. App. 536 (1928); *Keusch* v. *Morrison*, 240 App.Div. 112, 269 N.Y.S. 169 (1934); 52 CJS 473. Specific language should be included in the assignment transferring all rights in the security deposit.

REFERENCE: An assignment of leases and rents (FORM), 3 ALI-ABA Course Materials Journal 87 (1978).

20.30(b)   Assignment of Leases and Rents—Prepayment of Rent— Rent Reduction—Lease Cancellation

A problem of considerable importance is the extent to which a receiver or a mortgagee entering into possession is bound by rent reductions, prepayments of rents, and lease cancellations effected by the mortgagor for a cash consideration. Such agreements are standard devices by which hard-pressed mortgagors pocket the future earning capacity of the land and deliver to the mortgagee the empty shell of the mortgaged asset. Again, differences exist between the theory and lien theory states. The following are some of the applicable rules:

1. In title and intermediate theory states, when the lease is made subsequent to the mortgage, the mortgagee is not bound by advance rent payments made by the tenant to the mortgagor, and upon appointment of a receiver or the mortgagee's taking possession of the land, the tenant will nevertheless have to pay rent thereafter to such receiver or mortgagee, even though he has already paid his rent in advance to the mortgagor. *Rohrer* v. *Deatherage*, 336 Ill. 450, 168 NE 266 (1929). This rule follows from the rule that recording of the mortgage gives all the world, including subsequent tenants, notice of the mortgagee's rights, and these rights include the right to take possession on default. This rule is of special importance to a tenant who pays a large sum of money for the privilege of receiving a lease, for example, a tenant in a co-operative apartment, a tenant of commercial space who pays a large "bonus" for receiving his lease, or a tenant who plans to make substantial investments in alterations in reliance on his lease.

2. In title and intermediate theory states, if the lease antedates the mortgage, recording of the mortgage does not give the tenant notice of the mortgagee's rights, for recording of the mortgage gives notice only to those persons who acquire rights in the property after recording of the document. The question therefore arises, if the tenant, acting in good faith and in ignorance of the mortgage, prepays his rent to the mortgagor, and the mortgagor thereafter defaults, is this prepayment binding on the mortgagee, or must the tenant pay his rent again to the mortgagee? Some cases hold for the mortgagee and some for the tenant. *Anno., 1916 D Ann. Cas.* 200; 55 L.R.A. (N.S.) 233; 2 Jones, *Mortgages* 362 (8th ed. 1928). Arguably the best rule is that no abnormal prepayment of rent is good against the mortgagee. 2 Glenn, *Mortgages,* 952 (1943). The mortgagee can protect himself at the time the mortgage is signed by procuring an assignment of all existing leases and giving tenants notice at that time of his rights under such assignment.

3. In many lien theory states the mortgagee is bound by advance payments of rents made in good faith by the tenant to the mortgagor, and when the mortgagee's receiver takes possession, he will find himself unable to collect any rents from the tenant. *Smith v. Cushatt,* 199 Ia. 690, 202 NW 548 (1925); *Ottman v. Tilbury,* 204 Wis. 56, 234 NW 325 (1931).

4. But even in lien theory states, following the rule stated in No. 3, if, at the time the mortgage is made, the mortgagee obtains from the mortgagor an assignment of rents and leases and notifies the tenants thereof, the mortgagee will not be bound by any advance payments of rent made by the tenant to the mortgagor. Also, no rent reduction granted by the mortgagor after the tenant has notice of this assignment will be effective. *Franzen v. G. R. Kinney Co.,* 218 Wis. 53, 259 NW 850 (1935).

5. Where, at the time of making the mortgage, the mortgagor, by a separate instrument, assigns an existing lease to the mortgagee, and the lessee is notified of the assignment, the tenant and mortgagor cannot thereafter cancel the lease or reduce the rent so far as the mortgagee is concerned. On the mortgagee's taking possession, or on the appointment of a receiver, the tenant can be held to his lease. *Metropolitan Life Ins. Co. v. W. T. Grant Co.,* 321 Ill. App. 487, 53 NE2d 255 (1944); *Mercantile & Theatres Properties v. Stanley Co.,* 346 Pa. 343, 30 A2d 136 (1943); *Franzen v. G. R. Kinney Co.,* 218 Wis. 53, 25 NW 850 (1935); *Darling Shop v. Nelson Realty Co.,* 262 Ala. 495, 79 So2d 793 (1954). If there is no assignment of rents, and the lease is prior to the mortgage, a cancellation of the lease made by the mortgagor and lessee may be valid. *Metropolitan Life Ins. Co. v. W. T. Grant Co.,* 321 Ill.App. 487, 53 NE2d 255 (1944).

6. The courts are less likely to be sympathetic toward advance payments of rent made pursuant to a conspiracy entered into between the mortgagor and the tenant in an effort to deprive the mortgagee of the rents. *Boteler v. Leber,* 112 NJEq. 441, 164 A 572 (1933).

7. The courts are also very unsympathetic toward last-minute rent reductions granted by the mortgagor to the tenant on the eve of foreclosure. *First Nat. Bank v. Gordon,* 287 Ill.App. 83, 4 NE2d 504 (1936).

8. In an effort to attract mortgage money to the state, various states that previously held views hostile to the mortgagee's right to rents (Minnesota, Oregon, and Washington, for example) have enacted laws validating the assignment of leases and rents. Each such statute must be examined to determine what qualifications it has attached to the mortgagee's rights. The Minnesota statute followed the suggestions expressed in Note, *Proposed Changes in Minnesota Mortgage Law,* 50 Minn. L. Rev. 331 (1965-66). See also *In re Federal Shopping Way Inc.,* 457 F2d 176 (9th Cir. 1972) (discussing Oregon and Washington statutes).

20.31   Acceleration—Default—Curing

The mortgage and mortgage note usually provide that in case of any default the entire principal sum shall become immediately due and payable. This clause is known as the *acceleration clause*. If it is not present, the mortgagee must file separate foreclosure suits as each installment of the mortgage debt falls due and is defaulted. Manifestly, the acceleration clause is one of the most important terms of the mortgage.

There are two kinds of acceleration clauses, automatic and optional. The theory of the automatic clause is that the happening of the event, *ipso facto,* advances the maturity of the debt. The optional clause, as its name implies, merely gives rise to the ability of the lender to call the debt due. The latter form is preferable as it obviates those problems caused by accidental or minor defaults while it gives the lender the ability to protect its interest.

While we usually think of acceleration in terms of payment-type defaults, mortgages usually are so drafted as to allow acceleration for nonmonetary defaults, and courts have allowed a mortgage to accelerate because of a mortgagor's failure to keep a building in repair, 69 ALR3d 773, or failure to keep insurance in force. 69 ALR3d 774.

The operation of the acceleration clause upon the borrower's default may bring about a harsh result. Some courts, even when confronted with minor deviations caused by the borrower's mistake or inadvertence, find themselves powerless to avoid the strict application of the mortgage language. Other courts, finding themselves not so hamstrung, have gotten around the language either by holding its operation to be unconscionable in the given instance or by deeming some act of the mortgagee to have negated the impact of the language. *Continental Bank* v. *Eastern Ill. Co.,* 37 Ill. App.3d 148, 334 NE2d 102 (1975); Rosenthal, *The Role of Courts of Equity in Preventing Acceleration Predicated upon a Mortgagor's Inadvertent Default,* 22 Syr. L. Rev. 897 (1971).

> **EXAMPLE:**   Where an acceleration is declared only because of the mortgagor's failure to pay real estate taxes, the courts will allow the mortgagor to cure this default before foreclosure is filed. *Kaminski* v. *Longon Pub Inc.,* 301 A2d 769 (N.J. 1973); 31 ALR 731.

> **EXAMPLE:**   Acceptance of past-due interest payments may operate as a waiver of the mortgagor's right to accelerate upon a prior default. 97 ALR2d 997. This result is especially a reality in view of today's stress upon not treating the mortgagor unconscionably.

It is clear that consumerist, proborrower judicial attitudes have no use for the older decisions. Courts have begun to set accelerations aside on the ground of unconscionability. *Federal Home Loan Corp.* v. *Taylor,* 318 So2d 203 (Fla. 1976); *Miller* v. *Pac. First Fed. S. & L. Assn.,* 545 P2d 546 (Wash. 1976); *Streets* v. *MGIC Mtg. Corp.,* 378 NE2d 915 (Ind. 1978).

In other instances courts have refused to follow the letter of the acceleration clause.

EXAMPLE: A mortgage and note provided that in case of default the mortgagee could declare an acceleration "without notice to the mortgagor." The court set aside an acceleration declared without notice to the mortgagor. *White v. Turbidy,* 183 SE2d 363 (Ga. 1971). This is contrary to earlier decisions on this point. There is, however, a strong trend of statutes and case law to require such a notice. In effect, this gives the mortgagor an opportunity to cure defaults. A mortgagor must be given notice of an intended acceleration and a reasonable time to cure defaults. *Haase* v. *Blank,* 187 NW 669 (Wis. 1922). Some states allow the foreclosure suit to stand as notice of the mortgagee's election to accelerate, *Home Federal S. & L. Assn.* v. *LaSalle Natl. Bank,* 264 NE2d 704 (Ill. 1970), but better practice is to give formal notice, and such action is mandatory when foreclosure is by power of sale. *Crow* v. *Heath,* 516 SW2d 225 (Tex. 1974). *Contra, S & G Investment Inc.* v. *Home Federal S. & L. Assn.,* 505 F2d 370 (D.C. Cir. 1974).

EXAMPLE: A mortgagee had been in the habit of accepting tardy payments. The court held that he could not accelerate without giving the mortgagor a reasonable opportunity to pay. *Stinemeyer* v. *Wesco Farms, Inc.,* 487 P2d 65 (Oreg. 1971).

NEW LAWS: Legislatures in California, Colorado, Illinois, Minnesota, New York, Oregon, and other states have passed laws which, within defined time limits, give the borrower the right to cure defaults by paying the sums necessary to make the mortgagee whole. This right of the borrower to reinstate the mortgage will be found in the FNMA mortgage form.

FEDERAL LAW: Lenders operating under the federal usury preemption are required to give the borrower at least 30 days notice of intention to accelerate. *Quiller* v. *Barclays American Credit,* 727 F2d 1067, 764 F2d 1400, 1404 (11th Cir. 1984).

One important question relates to the problem of the mortgagee's rights under Chapter 13 of the Bankruptcy Code, a provision very commonly used by individuals who hope to get back on their feet and ultimately take care of their debts.

First of all, the mere filing of the bankruptcy petition operates as a *stay.* All foreclosures are stopped cold.

Then comes the question. Suppose the mortgagee has exercised the right of acceleration every mortgage contains and declared the entire mortgage debt due. Can the bankruptcy judge undo this and "unaccelerate" the mortgage debt? The decisions are in total confusion. Some say that the bankruptcy court cannot "deaccelerate" at all. Others say the bankruptcy court can "deaccelerate" at any time before judgment of foreclosure has been entered. 67 ALR Fed. 238. Other decisions say the court can "deaccelerate" at any time before foreclosure sale. 67 ALR Fed. 241. Others say the court can "deaccelerate" after sale and during the redemption period. 67 ALR Fed. 240. All agree that there can be no "deacceleration" after ownership has vested in the foreclosure purchaser. 67 ALR Fed. 236.

20.31(a)   Acceleration—Late Payment

If the mortgage specifies a period after which a "late payment" charge is imposed, a payment made before that period expires is timely and prevents acceleration. *Baypoint Mortgage* v. *Crest Trust,* 214 Cal. Reptr. 531 (Cal. App. 1985).

20.32   Deed of Mortgaged Premises

Generally, when mortgaged land is sold, the mortgage is paid and released during the process of sale for the reason that the existing mortgage usually does not meet the financing requirements of the buyer. For example, if land is sold for $15,000 and there is an existing mortgage of $13,000, which has been paid down to $60,000, the buyer will want a new mortgage of more than $6,000. Thus it becomes necessary to retire the old mortgage in the process of closing the sale. However, it is perfectly possible to sell mortgaged land without providing for retirement of the old mortgage. For example, where *A* owns land worth $15,000 on which there is a mortgage securing a debt of $5,000, the arrangement between seller and buyer can be that there will be a payment to the seller of the sale price ($15,000) less the amount of the mortgage debt ($5,000), in this case, $10,000. Obviously, the understanding here is that the buyer will pay the balance of the mortgage debt. In this situation, where the buyer is to pay the mortgage debt when and as it matures, the deed from the seller to buyer may take one of the following forms:

1. The deed may provide that it is subject to the mortgage, which the purchaser assumes and agrees to pay. This is called an assumption clause.
2. The deed may merely recite that the property is subject to the mortgage.
3. The deed may be a quitclaim deed with no subject clause.

The following rules apply:

1. When the deed of the mortgaged premises recites that the grantee *assumes and agrees to pay* the mortgage or *assumes* the mortgage, it imposes on the grantee personal liability for the payment of the mortgage debt. The mortgagee when he forecloses may obtain a deficiency judgment or decree against such grantee when the sale price is less than the amount of the debt. In this way the mortgagee may obtain a personal judgment against such grantee for the difference between the amount of the foreclosure sale and the amount of the mortgage debt.
2. Where the deed merely recites that the land is taken "subject to" the mortgage, the grantee is usually not personally liable for the payment of the mortgage debt. *Pearce* v. *Desper,* 144 NE2d 617 (Ill. 1957).
3. Where the mortgagor enters into a contract to sell merely his equity over and above the mortgage and thereafter gives the buyer a quitclaim deed, the buyer does not become personally liable to the mortgagee.

20.33   Assumption

When there is a shortage of mortgage money, the sale of mortgaged properties subject to an existing mortgage is commonplace. In the trade's jargon it is referred to as an *assumption*. The deal has become complex.

20.34   Assignment of Mortgage

Often a mortgagee wishes to sell his mortgage. In fact, many mortgages are originated for prearranged purchasers. The manner in which the transfer may be accomplished depends upon whether the mortgage in question is a deed of trust or regular mortgage. A deed of trust is usually given to secure a negotiable note which passes from hand to hand, very much as money. Such a note may be payable to the bearer. In that case, merely handing the note to the purchaser will be sufficient to transfer title thereto. Endorsement is unnecessary. If the note is payable to the order of a named person, that person must endorse the note over to the purchaser. In the case of a deed of trust securing negotiable notes, a sale of the mortgage is affected by properly transferring the notes by delivery or endorsement, depending on the character of the note.

In the case of a regular mortgage, it is necessary to execute an assignment, which is a brief form reciting that the mortgagee, the assignor, transfers and assigns the mortgage and mortgage note to the purchaser thereof, the assignee. The mortgage is identified by a recital of the names of the parties thereto, its date, the recording date, the book and page where the mortgage is recorded, and so on. The assignment should be signed by the mortgagee, acknowledged, delivered to the assignee, and recorded. The mortgage note, too, should be endorsed or delivered to the assignee along with the original mortgage.

The mortgage cannot be assigned except in connection with a sale of the mortgage debt. The reason for this is that the mortgage is incidental to and exists only for the purpose of securing payment of the debt. A person who does not own the mortgage debt can have no reason for obtaining the mortgage, and any attempt to assign the mortgage without a transfer of the debt is a nullity. *Commercial Products Corp.* v. *Briegel,* 242 NE2d 317 (Ill. 1968). The assignee of the mortgage must insist on receiving the mortgage note, since if the mortgagee has already transferred the mortgage note to someone else, he can no longer make a valid assignment of the mortgage.

On the other hand, whatever is sufficient to transfer the mortgage debt will transfer a mortgage given to secure it. This is because the debt secured by the mortgage is the principal thing and the mortgage is a mere security for its payment. Thus, if a regular mortgage secures a note, its transfer without an assignment of the mortgage will give the transferee the right to foreclose the mortgage. But as a practical matter, for the assignee's protection, it is necessary to obtain an assignment of the mortgage. The reason for this is that in the case of a deed of trust securing negotiable notes, everyone is supposed to know that it is likely that the notes will be sold. However, in the case of a regular mortgage securing a note payable to the mortgagee, unless an assignment of the mortgage is filed in the recorder's office, subsequent purchasers or mortgagees of the mortgaged premises are entitled to assume that the mortgagee continues to hold the mortgage note.

> **EXAMPLE:** Owner executed a regular mortgage to Lender #1 to secure a note payable to Lender's order. Lender #1 endorsed the note to Assignee but no assignment of the mortgage was recorded. Thereafter, Owner sold the mortgaged land to Lender #1, and Lender #1 entered a satisfaction of the mortgage on the public records. Lender #1 then mortgaged the land to Lender #2. It was held that Lender #2's mortgage was a first mortgage on the land, since when Lender #2 took his mortgage on the land, the earlier mortgage appeared from the public records to have been released by the apparent owner thereof. *Bowling* v. *Cook,* 39 Iowa 200.

When the mortgage secures a nonnegotiable note, a purchaser of the mortgage takes it subject to all defenses to which it was liable in the hands of the original mortgagee. *Holly Hill Acres Ltd.* v. *Charter Bank,* 314 So2d 209 (Fla. 1975). This means that if the original mortgagee has been guilty of fraud or some other conduct that would make it impossible for him to foreclose the mortgage, any person to whom he sells the mortgage will also be unable to foreclose.

> **EXAMPLE:** Owner mortgages his land to Lender to secure a nonnegotiable note for $5,000, but Lender never pays out the money to Owner. Lender sells the mortgage to Assignee. Assignee will be unable to foreclose the mortgage.

In time, American mortgage bankers began the experiment of having the mortgage secure a negotiable note. The experiment proved highly successful. In all states except Illinois, Minnesota, and Ohio, it is now the rule that *a holder in due course* of the negotiable note secured by a mortgage, that is, one who buys the note and mortgage in good faith before the debt is overdue and without knowledge of any infirmities, takes the mortgage as well as the note free from defenses that would have been available to the mortgagor against the original mortgagee. The theory is that negotiable notes, like money, should pass freely from hand to hand, without the necessity of any inquiry by purchasers thereof as to the possible invalidity of the paper. And since the mortgage is a mere security for the note, it should enjoy the same protection that the law accords to the note.

> **EXAMPLE:** Owner gave Lender a mortgage securing a negotiable note for $50,000 but never received any money from Lender. Lender sold the note and mortgage to Assignee before the due date of the note. Assignee can foreclose the mortgage even though Owner never received the mortgage money. As an innocent purchaser of a negotiable note, Assignee is protected against any defenses that exist between Owner and Lender.

A purchaser of a mortgage can also be protected against unknown infirmities existing as between the mortgagor and the original mortgagee by insisting that he be furnished a statement signed by the mortgagor stating that he has no defenses to the enforcement of the mortgage. This document is variously called a *waiver of defenses, estoppel certificate, no set-off certificate,* or *declaration of no defenses.*

Under standard mortgage practice, it is addressed to "all whom it may concern" and is signed by the mortgagor at the time the mortgage is signed.

The practical effect of a waiver of defenses is to give the assignee a legally enforceable mortgage even though the mortgage does not secure a negotiable note and the mortgagee could not have successfully foreclosed. For example, if the mortgagee had paid out no money or had received payment in full, he could not foreclose. But an assignee who receives a waiver of defenses can foreclose, since he received the mortgagor's written assurance that the mortgage is valid and enforceable. 59 CJS 531; 110 ALR 457.

> **EXAMPLE:**   Owner gave Lender a mortgage securing a note for $50,000, but never received any money from Lender. Lender sold the note and mortgage to Assignee before the due date of the note. Lender also delivered to Assignee a waiver of defenses signed by Owner. Assignee can foreclose the mortgage even though Owner never received the mortgage money. As an innocent purchaser relying on a waiver of defenses, Assignee is protected against any defenses that exist between Owner and Lender.

Before purchasing a mortgage, one should always check the public records for any prior recorded assignment of the mortgage, since in many states, where there are two or more assignments of the mortgage by the mortgagee, the first recorded assignment prevails.

The assignee should also obtain the mortgagee's evidence of title, assignment of chattel security agreements, if any, and other such papers.

The assignee of a mortgage may foreclose for the full amount due on the mortgage even though he purchased at a discount. 2 Jones, *Mortgages* § 997 (1928).

20.34(a)   Notice of Assignment

The purchaser of a note secured by either a regular mortgage or deed of trust should always give personal notice to the mortgagor that he has purchased such note. If he fails to do so, and the mortgagor afterward in good faith makes a payment to the original mortgagee, this payment will reduce the mortgage debt accordingly. This rule is generally followed where the mortgage note or bond is nonnegotiable.

Except in Illinois and Minnesota, it is the rule that the purchaser of a negotiable note need not notify the mortgagor of his purchase, and if the mortgagor continues to make payments to the original mortgagee, he cannot claim that the mortgage debt has been reduced thereby. This places the burden on the mortgagor of demanding production of the mortgage note and endorsement of each payment thereon.

In Illinois and Minnesota, even where the mortgage secures a negotiable note, the mortgagor may continue to make payments to the original lender until he receives notice of the assignment. *Napieralski* v. *Simon,* 64 NE 1042 (Ill. 1902). The Illinois–Minnesota rule is based on the inconvenience to the mortgagor of requiring production of the mortgage paper each time a payment is made on the mortgage debt.

Whenever notice of assignment is necessary, the notice should be given personally to the mortgagor. Merely recording an assignment of the mortgage ordinarily will not suffice. The mortgagor should not be subject to the burden of making constant searches of the records to see if the mortgage has been assigned, especially since it requires little effort for the assignee to serve a personal notice on the mortgagor. 89 ALR 196. However, any purchaser of the property from the mortgagor is usually required to take notice of such a recorded assignment. *Erickson* v. *Kendall,* 191 P 842 (Wash. 1920).

20.34(b)   Warehousing

There is usually a time lag between the date a mortgage is made to a homebuyer by a mortgage banker and the date it is sold to a permanent investor. The period will be longer when a construction loan is involved, shorter when the loans are simply awaiting packaging and sale to an investor or sale to a permanent lender. At times the mortgage banker has a commitment by a permanent lender to purchase the mortgage at a later date, say, when construction has been completed.

A mortgage banker borrows the money it takes to bridge the gap between the time he is paying the builder to build the home and the time a permanent investor will buy the mortgage. The mortgage banker arranges a line of credit with a commercial bank. The bank arranges to "buy" the individual mortgages, and the mortgage banker agrees to "buy" them back at the appropriate time.

To show the world that the commercial bank is in the picture, the individual mortgage notes are transferred to the custody of the commercial bank. Some banks insist that an assignment of the mortgages be recorded. The reason is obvious. The bank cannot loan millions to the mortgage banker while leaving all the documents in the apparent custody and ownership of the mortgage banker. One risk, of course, is that the mortgage banker might sell the mortgages to a third party.

> REFERENCE: *Rucker* v. *State Exchange Bank,* 355 So2d 171; *In re Staff Mtg. Corp.,* 625 F2d 281 (9th Cir. 1980); 104 U. Pa. L. Rev. 494; Madison & Dwyer, *The Law of Real Estate Financing,* 11–4 (1981).

20.35   Payment

The mortgagor, to release himself from personal liability on his note, must see that he pays the money to the holder of the note. This is also true of any purchaser of the mortgaged premises. He is bound at his peril to pay the debt to the one entitled to receive payment. Upon paying the mortgage note, the party should demand that the canceled note be delivered to him. This prevents any further transfer or negotiation of the note and is of particular importance where payment is made prior to the maturity of the note.

Payment also has the effect of destroying the mortgage lien to the extent of such payment. When the mortgage is paid in full, the lien is *ipso facto* extinguished. *American National Insurance Co.* v. *Murray,* 383 F2d 81 (5th Cir. 1967). However, it is customary to record a release, satisfaction, or discharge of the mortgage in order to clear the public records in the recorder's office.

20.35(a)   Payment to Agent

A mortgagor, before making payment to an agent of the mortgagee, should ascertain the agent's authority by inquiring of the mortgagee or by requiring the agent to produce a power of attorney from the mortgagee. *Coxe* v. *Kriebel,* 185 A 770 (Pa. 1936).

20.35(b)   Payment—Joint Mortgagees or Joint Sellers

Where a husband and wife own land jointly, sell it, and take back an installment contract or purchase money mortgage, the rule is that payment to either party is good payment. 70 CJS Payment § 4, 59 CJS *Mortgages* § 446. The party receiving payment can give a release of the mortgage. One would think that the buyer would feel more comfortable if this is spelled out in the documents. Of course, if the check is made payable to both, a different problem arises, namely, whether one party can endorse the other party's name. Again, the documents should cover this.

20.35(c)   Prepayment of Mortgage Debt

In the absence of an agreement to the contrary, the mortgagee has a contractual right to have his money earning the stipulated interest for the agreed period. *Dugan* v. *Grzybowski,* 332 A2d 97 (Conn. 1973). The mortgagor has no right to insist upon making payment before maturity, even by offering to pay the principal and all interest to the maturity date. *Peter Fuller Enterprises Inc.* v. *Manchester Sav. Bank,* 152 A2d 179 (N.H. 1959). Accordingly, it is to the mortgagor's advantage to provide in the mortgage and the mortgage note that the debt is payable *on or before* the due date, *Fortson* v. *Burns,* 479 SW2d 722 (Tex. 1972), or that the debt is payable in monthly payments of a stated sum *or more,* or payments are to *not less than* a given amount. *Peters* v. *Fenner,* 199 NW2d 795 (Minn. 1972). Also, a specific clause may be inserted conferring upon the mortgagor the privilege of prepaying the mortgage debt. This is known as a *prepayment privilege.* In corporate trust deeds securing issues of bonds, the comparable provision is that providing for *redemption* of bonds prior to their stated maturity dates. Such provisions enable the mortgagor to refinance when money is cheaper or to retire the mortgage where he has entered into a contract of sale that requests him to deliver title free and clear of any mortgage.

Occasionally a mortgagor whose mortgage does not have a prepayment clause defaults in his payments hoping to force the mortgagee to accelerate. Thereupon, he reasons, he can pay off the mortgage. The trouble is, it will not work. The mortgage usually has a clause in it stating that if the mortgagor defaults, the mortgage may foreclose as to the defaulted payments only, subject to the continuing lien of the mortgage as to the remainder of the debt. All the mortgagor succeeds in doing is to incur attorney's fees and foreclosure costs.

Where a mortgagor takes advantage of a mortgage provision that allows prepayments on any monthly payment date and suddenly becomes pinched for ready cash, he may contend that he has the right to skip payments until the prepaid amount is exhausted. This contention will not prevail. In effect, the prepayments are applied against the last payments falling due. *Smith* v. *Renz*, 265 P2d 160 (Cal. 1954). Some recent cases hold that where the mortgagor has been making prepayments, he will not be in default until these prepayments have been exhausted by application to current payments. *Bradford* v. *Thompson*, 470 SW2d 633 (Tex. 1971).

> **NEW DIRECTIONS:**   Various forms of limitations on prepayment penalties have found their way into the fabric of mortgage law. In some states prepayment penalties may be exacted only during the initial years of the loan, Cal. Civ. Code. §2954.9; or if the interest exceeds a certain rate, prepayment penalties are absolutely forbidden. Ill. Rev. Stat. 1975 Ch. 74 §4. In other states, the presumption has changed to the effect that the mortgage debt is prepayable unless the loan documents specify otherwise.

> **HUD MORTGAGES:**   HUD mortgages are usually required to carry a provision that permits the mortgagor to prepay and the imposition of a prepayment penalty is prohibited. See, for example, 24 CFR §§203.22(b) and 234.37(b). Federal Home Loan Bond Board (FHLBB) regulations provide that borrowers may prepay their home mortgage loans without a penalty unless there is an express penalty provision in the loan contract. Even when the penalty provision is expressed, it cannot exceed six months advance interest. 12 CFR §545.6–12(b).

Other typical approaches to the prepayment problem include:

1. Mortgage provisions that set out a sliding scale with either no prepayment allowed or a larger penalty imposed on prepayment during the early years of the mortgage and a decreasingly burdensome penalty as the mortgage matures.

2. The giving of a notice of intention to prepay prior to prepayment.

3. The allowance by some mortgagees of prepayment without penalty upon the sale of a house where the buyer finances his purchase through the same mortgagee, or where the mortgagor finances his new home through the same mortgagee.

20.35(d)   Prepayment Penalties—Acceleration by Lender

Many mortgages, notably large commercial mortgages, contain provisions calling for substantial monetary penalties to be paid in case of prepayment of the mortgage debt. Such provisions are valid. However, where the mortgagor defaults in his payments and the mortgagee declares an acceleration, a question arises. If the borrower is able to raise the money to pay the entire mortgage debt, must he also pay the prepayment penalty? Probably not, the default and acceleration being unintentional. *In re LDH Realty Corp.*, 726 F2d 327 (Cal. 7th 1984). Suppose the acceleration occurs because of a sale that violates the due-on-sale clause. Again, it seems that the mortgagee will not be permitted to collect the prepayment penalty. *Slevin Container Corp.* v. *Provident Fed. S. & L. Assn.*, 98 Ill. App.3d 646, 424 NE2d 939 (1981); *American Fed. S. & L. Assn. of Madison* v. *Mid America Service Corp.*, 329 NW2d 124 (S.D. 1983). New York and Virginia have laws that forbid collection of a prepayment penalty in residential due-on-sale situations. The philosophy evidently is that an involuntary acceleration ought not to trigger the prepayment penalty clause. It is this thinking that bars collection of the prepayment penalty if the debt falls due because of a fire or condemnation of the property by a public body. Friedman, *Contracts and Conveyances of Real Property* 647 (4th ed. 1985).

The FHLBB adopted a rule on prepayment penalties on November 10, 1985. 12 CFR 591. Where a *residential mortgage* contains a due-on-sale clause and also provides for prepayment penalties, and the mortgagor sells the property in violation of the due-on-sale clause, the lender must choose: He can either declare the debt due under the due-on-sale clause or he can collect the prepayment penalties. He cannot do both.

As to *commercial loans* the rule is inapplicable. At this time it is unclear what the courts and regulatory agencies will do with this situation. In *Slavin Container Corp* v. *Provident Fed. S. & L. Assn.*, 98 Ill. App.3d 646, 424 NE2d 939 (1981), the court held that a lender who accelerates because of a violation of the due-on-sale clause cannot collect a prepayment penalty because it is the lender who is forcing the prepayment. This suggests that where, in a commercial loan, the lender is determined to collect the prepayment penalty when a mortgagor sells in violation of the due-on-sale clause, the lender should consider doing nothing. He simply sits back and refuses to execute a release or satisfaction of the mortgage unless the prepayment penalty is paid. This involves a serious risk. Almost all states have laws that impose a financial penalty on a mortgagee who refuses to execute a release when the debt is paid. 56 ALR 335. Tender of the debt by the mortgagor also stops the running of interest. In some states a proper tender of payment extinguishes the mortgage. Osborne, *Mortgages* Ses. 294 *et seq.* A prudent lender might find these risks unacceptable.

20.35(e)   Payment—Late Charges

A *late charge* is, as the name implies, a customary charge made by the lender for the expense involved in processing and pursuing late payments. 63 ALR3d 50. If reasonable, it is valid and devoid of the taint of usury.

20.35(f)   Payment—Final Payment

When a final payment has been made on a mortgage, the landowner should insist on receiving a receipt stating that payment in full has been made. The landowner should also insist on receiving: a release in recordable form satisfying the mortgage of record; the canceled mortgage and note; all evidence of title and other loan documents held by the lender; and an endorsement from the hazard insurance company stating that the mortgage loss clause (giving the name of the lender as an additional party insured) has been released. This last requirement is quite important. Lacking this endorsement, the insurance company will make any check for loss payable to the mortgagee as well as the landowner. The owner then must go through the bother of obtaining the old lender's endorsement on the check, a task that may take some time.

20.36   Limitations

In all states, a promissory note ceases to be enforceable after a certain time if no payments are made thereon. Such a note is said to be barred by limitations. The period varies from state to state. In most states, the fact that the mortgage note is barred by limitations only prevents the obtaining of a personal judgment on the note and does not prevent foreclosure of the mortgage. But in other states, the mortgage is automatically barred whenever the mortgage note is barred.

In many states, if a period of twenty years elapses after the maturity date of the mortgage note, the mortgage is presumed to be paid. The mortgagee, however, may overcome this presumption by providing that the mortgage has not been paid, but has been kept alive by partial payments of principal or interest thereon. Since this rule makes it dangerous to disregard even an old recorded mortgage, some states go further and provide by law that after a stated period of time, the mortgage becomes void. The period varies from state to state. In Michigan it is thirty years; in Kentucky, fifteen years.

20.37   Extension Agreements and Modifications

Where the mortgagor and mortgagee agree to extend the maturity date of the mortgage note, the priority of the mortgage over those who took their interest between the recordation of the mortgage and the execution of the extension agreement remains undisturbed. The same is true when the earlier mortgage or note is replaced by another bearing a later maturity date. A different result follows, however, where in addition to merely extending the maturity date, the extension works a prejudice against the interests of the intervening interest holders.

EXAMPLE: As a result of an economic downturn, mortgagor's business activity and profits are sharply reduced. To cope with this problem, mortgagor and mortgagee agree to alter the payoff schedule on the mortgage covering mortgagor's plant. It is agreed that principal payments would be deferred for eighteen months, mortgagor only being required to pay interest for that period. The ultimate maturity date is thereby extended eighteen months. Priority over junior mortgagees remain the same. This is a valid extension.

EXAMPLE: Mortgagor and mortgagee agree to extend the maturity date and increase the interest rate. This agreement results in a split priority for the mortgage over junior lienors. To the extent of the unpaid principal and original interest, the mortgage is senior; to the extent of the increased interest, the priority will date from the modification date. This agreement results in a highly unusual priority problem: (1) the original mortgage principal and interest will have a first lien; (2) the second mortgage will take second place, subject only to (1) above;

(3) the increased interest will have a third lien on the property. *Bowen v. American Arlington Bank*, 325 So2d 31 (Fla. 1975).

A question arises whether the first mortgagee can overcome this handicap by language inserted in the first mortgage. No case has been discovered indicating that this can be done. Probably it is impossible. The granting of the extension is like an "optional advance."

> REFERENCE: Kratovil and Werner, *Mortgage Extensions and Modifications*, 8 Creighton L. Rev. 595 (1975).

> **HUD MORTGAGES:** Where the mortgagor defaults because of circumstances beyond his control, he may enter into a forbearance agreement wherein mortgage payments may be altered or suspended for a specified period. 24 CFR §203.340. Also, HUD may approve a modification of the amortization provisions by recasting the balance due over the original term of the mortgage or an extended term. 24 CFR §203.342. Recent cases have held that the HUD insured mortgagees must seek to aid the distressed debtor and, absent such efforts, foreclosure is not allowed. *FNMA* v. *Ricks,* 83 Misc.2d 814 (N.Y. 1975).

Where the mortgage has been assigned to FNMA or FHLMC, they must consent to any modification.

20.38   Release, Satisfaction, or Discharge of Mortgage

Although the payment of the mortgage debt discharges the mortgage, it nevertheless remains on the public records as a cloud upon the title until it has been released. The common method of releasing a mortgage or deed of trust is by execution, acknowledgment, delivery, and recording of a *release deed,* also variously called *satisfaction, discharge,* or *deed of reconveyance,* executed under seal by the trustee or mortgagee.

These formalities are necessary even though full payment has the effect of extinguishing the lien of the mortgage. Payment is not revealed by the public records, and without the recordation of a properly executed satisfaction or release deed, the mortgage remains a defect in title.

20.38(a)   Partial Release

When a mortgage conveys several distinct tracts of land, it is often provided in such a mortgage that on payment of a certain specified portion of the debt the mortgagor shall be entitled to a release of the mortgage as to a certain tract of land. Such a release is known as a partial release. In the absence of such a provision, the mortgagor is not entitled to any release of the mortgage except upon full payment of the mortgage debt. When a blanket mortgage is placed on an entire subdivision, such a provision is indispensable, since otherwise the subdivider could not furnish lot purchasers with clear title to their lots.

20.38(b)   Partial Release Schedule

Typically, the release clause will contain a schedule showing what lots may be released and the amount of payment for the lot or lots released. This must be set forth in accurate detail. *White Point Co.* v. *Herrington*, 73 Cal. Reptr. 885 (1968).

20.38(c)   Default

Unless the mortgage provides otherwise, the mortgagor can legally insist on a partial release even if he is in default in his mortgage payments. 41 ALR3d 7; 59 CJS 759. Hence it is best for the mortgagee to insist on a clause preventing this result.

> CLAUSE: No partial release will be issued if an uncured default in payment of principal or interest or breach of covenant exists hereunder.

20.39   Deed by Mortgagor to Mortgagee

Earlier, the deed absolute problem was described. There is a second type of deed absolute problem. At times a mortgagor will find that he is unable to pay the mortgage debt. In this event, the mortgagee may, of course, foreclose the mortgage. Foreclosure, however, usually costs the mortgagee time and money. He may wish to make some arrangement with the mortgagor for acquiring ownership of the land without the necessity of foreclosure. This is accomplished by means of an agreement between mortgagor and mortgagee whereby the mortgagor agrees to sell the land to the mortgagee for a small sum of money, and the mortgagee, in return, agrees to cancel the mortgage debt. The mortgagor thereupon gives the mortgagee a deed, and the mortgagee cancels the notes and releases the mortgage. The courts are inclined to be suspicious of such transactions, since the mortgagee is in a position to exert pressure on the mortgagor. To give validity to such a sale by the mortgagor, it must appear that the conduct of the mortgagee was, in all things, fair and frank and that he paid for the property what it was worth, and that he did not coerce the mortgagor into signing the deed. In order to protect himself, a mortgagee entering into such a transaction should take the following precautions:

> 1. He should examine the title to the land to make sure that no other liens, such as judgments or junior mortgages, attach to the land after the date of the mortgage.
> 2. A written contract should be entered into between the mortgagor and mortgagee. This contract should show that it was the mortgagor, not the mortgagee, who proposed the transaction. This renders it difficult for any court to hold that the mortgagor was coerced, since the agreement itself shows that he took the initiative in the transaction. The contract should also provide that the deed is given in full satisfaction of the mortgage debt. *Rooker* v. *Fidelity Trust Co.,* 109 NE 766 (Ind. 1915). In some states the same result is accomplished by putting a clause in the deed or in a separate affidavit.
> 3. The mortgage should be released and the mortgage and mortgage note canceled. If

the mortgage debt is not canceled, courts tend to regard the deed as merely additional security for the debt rather than an outright sale of the mortgagor's equity. 129 ALR 1495.

4. The mortgagee should not enter into any contract to resell or reconvey the land to the mortgagor, though he may safely give the mortgagor an option to repurchase the premises. 129 ALR 1473.

HUD MORTGAGES: A mortgagee in a HUD mortgage may acquire the security from a mortgagor by a deed in lieu transaction if the following conditions are met: (1) the mortgage must be in default at the time the deed in lieu is executed and delivered. (2) The credit instrument must be canceled or surrendered to the mortgagor and the mortgage must be satisfied of record. (3) The mortgagor must give a warranty deed and convey good marketable title. 24 CFR § 203.357.

As you can see, this section presents the problem of determining whether the deed was actually given with the intention to transfer the absolute ownership of the land or was given primarily as additional security, without the intention of extinguishing the mortgage.

20.40   Refinancing

Landowners tend to refinance their mortgages when interest rates drop more than 2 percent. This is possible if the mortgage documents permit prepayment. An alternative is to negotiate with the existing mortgagee. He would rather reduce the interest than lose a customer. Such modification is not possible where the mortgage has been sold in the secondary market.

20.41   Federal Programs

The federal government has several programs to help borrowers of lower income. The FHA program insures home mortgages of smaller amounts than those currently encountered on typical suburban homes. FHA requires a small down payment to be made by the purchaser. Like all government agencies, FHA has voluminous regulations that change constantly. The Veterans Administration (VA) issues mortgage guarantees that enable a veteran to buy a home with no down payment. The VA regulations also change constantly. Both FHA and VA have acquired homes by foreclosure and have programs for selling these homes. The Farmers Home Administration (FmHA) has a program for financing purchase of small farms. All these mortgages can be foreclosed in federal courts. Violation of a federal rule can be raised as a defense in a mortgage foreclosure on any of these mortgages. *FNMA* v. *Moore*, 609 Fed. Supp. 194 (N.D. Ill 1985). Whether state redemption laws apply to these foreclosure sales has not been settled. *U.S.* v. *Stadium Apartments Inc.*, 425 F2d 358 (9th Circ. 1970); *U.S.* v. *Victory Highway Village*. 662 F2d 488 (1982). The priority of federally related mortgages over other liens is a matter of federal law. *U.S.* v. *Kimbell Foods*, 440 U.S. 715, 59

L. Ed. 711 (1978). And whether or not a deficiency judgment can be entered is a matter of federal law. 56 Minn. L. Rev. 463.

Federal rules may require a lender to negotiate with or extend forbearance to a borrower before foreclosing. *Allison* v. *Block,* 723 F2d 631 (8th Circ. 1982); *Ferrell* v. *Pierce,* 785 F2d 1327 (Ca. 7th 1986).

CHAPTER 21

Real Estate Finance—
New Forms of Mortgages

21.01 In General

It is difficult to convey today the economic significance of the various new forms of mortgages unless one understands the conditions that made the new forms necessary. In the period from the beginning of the first Roosevelt administration (1933) to the early 1970's, interest rates fluctuated very little and there was little inflation. Then in the 1970's interest rates began to soar and to fluctuate and inflation hit the real estate market.

Hardest hit were the thrift institutions. These institutions found their portfolios loaded with thirty-year mortgages paying 8% interest or less. To obtain funds to operate, these same thrift institutions sold certificates of deposit bearing 12% interest or more. Inevitably many such institutions became insolvent.

Federal intervention. The problem, it is obvious, was too big for the states to handle. The federal government stepped in. A comprehensive law was enacted by Congress, the Garn-St. Germaine Depository Institution Deregulation Act, 12 USCA, Sec. 3801 (1982). The basic purpose of this law was to enable all lenders, state and federal, to make residential loans with interest that fluctuated so that the interest paid by lenders to their investors would track with the interest they charged their borrowers. 39 Bus. Law 1279.

Under this new law, all home lenders are given the power to issue home mortgages with fluctuating interest rates. The lender is required to select some "index". This index must be a regularly published statement of the fluctuations in interest on some recognized financial instrument, such as the treasury bills the federal government issues regularly. Such interest rates are published in the Wall Street Journal. The mortgage interest rate charged would be "a spread" of two or three percent, more or less, above the index, as the parties agree. To make this type of loan attractive to borrower, the starting interest (first year) is usually fixed at a rate slightly lower than charged on the old fashioned thirty-year mortgages. This is a "teaser" rate.

Because the interest rate on the new fluctuating rate mortgage is periodically adjustable, the mortgages are called Adjustable Rate Mortgages (ARM).

The ARM is used on homes, condominium units, co-op units, mobile homes and two, three and four-family dwellings.

21.02 Rate, Adjustment Period, and Margin

All interest rates change from time to time. Therefore the mortgage must state an *adjustment period.* With most ARMs, the interest rate and monthly payments change every year. The period between one rate change and the next is called the *adjustment period.* So, a loan with an adjustment period of one year is called a *one-year ARM,* and the interest rate can change once every year. All lenders tie ARM interest rate changes to changes in an "index rate." These indexes usually go up and down with the general movement of interest rates. If the index rate moves up, so does the mortgage rate in most circumstances, and the mortgagor will have to make higher monthly payments. On the other hand, if the index rate goes down, the mortgagor's monthly payment will go down.

The margin. To determine the interest rate on an ARM, lenders add to the index rate two or three percentage points called the "margin." The amount of the margin can differ from one lender to another, but it is usually constant over the life of the loan.

Many lenders today use the one-year Treasury bill as an index and also provide in their mortgages that the interest rate will be adjusted at one-year intervals. Adjusting every 3 years based on three-year treasury bills is also popular.

21.03 Negative Amortization

Several ARM loan formats involve negative amortization.

> **EXAMPLE:** In the typical loan, each monthly payment consists of two parts. One part is allocated to the interest due for the month. The remainder is allocated to reduce the principal. Suppose in a given ARM the interest moves up and down as interest rates on ninety-day Treasury bills move up and down. The interest rate on Treasury bills swings sharply upward. The entire monthly payment may be insufficient to pay the interest. If the amount of the monthly payment remains unchanged, the unpaid portion of the interest is added to the principal. With each monthly payment, the amount of the mortgage debt increases.

This creates several issues that must be resolved: (1) The loan-to-value ratio increases making the loan riskier from the lender's standpoint. (2) The increased principal may not have the same priority over intervening lien claimants as the original principal.

As is obvious, negative amortization that occurs where the early monthly payments are insufficient to pay the interest accrued that month presents a special problem. The mortgage tells us that the unpaid part of the interest is added to the principal. The borrower makes his monthly payments but his debt increases. No sensible borrower will sign a mortgage that permits this.

21.04 Interest Rate Adjustable Loans

Many forms of loans have developed to give lenders some ability to adjust the interest rate during the life of the loan. Although these loans have many names, variable-rate mortgages (VRMs), renegotiable-rate mortgages (RRMs), rollover mortgages (ROMs), adjustable mortgage loans (AMLs), and the like, they all have the common quality of allowing for a change in prevailing market interest rates paid to depositors to be passed on to the borrower. These loans tend to insure a positive spread for the lenders and transfer to borrowers the risk of increases in market interest rates.

A borrower should not assume that some form of adjustable loan is the only form of loan available. Some lenders still make fixed-rate loans, but they may charge a premium interest rate for such a loan. The borrowers must weigh the alternatives. If the borrower agrees to accept an ARM, he should not assume that all ARMs are the same. Borrowers should shop and analyze the differences between ARMs offered by various lenders. Inquire about many factors:

1. How are interest rate adjustments put into effect? Does the monthly payment change, the principal amount of the loan change, or the maturity of the loan change?

2. Will the interest rate move up and down according to some index, such as the interest paid on Treasury bills?

3. How frequently will rates change? As the index changes? Every month? Every six months? Every year? Every five years?

4. Are there minimum and maximum limits on interest rate movements?

5. What period of notice must be given to the borrower before a change will be allowed?

6. Are the borrowers charged a fee upon adjustment of the interest rates or refinancing with the same lender?

7. Must the lender offer to refinance at the conclusion of each adjustment period?

8. What index is used to determine the extent of any rate change?

9. Over what period is the loan amortized?

10. Is the loan prepayable at any time? If so, the borrower is free to take advantage of other financing that may become available.

11. What happens if the selected index pushes the monthly payments so high that all of the payment must be allocated to principal, thus forcing the interest to accumulate?

12. Are the mortgages acceptable to the secondary market?

13. Is a fixed-rate loan available? If so, compare the projected payments on the fixed-rate loan to the projected payments on the variable-rate loan. Of course, some assumptions will have to be made to make this comparison, and assumptions of economic expectations are often wrong, but some comparison is needed if an informed decision is to be made.

14. Is it possible that reasonably foreseeable increases in interest rates will cause the periodic payments to increase to such a level that will be only burdensome to the buyer?

15. How long does the borrower intend to hold the loan?

21.04(a)   Risks in Adjustable-rate Mortgages

It is obvious that the ARM creates risks not present in the fixed-rate mortgages. These risks include: (1) the inability of the borrower to handle payment increases, where an increase in the market interest rate compels an increase in the size of the monthly payment, and (2) the erosion of the equity due to negative amortization.

These risks can be minimized for the borrower by the inclusion in the mortgage of a stated maximum on the permitted increase in interest.

These loans must be looked at very carefully by borrowers. In standard mortgages every payment goes to reduce the loan balance and increase the borrower's equity. The addition of amounts to principal in an ARM can have a long-term impact on the borrower's financial planning and should not be taken lightly. Borrowers must carefully study these loans and shop for alternatives. Shopping for mortgage loans was always possible theoretically. In practice, it seldom occurred. The brief time allowed for closing a deal compelled the buyer to take the first loan offered, and competition assured that this would be much the same as any other loan offered. This is no longer true. A borrower might be able to live with *Index A,* but not *Index B.*

21.04(b)   Variable-rate Mortgages (VRM)

The VRM is an ARM and is almost standard in construction lending. These loans are usually tied to a prime rate, have no limit on interest rate movements, and cause the interest rate to increase or decrease simultaneously with movements in the prime rate.

Until not too long ago, the VRM was used only in commercial transactions. Indeed, it was largely forbidden in most consumer mortgages. The FHLBB, regulating federal savings and loan associations, largely outlawed VRMs for those lenders until 1979. Similarly, many states had statutes that prohibited interest rate increases during the life of the loan. Recent interest rate history has mandated the change in these laws that has occurred since 1978.

21.04(c)   Rollover Mortgage

In the renegotiable-rate loan, or rollover, the *interest rate* is set for a period of time, say three to five years, at which time the loan falls due. But the monthly payments are fixed as though the loan would mature on a thirty-year schedule.

Once the initial loan term is up, the loan is renegotiated in that the borrower may seek financing elsewhere or, if the lender permits, renew the loan at the original lender's new rate. This plan has been used in Canada for some time.

21.04(d)   The Index

With an ARM the interest rate changes periodically as some specified index changes, and monthly payments go up or down accordingly. Various indexes can be used.

From the lender's point of view, the index should reflect the lender's cost of funds, that is, the index should move up and down as the lender's cost of funds increases and decreases. From the borrower's point of view, an index that could move up so fast as to outstrip the borrower's ability to pay the loan should be avoided. Both borrowers and lenders are concerned with the volatility of the index. Does it quickly respond to changes in short-term interest rates or does it reflect long-term interest rate trends?

The indexes currently in greatest use are those based on the yield afforded by U.S. Treasury securities.

It seems appropriate at this point to explain the nature of these instruments. Treasury bills are short-term U.S. government IOUs maturing in three, six, or twelve months. They are sold at a discount rather than at face or par value.

EXAMPLE: An auction price of three-month Treasury bills may be $96.562 per $100 of face value giving an investor an effective yield of 14.28 percent.

Treasury notes and bonds are longer maturity debt instruments of the U.S. government that pay the investor a fixed interest on a semiannual basis. These instruments may be sold either at a discount or a premium thereby yielding the investor more or less than the stated interest.

EXAMPLE: The U.S. Treasury auctions a two-year note with a stated interest rate of 8.5 percent at $99.802 per $100 of par value. The effective annual yield to the investor is 8.61 percent.

If the index is based upon short-term rates such as three- or six-month Treasury bills, it will move up and down faster than if it is based on long-term rates. Conversely, an index based upon longer maturity securities such as three- or five-year U.S. Treasury notes is slow moving and will not rise or fall as quickly as market rates may move.

Other indexes are available, but these are difficult for borrowers to comprehend and should be explained by the loan officer to the borrower. Pamphlets are available that describe these indexes.

Let us look at the ARM loan when it is first made.

EXAMPLE: In our example we assume a thirty-year mortgage of $65,000 with an index based on a one-year Treasury note and a 2 percent margin. Let us assume that as of the date of the loan commitment such Treasury notes yield 10 percent. The margin is 2 percent. Therefore the initial ARM interest will be 10 percent plus 2 percent or 12 percent. The monthly payment will be $668.60. If at year's end T bills are yielding 11 percent, the mortgage interest climbs to 13 percent.

21.04(e)   Limits on Interest Rate Movement—"Caps"

If interest rates were to rise 5% per year, the ARM borrower would quickly lose his home unless the mortgage limited the amount his interest rate could increase. This is called a *cap*.

An interest rate cap places a limit on the amount an interest rate can increase. ARMs with caps may command higher rates than ARMs without them. Interest rate caps come in two versions: (1) *periodic caps*, which limit the interest rate increase from one adjustment period to the next; and (2) *overall caps*, which limit the interest rate increase over the life of the loan. The borrower wants both caps.

An ARM may have both a periodic and an overall interest cap. This is a very important point. The loan officer must explain: (1) the maximum increase in the interest rate each year, and (2) the maximum increase in the rate over the life of the loan.

21.04(f)   Payment Caps

Some ARMs include payment caps that limit the monthly payment increase at the time of each adjustment, usually to a percentage of the previous payment.

Ideally, for the borrower, the mortgage will have a cap on both interest and monthly payments. If the mortgage contains only a payment cap, negative amortization may result.

21.04(g)   Frequency of Interest Rate Movement

Depending upon the type of loan and its documentation, the interest rate may fluctuate simultaneously with interest rate index changes or only after a stated period, for example, six months or two years. In commercial mortgages, particularly construction loans, the loan rate often moves as the prime rate moves. As can be guessed, the frequency of adjustment is high in these types of loans.

Competition will probably force lenders to state a period during which a given rate must remain in force.

21.04(h)   ARM—Direction of Interest Rate Movements

The loan documents may provide that the interest rate may move both up and down with index movements. Are interest rate movements optional with the lender? Must the rate move down if the index moves down? The loan documents must answer these questions. In some cases the law requires downward movement if the index moves down.

21.04(i)   ARM—Implementing Adjustments

While often a change in the interest rate will be reflected in the level of monthly payments, other methods can be used to accommodate the interest rate change.

The term of the loan can be extended, thereby keeping the monthly payment level and reducing the amount of the payment that goes to repay principal. Obviously, this method has limits. Mathematically, it may not be possible to stretch the term to a length that will pay off the debt.

Lastly, the loan principal may be increased by keeping the payment level at the initial amount and adding any unpaid interest to the principal of the loan.

> **EXAMPLE:**   Assume an $80,000 ARM on a $100,000 home at an original rate of percent with an original amortization period of thirty years with interest rate adjustments every three years and no limit on the amount of the adjustment. The initial payment would be $948 per month. That would reduce the loan balance to $79,352.80 after three years. If the index increases to cause the loan rate to go to 16 percent, the interest payment alone on that balance would be $1,058.03. If the payment were to remain constant at $948 per month for the second three-year period, negative amortization would occur.

Because the mathematics of upward interest rate adjustments can create such a large mortgage debt, many lenders periodically reset the payoff schedules to fully amortize the loan over the remaining term. In a period of rising interest rates, this can greatly increase the monthly payment.

21.04(j)   Term of Loans

Federal regulations limit most loans to a maximum of forty years. 12 CFR Sec. 545.33 (a). Thus negative amortization can be avoided by "stretching" the term of the loan, leaving the monthly payments the same as the interest rate goes up, but not beyond forty years. A borrower must question the loan officer carefully concerning the treatment of negative amortization.

21.04(k)   Prepayment

An ARM mortgage often provides for prepayment without penalty or allows prepayment on payment adjustment dates. In any case, prepayment penalties are negotiable.

21.04(l)   Conversion

Many ARM mortgages provide that at some point the mortgage becomes convertible into a fixed-rate mortgage calling for interest at the current market rate for a fixed-rate mortgage. FNMA regulates the available conversion date. A conversion fee is often charged. Such mortgages may command a higher loan commission than other ARM mortgages.

21.04(m)   Description of the Mortgage Debt

Previous discussion has drawn attention to the rule that a mortgage must describe the mortgage debt accurately so that subsequent purchasers and mortgagees can determine what amounts are outstanding against the equity. The ARM mortgage secures a debt that is not easy to describe accurately. Nevertheless, the secondary market lenders have prepared riders that have satisfied the title insurance companies. The courts are almost certain to approve the fine draftsmanship characteristic of secondary market documentation.

21.04(n)   Future Advances Problems

Chapter 20 discusses the problems involved in future advances. Because the ARM secures a debt that may increase in the future by negative amortization, a future advance problem may be present. Barnett and McKenzie, *Alternative Mortgage Instruments,* Par. 4.05(2)(b), Par. 4–27 (1984). Again, the title insurance companies have come to the rescue by offering endorsements to their policies. These endorsements insure against the problems of future advances. Barnett & McKenzie, *supra,* A–86.

21.04(o)   Effect of Variable-rate Clauses on Parties Secondarily Liable

Frequently, mortgages have parties secondarily liable, with the borrower being primarily liable for payment of the debt. For example, in major transactions, it is not uncommon to have guarantors for the principal's obligation of payment of the debt. Similarly, endorsers and assignors may have secondary liability. Under traditional theories, an alteration of the obligation between the principal and the creditor will discharge the obligation of the secondarily liable parties. This should present no great difficulty in the variable rate mortgage context since careful draftmanship, even where the increase in the interest rate is optional, can continue the obligation of these parties notwithstanding the increase in the burden upon the primary debtor. Barnett, *Alternative Mortgage Instruments: How to Maintain Secured Lender's Status*, 96 Banking L. J. 6, 31 *et seq.* (1979).

21.04(p)   Truth-in-lending Law

It is important for a mortgage lender who is loaning on a variable-rate mortgage to observe the truth-in-lending law. If the lender fails to disclose that the interest rate is going to fluctuate as some stated index (e.g., interest in Treasury bills) fluctuates, the court may nullify the variable-rate clause, thus converting the mortgage into a fixed-rate mortgage. *Preston* v. *First Bank of Marietta*, 16 Ohio App.3d 4, 473 NE2d 1210 (1983).

21.05   Loans that Provide Lower Payments at the Beginning of the Loan and Higher Payments Thereafter

In many instances the borrower must have a lower payment at the outset of the loan to afford the house of his choice. Before selecting such a loan, the parties should look at the following:

1. Has the program been fully explained? Does the borrower understand exactly what the payments will be as the loan matures?
2. Does the borrower expect his income to increase as the payments are scheduled to increase? If not, are alternate payment schedules available that are more in line with the borrower's expected cash flow increases?

21.05(a)   Graduated Payment Mortgage (GPM)

The graduated payment mortgage is characterized by lower payments during the initial period of the loan and higher payments thereafter. Theoretically, as the

borrower's income increases, payments increase. The payment graduation schedule and the interest rate are set at the outset of the transaction. While payments
on this mortgage are lower during the initial years, the period payments level off
at a higher plateau than for a comparable level payment mortgage. The total
amount paid on this type of mortgage exceeds the amount that would be paid
on a level payment mortgage of the same amount for the same period of time.

EXAMPLE: A borrower under a 30-year, 8.5 percent, $30,000 GPM with pay-
ments increasing by 5 percent a year for the first five years with level payments
thereafter, would make monthly payments of $190.83 during the first year,
$200.37 during the second year, $210.39 during the third year, $220.91 during
the fourth year, $231.96 during the fifth year, and $243.56 thereafter. A level
payment mortgage of the same amount would have monthly payments of
$230.68. If both the GPM and the level payment mortgages run to maturity, the
borrower under the GPM plan will make principal and interest payments totaling $85,724.28; the borrower under the level payment plan will make principal
and interest payments totaling $83,044.80, $2,679.48 less than under the GPM
plan.

The increase in periodic payments in the years after the loan is originated
can cause strains upon the ability of the borrower to make payments if expected
increases in income do not occur or inflation in other areas of the economy
causes unexpected strains on the borrower's income stream.

A feature of this type of financing device is that initial payments are not of
sufficient size to fully pay the interest that accrues during any month. To the
extent that the initial payment is insufficient in this regard, additional principal
is created. Thus in the early stages of the payment schedule, the debt increases
rather than decreases. This is called *negative amortization.*

If the price of the home does not increase at an acceptable pace, the negative amortization feature of a GPM can cause the borrower an out-of-pocket expense upon the sale of the property. Frequently, these mortgages are low down
payment loans, and the "thin equity" of the borrower is made even thinner by
operation of the negative amortization aspect. Selling costs can quickly erode
whatever equity there is.

The advantages of negative amortization in a GPM are great.

EXAMPLE: On a $50,000 GPM mortgage bearing an initial 14 percent interest
the borrower can qualify with a salary of $19,768. On a fixed-rate mortgage the
salary needed would be $25,768.

Mortgage and note should state that the size of the monthly payment increases periodically and should contain a provision such as, "From time to time,
deferred interest shall be added to the principal balance outstanding on this
loan." This statement is made necessary by state laws requiring the character of
the debt or mortgage to be reflected in the recorded documents. Other state laws

require that the maximum amount to be advanced or secured by the mortgage be stated. Careful draftsmanship can solve these problems.

21.05(b) Disclosure

Not later than three business days after receiving a loan application for a home loan, the lender must furnish the borrower a disclosure statement. 12 CFR Sec. 545.33. The disclosure required is very detailed. The way interest and payments fluctuate if the loan is an ARM must be set forth. Information must be furnished as to a due-on-sale clause, late charges, escrows for taxes, and so on. Efforts are being made to provide a simple, easily understood form.

21.05(c) GPM—Usury Problems

The GPM may cause usury problems. If state law or policy forbids interest on interest and thus interest is treated not as being on an increased principal amount but rather as additional interest, the effective rate of interest will be increased and state usury laws could be violated. 37 ALR 325, 345 suppl. by 76 ALR 1484, 1487.

> **EXAMPLE:** The GPM is made at 10 percent, the maximum allowable interest rate. If state law will not recognize the concept of increasing the principal and charging interest on the increased principal, the effective rate of interest will be increased above 10 percent, and the usury law will be violated, absent, of course, any federal preemptive law applying to the situation.

21.06 Discounts and Buy-downs

A builder-seller often arranges financing for his buyers. As a sales gimmick he will arrange to pay funds to a mortgage lender over a period, often three years, and in return the lender will finance the buyer at below-market interest rates for these three years.

21.07 Reverse Annuity Mortgages

The reverse annuity mortgage (RAM) is designed to allow an elderly homeowner to convert his home equity into a cash flow that can be used to pay normal living expenses. Many elderly persons prefer to live out their lives in the home they have occupied for many years. In one version of this loan the lender purchases an annuity with the proceeds of the loan. A portion of the monthly annuity payment is used to pay interest on the mortgage. The remainder of the monthly payment is made to the borrower. It is a strange sort of mortgage, in which the mortgagee makes payments to the mortgagor. Of course, sooner or later the loan falls due and if the mortgagor is still alive, there must be a refinancing. This form of mortgage is the least used form of the ARM category. Barnett & McKenzie, *Alternative Mortgage Instruments,* Chap. 8. It derives its name from the fact that the lender at times purchases an annuity for the borrower, and under this mortgage payments are made by the lender to the borrower, just the reverse of the typical mortgage.

This mortgage requires the borrower (typically a widow) to guess her life expectancy and hope she does not outlive the maturity of the mortgage. Refinancing is very difficult for elderly people.

21.08   Growing Equity Mortgage (GEM)

The growing equity mortgage is used at times.

> **EXAMPLE:**   In one plan the interest rate is fixed at 11.875 percent for the first five years. In the sixth year the interest jumps to 12.625 percent and stays there for the remainder of the loan. Beginning in the seventh year, the monthly payment is increased by 7 percent each year for the remainder of the 16-year loan. This entire increase is applied to the loan principal. The mortgage so provides.
>
> The GEM is a poor idea. If interest on savings exceeds the mortgage interest, the borrower is better off with the *lower* interest rate. But it forces the borrower to make higher monthly payments, and this is a forced savings gimmick.
>
> FNMA regulates the type of GEM it is willing to acquire.

21.09   Shared Appreciation Mortgages (SAMs)

Over the past several years, inflation has greatly enhanced the return to developers and project owners while decreasing the economic return to the lender that has financed the equity buildup. Traditional permanent lenders have therefore altered their investment philosophy by seeking out new investment devices, including the outright purchase of a property, the partial purchase of a property, short-term loans, contingent interest provisions, indexed interest, and shared appreciation mortgages (SAMs).

In the SAM, the lender, as an inflation hedge, obtains a share of the appreciation of the property that is security for the debt. This is done in one of two general formats. In one, the lender finances the property, usually at below market rates, and at the same time takes an ownership interest in the property. In the other format, the borrower promises to pay the lender *contingent interest,* that is, interest that is payable only out of appreciation in the value of the property or, in the case of income property, out of the owner's proceeds from the operation of the property.

Where the contingent interest format is used, the lender must be careful in defining the income that is subject to the contingent interest application and establish a system to carefully monitor the income to determine that the proper amount of contingent interest is in fact being paid.

While SAMs are becoming an important form of financing for commercial projects, they are developing very slowly as forms of residential financing. This is so even though the lower interest rate means that buyers will have an easier time qualifying for the loans.

21.09(a)   SAM—Refinance Provisions

Some SAMs require a sale or refinance after a few years, often five or ten years, to "buy out" the lender's position. How is the value to be determined if the property is not sold? How are improvements to be factored into the valuation? How is the lender to be paid its share of the appreciated value of the property—by a cash payment or by addition to the loan principal? If the latter method is chosen, will the borrower be able to meet the debt service requirements of the larger loan?

21.09(b)   SAM—Ownership Considerations

Any lender embarking on a SAM program must consider the impact of the essential change in the nature of its status. Owners have liability for the operation of the property, different insurance needs, care that their partner is fairly accounting for the property's revenues, and so on. The lender is also in a somewhat dangerous position, because of the potential that junior lien claimants may contend that the quasi-equity position of the lender destroys any priority rights available to the lender upon foreclosure as against the junior lien claimant.

> **EXAMPLE:**   Buyer and Lender enter into a transaction where Lender finances the acquisition of a home and certain improvements (room additions and new roof) to be placed in the home. Through the shared equity device, these improvements will work to the Lender's benefit in that the value of the home will be increased. Even though the law of the state where this loan is made allows a true "Lender" priority interest in this regard against mechanic's lien claimants, that priority protection is not available to an owner. If the loan goes into default, mechanic's liens arising out of these improvements will be alleged to be prior to the owner/Lender's interest.

21.09(c)   SAM—Clogging the Equity

The old theory of clogging the equity has moved into the limelight with the SAM loan.

> **EXAMPLE:**   The SAM provides that the lender will receive contingent interest in the form of 40 percent of the profit on the sale of the mortgaged property in addition to the interest stated in the note.

EXAMPLE: As a hedge against inflation, the lender on a commercial property obtains an option to purchase the property.

The application of this ancient doctrine may invalidate the mortgagee's option or right to contingent interest. The theory is that the lender is exacting a *collateral advantage* in addition to the interest specified in the loan or somehow making the transaction more than a mortgage that can be repaid, returning the borrower to the position that it was in before the loan was made. This very complex problem is explained in Kane, *The Mortgagee's Option to Purchase Mortgaged Property*, in A.B.A. Real Prop., Prob. & Tr. L. Sect., *Financing Real Estate During the Inflationary 80s* (Strum ed. 1981).

This ancient rule should not find application in a transaction negotiated between a large developer represented by a team of experts and a large lender represented by a team of experts. These sophisticated parties should have the complete freedom to contract for the result they want in light of the economic realities they find in the marketplace.

REFERENCES: *Mac Arthur v. North Palm Beach Utilities Inc.,* 202 So2d 181 (Fla. 1967); *Smith* v. *Smith,* 82 NH 399, 135 A25 (1926); *Hopping* v. *Baldridge,* 130 Okla. 226, 266 P2d 469 (1928); *Coursey v. Fairchild,* 436 P2d 35 (Okla. 1967); *Griffin Co.* v. *Chicago,* 52 Ill. 130 (1869); 59 CJS Mortgages §113; 55 Am.Jur.2d Mortgages §85, §514; 2 Harv L. Rev. 459, 472.

21.10 Convertible Mortgages

A new type of mortgage (usually encountered in large-scale transactions) is the convertible mortgage. It starts out looking like the typical large-scale mortgage, but an option clause gives the mortgagee the privilege, at some future specified date, of converting the outstanding balance of the mortgage into a predetermined percentage of ownership of the property.

This type of provision is attractive to the borrower because it allows the borrower to retain all the tax benefits associated with ownership until the lender exercises the conversion option.

It is attractive to the lender because the lender exercises his option at a time when the property has proved itself to be viable and increasing in value.

There is some danger that the borrower will resist the conversion, claiming that a "clogging of the equity" is involved. There is also some danger that a bankruptcy trustee might refuse to honor the clause.

There is another type of convertible option used in home loans. A clause in an ARM mortgage gives the borrower the right, at some specified date in the future, to convert to a fixed-rate mortgage.

21.11 Participating Mortgage

In large mortgage transactions the lender may wish to participate in the income of the property, either net income or gross income. The share of income to be awarded the lender is stated in the mortgage or in a separate agreement. It is often described as "contingent cash flow participation." It presents many thorny legal problems. Among these problems are possible usury, possible unconscionability, possible clogging of the equity, and possible joint venture liability.

21.12   Deferred Interest Mortgage (DIM)

In the DIM, early payments not only fail to contribute to the amortization of principal, but also fail to cover all of the accrued interest. This results in negative amortization and the interest on interest problems. See §21–16.

21.13   Interest-only Mortgage

Under the interest-only mortgage, early payments do not contribute to the amortization of principal but fully pay any accrued interest. Either the mortgage is payable at a stated date, perhaps three to five years from its creation, or principal amortization is deferred until such later date.

21.14   Balloon Loans

Balloon loans are structured in one of two general ways. The loan is for a short term, with the payments including either interest-only or interest and principal amortized over a longer term with the whole loan payable at the end of the shorter term. At that time the loan is either renegotiated, refinanced, or paid off. This is really a form of ARM, giving the lender the chance to adjust the interest rate to current market conditions every three to five years.

The federal agencies and state laws regulate balloon notes. Balloons pose dangers to borrowers, and this should always be explained to a prospective borrower. The theory is that when a balloon comes due, new financing will be available at reasonable rates. This is a pure guess. New financing may be unavailable or may command high interest rates. Some borrowers have lost their homes for this reason and are suing the brokers who recommended balloon financing. Much balloon financing takes place when a seller takes back a second mortgage when he sells his home subject to an assumable first mortgage.

21.15   Fifteen-year FRM

A popular mortgage that is something of a novelty but not of the ARM type is the fifteen-year fixed-rate mortgage.

EXAMPLE: This mortgage is simply the old fixed-rate mortgage, but instead of paying out over a thirty-year period, it pays out over a fifteen-year period. Of course, to accomplish this, it calls for larger monthly payments. But since it reduces principal quickly, it reduces the total interest cost. Thus for a 12 percent, fifteen-year loan of $100,000 the monthly payment would be $1200.17.

On a thirty-year loan the payment would be $1067.26. But the total interest paid on a fifteen-year loan would be $116,030.60 as against $284,213.60 on a thirty-year loan.

Mortgage lenders like the fifteen-year loan. It does not lock them into a fixed-interest rate for thirty years. It is easier to sell in the secondary market.

21.16   Interest on Interest

The negative amortization feature of an ARM and GPM creates a legal problem of charging interest on interest.

EXAMPLE: To the extent that any monthly payment does not fully pay the interest due on the principal for that month, an addition to principal is made. Interest for the next month is then charged on the new principal balance which includes the amount added after the application of the last payment.

This practice is prohibited as being against the public policy of many states. See generally, 37 ALR 325, 332 suppl. by 76 ALR 1484, 1485. This should not be confused with the allowable process of settling an overdue debt by an agreement which capitalizes past due interest and charges interest on the new principal amount including that past due interest. *Hamilton* v. *Stephenson*, 55 SE 577 (Va. 1906); 37 ALR 325, 328 suppl. by 76 ALR 1484, 1485.

EXAMPLE: A loaned B $10,000 for one year with interest at 10 percent per annum. At the end of the year, B owed A $11,000, the $10,000 principal originally advanced and $1,000 in interest. B was unable to pay at that time, but, if given the chance, had a reasonable opportunity of fully repaying the debt upon the successful conclusion of a business transaction. A and B agreed, and a new note was executed for the $11,000 debt (the $11,000 being the principal on the new obligation, the amount upon which interest would be charged) with interest at 10 percent per year. This device is perfectly valid. It is distinguished from the graduated payment mortgage system which at the outset creates a program for automatically increasing the principal each month by the amount of unpaid interest and charging interest for that month on the increased principal amount.

The interest on interest prohibition is becoming less of a problem in the ARM and GPM setting as some states have enacted statues to facilitate the making of such mortgages. See, for example, Ill. Rev. Stat. Ch. 32 §794(e). These statutes generally exempt ARMS and GPMs from the interest on interest rule. See, for example, Burns Ind. Stat. Ann §28-1-21.5-7(b). Minn. Stat. Ann §47.201. This is obviously an area where federal preemption was necessary.

21.17   Intervening Liens

While it is a simple task for the borrower and lender to allow the property to stand as security for additional debt created by negative amortization, the retention of priority over other lien claimants for that additional debt is another matter. This is especially a problem where negative amortization is used. As long as the "advances" or additions to principal caused by the negative amortization are obligatory on the part of the lender, the priority of the ARM will be preserved against intervening lien claimants. Kratovil and Werner, *Modern Mortgage Law and Practice,* Sec. 11.02 (2d ed. 1981).

However, since under the ARM the lender may have the *option* of increasing the interest rate, the priority for all negative amortizations cannot be upheld under the obligatory advance theory.

The right of the lender to increase the mortgage debt as the index moves up poses a possible future advance problem, not only where negative amortization operates to increase the *principal* of the mortgage debt, but also where there is an increase in the *interest rate.*

No reliable body of law has as yet been developed in this area. Among the liens that may intervene between the recording of the mortgage and the increase in the mortgage debt are second mortgages, judgment liens, mechanic's liens, and federal tax liens. Barnett & McKenzie, *Alternative Mortgage Instruments,* p. 4–35 *et seq.* The simple solution, wherever title insurance is available, is for the lender to insist on a title insurance endorsement such as that shown in Fig. 4. FNMA requires this endorsement on all negative amortization mortgages it acquires.

21.18   Usury

An adjustable mortgage may become usurious if the index carries the rate over the usury limit. *Kin-Ark Corp.* v. *Boyles,* 593 F2d 361 (10th Cir. 1979). Another court has held that usury is not present even though the variable rate provisions at times carry the loan rate above the legal maximum if the parties contracted in good faith and without the intent to avoid usury laws. *McConnell* v. *Merrill, Lynch Pierce, Fenner & Smith,* 146 Cal. Reptr. 371 (1978). See, generally, Werner, *Usury and the Variable-Rate Mortgage,* 5 RELJ 155 (1976). This is the better view.

Absent an exemption or preemption, the lender must include a provision in the loan documents that the interest rate will not increase to a level above the maximum rate allowed by law.

21.19   Negotiability

The concept of negotiability protects a holder in due course of a promissory note from defenses that may be available against the original creditor. The ARMs are often, almost by definition, evidenced by nonnegotiable (as opposed to nonmarketable) notes. Where the sum is uncertain, as in the ARM, and where the buyer of the loan must refer to something outside of the note itself, that is, the index, to determine the interest rate, the note is not a negotiable instrument.

Attorneys' Title Guaranty Fund, Inc.

Policy No.:

NON-FIXED RATE MORTGAGE ENDORSEMENT

(a) The Fund hereby insures the insured against actual loss which the insured shall sustain by reason of any inaccuracies in the following assurances:

    1) The provisions of the insured mortgage authorized by the applicable Regulations contained in Title 12 of the Code of Federal Regulations, are valid and fully enforceable; and

    2) The priority of the lien of the insured mortgage shall not be impaired or diminished by reason of those changes in the rate of interest from time to time authorized by the insured mortgage when such changes in the rate of interest are made pursuant to the terms of the applicable Regulations contained in Title 12 of the Code of Federal Regulations; and

    3) Such lien continues as a mortgage lien securing the principal amount of indebtedness together with all interest having accrued thereon, including negative amortization if any.

(b) This endorsement does not insure against loss or damage by reason of failure of the insured to comply with the applicable Regulations contained in Title 12 of the Code of Federal Regulations.

(c) This endorsement does not insure against loss or damage based upon (i) usury, or (ii) any consumer credit protection or truth in lending law.

(d) This endorsement is made a part of the policy and is subject to all of the provisions of the Conditions and Stipulations and Schedules A and B; provided, however, that Exclusion from Coverage, Paragraph 3(d) shall not be construed to limit the assurances herein contained.

ATTORNEYS' TITLE GUARANTY FUND, INC.

By _Ward F. McDonald_

Ward F. McDonald
President

| DATED | MEMBER NO. | SIGNATURE OF ATTORNEY |

FUND FORM 218 (Rev. 5 82)
NON-FIXED END.

353

21.20   Mortgage-backed Securities

FNMA, FHLMC, GNMA, and other private companies have engaged in the issuance of various investment instruments backed by pools of mortgages. This practice is discussed in detail in Kinney and Garrigan, *The Handbook of Mortgage Banking* (1985). It is unnecessary to repeat here the scholarly analysis given in that treatise.

> REFERENCES: Gobel and Miller, *Handbook of Mortgage Mathematics & Finance Tables* (1981). A.B.A. Real Prop., Prob. & Tr. L. Sect., *Financing Real Estate During the Inflationary 80s* (Strum ed. 1981). This book is a must for every real property lawyer. HUD, *Alternative Mortgage Instruments Research Study* (1981). PLI, *Mortgages and Alternative Mortgage Instruments* (Sweat, Chmn. 1981). Public Information Dept., Fed. Res. Bank of N.Y., *The Arithmetic of Interest Rates* (1981). Brodkey, *AMIs: Let the Lawyers Work Out the Details,* 45 Legal Bull. 133 (May 1979). Kaplan, *Alternative Mortgage Instruments, the FHLBB Study,* in 1977 *FNMA Gen. Counsel's Conf.* 157.

21.21   Repo

Pending sale of a mortgage-backed security to an investor, a mortgage banker can obtain operating funds by selling the securities to a bank, with an agreement to repurchase them as they are sold to investors. The bank takes physical possession of the securities and an assignment executed in blank by the mortgage banker. The bank thus protects itself against a second sale by the mortgage banker to an innocent purchaser or the claims of a trustee in bankruptcy of the lender. It is important that the transaction be structured and documented as a sale to the bank with an option to sell the securities back to the mortgage banker.

CHAPTER 22

Real Estate Finance—
Due-On-Sale Clause

22.01 In General

The most controversial clause in mortgage law today is the due-on-sale clause. Let us begin with a simple, early version of this clause:

> In case of a *sale* of the mortgaged premises without the written consent of the mortgagee, the entire principal of the mortgage debt shall, at the election of the mortgagee, become immediately due and payable.

A word or two of history is needed. The mortgage lending that took place prior to the Great Depression was essentially balloon-note financing based on a bricks-and-mortar appraisal of the property. During the bad years of the Depression, mortgage lending ground to a halt. After President Roosevelt took office in 1933, there was a modest revival of home mortgage lending sparked by the introduction of FHA mortgage insurance and the creation of the federal savings and loan associations.

A new concept found its way into mortgage lending, namely, that the loan should be an amortized loan made to a creditworthy borrower. The borrower would have to be one who could "qualify" financially for the loan. As a corollary, the lender argued that he should be able to prevent the passing of the mortgaged property into the hands of an owner who was not creditworthy, who might allow the property to run down. Toward that end, the lenders began to insert the due-on-sale clause in their mortgages. Even FHA used the clause.

For many years the clause gave no difficulty. However, when inflation and interest rates began to skyrocket, a new problem developed. The thrift institutions found themselves saddled with old, low-interest loans. At the same time they were compelled to pay high rates of interest on certificates of deposit. Ultimately, the thrift institutions began to run into the red as the average cost of funds became higher than the average yield on the mortgage portfolio.

Again, we must turn back the clock to see what economic forces propelled the due-on-sale clause into such prominence that it became worthy of an entire chapter in this treatise.

In the previous chapter attention was directed to the incredible economic and financial changes that devastated this country beginning in the early 1970's. Inflation roared out of control. Interest rates began to soar and to gyrate. It became necessary for the federal government to step into the picture. It virtually abolished the old-fashioned state usury laws in the residential lending. It created a variable-interest-rate mortgage that permitted mortgage lenders to charge an interest rate that fluctuated and tracked with the interest rate lenders were paying on the short-term certificates of deposit they sold to investors. It vastly increased the amount of mortgage funds available for lending by allowing GNMA, FNMA and FHLMC to issue and sell to investors securities secured by pools of mortgages. And ultimately the federal government had to step in to control the due-on-sale clause.

The situation. As the situation began to develop in the early 1970's, thrift institutions and other lenders held in their loan portfolios many 30-year home mortgages bearing low interest rates, mostly six percent mortgages, but some seven or eight percent. Now market interest rate mortgages, those currently made, began to bear much higher interest, at times up to 16%. Let us take a typical example of how the due-on-sale clause influenced home sales.

> **EXAMPLE:**   Owner mortgages his home to Lender in 1969 for $50,000 at 8% interest. The mortgage contains a due-on-sale clause reading as follows: "In case of a *transfer* of the mortgaged premises without the written consent of Lender, the entire principal of the mortgage debt shall, at the election of the mortgagee, become immediately due and payable."
>
> In 1978 the mortgage has been paid down to $45,000. Owner is selling his home to Buyer for $70,000. Ordinarily the old mortgage is paid off when a home is sold. The buyer gets his own mortgage on terms that suit him. But the new mortgages made in 1978 carry an interest rate of 15%. Both Owner and Buyer would be better off if they allow the old mortgage to remain, for the debt of $45,000 will bear interest at only 8%. So the sale is arranged as an installment sale. Owner sells his equity of $25,000 for $5000 cash, balance of $20,000 payable in installments. If Lender threatens to invoke the due-on-sale clause and thus accelerate the mortgage debt, the answer will be, "No deed was made. Therefore this is not a *transfer.*" Thus creative financing was born.

22.02   Creative Financing

Not all mortgages contained due-on-sale clauses. While the savings and loan industry made use of these clauses, mortgage forms used by many insurance companies, banks, and FHA lenders did not contain this term. This set the stage for many "creative financing" transactions, especially when market interest rates were high and mortgage credit was generally unavailable. A seller eager to dispose of his home sold it subject to the existing mortgage. For the balance of the sale price he took cash and a second mortgage on the home.

EXAMPLE: Assume that the existing mortgage does not contain a due-on-sale clause. Buyer would purchase the $70,000 home subject to the existing mortgage with a $45,000 balance. The remaining $25,000 would be paid by Buyer giving a $5,000 down payment and giving a second mortgage to Owner for $20,000. Typically this mortgage would be due in three to five years.

If the existing mortgage contained a due-on-sale clause, buyer and seller were left with some options. Many deals were closed secretly in the hope that the lender would not discover the situation. Lenders became vigilant, watching more carefully the names of the payees on checks given to make the periodic mortgage payments and the names of the insured on the casualty insurance policies covering the mortgaged property for indications that a sale had taken place secretly. It was easier to keep the sale a secret when the seller and buyer entered into an unrecorded installment contract for the balance of the sale price over the balance of the mortgage.

Others simply defied the lender to enforce the due-on-sale clause. Some lenders took up the challenge and litigation followed. Some state courts refused to enforce the clause where the buyer was creditworthy; others sustained the use of the clause, even where the lender was using it as a device to increase the interest rate. While these battles were raging in the marketplace and the courtroom, states began to enact legislation, and a crazy-quilt pattern of laws resulted. The controversy continued. Federal associations challenged state laws and court decisions that seemed to limit their use of the due-on-sale clause.

REFERENCE: Roszkowski, *Drafting Around Mortgage Due-on-sale Clauses: The Danger of Playing Hide-and-Seek*, 21 R.P.P. & T. J. 23 (1986).

22.03   Federal Preemption—The Garn–St. Germain Act

Some lending corporations are organized under state law, others under federal law. To a considerable but poorly defined extent the federal lenders are governed by federal law. Federal savings and loans are largely governed by federal laws and federal regulations. For many years they have used and enforced the due-on-sale clause.

Federal regulations have stated unequivocally that enforcement of this clause is a federal matter. Nevertheless, beginning in 1976, California took the position that the clause could not be enforced by either federal or state institutions where the buyer was creditworthy. A number of states passed laws incorporating this point of view or their courts chose to follow the California reasoning.

At all events, the Supreme Court ultimately decided that *federal* savings and loan associations in invoking the due-on-sale clause were immune from *state* regulation or *state* court interference. *Fidelity Fed. S. & L. Assn.* v. *De la Cuesta*, 73 L. Ed.2d 664, 102 S.Ct. 3014 (1982). Of the many articles previously written on the subject, only a few had anticipated this result. See Kratovil, *A New Dilemma for Thrift Institutions: Judicial Emasculation of the Due-on-sale Clause*, 12 John Marshall J.

of Practice & Procedure 299 (1979); Kratovil, *Epilogue: Wellenkamp* v. *Bank of America,* 15 J.M.L. Rev. 435 (1982).

In September 1982, Congress enacted a law (The Garn–St. Germain Act) dealing in part with the due-on-sale clause. The Supreme Court's decision that neither state laws nor state court decisions can limit a federal savings and loan association's enforcement of the due-on-sale clauses in their mortgages gave the *federal* associations a competitive advantage over state associations. Congress therefore enacted a law allowing all lenders, state and federal, to exercise the due-on-sale clauses in their mortgage documents regardless of the buyer's creditworthiness. In effect, this permits the lender to demand increased interest as the price of consenting to the sale. 12 USCA Sec. 1701–j–3.

22.04   Federal and Other Limits on Triggering Events

Where the mortgaged property consists of fewer than five residential units, the Garn–St. Germain Law limits the lender's right to invoke, or "trigger," the due-on-sale clause. No matter what the mortgage may provide, acceleration will not be allowed under the due-on-sale clause in the event of:

1. The creation of a junior lien or encumbrance that does not relate to the transfer of the right to occupy the property.
2. The creation of a purchase money security interest for household appliances.
3. A transfer by devise, descent, or operation of law upon the death of a joint tenant or tenant by the entirety.
4. The granting of a leasehold interest of three years or less that does not involve an option to purchase.
5. A transfer to a relative resulting from the death of the borrower.
6. A transfer to a spouse or child of the borrower.
7. A transfer resulting from a divorce or legal separation by which the spouse of the borrower becomes an owner of the property.
8. A transfer to an intervivos trust in which the borrower is and remains a beneficiary and which does not relate to a transfer of rights of occupancy.
9. Any other transfer or disposition described in regulations prescribed by the Federal Home Loan Bank Board.

REFERENCE: 12 U.S.C.A. Sec. 1701 j–3.

Other controversies rage regarding the events that trigger the operation of the due-on-sale clause. The resolution of any such disputes is obviously tied to the language of the clause itself. While some clauses are well drafted from the lender's point of view, covering with great specificity the various events that will give rise to the operation of the clause, others are poorly drafted and require court construction for their application. There are, however, some instances in which the courts have given some guidance, and some common patterns have begun to emerge.

22.04(a)   Installment Contracts Causing the Clause to be Invoked

The federal law does not forbid the triggering of the clause when the landowner contracts to sell the land on the installment method. Indeed, the language of Garn–St. Germain leans toward permitting the clause to be invoked. Much of the debate in the state courts turns on the meaning of the word "sale." Does it mean only a cash sale, or does it also include a credit sale on the installment basis? Most of the decisions treat an installment sale as a "sale" as that term is generally used in the due-on-sale clause. 69 ALR3d 713.

22.04(b)   Junior Mortgages Causing the Clause to be Invoked

Some clauses are drafted broadly enough to include a second mortgage as an event that triggers the operation of the clause. This is common provision in large-scale mortgages. The theory is that revenue from a mortgaged property will be diverted to the payment of the second mortgage, and cash flow will not be sufficient to also support the first mortgage. Federal law now prohibits the application of a due-on-sale clause to the placement of a junior mortgage only on *residential* property.

Thus the law seems to have responded well to the economics of the situation. A homeowner is free to put a second mortgage on his home, and a life insurance company is free to accelerate a commercial mortgage if the developer places a second mortgage on the mortgaged property.

22.05   Window Period

The Garn–St. Germain Act provided for a "window period." This clause permitted the old state law, whether by statute or court decision, to continue to apply under certain circumstances. Arizona, Michigan, Minnesota, and Utah took advantage of this loophole. New Mexico took limited advantage of this exemption. The window period does not apply to a federal savings and loan association or a federal savings bank.

22.06   State Override of Federal Preemption

The Garn–St. Germain Act gave the states the option of moving out from federal control. To date, Maine, Massachusetts, New York, South Carolina, and Wisconsin have taken this course. Their regulations apply, of course, only to state institutions.

22.07   Prepayment Penalties

A federal rule prohibits a real estate lender from imposing a prepayment penalty or premium in connection with a residential loan upon acceleration of the loan or commencement of a foreclosure proceeding for violation of a due-on-sale clause. It also restricts a lender's right to impose a prepayment penalty or premium on a homeowner who proposes to sell his residence to a purchaser seeking to assume the existing loan. 12 CFR 591 (1985).

22.08 The Secondary Market

If a mortgage has been sold in the secondary market, whether the due-on-sale clause will be enforced is, of course, a decision that rests with the mortgage owner, FNMA, FHLMC, etc.

22.09 Installment Contract Containing a Due-on-sale Clause

An installment contract may contain a due-on-sale clause.

> **EXAMPLE:** Vendor enters into an installment contract to sell his home to Purchaser for $100,000, payable $10,000 cash and balance of $90,000 payable in monthly installments over a ten-year period. The contract provides that if Purchaser assigns his contract interest without Vendor's written consent, Vendor may declare the entire balance immediately due and payable. Probably the Garn–St. Germain Act applies to this clause. 35 Hastings L. J. 243, 266 (1983).

> REFERENCE: 52 Legal Bulletin 110 (1986) (discussing twenty-eight recent decisions on this clause).

In matters of national interest, Congress has the power to overrule state laws and court decisions. This is called "preemption." Garn–St. Germain is an instance of federal preemption.

> REFERENCES: 24 Ariz. L. Rev. 371; 36 Ark. L. Rev. 705; 100 Banking L. J. 772; 47 Mo. L. Rev. 725; 14 Pac. L. J. 1; 23 So. Tex. L. J. 357; 23 Santa Clara L. Rev. 291; 20 San Diego L. Rev. 897; 1982 So. Ill. U.L. Rev. 487; 17 U. of San Fran. L. Rev. 355; 23 Urb. L. Ann. 285.

CHAPTER 23

Real Estate Finance—
Sale Subject to Existing Mortgage

23.01   In General

For economic rather than legal reasons, a home sale usually involves the payment and release of the old mortgage obtained by the seller when the home was acquired and the placement of a new mortgage obtained by the buyer. Sometimes economic conditions are such that mortgages are difficult to obtain or, if obtainable, they bear such a high rate of interest that the buyer may not qualify, or he may be discouraged from purchasing the property. In those times the existing financing makes the home more salable or may even give value to the property if the old mortgage is at a comparatively low rate. For these reasons the buyer and seller may attempt to work out a deal to enable the old mortgage to remain outstanding and not be paid and released as a part of the transaction.

The first question, then, is this: Is it legally permissible to sell property without paying off the old mortgage? The answer is that this can legally be done except where the old mortgage contains an enforceable due-on-sale clause (see Chapter 22). In this chapter it is assumed that: (1) the old mortgage is *assumable,* that is, it contains no enforceable due-on-sale clause; or (2) the old mortgage contains an enforceable due-on-sale clause but the mortgage lender has consented to the sale.

23.02   Personal Liability of Seller to Lender after Sale

Where Owner mortgages his land to Lender, as has previously been stated, he customarily signs two important documents, namely, a promissory note and a mortgage securing the note.

The promissory note creates personal liability from Owner to Lender. If Owner sells the property to Buyer, Lender is not involved. His rights are not affected. Owner's personal liability to Lender continues. Lender's mortgage is unaffected.

All mortgage lenders have a printed form available that will change this. The form is designed for the signatures of Owner, Lender, and Buyer. It releases Owner's liability as of the date of his deed to Buyer. In turn, Buyer accepts personal liability to Lender for the balance of the mortgage debt. This is a commonplace transaction. Sometimes it is called a *novation agreement*. From the seller's point of view, this is the best possible result.

Concerning the personal liability of the buyer for payment of the mortgage debt, certain distinctions must be kept in mind.

In the first place, regardless of personal liability, if the old mortgage is not paid off in the process of closing the sale, the old mortgage remains, and if the payments on the mortgage are not made, the old mortgage can be foreclosed. The question here discussed, then, is whether in addition to foreclosing the mortgage, the mortgagee can obtain a personal judgment against the buyer.

EXAMPLE: The mortgage is in the sum of $80,000. The foreclosure sale price is $75,000. This is considered a part payment of the mortgage debt. Thus the mortgage debt, after the foreclosure sale, is $80,000 minus $75,000, or $5,000. Can the mortgage lender obtain a judgment against the buyer? If he can, he can levy on the buyer's automobile, his bank account, his appliances, and so on.

Absent a novation agreement there are two important documents that bear on this issue: the contract of sale and the deed to the buyer.

EXAMPLE: Owner owns a home. It is mortgaged to Lender. The contract of sale and the deed to the Buyer both recite that the land is subject to a mortgage to Lender, which Buyer does *not* assume or agree to pay. Here the only relevant documents state unequivocally that Buyer does not assume liability for the mortgage debt. Buyer has no personal liability for that debt.

EXAMPLE: Facts as in previous example, except that both documents provide that Buyer *does* assume and agree to pay the mortgage debt. Even though Lender, the mortgagee is not a party either to the contract of sale or the deed, Buyer becomes personally liable to Lender. The theories differ from state to state. The favorite theory is that Lender is the third-party beneficiary of a contract between Owner and Buyer. Buyer's liability to Lender attaches when Lender learns of the transaction and determines to hold Buyer liable.

EXAMPLE: Facts as in previous example, but contract and deed simply state that land is being conveyed "subject to" the described mortgage. The phrase that Buyer does assume and agree to pay the mortgage is absent. In all but one or two states, Buyer has no personal liability for the mortgage debt.

EXAMPLE: Facts as in first example, but neither the contract nor deed says anything about the mortgage. Again, Buyer has no personal liability for the mortgage debt.

See Kratovil and Werner, *Modern Mortgage Law and Practice,* Ch. 15 (2d ed., 1981).

Much of this discussion is quite academic in a number of states. During the Great Depression, personal judgments in favor of mortgagees bankrupted many persons.

EXAMPLE: In 1933 a mortgage for $100,000 is foreclosed. The foreclosure sale price is $5,000. The mortgagee obtains a personal judgment against the mortgagor for $95,000. This struck many legislatures as disgraceful. In many states, laws were passed totally abolishing deficiency decrees.

In addition, there are factors today which diminish the importance of personal liability. Before a foreclosure is begun, the lender makes every attempt to work the situation out without foreclosure. If the mortgage can be recast, with lower monthly payments that the landowner can handle, that will be done. If recasting the mortgage will not help, the majority of the deals are worked out by a deed in lieu of foreclosure, which, of course, includes a release of all personal liability.

23.03   Protection of Buyer

There are some steps a buyer should take when entering into a "sale-subject-to" transaction.

First, the mortgage must be read very carefully. If it contains a due-on-sale clause, the sale may entitle the existing mortgagee to foreclose and enforce the loan documents against both the land and the seller–original mortgagee. Some mortgages call for an automatic increase in the interest rate or the payment of a fixed sum when such a sale is made.

Second, a careful buyer will seek an *estoppel certificate* from the existing mortgagee. This certificate will typically state the principal and interest balance due, whether the loan is in default, that there are no late charges or penalties due, and the balances in the tax and insurance impound or escrow accounts.

Third, title insurance is indispensable since the seller's state of title must be evidenced and the buyer must have assurance of the state of title. The contract should specify who pays for the title search and list the permitted title objections.

Fourth, if the seller's monthly payments include payments to a tax or insurance impound or escrow account, those accounts should be assigned to the buyer with the seller given an appropriate closing statement credit for the account balances.

In general, the contract should contain the other provisions that are customary in local cash real estate transactions.

23.04   Protection of Seller–mortgagor

Where mortgaged land is sold without paying off the mortgage, it is necessary to provide carefully for the protection of the seller–mortgagor. As has been stated, the seller–mortgagor cannot get rid of his personal liability to the mortgagee merely by selling the mortgaged land. Now let us take a close look at an example previously given.

> **EXAMPLE:** Owner owns a home. It is mortgaged to Lender. Owner sells the home to Buyer. In the contract of sale and deed it is stated that the land is subject to a described mortgage which Buyer assumes and agrees to pay. In a situation like this, the law creates a scheme of priorities, so far as personal liability is concerned. It is said that Buyer is primarily liable to Lender and Owner is secondarily liable to Lender. This is the first step in applying the law of *subrogation*. If Lender chooses to pursue Owner, when default occurs, and succeeds in collecting the balance of the mortgage debt from Owner, then Owner steps into Lender's shoes as mortgagee. Owner can foreclose the mortgage against Buyer. This is for the reason that, as between Owner and Buyer, Buyer should have paid the mortgage debt. The result would be the same if the deed merely stated that the land "is subject to" the described mortgage without adding words of assumption. Here the courts say that use of the "subject clause" makes the land the primary fund for the payment of the mortgage.

All this is well and good, but it is better to have this and more in black and white. A carefully prepared document is needed, signed by Owner and Buyer when the sale to Buyer is made. It provides that if Owner is compelled by Lender to pay the mortgage debt, Owner is entitled to foreclose the mortgage against Buyer. But it goes further. It requires Buyer to pay the real estate taxes, keep up the insurance, keep the building in repair, and so on. If Buyer fails to make these expenditures, Owner is permitted to do so and to add such amounts to the mortgage. Owner is permitted to buy the mortgage at a discount and to enforce it for the full amount of the debt.

If the buyer is not to assume personal liability *to the mortgagee* for the mortgage debt, that ought to be spelled out clearly. Caution suggests the addition of a clause that the contract is only for the benefit of the parties thereto and not for the benefit of any third parties. This prevents the mortgagee from contending that one or more provisions of the sale contract were intended for the mortgagee's benefit.

23.05 Personal Liability of Buyer to Seller

Let us go back to an example previously given.

> **EXAMPLE:** Owner owns a home. It is mortgaged to Lender. Owner sells the home to Buyer. In the contract of sale and deed it is stated that the land is subject to a described mortgage, which Buyer assumes and agrees to pay. This is a promise that makes Buyer personally liable to Lender when Lender learns of the transaction. But this promise runs to Owner, so Buyer also becomes personally liable to Owner.

What this means, in practical effect, is that if Lender and Buyer get together to work out a deed in lieu of foreclosure, it will also be necessary to get Owner into the deal. Lender will release Owner's personal liability to Lender, and Owner will release Buyer's personal liability to Owner. Kratovil and Werner. *supra.* §40.04.

CHAPTER 24

Real Estate Finance—
Purchase Money Mortgages

24.01 In General

The purchase money mortgage is a venerable mortgage instrument.

> **EXAMPLE:** Seller conveys his home to Buyer for $60,000, Buyer paying $20,000 cash, and giving Seller a mortgage for the balance of $40,000. Notice that no outside bank is present in the transaction. Seller holds the mortgage and collects mortgage payments. The only cash involved is the $20,000 down payment. This is currently being called by realtors the *take-back* mortgage.

Second mortgages given by commercial second mortgage lenders have terms and bear interest according to current market conditions. The purchase money mortgage, in contrast, is given because the *seller* wants to sell the property. He will quote terms that enable him to sell, often with interest well below the market. Hence many second mortgages are often purchase money mortgages.

> **EXAMPLE:** Seller is selling his home to Buyer for $100,000. The existing mortgage has been paid down to $70,000. It has no due-on-sale clause. Thus only $30,000 remains to be financed if Buyer takes subject to the existing mortgage. Buyer can pay $10,000 cash; Seller takes back a purchase money second mortgage of $20,000.

24.02 Legal Advantages of Take-back Mortgage

The take-back mortgage is a favorite of the law.

> **EXAMPLE:** Seller sells his home to Buyer. Buyer is married to Wife, who is insane. Buyer needs a home for his children. Wife's signature would ordinarily be needed on any mortgage, as is true in most states involving home mortgages.

Buyer gives a take-back mortgage to Seller. It is good as gold without Wife's signature.

EXAMPLE: Seller is selling his home to Buyer. Buyer has had a tussle with the IRS and they have filed an income tax lien against his assets for $10,000. Buyer is contesting this lien. Ordinarily, this lien would cloud Buyer's title. But his purchase money mortgage to Seller has priority over the earlier IRS lien.

REFERENCE: Kratovil and Werner, *Modern Mortgage Law and Practice* § 19.04 (2d ed., 1981).

At times a third-party financial institution is advancing the money to pay the seller and wishes to claim the legal benefits given the purchase money mortgage. The law permits this. 59 CJS *Mortgages* § 231(c).

24.03   Income Tax Effect of Purchase Money Mortgages

The purchase money mortgage has traditionally offered certain income tax advantages. Where property is sold at a gain, income tax must be paid on that gain. This tax liability may be paid out of the proceeds of the sale. If property is sold on the installment method or through a purchase money mortgage, all of the sale proceeds will not be received to thereby generate the funds for the making of the tax payment. It is in this situation that the installment method of reporting taxable income is utilized.

EXAMPLE: Owner purchased a home for $100,000 in 1974. Owner sold the home to Buyer in 1986 for $300,000. Ignoring for the moment the potential applicability of other income tax rules relating to the treatment of gain on the sale of residential property, Owner would have taxable gain of $200,000, payable as part of his 1986 income taxes. If, however, Owner sold the home by taking a down payment of $50,000 and was in the highest income tax bracket, the down payment may not produce enough funds for payment of the tax. To avoid this result, Owner may elect to treat the taxability of the gain on the sale of the home on the installment basis. In this way each payment made by Buyer is considered, for tax purposes, to be made up of two components, one-third return of investment (which is not taxable) and two-thirds gain (which is taxable and for which the taxes will be payable in the year the payment is received).

The installment method of reporting has the obvious income tax benefit of avoiding the creation of income tax liability in a year in which cash flow does not facilitate the making of the tax payment.
The Tax Reform Act of 1986, now known as the Internal Revenue Code of 1986, brought sweeping changes to this area of the tax law. For the sale of property other than the taxpayer's personal use property, a complex set of formulas must now be used to determine whether and to what extent the taxpayer must report the gain on property sold under the installment method in the year of sale and subsequent years. The only exceptions to the use of these formulas relate to the sale of the taxpayer's personal use property, the sale of farm property, or

the sale of trade, business, or rental property where the sale price does not exceed $150,000.

The purchase money mortgage transaction offered a mechanism for the buyer and seller to adjust the amount being paid for the property between the sale price and the interest to be paid on the purchase money debt.

> **EXAMPLE:** Suppose that in the preceding example, the parties agreed that the mortgage shall bear interest at 2 percent. The adjustment of the interest rate and purchase price was a way to shift income to the more favorable capital gains treatment as an increase of the purchase price, as opposed to the treatment of the interest as ordinary income, which would have been taxed at a higher rate.

The federal government reacted to this by imposing certain minimum standards on the interest rates charged in connection with installment sales. Interest of at least 110 percent of the "applicable federal rate," which changes monthly, must be charged or the IRS will impute interest at a rate of 120 percent of the applicable federal rate. An exemption to this rule applies in the sale of farms for less than $1,000,000 and the first $250,000 of the sale price of principal residences.

Although these rules remain after the enactment of the Tax Reform Act of 1986, they no longer have their former impact because the Tax Reform Act also abolished capital gains treatment. With all income taxed at the same rate, there is no advantage to be gained by attempting to shift income between interest income and income from the sale of the property.

24.04   Usury and the Purchase Money Mortgage

There has been previous discussion of the juggling of interest rates and the amount of mortgage debt where a purchase money mortgage is involved. The same juggling process gives rise to a usury problem.

> **EXAMPLE:** Seller sells his home to Buyer for $100,000. Buyer pays $20,000 in cash and gives Seller a purchase money mortgage for $80,000. Obviously, the figures can be juggled. Seller can quote a price of $105,000, with a 10 percent interest rate, or a price of $100,000 with a 14 percent interest rate, having income tax consequences in mind. If the 14 percent exceeds the usury rate, it has nevertheless been held that there is no violation of the usury law. *Mandelino v. Fribourg,* 23 NY2d 145, 242 NE2d 823 (1979), 20 Syracuse L. Rev. 762; 91CJS *Usury* §18; 45 Am.Jur.2d Interest & Usury §126; 91 ALR 1105 (listing conflicting decisions). The philosophy here is that the parties can and do juggle the two components of the transaction, price and interest rate, and the economic consequences to the buyer are the same. Bear in mind that this problem often arises on second mortgages and that the usury law is usually different from that governing first mortgages.

24.05   Flexibility of Take-back Mortgage

The take-back mortgage is just as flexible as the parties wish to make it.

> **EXAMPLE:** Seller is selling Buyer a block of stores and taking back a purchase money mortgage, payable in monthly payments. The parties can agree that the monthly payments will fluctuate as cash flow fluctuates. And they can agree on a "balloon" maturity payment.

The mortgage can also provide for lower payments during the first three years of the loan, as is commonly done where a "buy-down" exists.

24.06   Discounting the Take-back Mortgage

The seller most often chooses to hold the take-back mortgage to maturity. After all, it's well secured. But if he needs to convert the take-back mortgage into funds, he will probably have to discount it.

> **EXAMPLE:** Seller sells his home to Buyer for $80,000. Buyer pays $20,000 cash and gives Seller a purchase money mortgage for $60,000, bearing 12 percent interest. A year later, Seller needs money. He sells the mortgage to Mortgage Investor, who will only pay $50,000 for the mortgage. This gives Mortgage Investor an effective annual yield of about 19 percent. This is the big disadvantage of the take-back mortgage. Investors who buy individual mortgages want substantial returns and insist on this discount.

24.07   FNMA Purchase

FNMA issues its private regulations from time to time. Under current regulations it will buy take-back mortgages as funds are available for this purpose. Inquiry should be made at a bank or savings and loan, and they will advise you as to the terms on which such sales can currently be made.

24.08   Hazard Insurance

Like any other mortgagee, the take-back mortgagee should insist that the standard mortgagee loss clause be attached to the fire insurance policy. The mortgagee may insist on holding the policy.

24.09   Due-on-sale Clause

The due-on-sale clause has previously been discussed.

Before any property can be sold without paying off the existing mortgage, such mortgage must be studied to see if it contains a due-on-sale clause. If it does, the mortgagee's consent to the transaction must be obtained unless the transaction falls in a category where the due-on-sale clause is inapplicable.

In any case, a seller selling with a take-back mortgage should insist that his mortgage contain a due-on-sale clause. The clause should be a broad form clause, covering such matters as installment contracts.

24.10 Balloon Notes

Perhaps the most popular device in the arsenal of creative financing draftsman is the balloon note. The mortgage is drafted with monthly payments as though the loan were to run for the usual thirty years. But at the end of, say, three years the entire debt falls due. This is the *balloon.*

The philosophy is that over the short run mortgage money will become more plentiful and interest rates will come down. This philosophy is open to question.

The Depression experience with such notes was so bad that savings and loan associations were forbidden to use balloon notes. Some states, such as Florida, have statutes that forbid certain types of balloon notes. *O'Neil* v. *Lorain Nat. Bank,* 369 So2d 378 (Fla. 1979). Consumer organizations oppose them. 1976 Am. Bar Found. Res. J. 35, 43. Regulation Z of the Federal Truth-in-Lending Act requires disclosure of the balloon. *Ibid.* at 84.

The danger, of course, is that the borrower will be unable to borrow funds elsewhere to pay the balloon and the holder of the mortgage will be in a position to exact harsh terms for a renewal. Also, borrowers under balloon notes will have to go into the market to compete with homebuyers and other borrowers when the balloon comes due. It is uncertain what that market will be when those loans are sought. Alternatively, the borrower will approach the seller for an extension. The seller–lender will then have much more bargaining power. He does not have a house to sell. There is no reason then for the seller–mortgagee to settle for a below-market interest rate. He may not want to give the extension, at any rate.

24.11 Call Provisions

As an alternative to the balloon note, there is the call provision, which gives the mortgage holder the right to declare the entire debt due and to foreclose if alternative financing is available to reasonable terms and the borrower refuses to avail himself of it. A form of such clause is found in Kratovil & Werner, *Modern Mortgage Law and Practice* § 19.09 (2d ed. 1981).

24.12 Deficiency Judgments

During the land sales boom of the 1920s, vacant land was sold at insane prices and huge purchase money mortgages were signed. When the Great Depression of 1929 began, thousands of mortgagors were subjected to large judgments obtained by the noteholders for a deficiency. These borrowers were forced into bankruptcy. As a reaction, many laws were enacted forbidding deficiency judgments in purchase money mortgages. 1960 Duke L. J. 1.

24.13 Form of Take-back Mortgage Transaction

The take-back mortgage documents do not differ greatly from normal real estate mortgage transactions. There is a mortgage, a promissory note, and, where appropriate, an assignment of leases and rents. If the mortgage is a junior mortgage, as is often true, the clauses needed in a junior mortgage are inserted.

Every purchase money mortgage ought to recite that it is a purchase money mortgage. And the deed to the buyer ought to recite that the grantor is taking back the mortgage as a purchase money mortgage. A purchase money mortgage, after all, enjoys priority over certain judgments, liens, dower, and homestead. The public records ought to reveal the true character of the mortgage so that the mortgagee is in a position to claim those benefits.

24.14   Truth-in-lending

When the purchase money mortgagee–seller is the typical homeowner who is not in the business of buying and selling real estate, the federal truth-in-lending law and other disclosure type statutes such as RESPA do not apply. 12 USCA § 2603.

24.15   Co-ownership Problems

Where a husband and wife own land as joint tenants or as tenants by the entireties, and they sell the land on an installment contract or take back a purchase money mortgage, questions arise as to the nature of their interest in the proceeds of sale.

> **EXAMPLE:**   Husband and Wife own Lot 1 in joint tenancy. They enter into an installment contract to sell Lot 1 to Buyer. This contract creates a new "chose in action," namely, a right to receive the purchase money. The question that arises is this: Is this "chose in action" owned in joint tenancy or in tenancy in common? The same question arises where a purchase money mortgage is involved. The decisions are in wild conflict.

> **SUGGESTION:**   If a joint tenancy is wanted, let the contract provide that the purchase price is payable to Husband and Wife as *joint tenants with the right of survivorship and not as tenants in common or as community property.* If a tenancy by the entireties is wanted, let the contract of sale, mortgage, and mortgage note read that the funds are payable to Husband and Wife as *tenants by the entirety and not as joint tenants or as community property.* Some states do not permit a tenancy by the entireties in personal property such as mortgages. 41 CJS *Husband & Wife* § 35.

24.16   Payment—Joint Mortgagees or Joint Sellers

Where a husband and wife own land jointly, sell it, and take back an installment contract or purchase money mortgage, the rule is that payment to either party is good payment. 70 CJS *Payment* § 4; 59 CJS *Mortgages* § 446. The party receiving payment can give a release of the mortgage. One would think that the buyer would feel more comfortable if this is spelled out in the documents. Of course, if the check is made payable to both, a different problem arises, namely, whether one party can endorse the other party's name. Again, the documents should cover this.

24.17   Contract Provisions

There are a number of legal problems involved in drafting a contract of sale where the seller is to take back a purchase money mortgage.

> **EXAMPLE:**   The contract of sale calls for the seller to take back a mortgage of $30,000 but states no interest rate, manner of payment, or other condition. The contract cannot be enforced if either party chooses to resist enforcement. It is "incomplete." *Sweeting* v. *Campbell,* 8 Ill.2d 54, 132 NE2d 523 (1956); 60 ALR2d 251.

The contract of sale for a transaction including a purchase money mortgage should contain the usual local provisions for cash sales, including, of course, permitted title objections. It should also set forth the following details: (1) Specific form of mortgage and note to be used. There is no such form as the "usual" form. (2) Who pays what charges (*e.g.,* who pays title insurance fee on the mortgage, recording fees, mortgage tax, if any, etc.). (3) Prepayment privilege, if any. A seller who hopes the buyer will prepay will use a sliding scale of prepayment fees, the cost of prepaying being small in the early years and higher in the later years of the loan. (4) Documents seller is to furnish (*e.g.,* statement by first mortgagee as to balance due, no existing defaults, amounts in tax and insurance escrow, etc.; also documents required by local junior mortgage statutes).

CHAPTER 25

Real Estate Finance—Junior Mortgages

25.01 In General

There is generally no legal limit on the number of mortgages a landowner can place on his property. Ordinarily, these mortgages will be ranked according to time under the legal rule that *prior in time is prior in right.*

EXAMPLE: Owner owns a home and mortgages it to Lender #1 in 1978. The mortgage is duly recorded. In 1979, Owner mortgages the same home to Lender #2. The mortgage is duly recorded. The mortgage of 1978 is a *first lien* on the property. The mortgage of 1979 is a *second lien.* If both mortgages go into default, both will be foreclosed. But foreclosure of the first lien wipes out the second lien. Lender #2 can prevent this by paying off Lender #1's lien. But if he doesn't do this, Lender #2's mortgage will be extinguished. That is why Lender #2's mortgage is customarily referred to as a *junior lien.* Foreclosure of Lender #1's mortgage (the senior lien) extinguishes the junior lien.

As is evident, the risk involved in lending on a second or junior mortgage is greater than in lending on a first mortgage. For this reason the interest rate is generally higher on a second mortgage. The usual rule governing all investments is that where the risk is greater, the return is higher. Conversely, where the return is high, be suspicious: the risk is greater. Also, customarily the junior mortgage has a shorter maturity than a first mortgage. The philosophy is that risk is reduced by compelling retirement of the junior debt over a shorter span of time.

Obviously, a junior mortgage is made only when there is an *equity* over and above the first mortgage.

EXAMPLE: Owner buys a home in 1978 for $80,000. He borrows $70,000 from Lender #1 and gives Lender #1 a first mortgage on the home. In 1982 the home value has risen to $100,000. Owner borrows $10,000 from Lender #2 and gives Lender #2 a second mortgage. The mortgage debts aggregate $80,000, but the combined loan-to-value ratio is 80%. This is safe, conservative lending.

25.02   Form and Contents of Second Mortgage

A second mortgage routinely contains clauses designed to protect the lender against the first mortgage. Some typical clauses are:

1. That the borrower will keep up the payments on the first mortgage and if he fails to do so, the second mortgage may make these payments, add the sums so paid to his second mortgage debt, and declare an acceleration of his debt.

2. That the second mortgage may, with the consent of the first mortgagee, buy the first mortgage at a discount and add the full face amount of the first mortgage to the second mortgage debt.

3. That if the borrower defaults in his first mortgage payments, the second mortgagee may declare an acceleration of the second mortgage debt and foreclose the mortgage.

4. That the surplus proceeds of any foreclosure sale over and above the amount needed to pay the first mortgage debt are assigned to the second mortgage. This is particularly helpful where a third party is the successful bidder at the foreclosure sale and bids more than enough to pay the first mortgage.

5. A covenant by the borrower reciting the total amount unpaid on the first mortgage and stating that no default exists under the first mortgage.

6. That the borrower will forward to the second mortgagee any notices received by the borrower from the first mortgagee or any public body. This enables the second mortgagee to prevent foreclosure of the first mortgage in some cases. The second mortgagee can make the payments on the first mortgage. Or if a public body is threatening action to close down the building for code violations, the second mortgagee can give the city assurances that all violations will be corrected.

7. That foreclosure of the first mortgage does not extinguish personal liability of the mortgagor on the note secured by the junior mortgage. 59 CJS *Mortgages* §§523, 704.

Of course, any junior mortgagee will want other protections. On commercial property he will demand an assignment of leases and rents. He will insist on a title insurance policy that shows the first mortgage he knows of as the only prior lien. He will want his name added to the fire insurance policy. Either the first mortgagee or the junior mortgagor should provide the junior mortgagee each month with proof of payment of the monthly first mortgage payment. The junior mortgagee should consider insisting on a due-on-sale clause in the mortgage. This is a necessity if the first mortgage contains such a clause. If the first mortgagee accelerates because of a sale of the property, the junior mortgagee will wish to do likewise.

If the first mortgage is an ARM, it should be checked for caps on interest and monthly payments.

25.03   Foreclosure Agreement with First Mortgagee

The second mortgagee may dicker with the first mortgagee and obtain a written agreement that the first mortgagee will give the second mortgagee a notice of any proposed first mortgage foreclosure. And even without the first mortgagee's consent, the second mortgagee may, in some states, record a notice requesting that he be notified of any foreclosure. This is done routinely in California, for example, where a deed of trust with power of sale is the common mortgage instrument and foreclosure is by the trustee's exercise of the power of sale without any court proceedings.

25.04   Subordination Provisions

Second mortgages usually contain a clause that if it becomes necessary to refinance the first mortgage, the second mortgagee will subordinate his mortgage to the new first mortgage. Because of the technicalities involved in all subordinations, this clause must be set forth in detail. See Kratovil and Werner, *Modern Mortgage Law and Practice,* chs. 30 and 38 (2d ed. 1981).

> **EXAMPLE:**   In 1975, Owner mortgaged his land to Lender #1 for $100,000 with 11 percent interest. In 1981 Owner gave a second mortgage to Lender #2 for $20,000 with 16 percent interest. A clause was included that Lender #2 will subordinate to any refinancing mortgage paying off Lender #1's mortgage. In 1982 Owner gave a refinancing mortgage to Lender #3 bearing 16 percent interest. A dispute will surely arise. Lender #2 will argue that a "refinancing" should bear the same interest as the loan refinanced. Lender #2 will also argue that his mortgage is not subordinated to any commissions, points, attorneys' fees, or title charges. Subordinations are usually interpreted rather narrowly. Draft the clause broadly. *Shane* v. *Winter Hill Fed. S. & L. Assn.,* 492 NE2d 92 (Mass. 1986).

25.05   First Mortgage Provisions

Many corporate first mortgages contain clauses dealing with second mortgage financing.

> **EXAMPLE:**   Owner gives a first mortgage to Lender in 1982 on his office building. Almost certainly this mortgage will contain a clause providing that Owner will place no second mortgage on the property and that if this clause is violated, Lender may declare his mortgage debt due and foreclose. This is the "due-on-encumbrance" clause. Some states, California, for example, have laws covering this situation.

The philosophy here is that placing a second mortgage on the property has two adverse consequences to the first mortgage, namely: (1) places an undue financial burden on the borrower and may create a default in the first mortgage payments, and (2) the second mortgagee may take action that will destroy leases that could be valuable to the first mortgagee.

Interestingly, in the numerous articles and decisions that discuss the due-on-sale clause there is no discussion of the corporate mortgage. One can conclude that the courts are compartmentalizing mortgage law. They are developing rules for home mortgages that have no application to corporate mortgages.

25.06   Statutes Governing Junior Mortgages

There are, of course, a variety of state laws governing junior mortgages.

EXAMPLE: Some statutes define consumer loans (e.g., loans for home repairs) and declare the mortgage void if made by an unlicensed lender. The philosophy here is that the state has a duty to the small borrower to see that reputable firms engage in second mortgage lending. Small borrowers usually do not consult lawyers. The opportunity to charge exorbitant fees is present. *Stubbs* v. *Security Discount Co.*, 407 A2d 1269 (N.J. 1979).

Or a law may forbid banks or insurance companies to make second mortgages. *National Bank* v. *Mathews*, 98 U.S. 62 (1878); *Jurgens* v. *Cobe*, 99 Ill. App. 156 (1900). Or the law may require a second mortgage to be so labeled in big print, so that any buyer of the paper will know he is buying a second lien. Ill. Rev. Stat. Ch. 121½ § 137.3(k).

A number of states have statutes invalidating certain junior mortgages.

EXAMPLE: The defendants became indebted to plaintiff's assignor for purchase of an automobile secured by installment sale and security agreement and collaterally secured by real estate mortgage. At issue was whether or not the mortgage is good under the Secondary Mortgage Loan Act. It was held that a real property mortgage may not be taken as additional security under the Retail Installment Sales Act. A mortgage on real estate given by the retail installment buyer in connection with the financing of an automobile is null and void and will be ordered discharged of record. *Girard Acceptance Corp.* v. *Wallace*, 76 N.J. 434, 388 A2d 582 (1978).

Various securities laws affect junior mortgages. There are consumer protection laws, protecting homeowners against sharp practices, such as kickbacks by building contractors to lenders. Some such laws declare the junior mortgage void. *Consumer Discount Co.* v. *Fuller*, 419 A2d 940 (Del. 1980). Today's lawmakers regard the highly regulated first mortgage lenders as responsible lenders, who can be trusted not to take advantage of borrowers. They tend to regard junior mortgage lenders as less reliable. They impose more stringent regulation.

25.07   Second Mortgage Companies

In many areas second mortgage companies are quite active. They are subject to licensing laws. Ill. Rev. Stat. Ch. 16½ Par. 601 *et seq.* They will buy second mortgages, usually at a substantial discount. This means that a home seller who takes back a purchase money mortgage must be prepared to suffer a loss if he is forced to sell his mortgage. These mortgage companies also carry on an active business selling second mortgages to investors. If I buy a second mortgage from a mortgage company, I will ordinarily enter into a written agreement with the company under which it collects the payments, checks the property to see that the first mortgage payments, taxes, and insurance premiums are paid, and in general maintains supervision of the loan, for which it receives a "service charge."

25.08   Prepayment

It is customary in some areas for a second mortgage to carry a prepayment privilege clause that stipulates a penalty of some sort, perhaps 80 percent of six month's interest, if the loan is prepaid, a not unlikely event. This produces a substantial return to the lender. Some second mortgages, especially purchase money mortgages, contain a clause requiring prepayment when regular bank financing is available. No prepayment penalty is charged. The terms of the financing are spelled out in detail.

Some states, Georgia, for example, permit junior mortgage lenders to use an add-on interest rate.

> **EXAMPLE:**   In an add-on loan a borrower who borrows $100 has the interest (say 9 percent) added on immediately so that his monthly or weekly payments include payments on the principal of $109 rather than one of $100. Obviously, the yield to the lender is in excess of 9 percent.

These loans, it is evident, collect at the outset, interest for the entire life of the loan. If the loan is prepaid, the portion of interest for the period from payment to maturity is technically unearned.

Some states, Georgia and Alabama, for example, require the application of the Rule of 78's in such a case. This is a complex rule that provides for rebate of part of the unearned interest. *Winkle* v. *Grant National Bank*, 601 SW2d 559 (1980). It is not well adapted to long-term loans.

Take the last example and suppose that the note has a prepayment privilege. Suppose that the borrower prepays on June 30, 1982. It is obvious that the $9.00 interest was intended to be spread over the entire year of 1982. Hence that portion representing interest from July 1, 1982, to December 31, 1982, is unearned.

Under this artificial rule, you divide the loan into 78 parts, allocating 12 to January, 11 to February, and so on, with 1 allocated to December.

You treat $12/78$s of the interest of $9.00 as being earned in January, an additional $11/78$s as being earned in February, and so on. If you add 12–11–10–9–8–7–6–5–4–3–2–1, you arrive at the sum of 78. Hence the name of the rule.

In our case you would take July (6), August (5), September (4), October (3), November (2), December (1), and add them, which equals 21. Now take $21/78$s of the $9.00. This is the refund to which the prepaying debtor is entitled.

25.09   Interest Rates

Local law concerning interest rates must be carefully analyzed where interest rates are concerned. State usury laws and the Uniform Consumer Credit Code come into play.

25.10   Rents

In large mortgages on commercial property the first mortgagee may insist that any junior mortgage provide that all rents collected by the junior mortgagee shall be held in trust for the first mortgagee and applied on the first mortgage debt.

25.11 Open-end Senior Mortgage

While the danger does not appear to be great, there is at least a possibility that where there is an open-end senior mortgage, advances may be made under the senior mortgage that could prime the junior mortgage. It is therefore advisable for the junior mortgagee who finds such a first mortgage on the public records to notify the first mortgagee of the making of the second mortgage. This will protect the second mortgagee against such advances.

25.12 Condo Assessments

A common provision in condo declarations is that the lien of assessments shall be subordinate to institutional *first* mortgages. Of course, the lien of assessments, since it relates back to the recording of the condo declaration, will enjoy priority over the lien of a junior mortgage. *Washington Fed. S. & L.* v. *Schneider,* 408 NYS2d 588 (1978).

25.13 Revolving Fund Mortgages

Revolving fund mortgages are almost always junior mortgages.

CHAPTER 26

Real Estate Finance— Wraparound Mortgages

26.01 In General

The wraparound mortgage, sometimes known as the *all-inclusive deed of trust,* made its appearance in large-scale commercial financing. It is a special type of junior mortgage. The typical junior mortgage is one that is added onto land already subject to earlier encumbrances. The face amount of the wraparound mortgage represents the total of the existing mortgages and the new money advanced under the wraparound. This compares to the face amount of a typical junior mortgage that states only the amount advanced under the junior mortgage. Since the debt stated in the wraparound mortgage is the total of the outstanding balances on prior mortgages plus the amount advanced under the wraparound mortgage, the wraparound lender charges interest on this total. This creates a yield far greater than the yield on an ordinary junior mortgage.

Also, because the debts are aggregated in this fashion, the wraparound mortgagee collects payments sufficient to pay the payments due on the prior mortgages and the wraparound mortgage. And the wraparound lender pays to the prior mortgagees the payments due on their mortgages.

EXAMPLE: Owner mortgages a shopping center to Lender #1 for $5,000,000 at 8 percent interest. Over the course of years, the loan has been paid down to $4,000,000. Owner now would like to borrow an additional $5,000,000 and the present value of the shopping center will support such a loan. The going rate of interest is 13 percent. Owner gives Lender #2 a second mortgage in the amount of $9,000,000 but Lender #2 only advances $5,000,000. Owner pays 13 percent interest on the entire $9,000,000 debt as part of the debt service on the $9,000,000 debt, Lender #2 acting as an intermediate collection agent for the servicing of the first mortgage to Lender #1. In this way, Lender #2 deducts the amounts due Lender #1, including amortization of principal and the interest payment of 8 percent and pays those monies to Lender #1. Lender #2 retains the 5 percent difference between the interest on the first mortgage and the interest payable on the wraparound. The result is a yield to Lender #2 of approximately 17 percent.

Under some forms of the wraparound mortgage, the full amount stated as the debt is not advanced to the borrower at the time the loan is made. Rather, the wraparound loan funds will be advanced as payments are made to reduce the amount of the first mortgage. Eventually, the underlying mortgage is paid and the payments are then all directed to retire the wraparound.

For the life of the wraparound, there is the danger that other liens will attach to the property and assert priority. To meet this danger, the wraparound lender relies heavily on the theory of subrogation. This is a legal doctrine under which one who pays money on a senior lien is often entitled to claim the benefit of the priority enjoyed by the senior lien.

EXAMPLE: At the time the mortgage to Lender #2 is executed, Owner and Lender #2 enter into an agreement providing that Lender #2 will be subrogated to Lender #1's prior lien position as to all payments made by Lender #2 to Lender #1. This is called *conventional* subrogation or subrogation by agreement. It is a technical concept, but is widely recognized. It gives Lender #2 all the priority that Lender #1's mortgage enjoys over intervening liens, that is total priority. Osborne, *Mortgages* §282 (2d ed. 1970).

Also the mortgage to Lender #2 provides, as it invariably will, that all payments made by Lender #2 to Lender #1 shall be protected and secured by the mortgage to Lender #2 to the same extent as any previous disbursements and advances made by Lender #2. This is valid and binding. *Boone* v. *Clark,* 129 Ill. 466, 21 NE 850 (1889). This is the rule of *tacking.* Mortgagees often pay real estate taxes and insurance premiums under such covenants, and the courts hold that such payments give the mortgagee a lien equal in dignity to the mortgage debt. *Reisman* v. *Jacobs,* 107 Ga. App. 200, 129 SE2d 338 (1962).

The wraparound today is used in residential financing as well as in commercial financing. In either case the objective for the lender is an increased yield, while the benefit to the borrower is a lower overall financing cost than would be obtained through complete refinancing.

It often develops that the underlying loan is not prepayable, or has such a low interest rate that prepayment is undesirable. The borrower arranges a wraparound loan package that has higher than normal yield to the seller–lender, while allowing the buyer–borrower to pay a lower rate than if the property was refinanced.

EXAMPLE: The rate on the underlying mortgage is 8 percent. Existing rates are 13 percent. The balance on the underlying mortgage is $50,000. The purchase price of the property is $100,000. The buyer can pay $20,000 down. Charging 11 percent, the seller finances the difference between the underlying loan balance and the down payment. The seller makes no actual advance of money, but sells the property, taking the down payment of $20,000 and obtaining a yield in excess of 15 percent, while the buyer, in effect, pays 2 percent below the market rate. The seller's yield is calculated as follows:

Interest on wraparound ($80,000 × 11%) $8,800
Interest on underlying ($50,000 × 8%)   4,000
Interest differential to wraparound lender $4,800

$$\frac{\$4,800 \text{ Interest differential}}{\$30,000 \text{ Amount ''advanced''}} = 16\%$$

The seller also gets the benefit of the use of the installment method of reporting gain for income tax purposes.

26.02   Usury

Unless the borrower is exempt from usury laws (e.g., when the borrower is a corporation), or if the lender is exempt (e.g., when the lender is a bank) or the loan is exempt (e.g., when the loan is a business loan), the transaction may come within the prohibitions of local usury law. If there is no local exemption, the question of usury may arise, especially if local law prohibits the lender from *receiving* more than the statutory maximum.

Beyond the statutory interest rate limitations, the common law prohibition against the exaction of unconscionable interest must be recognized and dealt with. While the stated interest rate is always under the statutory limit, the effective yield to the lender may increase the interest received by the lender on the funds actually advanced beyond the legal limit. This results from the lender's receipt of interest at the stated rate on the amount actually advanced plus the spread between the stated interest and the interest remitted to the first lienholder. Comment, 21 UCLA L. Rev. 1529, 1532 *et seq.* (1974); Note, 1972 Duke L. J. 785.

26.03   Wraparound Documents

For lenders who do not hold the original first-lien mortgage, certain borrower controls must be built into the wraparound mortgage instrument to prevent possible deterioration of the wraparound loan's first-lien status or its high yield.

The most important wraparound mortgage "clause" is the cross default provision. This is protective language, such that a default of the wraparound mortgage is considered a default of the first mortgage. This provision prevents the borrower from entering into an agreement with the first lender to keep the first lien current while defaulting on the wraparound mortgage. Likewise, any default on the first mortgage should be a default on the wraparound mortgage.

The wraparound contains covenants like those found in a second mortgage, also covenants like those in the first mortgage. As a result a default under the first mortgage will be a default under the wraparound.

The borrower should not be allowed to prepay the first mortgage. This will protect a high wraparound yield.

REFERENCES: Galowitz, *How to Use Wraparound Financing,* 5 Real Est. L. J. 107 (1976) (discusses mathematics involved). Gunning, *The Wrap-Around Mortgage,*

2 Real Est. Rev. 35 (1972). Yield Table for Wrap-Around Mortgages, Financial Pub. Co., 82 Brookline Ave., Boston, Mass. 02215. Comment, *The Wrap-Around Mortgage: A Critical Inquiry,* 21 U.C.L.A. L. Rev. 1529 (1974). The Magic Wrap Yield Charts, M.G.I.C., MGIC Plaza, Milwaukee, Wis. 53202. Kratovil and Werner, *Modern Mortgage Law and Practice* §§ 24.11 *et seq.* (2d ed., 1981).

CHAPTER 27

Real Estate Finance—Miscellaneous Devices—Ground Leases

27.01 Ground Rents—In General

Ground leases as a method of real estate finance have been commonplace in Maryland, Pennsylvania, and Hawaii and the practice is spreading.

27.01(a) Ground Rents—The Maryland System

In Maryland, leases are used in the *ground rent* method of financing. The chief characteristics of the Maryland ground rent leases are: (1) the landowner leases the land to the lessee for a period of ninety-nine years; (2) with a provision for the perpetual renewal of the lease from time to time as each ninety-nine-year period draws to a close, upon payment of a small sum of money called a *renewal fine;* (3) the lessee agrees to pay a certain sum of money (usually semiannually) as ground rent; and (4) the lease contains a provision that if the lessee makes default in his ground rent payments, the lessor may declare the lease void and evict the lessee. The lessee also agrees to pay the taxes on the property, and they are assessed to the lessee. The interest acquired by the lessee under the lease is regarded as personal property. His wife or widow has no dower in the leasehold estate.

Prior to 1884, the ground rents reserved by such leases were not redeemable by the lessee unless expressly so stipulated in the lease; but in that year and by subsequent laws, it was provided that the lessee, in leases subsequently executed, could pay the lessor the value of the lessor's interest and thus *redeem* the rent and become the owner of the property. The original lease and assignments thereof must be executed, acknowledged, and recorded in the same manner as deeds. The leasehold estate is subject to the liens of judgments against the lessee.

In practical economic effect, the relation of the lessee to the property is that of the owner of the land subject to the payment of the annual rent and the taxes; and his economic relation to the owner of the ground rent is much like that of a mortgagor paying interest on a debt where the principal never matures so long as the mortgagor pays the interest and taxes. The technical relation between the owner of the land and of the leasehold is that of landlord and tenant. *Jones* v. *Magruder,* 42 F.Supp. 193.

Such ground rents are bought and sold in Baltimore the same way mortgages are dealt in.

27.01(b)   Ground Rents—Improved Property

A Maryland case (*Packard* v. *Corporation for Relief of Widows,* 77 Md. 240, 26 Atl. 411) describes the operation of the ground rent system in a sale of improved property.

> **EXAMPLE:**   Landowner sold and conveyed his land to Buyer for $4,500. Buyer immediately leased to Tenant for a consideration of $1,000 cash, and rent payable at $210 which capitalized at 6 percent equals $3,500. Thus a margin of $1,000 was left to protect Buyer against loss in case he should be compelled to take the property back. It was held that this was not a mortgage, but was merely a ground rent.

The court pointed out, however, that in legal contemplation this lease was not a mortgage, since, while the lessee had the privilege of redeeming, he was not obliged to do so. Thus there was lacking the relation of debtor and creditor, which is the distinguishing characteristic of mortgage transactions.

27.01(c)   Ground Rents—Redemption

Originally, ground rents were divided into redeemable and irredeemable rents. An irredeemable rent was one in which there was no provision in the lease allowing the lessee to buy the land. A redeemable lease contained an option permitting the lessee to purchase the land on payment of a stipulated price. Legislation was passed in 1884 and subsequent years making redeemable all ground rents thereafter created. Thus, under laws passed in 1900, all long-term ground rents created thereafter are redeemable, at the option of the tenant, for a sum of money equal to the capitalization of the rent at a rate not exceeding 6 percent. However, irredeemable ground rents existing prior to the passage of these laws are still not subject to redemption. And, as heretofore pointed out, the landlord cannot compel the tenant to redeem.

27.01(d)   Ground Rents—Pennsylvania System

In Pennsylvania, ground rents are created by a deed of the land which conveys the legal title to grantee subject to the payment of rent to the grantor. *Jones* v. *Magruder,* 42 F.Supp. 193. A subsequent purchaser of the land must pay the rent thus stipulated, but he does not become personally liable therefor unless his deed provides that the grantee assumes and agrees to pay such rent. However, the grantee in the original deed remains liable for rents accruing even after his sale of the land. If default is made in payment of ground rent and the owner of the land obtains a judgment therefor, a sheriff's sale under his judgment wipes out all encumbrances and titles arising subsequent to the creation of the ground rent. Pennsylvania also has passed laws providing for the redemption of ground rents. *In re Crean's Estate,* 321 Pa. 216, 183 Atl. 915.

27.01(e) Ground Lease Financing

Today's ground lease financing is a relatively simple transaction.

> **EXAMPLE:** Builder builds a home on a lot he owns. He enters into a contract of sale and lease with Tenant, the purchaser. The contract calls for the usual title search. When that shows clear title in Builder, he is required at closing to give Tenant a deed to the *building* and a long lease of the land. The lease includes an option to purchase the land. The option price steps up each year, so that the annual increase in option price reflects the appreciation in land value and also exerts pressure on Tenant to buy as soon as he can command the resources. The lease is usually at a flat rental for fifteen years. The contract requires Tenant to execute a mortgage to *ABC Co.,* the company financing the transaction. By means of the mortgage, Tenant mortgages his leasehold estate and his option to purchase. Builder joins in the mortgage or signs a separate document subordinating his ownership interest to the mortgage. This process is called "bringing the fee under the mortgage." See Kratovil and Werner, *Modern Mortgage Law and Practice* Ch. 30 (2d ed. 1981). The result is that if the mortgage is foreclosed, *ABC Co.* acquires full ownership of the land. But since Tenant initially acquired only a lease of the land, he is permitted to make a substantially smaller down payment. But because Builder joins in the mortgage, the lender has total security. If Builder is in need of cash (as builders often are), he can make up a package of twenty or more such homes and sell the land to a syndicate at a discount.

The leasehold mortgage in this form can be sold to FHLMC.

The ground lease viewed from the land developer's perspective is a different and far more complex transaction. Kratovil, *Modern Real Estate Documentation,* Ch. 34.

27.01(f) Modern Developments in Ground Leases

There have been two recent developments in the area of ground rents and leases that have had some national attention.

The area of Irvine, California, was developed largely through the device of ground leases. When a purchaser bought a home, it was just that, the purchase of the home that was constructed on the land of the developer who leased the land to the homebuyer. Through this device the homebuyer had a lower initial cost because only the *home* was the subject of the purchase. Monthly housing costs included not only monthly mortgage payments, but also monthly rental payments made back to the developer. The developer retained the land, and the land cost was not included in the price charged to the homebuyer. The land was leased to the homebuyer pursuant to long-term leases, which were made at fixed rents based upon then current economic conditions.

The area became quite affluent and desirable. The price of housing greatly increased, and the homeowners naturally valued their homes and the lifestyle of the community. Then the leases began coming due. As the developer's successors began attempting to renegotiate the leases to what they believed were current values, homeowners realized that they were going to be paying significantly higher housing costs. Class action litigation ensued whereby the homeowners attempted to stop the landowner from terminating the rights of the homeowners and at the same time reduce the cost of renegotiating or buying out the landowner's interests. The matters were ultimately settled, but neither party obtained all that they had expected.

As indicated at the outset of this chapter, Hawaii is an area where ground rents have proliferated. The land came to be owned by a few who held the land in trust, leasing it to those who built homes and otherwise improved it. Hawaii found this to be a system of land ownership that it wanted to change, and for that reason it enacted a statute that allowed the landowners' interest to be taken by the lessee by way of eminent domain proceedings. This law was challenged and upheld in the United States Supreme Court. *Hawaii Housing Authority* v. *Midkiff,* 104 S. Ct. 2321 (1984).

27.02 Sale and Management Agreement—"Earn Outs"

An owner of an existing commercial property (e.g., shopping center, office building) may, for a variety of reasons, choose to sell the asset. Yet he may wish to extract some further benefit from the property, for example, through a long-term (five years) management agreement. The buyer may be willing to agree to such an arrangement because the seller has general expertise in the field and intimate knowledge of the project, its tenants, and its legal and construction problems. Such an arrangement may be attractive to foreign investors who wish to avoid daily management problems. It may also be attractive to pension funds. Such funds are no longer content with mortgage investments, since the interest return dwindles in value as inflation continues, while pension compensation must keep pace with inflation.

The management agreement may be tailored so that the buyer sets financial goals the project is expected to achieve, and the seller's continuing as manager is contingent on achievement of these goals. This would be particularly true of new projects.

New projects may be initiated for the express purpose of selling the completed project and the signing of a management agreement.

The contract of sale may provide for an adjustment in the sale price to take place after the closing of the deal. This adjustment may take place whether or not the seller retains a management position. It would be logical to use this "earn out" provision where the seller retains a management position and can control the economic destinies of the project. The adjustment will be in the form of seller's participation in the earnings of the project based on economic achievements set forth in the contract. The situation offers problems, since a seller retaining management control has an incentive to manipulate the project so as to reflect cash flow or rental achievements that will trigger his participation in the earnings. This suggests that the buyer may need to have some control over the management operation. This, in turn, poses other problems. If the two parties share control, the deal begins to look like a partnership or joint venture (with the attendant liabilities) and the seller-manager looks less like an independent contractor.

A like problem arises if the seller's share of the earnings is abnormally large. This again suggests joint venture.

Also, a seller may be liable to the buyer on some fraud or securities law theories.

27.03   Pledge of Beneficial Interest

In states that recognize the validity of the land trust there is a mode of financing that offers many advantages.

> **EXAMPLE:**   Owner owns Blackacre. He conveys it in 1979 to *XYZ Trust Co.,* as trustee, using a typical land trust documentation. The trust agreement designates Owner as sole beneficiary. Under the land trust documentation the beneficial interest is deemed personal property. In 1982, Owner wishes to borrow money. He applies to *ABC Bank* for a loan. The loan is worked out as a pledge of the beneficial interest. Owner executes a collateral note to the bank. This is a lengthy promissory note well known to all bankers who lend money on corporate stock as collateral. Technically, it is a pledge of personal property. It contains provisions authorizing the bank, in the event of default, to declare an acceleration of the debt, to hold a pledgee's sale in its own offices, and to bid at its own sale. As security, Owner assigns his beneficial interest to the bank. This assignment is on a form furnished by the bank. It is lodged with *XYZ Trust Co.* As is evident, since the bank now appears on the trust company's records as the purported owner of the beneficial interest, the trust company will not execute any deeds or mortages or honor any further assignments of the beneficial interest without the bank's consent. The property is "locked up." In case of default, the bank holds a quick pledgee's sale under the Uniform Commercial Code and bids in the beneficial interest. It places Blackacre up for sale. It finds a purchaser. It directs *XYZ Trust Co.* to make a deed to the purchaser at the closing of this sale and this is done. Everything is accomplished quickly and inexpensively. Nothing relating to the loan appears on the public records.

There is one warning. This type of deal will not work where the landowner deeds the land into the trust and simultaneously pledges the beneficial interest. This is treated as an attempted waiver of the equitable right of redemption, and under ancient principles of mortgage law the whole transaction is deemed a real estate mortgage. But those who deal in real estate find it convenient to keep their real estate holdings in a land trust. Hence this rule is no inconvenience.

REFERENCES ON PLEDGES OF LAND TRUST BENEFICIAL INTEREST: *Horney* v. *Hayes,* 11 Ill.2d 178, 142 NE2d 94 (1957) (60 Ill. B. J. 268, 55 Chicago Bar Rev. 64) (pledge of existing beneficial interest is valid as pledge of personal property); *Quinn* v. *Pullman T. & S. Bank,* 98 Ill. App.2d 402, 240 NE2d 791 (1968) (pledge made simultaneously with creation of land trust is ineffective as a pledge).

27.04   Vendor's Lien Reserved by Deed

In some states, a seller, in lieu of taking back a mortgage from the buyer, expressly reserves in his deed to the buyer a lien on the land to secure payment of the balance of the purchase price. Such a lien is called a *vendor's lien.* It is really a mortgage.

> **EXAMPLE:**   Landowner conveyed to Buyer by a warranty deed which warranted that title was free from all cumbrances excepting three certain notes executed by Buyer, for which a vendor's lien was retained until said notes and the interest thereon should be fully paid. The court held that this clause created a lien on the land. Such a lien is regarded as partaking of the nature of an equitable mortgage. It is really a mortgage and is governed by the same rules as a mortgage, and must be foreclosed as such. *Crabtree* v. *Davis,* 237 Ala. 264, 186 So 734 (1939).

Such liens are governed by many of the rules applicable to mortgages.

> **EXAMPLE:**   A promissory note was given by the buyer to the seller for part of the purchase price, and the deed recited that a purchase money lien was retained for the payment of the note. The court held that the fact that the payee of the note was not mentioned in the deed did not invalidate the deed. But under Kentucky law the deed must recite the amount of purchase price remaining due if the lien is to be valid against subsequent creditors and purchasers of the property. *Campbell* v. *Salyer,* 290 Ky. 493, 161 SW2d 596 (1942).

Such a lien enjoys priority over subsequent liens and encumbrances, and, like a purchase money mortgage, has priority over prior judgments against the purchaser. The grantee under such deed does not become personally liable for the purchase money, unless he has signed a promissory note or otherwise obligated himself personally to pay the debt. And a purchaser from such grantee does not become personally liable to the holder of the vendor's lien unless by his deed he assumes and agrees to pay the unpaid balance of the debt. The debt may be assigned, and the assignee will have the right to foreclose the lien.

27.05   Buy-down

Developers have engaged in the practice of "buying down" the buyer's interest rate. The developer pays a lump sum or agrees to pay a stated sum to a lender who agrees to finance the buyer's purchase. If the developer is committing to pay instead of paying, he may deposit a sum in the lender's savings account deposits as security for his advancing funds. The developer's money operates as an inducement to the lender to reduce the borrower's interest payments for a period of time, often one to three years.

Often, this is done on a sliding scale. The largest reduction in the buyer's interest rates occurs in the first year and the smallest in the third year. The obvious purpose here is to "hook" the buyer. Most people tend to think of their problems *now*, not three years from now.

At the end of the third year the mortgage payments move up to the market rate. Or in some cases there is a balloon at the end of the third year and the buyer must refinance.

Some concern has been expressed about this practice. The ads in the newspapers tell the public that the interest rate is a comfortable 9.5 percent, for example. But in fine print that follows we are told that this is for the first three years. Especially if there is a balloon, there is some concern that consumer type litigation may result.

FHA mortgages with a three-year minimum buy-down have been approved by HUD. GNMA will issue guaranteed securities secured by FHA buy-down mortgages. FNMA will purchase buy-downs. It is comforting, in a way, to see this government stamp of approval placed on the buy-downs. No doubt courts will be strongly impressed by this approval if the buy-downs come under fire.

Some lenders offer individual buyers the opportunity of buying down the interest rate on their mortgages by increasing the origination points paid.

CHAPTER 28

Real Estate Finance—Foreclosure and Redemption

28.01 In General

After default, today's lender exhausts all possibility of effecting a "workout," extension of time, moratorium on payment, sale of the property to a creditworthy buyer, deed in lieu of foreclosure, and the like. Any of these is preferable to foreclosure. If these alternatives fail and foreclosure becomes necessary, it is, of course, handled according to local law. Even after foreclosure has begun, a workout is possible until a foreclosure sale has taken place. Even after the foreclosure sale, perhaps half of the states allow the owner a period of redemption, permitting the borrower to retain ownership of the property until that period has expired. The foreclosure and redemption process are technical.

> REFERENCE: Kuhlin & Roberts, eds., *Real Estate Bankruptcies and Workouts,* (ABA 1983).

28.02 Types of Foreclosures

Methods of foreclosure vary from state to state. A common method involves a court proceeding filed by the mortgagee, called a foreclosure suit. In such suits the court orders a public auction sale of the property, and the sale is held by an officer of the court. Up to the time of the foreclosure sale, the mortgagor, his wife, any junior mortgagee, or even the mortgagor's tenant may come in, pay off the mortgage, and stop the foreclosure. This, you will remember, is the equitable right of redemption. In states that have statutory redemption, the highest bidder at the foreclosure sale usually receives a certificate of sale reciting that he will be entitled to a deed if no redemption is made. In states that do not have a statutory redemption period, the highest bidder receives a deed to the land, and this deed

389

gives him ownership of the mortgaged land, free and clear of the rights of the mortgagor.

28.03   Statutory Redemption

The equitable right of redemption is cut off by a sale under a foreclosure judgment, or decree, since that was the object of the foreclosure suit. After the foreclosure sale, in many states, an entirely different right arises, called the statutory right of redemption. Laws providing for statutory redemption give the mortgagor and other persons interested in the land, or certain classes of such persons, the right to redeem from the sale within a certain period, usually one year, but varying in different states from two months to two years after the sale.

Most statutory redemption laws were passed in a time when America was predominantly agricultural. Most mortgagors were farmers. When the weather was bad, crops failed, and foreclosures followed. It seemed logical to suppose that the next year might bring better weather and good crops. Hence laws created the statutory redemption period, usually one year, and usually the law was so worded that the mortgagor had the right to possession during that year.

At the expiration of the redemption period, if redemption has not been made, the purchaser at the foreclosure sale receives a deed from the officer who made the sale.

Statutory redemption is usually accomplished by payment to the officer who made the sale of the amount of the foreclosure sale plus interest. After redemption the mortgagor holds the land free and clear of the mortgage.

In a number of states there is no statutory redemption after sale. Immediately after the foreclosure sale a deed is given to the purchaser, and he thereupon acquires ownership of the land. In states that do not permit redemption after the foreclosure sale, provision is often made to permit the mortgagor to effect a redemption or discharge of the mortgage prior to the foreclosure sale.

28.04   Deficiency Judgment

A mortgage foreclosure sale is regarded as a payment of the mortgage debt in an amount equal to the sale price. If the foreclosure judgment, or decree, finds that there is $5,000 due to the mortgagee on his mortgage, and the property is sold for $4,500, the mortgage debt is thereby reduced by $4,500, leaving a deficiency of $500 due the mortgagee. Since by virtue of the promissory note that usually accompanies a mortgage, the mortgagor becomes personally liable to the mortgagee for the mortgage debt, the mortgagee is entitled to a personal judgment against the mortgagor for the amount of the deficiency.

In many states laws have been passed limiting the mortgagee's right to a deficiency decree.

28.05   Foreclosure by Exercise of Power of Sale

In many states mortgages may be foreclosed by exercise of a power of sale without resort to any court proceedings. If the mortgage is, in form, a trust deed, a provision will be found therein conferring on the trustee the power to sell the land in the event of a default in the mortgage payments. If the instrument is a regular mortgage, the power of sale is conferred on the mortgagee. However, in Colorado the power of sale must be exercised by an official known as the public trustee, in Minnesota the sale is made by the sheriff or his deputy.

In states where this method of foreclosure is employed, the mortgage or trust deed spells out the events of default that will give the trustee or mortgagee power to sell the premises, and it also sets forth the notice of sale that must be given and the other formalities that must be complied with in making the sale. The state law may also specify the notice of sale that is to be given. In some states, personal notice to the mortgagor is necessary, but in others, advertisement is sufficient. Some state laws provide that a notice of default must be recorded and a stated period of time must elapse thereafter before the sale is held. This gives the mortgagor a final opportunity to pay his debt.

At one time, concern was expressed over the validity of the power of sale in the aftermath of United States Supreme Court decisions which held that prejudgment seizures of chattels violated the due process clause of the fourteenth amendment. See, for example, *North Georgia Finishing, Inc.* v. *Di-Chem, Inc.,* 419 U.S. 601 (1975). The debate centered on whether power-of-sale foreclosures of real property were constitutional in the absence of prior notice and a hearing for the benefit of the defaulting mortgagor. Recent cases have upheld the nonjudicial power-of-sale foreclosure process. *Flagg Bros.* v. *Brooks,* 436 U.S. 149; 56 L.Ed.2d. 185; 28 De Paul L. Rev. 523; 27 Kan L. Rev. 674 (1978).

Consumer lobbies have succeeded in enacting amendments to the power-of-sale foreclosure laws of the various states. The new laws have been generally directed toward requiring that the borrower and other parties with an interest in the real estate be given a more effective notice of the impending foreclosure.

> **EXAMPLE:**   Prior law in Texas merely required the posting of a notice of the foreclosure at three public places for three weeks prior to the sale. Obviously, this method is not the best reasonable method of notifying the debtor of the foreclosure sale. The amendment to that law requires the posting of such notices at the local courthouse and a certified mail notice to the debtor. Vernan's (Texas) Ann. Civ. St. Art. 3810.

Unless the mortgage allows him to do so, the mortgagee cannot purchase the property at his own foreclosure sale, either in his own or his wife's name, or in the name of some third party, and if he does so, the sale may be set aside. *Mills* v. *Mutual B. & L. Assn.,* 6 SE2d 549 (N.C. 1940). The trustee in a deed of trust is likewise forbidden to purchase at his own foreclosure sale. However, the holder of the note secured by a deed of trust is permitted to purchase at the trustee's sale. Deed of trust forms usually expressly permit the trustee to bid at the foreclosure sale, and such provisions are valid. Experience indicates that there will be fewer lawsuits attacking a foreclosure sale if the sale is held by some impartial individual. A lender who uses some individual in his employment as trustee in his deeds of trust often finds it expedient to appoint some disinterested third party as trustee if foreclosure becomes necessary.

The sale is usually at public auction, and a deed is executed to the highest bidder. Whether or not redemption is allowed depends on the local law.

28.06   Foreclosure by Other Methods

Other methods of foreclosure—strict foreclosure, foreclosure by entry and possession, and foreclosure by writ of entry—are allowed in a small number of states. These involve technical procedures that are only of local interest.

28.07   Foreclosure—Conscionable Conduct

No matter what the method of foreclosure may be, lenders must always be mindful that today's courts protect consumers, and in the mortgage transaction the borrower is the consumer. Evidence of the protection given to borrowers may be found in recent cases requiring lenders to ascertain the reasons for default and make a concerted effort to avoid foreclosure by voluntary forbearance or recasting the mortgage. *FNMA* v. *Bryant,* 378 NE2d 333 (Ill. 1978); *Hamm* v. *Taylor,* 429 A2d 946 (Conn. 1981); 1976 Utah L. Rev. 327; *FNMA* v. *Ricks,* 372 N.Y.S. 485 (N.Y. 1975). While these cases may apply to a particular class of lenders (FHA and VA mortgagees) and have been undercut by subsequent proclamations by the Department of Housing and Urban Development, the decisions once again announce to lenders that conduct toward borrowers must be conscionable or foreclosure will not be allowed. Kratovil, *Mortgage Law Today,* 13 John Marsh L. Rev. 251, 265 (1980).

> **EXAMPLE:**   Borrower lost his job and fell four payments in arrears on his mortgage. Lender began foreclosure proceedings whereupon Borrower, once again employed, tendered the past due payments. Lender refused the tender because it did not include the attorney's fees incurred in beginning foreclosure. Foreclosure would not be allowed as Lender's conduct was unconscionable. *Brown* v. *Lynn,* 385 F. Supp. 986. (1974).

> REFERENCE: 53 Chi-Kent L. Rev. 703 (1976).

These decisions are reflections of not only the law but also the "fireside equity" practiced by many judges when they sit in foreclosure courts. Frequently, foreclosure will not be allowed unless the borrower is at least three or four payments behind and good faith settlement negotiations have produced no results.

28.08   FHA Foreclosures

FHA has a variety of rules relating to FHA–insured mortgages. The secondary market also has rules on this subject. In general, foreclosure of a first mortgage cannot, under FNMA rules, begin until at least three full monthly payments are past due. The FHA requires that the mortgagor must be given an opportunity to ask FHA to take over the mortgage. HUD regulations permitting a cure of default must be complied with. There must be a face-to-face interview between the mortgagor and mortgagee in an effort to work out the situation. The regulations will be found in 24 CFR 203.600, etc. These extensive regulations are discussed at length in *Associated East Mtg. Co.* v. *Young,* 394 A2d 899 (N.J. 1978) and *FNMA* v. *Moore,* 609 F. Supp. 194 (D.C. Ill. 1985).

    Courts are not in agreement as to the binding force of these regulations. There are actually three different lines of decision: (1) The regulations are binding on the courts; if they are not complied with, the foreclosure cannot proceed. *Associated East Mtg. Co.* v. *Young,* 394 A2d 899 (N.J. 1978); *Bankers Life Co.* v. *Denton,* 120 Ill. App.3d 576, 458 NE2d 203 (1983). (2) The regulations are not binding on the foreclosure court, but the court can "adopt" them as legal principles that must be obeyed. The result is the same as under (1) above. *Cross* v. *FNMA,* 359 So2d 464 (Fla. App. 1978); *FNMA* v. *Ricks,* 83 Misc.2d 814, 372 NYS2d 485 (1975). (3) The regulations are not binding on the court and can be totally ignored in the foreclosure. *Manufacturers Hanover Mtg. Corp.* v. *Snell,* 142 Mich. App. 545, 370 NW2d 401 (1985); *Barclay Bank* v. *Ruh,* 465 A2d 547 (N.J. 1983).

28.09   Relief

A diversity of federal and state programs exist offering troubled borrowers relief from foreclosure. A stay of the foreclosure is provided in Minnesota and Connecticut. HUD has provided relief. 24 CFR Part 203.640; *Ferrell* v. *Pierce* 743 F2d 454; *FNMA* v. *Moore,* 609 F. Supp. 194 (1985). Pennsylvania has created a Pennsylvania Housing Finance Agency to provide help. Farm mortgagors are entitled to relief. *Allison* v. *Block,* 723 F2d 631 (8th Circ. 1983); *Coleman* v. *Block,* 580 F Supp. 192 (N.D. 1983); *U.S.* v. *Henderson,* 707 F2d 853 (5th Circ. 1983).

    As an alternative to permitting the mortgage to foreclose, FHA may buy the mortgage. It then controls disposition of the mortgage.

    FHA also has a Temporary Mortgage Assistance Payment (TMAP) program that authorizes HUD to make the mortgage payments when the borrower's default is for causes beyond his control.

    In any case the regulations require the mortgager to obtain a face-to-face interview with the borrower in an effort to work out the situation before filing foreclosure. A "forbearance agreement" (postponing foreclosure) may be signed. The loan may be recast to provide for smaller payments.

28.10   Veterans Administration (VA) Foreclosures

In VA foreclosures the same conflict of opinion can be expected as is found in FHA foreclosures. *Rank* v. *Nemmo,* 677 F2d 692 (CA 9th 1982).

28.11   Bankruptcy Stay

Bankruptcy proceedings are designed to collect the debtor's assets and then either liquidate the debtor's estate or restructure the debt payment schedules to allow the debtor to continue. Under either course of action, the bankruptcy trustee needs time to study the value of these assets. When the bankruptcy petition is filed, however, the debtor is usually in the midst of lawsuits and foreclosures caused by defaults on his loans and accounts. To give the bankruptcy trustee the time needed to inventory and evaluate the assets, the bankruptcy law provides that the filing of the bankruptcy stays or prohibits the commencement or continuation of any proceedings against the bankrupt, including the enforcement of liens against the debtor's property. 11 USC § 362 (a). The stay stops such foreclosures until the creditor successfully petitions the court to vacate or modify the stay.

28.12   Bankruptcy Problems in Foreclosure Sales

In a recent case that startled the legal profession, a federal court set aside a mortgage foreclosure sale on the grounds that it was a fraudulent transfer under the Bankruptcy Code (11 U.S.C. Sec. 548) if it brought less than a "reasonably equivalent value" for the property. *Durrett* v. *Washington National Insurance Co.,* 621 F2d 201 (5th Cir. 1980). Some real estate lawyers have taken the term "reasonably equivalent value" to mean at least 70 percent of the fair market value of the property. Thus in practical effect, if this case is followed, the mortgagor has the ability to have the foreclosure sale set aside, even though state law gives the mortgagor no redemption rights after the sale. Of course, to accomplish this result, the mortgagor must file a bankruptcy, but that is an easy enough task to undertake if the mortgagor is so motivated.

The theory of the *Durrett* decision is applicable when: (1) the foreclosure sale occurred within one year prior to the filing of the bankruptcy petition; (2) the foreclosure sale price was less than the "reasonably equivalent value" of the property: and (3) the debtor was insolvent at the time of the foreclosure sale.

While lenders and their attorneys view this decision with alarm, many courts follow it. Fortunately, there is a respected decision reaching an opposite result. *In re Madrid,* 725 F2d 1197 (9th Cir. 1984). Also, the bankruptcy law itself contains certain protections for bona fide purchasers so that their title will not be divested in the event that the foreclosure sale is set aside on a *Durrett* theory. 11 U.S.C. Sec 550(b).

> **EXAMPLE:**   Mortgagor fell into default in the payment of his mortgage. The mortgaged property was worth $100,000 and the mortgage debt was $45,000. Mortgagee foreclosed upon the property, purchasing the property at the foreclosure sale for the amount of the mortgage debt, $45,000. Two months later, Mortgagee sold the property to Mr. Innocent who paid $100,000, the market value of the property. Five months later, Mortgagor filed a voluntary bankruptcy petition in a jurisdiction that followed the *Durrett* theory. Mr. Innocent would not be divested of his title.

REFERENCE: Zinman et. al., *Fraudulent Transfers According to Alden, Gross & Borowitz*, 39 Bus. Lawyer 977 (1984).

28.13   Bankruptcy—Effect on Redemption Rights

The problem often arises that the mortgagor files bankruptcy during the redemption period. If the redemption period is before the foreclosure sale, the automatic stay operates to suspend further proceedings, thus preventing the sale. A different situation is presented in those jurisdictions that have postsale redemption rights. If the mortgagor files a bankruptcy after the foreclosure sale, but before the running of the redemption period, 11 U.S.C. Sec. 108(b) extends the redemption period for sixty days from the commencement of the bankruptcy period if the period would have expired within that sixty day period. *In re Tynan,* 773 F2d 177 (7th Cir. 1985). Of course, if there was more than sixty days to run in the redemption period, that longer period will be available to the mortgagor–debtor.

28.14   Mortgagee as Purchaser at Foreclosure Sale

For several reasons the mortgagee is often the only bidder at the foreclosure sale. The mortgagee is allowed to bid up to the amount of the mortgage debt without producing any cash. The reason is obvious. If he were to pay cash, the officer holding the sale would have to hand the cash back to him in payment of the mortgage debt for, after all, the sale is held to raise money to pay the mortgagee. Again, in states that have redemption laws the highest bidder will not get ownership of or possession of the property until the redemption period is over, and then only if no redemption is made. Land speculators, who are the chief bidders at public land sales, are unwilling to have their money tied up for long periods with such uncertainty as to ultimate ownership of the property.

28.15   Mortgagee as Owner

Whenever and however the mortgagee becomes the owner of the property (either by foreclosure or deed in lieu of foreclosure), he must take all the precautions that an owner takes.

Immediately after the foreclosure sale, existing insurance policies must be endorsed to give protection to the mortgagee as an owner, or new policies must be obtained. Reliance on the old policy may be misplaced, since satisfaction of the debt by purchaser at the foreclosure sale or in the deed in lieu transaction satisfies the mortgage debt and may simultaneously extinguish the lender's protection. *Whitestone S. & L. Assn.* v. *Allstate Ins. Co.,* 270 NE2d 694 (N.Y. 1971). The necessity of other insurance such as liability, workman's compensation, dram shop, and so forth should be determined. Since foreclosure usually extinguishes any leases entered into after the mortgage, new arrangements should be entered into with the tenants. *Kage* v. *1795 Dunn Road, Inc.,* 428 SW2d 735 (Mo. 1968). A new owner's title insurance policy should be obtained, and the currency and amount of real estate taxes and assessment payments should be examined. Inquiry should be made of the desirability of retaining or releasing the building manager. The building itself should be inspected for conditions potentially dangerous to tenants, compliance with local, state, and federal safety laws as they apply both to employees and others, and conditions that could damage the building or hinder its marketability.

CHAPTER 29

Land Use Controls— Building Restrictions

29.01   Private and Public Controls Distinguished

Use of land is controlled in two ways, namely, through *private* controls and through *public* controls.

> **EXAMPLE:**   A buys 100 acres of farmland and divides it into 100 residential lots by means of a recorded plat of subdivision which specifies that all lots must be used only for the construction of single-family dwellings. This is *private* control of use of land by means of building restrictions.

> **EXAMPLE:**   The city of X adopts a zoning ordinance by which part of the city is zoned for residential use, part for stores, and part for industry. This is *public* control of land use.

Private land use controls rest on the philosophy that where private ownership of land is recognized, as it is in America, ownership of land includes the right to sell it on such terms as please the landowner, including the right to restrict the future use of the land in some way that seems desirable *to the seller*.

There is a parallel, but quite different philosophy, namely, that use of land must be controlled, not in the interest of private individuals as such, but in the public interest. Both methods coexist under our American law with some overlapping and some conflict.

Historically, private controls antedate public controls by many years. Hundreds of years ago in England, a landowner might have given away his land and included some whimsical or capricious requirements in his gift that, while legally enforceable, contributed nothing toward the practical control of land use.

> **EXAMPLE:**   Gifts on the following conditions were sustained by the courts: that the donor reside in the house on the land; that donee would lose the land if

he were educated abroad; that donee must always write his name "T. Jackson Mason"; that the minister of donee's church always wear a black gown in the pulpit. 65 U. of Pa. L. R. 527.

If you bought a home in those early days, there was nothing to prevent your neighbor from constructing a slaughterhouse, tannery, or other offensive use adjoining your dwelling. Thus matters continued until 1848, when the courts first evolved the idea that if a land developer deeds out all the lots in the subdivision with *identical* restrictions providing, for example, that only single-family dwellings are permitted in the subdivision, *any lot owner can obtain a court order preventing any other lot owner from violating this restriction.* This was one of the great milestones in the history of law.

The reader may be inclined to wonder why the courts took this drastic step in 1848. The answer is that this took place in the middle of the Industrial Revolution. Factories were springing up everywhere and threatened to engulf all residential areas. By creating these general plan restrictions, enforceable by any lot owner, the courts preserved residential areas from intrusion by factories.

29.02   Private Restrictions in General

Private restrictions fall into five main categories:

1. Whimsical or capricious restrictions imposed by the seller because of some whim or prejudice, such as a restriction that neither tobacco nor liquor shall be used on the premises sold or that there shall be no card playing on the premises.
2. Covenants for the benefits of land sold or land retained. These last are restrictions imposed by a landowner who owns two adjoining tracts of land and sells one of them.

> **EXAMPLE:**   *A,* owning Lots 1 and 2, with a house on Lot 1, sells vacant Lot 2 with a clause in the deed that no building shall be erected in the front thirty feet of the lot. This protects the view from the front of *A's* house. Or *A* could have sold the house lot, with a restriction that no buildings shall be erected on the front thirty feet of the lot retained.

3. Restrictions imposed by a subdivider or land developer with a view to making the subdivision attractive, such as a restriction that only single-family dwellings shall be erected in the subdivision. This is the most important category. These are the restrictions that create a *general plan.*
4. Affirmative covenants running with the land, discussed later herein.
5. Conditions. These are restrictions providing for a reverter of title if they are violated. They also are discussed later.

29.03   Creation of General Plan Restrictions

In order to attract lot purchasers, a subdivider or land developer often evolves a building scheme or *general plan* for restricting the lots in the tract undergoing development to obtain substantial *uniformity* in building and use. For example, the plan often contemplates that only residences shall be erected, thus excluding stores and industrial uses. The effect is to create a restriction that any lot owner may enforce against any other lot owner. Restrictions upon the use of property, imposed as a part of general plan for the benefit of all lots, give to the purchaser of any lot a right to enforce such restrictions against the purchaser of any other lot. Such restrictions are enforced on the theory that each purchaser buying with knowledge or notice of the general plan impliedly agrees to abide by the plan.

EXAMPLE: The map or plat of a certain subdivision provides that all the subdivision lots shall be used for residence purposes only. A, one of the lot owners, seeks to open a store on his lot. Any lot owner can obtain an injunction preventing A from using his lot for store purposes.

29.03(a)   Notice of General Plan

It must be stressed at this point that there are two important ingredients here: (1) the *general plan* created by the uniform restrictions, and (2) notice of the general plan created on recording, usually of the plat or declaration of restrictions.

General plan restrictions were originally created by incorporating identical restrictions in all deeds by the subdivider. *Field Ppties, Inc.* v. *Fritz,* 315 So2d 101 (Fla. 1976). This is not the usual practice today. The character that a particular development is to assume is planned at the same time that the acreage is first subdivided into building lots. The subdivider incorporates in the recorded plat or map of the subdivision itself uniform restrictions to which all lots are subject. Clearly the plan is general. *Case* v. *Morisette,* 475 F2d 1300 (1973). It is best to have each deed state, "subject to restrictions in recorded plat." And since every lot purchaser must take notice of the recorded plat, he has constructive notice of the restriction. Therefore any lot owner may enforce the restriction against any other lot owner. These building schemes have become so elaborate that often there is not enough room for them on the plat or map. Hence the restrictions are set up in a recorded *declaration of restrictions* recorded simultaneously with the plat and referred to in the plat. Legally this is as though the restrictions had been set forth in the plat. Subsequently, as sales of the lots are made, the deeds contain clauses stating that the land is subject to such recorded restrictions. Kratovil, *Building Restrictions: Contracts or Servitudes,* 11 John Marshall L.J. 465 (1978).

Of course, the privilege of creating restrictions is by no means confined to subdividers. Any landowner is at liberty to insert restrictions in his deed when he sells and conveys the land. An enforceable restriction may be inserted in a contract for the sale of land. The landowners in a particular area may enter into an agreement subjecting their land to restrictions.

To recapitulate, then, by way of a brief historical summary:

1. Private restrictions on the use of land became practical and workable when the general plan idea was invented by the courts in 1848. *Tulk* v. *Moxhay,* 2 Phil. 774, 41 Eng. Rep. 1143 (Ch. 1848).
2. At first land developers tried to create these general plans by placing uniform restrictions in their deeds to purchasers. This did not work satisfactorily, because the

restrictions were omitted on some deeds, and the plan was not "general." Virtually all lot owners must be subject to identical restrictions. 4 ALR2d 1364 (1949).

3. This last defect was taken care of when subdividers learned to put these restrictions in the plat of subdivision. Obviously, all lots in a platted subdivision are subject to the restrictions placed in the plat.

4. As restriction schemes became elaborate, they became too lengthy to place in a plat, and the "declaration of restrictions" was invented. The plat simply stated that "all land in this subdivision is subject to the restrictions incorporated in the declaration of restrictions recorded contemporaneously herewith." It became customary for the subdivider to include in each deed executed a brief statement that "all lots in the subdivision are subject to building restrictions in the Declaration recorded in Book _____ Page _____." Kratovil, *Building Restrictions,* 11 J. Marshall J. of Pract. & Pro. 465, 472 (1978).

5. To make sure that the restrictions were enforced, subdividers began to create home owners associations (HOAs). The declaration of restrictions conferred power on the HOA to enforce the restrictions.

6. Finally, subdividers began to include in the declaration a provision empowering the HOA to levy an assessment in each homeowner to create a fund for the enforcement of the restrictions. The declaration explicitly declared that an unpaid assessment was a lien on the land of the delinquent homeowner. The lien usually took effect as of the date of the recording of the declaration. *Bessimer* v. *Gerston,* 381 So2d 1344 (Fla. 1980); *Lakeland Prop. Owners* v. *Larson,* 121 Ill.App.3d 805, 459 NE2d 1164 (1984); *Prudential Ins. Co.* v. *Wetzel,* 212 Wis. 100, 248 NW 791 (1964).

29.03(b)   Enforcement of General Plan Restrictions

If a general plan restriction is violated, the court will issue an order (injunction) forbidding the violation. Anyone who disobeys the order can be jailed. Structures erected in violation thereof can be ordered demolished. *Stewart* v. *Finkelstone,* 206 Mass. 28, 92 NE 37 (1910). The general plan creates rights known as *equitable servitudes.* The *benefit* and *burden* of those equitable servitudes attaches to each lot in the subdivision. For a general plan restriction to be enforced, the one seeking enforcement need only show that the violator purchased his lot with notice of the restriction, either from a recorded document or from actual knowledge of the restriction. The question as to enforcement of a general plan type restriction, then, arises when one lot owner attempts to violate a restriction, and another lot owner seeks a court order prohibiting such attempted violation. The court will ask two questions: (1) Is there a general plan? (2) If there is, did the violator purchase his land with actual knowledge or with notice from the public records of the existence of the general plan? If the answer to these questions is in the affirmative, the restriction will be enforced, except in the situations hereafter discussed.

As to who may enforce a general plan restriction, any lot owner, or his tenant or mortgagee, or contract purchaser may do so. 51 ALR3d 556. As long as the subdivider owns any lot in the subdivision, he can enforce the restriction. However, when he has sold the last lot, he no longer has any economic interest to protect. Nearly all courts say that he thereupon loses his right to enforce. *Kent* v. *Koch,* 333 P2d 411 (Cal. 1958); *Canel Coal* v. *Indiana,* 78 Ind. App. 115, 134 NE 891 (1922).

The conscientious developer continues to want orderly development of his subdivision even after his last lot is sold. He will therefore create a home owners' association in the form of a nonprofit corporation at the time he creates his subdivision. The plat or declaration of restrictions confers on this association the right to enforce the general plan restrictions. As lots are sold, the lot owners become members of this association. They pay dues to the association, and a fund is thus formed to finance, among other things, a lawsuit if a violation of the restrictions is threatened. This device is valid. *Neponsit Property Owners Assn.* v. *Emigrant Industrial Svgs. Bank*, 278 N.Y. 248, 15 NE2d 793 (1938); *Merrionette Manor Homes Impt. Assn.* v. *Heda*, 11 Ill. App.2d 186, 136 NE2d 556 (1956).

29.03(c) Interpretation of General Plan Restrictions

The problem of framing restrictions that will carry out the intention of the subdivider is a difficult one. Much litigation has centered around this point.

29.03(c)(1) Location Restrictions

When the plat or map of a subdivision shows a line designated as a building line extending across the front portion of the subdivision lots, this is sufficient to create a building line restriction. No substantial parts of buildings may then be erected beyond the building line. Building line restrictions may also be created by restrictions in the deed. The purpose of a building line is twofold: to insure a certain degree of uniformity in the appearance of the buildings and to create a right to unobstructed light, air and vision. The fact that a small porch, awning, stoop, steps, or an overhanging bay window extends beyond the building line will not constitute a violation of the restriction.

In dealing with the interpretation of building restrictions, keep in mind that the courts are trying to discover and give effect to the intention of the subdivider. Where he leaves his intention in doubt, the court faces a difficult problem. It must be as practical as possible. Common sense must be applied. The literal language of the restriction must often be disregarded. Certainly, common sense dictates that minor violations of restrictions must be disregarded. The problem concerns where to draw the line. What, for example, is a "small porch"? However, a so-called bay window that is really the front wall of the house is a violation of the restriction. 55 ALR 332, 172 ALR 1324. Likewise, a carport is part of the house and is a violation. *Garden Oaks* v. *Gibbs*, 489 SW2d 133 (Tex. 1972).

CAUTION: When a restriction provides that no building shall be erected within a certain number of feet of the street line, it is the line where the lot meets the street that is meant. In other words, some plat of a subdivision shows this particular lot as fronting on some street. Where the lot ends, the street begins. Often enough, to be sure, the city paves only the middle part of the street strip, and laymen sometimes speak of this as the "street," which is erroneous. The street extends to the lot line and includes not only the roadway, but also the parkway or planted area, if any, sidewalks, if any, and so on. Building line restrictions are measured from the true street line, not from the curb line. *Trunck* v. *Hack's Point*, 204 Md. 193, 103 A2d 343 (1954).

29.03(c)(2)   Incidental Use

A use purely incidental to a permitted use is permitted.

> **EXAMPLE:**   Shop in hotel. *Blakely* v. *Gorin,* 313 NE2d 903 (Mass. 1974).

29.03(c)(3)   Residence Purposes

Many restrictions provide that "the land shall be used for residence purposes" or that "only residences shall be erected on this real estate." Under this type of restriction, any kind of building devoted exclusively to residence purposes may be erected, including a duplex house or an apartment building. 14 ALR2d 1376. If the restriction permits construction of only "private," "single," or "detached" residences, only single-family dwellings are permitted. *Flaks* v. *Wichman,* 128 Colo. 45, 260 P2d 737 (1953). But the renting of homes will be permitted. *Gilbert* v. *Shenandoah Valley Assn.,* 592 SW2d 28 (Tex. 1979).

29.03(c)(4)   History of Apartment Rule

When the general plan restriction was born in 1848, apartments were virtually unknown in most of America. The first apartments in Chicago, for example, appeared in the 1870s. In Detroit, the first apartment was built in 1892. It is not surprising, then, that the early restriction schemes, those antedating 1880, were drawn by subdividers and their lawyers on the blissful assumption that all that was needed was protection of homes against *factories.* The land was restricted to "residential use." When the construction of apartments began, it was discovered that the early restriction schemes were lacking in protection against *apartments.* Apartments are a residential use.

29.03(c)(5)   Condominium

A multifamily condominium is a violation of a restriction that forbids apartments. It is not a group of single-family dwellings. 65 ALR3d 1212.

29.03(c)(6)   Form

A good residential restriction might read as follows:

> **SUGGESTED FORM:**   Only one detached, single-family dwelling and private attached garage appertaining thereto shall be erected on each lot. No use shall be made of said premises except such as is incidental to the occupation thereof for residence purposes by one private family residing in a detached, single-family dwelling.

This form has the following advantages: The phrase "single-family dwelling" keeps out apartments and other multiple dwellings. Single dwellings will not do the trick because in some states, a restriction against single dwellings does not prohibit a duplex or apartment.

Vocabulary is important. A *duplex* consists of two single-family dwellings, each on its own lot, but sharing a party wall that straddles the line between the lots. A duplex is permitted on land restricted to residence purposes. 99 ALR3d 985. A *bi-level* is a two-story house designed for occupancy by one family. A *two-flat* is a building with two apartments, one above the other, designed for occupancy by two families. A two-flat is not a single-family dwelling. 14 ALR2d 1376. The use of the word "detached" keeps out duplexes or row houses. The stipulation as to occupation by one private family keeps out lodgers and prevents doubling up of families.

If a restriction merely specifies the type of building that can be built but is silent regarding the use of the building, an argument may be advanced that the building can be used for any purpose. As a rule, courts try to give effect to the obvious intention by holding that use of the structures must conform to the purposes for which it was erected. 155 ALR 1000.

> **EXAMPLE:** A restriction provided that "no structure shall be built except for dwelling purposes." A dwelling was erected. Later, the owner of the dwelling attempted to use it as a beauty parlor. The court held that the building could be used only for dwelling purposes. *Holderness* v. *Central States Finance Corp.*, 241 Mich. 604, 217 NW 764 (1928). Obviously, the restriction was badly drafted. If it had been properly drafted, litigation could not have arisen. Accord: *J. T. Hobb & Son* v. *Family Homes*, 274 SE2d 174 (N.C. 1981).

The restriction should restrict the use of the *land* as well as use of the *building*. Again, courts will usually come to the rescue by holding that the intention was to restrict use of both building and land.

> **EXAMPLE:** A restriction provided that no building erected on the land should be used for any purpose other than as a private dwelling place. The landowner attempted to use the vacant land as a parking lot. He contended that the restriction applied only to the use of buildings and therefore did not apply to vacant land. The court held that it was the intention to restrict use of both building and land. *Hoover* v. *Waggoman*, 52 N.M. 371, 199 P2d 991 (1948); 155 ALR 528, 1007. It has even been held that a restriction calling for only one detached *single-family* dwelling per lot impliedly forbids occupancy by two families. *Freeman* v. *Gee*, 423 P2d 155 (Utah 1967).

29.03(c)(7)   Duplex

Often one will hear the argument that a duplex is really two single-family dwellings connected by a party wall with one building on each lot. *Stephenson* v. *Perlitz*, 537 SW2d 287 (Tex. 1976); *Easterly* v. *Hall*, 182 SE2d 671 (S.C. 1971). To keep out duplexes, it is therefore advisable to have the restriction read that only one *de-*

tached single-family dwelling may be built on each lot. *Freeman* v. *Gee*, 423 P2d 155 (Utah 1967); 99 ALR 3d 985.

29.03(c)(8)   Business Purposes

When the restriction forbids use of the premises for business purposes, the following are not permitted: gasoline filling stations, billboards, and parking for business purposes. Especially in older deeds one is likely to find restrictions prohibiting use of the property for a "trade or business." Suppose a doctor uses a room of his home as an office for the practice of medicine. This would not violate such a restriction because the practice of medicine is not a *trade* or *business;* it is a *profession. Auerbacher* v. *Smith,* 19 N.J. Super. 191, 88 A2d 262 (1952); 21 ALR3d 641.

29.04   Senior Citizens

There are, of course, numerous subdivisions restricted to senior citizens. This is accomplished by means of general plan type restrictions in a declaration of restrictions. They are valid. *Riley* v. *Stoves,* 526 P2d 747 (Ariz. 1974); 68 ALR3d 1239.

> **SUGGESTION TO DRAFTSMAN:**   Since the old law frowns on restrictions on the *sale* of land, frame restrictions in terms of restrictions on *occupancy* since these present no legal problem. Because of the desperate housing shortage and the tendency of condominium developers to bar occupancy by children, the argument is being made that barring children is illegal. This is an unresolved issue. A genuine senior citizens community will probably survive attack. 100 ALR3d 241.

29.05   Defective Restrictions

Many restrictions are so poorly drafted that they fail to achieve their main purpose.

> **EXAMPLE:**   A restriction provided that "no flat roof dwelling house shall be erected." Since no other type of building was mentioned, a flat roof church could be erected. *Corbridge* v. *Westminster,* 18 Ill. App.2d 245, 151 NE2d 822 (1958).

You can see that many restrictions, particularly the older ones, are negative in form. They contain enumerations of prohibited uses, such as apartments and businesses. Such devices are doomed to failure. In the first place, nobody ever makes the list of excluded uses long enough, and nobody, of course, can cover the uses that do not even exist today but will crop up in the future. This is why, particularly for residential property, modern restriction plans simply specify the one type of permitted use, that is, "only detached single-family dwellings shall be constructed, and the premises shall be used only as a residence for one private family."

29.06   Plans of Buildings

Often a scheme of restrictions provides that no building shall be erected until the plans and specifications therefor have been approved by the developer or subdivider. Such provisions are valid, but any refusal to approve plans will be set aside by the courts if such refusal is capricious, arbitrary, or unreasonable. *Hannula* v. *Hacienda Homes*, 34 Cal. App.2d 442, 211 P2d 302 (1949); 19 ALR2d 1268; 47 ALR3d 1232.

29.07   Ingress and Egress for a Prohibited Use

Occasionally, a lot in a restricted residential subdivision is acquired by one who seeks to use it for the benefit of nonresidential land outside the subdivision. This is not permitted.

> **EXAMPLE:**   A plat restriction permitted only residential use of the lots. *X*, who owned a restaurant across the street from the subdivision, bought three lots in the subdivision, meaning to use them for access to the restaurant and parking. The court prohibited this. *Bennett* v. *Consolidated Realty Co.*, 226 Ky. 747, 11 SW2d 910, 61 ALR 453 (1928); 25 ALR2d 904.

29.08   Modification, Extension, and Release of General Plan Restrictions

If the right to modify general plan is not reserved in the deeds, plat, or declaration, it takes a unanimous vote of all lot owners (and probably also their mortgagees) to modify or release the restrictions. *Steve Vogli & Co.* v. *Lane*, 405 SW2d 885 (Mo. 1966); 4 ALR3d 570. This is rarely obtainable.

> **EXAMPLE:**   All owners but one signed a release of the restrictions. He was entitled to enforce the restrictions. *Evangelical Church* v. *Sahlem*, 254 N.Y. 161, 172 NE 455 (1930).

In recent restriction plans, subdividers have often included a clause giving themselves the right to waive or dispense with the restrictions as to some or all of the lots. This is dangerous. A number of courts have held that such a provision destroys the uniformity necessary to a general plan, and therefore the restrictions cannot be enforced by one lot owner against another. 19 ALR2d 1282.

When the right to modify the restrictions is reserved to the developer by the deeds, plat, or declarations, he may validly exercise this right. *McComb* v. *Harly*, 132 N.J.Eq. 182, 26 A2d 891; 4 ALR2d 570.

In providing for periodical extensions and modifications of the restrictions in the declaration, thought must be given to the voting arrangements.

> **EXAMPLE:**   There is a difference between "the owners of a majority of the lots" and "a majority of the lot owners."

Where the right to modify restrictions is reserved in the plat, declaration of restrictions, or deeds, any modifications voted by the required majority must be general in their nature.

> **EXAMPLE:**   A majority of the landowners voted to take one lot out of the restrictions so that a filling station be erected on it. This was invalid. *Riley* v. *Boyle,* 434 P2d 525.

Any amendment must be reasonable and must leave the plan basically intact. *Flamingo Ranch Estates* v. *Sunshine Ranchers,* 303 So2d 665 (Fla. 1974).

29.09   Mortgage Foreclosure

One must exercise care concerning any mortgage that is recorded prior in time to the declaration of restrictions.

> **EXAMPLE:**   Owner records a construction mortgage on some vacant but subdivided land to Lender. Thereafter Owner records a declaration of restrictions. He sells a few lots, and deeds are recorded to the buyers. These lots are released from the mortgage. Then he defaults on his mortgage, which is foreclosed. The restrictions are wiped out by the foreclosure. *Boyd* v. *Park Realty Corp.,* 137 Md. 36, 111 A 129 (1920); *Sain* v. *Silvestre,* 144 Cal. Reptr. 478 (1978). Prior in time is prior in right.

The construction mortgage should have stated that it was subject to a declaration of restrictions to be recorded later, or simultaneously with the recording of the declaration of restrictions Lender could have recorded a subordination of his mortgage to the restrictions.

29.10   Minor Violations

Earlier, it was stated that courts will not force removal of trivial encroachments. A court is a tribunal where revenge or punishment in the way of reprisal has no place. *Kajawski* v. *Null,* 177 A2d 101 (Pa. 1962). The courts will "balance the equities." *De Marco* v. *Palazzolo,* 209 NW2d 540 (Mich. 1973). If an unintentional minor violation of a restriction is involved, the courts will not compel its removal. This has been explained in connection with location restrictions. The same rule applies to other violations.

> **EXAMPLE:**   A restriction limited the height of buildings to twenty-five feet. By mistake, a landowner erected a building that was twenty-six feet high. The court refused to compel him to remove the offending one foot.

EXAMPLE: At times a lot owner will build his home so that it extends slightly over the front building line established by the building restrictions. In the process of balancing the equities, the court will consider that compelling removal of three or four inches of a home is a disastrous burden, but such removal does little for the neighbor. Removal is rarely ordered. Note that encroachments on a *neighbor's land* of three or four inches are serious. Encroachments over a *building line* are less serious.

29.11   Factors that Render General Plan Restrictions Unenforceable

In considering what factors render restrictions unenforceable, it is necessary, first of all, to distinguish between restrictions that do not provide for a reverter of title and those that do. We consider first the general plan type restrictions, which are traditionally enforced by means of an injunction, or court order, forbidding violation. Such orders are not granted lightly. Various circumstances are considered by the courts in determining whether such an order should be granted.

29.11(a)   General Principles

In determining the legal duration of a restriction, which is the subject matter of much of this section, keep in mind that courts are practical. Even if the restriction recites that it will exist "forever," courts are likely to terminate it when it has become useless. *Ferguson* v. *Zion Ev. Church*, 190 P2d 1019 (Okla. 1948).

29.11(b)   Change in Neighborhood

A court will not, as a rule, enforce a restriction by injunction when the neighborhood has so changed in character and environment as to make it unfit to continue the original use. 4 ALR2d 1111; 53 ALR3d 492; 26 CJS *Deeds* § 171. The court will "balance the equities." That is, it will not grant an injunction that will do the plaintiff little good but will do the defendant great harm.

EXAMPLE: A restriction provides that lots in the subdivision shall be used only for residence purposes. Gradually the neighborhood changes character, and stores and factories creep in. This often happens because no single homeowner wishes to incur the expense of hiring an attorney and litigating the right of his neighbors to violate the restrictions. When it becomes impossible to characterize the area as residential, courts will refuse to enforce the restriction on the ground that it is no longer possible to carry the original plan into effect. However, if the change in neighborhood affects only a part of the subdivision while the remainder is unchanged, the restrictions may be enforced in the area that remains unchanged. *O'Neill* v. *Wolf*, 338 Ill. 508, 170 NE 669. Suppose *A* owns a house in a restricted subdivision, but six blocks away, a number of violating structures are erected. *A's* acquiescence in these violations will not bar him from stopping a violation next door to him or in the same block. In other words, these previous violations are so remote from him that they do not constitute a change in his immediate neighborhood, nor could *A* be charged with undue neglect in enforcing his rights. *Meek* v. *Yarowsky*, 236 Mich. 251, 210 NW 226.

A question on which the courts are not in agreement relates to changes that occur outside the subdivision.

> **EXAMPLE:**   A plat restriction limits the subdivision to residential uses. As the surrounding area changes, many stores are built across the street from the subdivision. Some courts insist that the front tier of lots in the subdivision must hold the line and the restrictions continue in force. *Knolls Assn.* v. *Hinton,* 389 NE2d 693 (Ill. App. 1979); *Oritz* v. *Jeter,* 479 SW2d 752; 2 Am. Law Ppty. §9.39. Since it is not always easy to get people to buy homes across the street from the stores, other courts will allow changes of this nature to sway them in refusing enforcement of the restrictions. *Hecht* v. *Stephens,* 464 P2d 258 (Kans. 1970); *Exchange Nat. Bank* v. *City of Des Plaines,* 336 NE2d 8 (Ill. 1975).

29.11(c)   Numerous Violations

Even when the restricted neighborhood has not changed its general character, the right to enforce a particular restriction may be lost by abandonment. When the property owners in the subdivision have violated the restrictions and the violations have been so general as to indicate an abandonment of the original general plan, the restrictions will not be enforced. The reason for this is that the purpose of the restriction can no longer be carried out. It would be an injustice to a property owner to compel him to conform to a restriction that most of the other owners have violated when such enforcement would be of no benefit to the party seeking to enforce the restriction.

> **EXAMPLE:**   A building line was established across a block consisting of fifteen lots. On nine of the lots, buildings were erected that extended across the building line. The owner of a lot that had remained vacant began construction of a building that would also violate the building line. The owner of another vacant lot sought a court order to prevent this violation. The court order was refused. The value of the building line had been destroyed by the numerous violations. *Ewersten* v. *Gerstenberg,* 186 Ill. 344, 57 NE 1051 (1900).

29.11(d)   Abandonment

Even in the absence of numerous violations a landowner's acquiescence in violations of restrictions may render restrictions unenforceable. Restatement, Property §561; 26 CJS *Deeds* §169.

> **EXAMPLE:**   A plat restricts all the lots to single-family dwellings. Without protest by others, *A* builds an apartment building on Lot 5 and *B* builds an apartment building on Lot 7. *X* now seeks to build an apartment building on Lot 6, which is sandwiched between the existing apartments. He may do so.

And there may be a *partial abandonment.* This leaves the remainder of the restrictions enforceable. *Donahoe* v. *Marston,* 547 P2d 39 (Mont. 1976).

> **EXAMPLE:** A plat restriction provided that all lots were to be used for residence purposes and only single-family dwellings could be erected. A number of two-flats were erected. Now one lot owner wishes to put in a store. He cannot do so. *Noyes* v. *McDonnell,* 398 P2d 838. Likewise minor violations of a building line furnish no excuse for major violations. *Carter* v. *Conroy,* 544 P2d 258 (Ariz. 1976).

29.11(e)   Violations by Party Who Seeks to Enforce Restriction

One who violates a nonreverter type restriction in some substantial degree or manner cannot procure a court injunction restraining the violation of the restriction by others. Restatement, Property § 560; 26 CJS *Deeds,* § 169, p. 1163; 4 ALR2d 1142.

> **EXAMPLE:** A plat restriction permits only single-family dwellings to be erected. *A* constructs a two-flat. His neighbor, *B,* now seeks to erect a three-flat. *A* cannot prevent this.

29.11(f)   Delay in Enforcing Restrictions

Where a nonreverter type restriction, as distinguished from a condition, is involved, a person wishing to prevent a violation must act promptly.

> **EXAMPLE:** A subdivision plat contains a nonreverter type building restriction forbidding the construction of anything but single-family dwellings. *X,* who owns a house in this subdivision, observes that *Y,* another lot owner, is erecting a filling station. After construction of the station has been completed, *X* files a suit to have it demolished. The court will refuse to interfere. *X* has been guilty of undue delay. 12 ALR2d 394; 36 ALR2d 861, 870. Lawyers call such delay *laches.*

29.11(g)   Restrictions About to Expire by Lapse of Time

Many restrictions specifically state a time limit for their expiration. Suppose construction of a building that violates the restriction is begun a year or so before the restriction has expired by lapse of time. Here the courts may refuse to enforce the restriction for the simple, practical reason that to do so would be of little practical benefit.

29.11(h)   Statutes of Limitations

In some states laws have been enacted limiting the period of time for bringing a suit for *violation* of a building restriction.

> **EXAMPLE:** In Missouri, such a suit must be brought within two years after the date the restriction was violated. Sec. 516.095 Mo. Stat. New York has a two-

year limitation on building line violations; in Massachusetts the period is six years. In Massachusetts, building restrictions unlimited in duration expire after thirty years. Basye, *Clearing Land Titles* §143 (2d ed. 1970). In Colorado, a suit to enforce a restriction must be brought within one year from the date of violation. *Wolf* v. *Hallenbeck,* 123 P2d 412 (1942).

29.11(i)   State Laws Placing Time Limits on Enforcement of Restrictions

A number of states—Arizona, Georgia, Massachusetts, Michigan, Minnesota, Rhode Island, and Wisconsin, for example—have enacted laws providing that after the lapse of a stated number of years restrictions become unenforceable; *Payne* v. *Borkat,* 261 SE2d 393 (1979); *Baker* v. *Seneca,* 116 NE2d 325 (Mass.); Basye, *Clearing Land Titles* §143 (2d ed. 1970). And in all states having marketability of title laws, restrictions will expire after the permitted time unless kept alive by new recording as provided in the law. *Semachko* v. *Hopko,* 301 NE 2d 560 (Ohio 1973).

29.11(j)   Other Factors

Courts are more merciful when the violation is not willful but is due to accident or mistake, as where a surveyor makes an error, and as a result a building extends over a building line. They are also more merciful toward minor violations than they are toward major violations. Of course, if the party seeking to enforce the restriction has said or done something that would encourage the violator to go ahead with the violation, he will get no help from the courts.

29.12   Conditions

A condition is a restriction that is coupled with a *reverter clause.* This clause provides that if the restriction is violated, ownership reverts to the grantor in the deed.

> **EXAMPLE:**   Owner deeds a lot to Buyer with a provision forbidding sale or use of intoxicating liquor on the lot and that in case of violation, ownership reverts to Owner. In time the premises are sold to Buyer #2, who puts in a drugstore with a liquor department. Owner files a suit. The court will give the property back to Owner.

The outstanding characteristic of a condition is the fact that if it is violated, the grantor may get his land back by filing a suit to obtain possession. He need not pay any compensation for it. Any mortgages or other interests in the land created after the creation of the condition are extinguished if the condition is enforced, again without payment of compensation to the mortgagee. This rule operates so harshly that courts are reluctant to construe a provision as a condition. In nearly all states, if the restrictive provision is followed by a clause providing that in the event of a violation of the restrictions the title to land shall revert to the grantor in the deed, the restrictive provision is a condition. If the deed contains no reverter clause, that is, a clause providing for a reverter or forfeiture of title in the event of violation of the restrictions, the restrictive provision is usually a covenant. The nomenclature employed by the parties is by no means decisive as to the character of the restriction created.

> **EXAMPLE:** A deed contained this clause: "These presents are upon the express condition that the said premises shall not be used or occupied as a tavern or public house." There was no reverter clause. It was held to be a covenant. *Koch* v. *Streuter,* 232 Ill. 594, 83 NE 1072 (1908). Violation would not cause a reverter.

Occasionally, the condition is referred to herein as a *reverter type restriction.*

29.12(a)   Enforcement of Conditions

When a condition (that is, a reverter type of restriction) occurs in a deed but the condition forms no part of any general plan, enforcement is relatively simple. The condition can be enforced by the grantor in the deed, or, if he is dead, by his heirs. Other lot owners in the same subdivision cannot enforce the condition.

A recorded condition can be enforced against any subsequent purchaser or mortgagee of the land. Enforcement of a condition by the grantor in the deed containing the condition, or by his heirs, if he is dead, extinguishes all subsequent titles and rights in the land.

> **EXAMPLE:** Seller conveys a lot to Buyer #1 with a condition in the deed that the premises shall not be used for the sale of liquor. The deed provides that in the event of violation of this provision, title to the property shall revert to Seller. Buyer #1 sells and conveys the property to Buyer #2, who places a mortgage thereon to Lender. Thereafter, Buyer #2 leases the building to Tenant and the latter uses the property for the sale of liquor. Seller brings suit to recover the land on the ground that the condition has been violated. Seller will be allowed to recover the land and all buildings erected on it without payment of any compensation, and will have good title free and clear of the mortgage and lease.

For the above reason, mortgagees are often reluctant to loan money on land that is subject to a condition. In fact, many insurance companies, which are authorized by law to loan money on first mortgages only, cannot legally make a loan on land that is subject to a condition. The problem may be handled in a number of different ways.

> 1. The person who has the right to enforce a reverter (the grantor in the deed creating the condition, or his heirs) may always release the reverter outright to the landowner.
> 2. The person who has the right to enforce a reverter may *subordinate* this right to a mortgage by a document stating that the reverter right is *subject* to the mortgage. If the subordination is unequivocal, the mortgagee, when he forecloses, completely extinguishes the condition.

3. Many subdividers who place conditions in their deeds also include provisions in their deeds stating that the reverter right is subordinate to all mortgages. These provisions are broad in their terms and protect any mortgagee who may take a mortgage on the land.

4. In some instances title companies will insure against loss caused by a reverter of title.

29.12(b)   Factors that Render Conditions Unenforceable

In many states, especially where older court decisions are still followed, the factors discussed above that would prevent enforcement of a *nonreverter type* restriction have little application to conditions, that is, *reverter type restrictions.* For example, in nearly all states the grantor in a deed containing a condition, or his heirs, if he is dead, has the right to enforce a condition even though the neighborhood has so changed that enforcement is of little practical utility. In one or two modern states, however, the change of neighborhood rule is now also applied to conditions, and conditions will not be enforced where the neighborhood has changed. *Letteau* v. *Ellis,* 122 Cal. App. 584, 10 P2d 496 (1932); *Cole* v. *Colorado Springs,* 381 P2d 13 (Colo. 1963); *Koehler* v. *Rowland,* 275 Mo. 573, 205 SW 217 (1917); *Townsend* v. *Allen,* 250 P2d 292 (Cal. 1953).

Again, laws exist in every state allowing a certain time, often as long as twenty years, for the bringing of a suit to declare a reverter of title and to enforce a condition. This period of time runs not from the date of the deed containing the condition, but from the date the condition is violated. Often situations arise where, after the condition has been violated, no action has been taken to enforce the condition, and the landowner continues in possession, perhaps for several years. Mere delay in enforcing a condition, so long as the period allowed by law has not expired, does not, in most states, bar enforcement of a condition. But if the one who has a right to declare a reverter stands idly by, apparently acquiescing in the violation of the condition, sees valuable improvement being made by the landowner and delays proceedings to enforce the condition until after the improvements have been completed, some modern courts feel that this conduct is so unfair to the landowner that they refuse to enforce the condition. 39 ALR2d 1111.

29.12(b)(1)   Reverter Acts

In some states laws have been passed outlawing conditions after a certain specified period of time has elapsed from the date of their creation. *Trustees* v. *Batdorf,* 6 Ill.2d 486, 130 NE2d 111 (1955); *State Highway Div.* v. *Tolke,* 586 P2d 791 (Ore. 1978); *Caldwell* v. *Brown,* 553 SW2d 692 (Ky. 1977); 87 ALR3d 1011. But see *Bd. of Educ.* v. *Miles,* 15 NY2d 364, 207 NE2d 181, criticized in 1965 *Law Forum* 941. Marketability of title laws also have this result.

29.12(b)(2)   Nominal Conditions

A number of states have statutes that conditions may be disregarded when they become "merely nominal" or "without substantial benefit to the parties." Basye, *Clearing Land Titles* §143 (2d ed. 1970).

> **EXAMPLE:**   A subdivider deeded out all lots with a reverter clause against trade or business. After he had deeded out all lots he could not enforce the conditions. They had only nominal value to him. He could not be hurt by violations. *Ingersoll Engineering Co.* v. *Crocker,* 228 Fed. 845 (Mich. 1915).

29.12(b)(3)   Acquiescence in Violations

Sometimes a general plan is revealed by the existence of identical conditions in deeds. In such case, if the owner of the reverter right follows a course of conduct that results in numerous violations of the conditions, he will, in some states, be denied the right to enforce any of the conditions. 39 ALR2d 1133.

> **EXAMPLE:**   A subdivider sold all the lots in the subdivision by deeds containing conditions against sale of intoxicating liquor. Later, he voluntarily released this clause as to a number of lots, and saloons were built on the released lots. He was refused the right to enforce any of the unreleased conditions. *Wedum-Aldahl Co.* v. *Miller,* 18 Cal. App.2d 745, 64 P2d 762 (1937).

It can be seen that while the older and stricter court decisions freely allow the enforcement of conditions, the modern decisions are beginning to apply to conditions the same rules that they apply to nonreverter type restrictions.

29.13   Covenants Running with the Land

The topic covered in this section is best explained by an illustration.

> **EXAMPLE:**   Seller owns two adjoining lots, Lots 1 and 2. Seller sells Lot 1 to Buyer, and in the deed he inserts a clause stating that Buyer covenants to keep in repair the fence between the two lots. Lot 2 enjoys the *benefit* of this covenant. Lot 1 bears the *burden* of the covenant. Any subsequent owner of Lot 1 must comply with this covenant and will be liable to pay damages to the owner of Lot 2 if he fails to do so. Any subsequent owner of Lot 2 will be able to enforce this covenant. *Such an affirmative covenant runs with the land,* much in the same fashion as an appurtenant easement runs with the land, the *burden* of the covenant running with Lot 1 and the *benefit* running with Lot 2.

In issuing such orders, courts ignore all the technicalities that surround damage suits. As long as a property owner bought his land with notice, either actual or from the public record, that the land was bound by a covenant, he is subject to court injunctions compelling obedience. In modern times, in other words, the old-fashioned method of enforcing covenants by damage suits that may not be decided by a jury until years after the suit has been filed, and then may offer only a slim chance of persuading a jury or collecting the damages a jury may award, has given way to the new, effective method of enforcing a restrictive covenant by a judge's injunction order that may issue within a few days after suit is filed. *Affirmative covenants,* such as those requiring payment of assessments for maintenance of common grounds in a planned unit development, still pose the problems relating to covenants running with the land.

29.14   Racial Restrictions

Racial restrictions, that is, restrictions prohibiting use of occupancy by, or sale of, the land to persons other than members of the Caucasian race are discussed elsewhere.

29.15   Suggestions

If you are about to buy real estate, you are concerned with several questions about restrictions: (1) Do any restrictions exist that will hamper or prevent the use you intended to make of this land or prevent construction of the building you have in mind? (2) What does the contract of sale say about restrictions? (3) Assuming that you are buying improved real estate and therefore have no building problem, are there reverter clauses in the restriction under which you may lose your title or that may hamper your financing of the real estate? (4) If there are restrictions, and the restrictions are desirable from your point of view, do you get the right to enforce them against other property owners?

In answering question 3 above, keep in mind that if there is a condition containing a reverter clause, and some prior owner violated the clause by constructing the wrong type of building or by committing some other violation, the grantor in the deed containing the condition has the right to take the property away from you.

In answering question 4 above, keep in mind the rules stated in the text. Lot owners get the best protection when the restrictions are incorporated in the map or plat of the subdivision, since this leaves no room for doubt that there is a general plan. The lot owners get the least protection in cases where the restrictions are imposed by the subdivider, who includes conditions in his deed to the lot owners. Except in a few states, only the subdivider or his heirs can, as a rule, enforce such conditions, and the subdivider is likely to lose interest once he has sold all lots in the subdivision. Also, when the subdivider has created conditions, the lot owners must be prepared to go to him each time they mortgage their lands and buy from him a subordination of reverter. Mortgagees usually insist on this protection, and lot owners have no recourse but to pay for it.

If you are attempting to obtain the release of a restriction, you must keep in mind the rules regarding the persons who may enforce the restriction. For example, if you buy a lot in a subdivision and the plat or map of the subdivision contains a restriction that only single-family dwellings shall be constructed, it is a waste of time to obtain the consent of the owners of the two neighboring lots to the construction of a two-flat building, because any lot owner in the subdivision can block construction of such a building.

CHAPTER 30

Land Use Controls—Zoning and Building Ordinances

30.01 State Enabling Legislation

For the most part, cities have only such powers as are given them by the state legislature. In 1919, the federal government drafted a suggested state law called the Standard State Enabling Act, setting forth a *proposed law* that a state could pass. When enacted by a state, it would grant cities and villages the power to pass zoning ordinances. Few zoning ordinances were enacted because at the time it was thought by many that zoning was of doubtful validity. However, when in 1926 the Supreme Court surprisingly held that zoning did not violate the federal constitution, virtually all states passed laws identical with this Standard State Enabling Act. Cities proceeded to enact zoning ordinances pursuant to the powers granted by this Act. Thus in zoning law we are usually dealing with the validity or interpretation of city ordinances enacted under the powers granted by laws like this model act.

As a historical fact, the crash of 1929 and the Great Depression that ensued discouraged zoning activity. Then, World War II began, and real estate activity remained at a low level. But after World War II ended and the veterans began to return to America, a huge housing boom began, centered in the suburbs and the inexpensive farm land around them. The old residents fought to keep out the developers. Zoning came into its own.

Each state by now has enacted its own zoning law granting cities, villages, counties, and townships the power to enact zoning ordinances. A zoning ordinance must therefore conform to the statute. *FGL & L Property Corp.* v. *City of Rye,* 66 NY2d 111, 485 NE2d 986 (1985). A number of states have "home rule" cities that derive their power from the state constitution rather than state legislation. Such cities may enact zoning ordinances that do not conform to the state statute so long as they are reasonable.

30.02   The Ordinance—History of Zoning Ordinances

A zoning ordinance consists of two separate parts. One part contains the text of the ordinance, which refers to the other part, a map of the city outlining the various zones into which the city is divided. There will be single-family dwelling zones, of course. There will be some commercial areas. Many cities have industrial zones. The text of the ordinance refers to the various zones depicted on the map and outline the uses that may be made of the lots in that particular zone.

Since only residential uses are permitted in residential zones, residential use is known as a preferred use. Originally, all other zones were cumulative zones in that they permitted residences in commercial zones, for example, and stores and residences in industrial zones.

Modern zoning ordinances usually create a greater number of classifications. Residential districts may be divided into single-family districts and multi-family districts. Multi-family zones may be divided into *walkups* and *high-rise* (elevator building) zones. Commercial zones may be divided into retail and wholesale districts, industrial zones into heavy and light industry zones. Small stores may be permitted in apartment buildings and planned unit developments.

History of zoning ordinances.   The first zoning ordinance was adopted by New York City. Its purpose was to prevent the garment district from spilling over into the fashionable Fifth Avenue shopping area. But the real history of zoning began in 1926, when the Supreme Court held zoning valid. *Village of Euclid* v. *Ambler Realty Co.*, 272 U.S. 365, 47 S.Ct. 114, 71 L. Ed. 303 (1926). Historically, the Village of Euclid was founded by some land surveyors who liked the location they had surveyed and named the town after their favorite mathematician. Today, "cooky cutter" zoning that divides the municipality into rigid zones with rectangular lots in each zone, as was done in the Village of Euclid, is derisively referred to as "Euclidean zoning."

Early zoning ordinances generally divided the city into three zones: residential, commercial, and manufacturing. Only residences were permitted in residence districts. Both stores and residences were allowed in commercial zones. All types of uses were permitted in manufacturing zones. Attached to the ordinance was a map showing zone boundaries.

Since only residential uses were permitted in residential zones, residential use came to be known as a *preferred use.* All other zones were *cumulative zones* in that they permitted residences in commercial zones, for example, and stores and residences in industrial zones.

Modern zoning ordinances usually create a greater number of classifications. Residential districts may be divided into single-family districts and multiple-family districts. Multiple-family zones may be divided into *walkups* and *high-rise* (elevator building) zones. Commercial zones may be divided into retail and wholesale districts, industrial zones into heavy and light industry zones. Small stores may be permitted in apartment buildings and planned unit developments.

30.03   Noncumulative Zoning

Many zoning ordinances do more than keep industries and stores out of residential zones. They also exclude residences from commercial and industrial zones. Ordinances zoning certain areas exclusively for industrial purposes are fairly widespread and are valid. *Roney* v. *Board of Supervisors,* 138 Cal. App.2d 740, 292 P2d 529 (1956); *People ex rel.* v. *Morton Grove,* 16 Ill.2d 183, 157 NE2d 33 (1959); *Lamb* v. *City of Monroe,* 358 Mich. 136, 99 NW2d 566 (1959). Obviously, it is just as injurious to the welfare of the community to permit residential development of land needed for industrial expansion as it is to permit industrial expansion in residential neighborhoods. We must remember that the supply of usable land is limited, and zoning is the chief tool that communities utilize to insure wise use of our limited land areas.

Interestingly, however, there is a trend away from noncumulative or exclusive zoning.

> **EXAMPLE:**   Many zones are mixed-use zones. Stores are common in planned unit developments. Office buildings and theaters are often included in large planned developments.

30.04   Zoning—Validity—In General

Determining the validity of zoning is basically a state court function. The United States Supreme Court determined the *general validity* of zoning in *Village of Euclid* v. *Ambler Realty Co.,* 272 U.S. 365, 71 L. Ed. 303 (1926). It decided that a state, acting under its police power, could enact a zoning law and compel a landowner to accept a substantial reduction in his land value as long as there was a corresponding benefit to the public. Thereafter, in *Nectow* v. *Cambridge,* 277 U.S. 183, 72 L. Ed. 842 (1928) the Supreme Court decided that while a zoning ordinance could be valid *in general* it might work such a hardship as to a particular tract of land that it would be held invalid *as applied to that tract of land.*

> **EXAMPLE:**   A zoning ordinance zoned a triangular tract of land for residential purposes. This tract of land was cut off from other residential lots by railroad tracks and was entirely surrounded by property zoned for industrial use. It was worthless as residence property. The *zoning map,* in other words, put the land in the wrong zone. The court held that the zoning ordinance was not valid *as applied* to this triangle. Insofar as the zoning ordinance limits property to a use that cannot reasonably be made of it, it is invalid. *Tews* v. *Woolhiser,* 353 Ill. 212, 185 NE 827 (1933).

Having laid down some general principles, the Supreme Court thereafter refused for a long time to decide zoning cases, leaving the problem of deciding validity to the state courts. Thus, in discussing the validity of a zoning ordinance, we are discussing its validity *as applied to a particular tract of land* under state law. Each of the fifty states is pretty much at liberty to decide that issue under its own state constitution. The fact that most state constitutions are modeled after the federal constitution is no guaranty of uniformity. Far from it, for judges are people. The decisions exhibit a wild diversity, because judges entertain diverse views on what is proper zoning.

In the ordinary zoning case we are dealing with a particular tract of land. In general, the landowner is trying to put in an apartment, a planned unit development, a mobile home court, an industrial plant, and opposition is encountered. There are some approaches to this problem that reveal a degree of uniformity. Since the validity of zoning in general is beyond question, most of the litigation is over amendments or rezoning of a particular tract of land. Or a landowner attacks the zoning *map* that is attached to every zoning ordinance. He argues that his land is placed by the *map* in the wrong type of zone. Unsuitable zoning is illegal zoning.

There is an unspoken balancing process at work. The court considers the proposed rezoning. Is the new proposed use nuisancelike so that it is sure to be harmful to its neighbors? The odds are against it, if it is. Is it relatively benign, such as a strictly residential planned unit development? Its chances are good. Does it fit well into the pattern of existing uses so that its neighbors will not suffer too much? Very likely it will prevail. And so on.

30.04(a)   Validity—Factors to be Considered

In dealing with zoning validity one is faced with a variety of situations, namely: (1) the attack may be leveled against the entire ordinance, which is a rarity; (2) the attack may be leveled against the zoning ordinance *as applied* to a particular tract of land; (3) the attack may be leveled against the *granting or refusal* of (a) an amendment to the ordinance (rezoning), (b) a variance, or (c) a special exception. Passing for a moment item (1) above, the factors to be considered in all these situations are these:

1. The character of the neighborhood.

EXAMPLE: One who seeks to thrust an apartment, industrial plant, or mortuary in the midst of a neighborhood of single-family dwellings will not succeed. Conformity to surrounding uses is one of the objectives of sound zoning.

2. The extent to which property values are diminished by the particular zoning restriction and the extent to which the public is benefited.

EXAMPLE: An area is zoned single-family, but one vacant lot sits between two nonconforming apartments. No one thinking realistically would erect a house on this site. The owner must be permitted to erect an apartment. Under the concept of the police power, a landowner cannot be compelled to accept a harmful and sharp reduction in land value unless there is some corresponding benefit to the public. Here it is obvious that the vacant lot has zero value if zoned single-family. No public purpose is served. The land must be rezoned.

EXAMPLE: In the leading case of *Village of Euclid* v. *Ambler Realty Co.*, 272 U.S. 365 (1926), the village enacted a zoning ordinance under which Ambler's tract of sixty-eight acres fell into a single-family zone. This reduced its value from $10,000 per acre to $2,500 per acre. Nevertheless, there were residences to the east and west of the property, so that the zoning did indeed benefit large segments of the public. A landowner can be compelled to accept a reduction in land value if the ordinance is reasonable and there is a *benefit to the public.*

The philosophy here is that in a democracy the people grant to various legislative bodies the power to enact laws. But inherent in this grant of power is the limitation that the power must be exercised reasonably.

Another way of stating this rule is that the ordinance must not be *confiscatory as applied to the land in question.* If the land is in a residential zone, this requires proof that residential development is not feasible and that use of the property for any of the permitted purposes in the zone is likewise not feasible. *Wackerman v. Town of Penfield,* 366 NYS2d 718 (1975).

3. The extent to which removal of the existing limitation would affect the value of other property in the area.

EXAMPLE: In an area zoned for heavy industry, it was irrational to single out the petroleum industry and exclude it. The area was already permeated with odors from existing, legal plants. *Tidewater Oil Co. v. Mayor & Council of Carteret,* 193 A2d 413 (N.J. 1963). Here we find no *benefit to the public.*

4. The suitability of the property for the zoned purpose.

EXAMPLE: The land was zoned single-family but was located in a district predominantly business and industrial and was worth ten times more for these purposes than as residential. The zoning is invalid as applied to this tract of land. Here the harm to the landowner is great, and there is no benefit to the public. *Galt v. County of Cook,* 405 Ill. 396, 91 NE2d 395 (1950).

5. The existing uses and zoning of nearby property.

EXAMPLE: Other examples in this section provide good illustrations of this rule.

6. The length of time under the existing zoning that the property has remained unimproved considered in the context of land development in the area.

EXAMPLE: A tract of land was a vacant island surrounded by business buildings. It was zoned for parking. As such it remained in use as a parking lot for twenty-five years, although its value for office building use would be much greater. The ordinance was held invalid as applied to this land. *Vernon Park Realty v. City of Mount Vernon,* 307 N.Y. 493, 121 NE2d 517 (1954). As to this land the ordinance was *confiscatory.* Such well-located property would normally be developed in much less than twenty-five years. While a zoning ordinance need not zone property for its *highest* and *best use* (a phrase invented by land appraisers), this is a factor to be considered. Moreover an unspoken factor here is that cities often provide municipal parking lots and here, in effect, the city is forcing the landowner to furnish a *public* service. The land is reasonably adapted to office-building use. No reason can be given why it was not so zoned. Certainly its use for this purpose would be compatible with existing uses.

EXAMPLE: The land in question was zoned for residential use. For twenty years it remained vacant. During that period, development was totally stagnant. The only buildings in the area were a cow stable, a dairy farm, and a city incinerator. The property was worthless for residential purposes. The court held that the zoning was invalid as applied to the land. *Arverne Bay Cons. Co.* v. *Thatcher,* 278 N.Y. 222, 15 NE2d 587 (1938).

7. The relative gain to the public as compared to the hardship imposed on the landowner.

EXAMPLE: Some of the examples given above illustrate this principle aptly. Indeed, the example last given is an excellent illustration.

8. A city cannot validly zone private land for what are essentially public purposes.

EXAMPLE: City rezoned certain land for school purposes. *City of Plainfield* v. *Borough of Middlesex,* 69 N.J.S. 136, 173 A2d 785 (1961). City rezoned certain land as a wildlife preserve. *Morris Co. Land Imp. Co.* v. *Parsippany-Troy Hills Twp.,* 40 N.J. 539, 193 A2d 232 (1963). Both ordinances are invalid as applied.

9. Other factors are considered. If a city has planned the area carefully, a court will be hesitant to disturb the plan by forcing it to accept a use that disturbs the plan. If the city has been lax in enforcing its zoning law, it is likely to lose its zoning battles.

30.04(b)   Validity—Reasonableness as a Test

In recent times, much of the technical verbiage of the older cases has disappeared. The real test of the validity of zoning is its *reasonableness.* Disregard "taking property," "confiscatory zoning," and instead ask the question: Is the zoning totally unreasonable? An ordinance requiring all building lots in Manhattan to be of a minimum size of one hundred acres would be totally unrealistic. Our forefathers gave our legislatures the police power, that is, the power to pass laws, but not to act indiscriminately. If the regulation is totally unreasonable as applied to particular land, it is invalid. *Fred F. French Inv. Co.* v. *City of N.Y.,* 39 NY2d 587, 350 NE2d 381 (1976). Viewed in this light, the task of the courts becomes a good deal simpler and a good deal more sensible. When a court holds that a particular zoning decision is invalid *as applied* to a particular tract of land, it is holding that *in the circumstances* the zoning is unreasonable.

30.04(c)   Validity—Federal Courts' Role

As has been stated, this country has a federal Constitution. In determining whether a zoning law or local activity violates the federal Constitution, the United States Supreme Court has the final word. However, even if that court should hold that the federal Constitution has not been violated, that decision is of minor consequence in zoning law. Each state has its own constitution. What *that* constitution permits is determined by the *state courts.* Thus, an ordinance held "valid" by the Supreme Court is valid only so far as federal law is concerned. The State Supreme Court may hold the very same ordinance *invalid* as a violation of the *state constitution,* which becomes the final and binding decision. The federal court decisions get the headlines, but, in point of fact, they are of relatively minor importance. The United States Supreme Court has tended to ignore zoning altogether and, when it chooses to decide a zoning case, it takes such a liberal view that land developers have little to fear from the federal courts. Thus, it has been said that, "the exercise of sound discretion does not, of course, always require a slavish adherence to federal constitutional minimums." *State* v. *Smith,* 347 A2d 816 (N.J.). The United States Supreme Court has, in fact, encouraged the state courts to exercise their independence. *Oregon* v. *Hass,* 420 U.S. 714, 719, 46 L. Ed. 2d 313 (1975).

30.04(d)   Validity—Judgment Declaring Zoning Invalid

It is commonplace, of course, for a landowner to file a suit to have zoning declared invalid as to his land. Suppose he wins. The court must then make a further decision. (1) It can declare the zoning invalid as to the land and go no further. The land is then unzoned. A factory could be built. (2) Or suppose the landowner wants to erect an apartment. The court can rezone the land for apartment use. Purists dislike this approach. Zoning and rezoning are jobs for the legislature. (3) Or the court can send the case back to the city with an order that the land be rezoned. *Zaagman* v. *City of Kenwood,* 223 NW2d 146 (Mich. 1975); 25 S.D.L. Rev. 116.

30.05   Rezoning—Referendum

The Supreme Court has held that the federal Constitution is not violated by making rezoning subject to referendum approval by the people of the municipality. *City of Eastlake* v. *Forest City Enterprises, Inc.,* 416 U.S. 668, 96 S.Ct. 2358, 2361 (1976). This leaves the state courts free to deal with this problem as they choose. Some courts will follow the Supreme Court's view that this is simply returning power to the people. Other courts will hold the referendum device illegal.

> REFERENCES: 10 Akron L. Rev. 557 (1977); 28 Case W. L. Rev. 41 (1977); 82 Dick. L. Rev. 99 (1977); 23 Loyola L. Rev. 243 (1977); 91 Harv. L. Rev. 1528; 55 N.C.L. Rev. 517 (1977); 5 Fordham Urb. L. J. 141; 72 ALR3d 1030.

30.06   Zoning Exactions

The subject of *forced dedication,* whereby the municipality approves a plat only if the developer agrees to exactions of some sort, donation of land to the public, for example, occurs in connection with plat approval. See §27.04 *et seq.* Some municipalities make the same kind of exactions a condition to granting rezoning or a zoning variance or special exception.

This, predictably, will receive a mixed response in the courts. Most decisions will be favorable if the exaction is reasonable in the circumstances. *Sommers* v. *City of Los Angeles,* 62 Cal. Reptr. 523 (1967); *Board of Education* v. *Surety Developer,* 63 Ill.2d 193, 347 NE2d 149 (1975). *Unreasonable* exactions are a sneaky way of blocking development. They are invalid. *James City & County* v. *Rowe,* 216 Va. 128, 216 SE2d 199 (1975).

30.06(a)   Senior Citizens

It has been held to be unlawful to zone out senior citizens. *Shepard* v. *Woodland Twp. Planning Bd.,* 128 N.J. Super. 379, 320 A2d 191 (1974). It has also been held invalid in some states to limit occupancy to senior citizens.

> **NEW DIRECTIONS:**   The better modern rule is that a municipality may limit a particular residential zone to senior citizens. Their needs, curb ramps for wheelchairs, for example, are largely peculiar to the elderly. They need a zone that caters to their needs. *Taxpayers Assn.* v. *Weymouth Tp.,* 71 N.J. 249, 364 A2d 1016 (1976); *Hinman* v. *Planning and Zoning Comm.,* 26 Conn. Supp. 125, 214 A2d 131 (1965); *Maldini* v. *Ambro,* 36 N.Y. 481, 33 NE2d 403 (1975).

> REFERENCES: 31 Ark. L. Rev. 707 (1978); 5 Fla. St. U. L. Rev. 423 (1977); 76 Mich. L. Rev. 64 (1977); 6 Urb. Law. 685; 83 ALR3d 1084, 1103.

30.06(b)   Children

Zoning that restricts units available to families with children has been held invalid. *Duggan* v. *County of Cook,* 60 Ill. App.2d 107, 324 NE2d 406 (1975); *Malino* v. *Mayor of Glassboro,* 116 N.J. Super. 195, 281 A2d 401 (N.J. 1971); 24 De Paul L. Rev. 784 (1975). Ultimately, this law will have to be reconciled with the decisions sanctioning communities for senior citizens only.

30.06(c)   Churches

It is well established that a zoning ordinance must not exclude churches or synagogues from residential districts. 74 ALR2d 377.

30.06(d)   Schools

Public schools, of course, are not subject to zoning ordinances. *Hall* v. *City of Taft,* 47 Cal.2d 177, 302 P2d 574 (1956). The only controversy, then, relates to *private* schools. The courts are not in agreement on this question. The more general view is that private schools, like churches, cannot be excluded from residential areas. *Roman Catholic Welfare Corp.* v. *City of Piedmont,* 45 Cal.2d 32, 289 P2d 438 (1955). 11 *Miami L. Q.* 68.

30.07   Prohibitory Zoning

Two techniques are available when a village wishes to exclude unwanted uses, such as oil drilling. For example, the zoning ordinance may explicitly prohibit drilling for oil or extraction of minerals. 10 ALR3d 1241. Whether the exclusion will stand up depends on the circumstances surrounding the particular tract of land.

> **EXAMPLE:**   A landowner whose land adjoined the city dump applied for re-zoning that would permit oil drilling. Refusal of rezoning was held invalid *as applied* to this land. How could oil drilling possibly debase an area next to the city dump? 10 ALR3d 1241.

> **EXAMPLE:**   A landowner applied for rezoning to permit oil drilling. His land was so close to the city water well that it created danger of contamination. Refusal of rezoning was sustained *as applied*. 10 ALR3d 1241.

As can be seen in both examples, the court considered the validity of the zoning *as applied* to the particular tract of land.

Another technique simply fails to provide a home in the ordinance for the unwanted uses. *Hohl* v. *Leadington*, 37 N.J.L. 271, 181 A2d 150 (1962); *Wiley* v. *County of Hanover*, 163 SE2d 160 (Va. 1968). The result is the same regardless of the technique involved.

30.08   Development Control Zoning—Sewer, Water, and School Problems—Downzoning

In many cases villages have refused to rezone single-family zones to apartments or other such uses and have given as a reason the shortage of sewer, water, or school facilities. Or the village may engage in *downzoning*.

> **EXAMPLE:**   The village rezoned *A's* land from multifamily dwelling to a single-family dwelling because it lacked sewer facilities. This was held invalid. *West-wood Estates* v. *Village of South Nyack*, 23 NY2d 424, 244 NE2d 700 (1969). To like effect are *Appeal of Gersh*, 437 Pa. 237, 263 A2d 395 (1970) and *McGibbon* v. *Board of Appeals*, 340 NE2d 487 (Mass. 1976).

> **EXAMPLE:**   The town increased minimum lot size from 35,000 square feet to three acres and six acres because of lack of sewer facilities. The court upheld the ordinance but admonished the city that the change must be temporary only. *Steel Hill Development Inc.* v. *Town of Sanbornton*, 469 F2d 956 (1972). This is also *downzoning*.

It can be seen from the examples given that the efforts of some villages are bent toward holding the population stable, keeping things "as they are now," barring developers who bring in a new, unwanted population. And yet, at times, a genuine health problem or school problem exists. The cases, of course, are in utter confusion.

EXAMPLE: Downzoning by rezoning commercial to residential has been sustained. *Shelburne Inc.* v. *Conner,* 315 A2d 620 (Del. Ch. 1974). But rezoning of a single block to "zone out" apartments has been rejected as "spot zoning," *G. & D. Holland Const. Co.* v. *City of Maryville,* 12 Cal. App.2d 989, 91 Cal. Reptr. 227 (1970).

EXAMPLE: The desire of the villagers to keep the village rural does not justify increasing the minimum lot area from one to two acres and the minimum lot frontage from 100 to 200 feet. *Kavenesky* v. *Zoning Board,* 160 Conn. 397, 279 A2d 567 (1971); *Oakwood at Madison, Inc.* v. *Twp. of Madison,* 283 A2d 353 (N.J. 1971).

See 31 Hastings L.J. 103; 5 R.E.L.J. 311.

The situation seems to break down into several sharply conflicting points of view, namely: (1) the village cannot use its shortage of facilities as an excuse for refusal to grant proper rezoning, *Appeal of Kit Mar Builders Inc.,* 439 Pa. 466, 268 A2d 765 (1970); (2) the shortage in facilities is one factor that may be considered in refusing rezoning to the developer, *Adams* v. *Reed,* 123 So2d 606 (Miss. 1960); (3) the village may impose a zoning freeze of *limited* duration so long as it has a program for correcting the problem.

As can be seen, blanket, haphazard, unplanned restrictions, especially those of indefinite duration, are likely to be held invalid. However, if the development control zoning is carefully planned and is limited in time, it will be sustained by the courts.

NEW DIRECTIONS: The town of X adopts a zoning amendment under which erection of homes by a merchant builder would require a special permit. The standards for the issuance of special permits are framed in terms of the availability to the proposed subdivision of five essential facilities or services, specifically: (1) public sanitary sewers or approved substitutes; (2) drainage facilities; (3) improved public parks or recreation facilities, including public schools; (4) state, county, or town roads (major, secondary, or collector); and (5) firehouses. No special permit issues unless the proposed residential development has accumulated fifteen development points, to be computed on a sliding scale of values assigned to the specified improvements under the statute. Subdivision is thus a function of immediate availability to the proposed plat of certain municipal improvements, the avowed purpose of the amendments being to phase residential development to the town's ability to provide the above facilities or services. This was held valid. *Golden* v. *Planning Board of Town of Ramapo,* 30 NY2d 359, 285 NE2d 291 (1972). This is a celebrated case, and the technique has been used in many areas. This is *phased development zoning.*

A number of factors are to be considered. Perhaps the most important factor is one rarely mentioned in the court cases, namely, the suburbs want to stay the way they have been. They wish to exclude newcomers.

All one can say is that the trend seems to be toward the rule that these real or fancied shortages may enable a village to declare a brief moratorium on development, but sooner or later land that is suitable only for homes will be developed for homes. The villages cannot block this indefinitely.

REFERENCES: The problem of phased development or "sequential controls" is discussed at length in Freilich and Ragsdale, *Timing and Sequential Controls*, 58 Minn. L. Rev. 1009 (1974). See also Note, *Ramapo Township's Time Controls*, 47 N.Y. U. L. Rev. 724 (1972). See Ch. 27.

30.09   Downzoning

At times a village will rezone land from a high-value use, such as commercial, to a low-value use, such as homes. This is *downzoning*.

30.10   Bulk Zoning

Bulk zoning is zoning that regulates the size and shape of the buildings to be erected and their location on the land. The purpose of this type of zoning is to control population density, open space, and access to daylight and air. The ordinance requires that any building erected must leave specified areas along the front, side, and rear of the lot which must not be built upon.

30.11   Single-family Zones

It is axiomatic that in single-family zones only one house per lot occupied by a single family will be permitted. But as times change, customs change. Many couples choose to live together today without marrying. So the zoning definition of a "single family" has tended to change. Thus the area of controversy.

The family is perhaps the most revered institution in American life. Hence any ordinance that forbids members of the same family to live together is invalid.

> **EXAMPLE:**   A grandmother cannot be prohibited from living with her grandson. A brother and sister must be allowed to live together. Zoning cannot slice into the family itself. *Moore* v. *City of East Cleveland*, 97 S.Ct. 1932, 52 L.Ed.2d 531 (1977). As an example, when a family's breadwinner dies, the broader family comes together for mutual assistance. The law cannot forbid this. The law protects the extended family.

Litigation involving single-family zoning ordinances is common. Although there appear to be almost endless differences in the language used in these ordinances, they contain three principal types of restrictions. First, they define the kind of structure that may be erected on vacant land. Second, they require that a single-family home be occupied only by a "single housekeeping unit." Third, they often require that the housekeeping unit be made up of persons related by blood, adoption, or marriage, with certain limited exceptions. Although the legitimacy of the first two types of restrictions is well settled, attempts to limit occupancy to related persons have not been successful. The state courts have recognized a valid community interest in preserving the stable character of residential neighborhoods that justifies a prohibition against transient occupancy. Nevertheless, in well-reasoned opinions, the courts of Illinois, New York, New Jersey, California, Connecticut, Wisconsin, and other jurisdictions have permitted unrelated persons to occupy single-family residences notwithstanding the existence of an ordinance prohibiting, either expressly or implicitly, such occupancy. *Moore* v. *City of East Cleveland,* 52 L.Ed.2d 531 (1977).

> **EXAMPLE:** Such ordinances must not forbid unrelated widows—widowers, spinsters, or bachelors—from living together to share expenses. *State* v. *Baker,* 81 N.J. 99, 405 A2d 368 (1978).

As will be seen, groups of mentally retarded persons or orphans must be permitted to live in single-family homes.

30.12 Apartments

The leading case on zoning held that apartments may be excluded from single-family dwelling zones. *Village of Euclid* v. *Ambler Realty Co.,* 272 U.S. 365 (1926). The state courts have followed a like rule.

> **EXCEPTION:** A tract of land can be so located that *as applied* to that tract single-family zoning would be invalid, for example, a single lot located in a single-family zone between two large nonconforming use apartments.

30.13 Accessory Uses

Every zoning ordinance recognizes that certain uses different from, but incidental to, the main use prescribed in the zone are normal. Such uses are legalized under the name *accessory uses.* Many accessory uses are found in residential zones.

> **EXAMPLES:** Coin-operated washing machines and dryers in apartment buildings; also, pay telephones, beverage vending machines, postage vending machines, swimming pools, and skating rinks for which a charge is made are accessory uses. *Newark* v. *Daly,* 85 N.J.S. 55, 205 A2d 459 (1964). Likewise, a food shop in a large apartment hotel is often permitted. A private garage on the rear of a residential lot is universally permitted. A doctor expects to see patients in his home even though he lives in a residential area.

30.14 Performance Standards

Industrial zoning poses special problems. Older ordinances contain lengthy laundry lists of permitted uses. Modern ordinances tend to list standards that must be complied with concerning noise, glare, smoke, toxic matter, flammable matter, explosive materials, radioactive matter, and so on. Any use that complies is permitted.

30.15   Incentive Zoning

A rather recent development in zoning law is incentive zoning. This is a type of zoning calculated to induce the landowner to introduce amenities the city deems desirable. This type of zoning employs the floor area ratio concept (FAR).

> **EXAMPLE:** The floor area ratio of a building is the ratio which the floor area within the building bears to the area of the lot occupied by the building. For example, a building occupying 40,000 square feet of lot area in a zone allowing an FAR of 10:1 could have 400,000 square feet of total floor area in all the stories of the building. But if, for example, the building is located in San Francisco, an FAR bonus is given if the building affords direct access to the rapid transit system, and in such case it would be allowed additional square feet of floor area. 21 Syracuse L. Rev. 895. In short, FAR establishes a relationship between total land area and total floor space. Under a FAR regulation of 1:1, a developer could build a one-story structure covering the whole lot, a two-story structure covering half of the lot, or a four-story structure covering a quarter of the lot. Bartke & Lamb, *Upzoning,* 17 William & Mary L. Rev. 701, 705.

An extremely imaginative type of incentive zoning was developed in connection with the Lincoln Center for Performing Arts in New York City. The district zoning permitted developers 20 percent more floor space on provision of certain amenities, notably, pedestrian malls, galleries, covered plazas, and pedestrian-oriented circulation improvements. Elliott & Marcus, *From Euclid to Ramapo: New Directions in Land Development Controls,* 1 Hofstra L. Rev. 56. See also 21 Syracuse L. Rev. 895; 17 Wm. & Mary L. Rev. 701.

30.16   Change of Neighborhood

A change of neighborhood may invalidate existing zoning. *Manger* v. *City of Chicago,* 257 NE2d 473 (Ill. 1970).

> **EXAMPLE:** In an area zoned single-family the authorities made no effort to enforce the zoning. Stores crept in everywhere so that the few remaining vacant lots were surrounded by stores and were totally unfit for residential use. The area had become a business area. The village must permit stores on the vacant lots. *Scott* v. *Springfield,* 83 Ill. App.2d 31, 226 NE2d 57 (1967); *Vigilant Investors Corp.* v. *Hempstead,* 34 App. Div.2d 990; 312 NYS2d 1022 (1970).

The same result occurs where the city affirmatively causes the situation.

> **EXAMPLE:** The city fathers handed out variances so liberally that nonconforming stores in the area were allowed to expand all over the area. The few remaining lots cannot be held to single-family dwelling use. *Metrop. Bd. of Zoning Appeal* v. *Sheehan Const. Co.,* 313 NE2d 78 (Ind. 1974).

30.17 Nonconforming Uses

All zoning ordinances make some provision for continuation of nonconforming uses.

> **EXAMPLE:** To invalidate an existing store use in a residential area would be unconstitutional deprivation of property. This is a simple proposition.

There is a second type of problem involved here.

> **EXAMPLE:** An area is zoned for multifamily dwellings. A developer buys it and obtains a permit to construct an apartment. The neighbors become aware of the situation and persuade the village to rezone the area to single-family dwellings. *If construction has not yet begun,* there is, as yet, most courts say, no nonconforming use. Perhaps the developer can attack the new zoning on other grounds, but not on the ground that he has a nonconforming use.

Virtually all courts agree that *if construction has begun* under a valid permit, nonconforming use status has been achieved and construction may be completed even though the zoning is amended after commencement of construction and forbids erection of such a structure. *Lutz* v. *New Albany City Plan Comm.,* 101 NE2d 187 (Ind. 1951). The construction must be done in good faith and not hastily, simply to obtain nonconforming use status. In New York the construction must be substantial. *Reichenbach* v. *Windward at Southhampton,* 364 NYS2d 283 (1975).

A generous court has accorded nonconforming use status after a permit has been issued, survey made, site cleared, and ground leveled. *Griffin* v. *Martin County,* 157 Cal. App.2d 507, 321 P2d 148 (1958). Some courts have held that nonconforming use status was not attained where permit was issued, building plans made, and construction mortgage signed. *Paramount Rock Co.* v. *County of San Diego,* 40 Cal. Reptr. 74, 180 Cal. App.2d 217. *Contra: Hull* v. *Hunt,* 55 Wash.2d 492, 331 P2d 856 (1959).

This is one of the battling grounds of zoning law. All courts agree that constitutions protect only *vested rights.* They disagree on *when* rights vest. As can be seen, there are several points in time a court can choose:

1. Rights vest when a landowner has spent money planning construction in good faith even *before* a permit has issued.
2. No rights vest *until* a permit issues.
3. Some construction must take place *after* the permit issues.

A landowner who has achieved nonconforming use status need not apply to the city or take other affirmative action. The ordinance says that nonconforming uses are protected. Nothing else need be done. Rights are *vested,* that is, beyond attack by the city. The landowner need not apply for a variance or seek other confirmation of his rights.

An aspect of this problem is discussed further in § 30.18.

Zoning ordinances, in permitting nonconforming uses, permit ordinary repairs to be made, but they sometimes forbid *structural alterations* of a nonconforming building. A structural alteration is such as would change the physical structure of the building or would change an old building in such a way as to convert it into a new or substantially different structure.

> **EXAMPLE:**   A operated a milk plant which was a nonconforming use in a residential zone. His attempt to replace decayed wooden walls with brick walls was a prohibited structural alteration. *Selligman v. Von Allmen Bros. Inc.,* 297 Ky. 121, 179 SW2d 207 (1944). 87 ALR2d 99.

Nonconforming uses, it is felt, should be gradually eliminated. *Cole* v. *City of Battle Creek,* 298 Mich. 98, 298 NW 466 (1941). The theory is that zoning seeks to safeguard the future in the expectation that time will repair the mistakes of the past. However, the treatment a particular nonconforming use will receive if it seeks to increase or change its use appears to vary considerably owing to differences in zoning ordinances. 87 ALR2d 4.

Once a nonconforming owner abandons the use of his property for a nonconforming purpose, he loses his right to make a nonconforming use of the property and must thereafter use it only in conformity with the uses allowed to other properties in the neighborhood. Were the law otherwise, an owner could keep his property in a nonconforming class forever.

> **EXAMPLE:**   The owner of a nonconforming slaughterhouse took down the smokestack and definitely discontinued the slaughterhouse business. He thereby lost his right to make a nonconforming use. *Beyer v. Mayor of Baltimore,* 182 Md. 444, 34 A2d 765 (1943). Also where an old nonconforming house trailer was sought to be replaced by a new one, the change was refused because the old use had been abandoned. *Town of Windham* v. *Sprague,* 219 A2d 548 (Maine 1966).

But a mere temporary discontinuance of the nonconforming use, as when a landowner is temporarily unable to procure a tenant, will not constitute an abandonment of the right to resume such use. *Landay* v. *MacWilliams,* 173 Md. 460, 196 Atl. 293 (1938); 114 ALR 993.

If a nonconforming building is either fully or partially destroyed by fire or other casualty, many ordinances forbid rebuilding.

Recently, ordinances have been passed that attempt to place a time limit on the right to continue a nonconforming use. To the extent that the *amortization ordinances* prohibit continuance of the nonconforming use after the useful economic life of the building has come to an end, most courts would consider them valid. 42 ALR2d 1146.

The rule of invalidity *as applied* is, as one might expect, applied to amortization of nonconforming uses. Thus the court must consider: (1) the nature of the surrounding neighborhood to determine whether discontinuance of the use will have any beneficial impact and to determine if the nonconforming use, in fact, conforms to other nearby use; (2) the value and condition of the improvements on the premises to determine the quantum of damage if use is discontinued; (3)

the cost of relocation and all other costs of relocating the business; (4) whether the time allowed permits the landowner to make plans for the future of his business. *Harbison* v. *City of Buffalo,* 4 NY2d 553, 152 NE2d 42, 176 NYS2d 598 (1958).

30.18   Amendments to Zoning Ordinances—During the Permit Period

Under pressure from unhappy neighbors, a city may seek to amend its ordinance at the time a landowner is applying for a permit to build a building the neighbors find objectionable.

> **EXAMPLE:**   After *X* had applied for a permit to build a building that complied with a zoning set back line of 24 feet, the city passed an amendment changing the setback to 49 feet. The court sustained refusal of the permit. *Builders Const. Co.* v. *Daly,* 10 N.J. Misc. 861, 161 Atl. 189 (1932). Until construction begins, the property has not achieved status as a *nonconforming use.*

However, in other states courts will strike down an eleventh-hour attempt to block construction where a landowner has in good faith made plans and applied for a permit in reliance on an existing ordinance. These same courts, however, may sanction the refusal of a permit where the landowner is attempting to rush through a permit in the knowledge that the city is working on an amendment that would block the intended construction, *CT&TCo.* v. *Village of Palatine,* 22 Ill. App.2d 264, 160 NE2d 697 (1959). Note, Ex post facto zoning, 1971 *Urban Law Annual* 63.

If a landowner receives a building permit and commences substantial construction in reliance thereon, the city cannot amend the ordinance so as to block the construction described in the permit. *Prescault* v. *Wheel,* 132 Vt. 247, 315 A2d 244 (1974). Basic fairness is becoming the test.

> **EXAMPLE:**   *X* applied for and received a permit to build an apartment. He graded, excavated, and put in a foundation. The city then attempted to rezone the area to exclude apartments. *X* can go forward with his building. *Deer Park Civic Assn.* v. *City of Chicago,* 347 Ill. App. 346, 106 NE2d 823 (1952).

When the courts want to protect the landowner, they say his rights have *vested,* or the city is *estopped* to amend its ordinance. 50 ALR3d 596; 49 *id.* 13; 49 *id.* 1150.

30.18(a)   Amendments and Rezoning—Spot Zoning

Amendments to the zoning ordinance are constantly being sought by landowners whose land will thereby become more valuable. For example, land is more valuable for industrial or commercial purposes than it is for residential purposes, so rezoning of residential land for industrial purposes will greatly increase its value. Some of such rezoning is invalid. Particularly objectionable is *spot zoning,* where the city, by amendment of its ordinances, singles out and reclassifies one piece of property in a particular zone without any apparent basis for such distinction. 51 ALR2d 267; 48 Ore. L. Rev. 245.

> **EXAMPLE:** A zoning ordinance was amended to permit construction of a mortuary in a residential district. This was held invalid as spot zoning. *Mueller* v. *Hoffmeister Undertaking Co.,* 343 Mo. 430, 121 SW2d 775 (1938). 51 ALR2d 263.

Spot zoning rules. The following are some of the circumstances that will validate rezoning that, on the surface, appears to be "spot zoning."

> **EXAMPLE:** A large area was rezoned for shopping center purposes because it was at the hub of a natural traffic concentration pattern. *Temmink* v. *Baltimore County,* 205 Md. 489, 109 A2d 85 (1954). Traffic is the key to this problem. The same approach is applicable to supermarkets. *State* v. *East Cleveland,* 169 Ohio St. 375, 160 NE2d 1 (1959).

> **EXAMPLE:** Zoning of all four corner lots in a large residential district for commercial uses. Here the need for service business in a residential area is the key. *Marshall* v. *Salt Lake City,* 105 Utah 111, 141 P2d 704 (1943).

> **EXAMPLE:** Rezoning to permit apartments in an area of older homes, thus increasing tax revenues of city. *Rodgers* v. *Village of Tarrytown,* 302 N.Y. 115 (1951).

As can be seen, illegal spot zoning is basically a reclassification of a small area in such a manner as to disturb the surrounding neighborhood. It is a discordant and unneeded use. None of the examples fall in this category.

Where a real *change* in circumstances has taken place since the original ordinance was passed, an amendment that conforms the ordinance to the new circumstances will be valid.

> **EXAMPLE:** At the time the original zoning ordinance was adopted, the only structure in an area zoned industrial was a factory. Thereafter, many single-family residences were built in the area, but no new factories. To protect the homeowners, the area was rezoned for residential purposes, the old factory remaining as a nonconforming use. This is valid rezoning. *Atlantic Coast Line R.R. Co.* v. *Jacksonville,* 68 So2d 570 (Fla. 1953).

> **EXAMPLE:** Where an urban redevelopment displaced many families, creating a need for many units to house those displaced, a single-family dwelling zone could be revised to permit apartments. *Malafronte* v. *Planning Board,* 230 A2d 606 (Conn. 1967).

> **EXAMPLE:** *X* owned an area that was zoned commercial. A large city park was opened across the street. The city rezoned the area for apartments. This change in circumstances makes the rezoning valid. *People ex rel* v. *City of Chicago,* 2 Ill.2d 350, 118 NE2d 20 (1954).

Or where the original zoning was a *mistake* the city can in most states correct the error.

> **EXAMPLE:** A lot that was unsuitable, because of topography and soil conditions, for single-family dwellings was included in a single-family dwelling zone. To correct this error, the lot was rezoned for apartments. This is valid. *Eggebeen v. Sonnenburg,* 239 Wis. 213, 1 NW2d 84 (1941).

30.18(b)   Zoning—Amendments—Reliance Rule

In a number of states the rule is followed that protection ought to be given by the courts to those who bought land in reliance on existing zoning and that zoning must not be changed unless some change in neighborhood has taken place. *Northern Trust Co.* v. *Chicago,* 4 Ill.2d 432, 123 NE2d 330 (1954). 91 Harv. L. Rev. 1494.

> **EXAMPLE:** An area is built up with homes. There are a few scattered lots. One lot owner has his lot rezoned for apartments. The courts will invalidate this rezoning.

30.18(c)   Amendments—Conditional

At times a city has rezoned land with a condition in the ordinance that a certain type of building would be erected. Older decisions frowned on this. Cities, they said, should not bargain for legislation.

> **NEW DIRECTIONS:** Recent decisions sustain conditional amendments.

> **EXAMPLE:** A zoning amendment was granted on condition that the land be used for a synthetic gas production plant. It was held valid. *Goffinet* v. *Christian County,* 65 Ill.2d 40, 357 NE2d 442 (1976); 70 ALR3d 125. This is simply a matter of contract zoning now. As this grows more common, villages will be better able to control the quality of new construction. Of course, there will be decisions still that resist the idea. *Ziemer* v. *County of Peoria,* 33 Ill. App.3d 612, 338 NE2d 145 (1975).

Where the landowner fails to meet the conditions, the village may return to the original zoning.

> **EXAMPLE:** The village rezoned residential to industrial on condition that the property be improved with an industrial plant. He failed to comply. The village zoned the land back to residential. *McGowan* v. *Cohalan,* 361 NE2d 1025 (N.Y. 1971).

The problem here resembles the problem created by contract zoning. See § 30.24.

30.18(d)   Amendments—Rezoning Procedure

When a municipality passes an ordinance of general application, such as a law fixing a maximum speed limit, ordinarily this does not require notice to anyone unless some state law requires it. However, where *rezoning* of a tract of land is involved, that is, amending the zoning ordinance or the zoning map, the latest court decisions regard this more in the nature of a lawsuit between the owner of the land and his neighbors. Of course, every lawsuit requires notice to the landowners affected and gives them an opportunity to be heard. Progressive courts have held that as a matter of constitutional law an ordinance rezoning land requires notice to the neighbors and an opportunity to state their objections. *Fasano* v. *Board of Commissioners,* 264 Oreg. 575, 507 P2d 23 (1973); *Snyder* v. *City of Lakewood,* 592 P2d 371 (Colo. 1975); *Fleming* v. *City of Tacoma,* 81 Wash.2d 292, 502 P2d 331 (1972); *West* v. *City of Portage,* 221 NW2d 303 (Mich. 1974).

> **EXAMPLE:** In an area zoned single-family and improved largely by residences, one landowner proposes that the city rezone his land to multifamily. His neighbors must be given notice, and a hearing must be held. Many ordinances routinely provide for such notice and hearing. And the notice given must be a reasonable notice.

> **EXAMPLE:** A zoning ordinance provided that the zoning ordinance could be amended by publication of notice in a newspaper. This is invalid. Neighboring landowners can easily be found and given notice by name and by mailing. *American Oil Corp.* v. *City of Chicago,* 331 NE2d 67 (Ill. 1975). The rule is that rational planning prior to zoning change also requires such planning to precede the granting of a special exception or variance. *Kristenson* v. *City of Eugene Planning Comm.,* 544 P2d 591 (Ore. 1976). Listening to the neighbors helps the authorities to make a rational decision.

> **EXAMPLE:** There was a failure to give proper notice as required by the ordinance. The rezoning was held invalid. *Jarvis Acres, Inc.* v. *Zoning Comm.* 163 Conn. 44, 301 A2d 244 (Conn. 1972).

However, the great majority of the courts continue to treat rezoning as a legislative process. This means that there is no *judicial* requirement that neighbors be given notice and an opportunity to be heard before rezoning takes place. *State* v. *City of Rochester,* 268 NW2d 885 (Minn. 1978).

> REFERENCES: 73 Mich. L. Rev. 1341; 75 Mich. L. Rev. 983 (1977); 12 Willamette L. J. 45 (1975).

30.19   Variances

Even the best ordinance may cause unintentional hardship to particular tracts of land. Some elasticity is needed if these hardship cases are to be dealt with. Most ordinances create a board, usually called the *board of adjustment* or *board of appeals,* which is given the power to authorize individual property owners to deviate from the terms of the ordinances where literal compliance would cause *undue hardship or practical difficulties.* This authorization is called a *variance.* The courts have worked out a number of requirements that must be met if a variance is to be granted.

1. The hardship must be special and peculiar to the particular property.

EXAMPLE: A lot is so irregular in shape that if all the front, rear, and the side line restrictions were observed, no building at all could be built on the lot.

If the hardship complained of is a condition which affects all property in the district, the hardship is not special and peculiar to any lot in the area and no individual lot owner will be granted a variance.

EXAMPLE: Foul odors from a nearby industrial area exist in an area zoned as residential. No residential lot owner will be granted a variance to build a factory. A plea must be made to the authorities to amend the ordinance.

2. Hardship means that if the landowner complies with the provisions of the ordinance, he can secure no reasonable return from, or make no reasonable use of, his property. 29 N.C.L. Rev. 250. With respect to income property, a party seeking a variance must prove that the land in question, if devoted to its existing or any permitted use, will not yield a reasonable return. This involves a detailed showing of the price paid for the property, the taxes assessed, expenses of operation, annual income, and so on. Then if the net income earned is not a reasonable return on the amount invested, hardship is shown. *Crossroads Recreation* v. *Broz,* 4 NY2d 39, 149 NE2d 65 (1958). The landowner should also show that reasonable return cannot be anticipated from other permitted uses. *Forrest* v. *Evershed,* 7 NY2d 256, 164 NE2d 841 (1959). The fact that a man could make more money by devoting his property to another purpose is not legal hardship. Everyone knows that land is worth more for commercial or industrial purposes than it is for residential, and yet most of our land must necessarily be zoned residential.

3. The hardship must not be self-created.

EXAMPLE: A departs from the plans attached to his application for a building permit and builds his home five feet closer to the side lines of his lot than the ordinance allows. When the building inspector stops him, A applies for a variance. He will not get it.

EXAMPLE: The city in question has an ordinance specifying a minimum lot area. A owns a building on a legal size lot. He then sells the building and enough of the land so that the building still occupies a legal building site. However, the portion of the lot left to A is now less than legal size. He will not be given a variance to permit him to build. *Board of Zoning Appeals* v. *Waskelo,* 240 Ind. 594, 168 NE2d 72 (1960).

4. The proposed new use must not change the essential character of the neighborhood. It must be consistent with the general plan of the ordinance.

EXAMPLE: A variance will not be granted to permit introduction of a cemetery into an area zoned residential.

Some courts are so strict on this point that they will not allow a variance that changes the *use* permitted by the ordinance. In other words, they will allow deviation only from the area, height, and location regulations of the ordinance.

> **EXAMPLE:** Some courts will not permit a variance for an apartment house in a single-family area because this would be a *use* variance. *Lee* v. *Board of Adjustment,* 226 N.C. 107, 37 SE2d 128 (1946); 168 ALR 1.

However, most courts will permit a use variance where the hardship is great.

> **EXAMPLE:** A owns a vacant lot in a single-family dwelling zone, and nonconforming apartment building are his neighbors on both sides, that is, these buildings were built before the ordinance was passed and are allowed to continue in operation. He will be given a variance for the erection of an apartment building. The sound reason for this variance is that no one can be induced to build a single-family dwelling on such a building site.

In granting a variance, the zoning board may impose conditions. *Vlahos* v. *Little Boar's Head District,* 101 N.H. 460, 146 A2d 257 (1958); *Zweifel Mfg. Co.* v. *Peoria,* 11 Ill.2d 489, 144 NE2d 593 (1957); 49 ALR3d 492.

> **EXAMPLE:** The board may put in a condition that the architecture of the permitted building conform to the architecture of neighboring structures, or that certain areas be left open and landscaped.

A variance may be limited in time.

> **EXAMPLE:** A variance given for five years is valid. *Bringle* v. *Board of Supervisors,* 4 Cal. Reptr. 493, 351 P2d 765 (1960).

Questions may arise as to who may apply for a variance. Clearly the landowner may do so. A contract purchaser is also qualified. However, one who is merely negotiating for the purchase of the land cannot apply for a variance.

The larger the tract of land involved, the greater the likelihood a variance will be held invalid. *Topanga Assn.* v. *County of Los Angeles,* 113 Cal. Reptr. 836, 522 P2d 12 (1974). Large tracts should be dealt with by amendment.

30.20 Special Exceptions

A common provision in zoning ordinances authorizes the board of appeals to issue special permits for special purposes, such as public utility structures, churches, hospitals, private schools, clubs, or cemeteries. Obviously, institutions of this character must be located somewhere, but some control must be exercised by the zoning authorities over their location so that adverse effects on the other property owners will be held to a minimum. Typically, the ordinance may list a number of different uses that may be licensed "where public convenience and welfare will be substantially served." *Dunham* v. *Zoning Board,* 68 R.I. 88, 26 A2d 614 (1942). The distinction between special exceptions and variances is a technical one. In the case of variances, the board is given authority to authorize violations of the zoning ordinance in hardship cases. In the case of special exceptions, the ordinance itself lists certain cases in which certain special uses are to be permitted, and the board only determines whether facts exist to bring the particular case within the terms of the ordinance. *Stone* v. *Cray,* 89 N.H. 483, 200 Atl. 517 (1938). It is not necessary to show "practical difficulties or unnecessary hardship," as is true in variance cases. *Montgomery County* v. *Merlands Club,* 202 Md. 279, 96 A2d 261 (1953).

In some states the special exception is referred to as a *special use* or *special permit.* In others, it is called a *conditional use.*

30.21   Procedure on Variances and Special Exceptions

A landowner seeking a variance or special exception files a petition with the zoning board. This is not a court. It is an administrative body. It holds hearings like a court, but very informally. Notice of hearing is given neighbors, as required by the ordinance. If the issue is not controversial, as where a landowner wants to locate his carport two or three feet beyond the zoning lines, the hearing is perfunctory. If the landowner wants a special permit to put a gasoline service station in a residential area, a fight may develop, and competing expert witnesses will be called.

In any case, the landowner applies for his permit *before* he begins construction. Starting construction *before* the permit issues may result in an automatic refusal to issue the permit.

> REFERENCE: *Wiltshire* v. *Superior Court,* 218 Cal. Reptr. 199 (1985); 38 ALR3d 1967.

30.22   The Floating Zone

A *floating zone* is a special use district. No specific location is assigned to it in the zoning ordinance. When the need for such a zone arises, the same public body that enacts the zoning ordinance enacts an amendment to the ordinance carving a new zone out of some existing zone. It differs from the special exception in that, at least in the earlier ordinances, a zoning amendment passed by the city council or board of trustees was needed to create a floating zone.

Also in this unique type of zoning amendment, the usual rules applicable to zoning amendments are not applied. For example, in some states, for a valid zoning amendment one must show that a mistake was made in the original zoning ordinance or that the conditions have changed, requiring rezoning. This rule is inapplicable to floating zones. *Haldemann* v. *Board of Commrs.,* 253 Md. 298, 252 A2d 792 (1969).

> **EXAMPLE:**   Cluster housing in a planned unit development is often allowed to float to any part of the village.

There are a number of decisions sustaining the validity of the floating zone. *Rodgers* v. *Village of Tarrytown,* 302 N.Y. 115, 96 NE2d 731 (1951); *Huff* v. *Board of Appeals,* 214 Md. 48, 133 A2d 82 (1957); *Treme* v. *St. Louis County,* 609 SW2d 706 (Mo. 1980); *Cheney* v. *Village 2 at New Hope,* 429 Pa. 626, 241 A2d 81 (1968). There are a few cases to the contrary. *Rudderow* v. *Twp. Committee,* 114 N.J.S. 104, 274 A2d 854 (1971).

If one must hazard a guess as to the future of the floating zone, the conjecture must be that its prospects look bright. The initial hostility of planning officials has been converted to approbation. Mosher, *The Floating Zone: Legal Status and Application to Gasoline Stations,* 1 Tulsa L. J. 149, 156, 166, 167 (1964). The criticism that zoning amendments lend themselves to political influence is not well taken. It is a well-known fact that zoning ordinances traditionally zone large areas for single-family dwellings in the full knowledge that developers will come forward requesting apartment or other zoning, thus giving the authorities an opportunity to "take a look" at the developer and development.

This argument would invalidate all rezoning. Moreover, the antirezoning view can easily be circumvented under modern ordinances by allowing desired uses, such as research laboratories, to "float" into any zone on issuance of a special exception permit. *Summ* v. *Zoning Comm. of the Town of Ridgefield,* 150 Conn. 79, 186 A2d 160 (1962). Indeed, it has been frankly acknowledged that the special exception technique lends itself to the introduction of desirable uses into residential and other districts. *Lazarus* v. *Village of Northbrook,* 31 Ill.2d 146, 199 NE2d 797 (1964). Moreover, conditions may validly be attached to a special exception. *Houdaille Constr. Mats. Inc.* v. *Board of Adjustment,* 92 N.J. Super. 293, 223 A2d 210 (1967). In this manner the authorities can impose requirements that might be complied with prior to issuance of a building permit, such as greenbelt buffer areas. The proponents of floating zones, it appears, will surely carry the field.

REFERENCE: 80 ALR3d 95.

30.23   Planned Unit Developments—Cluster Housing

The planned unit development (hereafter referred to as PUD) is one of the novel ideas in housing. Such developments consist of town houses, homes, apartments (both garden and high-rise), or combinations of such buildings, all with common open areas and some with private recreation facilities. The advantages offered are:

1. Lower priced homes achieved by cost savings through more efficient land use and planning.
2. Small, private yards with a minimum of maintenance chores and a maximum of time and energy for recreational activities in the common areas.
3. Common areas of green open space providing an attractive setting.
4. In some cases shared facilities for swimming, golf, fishing, and so forth, and a recreation center for crafts, meetings, and other group activities.
5. Maintenance furnished by homeowners' association.

The phrase *cluster housing* means that the individual homes, usually party-wall row houses, or apartment buildings are grouped together on relatively small plots of land with large surrounding areas of land left open for common recreational use. The cluster form of development is economical because the clustering of houses with party walls reduces the cost of supplying utilities and roads. Often a PUD is placed in a floating zone.

The old-fashioned zoning ordinance with its rigid allocation of specific uses to specific zones, its building lines, and its minimum-area requirements does not lend itself to the PUD type of development. Cluster development calls for smaller homesites, the land subtracted from homesites being added to common areas. However, the PUD can be listed as a special exception in the zoning ordinance. Alternatively, the zoning ordinance may include a special section devoted to the PUD, calling it variously a *Community Unit Plan, Dwelling Groups, Group Housing, Planned Residential Development* or *Planned Building Groups.* Because approving a development of this sort involves a considerable exercise of discretion, it seems wise to provide that final approval of a special exception for a developer's proposal to create a PUD zone should rest with the city council, just as if an amendment to the zoning ordinance were being considered, and some ordinances so provide. *Rodgers* v. *Village of Tarrytown,* 302 N.Y. 115, 96 NE2d 731 (1951); *La Rue* v. *East Brunswick,* 68 N.J. Super. 435, 172 A2d 691 (1961); *DeMeo* v. *Zoning Comm.,* 148 Conn. 68, 167 A2d 454 (1961). The applicant for such zoning may, under many ordinances, be a government agency, since urban redevelopment plans sometimes call for a PUD.

Where cluster housing occurs in a residential zone that permits the type of housing planned for the PUD, it is simply a form of density zoning and offers no legal problems.

30.24 Contract Zoning

An application by a landowner for rezoning often results in bargaining with the planning board or the city's governing body. At times a formal covenant is entered into by the landowner and the city contemporaneously with the rezoning.

> **EXAMPLE:**   In granting rezoning of land from residential to shopping center use, the city exacted a recorded covenant from the landowner that he would maintain a buffer area of landscaped land between the center and adjoining residential land. This was held valid. *Buchholz* v. *City of Omaha,* 174 Neb. 862, 120 NW2d 270 (1963).

Some courts disapprove of contract zoning. The arguments against contract zoning are:

> 1. It is illegal to "bargain" for legislation. *Baylis* v. *City of Baltimore,* 219 Md. 164, 148 A2d 429 (1959). This argument is specious. Much of the legislation on our books was initiated and lobbied through by private interests. Moreover, the rezoning could have

been enacted without any conditions. *Church* v. *Town of Islip,* 8 NY2d 254, 168 NE2d 681 (1960). Why, then, would the imposition of beneficial conditions invalidate it? Also, since rezoning deals, as it often must, with particular parcels of land, it is difficult to legislate sensibly without taking cognizance of the special conditions relating to that particular parcel. *Ibid.*

2. The rezoning is not in accordance with the state zoning enabling act, which contemplates division of the city into zones plainly appearing on the zoning map. Contract zoning introduces a control of land use that appears in the recorder's office but does not appear on the city's legislative records. *Treadway* v. *City of Rockford,* 24 Ill.2d 188, 182 NE2d 219 (1962). Contra: *Goffinet* v. *Christian County,* 65 Ill.2d 40, 357 NE2d 442 (Ill. 1976); 63 Ill.B. J. 132.

It has been suggested that this sort of bargaining is commonplace and stands a good chance of acceptance if it is accomplished by means of "private restrictions" voluntarily created and recorded by the landowner. Hagman, *Wisconsin Zoning Practice,* 11 (1962). At least one court has accepted this suggestion.

> **EXAMPLE:**   The city of *X* suggests to *D,* a developer, that he record a declaration of restrictions restricting a specified area in his development for golf course purposes over a period of twenty-five years. He does this. In return the city rezones a part of the area from detached single-family dwellings to town houses. This arrangement is valid. *State ex rel Zupancic* v. *Schimenz,* 174 NW2d 533 (Wis. 1970).

At times a contract zoning ordinance provides that if the contract is breached, the zoning reverts back to the preexisting zoning. Such a provision is invalid in some states. *Stiriz* v. *Stout,* 210 NYS2d 325 (S.Ct. 1960). In other states, it is valid. *Goffinet* v. *Christian County,* 65 Ill.2d 40, 357, NE2d 442 (1976). Every legislative change of zoning requires a careful weighing of the need for such action in the light of the circumstances then prevailing. The automatic reverter provision is the antithesis of proper legislative consideration.

It remains impossible to make a definite statement of the law on this subject. Some courts reject contract zoning. Others permit it. Others permit a form of it. The trend is in favor of permitting contract zoning. *Goffinet* v. *Christian County,* 65 Ill.2d 40, 357 NE2d 442 (1976); 70 ALR3d 125.

> REFERENCES: 12 UCLA L. Rev. 897; 24 Maine L. Rev. 263; 1972 Urban L. Ann. 219; 67 Dick. L. Rev. 109; 23 Md. L. Rev. 121; 23 Hastings L.J. 825; 51 J. Urban L. 94; 1974 Planning, Zoning, and Em. Dom. Inst. (S.W. Legal Foundation) 121; 63 Ill. B. J. 132; 25 De Paul L. Rev. 616; 8 Loyola U. L. J. 642 (1977); 70 ALR3d 125.

30.25   Density—In General

Density zoning deals with a number of related items all designed to reduce density of residential occupancy, for example: (1) minimum lot size or area; (2) minimum frontage; (3) front, back, and side yards; (4) maximum lot coverage (open space zoning); (5) minimum building size. The general purpose, to prevent overcrowding, is a valid one. *Town of Durham* v. *White Enterprises Inc.*, 348 A2d 70 (N.H. 1975).

In large-scale residential developments, sophisticated density concepts are applied.

> **EXAMPLE:** The ordinance may divide up the residential area of the city into districts of differing residential density. Thus, if the zoning of a particular area permits single-family, duplexes, town houses, and apartments, the applicable zoning may permit a density of five dwelling units per acre. The developer, developing ten acres, let us say, can build fifty single-family units, or twenty-five duplexes, or five ten-unit buildings or one fifty-unit building. The usual lot size and building bulk restrictions apply unless combined with clustering.

Front, back, and side yards require no discussion since they occasion no problems. Bulk variances deal adequately with the situation. For example, when sprawling ranch homes became popular after World War II, zoning boards handed out front and side line variances by the thousands.

30.25(a)   Density—Minimum Lot Area

Many decisions sanction minimum area residential lot requirements. The theoretical legal basis for such zoning is that spacing buildings farther apart prevents the spread of fire and provides for ample light, air, and adequate sewage disposal. *Simon* v. *Town of Needham*, 311 Mass. 560, 42 NE2d 516 (1942); *Barnard* v. *Zoning Bd. of Town of Yarmouth*, 313 A2d 741 (Maine 1974). In a rural area, a minimum lot area of five acres has been sustained *as applied*. *Honeck* v. *County of Cook*, 12 Ill.2d 257, 146 NE2d 35 (1957). In connection with the validity of such zoning, courts consider the character of the area. A rural area *not in the path of development* is a favorable characteristic. Also favorable is the predominance of large tracts in single ownership; also the presence of historic sites. The presence of smaller lots in the neighborhood is unfavorable to the validity of the zoning. *Marquette Nat. Bank* v. *County of Cook*, 24 Ill.2d 497, 182 NE2d 147 (1962) (minimum area of 20,000 square feet held invalid where neighboring lots were 10,000 square feet in area); *Christine Bldg.* v. *City of Troy*, 367 Mich. 508, 116 NW2d 816 (1962) (requirement of 21,780 square feet held invalid where most lots were 15,000 square feet or less). Here the competitive disadvantage makes the larger lots virtually unsalable. Increase in minimum lot area is sometimes characterized as *upgrading*. Thus, an increase of minimum lot area from two acres to four acres has been sustained. *Senior* v. *Zoning Comm. of Town of New Canaan*, 153 A2d 415 (Conn. 1959). The courts have said that the maximum enrichment of developers is not a controlling purpose of zoning. *Ibid*.

In more recent times environmental factors (water pollution, for example) have been cited in favor of such zoning. *Steel Hill Development Inc.* v. *Town of Sanborton*, 469 F2d 956 (1st Cir. 1973).

This type of zoning faces the problem of *substandard* lots, that is, smaller lots platted and sold before the *upgrading* by zoning amendment. In general, the courts have required the city to issue building permits or to have invalidated the zoning as to such substandard lots. *Harrington Glen Inc.* v. *Municipal Bd. of Adjustment,* 243 A2d 233 (N.J. 1968); *Fulling* v. *Palumbo,* 21 NY2d 30, 286 NY2d 249 (1967); *Grace Bldg. Co. Inc.* v. *Hatfield Twp.,* 329 A2d 925 (Pa. 1974) (holding that lot owner cannot be required to buy adjoining lot in order to come into compliance with the amendment). *Contra, Grobman* v. *City of Des Plaines,* 322 NE2d 443 (Ill. 1975) (denying relief to owners of substandard lot where they refused adjoining owner's offer to purchase).

An occasional decision refuses to protect the purchaser of a substandard lot on the ground that his purchase of the lot was a gamble. He bought the lot fully aware that it was substandard, probably at a bargain price. *Phoenix* v. *Beall,* 524 P2d 1314 (Ariz. 1974). This is akin to *self-created hardship,* which is a valid basis for refusing a variance.

30.25(b)   Density—Minimum Frontage or Lot Size

Minimum frontage requirements have been sustained. *Clemons* v. *City of Los Angeles,* 36 Cal.2d 95, 222 P2d 439 (1950). With respect to such requirements, the problem of substandard lots has arisen quite frequently. Many ordinances exempt *previously platted lots* from this requirement. *Graves* v. *Bloomfield Planning Bd.,* 235 A2d 51 (N.J. 1967). In any case the courts have gone far in protecting substandard lots. *Milano* v. *Town of Patterson,* 93 NYS2d 419 (1947) (requirement of sixty-foot frontage inapplicable to previously platted twenty-three-foot lot). Courts have granted flexible relief. *Ziman* v. *Vill. of Glencoe,* 275 NE2d 168 (Ill. 1971) (court imposed three-foot side yard requirement). But a denial of a variance will be overthrown. A permit must be granted. *Jacquelin* v. *Horsham Twp.,* 312 A2d 124, 10 Pa. Comwlth 473 (Pa. 1973). As in the case of minimum area cases, occasionally relief is denied to a purchaser who buys *with knowledge* of the problem, *Klehr* v. *Zoning Bd.,* 320 NE2d 498 (1974 Ill. App.).

The owner of a substandard lot cannot be compelled to buy additional frontage. Nor can he be compelled to sell to a neighbor. *Smith* v. *Smith,* 53 N.J.S. 590, 140 A2d 58 (1958).

When an owner owns several contiguous substandard lots he must comply with the new frontage requirements. In effect, he must resubdivide the frontage into lots that comply with the new requirements. *Citizens Bank and Trust Co.* v. *City of Park Ridge,* 5 Ill. App.3d 77, 282 NE2d 751 (1972).

Checkerboarding is always struck down. This is a situation in which an owner of a number of contiguous platted lots conveys out alternate lots in order to qualify each substandard lot for a permit. Note, 16 Syracuse L. Rev. 612 (1965).

30.25(c)   Density—Minimum Building Area

Prescribing a minimum building area compatible with health requirements is within the police power. *Lionshead Lake, Inc.* v. *Twp. of Wayne,* 10 N.J. 165, 89 A2d 693, appeal dismissed, 344 U.S. 919, 73 S.Ct. 386, 97 L.Ed. 708 (1953) (requirement of 768 square feet for one-story building sustained). The only substantial issue in this area is whether such a requirement can occur on a *graduated basis,* with differing minimum building areas in differing residential zones. One court has rejected this approach. *Medinger Appeal,* 377 Pa. 217, 104 A2d 118 (1954). The logic of *Medinger* is superficially attractive. If a building area of 1,000 square feet suffices to protect public health, it is difficult to sustain a requirement of 1800 square feet in zone B. However, this approach overlooks the compatibility argument. Houses of differing value do indeed exist in the various areas of the city, and to keep new houses compatible with existing houses is a legitimate objective of zoning. *Garelick* v. *Board of Appeals,* 350 Mass. 289, 214 NE2d 60 (1966). The cases have been collected elsewhere. 9 ALR2d 1374, 1409. In line with the compatibility argument, a requirement of large houses in an area characterized by smaller homes could be invalid for that reason.

30.26   Exclusionary Zoning

One of the recent developments in zoning law is the appearance of the doctrine of *exclusionary zoning.* The attitude of the courts embracing this doctrine is, in large part, that the public welfare requirement of the police power does not stop at the city limits. Courts cannot think in terms of the welfare of the *municipality* and its present inhabitants in testing the zoning. In some states the *tight little island* concept of zoning is outmoded. Sager, *Tight Little Islands: Exclusionary Zoning, Equal Protection and the Indigent,* 21 Stanf. L. Rev. 767 (1969). The wants and needs of all the people living in the *region* must be considered. The poor people must not be zoned into the decaying central city and zoned out of suburbs. Some early decisions in this area struck down large lot zoning. *National Land and Investment Co.* v. *Kohn,* 215 A2d 597 (Pa. 1956); *Appeal of Kit-Mar Builders,* 439 Pa. 466, 268 A2d 765 (1970); *Board of County Supervisors of Fairfax County* v. *Carper,* 200 Va. 653, 107 SE2d 390 (1959). The inequitable aspect of such zoning, bearing heavily as it does on those who cannot afford to buy large lots, has long been the subject of discussion.

Now the battle is out in the open. The authorities, and they are numerous, are collected in *Township of Williston* v. *Chester Gale Farms, Inc.,* 300 A2d 107 (Pa. 1973). The *Williston* case also collects the authorities on exclusion of apartments from suburbia as a form of exclusionary zoning. Many poor people simply cannot afford to buy a house. The most important state court decision on zoning is *Southern Burlington County NAACP* v. *Twp. of Mount Laurel,* 67 N.J. 151, 336 A2d 713 (1975). Very often other courts have followed in the footsteps of the highly respected New Jersey Supreme Court. Therefore its influence has been felt nationwide. Mount Laurel is a "developing municipality," that is, one with a good deal of vacant land left. Its zoning ordinance was a rather typical suburban ordinance. The residential zones permitted only single-family dwellings. Apartments and mobile homes were not permitted. Over 4,100 acres were zoned exclusively for industry, even though only 100 acres were occupied by industry. These aspects tended to keep out the poor and were obviously so intended. The court held that virtually the *entire ordinance* was void because its entire scheme and plan were designed to keep out low- and moderate-income housing. This alone makes the case important. It holds, in effect, that the *typical suburban zoning ordinance is invalid.* The case holds, moreover, that the public benefit idea that sustains the validity of zoning ordinances in the first place is the public benefit of the *region. The zoning must benefit those who live outside the municipality, not simply the residents of the municipality. Outsiders have a right to travel into the municipality and then remain there. The municipality must accept a "fair share" of the disadvantaged. Urban League* v. *Mayor & City Council* 442 N.J. Super 11, 359 A2d 526 (1976) (invalidating 11 ordinances); *Surrick* v. *Zoning Board,* 476 Pa. 182, 382 A2d 105 (1977); 51 Temple L. Q. 764 (1978). It must adopt a new zoning map with smaller lots that the poor can afford. Space must be allocated, the court said, for apartments and mobile homes.

REFERENCES: 29 Rutgers L. Rev. 73 (1975); 30 *id.* 1237 (1977); 8 Seton Hall L. Rev. 460 (1977); 49 St. Johns L. Rev. 653 (1975); 45 U. Cinn. L. Rev. 115 (1976); 1976 U. Ill. L. For. 1; 37 U. Pitt. L. Rev. 442 (1975); 6 U. Mich. J. Law Ref. 290 (1973); 48 ALR3d 1210; 13 Wake Forest L. Rev. 13; 11 Suffolk U. L. Rev. 1; 52 Notre Dame Law. 48; 84 Harv. L. Rev. 1645; 6 Rutgers Camden L. J. 653; 86 Yale L. J. 385; 4 Fordham Urb. L. J. 147 (contrasting federal and state approaches); 8 Ind. L. Rev. 995; 7 Seton Hall L. Rev. 1.

In legal theory, the local governments of New Jersey should immediately have begun the process of amending their ordinances to conform to the Mt. Laurel decision. Instead they chose to ignore the decision. This was unwise. More litigation ensued and ultimately reached the New Jersey Supreme Court. This time the court dealt harshly with the local governments. It reiterated the earlier holding but made it clear that if the local governments failed to conform, the courts would take over the issuance of building permits. Evidently the local governments failed to act, for the New Jersey courts are issuing building permits to builders. Thus the zoning ordinances have been virtually nullified. *Southern Burlington County NAACP* v. *Twp. of Mt. Laurel,* 92 N.J. 158, 456 A2d 390 (1983); *J. W. Field Co., Inc.* v. *Franklin Twp.,* 204 N.J. Super. 445, 449 A2d 251 (1985).

The question is, how far will other states go in following New Jersey?

30.27 Inclusionary Ordinances

To insure that housing for lower income people will be built and widely dispersed, several communities (Fairfax County, Virginia; Montgomery County, Maryland; and Los Angeles, California) have adopted ordinances requiring developers to include a minimum amount of subsidized or low-cost housing in their projects. Kleven, *Inclusionary Ordinances—Policy and Legal Issues in Requiring Private Developers to Build Low Cost Housing,* 21 U.C.L.A. Rev. 1432 (1974). One such ordinance was held invalid. *Board of Supervisors* v. *Caper,* 214 Va. 635, 198 SE2d 600 (1973). But in California such ordinances are valid. 62 ALR3d 880.

REFERENCES: 33 Maine L. Rev. 29; 6 Urb. Law. 690; 62 ALR2d 880.

30.28 Effect of Zoning Ordinance on Restrictions

Restrictions contained in a deed, plat, or property owner's agreement are neither nullified nor superseded by the adoption of a zoning ordinance. *Chuba* v. *Glasgow,* 61 N.M. 302, 299 P2d 774 (1956); *Schwarzchild* v. *Wolborne,* 186 Va. 1052, 45 SE2d 152 (1947).

EXAMPLE: A deed provided that use of the land thereby conveyed was restricted to residence purposes. Thereafter, an ordinance was passed zoning this area for commercial purposes, and the owner attempted to construct a gasoline station thereon. It was held that the deed restriction would be enforced, and a court order was entered forbidding erection of the gasoline station. *Dolan* v. *Brown,* 338 Ill. 412, 170 NE 425 (1930).

However, a change of use in the zoning ordinance does help to show that a change in the neighborhood has taken place, and the court may well decline thereafter to enforce the building restrictions on the ground of change in neighborhood. *Goodwin Bros.* v. *Combs Lumber Co.,* 275 Ky. 114, 120 SW2d 1024 (1938); *Austin* v. *Van Horn,* 225 Mich. 117, 237 NW 550 (1931); 26 CJS *Deeds* § 171 (2).

NEW DIRECTIONS: The older zoning ordinances permitted residences to be erected in any zone (cumulative zoning). The newer ordinances, by and large, forbid residential uses in commercial and industrial zones. Where the earlier building restriction calls for residential use and later zoning ordinance forbids residential use, the zoning ordinance supersedes the restriction. *1.77 Acres of Land* v. *State,* 241 A2d 513 (1968); *Grubel* v. *MacLaughlin,* 286 F.Supp.24 (1968); *Key* v. *McCabe,* 54 Cal.2d 736, 356 P2d 169 (1960); *Blakely* v. *Gorin,* 313 NE2d 903 (Mass. 1974); Hagman, *Urban Planning,* 308.

30.28(a)   Mortgages

Zoning laws are binding on mortgagees. When a mortgagee loaned money for construction of a building that violated a zoning ordinance, the court refused to protect him although he was ignorant of the fact that the ordinance was being violated, since in dealing with real estate, all who are interested are required to take notice of zoning laws. *Siegemund* v. *Building Commissioner,* 263 Mass. 212, 160 NE 795 (1928). Accordingly, a mortgagee making a construction loan should satisfy himself that the contemplated improvement complies with existing ordinances. Otherwise he may find construction of the building halted by a court order after part of his mortgage money has been paid out.

30.29   Planning

City and regional planning figures prominently in the life of many communities today. State laws authorize the adoption by planning commissions of master plans. Such a commission plans for the systematic and orderly development of the community, with particular regard for the location of future major street systems, transportation systems, parks, recreation areas, industrial and commercial undertakings, and residential areas, the creation and preservation of civic beauty, and other kindred matters, all looking not only to the present, but with a view to the orderly development of the unbuilt, as well as the built-up areas.

Generally, at present, the formulation of a master plan is not a precondition to the enactment of a zoning ordinance. True, the zoning ordinance must be rational and bear within itself some evidence of logical planning, but if that is present, it suffices. *Angermeier* v. *Sea Girt,* 27 N.J. 298, 142 A2d 624 (1958).

NEW DIRECTIONS: Increasingly, the courts are looking for some comprehensive plan to guide them in their decision as to the validity of zoning. If there is a plan and the zoning or rezoning conforms to that plan, the courts are likely to sustain it. If the existing zoning is inappropriate when compared with an existing plan, the courts may strike it down. *Fasano* v. *Board of County Commrs.,* 264 Ore. 574, 507 P2d 23 (1973).

EXAMPLE: The plan showed the area was ideal for multifamily housing, but the ordinance zoned it as single-family. It must be rezoned multifamily. *City of Louisville* v. *Kavanagh,* 495 SW2d 502 (Ky. 1973).

NEW DIRECTIONS: If the municipality has no plan at all, the courts are likely to regard this as a good basis for striking down a zoning change. If the city has no plan, any change is, arguably, a planless change. *Forestville* v. *County of Cook,* 18 Ill. App.3d 230, 309 NE2d 763 (1974). Planless change creates a hodgepodge of incompatible uses. If the court is to decide the validity of a proposed zoning change, it is entitled to know the city's long-range plans for the general area. *Hall* v. *City and County of Honolulu,* 530 P2d 737 (Hawaii, 1975). This is one of the battlegrounds that will surely be fought on, hammer and tongs. The city fathers prefer to keep their plans secret, meanwhile zoning much land for single-family dwellings or industrial use, always intending to rezone the land when the "right" developer comes along and they have had a look at his proposals. If they must come out into the open and show on their plans that the area has a long-range future for multifamily dwellings, they will have a hard time rejecting rezoning for this purpose. At the same time the courts want to see "in public" what the long-range plans are so that they can make a rational decision on the score.

Among the states now requiring a city to have a plan are California, Florida, Hawaii, Kentucky, Michigan, Nebraska, Oregon, and Washington. The states in this category apply the rule to rezoning (amendment of zoning ordinance) and to variances and special exceptions. 40 ALR3d 372.

But most recent decisions continue to reject the notion that a prior plan must exist as a basis for valid zoning. *Quinn* v. *Town of Dodgeville,* 354 NW2d 747 (Wis. App. 1984) (citing many cases).

REFERENCES: 29 Fordham L. Rev. 635; 43 Geo. Wash. L. Rev. 120; 8 Natural Resources Law 455; 20 Law & Contemp. Problems 351; 74 Mich. L. Rev. 899 (1976); 73 *id.* 1341; 12 Syracuse L. Rev. 342; 116 U. Pa. L. Rev. 25; 35 Temple L. Q. 59; 7 Univ. of Mich. J. L. Ref. 516 (1974); 9 Urb. Law. Ann. 69 (1975); 6 Urb. Law. 686; 7 *id.* 731; 1977 Planning, Zoning, & Em. Dom. Inst. 1 (1977); 1978 *id.* 205; 10 Willamette L. J. 358 (1974); 12 *id.* 45; 40 ALR3d 372.

30.30   Enforcement of Zoning Ordinance

It is usually provided in the zoning ordinance that any property owner wishing to erect a building must first apply to the commissioner of buildings or other proper official for a building permit. Every such application must be accompanied by plans and specifications of the contemplated structure. The official inspects the plans and declines to issue the permit if a violation of the zoning ordinance is disclosed. If, despite the fact that the contemplated structure would violate the zoning ordinance, the building permit is nevertheless issued, any other property owner whose property would suffer special damage by erection of the proposed structure (for example, a neighbor) may, if he acts promptly, obtain a court order prohibiting the erection of the building. *Garner* v. *County of DuPage*, 8 Ill.2d 155, 133 NE2d 303 (1956). Although it is advisable to do so, the complaining property owner need not first request the public authorities to take action. *Fitzgerald* v. *Merard Holding Co.*, 106 Conn. 475, 138 Atl. 483 (1927). If the complaining owner acts promptly in asserting his rights, but construction of the building is nevertheless begun, the offending property owner may be ordered by the court to demolish the illegal portion of the structure.

> **EXAMPLE:**   Despite protests of an adjoining owner before the commissioner of buildings and the Zoning Board of Appeals, a permit was issued to a property owner to construct an apartment building that violated the zoning ordinance in that it did not have a one-foot setback for every nine feet or rise above a height of seventy-two feet. While litigation was pending to declare the permit invalid, the apartment building corporation proceeded with construction of the building. Eventually, the courts declared the permit invalid, and the adjoining owner filed suit to compel the corporation to reconstruct the building to conform to the zoning ordinance. It developed that such reconstruction could be accomplished only at a cost of $343,837.07. Nevertheless, the court ordered the building corporation to reconstruct the building to comply with the ordinance. *Welton* v. *40 East Oak St. Bldg. Corp.*, 70 F2d 377 (1934).

It is held in some states that if a permit is issued, and in reliance thereon erection of the building is begun, the city cannot thereafter enforce the zoning ordinance if it is discovered that the permit should not have been issued. *Shellburne Inc.* v. *Roberts*, 224 A2d 250 (Del. 1966). The law on this point is chaotic. 1971 Urban Law Annual 63.

> **EXAMPLE:**   The city allowed an apartment building to stand for over forty-three years although it violated the zoning ordinance. The city then sought to fine the apartment owner. It can do so. The long delay does not bar city action. The philosophy here is that important public rights ought not be lost by inaction of public servants. *G & S Mtg. & Invest. Corp.* v. *City of Evanston*, 264 NE2d 740 (Ill. 1970).

As to the matter of a court finding that the village is barred (estopped) from enforcing its zoning laws against a particular tract of land, this usually arises from some action of the village that encourages the landowner to make substantial expenditures in the belief that he is acting legally. The village then seeks to invalidate a previously issued building permit, change the law, or otherwise pull the rug out from under the landowner. Courts at times protect the landowner, perceiving the injustice of allowing him to spend money in a mistaken belief encouraged by the city. At times courts permit the city to block construction, often in the unspoken belief that bribery was present. At all events, the decisions are in chaos. In Illinois alone, the decisions number fifty or more.

REFERENCES: 1971 Urb. Law Ann. 63; 29 Hastings L. J. 658 (1978); 49 N.C.L. Rev. 197 (1970); 6 ALR2d 960.

CHAPTER 31

Land Use Controls—Group Homes

31.01 In General

Not too many years ago orphans found refuge in orphanages, and the mentally retarded were confined in insane asylums. The concept developed that these unfortunate persons would fare better if they were placed in family-type situations in residential neighborhoods. As a result, small groups of orphans were dispersed into neighborhoods to live with foster parents. Similarly, small groups of mentally disabled people were sent to live in a family-type setting with a supervisory couple. The trend was started, and public authorities and private groups began to acquire or lease large homes with inadequate thought to the legal problems involved.

We know, of course, that a purchaser or lessee of a home acquires it subject to recorded building restrictions. If the recorded restriction limits its use to single-family occupancy, the question arises whether a group of eight or ten mentally retarded children supervised by foster parents constitutes a "single family." Cases have arisen all over the country. The court decisions are conflicting. 41 ALR 4th 1216; 19 ALR 4th 730.

The same question arises where the home is in a single-family zone created by a zoning ordinance. Note, *Zoning for the Mentally Ill: A Legislative Mandate*, 16 Harv. J. of Leg. 853 (1979).

REFERENCE: Boyd, *Strategies in Zoning and Community Living Arrangements for Retarded Citizens: Parens Patriae Meets Police Power*, 25 Vill. L. Rev. 273 (1979–1980).

As is evident, a large home must be acquired or leased to house these groups. Neighbors will often be unhappy with their new neighbors and band together to litigate the legal right of the group home to be maintained. The court decisions are not harmonious.

448

31.02 Zoning

The first problem is likely to be a zoning problem. An essential element of this form of care is the establishment of the group home in an area of single-family homes. It naturally follows that these homes will be in single-family zones. The neighbors will argue that only a single family can occupy homes in this zone and that the group is not a single family.

> **EXAMPLE:**   A group of six mentally retarded persons living with two foster parents was held to be a "single family" within the meaning of the zoning ordinance. *Costley* v. *Caromin House Inc.,* 513 NW2d 198 (Minn. 1981).

There are quite a number of cases along this line. But there are some decisions holding that such a group is not a family.

Exactly the same problem arises with children who, for one reason or another, must live in a foster home.

> **EXAMPLE:**   A foster home for disabled children was held to be a family home. *Linn County* v. *Hiawatha,* 311 NW2d 95 (Ia. 1981).

Again, there are some decisions holding that unrelated children are not a family.

Many states have enacted laws that prohibit cities from barring these groups from residential neighborhoods. *Montgomery* v. *Bevilacqua,* 432 A2d 661 (R.I. 1981).

31.03 Building Restrictions

There are, of course, many thousands of building restrictions that limit occupancy to a "single family." Exactly the same problem of interpretation arises. *Jackson* v. *Williams,* 714 P2d 1017 (Okla. 1985). And, again, the courts cannot agree on whether a group of children living with foster parents is a family.

31.04 Constitutional Law

The Supreme Court has held that exclusion of a group home violates the constitution where the decision is thus made simply to please the neighbors and is purely arbitrary. *City of Cleburne* v. *Cleburne Living Center,* 87 L.Ed.2d 313, 105 S. Ct. 3249 (1980).

Many unanswered questions remain. It seems that the "law" does not compel a decision to go in favor of or against group homes. Human attitudes are involved, not law.

REFERENCE: Kratovil, Group Homes, 15 Real Estate Law Journal 223 (1987).

CHAPTER 32

Land Use Controls—
Land Development, Regulation,
Subdivisions, and Dedication

32.01 Dedication

Dedication involves the landowner's setting apart his land for some public use, followed by an acceptance of such donation by the public. Dedication is of two kinds—common law and statutory.

32.01(a) Common Law Dedication

No particular form is required for a common law dedication. It is not necessary that there be any written instrument. There must be an intention on the part of the landowner to dedicate his land to the public. He must, either by his words or acts, offer the land for some public use, and the public must accept the offer. On acceptance of the offer, the city acquires an easement in the land dedicated.

> **EXAMPLE:** A owned a tract of land. He fenced off the tract, locating the fence approximately thirty-three feet north of the south line of his land. This thirty-three-foot strip was used by the public as a road and was later paved by the city. A's acts showed an intention to offer the strip as a street, and the city's acts showed an acceptance of that offer. The city acquired an easement in the land for street purposes. Ownership of the street remained in A. 24 Baylor L. Rev. 592.

Once an offer of dedication has been accepted by the city it is irrevocable. 86 ALR2d 877. Whether it can be revoked *before* acceptance depends on the state law. 86 ALR2d 860.

If the intention to dedicate is lacking, there is no dedication.

> **EXAMPLE:** Suppose I own land abutting on a public street and have a store thereon located some five feet from the street line. To induce the public to look into my store windows, I pave the strip between the store and the street. This does not operate as a dedication of the strip as part of the street, for my intention here is simply to make a more profitable utilization of my private property, not to give it to the public. *Nickel* v. *City* 239 SW2d 519 (Mo. App. 1951).

For the same reason, any sign placed on such a strip indicating that the same is private property will prevent the creation of a dedication, even though the public is permitted to use such strip. 18 CJS 91. Some owners of private streets or alleys periodically place chains across the street or alley or imbed markers in the pavement to show an absence of intention to dedicate.

It is often said that land can be dedicated only by the true owner thereof. *O'Rorke* v. *City of Homewood,* 237 So2d 487 (Ala. 1970). This is true. Nevertheless, dedications can be and are made by owners whose land is subject to easements or other rights. 69 ALR2d 1236.

> **EXAMPLE:** *R* owned land over which *X*, a neighbor, had a recorded driveway easement. *R* filed a plat in which he included the driveway in a public street dedicated by the plat. This is valid. The city acquires its rights subject to the rights of *X* to continue to exercise his rights under the easement. This is simply an application of the rule that one acquiring an easement does not acquire the exclusive right to its use.

32.02   Subdivision Plats

Successful subdivision planning involves far more than the mere drawing of street and lot lines on paper; it includes the planning of neighborhoods. This planning begins with the selection of the raw land, the economical planning of streets, lots, and utilities, and the control of house design. After a plan has been arrived at, the lots, parks, and streets into which the land is to be divided are staked out by a land surveyor, and permanent monuments are placed at the corners of the subdivision. After this has been done, the surveyor plots on paper the manner in which the land has been subdivided. This is called *platting the subdivision.*

The plat is signed and acknowledged by the owner. If the land is mortgaged, the mortgagee must join in the plat. 63 ALR2d 1160. Then it is necessary to obtain the written approval of various city and other authorities. This approval merely signifies that the plat conforms to local law. After all this has been done, the plat is recorded in the recorder's office. It then constitutes an offer of *ownership* of the public places shown on the plat.

32.02(a)   Dedicated Areas

Plats often contain donations or dedications of areas for parks or schools. One common trouble with these dedications is their ambiguity.

SUGGESTIONS

1. Do you want to create rights in the general public or only in the lot owners in the subdivision? For example, if you mark a tract of land on the plat as "beach" or "park," is it intended that the *general public* may use the area, or is it intended that only *lot owners* shall use the area? The decisions are conflicting. 11 ALR2d 562. Make your intention clear. Place a legend on the plat as follows: "A perpetual easement appurtenant to each lot in this subdivision is hereby created for use of the area marked 'beach' as a private bathing beach only for owners of lots in this subdivision, members of their family, and guests. This must not be construed as a dedication to the general public. Ownership of the area is reserved to the subdivider and does not pass by any deed or mortgage of a lot."

2. To what *specific use* is the dedicated area to be put? For example, what is meant by such a general, ambiguous phrase as "public square"? Is it something like a park? Could a courthouse be built on it? A school? A church? A swimming pool? An athletic stadium? Spell out the specific use you want.

3. Who is to be the *legal owner* of the dedicated area? The city? The subdivider? The adjoining landowners? There is some advantage to putting ownership in the city. For example, it will usually rid the subdivider of the burden of paying taxes on the area and will relieve him of personal liability for accidents that may occur on the area. A plat of dedication may give only an easement. 11 ALR2d 549. Give the city a deed. Approval of a plat by a city is *not* an acceptance of ownership.

4. Is a *present gift* intended or merely some possible gift in the future? For example, what is meant by the phrase "reserved for park"? Or "proposed park"? *Anderson v. Tall Timbers Corp.,* 378 SW2d 16 (Tex. 1964). Does such a phrase create present rights in the lot owners or the city, so that the subdivider may not change his mind a year from now and build a house on the tract? Don't use ambiguous phrases.

5. Is the utility strip dedicated to the public? A plat often shows a strip across the rear of the lots marked *easement for public utilities.* Some courts feel that the use of the word *public* makes this a dedication to the public. *Nichol v. Village of Glen Ellyn,* 89 Ill. App.2d 467, 231 NE2d 462 (1967); but other courts disagree. *Island Homes v. City of Fairbanks,* 421 P2d 759 (Alaska 1966). This should not be left in doubt, for if the strip is not dedicated to the public, there is some control in the landowner over which companies come into that strip with their services.

SUGGESTION: Place a legend on the plat as follows: "A perpetual easement is hereby created in favor of all lot owners in this subdivision, over, under, and across the area marked *easement for public utilities* as an easement appurtenant to each lot in this subdivision for the installation, use, maintenance, repair, and replacement of public utilities, including sewer, water, gas, electricity, cable television, telephone and telegraph. Said areas are not dedicated to the public."

Even where the public authorities never accept a particular street, public park, or other public area so designated on a plat, any lot owner in the subdivision has a private right to have the area used as platted and may obtain a court order forbidding any other use. *Newton* v. *Batson*, 223 S.C. 545, 77 SE2d 212 (1953); *McCorquodale* v. *Keyton*, 63 So2d 906 (Fla. 1953).

Approval of the subdivision plat by the city or other public body is not an automatic *acceptance* of the streets, parks, and other public areas depicted on the plat. 26 CJS 479; 11 ALR2d 574. *Acceptance* is shown by the city's paving the streets, putting in sewers, and so on. 52 ALR2d 263. Therefore, if you want the city to assume *immediate responsibility* for these areas, you had best get the city council to pass an ordinance accepting this dedication. And if you want the city to have complete ownership of a park, for example, it is best to give the city a deed to the area and have the city council pass an ordinance accepting it, although in many states acceptance of a plat operates as a transfer of ownership to the city. Once an area has been dedicated, neither the subdivider nor the city can use the land for a purpose other than the dedicated purpose. *City of St. Louis* v. *Bedal*, 394 SW2d 391 (1965).

32.03   Subdivision Regulation—Plat Approval

During the real estate boom of the 1920s countless subdivisions were laid out with no thought for potential need. Plats were recorded showing streets and parks that never materialized. Lots were sold to ignorant people who had no notion of their true value. When the crash of 1929 arrived, lot sales stopped. The market for vacant lots totally disappeared. Real estate taxes were not paid. These premature subdivisions became a disaster area. 36 Mo. L. Rev. 1; 3 Urb. Law. 126; 17 N.Y. L. Forum 1050. Hence laws were passed requiring a developer to submit his plat for approval before it is recorded. *Kligman* v. *Lautman*, 251 A2d 745 (N.J. 1969). In general, the legal philosophy is that if a landowner chooses to subdivide his land and to record a plat for that purpose, the public can legitimately impose reasonable restrictions on his use of the public records to accomplish his objectives. Even more important, the community has a stake in avoiding the problems of unpaid taxes and unusable streets that premature platting creates and an even greater stake in preserving the health of the community through proper sewer and water installations. Proper traffic control is also a legitimate objective. *Forest Const. Co.* v. *Planning Comm.*, 236 A2d 917 (Conn. 1967).

Today subdivision of land is subject to strict controls. 86 Yale L.J. 385 (1977). The governing body of the city or village or a planning board may retain in its own hands the power to approve or disapprove proposed subdivisions, or, where the state law permits, this power may be delegated to a planning commission. Control over land subdivision is exercised over the entire city and often a surrounding area of several miles. *Prudential Co-op Realty Co.* v. *City of Youngstown*, 118 Ohio St. 204, 160 NE 695 (1928); 11 ALR2d 524. However, this power to *approve* plats of land outside the city limits does not confer power to *zone* the area outside the city. *City of Carlsbad* v. *Caviness*, 66 N.M. 230, 346 P2d 310 (1959). The city adopts regulations establishing standards of subdivision design, including regulations concerning utilities, streets, curbs, gutters, sidewalks, storm and sanitary sewers, fire hydrants, street lighting, street signs, and width, depth, and area of lots. No subdivision plat may be recorded unless it has been approved, and approval is withheld unless the plat complies with the regulations. In lieu of requiring installation of streets, utilities, and so on, before approval, the commission may accept a surety company bond guaranteeing that the installation will be made. It is impractical to install streets and then have them pounded to rubble as home construction goes forward.

Like zoning, plat approval is a type of land use control. But it is different from zoning. There are two separate laws.

NEW DIRECTIONS: Zoning and plat approval combined. There is a trend toward combining the functions of rezoning and plat approval. The developer proposes a development that requires rezoning and submits a plat that conforms to the rezoning.

If a subdivider records his plat without the required approval, he runs the risk that the planning board or the city may procure a court order stopping all sales. *Wrongful Subdivision Approval by the Plan Commission: Remedies of the Buyer and City,* 29 Ind. L.J. 408 (1954). Moreover, in most states the law forbids the recording of a plat unless city approval is endorsed thereon. And in many states, selling land in an unapproved subdivision plat is subject to a fine. In some states— California, Michigan, and New Jersey, for example—the buyer of a lot in an unapproved subdivision may change his mind, abrogate the sale, and get his money back. *Platting, Planning & Protection—A Summary of Subdivision Statutes,* 36 N.Y.U. L. Rev. 1214 (1961). In other states—Idaho, Iowa, Massachusetts, Michigan, Nebraska, Rhode Island, and Wyoming, for example—the buyer of a lot in an unapproved subdivision may sue the seller for damages. The contract of sale is not void. If the buyer wishes to enforce the contract, he may do so. *Bamberg* v. *Griffin,* 76 Ill. App. 138, 394 NE2d 910 (1979).

32.04   Forced Dedication

As the need for public control of platting gained acceptance, the pendulum began to swing steadily toward more rigorous controls. The cities, in addition to controlling the size and direction of streets, grading and paving, gutters and drainage, water and utility installation, and so on, began to insist on dedication of land for schools and parks and other contributions to the public. The requirements as to streets, sidewalks, sewer, and water have been upheld as valid. Yearwood, *Accepted Controls of Land Subdivision,* 45 J. of Urban Law 217 (1967). 36 Mo. L. Rev. 1; 73 Yale L. J. 119 (1964). The other requirements have aroused controversy.

When it comes to city exactions of great magnitude, such as those requiring the developer to contribute parks, school areas, and sewage treatment plans, the problems become very difficult.

The city has two great powers, the police power and the power of eminent domain. The police power is the power to pass reasonable laws for the good of the public. The power of eminent domain is the power to acquire land for public purposes by paying for it. Where forced dedication is employed and sustained, the court is saying that this is an appropriate situation for exercising the police power. This does not require the payment of any compensation. The decisions are not entirely consistent from state to state. That is evident from a review of the following examples.

The following exactions were held valid under the police power without the necessity for the payment of compensation:

EXAMPLE: An ordinance requiring the subdivider to dedicate ample streets to the city. *Ayres* v. *City of Los Angeles,* 34 Cal.2d 31, 207 P2d 1 (1949).

EXAMPLE: An ordinance requiring the subdivider to pave streets and install utilities, gutters, and storm sewers. *Brous* v. *Smith,* 304 N.Y. 164, 106 NE2d 503 (1954); *Petterson* v. *Naperville,* 9 Ill.2d 233, 137 NE2d 371 (1956); *In re Spring Valley Development,* 300 A2d 736 (Maine 1973); *Deerfield Estates Inc.* v. *Twp. of East Brunswick,* 286 A2d 498 (N.J. 1971).

EXAMPLE: The city required 4 percent of the platted area to be set apart for parks and playgrounds. This was held valid because the need for parks and playgrounds was created by the subdivider's activity. *Aunt Hack Ridge Estates, Inc.* v. *Planning Comm.,* 160 Conn. 109, 230 A2d 45.

EXAMPLE: An ordinance requiring subdivider to dedicate land or pay a fee in lieu thereof for park purposes. *Assoc. Home Builders* v. *City of Walnut Creek,* 94 Cal. Reptr. 630, 484 P2d 606 (1971). This case contains a valuable review of the law on the subject.

EXAMPLE: A city may require that a developer donate land for recreation purposes because the need was "specifically and uniquely attributable" to the development. *Frank Ansuini Inc.* v. *City of Cranston,* 264 A2d 910 (R.I. 1970); *Dept. Pub. Works* v. *Exchange Nat. Bank,* 334 NE2d 810 (Ill. 1975).

EXAMPLE: A developer was required to dedicate land for a school site. *Krughoff* v. *City of Naperville,* 68 Ill.2d 352, 369 NE2d 892 (1977).

Among regulations held invalid without payment of compensation are the following:

EXAMPLE: Ordinances requiring subdivider to donate land for schools, parks, and so on. *Ridgemont Development Co.* v. *East Detroit,* 358 Mich. 387, 100 NW2d 301. Contrary decisions on this point are: *Jordan* v. *Menomonee Falls,* 28 Wis.2d 608, 137 NW2d 442; *Billings Properties Inc.* v. *Yellowstone County,* 144 Mont. 25, 394 P2d 182 (1964); *Jenad Inc.* v. *Scarsdale,* 18 NY2d 78, 218 NE2d 673 (1966).

EXAMPLE: Ordinance requiring subdivider to contribute money for school or park. *West Park Ave. Inc.* v. *Ocean Twp.,* N.J., 244 A2d 1. *Berg Development Co.* v. *City of Missouri City,* 603 SW2d 273 (1980).

NEW DIRECTIONS: As can be seen, there seems to be a strong current trend toward sustaining these exactions. In part, this trend stems from the view that land developers buy land cheap because it is zoned agricultural. This is done deliberately by the municipality because it wishes to consider the desirability of the developer who comes in for rezoning to multifamily or commercial. Once rezoning is granted the land value shoots up astronomically. There is a feeling that the developer should share part of this increment or windfall with the municipality that conferred it.

REFERENCES: 8 Calif. W. L. Rev. 254; 52 Cornell L. Q. 871; 76 Dick. L. Rev. 651; 29 Okla. L. Rev. 155; 12 Syracuse L. Rev. 224; 26 U. Fla. L. Rev. 671; 27 U. Kans. L. Rev. 1; 9 U. Richmond L. Rev. 435; 2 Urb. Law 706; 43 ALR3d 862.

32.05   Development Rights

Professor John Costonis pioneered the idea of transferring development rights.

> **NEW DIRECTIONS:**   A developer owns a landmark building, which he plans to demolish so that he can erect a modern office building. The city negotiates with him and he transfers to the city his "development rights" in the old building. The city in turn grants him additional development rights on other land he owns in the area, so that he can build a more extensive building than the law otherwise allows. This is a great oversimplification, but it conveys the idea. *Development Rights Transfer and Landmark Preservation,* 9 Urban L. Ann. 131 (1975).

32.05(a)   Development Rights—Farm Land-transfer

A special problem exists with respect to farm lands.

> **EXAMPLE:**   *X* owns a farm that has been in his family for many years. As the nearby suburbs expand, his land becomes valuable for a development and his real estate taxes soar. For example, his land might be worth $1,500 per acre for farming, but $10,000 to $25,000 per acre for development. Under state law, all land must be taxed uniformly at its full market value. *X's* taxes will go up.

One solution to this problem is for the county to buy the farmer's development rights. He is paid the excess value above the $1,500 per acre. He gives the county a release of his development rights. He and his successors may continue to farm the land. However, no one can use the land for development for housing or purposes other than farming. This reduces the land value back to $1,500 per acre. This situation is currently happening in Suffolk County, on Long Island, and elsewhere.

This technique of purchasing development rights was first used to preserve scenic areas. It is now being used to preserve landmarks and farm lands. 12 Urb. Law. 3 (1980).

32.05(b)   Transfer of Development Rights

In many cities older buildings do not use all of the development rights that they would otherwise have available to them. For example, an old building of historical import may be developed only to the fifteen-story level. A developer today may be able to develop that parcel to a height of thirty-five stories. Thus there is an unused balance of development rights, which may be utilized by the landowner in a unique way. The development rights can be sold to an adjoining landowner who will add those transferred development rights to the development to be constructed on neighboring land. In this way a historic building can be preserved and its owner compensated for the unused development rights, which are transferred to another developer.

In yet another use of these development rights, a public facility, such as a museum or school, can be built with the unused development rights related to that parcel transferred or leased to an adjoining parcel to provide income to pay for the operation of the public facility.

REFERENCES: Pedowitz, *Transferable Development Rights*, 19 R.P.P.& T.L.J. 604 (1984); Richards, *Transferable Development Rights: Corrective, Catastrophe or Curiosity*, 12 R.E.L.J. 26 (1983).

32.06   Interstate Land Sales Act

The Interstate Land Sales Act, 15 USC § 1701 *et seq.*, and the regulations issued by the Office of Interstate Land Sales Registration (OILSR), 24 CFR § 1700 *et seq.*, were amended in mid–1980. The act requires that lots not be sold or leased until a *statement of record* is filed with OILSR and a property report is given to the buyer. The statement of record is a comprehensive document detailing the information relating to the property and its developer. The property report is a condensed version of the statement of record and is written in a question-and-answer format.

The act requires that the property report be given to the buyer before the contract is signed. If not, the contract may be revoked at any time during the next two years after the contract is signed. A violation of the act may lead to criminal penalties and a buyer may sue the seller for damages.

The following transactions are exempt from the act:

1. The sale or lease of lots in a subdivision containing fewer than 25 lots.

2. The sale or lease of any lots on which there is a residential, commercial, condominium, or industrial building, or the sale or lease of land under a contract obligating the seller to build within two years. This is an important exemption because it benefits homebuilders and developers who contract in good faith to build a structure within two years.

3. The sale of evidences of indebtedness secured by a mortgage or deed of trust on real estate.

4. The sale of securities issued by a real estate investment trust.

5. The sale or lease of real estate by any government or government agency.

6. The sale or lease of cemetery lots.

7. The sale or lease of lots to any person who acquires such lots for the purpose of engaging in the business of constructing residential, commercial, or industrial buildings or for the purpose of resale or lease of such lots to persons engaged in such business.

8. The sale or lease of real estate that is zoned or restricted to commercial or industrial development. 15 USC § 1702(a).

The following transactions are exempt from the disclosure and registration sections of the act but are subject to the act's antifraud provisions:

- The sale or lease of lots in a subdivision containing fewer than 100 lots.
- The sale or lease of less than 12 lots in a twelve-month period.
- The sale or lease of lots in separate unconnected parts of a subdivision, if the part of the subdivision contains less than 21 lots.
- The sale or lease of lots that are 20 acres or larger.
- The sale or lease of lots in a municipality or county that has set minimum development standards, if the subdivision meets local codes, each lot is limited by zoning or otherwise to single-family ownership, roads, water, sewer, and other utilities are available to the lot, the seller must give a deed within 180 days, after the contract is signed, title evidence is available, the buyer has made an on-the-lot inspection of the property, and there are no high-pressure sales techniques used to sell the lot.
- The sale or lease of a mobile homesite if the lot is sold or leased by one party and the mobile home is sold or leased by another.
- The sale or lease by a developer who is operating on an intrastate as opposed to an interstate basis if the lot is free and clear of liens, the purchaser has made an on-the-lot inspection, the contract contains an estimate of when roads, utilities, and amenities will be completed and the buyer has a seven-day "cooling off" period to revoke the contract.
- The sale or lease of lots to buyers within the same "standard metropolitan statistical area" if the same sort of technical requirements set out in the above exemption are met. 15 USC § 1702(b).

The act also regulates installment contracts that are not subject to one of the exemptions by forbidding a damage clause that results in the forfeiture of amounts paid by the buyer in excess of 15 percent of the purchase price or the seller's actual damages. 15 USC § 1703(b)(3).

32.07   Local Regulations

Regarding sales not covered by the Interstate Land Sales Act, most states have their local laws regulating lot sales. 21 Rutgers L. Rev. 720 (1967); Walter, *The Law of the Land: Development Legislation in Maine and Vermont,* 23 Maine L. Rev. 315 (1971).

32.08   Regulation of Land Sales—FTC

Because the Interstate Land Sales Act has not been very effective, the Federal Trade Commission (FTC) now regulates interstate land sales also, and to a considerable extent its regulations overlap the Interstate Land Sales regulations. Both regulations forbid deceptive advertising, unfair sales techniques, and unfair provisions in land sale contracts. The FTC feels that its ability to harshly punish developers who violate its regulations will deter fraud in the sale of vacant lots.

32.09   Development Regulation

An example of modern development regulation is the law adopted in Vermont.

EXAMPLE: Vermont's law provides for an Environmental Control Board and seven district environmental commissions. The latter agencies process permits that must be obtained for proposed developments of more than one acre in towns without duly adopted permanent zoning and subdivision regulations. In communities having these codes, permits are required for any development encompassing more than ten acres. Permits are awarded if the District Commission is satisfied that the proposed subdivision is found acceptable in four major aspects: that it will not unduly pollute air, land, or water; that it will pose no unreasonable burden on a community's capacity to deliver municipal services; that the application conforms to any duly adopted local, regional, and state plan; and that the project "will not have an undue adverse effect on the scenic or natural beauty of the area, aesthetics, historic sites, or rare and irreplaceable natural areas." As can be seen, this shifts land regulation away from the cities and villages.

Because of concern for the protection of the environment, scores of new laws and court decisions are appearing.

NEW DIRECTIONS: Because of concern for the environment, the land developer is or will be required to submit his plans to some public body that will grant him approval to go ahead only if no appreciable adverse effect on the environment will occur. *Friends of Mammoth* v. *Mono City Board,* 104 Cal. Reptr. 16. This will be especially true in offshore areas, swamplands, and wetlands.

EXAMPLE: A developer bought a wilderness area. The county refused a building permit because it wanted the land kept in its natural state. This action was held invalid. If the public wants wilderness areas preserved, the court thought it must condemn them. *Harbor Farms Inc.* v. *Nassau County Planning Comm.,* 334 NYS2d 412 (1972).

NEW DIRECTIONS: Among the recent developments in this area are statutes providing for state regulation of land use. Keep in mind that traditionally *cities* and *counties* regulated land use. Now the *state* is stepping in.

EXAMPLE: Hawaii has created a State Land Use Commission, which has divided the state into *urban, rural, agricultural,* and *conservation* areas; land use in each area is limited to the uses permitted by state laws.

Some state laws are pretty drastic.

EXAMPLE: In Delaware heavy industry is forbidden in a strip of coast land one to five miles wide.

EXAMPLE: Maine divides the state into *protection districts, management districts, holding districts,* and *development districts.* In protection districts, where presently development is negligible, the state will endeavor to preserve the present status.

Large-scale development is particularly vulnerable to state regulation. 56 Minn. L. Rev. 869.

EXAMPLE: In Maine and Vermont all large-scale developments are subject to state regulation. *In re Spring Valley,* 300 A2d 736 (1973).

NEW DIRECTIONS: Florida has enacted the Environmental Land and Water Management Act of 1972. Florida, of course, has vast expanses of marsh land, which developers can acquire cheaply. Such marsh land is essential to the health of the ecology. Florida divides the state into zones or areas. Thus there are areas of ''critical state concern.''

EXAMPLE: The act sets forth principles for development of areas containing or having a significant impact upon environmental, historical, natural, or archaeological resources of *regional* or *statewide* importance, such as Big Cypress Swamp, the Florida Keys, or a jetport, or a new community. Municipalities must adopt development regulations that comply with these regulations or the state will impose regulations on the area.

Then there are areas involving development of regional impact (DRI).

EXAMPLE: A large hospital, a large shopping center, or a large housing development. These areas are not mapped by the state but are so designated when a developer proposes to build a project of the type listed in the state law as a DRI. The developer is required to fill out an enormously complex application, hundreds of pages in length. It is then considered by the municipality and a regional planning agency. As is evident, the Florida scheme focuses on relatively large developments.

NEW DIRECTIONS: By contrast, in Vermont state controls apply to residential developments with ten units or more, and in Maine the magic number is twenty acres. A developer of a regulated project must often obtain two approvals, one from the state or a regional commission and one from the municipality. This applies, for example, to California, Vermont, Maine, and the coastal zones of New Jersey and North Carolina. Also there is a third factor, environmental control, which brings in a third agency, such as the one established under the Federal Clean Air Act. This agency handles shopping centers and new towns, where the concentration of automobile traffic creates air pollution. At times the regulations will conflict, with the Environmental Protection Agency (EPA) pushing for smaller parking areas (to restrict traffic) and the local agencies pushing for larger parking areas (to reduce traffic densities). Basically, this means that the expense of land development, including the cost of paying real estate taxes for as much as two years, goes up sharply.

REFERENCE: A good discussion of the law relating to the new problems of land regulation will be found in Leahy, *Environmental Issues in Local Land Use Regulation,* 11 RPP & TJ 457 (1976).

32.10   Phased Development—Moratoria—''No Growth''

Some municipalities have provided for phased development.

EXAMPLE: In 1966 the Town of Ramapo, New York, adopted a master plan that had been two years in the making for the future development of the town. It also adopted a comprehensive zoning ordinance. Nine-tenths of the town's unincorporated area was zoned residential. To implement the plan, the town enacted a capital budget for the construction of streets, parks, sewers, and so forth. This plan called for installation over an eighteen-year period, with specific phases to be completed at the end of the sixth and twelfth years. In 1969 an amendment to the zoning ordinance was adopted. This amendment required that a special permit would be necessary in order to construct a residence. When a permit was applied for, the zoning board would consider the area to be built upon, including availability of sewers, parks, schools, roads, and firehouses. Each item was assigned a point value. A minimum of fifteen points was required to qualify for a permit. If public facilities were lacking, the developer was at liberty to construct the needed facilities at his own expense. In this fashion, he could proceed with his development as soon as he acquired the required points. The town considered only its own needs. The area outside the town was ignored. A residential developer applied for plat approval. His plan did not conform to the permit requirements. He was turned down. The ordinance was held valid. *Golden* v. *Town of Ramapo,* 30 NY2d 359, 285 NE2d 291, 334 NYS2d 185, App. dsd. 409 U.S. 1003, commented on in 47 N.Y.U. L. Rev. 723 (1972). The scheme is called phased development.

A water-short municipality, after imposing a *moratorium on development,* must make a good faith effort to augment its water supply in order to permit the landowner, particularly the land developer, to proceed with erection of buildings. It is only after such efforts have proved fruitless that the hookup moratorium may be continued and, of course, development must stop because the water supply is unable to support added population. 27 Hastings L. J. 753 (1976). In short, a municipality can reasonably be expected to exert reasonable efforts. It cannot be expected to perform miracles.

NEW DIRECTIONS: "No growth" regulation. The town of Petaluma adopted a housing and zoning plan that specified that only 500 new home permits could be issued per year for five years. The federal courts sustained this. *Const. Ind. Assn. of Sonoma County* v. *City of Petaluma,* 522 F2d 897 (1975); 8 Urb. Law 748, 776; 6 Seton Hall L. Rev. 207; 20 S.W. L. J. 794. The court held that the concept of public welfare is sufficiently broad to uphold Petaluma's desire to preserve its small town character, its open spaces, and low density of population, and to grow at an orderly and deliberate pace. Obviously, some *state courts* disagree violently with this point of view, *Harbor Farms Inc.* v. *Nassau Planning Comm.,* 40 App. Div.2d 517, 334 NYS2d 412 (1972); 66 Ky. L. J. 99; 52 So. Cal. L. Rev. 1239, and are not bound by it.

EXAMPLE: In 1974 there came before the U.S. Supreme Court the question of the validity of an ordinance of the Village of Belle Terre on Long Island. The ordinance restricted land use to one-family dwellings, thus ensuring that the village would probably grow no larger than its population of 700 living in 220 residences. *Village of Belle Terre* v. *Boraas,* 416 U.S. 1536 (1974), 72 Mich. L. Rev. 508, 88 Harv. L. Rev. 41; 120. This decision totally ignores the enormous growth of population taking place in this country. It deals only with a claimed violation of the *federal Constitution.* Any state court is free to ignore it when determining whether a violation of the *state constitution* is involved. *State v. Baker,* 81 N.J. 99, 45 A2d 368 (1978).

EXAMPLE: Other courts have held no-growth ordinances illegal under state law. *Stoney-Brook Develop. Corp.* v. *Town of Penbroke,* 394 A2d 835 (N.H. 1978).

Remember that if a federal court holds that an ordinance does not violate the *federal* Constitution, the state courts remain free to hold that the ordinance violates the state constitution.

REFERENCES ON PHASED DEVELOPMENT: 4 Environ. Affairs 759; 9 Houston L. Rev. 189; 66 Ky. L. J. 99; 1 Pac. L. J. 461; 26 Stanf. L. Rev. 585; 63 ALR2d 1184.

32.11   Recapitulation—Moratoria

The decisions relating to moratoria are quite inconsistent. Where there is a genuine present danger to the public health, a *temporary* moratorium is valid.

EXAMPLE: The existing sewage system could not handle any additional buildings. Development may be halted *temporarily* by the city while the system is expanded. *Lom-Ran Corp.* v. *Dept. of Environ. Prot.* 394 A2d 1233 (N.J. 1978).

The key words here are (1) present danger, (2) *temporary moratorium,* and (3) expansion of existing facilities. The reasoning is elementary. A landowner has the constitutional right to put his land to use. A municipality cannot force a landowner to leave his land vacant indefinitely. The federal Constitution protects a landowner's ownership of property. But ownership connotes a right to put the land to use. In the exercise of its police power, a local government can act to protect health. But somewhere along the line the landowner must be given the right to use his land for some purpose. Land developers frequently encounter questionable conduct on the part of public officials, including delays in acting on applications for building permits, the installing of sewer installations, and encouragement of septic field construction that provides an excuse for large lot zoning that limits newcomers to the well-to-do who can afford large lots. See 32 Maine L. Rev. 29 (1980). The moratorium must be temporary and reasonably limited as to time. *Wheeler* v. *City of Pleasant Grove,* 746 F2d 1437 (11th Circ. 1984); *Schavone Const. Co.* v. *Hackensack,* 486 A2d 330 (N.J. 1985); *Smoke Rise Inc.,* v. *Washington Comm.,* 400 F.Supp. 1369 (1975); *Collura* v. *Town of Arlington,* 329 NE2d 733 (Mass. 1975); 32 Maine L. Rev. 29 (1980).

The opposition of existing communities to any growth is reflected in various other measures. Counties around San Francisco have minimum requirements of 20, 40, and even 60 acres per home in agricultural areas. Local governments draw up boundaries beyond which they will not extend utility lines. Other communities impose a substantial hookup charge of up to $5,000 per home on furnishing of public services.

All these steps together with those discussed in the zoning chapter are but aspects of the great battle of the 1980s, the battle between existing communities and developers who would like to open them up to low-income persons.

REFERENCES ON "NO GROWTH" REGULATION: 3 Fordham Urb. L. J. 137 (1974); 26 Hastings L. J. 845 (1975); 6 Seton Hall L. Rev. 207; 30 S.W. L. J. 794; 19 Villanova L. Rev. 703 (1974); 26 U. of Fla. L. Rev. 750; 8 Urb. Law 748, 776; 62 Ky. L. J. 99 (1977–78); 52 So. Cal. L. Rev. 1239 (1979); 12 U. San. F. L. Rev. 357 (1979).

32.12   Moratoria—Sewer and Water Problems

Some municipalities have resorted to the moratorium to stop unwanted construction.

EXAMPLE: Cities that lack adequate sewer or other facilities have imposed a moratorium on issuance of building permits. If the time period is reasonable and the city has a definite plan for solving the problem, the moratorium has been sustained by some courts. *Smoke Rise Inc.* v. *Washington Suburban San. Comm.,* 400 F.Supp. 1369 (1975) (sustaining five-year moratorium); Fairfax County, Virginia, tried a "no growth" moratorium approach, but lost. The Virginia Supreme Court held that permits *must* be issued to land developers. *City of Richmond* v. *Randall,* 205 Va. 506, 211 SE2d 56 (1975).

One writer takes the following position on moratoria; (1) the moratorium is valid if an actual emergency exists and a law or ordinance authorizes the moratorium; (2) the moratorium must be limited in time; (3) the city must have a program to end the emergency; (4) it is up to the court, not the village, to determine if these requirements exist. *The Thirst for Population Control,* 27 Hastings L. J. 753.

EXAMPLE: In Colorado an interesting situation arose. The county in question required that the developer make arrangements for water and sewer service before receiving approval for his residential building plans. The city of Boulder was the only provider of sewer and water in the entire area, including land outside the city. The developer applied for such service and was refused, although it could readily be furnished. The court held that the city must furnish the sewer and water. The county and the city had contrived a situation between them under which the developer could not go ahead without sewer and water, but the city, the only provider, could refuse to furnish these services. Plainly, this indefinite ban on development violates the developer's rights under the state constitution. *Robinson* v. *Boulder,* 547 P2d 228 (Colo. 1976), commented on in 5 Real Estate L. J. 170.

However, a moratorium on building permits for a reasonable time, while the city attempts to cope with the problem, is valid. If during that time it is established that there simply is no water available for further building, for example, the city can make the moratorium permanent. "You cannot get blood out of a turnip, and you cannot get water out of a dry well."

32.13   Estoppel—Vested Rights—Development Agreements

There has always been a reluctance to apply estoppel where a government body is involved. However, in land development matters courts are increasingly resorting to this doctrine.

> **EXAMPLE:** In zoning cases where a city has issued a permit to a developer and he has, in reliance on a building permit, expended substantial sums (hiring an architect, obtaining a loan commitment, signing a construction contract) but has not as yet achieved nonconforming use status the courts will, at times, hold the city estopped to cancel the permit. This is simply a legal way of stating that in the circumstances it would be unjust to permit a cancellation of the permit. Here the courts are balancing the obvious injustice to the developer against the public policy favoring an orderly development of land use that permits a city to alter its plans as circumstances indicate the desirability of doing so. Obviously, courts will differ in their approach to the problem. 29 Hastings L. J., 623, 651. The problem is enormously complicated where several different public bodies issue permits for different aspects of the development.

While the courts often approach this problem in terms of a question whether the developer's rights had "vested," it is hard to distinguish this view from the rule that protects nonconforming use status. If a final permit has issued, and substantial commitments were made in reliance on a final permit, the courts have to protect the developer.

> **EXAMPLE:**   A developer expended $2,800,000 after the county had approved his plat. He had not obtained a final permit for the work. The court refused to protect the developer, since he had not obtained a final permit. *AVCO Community Developers Inc.* v. *South Coast Regional Commr.,* 17 Cal.3d 785, 553 P2d 546, 132 Cal. Reptr. 386 (1976), *cert. den.* 429 U.S. 1083 (1977).

The *Avco* decision led to dissatisfaction. Ultimately, California passed a law under which a developer can enter into an agreement with the local government. If the developer proceeds in good faith to comply with the agreement, his rights cannot be revoked. Kessler, *The Development Agreement,* L. J. of Land Use & Env. Control 451 (1986). Holliman, *Development Agreements and Vested Rights in California,* 13 Urb. Law. 44 (1981); 54 Ore. L. Rev. 103. Perhaps similar laws will be enacted elsewhere. Especially where the developer has expended substantial sums with the encouragement of local government, the idea is gaining ground that "every citizen has the right to expect that he will be dealt with fairly by his government." *Hollywood Beach Hotel Co.* v. *City of Hollywood,* 329 So2d 10 (Fla. 1976).

> REFERENCE: Kratovil, *Eminent Domain and Some Land Use Problems,* 34 De Paul L. Rev. 587 (1985).

32.14   Regulations Preserving Light, Air, and View

There is a growing body of opinion that blocks of boxy high-rise office buildings are destroying the attractiveness of downtown areas. Some cities are taking action. In Austin, Texas, building height is restricted where view of the state capitol dome would be obstructed. In Denver, height restrictions have been imposed to preserve views of the Rocky Mountains. San Francisco has elaborate regulations designed to reduce shadows on sidewalks. 17 Urb. Law 851 (1985). Slender, tapered buildings are encouraged.

REFERENCE: 12 Ecology L. Q. 511 (1985).

CHAPTER 33

Land Use Controls—
Wetlands, The Public Trust,
Beaches, and Navigable Waters

33.01   Definition of the Problem

There are two types of wetlands. *Inland wetlands* are marshes such as those found in every state of the union. *Coastal wetlands* are *estuarian* lands (salt marshes). An estuary occurs where an arm of the sea (salt water) extends inland to meet the mouth of the river (fresh water). The tides alternately flood and expose tidal marshes. Both types of wetlands are shallow. Land development is possible through "dredge and fill" operations. It is only recently that we have come to realize that our very national existence depends upon these wetlands and that these wetlands are disappearing as building construction goes forward. Wetlands are an important natural resource because:

1. Wetlands are nature's way of controlling floods. Wetlands act as giant sponges, absorbing vast amounts of water and releasing it gradually. Paving the area creates a flood problem. Estuarian lands, with their mixture of peat, bog, moss, and so forth, absorb the moisture from incoming storms.

2. Inland wetlands maintain ground water at proper ground water levels. If this ground water is drained, a desert may result.

3. Estuarian lands are an important source of food supply. Carbohydrates and vitamins wash out to sea from the estuaries and greatly increase the number of fish and oysters that the ocean can produce. By far the greater quantity of ocean fish depends for survival on the estuaries. The deep sea, by and large, is empty of fish. A great many ocean fish can reproduce only in the estuaries. The classic illustration is that of the salmon that come back to the stream of their birth and go upstream to spawn. The fishermen, the fishing villages, and the tourist trade depend upon the estuaries. Wild fowl, such as ducks and geese, cannot exist without the wetlands. They are necessary for reproduction, migration, and as winter feeding grounds. In these areas, hunters bring in substantial local revenue.

4. Wetlands absorb polluted air and water and make them clean and wholesome.

A court decision points up the legal problems that arise in the wetlands area.

> **EXAMPLE:**   Ronald and Kathryn Just, land developers, bought a large tract of land in Wisconsin. When their plans became public knowledge, Marinette County passed an ordinance making any reasonable use of wetlands land impossible. Cranberry picking and other low- or no-income activities were permitted. When the Justs went ahead in defiance of the law, they were stopped by the courts. The Wisconsin Supreme Court sustained the law. *Just* v. *Marinette County,* 56 Wis.2d 7, 201 NW2d 761 (1972), *cert. den.* U.S. S.Ct. The land was thus rendered worthless. The court, in a ruling contrary to hundreds of previous decisions, said that a landowner has no constitutional right to develop his land! The dilemma is plain. If all developers are allowed to develop wetlands, the landowners are protected from loss of land value, but the surrounding country may be damaged.

The *Marinette County* case clearly presents a problem that exists in American constitutional law. Each government body has two powers that frequently come into conflict, the *police power* and the power of *eminent domain.*

> **EXAMPLE:**   X owns Blackacre. The city wants this land for a street. The city files a petition under its power of eminent domain. A jury fixes the value of the land, the city pays it to X, and the street is installed. This is an exercise of the power of eminent domain. No controversy exists.

Each public body also has *police power,* the power to govern. This is the great power of government, but it has its limits. The city, for example, can take *X's* land in the preceding example for a street because *X* refuses to sell. But it must exercise the power of eminent domain to do so.

The situation is complex. The greater the need for preservation of the public safety in a given situation, or the closer the landowner's use approaches the nuisance level, or the greater the threatened harm, the closer the courts come to permitting the city to reduce the landowner's land value without paying him compensation.

> **EXAMPLE:**   In the city of Los Angeles a residential section expanded until it closely approached a brickworks that gave off a foul odor. The city passed an ordinance making brick-making illegal in the city. The courts upheld the decision because, in balancing the harm to the public against the gain to the public, it was clear that the gain to the public outweighed the benefit to the brickmaker, even though the land was reduced to zero value.

> **EXAMPLE:**   In the city of San Francisco a disastrous fire broke out. To save the balance of the city, the fire department dynamited a row of buildings to create a fire break. The city does this under the police power. It need not pay a penny of compensation. *Surrocco* v. *Geary,* 3 Cal. 70 (1853). The police power was properly exercised because of the great public danger.

The question arises: In the wetlands situation, is the danger to the public so great that filling in the wetlands would cause a calamity? If so, arguably the city can exercise its police power, its power to regulate and pay no compensation. If the danger does not reach these proportions, it must compensate the landowner.

This is a very great simplification of the problem over which the courts and scholars have fought bitter battles in the last few years. There is an almost total lack of agreement, and here we can merely draw attention to a few of the conflicting points of view.

33.01(a)   The Decisions

The decisions, of course, are conflicting:

33.01(a)(1)   Prodeveloper Decisions

Morris County Land and Imp. Co. v. *Twp. of Parsippany-Troy Hills,* 40 N.J. 539, 193 A2d 232 (1963). Here the township had amended its zoning ordinance to create a meadowlands zone designed to preserve the swampland for flood control purposes. Only minor uses were permitted, such as commercial greenhouses. The landowneer wished to develop his land for intensive commercial development. The court held for the developer.

State v. *Johnson,* 265 A2d 711 (Maine 1970). The state of Maine passed a wetlands law. The state court held that the preservation of wetlands was a laudable purpose but that the cost must be publicly borne. The landowner must be paid by the state if his development rights are to be taken away. See also *Mac Gibbon* v. *Board of Appeals,* 350 Mass. 635, 255 NE2d 347 (1970).

33.01(a)(2)   Antideveloper Cases

Sibson v. *State,* 336 A2d 239 (N.H. 1975) and other cases follow the lead of *Just* v. *Marinette County. Sibson* involved a denial of a building permit that was to cover four acres of salt marshland that was part of a one-hundred-acre tidal wetland. The court sustained this denial because of the harm to the public. See also *Brecciaroli* v. *Connecticut Commr. of Environmental Protection,* 36 Conn. L. J. 42, p. 4 (S.Ct. Jan. Term 1975); *Potomac Sand and Gravel Co.* v. *Governor,* 293 A2d 241 (Md. 1972); *S. Volpe & Co., Inc.* v. *Board of Appeals,* 348 NE2d 807 (Mass. App. 1976); *State* v. *Reed,* 78 Miss.2d 1004 (N.Y.)

33.02   Environmental Factors

A final obstacle to land development in marshes is the emergence of the concept that environmental factors must be considered before a "dredge and fill" permit is issued. *Zabel* v. *Taub,* 430 F2d 199 (5th Circ. 1970), *cert. den.* 401 U.S. 910 (1971).

33.03   Conclusions on Wetlands

It is difficult to extract rational rules out of all this, but certain things are plain with respect to *Just* v. *Marinette County.* The Wisconsin court's view that a landowner has no constitutional right to develop his land cannot possibly be correct. How would this country have reached its present state of development if this is the law? Who will buy vacant land if it can be taken from him without payment of a penny of compensation? Definitely, it should not be the law. There is a vast body of law on purchase and condemnation of development rights. Ironically, Wisconsin has pioneered in the purchase of development rights and is still doing so in acquiring scenic easements.

Also, the court failed to require evidence of the facts demonstrating the impact that the proposed development would have on the area in question. How can a rational decision be made if the facts are not known?

Obviously, all these cases should be decided on their particular facts. Siegan, *Other People's Property,* 102 *et seq.* (1976). This last is the approach in zoning law, where each case is tested by looking at the ordinance *as applied* to the particular tract of land.

The choice is a difficult one, and the solution to the problem is nowhere in sight. State courts will differ. The United States Supreme Court is unpredictable. If unlimited development is permitted, the fishing and resort industries will be destroyed without compensation. The danger to the public is very great. If the owners of marshlands and estuarian lands are not permitted to develop their properties, the loss to them is also very great. Here is a choice between two very great evils. Some courts will pick one side, other courts will pick the other.

33.04   Compensable Regulations

One solution to the problem in which land developers are pitted against the public, and the evidence shows that proceeding with the development would cause great pubic harm, is to combine the two great powers of government, the police power and the power of eminent domain. Comment: *Compensable Regulations: Outline of a New Land Use Planning,* 10 Willamette L. J. 451 (1974). Rhode Island has already passed a law to compensate landowners for restrictions on the development of wetlands. *Ibid,* p. 454. Under this system the landowner receives *some* compensation for the restrictions placed on his right of development, but not the full market value of the land. Of course, developers are unhappy with this solution. The environmental enthusiasts are also unhappy. But the fact of the matter is that the landowner is entitled to some payment, and tax money is not available to buy all these lands at market value. In legal effect, this is quite similar to the *scenic easement* or *development rights easement* discussed earlier. The landowner retains ownership of the land, is entitled to make some use of the land, but is not entitled to develop it. Anything less than this offends our sense of what is fair and just.

33.05   The Public Trust Doctrine

Some states have used a different approach to avoid paying the landowner compensation.

> **EXAMPLE:**   In *International Paper Co.* v. *Mississippi State Highway Dept.,* 271 So2d 395 (Miss. 1973), a landowner claimed ownership of an island in the Pascagoula River because a prior owner, from whom he had purchased the island, had received a grant from the state. The state of Mississippi argued and its supreme court held that ownership of all tidelands, the spaces between ordinary high- and low-water mark, the bed of a bay, and all bodies of land arising from the bay floor are forever held in a public trust by the state. Such land cannot be sold to private persons. Of course, since the state owns the land it can control whatever is built thereupon. A number of states follow this public trust rule. Its application, currently, is hard to predict.

> **EXAMPLE:**   The owner of land abutting on the ocean sought to fill and develop the tidelands abutting this property. The court held the power of the state to control its navigable waters and the land beneath them was held in a public trust and was within the absolute control of the state. *Marks* v. *Whitney,* 6 Cal.3d 251, 491 P2d 374, 98 Cal. Reptr. 790 (1971). This was true even though a prior owner had purchased the submerged land from the state.

33.06   Navigable Waters

Another approach to the problem rests upon the claims of the federal and state government to control of navigable waters. It is, of course, elementary that both government bodies have and exercise control over navigable waters. What is surprising is the position they maintain, sustained by the courts, that waters "once navigable, always navigable." *U.S.* v. *Stoeco Homes,* 359 F.Supp. 672 (D.N.J. 1973). Thus, even though land under navigable water was filled and built on as long as one hundred years ago, it is still navigable, and either public body can compel removal of the improvements. Navigable water is subject to federal and state *servitudes.* It is elementary that either government can halt construction if it can show that the construction is on "navigable waters." In this context, water is "navigable" if it is or once was navigable, or if it is or once was part of the tidelands and marshlands of the aquatic ecosystem surrounding the navigable water. *Potomac Sand and Gravel Co.* v. *Governor,* 266 Md. 358, 293 A2d 241 (1972).

> **EXAMPLE:**   Landowner wanted to dredge in the navigable waters of Boca Ciega Bay in order to create a trailer park. The permit was denied by the United States because construction would have a destructive effect on wildlife. *Zabel* v. *Taub,* 430 F2d 199 (5th Cir. 1970).

> **EXAMPLE:**   Where the builder erected mobile homes on coastal marshland without a permit, he was compelled to remove them. *U.S.* v. *Moretti,* 478 F2d 418 (1973).

33.07   Beaches

Since the history of this country began, it has been assumed that one who buys lands abutting on waters, navigable or nonnavigable, has the right to enjoy the beach as his private domain. In lands abutting on tidal waters, this right generally stops at the highwater mark. Landward of that line the public has no right to picnic or stroll. *In re Opinion of Justices*, 313 NE2d 561 (Mass. 1974). In recent times the courts have suddenly discovered that the public should be allowed to use and enjoy these beaches and have evolved a variety of theories that would enable the public to enjoy such rights, much to the disgust of riparian landowners who paid vast sums of money for their riparian rights and the right to enjoy these beaches in privacy. Some remarkable legal decisions have been handed down in order to enable the public to enjoy the beaches.

> **EXAMPLE:**   In California it has been held that where a riparian landowner over a five-year period made no objection to the use of his beach by the pubic, there exists an *implied dedication* to the public, and the landowner must allow public use. The reference here is to the beach area above high-water mark, where ordinarily the public has no rights. *County of Orange v. Chandler-Sherman Corp.*, 126 Cal. Reptr. 765, 5 S.W.U. L. Rev. 48 (1973); 11 Santa Clara L. Rev. 327.

> **EXAMPLE:**   In Oregon the courts have held that the public has a *customary right* to the use of the dry sand area. *State ex rel Thornton v. Hay*, 462 P2d 671 (Oreg. 1969).

> **EXAMPLE:**   In New Jersey it has been held that land contiguous to a beach is unique and therefore subject to strict zoning. *Frankel v. Atlantic City*, 63 N.J. 333, 307 A2d 562 (1973). This makes sense. Any person buying beach property ought to recognize that the public will want it kept free from undesirable uses.

> **EXAMPLE:**   Under the "public trust" rule, Massachusetts holds that land *below* the high-water mark, even though sold by the state to a private landowner, remains subject to the public rights of fishing and navigation. *In re Opinion of the Justices*, 313 NE2d 561 (1974).

No doubt other states will reach out into the beaches under some theory or other to give the public rights therein. As can be seen, the California rule punishes the "nice guy." The Oregon rule, discovering a customary right after millions have been spent by purchasers of riparian land, seems unfair. The fact is, that private landowners are now being punished for years of public neglect.

REFERENCES: 4 Seton Hall L. Rev. 662 (1972); 1978 ABF Res. J. 397 (1978); and 86 Harv. L. Rev. 1582 (1972) discussing *Just v. Marinette County*; Large, *This Land is Whose Land? Changing Concepts of Land as Property*, 1973 Wis. L. Rev. 1039 (especially valuable discussion); 58 Va. L. Rev. 876 (1972) (valuable); Hill, *Coastal Wetlands in New England*, 52 Boston U. L. Rev. 724 (1972); Binder, *Taking Versus Reasonable Regulation: A Reappraisal in Light of Regional Planning and Wetlands,* 25 U. of Fla. L. Rev. 1, (1972) (valuable); Kramon, *Section 10 of the Rivers and Harbors Act: The Emergence of a New Protection for Tidal Marshes,* 33 Md. L. Rev. 229 (1973) (valuable); Morris, *Federal Navigation Servitude; Impediment to the Development of the Waterfront,* 45 St. Johns L. Rev. 189 (1970); 44 Notre Dame Law. 236 (1968); 4 Land & Water L. Rev. 521 (1969); Bartke, *The Navigational Servitude and Just Compensation—Struggle for a Doctrine,* 48 Oreg. L. Rev. 1 (1968); 52 Notre D. Law 1015 (1977). See also 6 Fla. St. U. L. Rev. 983 (1978); 8 R.E.L. J. 166 (1979); 15 San Diego L. Rev. 1241 (1978); 29 S.C.L. Rev. 627 (1978).

CHAPTER 34

Land Use Controls—
Historic Buildings and Areas

34.01 In General

Federal law provides for the registration, in an official list, descriptions of buildings worthy of preservation for historic or architectural value. 16 USCA Sec. 461, 16 USCA Sec. 470. Each state has a procedure for submitting a building worthy of listing. The Secretary of the Interior may also designate a building if it has "*national* historical significance."

Income tax benefits are available for expenditures incurred in rehabilitating historic buildings. Rehabilitation must follow federal standards. State laws and city ordinances also provide for preservation of historic buildings.

Where local law allows the designation without the owner's consent, litigation may result, since often the landowner can greatly enhance his revenue by demolishing an old building and erecting a larger, modern structure. Local laws may forbid demolition or structural alteration.

Historic areas, as distinguished from historic buildings, are often designated under state law, often by the use of zoning power as was done in the case of the area surrounding the Abraham Lincoln home in Springfield, Illinois.

The literature on preservation of historic areas and landmarks through zoning is extensive. See, for example, *Bibliography of Periodical Literature Relating to a Law of Historic Preservation,* 36 Law and Contemp. Prob. 442 (1971); also, *Symposium of Historic Preservation,* 36 Law and Contemp. Prob. 309–444 (1971); *Martha's Vineyard: The Development of a Legislative Strategy for Preservation,* 3 Environmental Affairs, 396 (1974). Of interest also is *Rebman* v. *City of Springfield,* 111 Ill. App.2d 430, 250 NE2d 282 (1969) (sustaining establishment of historical zone around the Abraham Lincoln home in Springfield and citing many cases holding that the preservation of historical areas is well within the concept of public welfare). To like effect are *M. and N. Enterprises Inc.* v. *City of Springfield,* 111 Ill. App.2d 444, 250 NE2d 389 (1969), and *Fitzpatrick* v. *City of Springfield,* 10 Ill. App.3d 317, 293 NE2d 712 (1973). Where the economy of the area depends on tourism engendered by the historic quaintness of the area, the zoning is likely to be sustained. 63 Columb. L. Rev. 708, 720. Historic zoning prevents changes in the historic nature of the area.

Landmarks consisting of isolated buildings present a different problem. Note: *Landmark Preservation Laws: Compensation for Temporary Taking*, 35 U. of C. L. Rev. 362 (1965).

> **EXAMPLE:**   In *Lutheran Church in America* v. *City of New York*, 345 NY2d 121, 304 NE2d 371 (1974), an attempt to freeze an individual landmark that was located in a high economic development area failed.

The constitutional issue can be avoided, of course, by payment of compensation. It has been argued that the city could condemn a development easement by paying an award equal to the difference between the fair market value of the land before taking (when the landowner would have the right to demolish and construct to the highest and best use) and the fair market value immediately after taking the development easement. Note: *Landmark Preservation Law: Compensation for Temporary Taking*, 35 U. of Chicago L. Rev. 362 (1965). Such a device is virtually certain to stand up if attacked in the courts.

Predictably , *area zoning* will fare better than the freezing of individual *landmarks. Fred F. French Inv. Co.* v. *City of New York*, 39 NYS2d 587, 350 NE2d 381 (1976); *People* v. *Ramsey*, 28 Ill. App.2d 252, 171 NE2d 246 (1960).

The New York courts appear to have introduced a new idea on the subject of landmark preservation.

> **EXAMPLE:**   The owners sought to construct an office building on the site of the Grand Central Terminal, a landmark building. The courts sustained the city's refusal to grant a permit. The court took the position that Penn Central, the landowner, owned other real estate in the vicinity of the terminal that would lose value if the terminal were not in operation. This is a new idea. You do not just look at the landmark property to see if it is operating at a loss. You look at the landowner's real estate in the vicinity to see how it would be affected by demolition of the landmark.

Part of the city scheme was to transfer the terminal's development rights to nearby Penn Central land.

The New York high court declared the scheme valid in *Penn Central* v. *City of New York*, 42 NY2d 324, 366 NE2d 1271 (1977), affirmed, 438 U.S. 104. Thus we have here a state court's view of validity as measured under a state constitution, and the federal view as measured under the federal Constitution. A more detailed look at the facts is needed.

In 1967 the Landmark Preservation Commission declared Penn Central Terminal a landmark. Penn Central proposed a plan for erecting an office tower above the terminal. Permission was refused. The city proposed to transfer development rights to other Penn Central properties.

Both the New York court and the United States Supreme Court ruled in favor of the city. What is important here is what the courts did not dispose of. In the first place, Penn Central owns other properties in the vicinity of the terminal that derive their value from proximity to the terminal. In other words, the situation as it existed *before* the development scheme was initiated was a situation that was not harming Penn Central seriously. Penn was making money, and constitutional law does not guarantee any landowner more than a reasonable return. People enthusiastic about landmark preservation have hailed the decision. It is an important decision. But much more litigation will be needed before the law can be regarded as settled.

REFERENCES ON PENN CENTRAL IN SUPREME COURT: 8 Capitol U. L. Rev. 553; 11 Conn. L. Rev. 273; 1979 Detroit Coll. L. Rev. 143; 7 Ecology L. Q. 731; 92 Harv. L. Rev. 222; 25 Loyola L. Rev. 205; 14 New England L. Rev. 317; 5 Ohio North L. Rev. 719; 47 U. Cin. L. Rev. 654; 1978 U. Ill. L. F. 927; 18 Washburn L. J. 404.

REFERENCES ON PENN CENTRAL IN NEW YORK COURTS: 42 Albany L. Rev. 523; 57 B.U. L. Rev. 931; 27 Buffalo L. Rev. 157; 78 Columb. L. Rev. 134; 6 Fordham Urban L. J. 667; 91 Harv. L. Rev. 402.

CHAPTER 35

Homeowners' Association

35.01 In General

The homeowners' association (HOA) is an interesting legal creature. It derived its early utility in connection with enforcement of general plan building restrictions in the old-fashioned subdivision of single-family dwellings.

> **EXAMPLE:** Developer plats a subdivision of 100 lots and in the accompanying declaration of restrictions creates a restriction that only single-family dwellings shall be erected and a fifteen-foot front building line shall be observed. The declaration also provides that *XYZ Corp.,* a nonprofit corporation whose members are the lot owners in the subdivision, shall be empowered to enforce the restrictions and shall collect an annual assessment from each lot owner. Ultimately, Developer sells out all the lots. He now has lost interest in protecting the lot owners. Lot Owner begins construction of a store that will come all the way to the street line. Any one homeowner might be disinclined to hire a lawyer and engage in litigation. However, *XYZ Corp.* warns Lot Owner to discontinue construction and to remove the foundations he has constructed. Lot Owner knows this is no empty threat. He complies.

35.02 Legal Form of Association

The homeowners' association is a form of private government. Gibson & Simms, *New Community Development,* 11 Washburn L. J. 227, 230 (1972). There is something of a misnomer here. Although real estate personnel talk of a "homeowners' association" they are most often actually referring to a not-for-profit corporation organized pursuant to the declaration of restrictions, easements, liens, and covenants. Hyatt, *Condominiums and Home Owner Associations* 7 (1985). *Merrionette Manor Homes Improvement Assn.* v. *Heda,* 136 NE2d 556 (Ill. 1956); *Garden Dist. Prop. Owners' Assn.* v. *New Orleans,* 98 So2d 922 (La. 1957); *Neponsit Property Owners' Assn.* v. *Emi-*

grant Industrial Savings Bank, 15 NE2d 793 (N.Y. 1938); *Rodruck* v. *Sand Point Maintenance Comm.,* 295 P2d 714 (Wash. 1956).

Unincorporated associations must be avoided, for traditionally these have very little in the way of legal existence or status. *Moffat Tunnel League* v. *U.S.,* 289 U.S. 113 (1933); 40 Ind. L. J. 420 (1964). Unincorporated associations cannot own land or bring lawsuits. Also, in any unincorporated association, the members have the risk of unlimited liabilities, for example, for personal injuries. Likewise, an unincorporated association cannot hold ownership of land. *Delaware L. and Dev. Co.* v. *First Church,* 147 A 165 (Del. 1929); Ford, *Dispositions of Property to Unincorporated Non-Profit Associations,* 55 Mich. L. Rev. 67, 235 (1956).

As with any corporation, there are bylaws and a corporate charter. In the beginning the developer and his associates are the members of the corporation. A nonprofit corporation, be it noted, has *no shareholders;* it has *members.* As homes are sold each homeowner automatically becomes a member of the corporation.

35.03   Membership

The membership in the HOA is automatic. Each unit purchaser automatically becomes a member and his membership passes automatically to his purchaser. *Paulinskill Lake Assn.* v. *Emmich,* 397 A2d 968 (N.J. 1978).

35.04   Meetings

Every corporation holds meetings. All corporate business of importance is conducted at these meetings. The association's board of directors usually meets monthly. The entire membership meets at least once a year, when the annual budget is discussed.

As is true of all corporations, proper notice must be given to all directors of a directors' meeting. Failure to do so invalidates the meeting and the action taken at the meeting. *State* v. *D. A. Davidson & Co.,* 517 P2d 722 (Mont. 1973). Likewise, proper notice must be given of any unit owners' meeting.

35.05   Association as a Vehicle for Enforcing Restrictions, Liens, and Covenants

In any land development where both a homeowners' association and a declaration exist, the right of enforcement of restrictions, liens, and covenants is transferred by the declaration to the association. *Merrionette Manor Homes Improvement Assn.* v. *Heda,* 136 NE2d 556 (Ill. 1956); *Garden Dist. Prop. Owners' Assn.* v. *New Orleans,* 98 So2d 922 (La. 1957); *Neponsit Property Owners' Assn.* v. *Emigrant Industrial Savings Bank,* 15 NE2d 793 (N.Y. 1938); *Rodruck* v. *Sand Point Maintenance Comm.,* 295 P2d 714 (Wash. 1956); 8 Urb. Law Annual 169. Subsequent owners of the land become burdened with the restrictions of these declarations and covenants and obtain the benefits of the association. *Lincolnshire Civic Association Inc.* v. *Beach,* 364 NYS2d 248 (1975).

At times, it is suggested that the association is acting as agent of the property owners. *Neponsit Ppty. Owners' Assn.* v. *Emigrant Ind. Sav. Bank,* 15 NE2d 793 (N.Y. 1938). At other times it is suggested that it is acting as a third-party beneficiary of the covenants in the declaration. *Anthony* v. *Brea Glenbrook Club,* 130 Cal. Reptr. 32 (1976). 40 Ind. L. J. 420, 430 (1964). Or it is acting as the assignee of the developer. *Ibid.* Occasionally, it is simply said that the association is a "convenient instrument by which the property owners may advance their common interests." *Neponsit Property Owners' Assn., Inc.* v. *Emigrant Ind. Sav. Bank,* 15 NE2d 293 (N.Y. 1938); Note, 24 Cornell L. Q. 133 (1939); *In re Public Beach, Borough of Queens,* 199 NE 5 (N.Y. 1935). It does no harm to combine all these thoughts into the declaration.

35.06   Other Uses of the Homeowners' Association

Once the HOA had been invented by lawyers and approved by the courts, other uses were found for this device. In a condominium the HOA *operates* the property and performs all of the customary business functions traditionally performed by the landlord. Each condominium unit owner automatically becomes a member of the HOA and votes to elect its board of directors. In a planned unit development (PUD), the HOA *owns and manages* the common areas and often provides exterior maintenance of the individually owned home units. In modern condominiums, if the building contains stores as well as residential units, ownership of the stores may be vested in the HOA and leased to storekeepers, or the stores may be a part of a separate condominium with its own separate owners' association.

35.07   The Documents

In determining the powers, functions, title, rights, and duties of the HOA, its board of directors, and its officers, one consults:

1. the declaration,
2. the corporate charter of the HOA, and
3. the bylaws of the HOA.

EXAMPLE: The bylaws of a condominium forbid any unit owner to rent his unit to a tenant. The HOA may obtain an injunction against any unit owner who rents out his unit. *Le Fevre* v. *Ostendorf,* 275 NW2d 154 (Wis. 1978).

The bylaws represent a form of private lawmaking, and unit owners agree to be bound by the bylaws when they choose this type of ownership.

These documents are also the source of many rights and duties of the members. The members are also obliged to obey the rules adopted by the board of directors.

EXAMPLE: The rules of a condominium forbid leaving baby buggies in the lobby. The HOA may enforce this rule.

All parties are bound by the relevant statutes and court decisions of the state and the ordinances of the local government pertaining to such developments.

35.08   Power of HOA—Statutes-Regulations

In addition to the powers granted to the HOA board by the declaration, the board has all the powers granted to such boards by the state law relating thereto. 13 ALR4th 598. Some such grants contain broad language, giving the board all the powers necessary or convenient for the operation of the development.

As with condominiums, there are various forms of disclosures required of developers of projects where homeowners' associations are involved. These regulations may be on the federal level, on the state level as required by state land sales acts or subdivision laws, or on the local level as required by county or municipal ordinance. In some instances there may even be regulation directed specifically at offerings of memberships in homeowners' associations. Parness, *Homeowners' Associations: Consideration for the Practicing Attorney,* 46 N.Y.S.B.J. 357, 360 (1974). The task for the developer and his attorney is to determine which regulations apply, and to comply with their requirements.

> RECENT REFERENCES: 5 ALI-ABA Course Materials Journal 93 (1981); Hyatt, Condominiums and Home Associations (1985) (treatise of great value by outstanding authority); 130 U. Pa. L. Rev. 1519 (1982); 94 Harv. L. Rev. 647 (1981); 34 U. of Fla. L. Rev. 218 (1981); 8 ALR4th 1987.

35.09   Liability of Association

In a condominium and PUD the HOA has *control* of various areas. With control goes liability.

> **EXAMPLE:**   Directors were held liable for a criminal assault on a unit owner. *Odar* v. *Schroct,* 202 Cal. Reptr. 457 (1984). See 45 ALR3d 1171. Directors are liable for racial discrimination. *Tilman* v. *Wheaton-Haven Assn.,* 517 F2d 114 (4th Circ. 1975). Directors are liable to a unit owner for injuries suffered owing to negligent maintenance of common areas. *Admiral's Port Assn.* v. *Feldman,* 426 So2d 1054 (Fla. 1983).

Obviously, liability insurance for the association and its directors is a must.

35.10   Master Association

Many developments take place in stages. Often, the reason for this is a practical business judgment. If phase one sells out nicely, the developer moves on to phase two, and so on. It is a matter of convenience for each phase to have its own association but to place a master (or umbrella) association over the entire project.

The master association employs a general manager and provides services needed for the entire project, such as bus transportation.

35.11   Stages in Transfer of Control of Common Areas

One can think of the transfer of control over a PUD development as taking place in phases. First comes the phase of land acquisition and assembly. Next comes the rezoning and plat approval stage. Next comes the preparation, execution, and recording of the declaration. Up to this moment the declaration lacks legal efficacy, for the developer owns all the land. Easements, covenants, and restrictions require divided ownership, with one property owner enforcing his rights against others. Finally comes the phase when the developer makes deeds to lot purchasers, subjecting the lots sold and the lots retained by him to the scheme of restrictions, covenants, and easements, and beginning the transfer of control to the homeowners.

At this stage, the HOA is still under the control of the developer with its officers and directors often being the developer, his family members, and agents. As the lot or homesite sales proceed, under the declaration and corporation documents, the developer's representation decreases, until ultimately the developer's rights are phased out. By establishing the association, the developer has absolute power in the beginning stages of growth of the development. By appointing the first board of directors he maintains effective control for the first several years of development. As development continues, however, the control of the board shifts to the owners through their ever-increasing vote.

When the homeowners have gained control, they may adopt their own by-laws to reflect their experiences and accomplish their purposes.

35.12   Standing to Sue

There is a principle of law that requires a plaintiff who files a suit to have a sufficient interest in the property involved to qualify him to bring the suit. Current statutes take this into account, and although there are earlier decisions to the contrary, current decisions allow the HOA to bring various kinds of suits.

> **EXAMPLE:**   An HOA had standing to sue the developer-builder for defects in the building. *Briarcliffe West Townhouse Owners Assn.* v. *Wisiman Const. Co.*, 118 Ill. App.3d 163, 454 NE2d 363 (Statute was later amended to make clear that this was the law); *Quail Hollow East* v. *Donald J. Scholz Co.*, 263 SE2d 12 (N.C. 1980).

Of course, there are quite a number of cases holding that the HOA lacks standing to sue. 69 ALR3d 1142. Much depends on the type of suit involved.

> REFERENCES: *The Homes Association Handbook, Technical Bulletin* 50 (1964), and *Community Builders Handbook,* both published by Urban Land Institute, 1200 18th Street, N.W., Washington, D.C. 20036; 9 San Diego L. Rev. 28; 8

Urb. Law Ann. 169 (1974); 123 U. Pa. L. Rev. 711 (1975); 43 U. Chgo. L. Rev. 253 (1976). 5 ALI-ABA Course Materials Journal 93 (1981); Hyatt, *Condominiums and Home Associations* (1985) (treatise of great value by outstanding authority); 130 U. Pa. L. Rev. 1519 (1982); 94 Harv. L. Rev. 647 (1981); 34 U. of Fla. L. Rev. 218 (1981); 8 ALR4th 1987.

CHAPTER 36

The Declaration of Restrictions, Easements, Liens, and Covenants: The Master Deed

36.01 In General

In today's land transactions property rights of considerable complexity are generated. This is true particularly of the condominium, the planned unit development (PUD), and the townhouse. Supplementing the local zoning ordinance in such development there will be found a scheme of private building covenants, easements, liens, and restrictions. The landowner in a condominium or PUD will covenant to do a number of things, for example, to pay maintenance assessments, which are foreclosable liens on the homesites or apartments. Each landowner in a condominium, PUD, or townhouse will enjoy a number of valuable easements over his neighbors' property, and his own property will be subject to easements in favor of his neighbors. There is general agreement among property lawyers that these detailed rights should be set forth in a *declaration of restrictions, easements, liens, and covenants,* and that only relatively brief reference should be made to them in the deeds of conveyance. *Leverton* v. *Laird,* 190 NW2d 427 (Iowa); Hyatt, *Condominiums and Home Owner Associations,* 8 (1985). In the case of condominiums this document is, in some states, referred to as the Master Deed.

The legality of this device rests upon the rule that if a recorded document, such as a deed, makes reference to another document recorded in the same office, the two are read together. Thus the provisions of the declaration are treated legally as "set out" in the deed. 82 ALR 412, 416; *Strickland* v. *Overman,* 181 SE2d 136 (N.C. 1971).

36.02 History of the Declaration

We can now profitably look back at the historical development of this important declaration document. Originally, in creating general plan restrictions, the subdivider utilized deeds containing identical restrictions. This proved impractical.

EXAMPLE: Subdivider records a plat dividing his land into 200 lots. He conveys 150 scattered lots by deeds containing identical restrictions. Subdivider dies. His heirs proceed to sell the remaining 50 lots to anyone who is willing to buy. No restrictions appear in the deeds. Obviously, there is no general plan. The required uniformity is lacking.

Prudent developers began to place the restriction in the recorded plat of subdivision. This served two purposes. Since the plat covers *all* lots in the subdivision, a general plan of restrictions is revealed. And since a plat is a recordable document, its recording imparts constructive notice of the restrictions.

As time wore on, restriction plans became complex and lengthy. Physically, there was no room on the face of the plat for these complex restrictions. Hence the subdivider simply placed on the plat a legend stating: "All land in this subdivision is subject to the restrictions appearing in a Declaration of Restrictions recorded contemporaneously herewith." When the plat was handed to the recorder, it was accompanied by a separate typed document, called a *Declaration of Restrictions,* setting forth the restrictions and a statement that they were to be treated as part of the plat. This declaration was signed by the subdivider and duly notarized. This procedure is called *incorporation by reference.* It is quite valid.

When planned unit developments and condominiums came along, a need was perceived for legal machinery to enforce the assessments needed to operate the common areas. The declaration was again utilized, this time to create (1) the lien of the assessments and (2) the covenant by the unit owner to pay it. The declaration is now serving additional purposes.

Finally, some legal body was needed to enforce restrictions, collect assessments, and operate the condominium and the PUD. So the homeowners' association was created and brought into the declaration.

As is evident, over a long period of time the declaration evolved into a very useful document.

36.03   Declaration and Other Document Provisions

The homeowners' association declaration in a PUD is modeled in part after the condominium declaration, which in turn is modeled after the declaration used to create building restrictions.

In both the condominium and the PUD, buyers like to see some limit on the increase in annual assessments, but there should be a provision that a stated percentage of unit owners can, at a regularly called meeting, authorize an expenditure that exceeds the maximum. If the roof leaks, for example, it must be fixed regardless of cost.

Every set of bylaws should state a percentage of the membership that will constitute a quorum. It is best to keep this percentage low. Members tend to shun these meetings. A member who monopolizes meeting time with irrelevant trivia can make meetings tiresome and boring.

The association should hold meetings in strict accordance with its bylaws and elect officers at the proper time. The elected secretary should keep careful custody of the association books and papers, insurance policies, and so forth. In a PUD the common area will be covered by title insurance in the name of the association. Of course, the association will take out liability insurance. It will take out hazard insurance on buildings owned by the association, for example, on recreation buildings. In a condominium it will take out liability and hazard insurance.

If the local law requires the lien of an unpaid assessment to be recorded, the secretary attends to this and keeps the recorded notice of lien in his records. The bylaws will provide for interest on delinquent assessments.

Of course, assessments cannot be levied if the purpose is one not authorized by the documents. *Spitser* v. *Kentwood Home Guardians,* 24 Cal. App.3d 215 (1972).

The declaration is now a standard real estate document, used for creating easements, building restrictions, planned unit developments, and condominiums. Kratovil, *Building Restrictions—Contracts or Servitudes,* 11 John Marshall J. of Practice and Procedure 465 (1978). When recorded, it imparts constructive notice. *Bessemer* v. *Gersten,* 381 So2d 1944 (Fla. 1980); *Lake Sherwood Estates* v. *Continental Bank,* 677 SW2d 372 (Mo. 1984); *Seaton* v. *Clifford,* 100 Cal. Reptr. 779; *Strickland* v. *Overman,* 181 SE2d 136 (N.C. 1970); *Preston Tower Condo Assn.* v. *S. B. Realty,* 685 SW2d 98 (Tex. 1985).

36.04 Amendments

All declarations contain clauses permitting the declaration to be amended. Invariably this clause sets forth a procedure to be followed. This procedure must be followed or the amendment will be void. *Wolinsky* v. *Kadison,* 114 Ill. App. 3d 507, 449 NE2d 151 (1983).

> **EXAMPLE:**   The declaration calls for a two-thirds vote of *all* board members to create an amendment. A bare majority vote for the amendment. It is void.

An amendment must also be reasonable. An unreasonable amendment will be declared void. *Crest Builders Inc.* v. *William Falls Assn.,* 74 Ill. App. 3d 420, 393 NE2d 107.

In general, a purchaser of a lot, unit, or condominium apartment is treated as relying on the declaration that exists on the public records when he buys his property. Any amendment adopted *after* he has recorded his deed may not be binding upon him. *Streams Sports Club* v. *Richmond,* 99 Ill.2d 182, 449 NE2d 151 (1983); *Breene* v. *Plaza Towers,* 310 NW2d 370 (N.D. 1981). However, if the clause permitting amendments states that it will retroactively bind prior purchasers, such purchasers will be bound. That is part of the contract they agreed to. *Kroop* v. *Caravello Condo Inc.,* 323 So2d 307 (Fla. 1975); *Seagate* v. *Duffy,* 330 So2d 484 (Fla. 1976). Although there is a governing law, as in the case of condominiums, the law may expressly give the board the power to adopt amendments and make them binding on *all* unit owners. This, of course, governs.

Once a declaration has been recorded and some deeds issued by the developer, he is powerless to change the easements or other provisions of the declaration unless the declaration so provides. *Horvorka* v. *Harbor Island Owners Assn.,* 356 S.E.2d 453 (S.C.App. 1987).

36.05   Restrictions

Since all that is needed to create enforceable building restrictions or easements is a recorded document that gives public notice of such restrictions or easements, a recorded declaration will suffice for this purpose, when followed by deeds referring thereto. *Spencer* v. *Poole,* 207 Ga.155, 60 SE2d 371 (1972). *Davis* v. *Huguenor,* 408 Ill. 468, 97 NE2d 295; *Kosel* v. *Stone,* 146 Mont. 218, 404 P2d 894; *Lawrence* v. *Brockelman,* 155 N.Y.S.2d 604; 4 ALR2d 1364.

There will be restrictions as to the homesites or apartments and restrictions as to the common areas. For obvious reasons the developer must not retain the right to modify the restrictions. This may destroy the general plan and render the restrictions unenforceable. 19 ALR 2d 1282. Also the declaration must be recorded before any deed or mortgage is recorded, for any deed recorded before the declaration will not be subject to the restrictions, easements, or other rights created by the declaration. All deeds are expressly made subject to the declaration.

The fact that complex building restrictions can be created by a declaration of restrictions in no wise prevents the creation of restrictions by insertion thereof in the plat of subdivision. Indeed, that is the logical place for insertion of simple building restrictions. The declaration, as a means of creating building restrictions, is a modern innovation. It must be remembered that a plat of subdivision, although it is a physically large document, has the map of the subdivision thereon occupying about 90 percent of the space. Moreover, all the language on the face of the plat is hand-lettered by the surveyor. It is this factor that makes it convenient to use a separate typewritten declaration, often running ten pages or more where valuable homesites are involved.

REFERENCE: Kratovil, *Building Restrictions—Contracts or Servitudes,* 11 John Marshall L. J. 465 (1978).

36.06   Easements

Since the law does not specify any particular form an easement must take, the creation of easements by means of a recorded declaration followed by a deed containing grants and reservations of the easements is universally recognized as a proper means of creating easements. The right to use the common areas must be accomplished by the creation of easements and covenants. It should not be done by *dedication.* A dedication is a giving of rights to the *public.* Hence use of the word *dedication* is to be avoided for this word has no place in the creation of private, as distinguished from public, rights. *Drye* v. *Eagle Rock Ranch, Inc.,* 364 SW2d 196 (Tex. Civ. App.)

When a tall building is divided into office space (lower floors) and residential apartments (upper floors) the declaration of easements is quite complicated. It is accompanied by or incorporated into an operating agreement, which sets out the duties of the party who is to operate the elevators, repair water pipes and electrical systems, and so forth.

36.07   Phased Development

It is quite possible to develop an area in several stages. This is a convenience to the developer. He can limit his investment to stage one, and, if it is not a success, he need not develop additional stages. The additional, undeveloped stages can be sold as raw land. It then becomes important to assure that the building restrictions on stage one do not "pour over" into the future undeveloped stages.

However, as to the common elements, for example, the swimming pool in stage one, the declaration should make clear whether or not the developer has the power to bring in several successive stages, all of which will share the use of the pool.

36.08   Party Walls

Where party walls are involved, as in the townhouse, the declaration will contain a detailed provision regarding same, including a provision that the cost of reasonable repair and maintenance shall be shared by the owners who make use of the wall in proportion to such use.

36.09   Lien of Assessments

Both in the condominium and the PUD, the homeowners' association will want a provision in the declaration giving it the right to levy assessments on the homeowner for maintenance of the common areas.

36.10   Lien and Assessment—Priority with Respect to Mortgages

In both the condominium and the PUD there will usually be two liens, the lien of the mortgage on the home or apartment, and the lien of the assessments. Obviously, a question will arise as to whether foreclosure of a mortgage will wipe out delinquent assessment liens or vice versa.

All states have *condominium* laws. All these laws deal with assessments, so that the condominium assessment is pretty largely a statutory lien at this time. Probably the statute sets forth the requirements for the creation of the lien and assigns it a priority as respects other liens. The condominium declaration adds other provisions regarding assessments. In making assessments the board must comply with the statute and the declaration. The priority of a first mortgage over an assessment lien depends on the state law and the language of the declaration.

As regards the *PUD*, as of this writing there are very few state laws governing the priority of the assessment liens. And as to simple subdivisions, the assessments levied to enforce building restrictions are not governed by any laws or ordinances.

In any case the declaration is likely to contain a clause giving the first mortgagee a lien prior to that of the assessments and this clause is likely to prevail.

36.11   Covenants

When the declaration is recorded and when deeds are given to purchasers, the declaration becomes a covenant running with the land. The benefits and burdens accrue automatically to subsequent purchasers. *Pepe* v. *Whispering Sands Condominium.* 351 So2d 755 (Fla. 1977).

36.12   Association as a Vehicle for Enforcing Restrictions, Liens, and Covenants

The enforcement of *restrictions, liens,* and *covenants* can legally be transferred through the declaration to an association or corporation formed by the home or apartment owners. *Merrionette Manor Homes* v. *Heda,* 11 Ill. App.2d 186, 136 NE2d 556; *Neponsit Property Owners' Assn.* v. *Emigrant Industrial Savings Bank,* 278 N.Y. 248, 15 NE2d 793; *Rodruck* v. *Sand Point Maintenance Comm.,* 40 Wash.2d 565, 295 P2d 714.

36.13   Deed Clauses to Implement the Declaration

To fully implement the declaration, it is necessary to insert a clause in the deed to the homebuyer or apartment buyer. Such a clause might be:

> **SUGGESTED FORM:** Subject to Declaration of Easements, Restrictions, Liens, and Covenants dated _____ and recorded in the Office of the Recorder of Deeds of _____ County, as Document No. _____ which is incorporated herein by reference thereto. Grantor grants to the Grantee, his heirs and assigns, as easements appurtenant to the premises hereby conveyed, the easements created by said Declaration for the benefit of the owners of the parcel of realty herein described. Grantor reserves to himself, his heirs and assigns, as easements appurtenant to the remaining parcels described in said Declaration, the easements thereby created for the benefit of said remaining parcels described in said Declaration, and this conveyance is subject to said easements and the right of the Grantor to grant said easements in the conveyances of said remaining parcels or any of them, and the parties hereto, for themselves, their heirs, personal representatives, and assigns, covenant to be bound by the covenants, restrictions,, and agreements in said document set forth. Said covenants and restrictions are covenants running with the land both as to burden and benefits, and this conveyance is subject to all said covenants and restrictions as though set forth in full herein. The land hereby conveyed is also subject to the liens created by said Declaration, and same are binding on the grantees, their heirs, personal representatives, and assigns. All of the provisions of said Declaration are hereby incorporated herein as though set forth in full herein.

In some decisions it has been held that the filing of the declaration would suffice to create restrictions even though they were not mentioned in the subdivider's deeds. *Kosel* v. *Stone,* 146 Mont. 218, 404 P2d 894; *Steuart Transp. Co.* v. *Ashe,* 304 A2d 788 (Md. 1973). But in California precisely the opposite has been held. There the declaration is totally ineffective unless the deeds refer to it. *Smith* v. *Rasqui,* 1 Cal. Reptr. 478. However, it suffices to state in the deeds that the land is "subject to covenants, conditions, restrictions, and easements of record," *Seaton* v. *Clifford,* 100 Cal. Reptr. 779; *Davis* v. *Huguenor,* 408 Ill. 468, 97 NE2d 295. Or it may be stated in the deed that it is subject to restrictions contained in the Declaration recorded in Book _____, Page _____. *Lake St Louis Assn.* v. *Ringwald,* 652 SW2d 158 (Mo. 1985). Obviously, the full suggested form should be used.

A different rule is applied if all of the restrictions, liens, and covenants are included in a recorded plat of the subdivision. The usual rule is that a deed describing the land conveyed as a lot in a recorded subdivision automatically is treated as if the plat were attached to and formed part of the deed. After all, how can you possibly locate your lot without looking at the plat? And if you look at the plat you are bound to see the restrictions. The same rule applies if the plat states *on its face* that all lots are subject to restrictions set forth in a declaration "recorded contemporaneously herewith." *Spencer* v. *Poole,* 207 Ga. 155, 60 SE2d 371.

Where the owner of a condominium apartment, PUD unit, or town house is placing a mortgage on his property, a clause is inserted in the mortgage along the following lines:

> **CLAUSE:** Subject to Declaration of Easements, Restrictions, Liens, and Covenants dated _____ and recorded in the Office of the Recorder of Deeds of _____ County in Book _____ page _____ as Document No. _____ , which is incorporated herein by reference thereto. Mortgagor grants to the mortgagee, its successors, and assigns all rights of every description created by said Declaration for the benefit of the mortgaged premises, same to run with the mortgaged land. The provisions of said Declaration regarding liens of assessments are also incorporated herein by reference thereto.

36.14 Sale by Homeowner

The declaration should provide that upon sale of a home or apartment, the seller shall not be liable for assessments levied or covenants or restrictions breached thereafter. Unless this clause is included there is a legal possibility of continuing liability.

36.15 Membership Corporation

The declaration will set forth who the members are to be in the home association created for a PUD or for a condominium.

36.16   Marketable Title Acts

Under the Marketable Title Acts, rights in land—including covenants, restrictions, private assessment liens, and, in some instances, easements also—terminate after a stated period of time unless fresh recordings are made to keep these interests alive.

> REFERENCE: For sample declaration of restrictions for detached single-family dwellings see FHA Land Planning Bulletin No. 3—Protective Covenants Data Sheet 40, also Sample Form Protective Covenants, both set forth in the Appendix to *Community Builders Handbook,* published by Urban Land Institute, 1200 18th Street, N.W., Washington, DC. 20036.

CHAPTER 37

Planned Unit Developments

37.01 The Planned Unit Idea

The planned unit development (PUD) may consist of attached homes, detached homes, condominiums, garden and high-rise apartments, or combinations of such buildings, all with common open areas and sometimes with private recreation facilities. The developer is permitted to construct more units per acre than is allowed under a standard lot and block subdivision. This more efficient land use results in lower prices for buyers. The purchaser is free of the work and worry of outside maintenance, which is often transferred to the homeowners' association. Small private yards and shared recreation facilities reduce the chores associated with any particular unit and give the owners a place for relaxation and enjoyment. The municipality benefits in that the streets and utilities, which are generally the municipality's responsibility to repair, replace, and maintain, are often privately owned and maintained by the property owners. 32 Maine L. Rev. 29 (1980).

The PUD is created by recording a plat of subdivision which delineates the building lots and common areas and the recording of a declaration of covenants, conditions, and restrictions that (1) sets forth the rules governing the property, (2) creates an association which may hold title to the common areas, (3) provides that membership in the association is automatic upon the purchase of a unit, (4) establishes voting rights and the rights of the owners to use the common areas, and (5) sets out the obligation of unit owners to pay assessments to defray expenses for the maintenance of the common areas and that such assessments are a lien on the unit until paid.

37.02   Cluster Housing

The phrase *cluster housing* means that the individual homes, row houses, or apartment buildings are grouped together on relatively small plots of land with large
surrounding areas of land left open for common recreational and park developments. The cluster form of development is economical because the clustering of
houses reduces the cost of supplying utilities and roads.

37.03   Creating a PUD

Before the first lot is sold, the developer obtains zoning and subdivision approval, incorporates the nonprofit homeowners' association (HOA), and records
the land subdivision plat and declaration of covenants and easements for all of
the land in the planned unit. His plat identifies (1) property to be transferred to
public agencies, such as any proposed public streets, (2) the individual homesites,
(3) the common areas to be transferred by the developer to the home association,
and (4) any other parcels, such as a church site or shopping center, to be kept by
the developer or transferred to others.

   Recorded contemporaneously with the plat is a *declaration of easements, covenants, restrictions, and liens.* It is hereafter referred to as the *declaration.*

37.04   Zoning

Most states accept the notion of PUD zoning, with its novel mixed use and floating zone concepts. 5 Rohan, *Zoning and Land Use Controls,* Ch. 32. At least fifteen
states have enacted laws on the subject. *Ibid.* The legislation was designed to encourage local governments to tailor their regulations to local needs. *Ibid.* Necessarily, bargaining takes place between local government and developer to reach
agreement as to unit size, use mix, and so on, so that contract zoning is also
involved. *Rutland Environmental Protection Assn.* v. *Kane County,* 31 Ill. App.3d 82,
334 NE2d 215 (1975). In short, all the zoning novelties are present and find acceptance. Often the PUD ordinance is part of the zoning ordinance. *City of Urbana*
v. *County of Champaign,* 27 Ill. Dec. 777, 389 NE2d 1185 (1979).

   On the whole, the modern decisions are likely to sustain the validity of PUD
zoning even though it is a far cry from "cooky-cutter" single-family dwelling zoning, 43 ALR3d 888, and even though the density requirements are different from
those applicable to conventional subdivisions. *Peabody* v. *Phoenix,* 485 P2d 565
(Ariz. 1971).

37.05   Plat Approval and Zoning Combined

It is evident that where a local government is called upon to assign a floating
zone area to a PUD, it is almost impossible to separate the plat approval process

from the rezoning process. Hence many local governments have adopted a unitary approval process that combines the two operations. 29 Hastings L. J. 647.

The PUD is often authorized by means of the grant of a *special exception permit* under the local zoning ordinance. Usually the zoning ordinance contains an elaborate section listing the requirements for the granting of the special permit. Developers usually submit a rough draft of the development scheme and thus obtain the city's views as to what would be acceptable. Commonly the ordinance provisions also list the requirements for plat approval, and the same department considers the special permit application together with the request for plat approval. At times a rezoning may be needed, and a petition for rezoning must be filed and appropriate notices given to adjoining owners.

At some point there will be a hearing before the zoning board, and opponents of the development will be given an opportunity to present their case.

37.06   The Common Area

The documents should convey ownership of the common area to the HOA. Indeed, a PUD ordinance may require that ownership be vested in the HOA. The plat of a PUD and the declaration creating it will contain easements granting the unit owners various easements in the common areas. The village may condition its approval of the plat on the assumption by the HOA of the obligation to maintain the common areas, particularly any roads that connect with city streets.

Since it is imperative that the common areas be kept in the ownership of the homeowners' association and not dedicated to the public, the recorded plat must bear on its face a legend relative to all the common areas indicating that the area is *not* dedicated to the public and that its ownership is reserved to the developer (who later will deed it to the association). If such a legend is lacking, courts may hold that any area having the appearance of common grounds is, by implication, dedicated to the public. However, since the homebuyers will want the developer to deed the land to the home association, an agreement to do so should be contained in the plat or in the accompanying declaration or in a separate contract. Also, appropriate language must be incorporated in the text of the plat to indicate that the individual homeowners take easements in the common properties but no ownership therein. This means that the legend on the plat should be quite comprehensive as:

> Full ownership of the tracts marked *park, playground, private lake, and golf course* (describe all other such areas) is retained in *ABC* (the developer) for ultimate conveyance to *XYZ,* a nonprofit corporation whose membership will be comprised of homeowners in this development, all according to the provisions of the declaration of restrictions, easements, liens, and covenants filed contemporaneously herewith, and made a part of this plat. Conveyances of lots in this subdivision shall not be deemed to convey title to any part of the retained areas. Said areas are not dedicated to the public. With respect to the total area embraced in this plat, and all parts thereof, easements, covenants, liens, and restrictions are created in and by the declaration aforesaid.

37.07(a)   Common Areas—Agreement of Developer to Convey to Home Association

The declaration will contain an agreement that not later than a set date, the developer will convey the common areas to the homeowners' association. The declaration should be signed as *accepted* by the homeowners' association so that it can enforce this agreement.

37.07(b)   Common Areas—Easements—Paramount Rights of Home Association

The declaration should create easements in favor of all of the homeowners in the development for access over the private walks ad streets, for utilities, water, sewers, and other services, and for use of the common areas, and so on, but it should make such easement grant expressly subject and inferior to certain rights of the homeowners' association. These rights should include the right of the association to exercise, free and clear of all private rights created in the homeowners, the following rights: (1) the right of the association to suspend the enjoyment of the common areas by any homeowner and the furnishing of services by the association (garbage removal, furnishing water, and so forth) to the delinquent homeowner while his maintenance assessments remain unpaid; (2) the right to manage, maintain, and control the common areas for the benefit of the homeowners, and to promulgate reasonable rules toward this end; (3) the right to dedicate part or all of the common properties to the public for public use; (4) the right of the homeowners' association to charge reasonable admission and other fees for the use of the common areas.

37.07(c)   Common Areas—Artificial Lakes

In some planned developments an artificially created lake is one of the attractive common facilities. It is quite clear that neither the public nor any public body has any rights whatever in lakes so created. The developer has the legal right to reserve to himself the right to dictate who may use the lake, or he may grant this right to the homeowners. *Mayer* v. *Grueber,* 138 NW2d 197 (Wis. 1965); *Thompson* v. *Enz,* 154 NW2d 473 (Mich. 1967).

37.08(a)   The Declaration—Building Restrictions

The declaration will establish a comprehensive general plan of restrictions governing minutely the structures and uses permitted in the development, both on the homesites and on the common areas. The plat or declaration should also vest in the home association the right to pass upon the plans of any structure to be erected by any home buyer or any alterations to the exterior of any building. 40 ALR3d 864.

37.08(b)   The Declaration—Covenants

The declaration will contain covenants binding on each homeowner to pay the assessments levied on his lot for maintenance charges, which covenants create a *personal liability* on which a personal judgment can be obtained by the association against a defaulting homeowner. It will also contain covenants by the homeowners' association to (1) maintain and operate the common property; (2) administer architectural controls; (3) enforce other covenants; and in some cases (4) maintain all or part of the exterior of individual homes. The covenants provide for amendments, but any amendment requires a vote of the homeowners.

37.08(c)   The Declaration—Lien for Maintenance

The declaration provides for the imposition of a maintenance assessment on each lot in the development. Homeowners' associations tend to operate somewhat informally. The danger here is that if procedures grow too lax (meetings held on days other than those set in bylaws, notice of meeting lacking or defective, and so on), the assessments made by the association may be declared invalid. *Noremac, Inc.* v. *Centre Hill Court, Inc.,* 178 SE 877 (Va. 1935).

37.08(d)   The Declaration—Restraints on Sales

Any provision in the declaration or deeds that a homeowner cannot sell his lot except by consent of a majority vote of the association is invalid. Such a clause is an illegal restraint on alienation (sale). *Mountain Springs Assn.* v. *Wilson,* 196 A2d 270 (N.J. 1963). Also invalid is any clause where only a member of the homeowners' association can purchase a homesite. *Ibid.* Nor can the declaration or by-laws of the association provide that sales by a homeowner to a future purchaser can only be made to a purchaser approved by the association. *Tuckerton Beach Club* v. *Bender,* 219 A2d 528 (N.J. 1966). No refusal to sell can be racially motivated. *Sullivan* v. *Little Huntington Park,* 396 U.S. 229 (1969). It is safe to provide that any homesite purchaser automatically acquires membership in the homeowners' association as a normal incident of home ownership. Other acceptable provisions are discussed in Chapter 38 on condominiums.

37.08(e)   The Declaration—Other Provisions

The declaration should also contain, among other things, the following:

1. The name of the PUD and the HOA. A detailed paragraph on the creation of the HOA is needed, listing the obligations of the HOA to operate the PUD and the rights and duties of the unit members. The HOA should be a state-chartered, nonprofit corporation. Each unit owner is automatically a member of the HOA.

2. A legal description of the land included in the PUD.

3. A description of each unit.

4. A description of the common elements or areas, and a contract by the developer to convey them to the HOA at a specified time.

5. Restrictions on use of the units and the common areas.

6. As in the condominium, a careful provision should be included in the declaration, providing for the procedure to amend the declaration.

7. The declaration should set forth the powers of the HOA. These should be included in the HOA corporate charter also.

8. Provision should be made in the declaration for the levying of assessments by the HOA. The lien and priority of such assessments must be set forth in detail.

9. The developer's warranties of the building can be included in the declaration, as well as the limitations the developer chooses to place on the warranties. The declaration may provide that a deed of the unit carries the benefit of the warranties.

In some states the *statutes* specifically regulate the documents creating the PUD. See Sec. 2–101 Uniform Planned Community Act. Where this is the case, all the requirements of the statute must be complied with. However, in many (probably most) states, the PUD is regulated by local *ordinance*. Many developers find that the condominium statute has grown so complex with its regulations and disclosure requirements that it is easier to work with the local governments under a PUD ordinance.

37.09   Mortgage Problems

A mortgage on a PUD homesite should contain a covenant of the mortgagor to pay all assessments and a covenant not to vote to amend the declaration without the mortgagee's written consent.

If there is a prior blanket mortgage, the mortgagee should consent to the creation of the PUD and amend the prior mortgage to allow partial releases from the lien of that mortgage as units are sold.

A standard FNMA mortgage may be used to finance the purchase of a PUD unit, but it must have a PUD rider as shown on p. 496.

37.10   Taxes on Common Areas

The common areas have no sales value to a third party. They are encumbered with easements that render them valueless to any purchaser. The value of the common areas is reflected in the increased value they contribute to the residential areas. Hence the tax assessor should not assess the common areas at the value they would have if unencumbered by easements. *People* v. *O'Donnel,* 139 App. Div.

PLANNED UNIT DEVELOPMENT RIDER

2629

THIS PLANNED UNIT DEVELOPMENT ("PUD") RIDER is made this........................day of ...., 19...., and is incorporated into and shall be deemed to amend and supplement a Mortgage, Deed of Trust or Deed to Secure Debt (herein "security instrument") dated of even date herewith, given by the undersigned (herein "Borrower") to secure Borrower's Note to.................................... ....(herein "Lender") and covering the Property described in the security instrument and located at..
(Property Address)

.... The Property comprises a parcel of land improved with a dwelling, which, together with other such parcels and certain common areas and facilities. all as described in........................... .... (herein "Declaration"), forms a planned unit development known as.................................. ....
(Name of Planned Unit Development)

(herein "PUD").

PLANNED UNIT DEVELOPMENT COVENANTS. In addition to the covenants and agreements made in the security instrument, Borrower and Lender further covenant and agree as follows:

A. PUD Obligations. Borrower shall perform all of Borrower's obligations under the: (i) Declaration; (ii) articles of incorporation, trust instrument or any equivalent document required to establish the homeowners association or equivalent entity managing the common areas and facilities of the PUD (herein "Owners Association"); and (iii) by-laws, if any, or other rules or regulations of the Owners Association. Borrower shall promptly pay, when due, all assessments imposed by the Owners Association.

B. Hazard Insurance. In the event of a distribution of hazard insurance proceeds in lieu of restoration or repair following a loss to the common areas and facilities of the PUD, any such proceeds payable to Borrower are hereby assigned and shall be paid to Lender for application to the sums secured by the security instrument, with the excess, if any, paid to Borrower.

C. Condemnation. The proceeds of any award or claim for damages, direct or consequential. payable to Borrower in connection with any condemnation or other taking of all or any part of the common areas and facilities of the PUD, or for any conveyance in lieu of condemnation, are hereby assigned and shall be paid to Lender. Such proceeds shall be applied by Lender to the sums secured by the security instrument in the manner provided under Uniform Covenant 9.

D. Lender's Prior Consent. Borrower shall not, except after notice to Lender and with Lender's prior written consent, consent to:

(i) the abandonment or termination of the PUD;

(ii) any material amendment to the Declaration, trust instrument, articles of incorporation, by-laws of the Owners Association, or any equivalent constituent document of the PUD, including, but not limited to, any amendment which would change the percentage interests of the unit owners in the common areas and facilities of the PUD;

(iii) the effectuation of any decision by the Owners Association to terminate professional management and assume self-management of the PUD; or

(iv) the transfer, release, encumbrance, partition or subdivision of all or any part of the PUD's common areas and facilities, except as to the Owners Association's right to grant easements for utilities and similar or related purposes.

E. Remedies. If Borrower breaches Borrower's covenants and agreements hereunder, including the covenant to pay when due planned unit development assessments, then Lender may invoke any remedies provided under the security instrument, including, but not limited to, those provided under Uniform Covenant 7.

IN WITNESS WHEREOF, Borrower has executed this PUD Rider.

_____
—Borrower

_____
—Borrower

496

83, 124 N.Y.S. 36 (1910); *Matter of Crane-Berkely Corp.* v. *Lavis,* 238 App. Div. 124, 263 N.Y.S. 556 (1935).

There is no guarantee of this result until the matter has been worked out with the local assessor. Assessors tend to be rather independent individuals. Basically, the *problem* is one of persuasion.

CHAPTER 38

Condominiums

38.01 In General

In the past two decades, the condominium has sprung from near obscurity to become a common form of property ownership. Interest rates and the cost of new housing may drastically curtail the ability of the American public to purchase detached housing. The townhouse, cluster homes, and apartments become obvious alternatives. If those living units are to be individually owned, the condominium form of ownership is an apt vehicle.

The condominium form of ownership may be best explained by comparing it to rental apartments. A typical apartment building consists of apartments, lobby, halls, stairways, roof, building walls, garage, grounds, walks, and drives surrounding the building. The apartment is the private domain of the occupant. Its use is not shared with other occupants. But the other areas (lobby, halls, stairways, roof, walls, grounds, walks, drives), the *common elements,* are owned by the landlord and shared by the tenants. In the condominium, the ownership follows this simple pattern. The apartment is purchased and becomes the exclusive domain of the owner, but *ownership* and *use* of the common elements are shared with all other apartment owners.

> **EXAMPLE:** Developer acquires a tract of land and obtains a construction loan for the construction of a 50-unit condominium project. The units are identical. The building is built and Purchaser contracts to buy Unit #1. Purchaser really is buying Unit #1 plus a percentage interest in the common elements. Technically, the unit is bounded by the inner surface of the apartment walls and the common elements include everything in the project that is not part of a unit, that is, the ground the project is built on, the air space above it, the outside walls of the project, walls between the units, its foundation and roof, the basement, stairs, elevators, foyers, swimming pool, janitor's apartment, water tanks, fire escapes, heating plant, air conditioning system, and so on. Purchaser receives a deed

that makes him owner of Unit #1 and of an undivided percentage interest in the common elements.

The purchaser will thus own the unit just as if it were a separate house and will become an owner in common of the *common elements* with fellow unit owners. When the purchase closes, the construction mortgage will be released from Unit #1 and its undivided share of the common elements. If Purchaser finances the purchase of Unit #1, the lender will have a mortgage lien against Unit #1 and its share of the common elements.

Condominiums are not limited to apartments. Cluster homes, townhouses, commercial structures of office and other uses, campsites, parking spaces, hotels, and other projects have been submitted to the condominium form of ownership.

38.01(a)   Uniform Condominium Act

The National Conference of Commissioners on Uniform State Laws have drafted a proposed uniform law, the Uniform Condominium Act (UCA) regulating the field of condominium law. A version of this law has been adopted in Arizona, Louisiana, Maine, Minnesota, Missouri, Nebraska, New Hampshire, New Mexico, Pennsylvania, Rhode Island, West Virginia, and Wisconsin. It contains a conversion article that extends protection to tenants. It requires disclosure of information and warranties of the building.

How far this law will progress is hard to say. Local governments have diligently sought to protect tenants against conversions, and they are fighting legislation that will restrict their powers. The commissioners are also drafting alternative legislation. Many of the good ideas in UCA are already part of existing law.

38.01(a)(1)   Public Offering—Statement

The UCA and some of the newer condominium laws require the developer to file with the state's real estate commission and deliver to each purchaser of a unit a public offering statement. This is a complex document that summarizes the law, the operational system of the condominium, and the facts concerning the physical condition of the building as revealed by an engineer's inspection. It also sets forth each tenant's right to purchase the unit in which he resides. The description of the assessments procedure is quite detailed.

38.02   Basic Documents

Several basic documents are necessary pertaining to a condominium.

38.02(a)   Basic Documents—Declaration

The condominium declaration is the basic organic document or constitution for the condominium. It spells out the extent of the interest that each purchaser acquires and the rights and liabilities of the unit owners. *Pepe* v. *Whispering Sands Condo. Assn., Inc.* 351 So2d 755 (Fla. 1977). Once the declaration is recorded, the last act in creation of the condominium is accomplished and the condominium comes into existence. *State S. & L. Assn.* v. *Kauaian Dev. Co.*, 445 P2d 109 (Hawaii 1968).

State laws require the declaration to contain:

1. The name of the condominium.

2. A description of the property being submitted to the condominium form of ownership. A traditional legal description is used here.

3. A description of each unit. The condominium survey is a three-dimensional marvel of far greater sophistication than the two-dimensional version. It has to be. Condominium units are often cubes of air space, but it is necessary to describe these pieces of real estate with the same precision with which parcels of land are described.

There are three methods by which a unit of air space can be described:

1. *The subdivision plat method.* A plat of subdivision of air space and the air lots representing the individual units is recorded by means of a drawing. This will permit conveyance of a particular unit by its number, as shown on the plat.

2. *The land and apartment survey.* A survey is first made of the land, showing the location of the building. Space surveys of each unit on each floor are then made showing the elevation of the floor and ceiling surfaces, the dimensions of the inside surfaces of the walls of each unit, and their location with reference to the boundaries of the land projected vertically upward.

3. *Floor plan method.* In lieu of individual apartment surveys, a survey can be made of the land showing the location of the building. This is attached to floor plans showing each unit's location, dimensions, and elevation from the ground floor surface, with a certification by the architect that the building was built substantially in accordance with the plans.

One difficulty with these methods is that the typical condominium unit is an apartment in a multilevel building.

PROBLEM: How does one describe the perimeters of an apartment located, let us say, on the twentieth floor of an apartment building? How does one describe with legal accuracy the exact height above ground level of the floor and ceiling of the apartment? Remember that a condominium unit is basically a cube of space. Space is considered to be land that can be deeded and mortgaged. But it is harder to describe than a simple two-dimensional tract of land, such as a lot on which a house has been erected. As regards the house lot, the surveyor can go on the tract of land and place monuments or markers at the lot corners. But one cannot plant markers in the sky. Hence, the problem.

One part of the problem is simple. The surveyor can depict on the ground the proposed perimeters of the apartment unit and then state that such perimeters extend upward indefinitely. To grasp this idea, imagine a rectangular lot, with stakes at all four lot corners. Then imagine the lot line thus created as extending up to the sky. Now you have the perimeters of the lot, however high you can go, since surveyors, given the outlines of a tract of land at ground level, can, by use of instruments, extend the lot lines upward to the heavens.

The other problem is more difficult. Legally, one cannot measure the height of the floor and ceiling from "the ground." The ground is not a stable and definite legal marker. Indeed, in the process of erecting a building, the construction crew invariably levels and changes the grade of the ground. Many condominium apartments are contracted for sale before construction begins.

Engineers have solved this problem.

EXAMPLE: In Chicago, for example, the city, by ordinance, has established an artificial horizontal plane beneath the surface of the entire city. This plane is uniform throughout the city. At many places throughout the city, concrete markers are placed extending about six feet downward from the sidewalk. The sidewalk is used because its grade is rarely altered. Each such monument contains a legend, stating, for example, "twenty feet above Chicago City Datum." The *Datum* is the artificial legal subsurface that extends at the same level throughout the entire city. The markers are called *Bench Marks*. There are hundreds scattered throughout the city, each identified by location and number. Now a surveyor, plotting a condominium unit on the twentieth floor, can show on his survey that the floor of the apartment is located ____ feet above Chicago City Datum as established by Bench Mark ____. The same is done with the ceiling. With this system, establishing vertical boundaries is a simple task for the surveyor.

The United Geodetic Survey has established its own *datum* and *bench marks*. Some surveyors prefer to use these because they are considered more accurate than city datum and city bench marks.

4. A description of the common elements.

5. A description of the limited common elements.

6. A statement of the share of each unit owner in the common elements. This share should be expressed as a percentage rather than a fraction. These shares are allocated upon several bases. In California, each unit, irrespective of its size and value as compared to the other units, has one equal share with the other units. Cal. Civ. Code §1353(b). In Illinois, the shares are computed on the basis of the value of the unit as compared to the value of the project as a whole. Ill. Rev. Stat. Ch. 30, §304(e). Other states have more complex formulas for allocation. Va. Code Ann. §55–79.55.

7. If the condominium is to be a phased or add-on condominium, the declaration should give the option to add additional property to the condominium, state any limitations on the developer's ability to bring other land under the declaration, and set forth the manner of allocation of common elements, voting rights, and charges for common expenses, upon the joinder of the additional property. See Ill. Rev. Stat. Ch. 30, §325.

8. If the condominium is a leasehold condominium, the declaration should identify the lease and state the unit owner's rights upon the termination of the lease.

There are other provisions that state law does not require the declaration to contain but they properly belong in the declaration because they affect the basic rights of the unit owners. They include:

1. A provision that ownership of an apartment and of the owner's share of the common elements shall not be severed or separated and that any conveyance or mortgage of the one without the other is prohibited. Also, that any partition suit with respect to the common elements is forbidden.

2. A provision giving the condominium association the right to levy assessments on the apartment owners for maintenance, and so forth, and creating personal liability on the unit owner plus a foreclosable lien on each apartment for any delinquency in paying the assessments applicable to each apartment unit, and stating the maximum assessment permitted.

3. Provision that in the event of total or substantial destruction of the building by fire or other hazard, or where the property reaches obsolescence, a stated percentage of co-owners' votes shall determine whether to rebuild or sell the property. A number of states have laws on this point.

4. A grant of easements to each apartment owner giving him rights of ingress and egress and other easement rights. As time goes by, buildings often settle. Thus the condominium unit sinks slightly into the common elements (the interior of walls, floors, and ceilings), and common elements encroach into the units. To dispose of this problem, the condominium declaration provides that as the building settles, the unit owner enjoys an easement to occupy the area not assigned to him by the surveys. Comment, 50 Calif. L. Rev. 299, 303 (1962). In tall buildings, the upper floors sway a good deal in a high wind. This is readily perceived when the water in the wash bowl sloshes around and chandeliers hung on chains sway perceptibly. Obviously, a unit in this area trespasses into the air space (common element) surrounding the building. It is probably a good idea to include a "sway easement" in the declaration.

NEW LAWS: Encroachment easements exist by virtue of statute in some states thereby allowing an easement for encroachment where the encroachment is the result of a deviation from the plat and plans of construction, repair, renovation, restoration, or settling or shifting. This statutory easement will not protect unit owners in the event of their willful or intentional misconduct, or exculpate the contractor from liability for reason of failure to comply with the plans. Code Va. §§ 55–79.60.

5. A provision is needed stating that all easements, covenants, and agreements in the declaration run with the land. Some statement is also needed that the benefit and burden of these covenants run with each unit. A provision should be included that when any apartment owner sells, his personal liability for future breaches of these covenants ends with the sale.

6. The condominium owners want to have the ability to control occupancy to avoid the presence of incompatible neighbors. Such control seems to be permitted in some states. 17 ALR4th 1247. *Rights of first refusal* are valid. These give the association the right to buy the unit at the same price a buyer from the unit owner is willing to pay. Practically speaking, these rights are rarely used because the association does not have the funds to make the purchase. Logistically, the unit owner's contract with a buyer must provide for this contingency, and the title company and buyer may require proof that the association was given notice of the sale and did not choose to exercise its right. The right of first refusal is vanishing. FNMA opposes its use. It lends itself to racial discrimination. Another declaration provision prohibits occupancy of the unit (not transfer of the unit) until the occupant is approved by the board. Ross, *Condominiums and Preemptive Options: The Right of First Refusal,* 18 Hastings L. J. 585 (1967). Of course, these provisions cannot be used as a means of racial discrimination. 50 Calif. L. Rev. 299, 317 (1962). The right of first refusal should not apply to a sale made

by a mortgagee who has acquired title through foreclosure. See generally *Backus* v. *Smith,* 364 So2d 786 (Fla. 1978); *Hoover & Morris Development Co.* v. *Mayfield,* 212 SE2d 778 (Ga. 1975); *Gale* v. *York Center Community Cooperative Inc.,* 171 NE2d 30 (Ill. 1961); *Lake Shore Club* v. *Lakefront Realty Corp.,* 398 NE2d 893 (Ill. App. 1979).

Reasonable restrictions against the occupancy of units by children under a specific age are probably valid. 100 ALR3d 241; *White Egret Condominium Inc.* v. *Franklin,* 379 So2d 346 (Fla. 1980). Some comment on this point must be made. The matter is one of state law. It does not follow that this rule will win acceptance in all states. States in the Sun Belt retirement areas are much more likely to sanction barring children than states like Massachusetts or Rhode Island. State laws forbidding all types of discrimination, including age discrimination, are being widely enacted. These laws may well prohibit restraints against occupancy by children. A social problem of major proportions is developing.

7. The unit owner's right to lease is a hotly debated issue. While estimates vary, somewhere between 25 percent and 33 percent of condominium apartment units are owned by investors who rent their units to tenants. Increasing opposition to this practice focuses on the alleged inattention of the investor to condominium affairs. He attends no meetings and serves on no committees. He is indifferent, it is alleged, to tenant conduct that annoys owner–occupants and makes the building less desirable.

Restriction on the renting of units is valid, if done properly. *Seagate Condominium Assn., Inc.,* v. *Duffy,* 330 So2d 484 (Fla. 1976); *Kroop* v. *Caravelle Condominium, Inc.,* 323 So2d 307 (Fla. 1975). Probably a significant restraint of this character ought to be included in the declaration. Courts may refuse to apply the restriction in hardship cases, as where an owner dies and it is convenient to rent the unit while the estate is in probate. Indeed, it would be wise to except this and other hardship cases explicitly, so as to discourage courts from holding the entire restriction void for lack of reasonableness.

Unit owners who rent should not use printed tenant-type leases without amendatory language. Ordinary apartment leases contain provisions not suitable for condominiums, such as landlord will furnish heat, hot water, and so on. The tenant's obligation to care for ordinary repairs should be spelled out. Often, the association requires that all leases be on a prescribed form that causes the tenant to be aware of and agree to conform to the building rules.

Resort type condominiums present special problems. Suppose you put a clause in the declaration that rentals shall be for a minimum of two weeks. This type of restriction eliminates the danger of a motel type operation. But if the restrictions on renting get too strict, there is the danger that more and more units will be sold to permanent residents, who may amend the declaration to eliminate renting altogether. This, of curse, is bad for those who bought the units basically for investment purposes, hoping to profit through renting the unit most of the year.

8. Most declarations have a clause obligating each unit owner to abide by all the rules or bylaws promulgated by the homeowners' association. Needed flexibility is obtained in this way since new and necessary rules can be enacted through the simple majority vote of a quorum, instead of a majority of the apartment owners. It is important that a method of enforcement exists for these rules. The declaration should allow the association to obtain injunctive relief. In this way the association may, in a serious case, have the court order the violation to cease.

9. The declaration should give the unit owners the right to amend the declaration and provide that the amendment will be binding upon all present and future owners. The declaration should state the procedure for amendment and the number of unit owners who must vote on the amendment for it to become effective.

38.02(b)   Basic Documents—Amendments to Declaration

The subject of amendments to the declaration has been generally discussed in Chapter 36. If you refer to that discussion you will see that some courts have taken the position that the declaration is like the constitution of the condominium. Those who buy units in reliance on a recorded declaration cannot be deprived of their rights under that declaration by a subsequent amendment. *Pepe* v. *Whispering Sands Condo Assn.*, 351 So2d 755 (Fla. 1977). But if the declaration specifically permits amendments to be retroactive, other courts allow retroactive amendments. *Crest Builders Inc.* v. *Willow Falls,* 74 Ill. App.3d 420, 393 NE2d 107 (1979).

To illustrate the point, let us assume that when you buy your condominium unit, you have a pet dog, and the documents are silent on the subject of pets or retroactive amendments. The courts will not let a subsequent amendment deprive you of your pet. But if the declaration permits retroactive amendments and an amendment bars pets, you may have to give up your pet.

38.02(c)   Basic Documents—Deeds

The individual deed of a unit need not necessarily be a complex document insofar as its legal description is concerned. The basis for such description will already have been provided by: (1) recording of the subdivision plat; (2) recording of the declaration to which were appended the land and apartment surveys containing legal descriptions of the various apartments; or (3) recording of the declaration to which were appended the land survey and building floor plans, in which case the legal descriptions of the apartments will have been set forth in the declaration.

Thus, in the deed, the legal description of the individual apartment could be as follows:

> **PARCEL I:**   The absolute and indefeasible fee simple title to the parcel of land, property, and space designated as Apartment Parcel 100 in the plat of subdivision recorded in the Recorder's Office of _____ County, _____ on November 1, 19____ as document No. 123456 (or: "in the Declaration recorded, etc." as the case may be).

The description of the common elements could be as follows:

> **PARCEL II:** The absolute and indefeasible fee simple title to an undivided ____ percent interest in the land, property, and space known as Lot 1 in Block 1 in Jones Subdivision, in Section _____, Township _____ North, Range _____ East of the _____ Principal Meridian, excepting from said Lot all the land, property, and space designated as Apartment Parcels 1 to 100, both inclusive, in the plat of subdivision recorded in the recorder's Office of _____ County, _____ on November 1, 19____ as Document No. 123456 (or: "in the Declaration recorded, etc." as the case may be).

The apartments excepted in Parcel II should, of course, consist of all the family units in the building. Should there be any units that are intended to be rented for commercial facilities, they should not be included among the apartments excepted, since they would be classed as part of the common elements.

An additional paragraph could be included in the developer's deed to the first purchaser of an apartment, conveying all the rights, benefits, easements, privileges, options, and covenants created by the declaration. It will do no harm to repeat in this clause the statement that these run with the land, for it is this document that gives life to the covenants.

Because of a dearth of modern cases touching on the specific question of whether ownership of the space occupied by an apartment or upper floor in a building would survive destruction of the building, it would be advisable to include in the deed a provision that it is the intention of the parties thereto that the ownership rights thereby conveyed shall so survive.

38.02(d)   Basic Documents—Bylaws

The bylaws generally control the internal government of the associations. Bylaws will provide for:

1. The election of a board of managers, their term of office, powers and duties, and the election of officers of the board (i.e., president, secretary, treasurer).
2. Notice to the unit owner of the proposed adoption of the annual budget.
3. A yearly accounting to unit owners.
4. Notice to unit owners of board meetings.
5. Quorum requirements for both board and unit owners' meetings.
6. Number and method for calling unit owners' meetings.
7. The maintenance, repair, and replacement of the common elements.
8. The furnishing of a statement of account of any unit owner stating the amount of any unpaid assessments or other charges.
9. The adoption of rules and regulations for the use of units and common areas.

As long as bylaws are reasonable they are binding. *Ryan* v. *Bapitiste,* 565 SW2d 196 (Mo. 1978); 48 St. Johns L. Rev. 1028.

Most bylaws are modeled on the federal models. 15A Am.Jur.2d *Condominiums,* Sec. 16. The federal model, like everything federal, is complex and often hard to understand. It is best to put important provisions (such as those forbidding children) in the declaration. The bylaws are easy to amend. But when you make it easy to strip a unit owner of his rights, you invite litigation.

REFERENCE: Am.Jur.2d Legal Forms, *Condominiums,* Sec. 64.54.

38.02(e)   Basic Documents—Rules and Regulations

Rules and regulations upon the use of the units and the common areas promote the communal nature of the condominium. 15A Am.Jur.2d *Condominiums and Co-*

operative Apartments Sec. 16. If they are reasonable, consistent with the law, and enacted in accordance with the bylaws, they will be enforced. Hickock, *Promulgation and Enforcement of House Rules,* 48 St. Johns L. Rev. 647 (1981). These are usually contained in a separate document.

Examples of common subjects of these rules include:

1. A rule prohibiting alcoholic beverages in the clubhouse area is valid. *Hidden Harbor Estates, Inc.* v. *Norman,* 309 So2d 180 (Fla. 1975).

2. A rule prohibiting the use of washing machines in individual apartments is a valid means to prevent water damage to other apartments. *Forest Park Cooperative, Inc.* v. *Hellman,* 152 NYS2d 685 (1956).

3. Reasonable security rules are valid.

4. Restrictions against pets are valid. *Dulaney Towers Maint. Corp.* v. *O'Brey,* 418 A2d 1233 (Md. 1980). If the prohibition of pets on the property is adopted after pet owners have taken up occupancy, a lawsuit may develop. To avoid this problem, amendments often permit existing pets to remain.

5. It is also valid to require that each condominium owner keep his apartment in repair at his own expense but not to interfere with the exterior of the building or any of the common elements.

6. A rule forbidding overnight parking in driveways has been held reasonable. *Hollman* v. *Mission HOA,* 556 SW2d 632 (Tex. Civ. App. 1977).

38.02(f)   Basic Documents—Corporate Charter

Every condominium declaration refers to a homeowners' association (HOA), which is simultaneously created. This is a corporation with its charter issued by the state. The charter lists in detail the powers of the HOA. Usually it includes a blanket power to do all the things necessary or convenient for the operation of the condominium. In addition, the state condominium statute lists powers that the HOA enjoys even though they are not all listed in the charter. Every state law gives the HOA the power to adopt bylaws and lists in detail the matters that can be covered by the bylaws. Thus included in the "contract" that defines the unit owner's rights and duties are the declaration, the bylaws, the local condominium law, the HOA charter, the local corporation law, the rules adopted by the board, and the decisions made at meetings of the board and unit holders.

38.03   Procedure

Condominium procedure is governed, as has been said, by the condominium declaration, the corporate charter of the HOA, the local statute relating to such corporations, the corporate bylaws, and the rules adopted by the board. In addition, the local condominium statute may set forth procedural requirements for the annual meeting, enforcement of assessments, and so on. 94 Harv. L. Rev. 647. And where court enforcement of the condominium documents is sought by the HOA or a unit owner, some courts treat this as a matter that is subject to constitutional requirements, such as notice and hearing. In this way the "private government" of the condominium is subjected to judicial scrutiny in somewhat the same fashion as local government action. 94 Harv. L. Rev. 647.

38.04   Assessments

Every condominium and homeowners' association needs funds to maintain the common areas, staff the project, create reserves for the periodic replacement of major components, and so on. Assessment against the unit owners provides these funds. The owners make monthly payments to fund the association budget, providing an orderly flow of funds to pay bills as they come due.

The declaration should establish the assessment process and a collection mechanism for past-due payments. The declaration should allow the association to sue the delinquent unit owner and foreclose against the unit. In some jurisdictions, the delinquent assessment lien can be foreclosed by the power-of-sale foreclosure process, a quick remedy that does not require court proceedings. To make the association whole, the declaration should provide that delinquent installments bear interest at the highest allowable legal rate, and attorneys' fees and other costs incurred by the association in the collection process are added to the amount of the delinquent installment.

The possibility of foreclosure gives rise to a priority conflict between the association and unit mortgagees. In the typical situation, a condominium declaration is recorded to create the units and establish the lien against the units for assessments. Units are sold, and buyers finance their purchase with mortgages. If state law or the documents do not provide otherwise, the foreclosure of delinquent assessments will extinguish the mortgage, even if the delinquency occurs after the date of the mortgage. *Prudential Ins. Co.* v. *Wetzel,* 248 NW 791 (Wis. 1933); *Washington Fed. Sav. & L. Assn.* v. *Schneider,* 408 NYS2d 588 (1978); *Bessemer* v. *Gersten,* 381 So2d 344 (Fla. 1980). Though a contrary result has been reached under particular statutory language. *Brask* v. *Board of St. Louis,* 533 SW2d 223 (Mo. 1976). This is obviously a situation that chills unit sale financing and works against the long-term best interests of the condominium. A simple provision in the declaration subordinates the assessment lien to first mortgage financing while requiring the foreclosing lender to pay assessments incurred after completion of foreclosure. Kratovil and Werner, *Modern Mortgage Law and Practice* § 26.02 (2d ed., 1981). The secondary market requires such a provision.

> **EXAMPLE:**   Lender financed Buyer's purchase of a condominium unit. If the suggested clause is in the declaration, Lender's lien will be prior to assessment liens against Buyer. If Buyer does not pay the mortgage as installments come due, the assessments will probably also go into default. Lender can foreclose and the purchaser at the foreclosure sale will take the title free of assessments due before the sale date. The buyer at the foreclosure sale, even if the lender is the buyer, will take the title subject only to the lien for those assessments that come due after the foreclosure sale date.

State laws invariably contain provisions regarding the priority of assessment liens.

In some states, Illinois, for example, a delinquent unit owner can be evicted just like a delinquent tenant.

The assessment lien process is binding on the original and all subsequent buyers of the units, *Kell* v. *Bella Vista Village Property Owners Assn.,* 528 SW2d 651 (Ark. 1975), and the assessment percentages allocated to the various units cannot be changed without a unanimous vote unless the declaration clearly provides otherwise. *Thiese* v. *Leland House Assn.,* 311 So2d 142 (Fla. App. 1975).

The question of what may be a proper subject of an assessment expense is sure to generate interest and litigation. To date, the courts have given wide latitude to the association as long as it exercises its judgment in good faith for the benefit of the project. 77 ALR3d 1290.

> **EXAMPLE:** The association may purchase a unit for the resident manager of a large complex so he will be available at all hours. An assessment may be levied for this purpose.

As in all cases involving the validity of corporate action, every condominium assessment levied by the board of directors is subject to scrutiny to determine if the power to levy the assessment for the particular purpose was one within the powers conferred on the HOA. In this instance it is necessary to examine the corporate charter of the HOA, the corporation statute under which it operates, and the condominium declaration. The declaration, as the great bill of rights of the unit owners, may limit the powers the corporation might otherwise enjoy. 77 ALR3d 1290.

38.05   Termination Due to Destruction of Building

The situation where the building is destroyed by fire or other casualty varies from state to state. Where rebuilding takes place with adequate insurance funds, the problems are not excessively complex. Where, however, a percentage of the owners have the right to vote to sell the property and divide the proceeds, problems exist unless the state law spells out a program. This has been done in some states, for example, New York, Hawaii, Mississippi, Nevada, Illinois, and Missouri.

38.06   Operational Aspects—New Condominiums

A number of steps must be taken to put a new condominium in operation. Among them are: (1) the election, in accordance with the bylaws, of a governing board by the unit owners; this usually takes place when about 75 percent of the units have been sold and occupied; (2) election of officers; (3) appointment of committees; (4) transfer of control from the developer to the newly elected board; (5) hiring of a new building manager, if it is desired to replace the developer's manager who has functioned from the date of first occupancy to the date the first board was organized; (6) review of insurance placed by developer; (7) review by the board of the completion of the building in accordance with plans and specifications; (8) adoption of rules governing swimming pools, pets, parking, and so forth. Hennessey, *Practical Problems of Residential Condominium Operation*, 2 Conn. L. Rev. 12 (1969).

Upon the transfer of control from the developer to the unit owners, many documents must be turned over to the new board, such as corporate record books, financial records, insurance policies, and management contracts.

After the completion of the building, normal operations include preparation of budgets by the Budget Committee, setting of assessments by the board, annual audits, approval of sales by unit owners, repair of building, etc. 2 Conn. L. Rev. 12. The common elements are operated and controlled by the board and the manager hired by the unit owners in accordance with the rules adopted by the unit owners.

38.07   Board of Directors

As in the case of any corporation, the board of directors controls the destiny of the building. It meets at least monthly. It appoints committees and hears committee reports. Often, its meetings are open to unit owners. Their complaints and suggestions are heard. The annual budget is a major concern. Fixing assessment rates and enforcing assessments against delinquent owners is another major concern. Dealing with repairs and replacement contracts in larger amounts than those entrusted to the manager is another concern. Hiring manager, auditor, and legal counsel will be a board matter, while hiring less important personnel, e.g., security guards, may be left to the manager. Procuring insurance is a board responsibility. Adopting rules (swimming pool hours, etc.) is a board matter. Bonding employees who handle money is also a board concern.

38.07(a)   Committees

A variety of committees will serve under the board of directors. There may be an Acceptance Committee. Its task is to review the building, possibly with the help of an architect, to establish what defects, if any, exist that require correction. The Maintenance Committee deals with maintenance problems after the building has been accepted. The Finance Committee reviews budget proposals with the help of the manager and condo auditor and proposes annual budgets.

38.08   Common Elements

The common elements include every part of the condominium project that is not a unit.

> **EXAMPLE:**   A one-acre parcel of ground is developed as a condominium parcel. The building that houses the units covers one-half of the acre. The remainder of the land surface is devoted to the pool, driveway, green areas, and a clubhouse, all of which are common elements. So also are the lobby, elevators, stairways, roof, etc. of the building, every part of the building that is not a unit.

The air space above the condominium is a common element, as is the ground below it.

These common areas are for the common use of all unit owners and are often subject to rules and regulations regulating their use for the mutual enjoyment of all owners.

38.08(a)   Limited Common Elements

Some state laws permit a class of common elements known as *limited common elements.* These are common elements used by less than all unit owners, such as parking area assigned to a unit. These are used exclusively by the unit owner whose unit they serve. Even though these areas are not for the use of all unit owners, they are subject to controls by the condo association.

> **EXAMPLE:**   Limited common elements were originally built as screened enclosures. The unit owner remodeled the area by installing jalousie windows in lieu of the screens. The jalousies had to be removed. *Sterling Village Condominium, Inc.* v. *Breitenbach,* 251 So2d 685 (Fla. 1971).

38.08(b)   Common Elements—Invasion by Unit Owners

Many town houses with their location at ground level are being developed as condominiums. These present a temptation for a unit owner to invade the common elements.

> **EXAMPLE:**   The building in question was a one-story town house project with units separated by party walls. One unit owner decided to expand his unit, adding a story and excavating beneath the ground floor to add a workshop. The HOA stopped this. It was an invasion of the air space, a common element and the subsurface, also a common element. *Makeever* v. *Lyle,* 609 P2d 1084 (Ariz. 1980). But a small storage cabinet may not be deemed a violation. *Mission Hills Condo Assn.* v. *Penashio,* 97 Ill.App.3d 305, 431 NE2d 221 (1981).

38.09   Real Estate Taxes

The real estate taxation issues relating to condominiums are simple but very important.

Before a particular condominium is created the real estate is taxed as a whole.

> **EXAMPLE:**   A vacant piece of land has one tax bill; an apartment house has one tax bill.

When these properties are developed into condominiums, either through new construction or conversion, the tax bills must be split. Technically, the tax assessor *assesses* each condominium unit and its share of the common elements separately from every other unit and its share of the common elements. The laws of most states specifically require this separation of units for real estate taxation purposes.

The condominium owner must determine that this form of separate taxation is in place or, in the case of a new development, being processed. Otherwise, a delinquency in the payment of part of the taxes could result in delinquencies on the entire project. If the *tax division* is properly done, a unit owner need not be concerned with tax delinquencies affecting any other unit, because a tax sale affecting other parts of the development does not affect his ownership interest. *400 Condo. Assn.* v. *Tully,* 79 Ill. App.3d 686, 398 NE2d 945 (1979). See generally 71 ALR3d 952.

The problem of assessing for tax purposes a newly converted apartment building is complex.

> **EXAMPLE:**   A rental apartment having 100 apartments, if sold as a rental apartment, has a market value of $1,000,000. If sold to a converter, it might sell for $1,500,000. Converters often pay a premium price. The converter, in turn, sells the 100 units at $30,000 each. As is evident, this gives the building a value of 100 times $30,000, or $3,000,000. Obviously, each unit owner is entitled to his own individual tax bill. But the aggregate of the tax bills will be higher than the old tax bill on the building when it was a rental. Meanwhile, the developer makes an estimate of what the tax bill will be. Often, this is a "low ball." It is deliberately understated. Any contract of sale made before the actual tax is fixed should provide for an escrow of a sum of money to cover a reprorating of taxes when the actual tax bill issues. But the buyer should be warned that as other conversions in the vicinity push the values up further, the tax bill is likely to increase.

38.10 Mortgages

The particular nature of a condominium causes the lender to be concerned with the questions that relate to any real property loan, plus:

> 1. The mortgage should provide: (a) that the unit owner's breach of a covenant of the declaration or the failure to pay assessments as they come due are defaults under the mortgage giving rise to the mortgagee's right to accelerate and foreclose; (b) that the mortgagee may pay delinquent assessments and add those sums to the mortgage debt; and (c) that the mortgagor will not vote to amend the declaration without the mortgagee's consent. The FNMA and FHLMC have developed a Condominium Rider for attachment to their uniform instruments that adequately covers these points.
> 2. Any limitation on sale or rental of a condominium unit or any right of first refusal should be expressly inapplicable to a lender who buys the unit at his foreclosure sale or who takes a deed to a unit in lieu of foreclosure.
> 3. On a newly constructed or converted condominium, outsale lenders will likely insist on a presale requirement as a condition to funding any outsale loans. The percentage of required sales ranges from 25 percent to 50 percent. The presale requirement causes the sale contracts to be contingent upon the firming of financing for the outsales.

4. Because financing a condominium unit is really financing part of the building as a whole, the legal framework of the condominium must be examined. An endorsement to the lender's title insurance policy can be obtained to insure that the condominium has been legally created in conformity with state law.

5. The developer is dependent upon sales, and sales can only go forward if the outsale lenders find the loans acceptable. The lenders, in turn, look to see if the loans are acceptable on the secondary market and to the FHA.

REFERENCES ON CONDOMINIUM FINANCING: Fegan, *Condominium Financing,* 48 St. Johns L. Rev. 799 (1974); Jackson, *Lenders; What Your Attorney Should Check in Condominium and PUD Documentation,* 1 #6 Lending Law Forum 2 (May 1976); Sakai & Reskin, *Leasehold Condominiums,* 2 Conn. L. Rev 37 (1969); Vishney, *Financing the Condominium,* 1970 Law Forum 181; Whitman, *Financing Condominiums and Cooperatives,* 13 Tulsa L. J. 15 (1977); Zinman, *Condominium Investments and the Institutional Lender—a Review,* 48 St. Johns L. Rev. 749 (1974).

A rider to be attached to FNMA/FHLMC uniform mortgage instruments is shown on p. 513.

38.11   Phased Construction

Construction lenders and common sense require that large projects be constructed in stages rather than all at once. The later stages are built and when sales volume justifies their construction.

Phasing also eliminates some problems with the legal logistics of setting up the condominium. Geis, *Representing the Condominium Developer: Tending the Paper Jungle,* 10 R.P.P.&T.J. 471 (1975). Many construction loan documents have presale requirements to be met before partial releases will be available to allow unit sales to close. For example, the lender may require 40 percent of the units to be sold before partial releases for the units will be given. If the total project is 200 units, 80 will have to be sold before closings can occur to give the developer the needed funds to pay down the construction loan and keep total interest costs at a minimum. If the project is built in phases, only 20 units need be sold before sales can close.

While phasing eliminates some problems, it creates other documentation problems which can be solved. Kratovil, *Modern Real Estate Documentation,* § 809 *et. seq.* (1975). Each phase will have its own condominium association. There will also be an *umbrella association* to manage the recreational and other facilities that serve the entire project. It is also important that the documentation set forth the complete plan for the phasing in of new units and the exact reallocation of each unit's common element percentage as new units are added. Fegan, *Condominium Financing,* 48 St. Johns L. Rev. 799, 810 (1974).

38.12   Leasehold Condominiums

Under the original condominium laws of most states, a condominium could not have been created on a leasehold estate. Statutory revisions have accommodated

CONDOMINIUM RIDER

THIS CONDOMINIUM RIDER is made this .... day of ...., 19........, and is incorporated into and shall be deemed to amend and supplement the Mortgage, Deed of Trust or Security Deed (the "Security Instrument") of the same date given by the undersigned (the "Borrower") to secure Borrower's Note to .... (the "Lender") of the same date and covering the Property described in the Security Instrument and located at:

....
[Property Address]

The Property includes a unit in, together with an undivided interest in the common elements of, a condominium project known as:

....
[Name of Condominium Project]

(the "Condominium Project"). If the owners association or other entity which acts for the Condominium Project (the "Owners Association") holds title to property for the benefit or use of its members or shareholders, the Property also includes Borrower's interest in the Owners Association and the uses, proceeds and benefits of Borrower's interest.

CONDOMINIUM COVENANTS. In addition to the covenants and agreements made in the Security Instrument, Borrower and Lender further covenant and agree as follows:

A. Condominium Obligations. Borrower shall perform all of Borrower's obligations under the Condominium Project's Constituent Documents. The "Constituent Documents" are the: (i) Declaration or any other document which creates the Condominium Project; (ii) by-laws; (iii) code of regulations; and (iv) other equivalent documents. Borrower shall promptly pay, when due, all dues and assessments imposed pursuant to the Constituent Documents.

B. Hazard Insurance. So long as the Owners Association maintains, with a generally accepted insurance carrier, a "master" or "blanket" policy on the Condominium Project which is satisfactory to Lender and which provides insurance coverage in the amounts, for the periods, and against the hazards Lender requires, including fire and hazards included within the term "extended coverage," then:

(i) Lender waives the provision in Uniform Covenant 2 for the monthly payment to Lender of one-twelfth of the yearly premium installments for hazard insurance on the Property; and

(ii) Borrower's obligation under Uniform Covenant 5 to maintain hazard insurance coverage on the Property is deemed satisfied to the extent that the required coverage is provided by the Owners Association policy.

Borrower shall give Lender prompt notice of any lapse in required hazard insurance coverage.

In the event of a distribution of hazard insurance proceeds in lieu of restoration or repair following a loss to the Property, whether to the unit or to common elements, any proceeds payable to Borrower are hereby assigned and shall be paid to Lender for application to the sums secured by the Security Instrument, with any excess paid to Borrower.

C. Public Liability Insurance. Borrower shall take such actions as may be reasonable to insure that the Owners Association maintains a public liability insurance policy acceptable in form, amount, and extent of coverage to Lender.

D. Condemnation. The proceeds of any award or claim for damages, direct or consequential, payable to Borrower in connection with any condemnation or other taking of all or any part of the Property, whether of the unit or of the common elements, or for any conveyance in lieu of condemnation, are hereby assigned and shall be paid to Lender. Such proceeds shall be applied by Lender to the sums secured by the Security Instrument as provided in Uniform Covenant 9.

E. Lender's Prior Consent. Borrower shall not, except after notice to Lender and with Lender's prior written consent, either partition or subdivide the Property or consent to:

(i) the abandonment or termination of the Condominium Project, except for abandonment or termination required by law in the case of substantial destruction by fire or other casualty or in the case of a taking by condemnation or eminent domain;

(ii) any amendment to any provision of the Constituent Documents if the provision is for the express benefit of Lender;

(iii) termination of professional management and assumption of self-management of the Owners Association; or

(iv) any action which would have the effect of rendering the public liability insurance coverage maintained by the Owners Association unacceptable to Lender.

F. Remedies. If Borrower does not pay condominium dues and assessments when due, then Lender may pay them. Any amounts disbursed by Lender under this paragraph F shall become additional debt of Borrower secured by the Security Instrument. Unless Borrower and Lender agree to other terms of payment, these amounts shall bear interest from the date of disbursement at the Note rate and shall be payable, with interest, upon notice from Lender to Borrower requesting payment.

BY SIGNING BELOW, Borrower accepts and agrees to the terms and provisions contained in this Condominium Rider.

this gap in many but not all states. See, for example, Fla. Stat. Ann. § 718.401; Va. Code Ann. § 55-79.54(e). Sakai & Reskin, *Leasehold Condominiums*, 2 Conn. L. Rev. 37 (1969).

Buyers purchasing units built upon a leasehold estate should take extra precautions. Proper care should be taken to insure that individual unit owners can protect their interests by making their separate payments of the lease rentals. This may be accomplished by a lease clause allowing a forfeiture to be lodged only against those unit owners in arrears in lease payments. State law may offer some protection in this regard. Va. Code Ann. § 55-79.54. The duration of the underlying ground lease must also be checked.

38.13   Developer Control

When the condominium is first created by the recording of the declaration or master deed, the developer owns all of the units and all of the common areas and is the board of directors. Even as units are sold, the developer continues to own the unsold units and have the power within the association that is attributable to ownership of the unsold units.

> **EXAMPLE:**   The developer has sold 25 units of a 100-unit condominium project. The developer retains 75 percent of the vote, an enormous power.

Some developers have used this period to their benefit at the expense of unit buyers. Expenses may be loaded toward unit buyers without the developer contributing his fair share. As the holder of the power to contract for the condominium project, some developers would, on behalf of the condominium, make a "sweetheart" contract with a corporation controlled by the developer.

> **EXAMPLE:**   The developer, as president of the condominium board, would make long-term contracts with: the developer's management company to manage the complex; the developer's janitorial company to clean and maintain the common areas; the developer's landscaping company to manicure the lawns in the summer and plow snow in the winter.

Perhaps the most notorious of these practices was the recreational lease.

> **EXAMPLE:**   The condominium documents would be drafted to exclude the recreational area: that is, clubhouse, swimming pool, pool deck, stairway to beach, and so on. These areas would not be common elements, but would be owned by the developer who in turn would enter into a long-term lease with the condominium board, with the developer signing as president of the board.

These arrangements generated a lot of litigation as the unit buyers tried, often without success, to break these agreements. 73 ALR3d 613.

At times these cases have been decided on narrow technical grounds that reveal an absence of imagination on the part of the courts.

> **EXAMPLE:**   Before any units were sold, Developer entered into a management agreement with a wholly owned subsidiary. The agreement was highly

unfavorable to the unit owners. The court sustained the agreement on the ground that no unit owner was injured when the agreement was signed. The court completely disregarded the modern development of the law of fraud, which allows recovery where injury to subsequently interested parties can reasonably be anticipated. *Lyons* v. *Christ Episcopal Church,* 71 Ill. App.3d 257, 389 NE2d 23 (1979).

The better rule forbids self-dealing by the developer and invalidates such contracts. *Avila South Condo. Assn.* v. *Kappa Corp.,* 347 So2d 599 (Fla. 1977).

The unit owners have, with mixed results, even attempted to use the antitrust laws to avoid these arrangements. *Spitz* v. *Buckwald,* 551 F2d 1051 (5th Cir. 1977); *Miller* v. *Prandos,* 529 F2d 393 (5th Circ. 1976). See, generally, Lewis & Jessell, *The Condominium Recreational Lease Controversy,* 9 RELJ 7 (1980).

The unit owners have found the real answer in both the market and the legislature. In several areas, units with recreation leases simply will not sell. Many states have amended their condominium laws in two ways. A specific time has been established for the developer to turn control of the property over to the buyers. See Ill. Rev. Stats. Ch. 30, § 318.2; Va. Code Ann. §55-79.74. Contracts and leases made by the developer are cancelable by the owners when they take control. See Ill. Rev. Stats. Ch. 30, § 318.2; Va. Code Ann. §55-79.74; 15 USC § 3607.

The courts have also begun to treat the developer as having special fiduciary duties toward the unit buyers. *Gov. Grove Condo Assn.* v. *Hill Dev. Co.,* 414 A2d 1177 (Conn. 1980); 73 ALR3d 613.

38.14   Liability of Developer for Defects

As is the case with respect to any newly constructed residence, the developer–builder implicitly warrants to the first purchaser of a condominium unit that the building and the unit are fit for occupancy and free from obvious defects. *Tassan* v. *United Development Co.,* 410 NE2d 902 (Ill. 1980); 50 ALR3d 1071.

38.14(a)   Fraud and Nondisclosure

The law of fraud, including nondisclosure, is much the same with respect to sales of condominium units as it is with respect to any land sale.

> **EXAMPLE:**   Condominium Developer held liable for failure to disclose known structural defects. *Cooper* v. *Jeone,* 128 Cal. Reptr. 724 (1976); *Gov. Grove Condo. Assn.* v. *Hill Dev. Corp.,* 414 A2d 1177 (Conn. 1980).

38.15   Association—Suits

It frequently develops that the condominium unit owners, individually or collectively, participate in a lawsuit. These suits often involve the buyer's complaint against the developer for faulty construction or to avoid a "sweetheart" contract made by the developer with the association while he was in control of the project.

Suits may also be generated by the business transactions of the association, that is, service contracts such as trash removal, extermination, and the like, or the real property rights relating to the project as a whole, that is, the encroachment of a neighboring project onto the common elements.

These suits are easier if the association can be the plaintiff rather than all members of the association. Generally, this is not allowed, but there are some exceptions to this rule. 72 ALR3d 314. The association can bring suits if:

1. The association owns the property that is the subject of the suit. *Raven's Cove Townhomes, Inc.* v. *Knuppe Development Co., Inc.,* 171 Cal. Reptr. 334 (1981).

2. A statute confers *standing to sue* upon the association, Ill. Rev. Stat. Ch. 30, §318.3, as construed in *Tassan* v. *United Development Co.,* 88 Ill. App.3d 581, 410 NE2d 902 (1980), regarding condominium unit owners' association. See also Cal. Code Civ. Pro. §374.

3. The suit is to rescind, reform, or seek recovery arising out of unconscionable provisions in recreation leases made while the developer was in control of the association. 15 USC §3608.

This is a developing area of the law and local law must be thoroughly reviewed before any action is taken.

38.16 Liability for Injuries—Liability Insurance

The condominium owners are owners and occupants of the common elements. As such owners and occupants, they become liable for injuries sustained by third parties to the same extent as any other owner. This liability corresponds to the liability of a landlord for proper maintenance of facilities enjoyed in common by the tenants, such as common stairways. It is this rule that makes it important for the condominium to have adequate and comprehensive liability insurance. Workmen's compensation, elevator liability insurance, and the like are also needed. Knight, *Incorporation of Condominium Common Areas? An Alternative,* 50 N.C.L. Rev. 1, 6 (1971). A closer question relates to the possible liability of the apartment association to a condominium owner.

EXAMPLE: *A,* a condominium owner, sustains injuries because of a negligently maintained common stairway. He sues the apartment association. By the modern rule, he will be allowed to recover his damages. *White* v. *Cox,* 95 Cal. Reptr. 265 (1971); Note, 25 Vand. L. Rev. 271 (1972). The theoretical legal problems are: (1) As an owner, *A* is, in effect, suing himself. (2) There are technical problems in suing an unincorporated association. In some states one or the other of these obstacles may prevent lawsuits of this nature.

The unit owners would also be liable to the injured party in proportion to the share of common elements each owns. 39 ALR4th 98.

38.17 Insurance

Insurance of the condominium is a problem that can be solved through coordination of efforts.

Each unit owner can obtain fire and other hazard insurances on his apartment and its share of the common elements. Note the problem in insuring a
condominium unit, which is a cube of air space. Should a loss occur, the damage
to the common elements must be repaired as a single enterprise for the benefit
of all owners. The *master policy* covers the common elements. The laws of some
states require that the condominium board obtain insurance on both the common elements and the units. See Ill. Rev. Stat. Ch. 30, § 312. It is extremely important that a dovetailing of coverage exist between the unit and master policies so
that as far as any unit owners are concerned, the entire structure and range of
risks are covered. This proper match of policies avoids a conflict or gap in coverage for such items as partitions, floor coverings, wall coverings, furniture, and
fixtures. This problem can be avoided if the new standard form policies are used,
and the association and unit owners purchase a package of coverage from the
same broker who then tailors the unit owners' policies to meet individual needs.

The standardized master policies (MLB-29 through MLB-29D) provide coverage for the common elements, which, when properly used with the unit owners'
policy (HO-6), constitute the basis for a well-rounded insurance program. The
HO-6 covers the amount of the interior of the unit not covered by the master
policy, and personal liability coverage. Rohan, Reskin, & Sanchisico, *Recent Development in the Field of Insurance of Condominiums Project,* 48 St. Johns L. Rev. 1084
(1974). These master policies waive the subrogation rights of the insurer as
against any unit owner.

EXAMPLE: A, the owner of Unit 12, falls asleep while smoking. The resultant
fire causes smoke and water damage to the hallways. The master policy insurer
could pay the loss to the association and by virtue of subrogation rights proceed
to recover for the loss as against A. The waiver of the subrogation right prevents
this from happening. The loss is paid by the insurance company and the matter
is over.

Many lawyers feel that losses to the common elements should be paid to
the insurance trustee named in the condominium declaration. The trustee is then
authorized by the declaration to *adjust* the loss, that is, to agree with the insurance
company as to the amount of loss and be exclusively entitled to hire contractors
to rebuild the common elements.

The HO-6 policy provides coverage for $1,000 of unscheduled personal
property, and $1,000 of unit owner's additions and alterations (fixtures, installa-
tions, or additions comprising the part of the building within the unfinished
interior surfaces of the perimeter walls, floors, and ceilings of the units). The
coverages may be increased by a special endorsement that can be tailored to meet
the individual needs of the unit owners.

Some points to remember: (1) The unit owner may want an endorsement
(Loss Assessment Coverage) to protect him against personal liability if the building's liability insurance is inadequate.

EXAMPLE: A brain surgeon visiting the building trips on loose flooring in the
lobby and is permanently injured. He recovers a judgment of $1,500,000 against
the HOA. The HOA carries only $1,000,000 liability insurance. It must levy an
assessment of $500,000. Remember that each of the unit owners owns a per-

centage of the defective floor and is personally liable for such injuries. The endorsement in question covers this assessment.

(2) The HOA's liability insurance provides no coverage for injuries sustained in the unit itself. (3) The HOA's insurance does not cover a cabana, storage shed, and so on, owned solely by the unit owner. (4) The HOA's insurance is probably an all-risk policy. Among the common exclusions in such policies are earthquakes, floods, water damage that occurs over a period of weeks (as from small roof leaks), termite damage, wear and tear, and explosion of boilers. (5) The unit owner needs Additional Living Expense Coverage for the cost of hotel and meals while his unit is untenantable owing to fire or other damage. (6) The unit owner needs his own coverage for theft or damage to his personal effects, furniture, furs, stereo, cameras, and so on. This should be the replacement value type. The other type covers value less depreciation. (7) The HOA should buy plate glass coverage if there are many large windows. (8) The HOA needs fidelity coverage on its treasurer and manager, all persons who handle money. (9) The HOA needs workmen's compensation and employer's liability coverage on its guards, maintenance men, and manager. (10) The unit owner's policy should be in the same company used by the HOA. There have been cases where two companies were involved and each pointed the finger at the other. (11) The unit owner may want a medical payments endorsement to cover injuries in his unit for which he is technically not liable, as where a baby sitter suffers burn injuries while fixing a snack. (12) Since many condominiums provide parking in garages controlled by the HOA, special garagekeeper's legal liability coverage is needed, to protect the HOA on loss of cars by theft, fire, and so forth. (13) If the HOA operates a snack bar or vending machine it needs products liability coverage to cover claims for illness due to contaminated food, etc. (14) If the HOA provides a car, uses a pickup truck, or the like, the usual motor vehicle insurance is needed. (15) Officers and directors want officers and directors liability insurance protecting them against various liabilities, such as failure to take out insurance and a loss occurs, or a unit owner sues for libel, slander, or invasion of privacy because his name has been posted in the lobby as delinquent in his assessments. Some directors feel that liability coverage is not needed where the HOA indemnifies them against liability, as is customary. This is a mistake. The insurance money will be needed by the HOA to pay the claim if the directors are found to be liable. (16) As in other insurance, the HOA can save money by purchasing an insurance policy with a deductible. Liability coverage may carry a deductible as high as $2,500. The wisdom of such a purchase is debatable. One important benefit of liability coverage is the fact that the company is obligated to defend lawsuits at its expense. The expense and nuisance of defending a lawsuit for an amount less than the deductible is considerable. As to deductibles in the hazard insurance part of the policy, a different problem surfaces. If the damage is only to the unit, the deductible is borne by the unit owner. If the damage is to the building, the loss is borne by the HOA.

Of course, some cases present difficult problems.

EXAMPLE: A roof is damaged by storm and rain damage to several units results. Here the deductible must be spread among the HOA and unit owners involved.

It is important to remember that basically no lawyer can hide behind the insurance agent. He can listen to the agent's recommendations, but if there is a gap in coverage, the lawyer is liable.

38.18   Title Insurance Requirements

A prudent purchaser of a condominium apartment will demand a title insurance policy. Preferably, it will contain specific coverage against mechanic's liens. It should also contain assurance that there are no delinquent condominium assessments, for such condominium assessments are, by law, a foreclosable lien on the apartment. In this connection, the management group furnishes the title company a certificate that all assessments have been paid, and the title company takes the risk of any inaccuracy in this certificate. The title company, in addition to making its usual search of the public records, also searches for assessment liens filed by the management group, for in some states these must be recorded. The title company also satisfies itself that the right of first refusal has been properly eliminated, and its policy insures the purchaser on this score. To supplement this coverage, the purchaser should demand a letter from the secretary of the condominium's board of directors that no unusual special assessments are in contemplation, for an apartment may go on the market because its owner wishes to avoid payment of a large assessment, for example, for automatic elevators.

In some areas it is commonly required by purchasers and mortgagees of condominium units that the title company insure that the condominium complies with the local statute. By special request, this assurance is procurable everywhere.

38.19   Regulation

There are various ways that condominiums are regulated. Building codes, zoning laws, and private building restrictions apply. Some laws are addressed solely to condominiums regulating their creation and sale. In some states, this is the same format used to regulate any other subdivision, requiring approval of public authorities. For example, in California, a "final public report" issued by the real estate commissioner must be given to a purchaser of a condominium or other subdivided land before a purchase contract is made. Cal. Bus. & Prof. Code § 11018.1. This report reveals all sorts of information about the project, including condition of title, soils condition, flood problem, nearby schools, and the like. Through these laws the state or local governments exercise their police powers to protect the health, safety, and well-being of local residents under the theory that disclosure of vital information to prospective purchasers allows them to make an informed decision. 123 U. Pa. L. Rev. 639 (1975).

38.20   Zoning

Some municipalities have tried to "zone out" condominiums. In this way a municipality might attempt to enforce a zoning ordinance to block a conversion of an apartment structure to condominiums. Any zoning ordinance that seeks to ex-clude condominiums while permitting similar tenant-occupied buildings is in-valid. Zoning must deal with land use, not land ownership. *Claridge House One Inc.* v. *Borough of Verona*, 490 F.Supp. 706 (D.C. N.J. 1980); 71 ALR3d 866.

38.21   Conversion

In the past we have seen the conversion of hundreds of thousands of rental units into condominiums and cooperatives. Several factors have caused this wave of conversion activity. Increasing costs have tended to make apartment building construction and ownership an uneconomic business. It becomes espe-cially unattractive when the value of a structure as an apartment building is com-pared to the total value of the apartment units in the structure. Indeed, the profits of successful conversion have caused developers to convert structure after structure in prime areas, such as Chicago's Lake Shore Drive area and the Gold Coast of Florida.

From the tenant–potential unit owner's point of view, the economic advan-tages and disadvantages are complex and difficult to analyze. It is almost univer-sally true that the gross costs of unit ownership are more than the costs to a tenant of the same unit. These costs may be offset by the equity buildup caused by principal payments against the mortgage debt and appreciation in the value of the unit—a very substantial factor, in many cases. It is also probable that the cost to the purchaser of a unit in a converted building will be less than the cost to purchase a comparable unit if it had to be built today. The income tax advan-tages to the unit buyer must also be factored into the equation.

One other point of view must be considered. The municipality where the condominium is has a stake. Economically, real estate taxes will probably increase upon conversion. Politically, the city must determine whether the interests of renters and low-income tenants should be fostered or should ownership of a stake in the community be fostered. The debate rages on.

38.21(a)   Conversion Legislation

The wave of conversion activity has brought about a hue and cry of opposition. Tenants, especially senior citizens and handicapped persons, have excited the sympathies of the legislatures to enact statutes and local ordinances that in one way or another protect the preconversion occupants of the structure. Unit pur-chasers have also benefited from the flow of recent legislation.

Although the federal government has not specifically legislated in this area, Congress has suggested that states and local governments require that tenants be given adequate notice of the conversion and the first opportunity to purchase converted units. 15 USC § 3605.

In considering the resultant regulation, it must be remembered that the legislative bodies were reacting to and trying to serve several goals, including the preservation of the community's housing goals (i.e., fostering ownership or tenant rights; the protection of tenants from displacement without the adequate opportunity to find replacement housing; protection of unit purchasers).

While the outright prohibition of conversion is invalid, *Zussman* v. *Rent Control Board,* 326 NE2d 876 (Mass. 1975), regulation of the conversion process is allowed. *Grace* v. *Town of Brookline,* 399 NE2d 1038 (Mass. 1979). While the form of regulation varies from community to community and reference is directed to local laws and ordinances, the regulations often include: moratoria barring conversion for a period; tying government approval of the conversion to apartment vacancy rates; requiring the rent control board's approval of the conversion; requiring a notice to the tenants prior to the conversion of their units; requiring that tenants receive preemptive options to purchase their units, any unit in the building, or even the entire structure; requiring approval of the conversion by a percentage of the tenants; giving senior citizens and handicapped tenants the right to remain as tenant for extended periods of time after the conversion; *Troy Ltd.* v *Renna,* 727 F2d 287 (1982); *Briarwood Properties* v. *City of L.A.,* 2 M. Cal. Reptr. 849 (1985); *Mountain Management Corp.* v. *Himmant,* 492 A2d 693 (N.J. 1985); requiring the converter to replace the rental units taken from the community by the conversion; giving displaced tenants relocation assistance; and disclosing the physical condition of major structural components of the structure and proposed budgets, past operating statements, and amounts recently spent for repairs to prospective purchasers. 1980 Duke. L. J. 306: 8 Fordham Urb. L. J. 507 (1980); 78 Mich. L. Rev. 124 (1979); 15 New England L. Rev. 815 (1980); Casazza, *Condo Conversion* 1982).

38.21(b)   Areas of Concern for Unit Purchasers

The unit purchaser of a converted unit has some concerns in addition to those of the purchaser of a new unit.

The physical condition of the units and the structure as a whole is of grave concern. The report of a reputable engineer is essential as are pest control reports. Warranties will not generally be available for the structure and its components except for work recently done in connection with the conversion. Unless the appliances were replaced in the upgrading of the building for the conversion, they will not have warranties.

38.21(c)   Preconversion Considerations

In addition to the ever-present market analysis, the converter must analyze several other factors in deciding to purchase a project for conversion.

The impact of conversion and tenant's rights laws and ordinances must not be taken lightly. The tenants have awesome power under these laws. The marketing effort can be stopped dead by the legal and political acts of opponents to the conversion. If sales stop while expenses continue, the result is disaster for the converter.

Can the underlying mortgage against the property be paid and how can those payments be made?

> **EXAMPLE:**   An owner of an apartment building wants to convert it to condo-
> miniums. The building is encumbered with an existing mortgage that permits
> no prepayment. Conversion is effectively blocked until the lender can be per-
> suaded to accept a prepayment, for which he may well extract a substantial
> prepayment charge.

The existing mortgage may not be prepayable until a later date or the prepayment penalty may be reduced as the loan ages. Nonetheless, the converter wants
to sell the units at an earlier date. Title insurance companies solve this problem
by issuing policies that "insure over" the existing mortgage. To do this the companies require a deposit of cash or triple-A securities that can be used to retire
the old mortgage at its earliest due date. Of course, this underlying loan must
not have a due-on-sale clause.

Any new financing must provide for partial payment as units are sold.
Often, lenders require that a minimum of 25 to 30 percent of the units be sold
before the first of the partial releases are available.

> **EXAMPLE:**   In a 100-unit conversion, the lender may require that 30 units be
> sold and closed with a stated portion of the closing proceeds applied to the loan
> before the partial release clause becomes effective.

This necessitates a volume closing at a title company when the documents and
funds for the 30 units are deposited, and, when all 30 units are ready to close,
the appropriate partial releases of the underlying loan are recorded and the loan
payment made by the escrowee. Thereafter, partial releases are available as individual units close.

The assumption of existing encumbrances may greatly assist the converter's
payment of the building's purchase price, but additional financing is needed to
pay the balance of the acquisition costs and the costs of conversion, such as attorneys' fees, title costs, engineering work, refurbishment, and marketing expenses.

During the time between the signing of the contract and the closing, the
converter wants to be able to begin the preliminary work in anticipation of the
conversion. For the developer, this is an important period of time; his interest
meter is not yet running. The more preliminary items that can be cleared during
this preclosing time, the less the cost of the conversion. To this end, the building's
purchase contract should give the converter: (1) access to the property for the
converter's own staff, his engineer and surveyor; (2) the ability to communicate
with the tenants; (3) access to tenants' lease files; (4) control over leasing activity;
and (5) access to operating information (i.e., service contracts, utility charges).

The physical condition of the property and its components, i.e., elevators,
climate control system, roof, etc., must be carefully analyzed.

The tenant roster and rent roll should be examined. Here the goal is to
determine the rights of the existing tenants. Any purchaser of the property will
take subject to these rights. Second, an analysis of the tenant roster and rent
levels may give some insight into the willingness of existing tenants to purchase
units.

Operating statements for recent years will aid in determining the level of
assessments to unit buyers, give evidence of repairs and maintenance, and per-

haps reveal any special problems that the building may have, i.e., an unusual insect problem.

The condominium documents should comply with the requirements of GNMA, FNMA, FHLMC, and so on. If not, the units will not be acceptable to permanent lenders because they will not be marketable in the secondary mortgage market. See Kratovil & Werner, *Modern Mortgage Law and Practice* § 26.09 (2d ed. 1981).

An interim loan will be necessary to finance conversion costs. The interim lender will require an end loan commitment to finance outsales to retail buyers. Outsales also necessitate a partial release clause in the interim loan.

The converter should require that the loan documents allow the rental of unsold units during the conversion process to generate funds to help the converter meet expenses.

38.22   Securities Law Problems

Many condominium developments are leisure-oriented projects in vacation areas. The unit purchaser intends to live in the unit for part of the year and hold the unit available for rent for the rest of the year. A managing agent is hired to rent out the various units. Taxpayers in high-income brackets had been attracted by the tax deductions for taxes, mortgage interest, maintenance charges, insurance, and depreciation. This form of operation, however, raises the specter that the development may be subject to both federal and state securities laws.

The Securities Exchange Commission has taken the position that the offering of a condominium must be in compliance with the registration and prospectus delivery requirements of the securities laws if any one of the following are found:

> 1. The condominiums, with any rental arrangements or other similar service, are offered and sold with emphasis on the economic benefits to the purchaser to be derived from the managerial efforts of the promoter, or of a third party designated or arranged for by the promoter.
>
> 2. Participation in a rental pool arrangement is offered. In a rental pool, all rents are collected by the manager and divided equally among unit owners.
>
> 3. The offering of a rental or similar arrangement whereby the purchaser must hold his unit available for rental for any part of the year must use an exclusive rental agent, or is otherwise materially restricted in his occupancy or rental of his unit. Securities Act Release No. 5347, CCH Fed. Sec. L. Rept., par. 79, 163 (1973).

Registration requirements may also be mandated by state securities or *Blue-Sky* laws.

> **EXAMPLE:**   An agreement for the sale of one of six units in a condominium project requires that the buyer enter into an exclusive management and rental agreement. Personal use of the unit was limited, in that the time for use had to be reserved far in advance; the owner had to maintain his unit in a rentable condition and had to pay a flat monthly fee for promotional activities to stimulate rentals. Promotional materials emphasized the investment rather than the

residential aspects of ownership. The court found that state securities laws had been violated. *Lowery* v. *Ford Hill Investment Co.,* 556 P2d 1201 (Colo. 1976).

Not all rental arrangements fall under the securities laws such as when the units are not sold with an emphasis on the economic benefits befalling the purchaser from the managerial efforts of others. A unit buyer may enter into a *non-pool* rental arrangement with an agent who is not designated or required to be used as a condition of purchase whether or not the rental agent is affiliated with the developer.

EXAMPLE: A developer offers condominium units in an ocean-front high-rise building. The sales emphasis is on the resort aspects of the development, and not on appreciation and return on investment caused by the developer's affiliate real estate management company's activity. In fact, no rental pool agreement is part of the package. The developer does, however, have a local real estate corporation that will, if asked, attempt to rent individual units for periods specified by the owners. No rental pool arrangement is available. No securities law registration is required. See generally, *Joyce* v. *Richie Tower Properties,* 417 F.Supp. 53 (1976).

REFERENCES: Burnman and Stone, *Federal Securities Law and the Sale of Condominiums, Homes and Homesites,* 30 Business Lawyer 411 (1975); Rohan and Reskin, *Condominium Law and Practice,* Ch. 18.

38.23   Timesharing Condominiums

In the mid-1970s a new form of condominium ownership, the timesharing condominium, was developed. Found in vacation areas where ownership of the unit for the entire year is unnecessary, expensive, and burdensome for many people, the timesharing concept allows the buyer to purchase a time slot of ownership. The original timeshare developments were in waterfront and recreational vacation areas. Today, we see the concept spreading into urban vacation areas such as New York, San Francisco, and New Orleans.

For the developer, the profit potential is large.

EXAMPLE: A unit in a resort condominium may sell for $100,000. A two-week period of ownership of that same unit may sell for $10,000. Obviously, if all two-week periods can be sold for $10,000, the developer will sell the unit for $260,000. This is not always the case. Recreational and vacation areas are usually seasonal. Only the prime weeks can be sold for the top dollar. The remainder of the year usually sells for rather steep discounts. Marketing costs of timeshare condominiums are usually greater than for nontimesharing units. So are the risks.

For the unit buyer, the property, which would normally be used only occasionally, can be purchased at a much lower price; the lodging costs of vacations are somewhat stabilized; income tax deductions for real estate taxes and interest payments are available; and ownership burdens are generally reduced while the possibility of gain from appreciation continues. If the owner cannot use the occupancy period, it may be rented, often through the building manager, or, if the owner grows tired of vacationing in the same place every year, the use period can be swapped through nationwide exchange programs for periods in other timeshare condominiums all over the world.

Through the timesharing device, the buyer uses the unit for an agreed segment of the year with other buyers having the use of the unit for other segments. There are three basic formats used to allocate these ownership rights. First, in the *time-span* or *tenancy in common* format, the buyers are deeded an undivided interest in a particular unit as tenants in common with other buyers of the unit. At the same time, the buyers agree to limit their use of the unit to a designated time period.

Second, in the *interval ownership* format, purchasers are granted an estate for years for the agreed time period each year. This revolving estate for years lasts for the expected useful life of the project. At that point, all owners become tenants in common of the whole property.

Third, under a *vacation license*, the developer retains ownership and agrees to allow the buyers to use the premises for a stated period for a given number of years.

Some states have enacted legislation to specifically authorize and regulate timesharing condominiums. See, for example, Fla. Stat. Ann. §718.103 *et seq.*, 6 ALR4th 1288. Also, a Uniform Real Estate Time-share Act has been promulgated by the National Conference of Commissioners on Uniform State Laws. Burek, *Uniform Real Estate Time-Share Act,* 14 R.P.P.& T.J. 683 (1979). See 10 Wm. Mitchell L. Rev. 13(1978).

Legislation of this type is necessary to resolve some of the legal problems that are unresolved in this relatively new form of ownership.

The management of a property of this kind is very important. The unit owners are truly absentee owners. They come to the property for two weeks every year only to return a year later. If a top-flight management company is not in control of the project, it may deteriorate rapidly, taking away many of the joys that the owner anticipated during his use period.

38.23(a)   Timesharing Condominiums—Declaration

The declaration for the timesharing condominiums must address itself to the following special matters:

1. Use and service periods with relevant undivided interests in the common elements.
2. Exclusive right to use, and occupancy of each of the timesharing owners for their relevant periods.
3. Collection and payment of costs such as telephone charges, firewood, repairs attributable to any owner's use, and common costs.
4. Waiver of right to partition.

This waiver goes beyond the waiver contained in the declaration of a non-timeshare condominium by waiving the right to partition between the various time segment owners of a particular unit.

> REFERENCES ON TIMESHARING CONDOMINIUMS: Burek, *Timesharing: Pie in the Sky,* Chicago Title Ins. Co. Lawyer's Supplement to the Guarantor (July–Aug. 1979); Malleris, *Five Legal Hurdles in Time-Share Ownership,* 8 #2 Real Est. Rev. 97 (Summer 1978); Merritt & Cowan, *Time-Sharing Ownership of Vacation Residences,* 1 #4 ALI–ABA Course Mat. J. 89 (1977); *Resort Timesharing: A Consumers' Guide* (1981) by the American Land Development Association.

The advantages of owning a commercial condominium are: (1) rent increases are avoided, but increases generally occur in the assessments as costs generally increase; (2) an owner cannot be evicted to make room for more important tenants; and (3) well located and constructed units tend to increase in value. Commercial condominiums also have disadvantages, which include: (1) the owner is locked into a particular location; (2) additional space is more difficult to obtain, if needed; (3) rent is totally tax deductible while commercial condominium owners are limited to tax deductions for mortgage interest, taxes, depreciation, and maintenance expenses; and (4) funds otherwise available for inventory and business expansion are tied up by the commercial condominium purchase.

38.24 Income Taxes

The income tax treatment of a condominium is the same as the income tax treatment of a house. The two are treated the same both for ownership deductions purposes and gain on sale purposes. The special vacation home deduction rules apply equally to both.

38.25 Suggestions for the Purchaser of a New Condominium

1. Do the condominium documents conform to state law? If not, dangerous consequences may result. For example, the tax assessor may refuse to separately assess the unit. This problem can be solved by obtaining an endorsement to the unit buyer's title insurance policy insuring that a condominium has been created in accordance with state law.

2. Determine whether the purchase contract gives the developer the right to cancel if a stated percentage of the units are not sold. Check to see how many units are sold to determine whether such clause is likely to be invoked. The buyer may change position by selling existing property, subletting an apartment, and so on, or incur expense by paying loan application fees only to be frustrated if the developer invokes this clause.

3. Check whether the burden of assessments for maintenance, and so forth, falls entirely on the apartments sold or is shared by the developer in proportion to the apartments remaining unsold and still owned by the development. In general, of course, the entire subject of assessments and the factors that make up the assessment level—maintenance costs, payroll expenses, cost of keeping up the recreational facilities, reserves, and so forth, should be studied.

Obtain a copy of the proposed budget. Is it realistic? How many months of advance assessments must be paid by the buyer at the closing? In trying to "sweeten" a deal for a prospective buyer, a developer may price the unit to include a prepayment of assessments for a period, say six months. Unless the developer controls the association and, on behalf of the association, credits the buyer's account, the developer's acts will not bind the association. When the developer passes control over the board to the unit owners, they may not share in the developer's attitude or largess and take action against the buyer for delinquent assessment payments.

4. Check whether the voting rights of the sold apartments give the apartment purchasers at least a minority representation in the homeowner's association. For example, if a majority vote of the apartments in the building can elect a home association board of directors, the developer will have absolute control until a majority of the apartments are sold.

5. Check whether the documents require all purchasers to get their financing from a specified mortgage lender and, if so, what the lender's terms are likely to be.

6. Consider whether the prospective occupancy is such that the membership is likely to vote future assessments for maintenance and renovation in excess of your financial abilities as a purchaser.

7. The early contracts of sale for a condominium apartment will permit the developer to amend or modify the declaration but should not permit him to increase the buyer's assessments, or to increase the apartment cost, or to reduce the seller's obligation to pay the expenses on unsold apartments.

8. The contract of sale may state that the purchaser's rights are subordinate to the construction mortgage. This is necessary for the mortgagee's protection. *State Savings and Loan Association* v. *Kauaian Develop. Co.*, 445 P2d 108 (1968).

9. Determine what is done with your deposit or earnest money. The most conservative approach is to require that it be held in escrow. Many buyers who did not protect themselves had their deposits lost when the developer got into financial difficulty. Legislation in some states requires the deposit of these funds into a separate escrow account. See Fla. Stat. Ann. § 718.202; Va. Code Ann. § 55-79.95.

10. What is the reputation of the management firm? Determine the duration of the management contract, keeping in mind that long-term contracts may lock you into inefficient management. How much authority is delegated to the manager by the association? Too much delegation strips the unit owner of a voice in the running of the project. Who does the hiring and firing of employees? If the board interferes, favoritism can creep in and efficient management becomes difficult. Pay scales of employees should track with pay scales generally.

11. Has the board met regularly and have there been genuinely democratic elections so that no clique runs the operation? In this connection, check the bylaws for duration of the term of board members. Check the present composition of the board. Lawyers and accountants, for example, are likely to do a better job in running the building than nonprofessionals.

12. Look into the physical attributes of the unit. When the purchase is made in reliance upon a model apartment, drawing, or promotional material, there is an obvious need to compare the delivered product with the model. Do carpeting, draperies, furniture, and other furnishings in the model go with the unit? Where the unit is not completed, room dimensions, carpet grade, landscaping, finish hardware, appliance quality, and so on must be established. Before the contract is signed, the particulars of the finished product must be agreed upon and reduced to writing. What of the physical nature of the building and the unit? Is it well constructed, soundproof, and so on? Does the structure conform to local zoning ordinances and private restrictions?

Is the unit located near the noisy parts of the building, lobby, elevators, trash chute, and so forth? What parking and storage space is allocated to the particular unit? Determine whether the common elements include the recreation areas (swimming pool, tennis courts, and so forth) or whether they are excluded from the condominium, retained by the developer, and then leased to the association on a long-term basis.

13. What is the developer's reputation? Go to other projects the developer has completed. Talk to the residents.

14. What type of insurance does the association buy for the building? What type of insurance does the unit owner have to buy?

15. Are children and pets allowed?

16. What are the rules about window coverings, balcony furnishings, physical changes of the units?

17. If the property is being bought as an investment, other factors must be considered. Are there restrictions on leases? Must a uniform lease form be used? Do you have the ability to check the credit of potential renters? Are you going to turn the property over to a management agent? Will rentals cover ownership costs (i.e., mortgage payments, taxes, insurance, assessments)?

18. The assessment problem is complex.

EXAMPLE: A rental apartment having 100 apartments, if sold as a rental apartment, has a market value of $10,000,000. If sold to a converter, it might sell for $12,000,000. Converters often pay a premium price. The converter, in turn, sells the 100 units for $180,000 each. As is evident, this gives the building a value of 100 times $180,000 or $18,000,000. Obviously, each unit owner is entitled to his own individual tax bill. But the aggregate of the tax bills will be higher than the old tax bill on the building when it was a rental. Meanwhile, the developer makes an estimate of what the tax bill will be. Often this is a "low ball," deliberately understated. Any contract of sale made before the actual tax is fixed should provide for an escrow of a sum of money to cover a reprorating of taxes when the actual tax bill is issued. The buyer should be warned that as other conversions in the area push values up, the tax bill is likely to increase.

19. Review the basic condominium documentation, such as declaration, bylaws, and lease rules. Will you enjoy living under those rules? Will you enjoy group living generally?

38.26   Resales of Condominium Units

While many states require the developer to disclose certain information to prospective buyers, some states now require disclosures on resales of a unit by an ordinary unit owner. See Ill. Rev. Stat. Ch. 30, § 322.1; Va. Code Ann. § 55-79.97. The required disclosures include the basic condominium documents, a statement of anticipated capital expenditures, a statement of the status of the reserve fund, a statement of the fiscal condition of the association, a statement of the status of pending suits involving the association, a statement of insurance coverage, and a statement of the amount of unpaid assessments against the unit.

CHAPTER 39

Cooperatives

39.01 In General

In a condominium the buyer receives a *deed* to the apartment. In a cooperative the buyer receives shares of stock in the building corporation and a lease or an assignment of the seller's lease of the apartment being sold.

To explain, let us look at an example:

EXAMPLE: Sponsor buys a tract of land that is zoned for apartment purposes. He places title in a corporation. He owns all the stock. He obtains an ordinary mortgage and builds an apartment building. At this point he has in his files a title insurance policy showing that his corporation owns clear title to the property subject only to one large mortgage.

Suppose the apartment building contains 100 identical apartments. Sponsor can now sell one share to First Buyer and have that sale and assignment recorded on the books of the corporation. A one-share stock certificate is issued to First Buyer. Sponsor has his corporation give a 99-year lease (proprietary lease) to First Buyer of one apartment. A memorandum reciting the making of this lease is recorded in the Recorder's office. First Buyer pays in cash the purchase price for the stock and lease. He moves in. The deal is complete.

As can be seen, First Buyer acquires his title subject to the large mortgage that covers the building. His lawyer may obtain a photocopy of Sponsor's title policy. First Buyer may or may not receive a title policy covering the lease he has received.

39.02 The Formative Documents

There is a corporate charter for the corporation that owns the building. In addition to the usual terms of a charter, this document contains special provisions needed for cooperatives.

A form of corporate charter for a cooperative corporation is set forth in 5 Am.Jur Legal Forms 2d, *Co-ops,* p. 390, Sec. 70.23. Special laws exist in some states for the incorporation of cooperative corporations. 61 Harv. L. Rev. 1707. A checklist for the contents of the corporate bylaws will be found in 5 Am.Jur. Legal Forms 2d, *Co-ops,* Sec. 70.31. The bylaws often provide that the board of directors shall adopt a form of lease so that all leases are uniform in content. 5 Am.Jur. Legal Forms 2d, *Co-ops,* Sec. 70.33. The bylaws provide that a cooperative lease can be assigned only in compliance with the terms of the lease. As can be seen, it is the practice to require the consent of the landlord to any assignment. The landlord is the building corporation, and its directors are elected by the tenant stockholders, so that the tenants can, to a considerable degree, control the occupancy of the building.

The Uniform Common Interest Ownership Act has been drafted and promulgated by the National Conference of Commissioners on Uniform State Laws. Although this Uniform Act has not yet been enacted by any state, and therefore discussion of it here is premature, the act is noteworthy in at least one respect. It provides for the creation of a cooperative by a declaration in much the same way as a condominium is created.

39.03   The Blanket Mortgage

As stated, the building and land are subject to a large mortgage. All present and future leases contain clauses specifically making the lease subject to this mortgage and all future mortgages. This means that every tenant takes subject to the possibility of loss of their investment by foreclosure. This occurred during the Great Depression. If, for example, 10 percent of the tenants are unable to pay their rent, there is not enough money coming in to make the mortgage payments. The mortgage is foreclosed and all leases are extinguished. The apartment becomes a rental apartment.

39.04   The Lease

The lease is called a proprietary lease because it runs for a long term. A form will be found in 5 Am.Jur. Legal Forms 2d, Sec. 70.59.

The lease does not state a fixed rental to be paid each month. Instead the landlord board each year fixes an amount that will be needed to pay the expenses of the building, mortgage debt service, insurance, operating expenses, and so on. A limit may be placed on the amount of rent that can be charged. In recent leases the tenant is given the right to pay a fee and surrender his lease to the corporation, thus terminating his liability for rent.

The board's consent to the assignment of a lease is needed under the lease provisions on any such assignment being made. This consent cannot be withheld arbitrarily. *Sanders* v. *Tropicana,* 229 SE2d 304 (N.C. 1976); *Mowatt* v. *1540 Lake Shore Drive Corp.,* 385 F2d 135 (7th Circ. 1967); *Logan* v. *3750 North Lake Shore Dr.* 17 Ill. App.3d 584, 308 NE2d 278 (1974). For example, a refusal of consent based solely on racial grounds would not stand up in court. Arbitrary refusals seem to be allowed in New York. *Weisner* v. *791 Park Ave. Corp.,* 6 NY2d 426, 160 NE2d 720 (1950). In California, landlord's consent is not required.

The lease provides that it is subject to any future mortgage placed on the building by the landlord corporation. A mortgage usually requires a two-thirds vote of the tenants. This clause facilitates refinancing of the existing mortgage.

It is significant that both a tenant's interest under a lease (his *leasehold*) and shares of stock are legally considered to be personal property. Thus a sale of a cooperative apartment is a sale of personalty.

> **EXAMPLE:** *R* entered into a contract to sell his cooperative apartment to *E*. *E* made an earnest money deposit as is common in sales of land. *E* failed to go through with the deal. *R* declared the earnest money forfeited. *E* sued *R*, and the court held that since a sale of personalty was involved, damages must be determined under the Uniform Commercial Code, which confine the seller's damages to loss on resale to another party and incidental expenses. *Silverman v. Alcoa Plaza Associates*, 323 NYS2d 39 (1971); 21 Buff. L. Rev. 555 (1972); 29 Wash. & Lee L. Rev. 189 (1972).

There are, of course, many other legal consequences of this rule. For example, on the death of an apartment owner, his leasehold and shares pass to his administrator or executor rather than to his heirs. As a result, a simple, informal sale by the executor or administrator is possible without the difficulties attendant upon sale of land owned by a deceased person. See *State Tax Comm* v. *Shor*, 371 NE2d 253 (N.Y. 1977).

39.04(a)   Stock and Lease Inseparable

The lease provides that ownership of the lease and of the stock must always be in the same person.

39.04(b)   Lien on Stock

The corporation retains a lien on any stock where the apartment owner is delinquent in his payment.

39.05   The Trust Form

In Illinois, title to a cooperative is often placed in a land trust. The tenants receive certificates of beneficial interest under the land trust. A managing committee takes the place of a corporate board. This can be done in any state that recognizes land trusts.

39.06   Securities Problem

In the cooperative apartment complex that is purchased for residential purposes, there appears to be no problem with entanglements caused by the Federal Securities law.

> **EXAMPLE:**   In a large New York cooperative, prospective purchasers made a recoverable deposit on their apartments by buying shares of stock in the non-profit housing corporation that held title to the property. The shares of stock were allocated to purchasers on the basis of the number of rooms in their apartment. When the tenant wanted to move out, he had to offer his stock back to the corporation at the initial selling price. The court found that the mere description of the certificates as "stock" did not render it a security subject to the Federal Securities Law. Noting that the purchasers intended merely to acquire a residential apartment for personal use rather than an investment for profit to be derived from the managerial efforts of others, the court found no security present. *United Housing Foundation, Inc.* v. *Forman,* 421 U.S. 837 (1975). For similar reasons, state Blue Sky laws are inapplicable. 1978 Law Forum at p. 789.

39.07   Conversion

In some areas, particularly New York, apartment buildings are being converted into cooperatives as well as condominiums. Because New York probably has more cooperative units than the remainder of the country, it has a very sophisticated cooperative conversion law. Because the cooperative development is both a mix of real estate and corporation concepts, the law has aspects of both bodies of law. *Richaras* v. *Kaskol,* 32 NYS2d 524, 300 NE2d 388 (1973).

> **EXAMPLE:**   Purchasers must be given a cooperative prospectus or offering plan approved by the attorney general in much the same way that a stock offering is approved. N.Y. Gen. Bus. Law Act 23A.

39.08   Warranties of the Building

The cooperative unit owner sufficiently resembles an ordinary tenant so that he is entitled to the benefit of the warranties of the building that characterize an ordinary residential landlord and tenant relationship. *Suarez* v. *Rivercross Tenants, Corp.,* 438 NYS2d 164 (1981).

39.09   Sale of Cooperative Apartment

The following suggestions may be appropriate for sellers and purchasers of existing cooperative apartments:

1. Obtain title evidence as hereafter suggested. Supplement this by getting an affidavit from the secretary of the corporation to the effect that the condition of title remains today as it was on the date of the title evidence which your lawyer examined and that no lawsuits are presently pending or threatened against the corporation.

2. Since you are buying the lease and stock of the present tenant, get the secretary of the building corporation to sign an affidavit stating: (a) that the stock is in fact owned by your seller and is fully paid for; (b) that the lease is owned by your seller, free of any subleases; (c) that the stock and lease are free from any assessments other than the

current ones shown on the financial statement submitted to you by the corporation; (d) that the stock is free of restrictions on its transfer or those restrictions have been satisfied, 99 ALR2d 236; (e) that no defaults have occurred in the lease being sold or in the building's mortgage payments; (f) that none of the other tenants is currently behind in his payments; (g) that no proposal to remodel the building or increase assessments has come before the directors within the past year, for this may be why your seller is moving out; (h) how much space is rented to persons other that tenant–stockholders, for if this figure gets too high, you may lose your income tax benefits; and (i) what insurance is carried presently. Get a certified copy of the cooperative charter and bylaws and the directors' resolution authorizing your seller to sell you his lease and stock, for all cooperatives restrict the right of the tenants to transfer their rights. Have your lawyer check the lease that you are about to buy and explain to you the restrictions (on remoldeling of apartments, for example, or the right to sell, sublease, or operate a business in the apartment) and liabilities (special assessments, for example) that it creates. Have him explain what maintenance costs you must pay yourself, such as decorating.

3. It is quite important that an apartment seller who lists his apartment with a real estate broker for sale insert the *no deal, no commission clause* in the listing. This is important because if the cooperative board turns down the purchaser, the seller does not want to be liable for a commission.

4. It is important that the contract of sale specify what appliances and other articles go with the sale of the apartment. The sale does not include these articles unless so specified, and normally they do not belong to the building corporation. The contract should also contain various warranties by the seller, such as a warranty that he owns the shares and lease and will so continue at closing, free of any liens or adverse interests, including mechanic's liens, that the shares are fully paid for, that no lease defaults will exist at closing, that the seller has no knowledge of building code violations, if any, or proposals to increase apartment assessments. For the seller's protection, the contract states that it is subject to approval by the co-op board, and that if the approval is refused, the buyer obtains return of his deposit. The contract clause as to closing costs requires some special attention. The seller normally agrees to pay the corporation's charges for transfer of the shares and lease.

If the buyers are husband and wife who wish to own the apartment in joint tenancy, the contract of sale should so state, and special language may be needed because of the personal property nature of the lease and shares.

EXAMPLE: In Illinois a deed of land to A and B "in joint tenancy" creates a joint tenancy. But to create a joint tenancy in shares and a leasehold probably requires the phrase "as joint tenants with the right of survivorship and not as tenants in common."

5. In states where a judgment against the owner of a leasehold creates a lien thereon, it probably will be necessary to have a title company make a search for such judgments.

REFERENCE: Rohan, *Co-op Apartment Transfers,* 19 Sta. L. Rev. 978 (1967); Schlesinger, *A Checklist For The Purchase Of A Cooperative Apartment,* 1 #1 Practical Real Estate Lawyer 33 (1/85).

A buyer planning to buy into a cooperative needs to check quite a number of other things, for example: (1) Is the building mortgage a low–interest rate loan that will soon mature? If it is, the new loan will call for higher interest and the monthly rent will increase. (2) Are there adequate reserves that could be used to meet emergency repairs? (3) Does the building have a tax exemption that will soon expire, thereby pushing up the rent? (4) Is at least 80 percent of the cooperative gross income derived from tenant–shareholders? If not, shareholders lose income-tax deductions for the building's taxes and mortgage interest. (5) Will the cooperative's documents and the board both allow apartment purchase to be financed by a pledge of the stock the purchaser acquires? Some older cooperatives do not permit share financing. (6) Will renovation contemplated by the purchaser be permitted? This is a thorny problem because the board cannot approve the alterations unless it sees the plans in some detail. In other words, the purchaser must hire an architect and may then may find he will not be permitted to do the work he considers indispensable to his happiness. (7) Will the building forbid use of appliances such as microwave ovens or computers? Many older buildings have inadequate electrical wiring.

Title insurance is available in some areas on sales of a cooperative. The insurer examines the chain of title, the formative documents, the lease, the assignment, and the mortgage documents on the apartment purchase. The title insurer will also require a certificate that the blanket mortgage is not in default and that the lease is in good standing.

If title insurance is not available on the purchase of the apartment, the seller may be able to furnish a photocopy of the existing title policy covering the entire building. This will probably be several years old. Title and abstract companies sell searches showing briefly what has happened since the policy was issued as reflected on the public records and in the Uniform Commercial Code filings. For example, if the mortgage debt was increased, such a recorded modification will be shown on the searches. Unpaid taxes will be shown also, and so on. 46 St. Johns L. Rev. 632, 656.

Both the real estate records and the Uniform Commercial Code records should be searched. In either place a filing may be made that affects the apartments.

The buyer receives a copy of the bylaws and the rules the board has adopted.

Some corporations impose a transfer fee, which may be substantial, on any assignment.

After closing, the secretary of the board should certify that the assignment of lease and stock have been duly recorded on the corporate records. The buyer receives his stock certificate, his assignment of lease, a copy of the lease, a bill of sale for the appliances, and other customary documents.

The sale contract should require the seller to deliver the keys and a vacant apartment at closing.

Insurance is carried by the corporation and by the individual tenant much as in the case of condominiums.

39.09(a)   Mortgage Loans on Sales of Cooperative Apartments

The problem of obtaining a mortgage loan when buying an apartment is great. 46 St. Johns L. Rev. 632. It is a second mortgage, of course, and the blanket first mortgage is apt to be a big one. Many sales are for cash. This is possible because the blanket mortgage is often so big that the seller has only a small equity that the buyer can handle for cash. The buyer who must borrow must seek out a lender who is making cooperative loans. These lenders have routine and printed forms. FNMA requires assurance that the cooperative corporation has marketable title. This process is much like that involved in a sale of the apartment. The stock and the lease are assigned to the lender. The buyer signs a collateral note (with the lease and stock as collateral) that qualifies as a security agreement under the Uniform Commercial Code, and a financing statement is filed under UCC requirements.

The lender also requires of the corporation an agreement that the corporation will not, while the mortgage is in force, permit any further assignment, sublease, agreed termination, agreed modification, or junior mortgaging of the lease. The corporation agrees to notify the lender of any default in the payment of rent and to give the lender an opportunity to cure that default. A sore point is the continuing need of the lender to obtain the landlord's consent to the sale of an apartment acquired by foreclosure.

If the lease is of recent vintage, the lender will want a certified copy of the board resolution authorizing the lease. The lender will probably want a memorandum of the lease to be recorded. The assignment of the lease to the lender and the landlord's consent to the assignment are also recorded.

Truth in Lending and Real Estate Settlement Procedures Act (RESPA) apply to these cooperative loans.

39.09(a)(1)   The Secondary Market

FNMA is buying cooperative loans in a number of states. Its requirements are not burdensome. Emphasis is on showing that the corporation has good, marketable title to the project, and that the lender has checked all changes since the title policy was issued. The lender's documents must require notice by the corporation of: any actual or threatened condemnation; receipt by the corporation of nonrent income exceeding IRS rules; and any defaults in rent. These are requirements that any lender can live with.

39.10   Condominium and Cooperative Ownership Compared

There are significant legal and practical differences between the two types of apartment ownership.

1. The condominium owner holds title to the unit. In the cooperative, the owner buys shares in the cooperative apartment corporation that owns the building and enters into an occupancy agreement or proprietary lease for a particular apartment.

2. The mortgage on a condominium unit covers only the unit and its share of the common elements. In a cooperative, the mortgage covers the entire property. If any substantial number of tenants default, the foreclosure would wipe out all tenants. To avoid this result, the nondefaulting unit owners would have to carry the defaulting owners.

The advantage the condominium enjoys with respect to mortgage financing should make it easier to sell or resell than a cooperative, since it enlarges the number of potential buyers.

> **EXAMPLE:**   *A* owns a condominium apartment which he can sell to *B* for $130,000. *B* can obtain a mortgage loan of approximately $100,000, so that he needs only $30,000. *A's* existing mortgage, whatever its amount, would be paid off in the process, just as if *A* were selling a house. If *A* were selling a cooperative in a comparable building on which the building mortgage had been paid down to 50 percent of the property value, *A* would be selling his apartment equity for cash subject to the building mortgage, and he would have to find a buyer who has cash, for many lenders do not lend on cooperatives. However, loans are now available in some states.

If a person desires a debt-free shelter, as many senior citizens do, a condominium purchaser can pay cash for his apartment, as many purchasers do. A cooperative purchaser has no choice but to accept his apartment subject to the mortgage on the building.

The condominium, since it is owned by many people, not by a single corporation as in the case of the cooperative, has no feasible way of putting a mortgage on the building in its later years when remodeling or repairs are needed.

> 3. Cooperative leases provide that the lease may be terminated for failure to meet a monthly assessment or because the apartment owner has become bankrupt or been guilty of objectionable conduct. *Green v. Greenbelt Homes Inc.,* 232Md.496, 194 A2d 273. The condominium owner is more secure in this regard.
>
> In a cooperative, the apartment owner has the right to leave. If he has bad luck and cannot keep up his monthly payments, he can sublease his apartment, sell it, or at the worst, give it back to the landlord corporation. The modern cooperative lease gives the lessee the right to cancel the lease after a specified number of years by surrendering his stock and his lease to the landlord corporation. In the condominium the owner, having signed a note and mortgage, has no right simply to "walk away." In case of default and foreclosure, there is always the possibility of a deficiency judgment.
>
> Another advantage that the cooperative possesses is the ease with which one can control the type of neighbors one will have in the building. In the cooperative the lease provides that it cannot be assigned or subleased except with the written consent of the landlord corporation. The stock certificate provides that it can be transferred only in connection with an authorized transfer of the lease. This method has the advantage of simplicity and unquestioned legality. *68 Beacon St.* v. *Sohier,* 194 NE 303 (Mass. 1935); *Weisner* v. *791 Park Ave. Corp.,* 160 NE2d 720 (N.Y. 1959).
>
> Every cooperative board has an admissions committee. This committee reviews the application of a prospective tenant for permission to buy into the building. It reports to the board, which gives final approval or refusal. The board policy, reflected in a board resolution concerning stated financial requirements, for example, will be helpful in cases where a refused applicant charges discrimination. The board can simply point to their official policy and the failure of the applicant to meet the stated requirements. Many cooperatives look at the applicant's entire package, contract of sale, mortgage application, references, and so on, before scheduling a personal interview. If the applicant cannot meet financial requirements, he need not be humiliated by appearing before the board.

Each owner of a condominium apartment holds his apartment subject to a right of first refusal should he desire to sell. Such a right of first refusal is probably valid. *Gale v. York Center Community Co-operative, Inc.*, 171 NE2d 30 (Ill. 1961). However, the method is clumsy. Also, since it calls for the apartment owners to buy the apartment at the price the selling apartment owner can obtain from an outsider, it requires a special assessment on the apartment owners.

Getting rid of an owner who defaults in his monthly payments or fails to abide by the bylaws is easier in the cooperative than in the condominium. Just as an ordinary lease can be terminated for default in rent or breach of covenant, so also a cooperative lease can be terminated for like grounds and the cooperative lessee evicted by quick and inexpensive forcible detainer proceedings. *Green v. Greenbelt Homes, Inc.*, 194 A2d 273 (Md. 1963). In a condominium, if a particular apartment owner fails to pay his monthly assessments, a lien on his apartment can be foreclosed, just as a mortgage is foreclosed, but the proceeding is costly and time consuming. Making the condominium owner behave, when his conduct becomes objectionable, is difficult.

4. In the condominium, the tax assessment is an individual assessment on the unit and its share of the common elements. As long as the tax on a particular unit is paid, failure of other unit owners to pay their taxes does not affect the nondelinquent unit. In the cooperative there is one tax bill on the entire building. If some owners do not pay their share, the others must carry the entire load or face tax foreclosure proceedings.

5. In a cooperative, work and materials ordered by one tenant can result in a mechanic's lien against the entire building. In a condominium the lien is confined to the apartment where the work was done.

6. Where for one reason or another it becomes advisable to sell the building and the tenants wish to do so, this can be accomplished in cooperatives by a vote of a percentage of the shareholders (who, of course, are the tenants). A two-thirds vote usually suffices. In the case of a condominium, sale of the building is apt to require a unanimous vote, except in certain special situations, as where the building is destroyed by fire.

7. Both the condominium owner and the cooperative owner have the right to defer payment of income tax on a capital gain where the apartment is sold at a profit. Both have the same right to deduct from income for income tax purposes all payments made on mortgage interest and real estate taxes.

39.10(a)   Additional Benefits of Cooperatives

In recent times benefits of the cooperative form have surfaced, indicating that cooperatives will gain greater acceptance. These are:

1. *Real estate taxes.* When a condominium is created, the tax assessor assesses each unit separately. As a result, the total of the tax assessments is far greater than the assessed value of the building viewed as a rental building. A co-op, being a rental building, enjoys the lower tax assessment.

2. *Regulations.* Except in New York, cooperatives are not heavily regulated. Condominium regulations, on the other hand, grow more complex each year.

3. *Legislation.* Condominium conversion legislation is deliberately harsh so as to discourage conversion. This harsh legislation is inapplicable to cooperatives.

ADDITIONAL REFERENCES ON COOPERATIVES: Rohan and Reskin, *Cooperative Housing Law and Practice* (1978); Clurman and Hebard, *Condominiums and Coops* (1970); Kehoe, *Cooperatives and Condominiums* (1974); Fifkin, *Co-op Proprietary Leases,* 51 N.Y.S.B.J. 290 (1979); Hennessey, *Cooperative Apartments and Town Houses,* 1956 U. Ill. L. Forum 22; Isaacs, *To Buy or Not to Buy, That Is the Question: . . . What is a Cooperative Apartment?,* 13 Record of N.Y.C.B.A. 203 (1958); McCullough, *Cooperative Apartments in Illinois,* 26 Chi-Kent L. Rev. 303 (1948); Whitman, *Financing Condominiums and Cooperatives,* 13 Tulsa L. J. 15 (1977); 61 Harv. L. Rev. 1407 (1948); 111 U. Pa. L. Rev. 638 (1963); 68 Yale L. J. 542 (1959); 8 Fordham Urban L. J. 345 (1980) (maintenance and repairs); 46 St. Johns L. Rev. 632 (financing symposium); 38 Geo. Wash. L. Rev. 958 (low income co-ops); 12 U. of Miami L. Rev. 13; 16 *id.* 305. 2 U. of Conn. L. Rev. 30; 50 Calif. L. Rev. 299; 19 Stanf. L. Rev. 978; 18 *id.* 1323; 21 Buffalo L. Rev. 555 (sale 1973); 40 U. of Cin. L. Rev. 40 (1971); 29 Wash. & Lee L. Rev. 189 (1972); 49 Harv. L. Rev. 158; 1978 Law Forum 76a.

MODEL ACT: Uniform Law Commissioners Model Real Estate Cooperative Act, August 7, 1981.

CHAPTER 40

Townhouses

40.01 In General

Land is the single largest cost component in any housing development. As a result, there is an indirect correlation between the density of a development and the cost of the housing units. A developer can hold down the selling price of the housing units by increasing the density of the development. Thus if land costs $50,000 per acre, the land cost per housing unit in a project with one house per acre is $50,000 per house. If the density is increased to two houses per acre, the land cost per housing unit goes down to $25,000 per unit.

The greatest density comes, of course, in the high-rise development. Townhouses or cluster housing presents an alternative that is denser than the single-family detached housing development, but not as dense as the high-rise. In the past, this higher-density project would have been accomplished by building rows of attached houses facing the street. The development concept matured, and townhouse projects were next built with the rows of units being built at right angles to the street. Today, we see more changes, and these projects are constructed with housing units built in clusters, on top of one another, on top of or as a part of multiuse projects, or as multiple-unit buildings that have the appearance of a single large house.

Whatever the development scheme, there are some common features to this form of development. There is extensive use of shared walls. This form of development makes extensive use of easements and restrictions. Frequently, these will be found in a document called the *Declaration of Covenants, Conditions, Restrictions and Easements*. Since the walls are party walls, easements must exist for their construction and use. Also, all of the housing units, except those closest to the street, will need easements of ingress and egress. Easements are also needed for common gutters and downspouts, common sewers, water pipes, electric lines, telephone wires, cable television lines, and so forth.

In the past, it was not unusual for some builders to develop projects of this type with complete indifference to their unique legal requirements. Units would be sold without any mention of the needed easements. Probably implied easements exist for all of the necessary common uses. *Gilbert* v. *Chicago Title and Trust Co.,* 131 NE2d 1 (Ill. 1956). Obviously, the declaration of easements is the better way of handling this issue.

The true townhouse functions without a home association. If a home association is included, it is formed as a condominium and is therefore subject to the local condominium laws, and the easements are found in the condominium declaration. The condominium form of ownership also has the advantage of offering a defined body of law and documentation for governing the use and occupancy of the development as time goes by.

If there are to be common areas owned by the homeowners' association, the development is treated in this text as a planned unit development and its legal aspects are discussed in that chapter.

In some states the townhouse development, with its dwelling units and common areas, is depicted on a recorded plat. In other instances the boundaries of the units and common areas are depicted on a map attached to the declaration.

The typical old townhouse development had only a few units and operated without the benefit of a homeowners' association. This form of organization, or lack of organization, has its drawbacks. For example, each unit would carry its own fire insurance. If a unit was severely damaged by fire, the mortgagee on that unit might choose to apply the insurance money to the reduction of the mortgage debt and not the rebuilding of the townhouse. This event has obvious and detrimental effects on neighboring units. Their salability is severely impaired, and the complex is left with a very visible scar. There is also no organization to enact rules and regulations for the common good of all of the development or to take action against the unit owner or occupant who acts in a manner unacceptable to the rest, as would be the case where a unit owner kept junk cars on the front lawn.

REFERENCES: Krasnowiecki, *Townhouses with Home Associations: A New Perspective,* 23 Penn L. Rev. 711 (1975); Krasnowiecki, *Condominiums Compared to Conventional Subdivisions with Homes,* 1 R.E.L.J. 323 (1972).

The changes in nomenclature are interesting. They started out as "row houses," became "town houses" and now are called "patio homes" or "carriage houses."

CHAPTER 41

Office, Research, and Industrial Parks

41.01 History and Purpose of Office and Industrial Parks

The history of office and industrial parks is comparatively modern when com-pared to the history of real estate law. To be sure, there are older industrial parks such as the Central Manufacturing District and the Clearing Industrial District in Chicago. But as the surge to the suburbs took place after World War II, the industrial developer appeared as a much larger force on the development scene. Today, as communities strive to attract high-technology industry to employ their workforce and to build a tax base—or rebuild the tax base that was damaged when smokestack industries closed their doors—the office and industrial park is staging a strong comeback. A drive down the streets of Silicon Valley will provide demonstrable evidence to the present-day uses of these facilities.

The developer of these facilities takes on an important role.

EXAMPLE: Developer assembles tracts of land zoned for farm and residential purposes. He persuades the local municipality to rezone the property for his intended use as an office and light industrial park. Developer then brings sewer, water, and other utilities to the site. The soil has been checked and arrange-ments for transportation facilities made. The developer records a declaration of restrictions that calls for a property owners' association. As the developer sells or leases tracts for office and industrial use, he can assure each business owner that all legal problems and development headaches have been solved. The busi-ness owner is left to the task of building or leasing his office or plant and com-mencing operations. The disadvantages are really disguised advantages. The fa-cility is required to observe setback lines, to landscape its facilities, and to screen off its trash heaps and truck docks. This can be costly, but these require-ments enhance the value of the property. Moreover, the owner knows that neighboring business will be subjected to the same scrutiny.

41.02   Advantages of Office and Industrial Parks

Parks of this kind offer many advantages to the small business owner: (1) Precious time is not taken up by site preparation or land assembly. The site, with all utilities, is presented to the businessman for use in the business. (2) Zoning problems are minimized. While the zoning and building codes must be checked to determine that they will not be violated by the particular use contemplated by the individual businesses, the developer has had the property rezoned to allow the general run of contemplated businesses. (3) There are no title problems. The developer has usually obtained a clear title policy showing that there are no objectionable building restrictions or easements to complicate the businessman's life. (4) There are operating economies. For example, the cost of a common sewage plant will be shared by all users. There may also be a shared security force and other shared services. (5) The park is usually protected by building restrictions established by the developer. For example, the developer would have established building lines so that there is ample open space surrounding each business. The developer or an architectural control committee may have the right to pass upon all building plans to assure each owner an aesthetically pleasing environment developed along a consistent architectural theme. This allows the business owner to omit the precaution of buying excess land to insulate the business from undesirable neighbors. (6) The business owner may have an opportunity of preserving working capital by accepting a build-lease arrangement with the developer or which the developer has arranged through a financing operation.

41.03   Continuing Management Responsibility

Owners of sites in industrial and office parks insist upon a continuing responsibility for the enforcement of site restrictions. This is usually accomplished by the formation of a property owners' association, which is given the legal right to enforce the restrictions set forth in the declaration of covenants, conditions, and restrictions.

41.04   Types of Parks—Legal Aspects

The developer of property of this kind works in one of several ways. Under one format, the developer assembles the land, obtains the proper zoning, brings in the needed utilities, and constructs the roadways and other common facilities. Lots are then sold to the business owners who in turn construct the buildings needed to suit their operations. In another development format, the developer does all of the above and also enters into contracts with the business owners to construct buildings to the owner's specifications and lease the facility to the business. In yet another format, the developer will construct building shells without yet having buyers. When buyers are found, the needed interior work will be done to outfit each property to the buyer's specifications.

The legal aspects of all of these formats are discussed in the various chapters of this book. For example:

1. The zoning must be checked to be sure that it will accommodate a wide variety of office and industrial uses, together with the necessary ancillary uses for a property of this kind. For example, does the zoning permit the fast food restaurant that will be needed to support an active park? Depending upon the park's size, a hotel may be needed. Will the zoning permit such a use?

2. A declaration of covenants, conditions, and restrictions will be filed with the plat. This will define the uses that are permitted within the park.

3. A property owners' association will be formed to enforce the restrictions.

4. The subdivision plat will be submitted to the public officials involved in the planning process and the necessary approvals obtained. The plat will be recorded before any lots are sold.

5. Arrangements will be made to bring utilities to the site.

6. Often these properties, especially office parks, are developed with common walls between the businesses. This brings many of the theories of townhouse development into play.

When a lot is sold, the developer may wish to reserve an option to repurchase the land within a given number of years at the purchase price if the land remains vacant. This is often done to discourage the purchase of such lots by speculators who are not going to build and use the premises.

41.05   Public Assistance

The need for commerce to provide employment, establish a tax base, and generally contribute to the economic life of a community has led to the enactment of various state laws and local ordinances. These enactments are intended to give businesses the economic incentive to locate their enterprise within a particular area. The form of incentives varies from the governmental purchase of the land for lease to the business, the provision of free offsite and utility service to the property, the reduction of real estate taxes for a stated period, and low interest rate loans, to the more creative devices such as the training of the community's work force for the future employer's needs. Whatever the incentives may be, the competition among communities and even states for the attraction of business is keen, and no developer should overlook the economic advantages that may be available from these sources.

41.06   Research Facilities

Light industry and office and administrative functions are often found in parks in combination with research facilities. The presence of research facilities staffed by highly educated people requires that the park have a campuslike atmosphere with green areas of open space and be located near cultural facilities.

CHAPTER 42

Building Construction and Building Warranties—Mechanic's Liens

42.01 Construction Contracts

There are different types of construction contracts:

1. I own a lot and hire you to build a house according to certain plans and specifications prepared by my architect. This is a construction contract only.

2. You are a subdivider and builder. I pick out a site in your subdivision, and you contract to build a house (like one of your model homes, perhaps) and deliver the house and lot at a specified price. This is a contract for the sale of land and for the construction of a house. Both the law of sale contracts and the law of construction contracts are applicable to this situation.

3. You are a subdivider and builder, and I decide to buy a house that I find under construction in your subdivision. This is essentially the same as No. 2 above.

Situations 2 and 3 above involve the *sell-and-build* type of contract. The contract is one for the *sale of land* and also for the *construction of a home. Dieckman* v. *Walser*, 144 N.J.Eq. 382, 168 Atl. 582 (1933). It must comply with the requirements of law as to both types of contracts.

EXAMPLE: *R* contracted to sell *E* a lot and build a home thereon. The contract of sale portion was complete, but there were no plans or specifications giving the details of the building. The contract was invalid. *Griesenhauer* v. *Bellea Lake Development Co.*, 421 SW2d 785 (1967).

A contract to build a home "like" the model the buyer has inspected is a contract to build a home with all the inadequacies of the model.

42.02   Types of Sell-and-build Contracts

The are several types of sell-and-build contracts.

> **EXAMPLE:**   Seller contracts to sell a lot to Buyer. The contract requires that Buyer apply for a mortgage loan of $75,000, and is contingent on the procuring of this loan. When the loan is obtained, the deal is to be closed, deed and mortgage recorded, and thereafter Seller is to construct the building, using the mortgage money for this purpose. After the closing of the deal, the contract between the parties is simply a construction contract.

> **EXAMPLE:**   Seller contracts to sell a lot to Buyer, to erect a house thereon, and when the house has been completed, to deed the completed house and lot to Buyer. Here Seller will get his own construction loan, build the building with his own construction loan proceeds, and deliver the completed package to Buyer. This has some advantages to Seller. The handling of the construction disbursements does not involve Buyer, whereas in the previous example Seller must go to Buyer for documents every time a construction disbursement is to be made. After all, in the previous example, it is Buyer's money, loaned to him by the mortgagee, that is being used for construction.

> **SUGGESTION TO HOME BUYER:**   When you buy from a professional sub-divider and builder, you are often dealing with a person who does not yet own the land that he is selling you. He may have only an option or contract to buy the land. If the builder runs into financial difficulties, he may never be able to pay up his option or contract or be able to transfer ownership to you. Moreover, as financial troubles develop, mechanic's liens are filed and mortgage foreclosures instituted. In such case you will find that the possibility of obtaining ownership or getting your money back is nil. Therefore, it is best for you to get a deed and title policy to the property as early as possible, before you have put too much money into the house.

42.02(a)   Sell-and-build Contracts—Signatures

Some sell-and-build contracts contain a clause that the seller is not bound unless an officer of the seller corporation signs for the corporation. Obviously, the buyer should not accept a contract signed only by a salesman. Indeed, it is always advisable to insist on an officer's signature.

42.02(b)   Sell-and-build Contracts—Mortgage Clauses

Every sell-and-build contract has a clause requiring the buyer to apply for a mortgage loan. The deal will go one of two ways.

> **EXAMPLE:**   Builder will convey the land to Buyer who puts on a mortgage, and Builder uses the proceeds of the loan to build the home.

> **EXAMPLE:** Builder has Buyer apply for a mortgage loan. As soon as the lender has approved Buyer for the loan, Builder puts a construction mortgage on the lot and uses the proceeds of this loan to build the home. When the home is completed, Buyer signs the permanent mortgage, the proceeds of which are used to pay off both Builder and the construction loan.

In either case the buyer must qualify for a mortgage loan, so the contract calls for him to apply for a mortgage loan; the deal is off if he fails to qualify.

42.02(c)   Delay in Completion

A prospective buyer should read the contract before signing it. The time set for completion is an important matter to a buyer who is planning to sell his present home. Carefully read the clause that gives the builder additional time to complete. It may be so broad that the completion date is virtually meaningless.

42.02(d)   Sell-and-build Contracts—Subordination of Contract to Construction Loan

Many sell-and-build contracts contain a clause subordinating the contract to any construction mortgage put on the property by the builder.

> **EXAMPLE:** Builder sells a lot to Buyer under a contract by which Builder will build a home for Buyer like a model home he has displayed to Buyer. Builder will now put a construction loan mortgage on the lot to Lender. Probably Lender will want to see the contract to make certain that the land is under contract and also to see the sale price. Having actual notice of the contract, Lender's rights would be subordinate to Buyer's rights, and a deed from Builder to Buyer could wipe out Lender's mortgage. Therefore the contract will state that Buyer's rights are subordinate to Lender's lien.

42.02(e)   Sell-and-build Contracts—Builder Liability

Obviously, the seller–builder in a sell-and-build contract has all the liabilities of a building contractor. *Jones* v. *Galewood*, 381 P2d 158 (Okla. 1963).

42.03   Mechanic's Liens

Mechanics and materialmen are persons who furnish labor or materials in the construction of improvements on land. A mechanic or materialman who has furnished such labor or material on the landowner's order can, by complying with certain formalities, acquire a lien on the land and improvements in question if the landowner fails to pay him. The lien is called a *mechanic's lien,* and the person furnishing the work or material is the *mechanic's lien claimant.* These liens resemble mortgages and in many states are foreclosed in the same manner as mortgages.

Generally, lienable work and materials must be such as become a permanent part of the building structure. Thus medical care furnished an employee of the contractor, even if the injury was suffered on the building site, is not lienable. Printing, stationery, and telephone service furnished to the contractor are not lienable. Nor is the furnishing of tools, machinery, cranes, hoists, and so forth, lienable, for those do not become a permanent part of the building.

42.03(a)   Performance by Contractor

In general, where the general contractor seeks to assert a lien, he must show that the contract was *substantially performed* by him. 57 CJS 605. Likewise, any subcontractor seeking to assert a lien would have to show that his job was substantially performed by him. Where the contract specifies that no payment will be made without production of an architect's certificate, a general contractor claiming a lien must be able to produce the certificate. 57 CJS 606.

42.03(b)   Inception and Priority of Lien

The law as to the particular time when a mechanic's lien attaches to the land varies from state to state.

42.03(c)   Notice of Lien

In many states, laws require a mechanic's lien claimant to file a notice of his lien in some public office within some specified time, usually within some period after completion of the work. Usually it is required that this notice state the amount claimed to be due, the name and address of the claimant, the type of improvement, a description of the land, and the name of the landowner or landowners. 52 ALR2d 12, 27 ALR2d 1169.

42.03(d)   Waiver and Release of Lien

As construction or repair work goes forward, liens attach to the land. Both the landowner and any mortgagee involved naturally want to get rid of these liens, which can be accomplished by procuring waivers of their liens from the parties furnishing labor or material. There are *partial waivers* and *final waivers*. Suppose that a subcontractor, such as a plumbing, electrical, or plastering subcontractor, has finished half his job and wants to be paid for that half. When the homebuilder pays him, he demands from the subcontractor a waiver of his lien for the work and materials furnished. This waiver recites that it waives all liens for *work and materials furnished*. This means, of course, for work and materials furnished *up to the date of the waiver*. No lien is waived as to the work still to be done. When final payment is made to that particular party, the homebuilder demands from him a final waiver, which waives all lien *for work and materials furnished or to be furnished* meaning that he has no lien at all on the land or buildings. Even if he must come back to repair or replace defective work or material, he can claim no lien on the property, which is important, because the objective is always to get the building built at the price and at the bids submitted by the various mechanics. There is trouble ahead if any of the mechanics is legally able to assert a lien for a sum greater than the amount he agreed to work for.

When a mechanic has filed a lien claim in some public office as required by law, it becomes necessary, when his claim has been paid or settled, to release his lien from the public records. As a rule, the waiver form is not appropriate for this purpose. Instead, a form called *release of mechanic's lien* is used. It is very similar to a release of mortgage and is filed in the same office where the lien claim has been filed.

42.03(e)   Time Limit on Enforcement of Lien

It is usually provided that a mechanic's lien ceases to exist unless steps are taken to enforce or foreclose it within a specified time, usually one or two years, after the filing of the lien claim.

42.04   Extras

Extras are probably the largest factor creating disputes between owners and contractors. There is a propensity on the part of some contractors to bid low in order to get the job and then try to bail their way out of a losing job by claiming extras. Also, an owner is frequently "inspired" during the course of construction and orders changes or extra work and materials indiscriminately without a definite understanding as to the cost. A contractor who is providing extras does not have to make a competitive bid in order to obtain the work. There is therefore a tendency on the part of some contractors to charge more money for extras than the ordinary markup used in bidding for work. The contract should therefore specifically require that all extra charges must be reduced to a written instrument, signed by the owner, describing the work to be performed and the amount to be paid. Such a provision is valid. 2 ALR3d 631. In the interest of both the contractor and the owner, this procedure should be religiously followed. The owner's architect has no power to waive this provision of the contract. He cannot order extras verbally. 2 ALR3d 686. However, if the owner himself verbally orders the extra work, he is liable. 2 ALR3d 658. By ordering the extras verbally, the owner has waived the provision requiring a change order to be in writing. Also, the contract should require the owner to deposit additional funds with the mortgage lender in order to assure the contractor and the mortgage lender that there will be adequate funds to complete the building when extra work or materials are ordered.

In addition to disputes with respect to the cost of extras, disputes often arise as to whether or not a given item is an extra or is included under the original contract. If the plans and specifications made a part of the contract are sufficiently detailed, the possibility of a dispute over whether a particular item is an extra can be minimized.

42.05   Progress Payments

If I hire you to erect a building on my land, the contract will almost certainly fix a total price for the entire job. However, your subcontractors will not wait for their money until the building is finished. Therefore, the contract will call for *progress payments* to the general contractor and the subcontractors as the building goes up. A widely used formula provides for a payment of 35 percent of the proceeds to the contractor when the house is under roof, 30 percent of the contract price when the house is plastered, and the balance of 35 percent when the building is completed and accepted by the owner. However, the contract often provides that only 85 percent of the full amount of a progress payment due the *general contractor* is payable when the progress payment falls due. The owner holds back 15 percent of each payment due the general contractor (often called a *retention*) until the building has been completed and accepted by the owner with all lien waivers produced. On big jobs the contract will call for retention on work done by the bigger subcontractors. After all, you cannot tell whether heating or air conditioning will work until you try it, and if it doesn't, the retention is an effective inducement to get the necessary repairs done.

As a progress payment is demanded, the contract often calls for an inspection to be made by the owner's architect, who certifies that the work and material for which payment is claimed are in place and in accordance with the contract. If the owner has no architect, this inspection should be made by the mortgage lending institution.

Failure of the landowner to make a progress payment is a material breach of the contract. It entitles the contractor to suspend work until payment has been made. *Watson* v. *Auburn Iron Works, inc.*, 318 NE2d 508 (Ill. 1974).

42.06   Mortgage Money

Any builder who builds on contract for a landowner should insist that the landowner have a definite commitment for a satisfactory construction mortgage loan before construction begins, and the construction contract should be made subject to this condition.

SUGGESTION TO BUILDER: Require the landowner to furnish you a photostatic copy of the lender's commitment to make the mortgage loan.

42.07   Cash Down Payments from Homebuyers

Builders usually insist that the homebuyer make a cash down payment. What to do with it is the question. Homebuyers are often reluctant to pay a builder a large sum of money before construction has begun. And builders are often reluctant to start construction when they have no assurance that the homebuyer will be able to come up with the money. One solution is to have the homebuyer deposit his money with the mortgage house that is financing construction. This is acceptable to the mortgage house, for under the typical construction loan agreement, this deposit is used for the initial stages of construction, and the mortgagee's loan money is not used until later stages of construction have been reached. Another idea is to deposit the buyer's money with some bank as escrowee, with directions to turn the money over to the builder as specified stages of construction are reached.

> **NEW LAWS:** In some states (New York, for example), laws require the builder to keep the buyer's deposit in an escrow. In other states a builder who diverts the deposit to another job is guilty of a crime. *State of Washington* v. *Thomas William McDonald,* 463 P2d 174 (Wash. 1969).

42.08   Substantial Performance

If a building contractor finishes the building in strict accordance with the plans and specifications and in a good and workmanlike manner, he is, of course, entitled to collect the full contract price. However, it is virtually impossible to complete a building contract in strict compliance with every tiny requirement of the plans and specifications. If the builder performs substantially according to the contract, he is entitled to collect the contract price, less a deduction that will compensate the owner for the builder's deviations from the contract. Substantial performance is hard to define. If the owner gets substantially the building that he contracted for, and the deviations are trifling and unintentional, there is substantial performance. For example, if I hire you to build a house according to my plans at a price of $120,000, and you fulfill your contract except that two rooms have the wrong wallpaper, which it would cost $1,000 to remedy, clearly there is substantial performance, and you are entitled to collect $119,000. The following are illustrations of cases where substantial performance was found lacking.

> **EXAMPLES:**   (1) The footings were inadequate for wet ground, so that the foundations sank and the floors sagged. *White* v. *Mitchell,* 123 Wash. 630, 213 P. 10 (1923); (2) the contract called for a six-room house, and the builder, erected a five-room house; (3) the foundations and walls of the house cracked immediately after completion of construction due to a soil condition that the builder did not properly correct. *Newcomb* v. *Schaeffler,* 131 Colo. 56, 279 P2d 409 (1955); (4) in New York it is generally held that if the deviations amount to more than 10 percent of the contract price, substantial performance is lacking. *Rochkind* v. *Jacobson,* 110 NYS 583.

If you contract to erect a building for me and your performance is less than substantial, one of several consequences is possible:

> 1. If I am in a generous frame of mind, then even though the building is not the kind that you agreed to build, I may accept the building as a complete and satisfactory substitute for the building contracted for. Here I must pay the full contract price. No

deductions are allowed because of the defects. *Zambakian* v. *Leson,* 77 Colo. 183, 234 P. 1065 (1925).

EXAMPLE: As the building went up, the owner inspected it and noticed the deviations from the contract. But he moved in, telling the builder that the building was satisfactory and that the contract price would be paid. This is full acceptance. All deviations were waived. *Hooper* v. *Cuneo,* 227 Mass. 37, 116 NE 237 (1917).

Often in these cases, the owner has with full knowledge of the defects paid the entire contract price. Since this is full acceptance, he cannot thereafter sue the builder for damages because of defects he knew about when he paid his money. *Houlette & Miller* v. *Arntz,* 148 La. 407, 126 NW 796 (1910). And there are always words, acts, or both on the landowner's part indicating full acceptance of the building. *Aarnes* v. *Windham,* 137 Ala. 513, 34 So 816 (1903). Often the builder has a printed form that he asks the landowner to sign. This form recites that the building has been constructed in complete conformity with the contract.

2. Owner may accept the building as substantial performance but reserve the right to deductions because of the deviations.

EXAMPLE: The owner discovers defects as the building goes up, protests the defects, but continues to proceed with the builder on the basis and assumption that their contract is still in force. *Otto Misch Co.* v. *E. E. Davis Co.,* 241 Mich. 285, 217 NW 38 (1928). The builder gets the contract price, less a deduction to compensate for the deviations. *Gray* v. *Wood,* 220 Ala. 587, 127 So 148 (1930); 17 CJS 1101, 1105.

3. I simply move into the building because it is on my land and I cannot avoid it. My attitude at all times after discovering the defects is that the builder has breached his contract and ought not to be paid anything. Most courts will nevertheless award the builder the value of the building, on the theory that it must be worth something to the landowner and that to give the builder nothing would be unduly harsh. Other courts, however, are less merciful with the builder. They say that I have a right to use my own land and the buildings on it, and since the builder's performance fell short of substantial performance, he is entitled to nothing. 5 Corbin, *Contracts* 551; 107 ALR 1411.

4. If I demolish the structure, or refuse to make any use of it, in most states the builder will be unable to collect a penny. 3 Corbin, *Contracts* 790.

42.09   Liability of Seller–Builder for Defects in Land or Building

The subject of liability of the seller–builder for defects in land or building has grown tremendously in *recent* years.

The obligations of the seller of a *new* house under the old law differed from those of the seller of an *old* house. The obligations of the seller of a *completed* house differed from those of the seller of a house yet to be constructed. One who sells a house *to be constructed* has *builder liability.* One who sells a *completed* house does *not*, at least under some older cases. Suppose you, as a builder, have a house in the process of construction. *X* sees it and signs a contract to buy it. You have *builder liability* to *X*. As long as the seller has workmen on the job, the house is not fully completed, and therefore when the house is sold, the contract is treated as though it were a contract (1) to sell the land and (2) to finish the house. In short, it is a sell-and-build contract. Builder liability means that the courts hold the builder on two implied warranties: (1) *he must build in a good and workmanlike manner;* (2) *the structure when completed must be reasonably fit for its intended purpose.* *Markman* v. *Hoefer,* 252 Iowa 118, 106 NW2d 59 (1960).

> **EXAMPLE:**   Exterior stucco peeled off soon after the house was completed. The builder is liable. He has failed to build in a good and workmanlike manner. The same would be true if the concrete footings were faulty and the building settled, causing cracked plaster and ill-fitting doors. 4 Western Reserve L. Rev. 361.

In addition to liability on the two implied warranties, a builder is liable for failure to use ordinary care and skill. This is called *negligence liability.* For example, a builder must use ordinary care in the selecting of building materials, and if he should carelessly select beams of inadequate strength, he would be liable for injuries resulting from collapse of the house.

There was an obvious defect in the law, as stated above. Under the old law, the seller of a *completed house* had no builder liability for defects in the building.

Often, but not always, builder liability on implied warranties is employed to hold a builder liable for *defects in the building*. Negligence liability is employed to recover for *personal injuries* resulting from defective construction.

42.09(a)   Liability of Builder–Seller for Defects in Building and Injuries Suffered as a Result of Defects in New Building

After World War II ended and the veterans began to return home to marry and look for homes, a tremendous building boom ensued—the greatest homebuilding surge in world history. Unscrupulous builders built shoddy homes. In the decade from 1954 to 1964, when the building boom was at its height, hundreds of magazine and newspaper articles appeared about the miserable homes foisted on veterans. The old law was basically "let the buyer beware." Look before you buy. Of course, the unscrupulous builders were clever at hiding the defects. Who looks behind the drywall or beneath the foundation? So the courts changed the law.

> **NEW DIRECTIONS:**   Beginning in 1964, the courts began to throw the old rules overboard. They began to hold that in every sale of a newly completed residence by a builder–seller there is an *implied warranty* that the home was built in a workmanlike manner and is fit for habitation. *Carpenter* v. *Donohoe,* 154 Colo. 78, 388 P2d 399, 402 (1964); *Bethlahmy* v. *Bechtel,* 415 P2d 698 (Idaho 1966); *Waggoner* v. *Midwestern Develop., Inc.,* 154 NW2d 803 (S.D. 1967); *Moore* v. *Werner,* 418 SW2d 918 (Tex. Civ. App. 1967); *Humber* v. *Morton,* 426 SW2d 554 (Tex. 1968); *Theis* v. *Heuer,* 280 NE2d 300 (Ind. 1972)(citing many articles); also *Tavaros* v. *Horstman,* 542 P2d 1275 (1976). The philosophy here

is that the average buyer of a new home is ill-equipped to detect the defects and shortcomings of jerry-built construction. It is likely that all states will come to this point of view in time. 25 ALR3d 383. At this writing the new rule has been adopted in more than 40 states.

It is now the rule that a builder–seller of a residence completed or in the process of construction, implicitly warrants to his purchaser that the house was, in its major structural features, constructed in a good and workmanlike manner. That is, the structure is of reasonable quality, is reasonably fit for its intended purpose, and is free of building code violations. The theories behind this rule are that the buyer of a new house relies on the skill of a seller–builder, that the buyer is incapable of detecting defects in construction, and that most defects in construction are hidden from view.

At first the courts applied their new rule only to the original purchaser who bought from the builder–seller. But the veterans, reordering their lives, and in the quest for new job opportunities, often moved and sold their homes after a brief residence, and the hidden defects came to light when a new purchaser acquired the home.

The more recent cases hold that a second purchaser can also sue a builder–seller for defective construction. *Richards* v. *Powercraft Homes, Inc.,* 678 P2d 472 (Ariz. 1984); *Redarowicz* v. *Ohlendorf,* 92 Ill.2d 171, 441 NE2d 224 (1982), 10 ALR4th 385. The implied warranty given the original purchaser carries over automatically to the second purchaser.

Likewise, the second purchaser can hold the builder liable because the defects were due to the builder's carelessness. The builder must have foreseen that subsequent purchasers would suffer from defective construction. *Cosmopolitan Homes Inc.* v. *Weller,* 663 P2d 1041 (Colo. 1963).

REFERENCES: 8 RELJ 303 (lists decisions in 38 states as recognizing implied warranty on part of builder–seller, and 10 states as not having addressed the issue). On sales "as is" see *Century Display Co.* v. *D. R. Wagner Const. Co.,* 376 NE2d 993 (Ill. 1978); the implied warranty rule does not apply to commercial buildings, see *Dawson Industries* v. *Godley Const. Co.,* 29 N.C.App. 270, 224 SE2d 266 (1976); the rule applies to sale of condominium unit, see *Tassan* v. *United Dev. Co.,* 88 Ill. App.3d 581, 410 NE2d 902 (1980) and to sale of co-op; *Suarez* v. *Rivercross Tenants Corp.,* 438 NYS2d 164 (1981), and to sale of leasehold, *Lemlee* v. *Breedon,* 462 P2d 470 (Hawaii 1969); as to effect of disclaimer of liability see *Herbly* v. *Dunbar Bldg. Corp.,* 415 NE2d 1224 (Ill. App. 1980).

The rule holding the builder–seller liable means the home must be fit for habitation, that the water will not seep in, that the indoor plumbing will work, that the foundation and walls will not crack, that the well will deliver ample supplies of potable water and so on.

The last edition of this book referred to 8 Real Estate Law Journal 303 as listing 35 states following the new rule of implied warranty on the part of a seller–builder. A more recent article lists Maine, Montana, Tennessee and West Virginia as joining this group of states. 20 ABA Real Property, Prob. & Tr. J. 933, 938 (1985). In addition to court decisions holding the builder liable, there are state laws in almost one-third of the states imposing warranty liability on condo-minium developers. *Ibid.* 939–943. State laws should be consulted in all warranty situations.

To sum up at this point:

1. The buyer hires a builder who agrees in the contract to construct a home of a specified description; the builder must do his job *carefully*. If he fails to do so, he must either repair the *faulty construction* or be liable for damages. This liability runs to the party who hired the builder. The philosophy is simple. If I hire you to do a job, the law says you must do your work carefully. Notice the timing. Buyer enters the picture *before* the house is completed.

2. If a professional builder erects and *completes* a home that contains defects, especially hidden defects, he is liable to the first purchaser of the *completed* home for damages.

In the interest of completeness and clarity of understanding, we must weave in here some additional aspects of the law on this and closely related topics.

3. With respect to No. 1 above, many courts today are likely to permit a *second* purchaser of the home to recover for the defects in the home. *Simmons* v. *Owens,* 363 So2d 142 (Fla. 1978); *Gates* v. *Jag, Inc.,* 314 N.C. 276; 333 SE2d 222 (N.C. 1985)(citing cases in many other states); *Cosmo Hames, Inc.* v. *Weller,* 663 P2d 1041 (Colo. 1983); 10 ALR4th 385.

EXAMPLE: Builder, operating in termite territory, builds a frame house that rests on the ground instead of being elevated above the surface of the ground. He sells the house to Purchaser who sells it to Second Purchaser. Termite damage is found. Second Purchaser can sue Builder.

And in No. 2 above involving sale of a completed house, Second Purchaser is permitted to sue Builder in most states. After all, the law is concerned with taking care of the homeowner who suffers loss from faulty work. Whether it's the first or second purchaser is of no consequence.

4. Remember that one who sells real estate is guilty of fraud if he fails to disclose a known defect. The professional builder always knows of defects in the building. He put them there. This liability runs only to his purchaser.

Now you can see that when a client comes to a lawyer with a case involving a defect in a new home, the lawyer must select carefully the theory of liability he will urge upon the court. What works in one state may not work in another.

REFERENCES ON IMPLIED WARRANTIES IN THE SALE OF NEW CONSTRUC-TION BY BUILDER: 25 ALR3d 383; 16 ALR4th 1246; 10 Am. Jur. P.O.F. 2d 111.

Turning our thinking now to *personal injuries* resulting from faulty construction, a new set of rules comes into play. Now we are concerned with the *seller's* liability, whether or not he is the builder.

The seller may be liable because he knew of a hidden defect that created a danger to occupants.

> **EXAMPLE:**   Seller knows that there is a dangerous break in the flooring of a dark closet. Seller also knows that it is unlikely that Buyer will discover the danger. Seller fails to warn Buyer. Buyer's wife is injured while hanging clothes in the closet. Seller is liable. *O'Connor* v. *Altus,* 123 N.J. Super. 379, 303 A2d 329 (1973), citing Restatement *Torts* 2d §353.

> **EXAMPLE:**   There is an unused well on the property which Seller has covered with sod. Wife of Buyer steps on the sod and the rotten boards break, plunging her into the well. Seller is liable for failure to warn Buyer. *Cooper* v. *Cordova Sand Co., Inc.,* 485 SW2d 261 (Tenn. 1972).

The *builder* is going to be liable if he constructs a dangerous structure. *Inman* v. *Binghamton Housing Authority,* 3 NY2d 137, 143 NE2d 895 (1957).

> **EXAMPLE:**   The child of a tenant in an apartment building was injured in a fall from a defectively constructed porch. The builder was held liable. See discussion, Kratovil, *Cardozo Revisited: Liability to Third Parties; A Real Property Perspective* 7 U. of Puget Sound L. Rev. 259, 286 (1984).

The idea of *products liability* arose in the sale of chattels.

> **EXAMPLE:**   Buick Motor Company manufactured a defective automobile. This was sold to its dealer, who sold it to X. X suffered injuries owing to the defects and recovered damages from Buick. *MacPherson* v. *Buick Motor Co.,* 217 N.Y. 382, 111 NE 1050 (1916).

Prior to 1916, a person could sue only the person who sold him a defective product, for example, the car dealer. Now it is possible to sue the manufacturer. In its modern version as expressed in some decisions, products liability does not require the injured party to prove carelessness in manufacture. All that is needed is to show that the product was defective and that *bodily injury* resulted. The philosophy is that the manufacturer is better able to stand the loss than the injured party. He can raise his prices or take out insurance against such risks. *Greenman* v. *Yuba Power Products Inc.,* 59 Cal.2d 57, 377 P2d 897 (1963); 76 Yale L. J. 887.

This view is beginning to appear in real estate law.

> **EXAMPLE:**   Builder erected a home that had a defective hot water system. The home was sold to Buyer, who rented it to Tenant. Tenant's son was scalded. Builder was held liable. *Schipper* v. *Levitt & Sons, Inc.,* 44 N.J. 70, 207 A2d 314 (1965), noted in 51 Cornell L. Q. 389; 19 Okla. L. Rev. 417; 41 Wash. L. Rev. 166.

This liability extends only to those "in the business" of building. It would not apply to a homeowner selling his own home. 21 Hastings L. J. 483.

One important aspect of products liability is that it extends beyond the *first purchaser* of the house. *Cooper* v. *Cordova Sand & Gravel Co., Inc.,* 485 SW2d 261 (Tenn. 1972).

> **EXAMPLE:**   Builder built a house and sold it to Buyer #1 who later sold it to Buyer #2 whose infant son was injured because of defective construction. Builder is liable. *Wright* v. *Creative Corp.,* 498 P2d 1179 (Colo. 1972).

42.10   Express Warranties

So far we have been talking about implied warranties. These involve situations where the documents are totally silent concerning the liability of the builder or seller for defects in the building. Yet the courts read "warranties" against defects into the contract.

In addition, there are express warranties. These are guarantees that state in so many words that the warrantor will correct any defects at his expense. There are a variety of such warranties.

42.10(a)   Express Warranties—New Homes

The National Association of Home Builders is an association of fine builders, engaged in constructing quality homes. Even quality homes develop defects and homebuyers need protection against them. To serve these buyers there exists the Home Owners Warranty Corporation, 2000 L Street, N.W., Washington, D.C. 20036. This company issues a warranty on new homes. This warranty offers rather broad protection for two years and protection against major structural defects, guaranteed by an insurance company, for a period of ten years. Subsequent purchasers are also protected. The major coverage is for the first year and is described in detail in the warranty.

42.11   FHA and VA Warranties

There are laws allowing FHA and VA to compensate buyers if their new homes develop certain structural defects. These agencies may correct the defect, pay the homeowner to have it corrected, or acquire the building by buying it from the owner. FHA and VA require the buyer to file his claim within eighteen months of purchase. See FHA Reg. 24 CFR Sec. 200,500. Where new residential construction is approved for HUD mortgage insurance prior to the beginning of construction, the builder is required to deliver to the purchaser a warranty that construction was carried out in accordance with the plans and specifications. 12 USC 1701j-1. While technically this is not the same as the responsibility the courts have placed upon builder–sellers, many defects occur because of the builder's noncompliance with the plans and specifications.

> **EXAMPLE:**   A foundation may crack because it was installed over ground that did not meet the compaction requirements of the specifications or because concrete of a lesser grade than required in the specifications was used. Furthermore, specifications usually require that work be done in a workmanlike manner.

VA has an almost identical warranty.

Both warranties are good for one year from date of completion.

The VA has requirements for warranties of good construction if it is to insure the mortgage loan. These requirements are:

1. An insurance-backed warranty for one year against defects caused by poor materials or workmanship.

2. A similar warranty for the first two years against faulty electrical, plumbing, and heating and cooling systems.

3. Direct insurance coverage for years three through ten against structural defects.

4. A system for handling disputes with builders and, if necessary, arbitration arranged by the American Arbitration Association or a similar group. 38 USAS § 1805.

42.12 Seller's Warranties

Of course, one frequently encounters warranties by the seller of a used home. Often they relate to the heating, air conditioning, electrical, water, and drainage systems. Often they are placed in the contract of sale. If so, they survive the closing of the deal. They are not *merged* into the deed. *Rouse* v. *Brooks*, 66 Ill. App.3d 107, 383 NE2d 666 (1979). The better practice is to provide in the contract that these warranties shall survive the closing.

42.13 Consumer Product Warranties

Typically, a builder incorporates into his structure various items that fall under the term "consumer products" as defined by the Magnuson–Moss Warranty Act. 15 USC § 2301 *et seq.* Because of this law, he must, prior to the sale of any consumer product that is covered by a warranty, fully, conspicuously, and understandably disclose the terms of the warranty and whether it is "full" or "limited" in terms of its duration. 15 USC §§ 2302, 2303. The Federal Trade Commission has taken the position that the act applies to separate items of equipment attached to real property whether or not they are fixtures under state law. The key to understanding the separateness test lies in the distinction between the physical separateness of an item and the separate function of that item.

> **EXAMPLE:** A furnace has a mechanical, thermal, or electrical function apart from the realty, whereas roofing shingles have no function apart from the realty. When sold by a builder to a home buyer as part of the home, the furnace is covered by the act and the shingles are not.

Using this test the FTC has decided that the following consumer products are covered by the act when they are sold as part of a home: boiler, heat pump, electronic air cleaner, exhaust fan, thermostat, space heater, furnace, air conditioning system, humidifier, central vacuum system, smoke detector, fire alarms, fire extinguisher, garage door opener, chimes, water pump, intercom, burglar alarm, electric meter, water meter, gas meter, gas or electric barbecue grill, whirlpool bath, garbage disposal, water heater, water softener, sump pump, refrigerator, freezer, trash compactor, range, oven, dishwasher, oven hood, clothes washer, clothes dryer, ice maker.

Using the same test, the FTC has found that the following are not consumer products when sold as part of a home: radiator, convector, register, duct, cabinet, door, shelving, windows, floor covering, walls or wall covering, ceiling, vanity, gutter, shingles, chimney and fireplace, fencing, garage door, electrical switch and outlet, light fixture, electric panel box, fuse, circuit breaker, wiring, sprinkler head, water closet, bidet, lavatory, bathtub, laundry tray, sink, shower stall, plumbing fittings, medicine cabinet.

A last category or group contains separate items or equipment that are consumer products under the act when sold as part of a condominium, cooperative, or multiple-family dwelling because they are not normally used for personal family or household purposes within the meaning of the act: fusible fire door closer, TV security monitor, emergency backup generator, master TV antenna, elevator, institutional trash compactor. FTC advisory opinion 12/17/76, *CCH Trade Regulation Reports,* par. 21245.

Even though the builder does not make these pieces of equipment himself, he is nonetheless bound by the disclosure sections of the act because he is a "supplier" under the terms of the act. 15 USC § 2301(4).

The builder can comply with the terms of the law by clearly and conspicuously displaying the text or a quote of the text of the written warranty covering the consumer product in close conjunction to each warranted product; or by maintaining in each of the seller's locations an indexed binder containing copies of all warranties on consumer products; or, if the warranty text is printed on the product box, by displaying the package.

> **EXAMPLE:** When the builder incorporates into his structure dishwashers, disposals, ranges, refrigerators, and range hoods he should either display next to, or taped onto the appliances, copies of the warranties given by the manufacturer of those applicances or keep in his model office a binder which contains those warranties. This binder should be displayed in a conspicuous place and potential buyers should be afforded the opportunity to review its contents prior to the sale. The builder should make similar disclosure of his own warranty if that warranty covers the consumer products.

> REFERENCE: Peters, *How the Magnuson–Moss Warranty Act Affects the Builders/ Seller of New Housing,* 5 R.E.L.J. 338 (1977).

42.14   Warranties of Used Homes

The National Association of Realtors has a nationwide program of warranties issued in connection with the sale of used homes. Other organizations also offer warranties. Cost of the coverage, usually borne by the seller, ranges from $65 to $450. Most plans call for an inspection by the warrantor. Items covered usually include central heating and cooling systems, interior plumbing, electrical systems, roof, walls, ceilings, water heaters and softeners, and built-in appliances. Obviously, a buyer who wants such a warranty should require the contract of sale to specify it.

42.15 Broker's Warranties of Used Homes

Some big brokerage firms (Century 21 Real Estate Corporation, for example) provide warranties where a home is sold by one of their brokers.

42.16 Disclaimer of Warranties

It is difficult for a seller to disclaim warranties. *Peterson* v. *Hubschman Const. Co.*, 76 Ill.2d 31, 389 NE2d 364 (1979); *Schoeneweis* v. *Herrin*, 110 Ill. App.3d 800, 443 NE2d 31, 66 Ill. Dec. 513 (1982); 65 Chicago Bar Record 364 (giving suggested form of disclaimer).

What this means, in brief, is that if the builder states in the fine print of the contract that he makes no guarantees whatever as to the presence or absence of construction defects, the courts will ignore this. It really takes a separate agreement, with the statement clearly made therein, that he accepts no responsibility for defects in construction.

CHAPTER 43

Rehab

43.01 In General

There is a national enthusiasm for buying old buildings and restoring them to their former glory, but with modern plumbing, heating, and electricity. Rehabilitation of older buildings is occurring both to residential and commercial structures. These buildings are typically closer to the core of the city where cultural and business activity is centered. The aesthetic and economic advantages are a powerful draw to this form of real estate.

If the structure has a strong shell, as is typical with older brick or stone structures, such as Georgetown row houses, the costs of acquisition and rehabilitation may be considerably less than the cost of new construction. When the income tax treatment of rehab expenses and favorable loan terms are considered, the economics of rehabilitation are even more attractive.

43.02 Appraisals

Increasingly, as home values skyrocket, professional appraisals are required by lending institutions. Appraisers have a number of professional organizations. One is the American Institute of Real Estate Appraisers, affiliated with the National Association of Realtors. It confers the prestigious title Member Appraisal Institute (MAI). There is also the American Society of Appraisers and the Society of Real Estate Appraisers.

The role of the appraiser in large construction is well understood. But a great expansion in the use of appraising is taking place as the rehabilitation process continues to assume increasing importance in home renovation. Among other things the appraiser will consider: an economic analysis of the neighborhood; street patterns and the width of streets; convenience to public transportation; the availability of stores and service establishments; community or neighborhood organizations; density of population; degree of home ownership; rent and income levels; and zoning, building codes, and other regulations restricting design or use.

43.03   Architect's Role

The architect has an indispensable role in the rehab process. His first step is to conduct a feasibility study and provide a realistic estimate of the cost of the rehab, including the cost of bringing the structure into compliance with current building codes. These estimates are based upon actual costs of the same or similar work performed on similar structures and can be made only after a complete detail of exactly what construction work is to be done has been made.

The architect will also help you find a reliable contractor. They are scarce. Then loan funds will be disbursed by the lender to the contractor on his production of the architect's approval of the work done and waivers of mechanic's liens by trades involved in the work.

43.04   Building Codes

Although building codes are intended primarily for new construction, they are also applied to rehabilitation projects through two widely used regulatory "trigger mechanisms"—the "25/50 percent rule" and change of occupancy requirements. These are called trigger mechanisms because they "trigger" the application of new construction code requirements onto a rehabilitation project.

The 25/50 percent rule, usually one of the administrative requirements of a typical building code, requires that when the cost of the rehabilitation work to be done exceeds a stated percentage (usually 50 percent) of the value of the building (which, for many urban buildings, may be very low), the entire building must then be brought up to new construction code requirements.

Since most U.S. buildings no longer meet new construction oriented codes (because the requirements in those building codes generally have been increased over time), the imposition of the 25/50 percent rule can and does add costs to the rehabilitation project.

The change of occupancy requirement, also usually one of the administrative requirements contained in a typical building code, states that when the occupancy of a building is changed, then the entire building must be brought up to the new construction requirements contained in the building code. An occupancy change, for example, could involve the conversion of a large, old single-family residence into a multifamily residence, a care facility, or a retail store.

NEW DIRECTIONS: Several cities have enacted revised building ordinances that have taken some of the rigidity out of the old codes that were primarily enacted to control new construction. These new rehab codes are often written in simplified language understandable to the layman and provide for the creation of a board to grant exceptions from code requirements if the rehabber's proposal will be equal to or better than the code requires.

43.05   Building Restrictions

Sometimes the building restrictions applicable to a particular piece of property prohibit certain changes or additions. Review the title policy to see if such restrictions exist. If so, obtain a full copy of the restrictions and any amendments to the restrictions from the recorder's office and have them reviewed by an attorney to see if the contemplated improvements can be made without violating the restrictions.

43.06   Zoning Ordinances

Zoning laws determine how land and buildings can be used. They regulate such things as the amount of land coverage buildings may occupy, front, side, and back setbacks, and the heights of fences and hedges. The local building department should be contacted to determine whether the contemplated work will be in compliance with the zoning laws and, if not, how the work may be changed to accomplish the goals of the rehabber, yet satisfy the requirements of the zoning laws.

43.07   The Contractor

Getting a reliable contractor is a must on any substantial rehab job. The National Home Improvement Council, 11 E. 44th Street, New York, N.Y. 10017, will give you a list of their members. There are local branches, such as the Professional Remodelers Assn., 20 E. Delaware, Chicago, Ill., who can give an up-to-date list of local members. Membership provides a measure of assurance of honesty and competence. Checking with the local Better Business Bureau also helps. Checking with customers who have had recent work done is a must. Your bank or thrift institution that will finance the work is a good source of names. Your lawyer will check to see that your contractor is licensed, if local law requires. Some states have good regulations.

> **EXAMPLE:**   The California licensing law requires a home improvement contractor to pass an examination and pay a license fee of $2,000. If two complaints are lodged against a contractor he loses his license. Nevada, Arizona, Oklahoma, Florida, Virginia, Michigan, and other states have licensing laws.

Of course, if you are hiring an architect he is sure to know the reliable contractors.

The Home Owners Warranty Corp., 2000 L St. N.W., Washington, DC, 20036, will give you a list of remodelers who can furnish you the HOW–insured warranty on the completed job. This is a reputable organization. The HOW organization has the answers to the following questions concerning the contractor:

- Does he have a legitimate business address and phone number?
- Is he licensed and bonded? Many states and local jurisdictions require licensing. Find out the requirements in your area and verify that the contractor has met them.

- Does the contractor offer a warranty on his work? If so, what does it cover? Is it insured?

43.08   Contractor's Bonds

Bonding companies write bonds insuring that the contractor will complete the job. However, most small contractors are not bondable. Incidentally, if you ask the contractor if he can get a bond, and he answers affirmatively, get the bond even if you must pay for it yourself. As discussed elsewhere, you really get two bonds for the price of one.

43.09   The Job Contract

When you are ordering a job done, it is best to put as much detail as you can into the contract. Of course, architects do this routinely. But many jobs will be ordered by you alone. It is customary to state the number of inches of crushed stone, the name and model of the faucet, the catalogue number of the chandelier, and so on. State that all work must conform to the building code and will be redone at the contractor's expense if the city inspector orders it redone, as occasionally happens. State that before commencement, the contractor will furnish you satisfactory proof that he has workmen's compensation and public liability insurance and is a licensed contractor. Manufacturers and dealers often furnish product warranties. Ask the contractor to list all warranties he expects to receive and list these as items to be delivered at completion of job. The contract should also set out the start and completion dates.

43.10   Payment

Many contractors ask for a down payment. If you have checked the contractor's references and they are satisfactory, you can agree to pay him a small amount down, say 15 percent. He gets credit from suppliers but will need to pay wages to his workmen. On bigger jobs a final payment on the order of 15 percent will be made after completion of the job. The difference is often paid as the job goes forward.

43.11   Lien Waivers

As work is done, the trades expect to be paid. An architect or other job supervisor checks the job first. He determines that the work has been done properly and in accordance with the contract and specifications. This supervisor also indicates how much money each trade is entitled to receive. Normally, the contract calls for holdbacks or retentions. *Holiday Develop. Co., & J. A. Tobin Const. Co.,* 549 P2d 1376 (Kans. 1976); 107 ALR 960; 54 ALR3d 848. A common retention is 10 percent of the amount due. As each trade is paid, a mechanic's lien waiver is demanded for the work done. When a trade completes its work, a final mechanic's lien waiver is demanded.

43.12   Bid and Specification Analysis

The building inspector may undertake to review the bids if you have no architect. This is important. A subcontractor is not required to do anything other than what his bid, including the specifications, requires him to do. Analyzing specifications for completeness is important.

43.13   Permits

Some fly-by-night contractors never obtain building permits. This may lead to heavy fines if this is discovered by the Building Department. An architect will not permit work to begin until he has verified that proper permits were obtained.

43.14   Rehab Supervision

If you do not plan to have the rehab work supervised by an architect, you may be able to hire a building inspector to do the job. Some inspectors will even give estimates of job cost, which can be used to check the general contractor's bid. Of course, a general contractor undertakes in his contract to supervise the work of the subcontractors.

   If the rehab work is being conducted in a home that is occupied, the owner should make it clear that the contractor is to respect the fact that he is working in the owner's home. While it is often foolish to expect too much in this regard, the owner should make it clear that it is expected that the contractor will: arrange a schedule so that the owner will know when the work crew will and will not be on the premises; clean up every night; lay drop cloths and install other protective padding to protect floors and walls; block off work areas with plastic sheeting taped over doors; and take other protective measures to reduce the inconvenience and dirt resulting from the work of improvement. However, the owner should realize that there will be a good deal of dirt and inconvenience resulting from the work no matter how attentive the contractor may be.

43.15   Insurance

On a substantial job, talk to an insurance agent. He may recommend that the job be covered by special insurance ("builder's risk"). At completion, your home insurance should be increased to cover the value added by the job.

43.16   Loans

Many lenders advance the funds only after the rehab job has been completed. FHA insurance may be obtained for rehab loans before the job begins. Long-term, low-interest loans may also be available under various government programs.

Bear in mind that the rehab lender who finances the job has several risks to weigh, namely: (1) the value of the building as is, (2) the value to be added by the rehab job, and (3) the ability of the contractor to do the job properly.

It may be possible to get a loan commitment that will become effective when and if the rehab job has been completed. A short-term loan is then obtained from a rehab lender, who will rely on the other loan commitment for ultimate payment. The rehab lender will make periodic inspections so that he is satisfied with the progress and get proper mechanic's lien waivers at each stage of the job.

The giant purchasers of mortgages, FNMA, and FHLMC, have announced a program and prepared a required mortgage form for rehab loans. Randolph, *The FNMA/FHLMC Uniform Home Improvement Loan Instruments: A Commentary and Critique,* 16 A.B.A. Real Ppty., Prob. & Tr. J. 546 (1981). This informative article explains all the legal and practical ramifications of these instruments. It is must reading, since all mortgage lenders will wish to tailor their loans so that they are available for sale in the secondary market.

43.17   Closing Observations

Your neighborhood broker will be glad to give you an opinion as to how much your planned rehab could add to the value of your home. Your architect cannot read your mind. Cut pictures out of magazines to show the architect what you want. Have a written contract with your architect. The American Institute of Architects (AIA) has a form, but it is heavily loaded in favor of the architect. Have your lawyer tailor a form for you. Architect's fees run between 10 and 15 percent of the cost of the project. Billing is in installments as construction takes place. Put a completion date in the contract, but keep in mind that no job is ever completed in time.

CHAPTER 44

Mobile Homes

44.01 The Mobile Home Contrasted with the Stick-built Home

Massachusetts Institute of Technology has called the mobile home industry "the most efficient building industry in the world." Bernhardt, *Building Tomorrow* (1978). The industry has the capacity to produce low-cost high-quality shelter that complies with strict federal standards. Most mobile homes are sold fully equipped with major appliances, furniture, draperies, lamps, and carpeting all included in the purchase price. Optional features include air conditioning, dishwasher, disposals, and other items typically found in a modern home. Warranties on components are available.

By federal law, the "mobile home" is now referred to as a "manufactured home." This chapter will deal with purchase of a new manufactured home.

44.02 Chattel Aspects

A manufactured home resting on land owned by one other than the homeowner has often been, for that reason, deemed to remain a chattel. *Farmers Union Mut. Ins. Co.* v. *Denniston*, 376 SW2d 252 (Ark. 1964); *In re Estate of Horton*, 606 SW2d 792 (Mo. App. 1980). This is in keeping with a general fixture law that a chattel placed on land owned by a third person remains a chattel, since it would be unrealistic to attribute to the homeowner an intention to make the home the property of the landowner.

44.03 Fixture Aspects

On the other hand, a manufactured home owned by *A* and placed by him on his land is a fixture and is part of the land. Normally, the intention to make the manufactured home a fixture is revealed by the removal of wheels, its attachment to a permanent foundation, and the use of permanent utility connections. *George* v. *Commercial Credit Corp.,* 440 F2d 551 (7th Cir. 1971); *Bell* v. *City of Corbin City,* 395 A2d 546 (N.J. 1978); *State* v. *Work,* 449 P2d 806 (Wash. 1969). Such homes are purchased in home-and-land deals in much the same way as stick-built homes.

44.04   Federal Controls

The construction of manufactured homes is now controlled by the federal government under the National Mobile Home Construction and Safety Standards Act, 42 USC §§ 5401, *et seq.* 24 CFR Part 280 *et seq.* This code is promulgated by HUD, but it varies throughout the country to meet geographic conditions. Elaborate federal safety factors are set forth. Inconsistent state laws and ordinances are ineffective. Each home is inspected at the factory where a plate is installed showing that the home complies with federal law.

44.05   Mortgage Sources

On the home-and-land type of deal, traditional mortgage financing is available, for example, from a savings and loan association, which will loan up to 90 percent of the total cost of land, home, setup charges, sales tax, and so forth. FHA and VA loans are available. The mortgages are sold in the secondary market to GNMA and FNMA. These loans, in turn, are pooled, securities issued against the pool, and sold to investors.

Because some states continue to view a manufactured home as having personal property characteristics, it may be necessary in such states to have the mortgage noted as a lien on the certificate of title. 7A Am.Jur.2d Automobiles Sec. 31. It may also be necessary for the lender to hold the certificate of title. *Ibid.* Sec. 39. The law in this area is garbled and complicated. Welsh, *Security Interests in Motor Vehicles,* 37 U. of Cincinnatti L. Rev. 265, 286. See *In re Circus Time Inc.* 641 F2d 39 (Cal. 1st 1981) and UCC § 9-302(3). A person who buys a new home from a dealer is buying personal property. A search should be made for Uniform Commercial Code security filings. Title insurance companies check into this before issuing their policies. It is wise to consult with the title company as to its requirements before drawing the sale and mortgage documents. In general, on homes that are located on land owned by the owner of the manufactured home, the title company requires proof that the home is permanently connected to the land— that it is connected to sewer, water, electricity, and gas, and that the owner has signed and recorded an affidavit that it is his intention that the home be a fixture and part of the real estate.

FNMA requires that the purchase of the land and the home be a single real estate transaction; that the financing be evidenced by a mortgage recorded in the land records insured by title insurance containing ALTA Endorsement Form-7 Manufactured Housing Unit; that no chattels, furniture, appliances and so on, be included in the mortgage financing; and that the land and home be taxed as land.

44.06   Usury—Federal Preemption Act

The federal usury preemption law applies to manufactured housing. However, to become entitled to the protection of this law the security instrument must contain provisions requiring a thirty-day notice before foreclosure is instituted. Lacking this provision, the security is subject to state usury laws. *Grant* v. *Gen. Elec. Credit Corp.*, 764 F2d 1404 (11th Circ. 1985); 41 Bus. Law 1050 (1986).

44.07   Furniture

Traditionally, mobile homes were sold complete with furniture, carpeting, draperies, and so on. Furniture, of course, is personal property. Where this practice is followed and the home and lot are sold and financed as real estate, a chattel filing under the UCC will accompany the mortgage. This practice is less prevalent today than formerly.

44.08   Building Restrictions

The areas of manufactured housing law that have given rise to much litigation involve building restrictions and zoning. Initially, it should be noted that many of these cases involve an isolated home placed on a lot in a community of stick-built homes. This is a situation which provokes litigation. It is improbable that the new manufactured housing developments will trigger any great volume of litigation.

Many older restrictions prohibit "trailers." Often the litigated case lacks an adequate description of the type of structure involved. It cannot be determined, for example, if the modern double-wide home was involved.

At any rate, there are decisions to the effect that a manufactured home of one kind or another cannot be erected where the restrictions prohibit *trailers.*

The more modern, better-reasoned decisions hold that a typical manufactured home constructed on the owner's land does not violate a restriction forbidding trailers. *Hussey* v. *Ray,* 462 SW2d 45 (Tex. 1970); *In re Willey,* 120 Vt. 359, 140 A2d 11 (1958); *Manley* v. *Draper,* 44 Misc.2d 613, 254 NYS2d 739 (1963); *North Cherokee Village* v. *Murphy,* 248 NW2d 629 (Mich. App. 1977); *Morin* v. *Zoning Board,* 102 R.I. 457, 232 A2d 393 (1967); *Douglas Twp.* v. *Badman,* 206 Pa. Super. 390, 213 A2d 88 (1965); *Heath* v. *Parker,* 93 N.M. 680, 604 P2d 818 (1980). The last case is significant. The home involved a structure containing three bedrooms, two full baths, 1,440 square feet of floor space, a patio, a 200-square-foot porch, and a 672-square-foot two-car garage. The court commented on the fact that this structure was more handsome and more livable than many stick-built homes. This is obviously the way court decisions will tend. The restrictions using the word "trailer" were framed in an older time, when the double-wide manufactured home was unknown.

44.09   Zoning

The zoning decisions are numerous and conflicting.

First of all, there are decisions holding that it is a violation of constitutional law to attempt, directly or indirectly, to bar a poor person's access to the suburbs by excluding manufactured housing. *Meyers* v. *Board of Supervisors*, 394 A2d 669 (Pa. 1978). The great leading case on this point is *Robinson Twp.* v. *Knoll,* 410 Mich. 293, 302 NW2d 146 (1980). In that case a township zoning ordinance attempted to exclude mobile homes except in mobile home parks. The court held this aspect of the ordinance was invalid. The court pointed out that manufactured housing has undergone drastic change and improvement since the days of "trailers"; that many mobile homes compare favorably in appearance, plumbing and health factors with stick-built homes; and that Vermont by statute forbids discrimination against mobile homes.

The authors feel that within the next decade the Michigan view will be the prevailing view in this country. At least one authority feels that states will step in with *state laws,* as has taken place in California, to invalidate *city ordinances* that exclude manufactured housing. 55 Cornell L. Rev. 491, 514.

Second, the particular tract of land may be such that a zoning ordinance barring manufactured housing would be invalid as applied. Such homes might provide the only reasonable use for the land. *Czech* v. *City of Blaine,* 253 NW2d 272 (Minn. 1977).

REFERENCE: 54 Am.Jur.2d. *Mobile Homes* §13.

44.10   Exclusionary Laws and Ordinances

The suburbs are quite generally hostile to the introduction of manufactured housing. Most of their exclusionary ordinances are illegal.

> **EXAMPLE:** An ordinance limiting manufactured housing developments to four new units per year was discriminatory and void where stick-built homes were not so limited. *Begin* v. *Inhabitants of Sabaltus,* 409 A2d 1269 (Maine 1980).

44.11   Antitrust

Park owners have at times enacted rules barring homeowners where the home was not purchased from the park owner. This is called a *closed park.* Probably this is a *tie-in sale,* illegal under the antitrust law.

44.12   Taxes

In past times, manufactured homes were taxed as motor vehicles or personal property. 71 Yale L. J. 71, 705. Nine states place a use tax on mobile homes. 21

DePaul L. Rev. 1008, 1011. Some states levy a license fee. *Ibid.* Where the land-owner owns the home, it is often taxed as real estate. 21 DePaul L. Rev., 1008, 1012. Any discussion of this problem seems pointless at this time. If manufactured housing goes into land developments where land and home are sold as a unit, these must be taxed as real estate. See 7 ALR4th 1016.

44.13 Warranties

Warranties vary among different manufacturers. All retailers are required to have copies of the manufacturer's warranties that are offered on the homes they sell, and they will make them available to buyers upon request. By reading the warranty before purchase, the buyer can make sure the home is covered by adequate warranty protection. The manufacturer's written warranty usually covers substantial defects in: workmanship in the structure; factory-installed plumbing, heating, and electrical systems; and factory-installed appliances.

A retailer may offer a written warranty on a home. While all written warranties are not alike, the typical retailer's warranty will state: the terms of the warranty; what must be done to keep the warranty in effect; what can reasonably be expected from the retailer; and that the home has been installed according to the manufacturer's specifications and local regulations.

The warranty will also guarantee that the home has a HUD inspection seal and that the optional appliances have been properly installed.

The appliances also will be covered by warranties. In many cases, these warranties, along with use and care manuals, are provided by the individual appliance manufacturers. In addition, some states require that the home manufacturer's warranty cover the appliances that come with the home.

CHAPTER 45

Landlord and Tenant

45.01 In General

In the centuries following the Battle of Hastings (1066), when William the Conqueror crushed the English armies and became king of England, the feudal system of real estate law that prevailed in a large part of continental Europe became part of the English way of life. Its intricacies are a twice-told tale and need not be repeated here. We must, however, look at the bottom rung of the social and economic ladder. Here we find the landlord renting a small farm to a tenant. Rent was often paid in the form of a share of the crops. Indeed, sharecropping still exists, though on a small scale. The house in which the tenant lived was a primitive structure. The tenant worked with primitive tools. He was a jack-of-all-trades and could repair almost any defect in house or tools. In 1588 England defeated the Spanish Armada; its ships began their long rule of the oceans of the world, and England became a trading nation. The formation of modern trading law (contract law) began. But in the meantime, the law of landlord and tenant had been formed. Basically, it was prolandlord law. The tenant took the premises as he found them, and the landlord had no obligation of repair.

Then, with the coming of the steam engine about 1800, the Industrial Revolution changed the face of England. Many men worked in factories. Such a worker was not a jack-of-all-trades. Tenement buildings, the predecessor of the modern apartment, began to appear as cities grew up around the factories. Still, the courts applied the old agricultural landlord and tenant law to the new state of affairs. Beginning about 1970, the courts began to reexamine their thinking. *Javins* v. *First National Realty Corp.*, 428 F2d 1071, *cert. den.* 400 U.S. 925 (1970). Several things became evident. The tenant, since he was not a jack-of-all-trades, lacked the skill to make repairs. Repairs, by and large, were beyond the means of the low-income tenant. Obviously, no bank would loan the low-income tenant money to make repairs. The defect might spring up in an area of the apartment to which the tenant had no access.

Modern courts made a 180-degree turn in their thinking on the law applicable to residential renting. They began to regard the renting of an apartment basically as a *contract* for the furnishing of services, including the service of maintaining the structure in a habitable condition, free from building code violations. This development made all the flexibility that is characteristic of modern contract law available to the courts. This change of thought is surely the law of most states.

Meanwhile, the law relating to stores, industrial plants, and commercial leasing remained as it had been. Tenants of these structures had the sophistication to protect themselves.

The Uniform Residential Landlord and Tenant Act (URLTA) has been drafted to protect tenants. It places obligations on the landlord, such as complying with building codes and keeping common areas in a clean and safe condition. It gives the tenant the right to withhold rent if the landlord fails to perform. It forbids harassment or retaliation by the landlord. A version of this law has been enacted in Alaska, Arizona, Delaware, Florida, Hawaii, Kentucky, Nebraska, New Mexico, Oregon, and Washington. Other tenant protection laws have been enacted in Massachusetts, New Jersey, Texas, and New York. More such legislation is on the way.

As is evident, the law of landlord and tenant is progressing steadily toward a compartmentalization. The law for residential tenants is developing safeguards that do not exist, for example, with respect to business tenants. 54 Cal. L. Rev. 670 (1966); 41 U. Colo. L. Rev. 541 (1969): 54 Georgetown L. J. 519 (1966); 5 Suffolk L. Rev. 213; 46 Yale L. J. 508; 6 Wake Forest L. Rev. 119; 1968 Wash. U. L. Q. 461 (1968).

45.02   Leases and Periodic Tenancies

The relationship of landlord and tenant may exist by virtue of a formal, written *lease* or of a periodic tenancy, such as a *tenancy from month to month*.

> **EXAMPLE:**   Tenant sees an "apartment for rent" sign on a building, goes in, makes a verbal arrangement with the owner for the rental of an apartment, pays his first month's rent, and later moves in. He is a *tenant from month to month*.

> **EXAMPLE:**   Facts as above, but the landlord and tenant, instead of agreeing verbally, sign a lease for one year. Tenant is a tenant under a lease.

One important difference between leases and periodic tenancies relates to the rights and liabilities of the parties during the existence of the landlord–tenant relation. When the relation of landlord and tenant exists without a written lease, the law implies certain rights and liabilities on the part of both. In a *month-to-month tenancy*, for example, the tenant is entitled to the exclusive possession of the rented premises, and the landlord has no right to enter thereon for the purpose of making repairs. But in many leases, the parties expressly agree that the landlord shall have this right. In other words, a lease is a contract, and most of the rights and duties of the parties are governed by the provisions of the contract, whereas in a month-to-month tenancy the rights of the parties are governed by rules of law.

Another difference between a lease and a periodic tenancy relates to the termination of the tenant's right of occupancy. In the case of a lease, at the expiration date fixed in the lease, the tenant need not give notice to the landlord before moving out, nor is any notice needed by the landlord to the tenant. In the case of periodic tenancies, certain notices must be given in order to terminate the tenancy.

45.03   Tenancy from Month to Month

The tenancy from month to month is generally created when no definite term of letting is specified by the parties and the rent is payable monthly. This kind of tenancy is very common. A tenant who pays rent monthly and has no lease is a tenant from month to month.

A tenancy from month to month cannot be terminated except by giving notice. That is, the landlord cannot evict the tenant unless he first gives the tenant the notice required by law, and the tenant continues liable for rent unless he gives the landlord the required notice. In many states a month's or thirty days' notice is required, but the period varies from state to state.

The notice to terminate a month-to-month tenancy must state a proper termination date, and must give the tenant the full number of days' notice to which he is entitled.

> **EXAMPLE:**   Landlord rents an apartment to Tenant on a month-to-month tenancy beginning as of the first of the next month. In the state in question a landlord must serve a thirty days' notice to terminate such a tenancy. After some months, Landlord serves a notice on November 1 terminating Tenant's tenancy as of November 30. The notice is void. It gives Tenant less than thirty days' notice. Landlord will lose the eviction suit and must serve a new and proper notice.

45.04   Tenancy from Year to Year

A *tenancy from year to year* is one that continues for a year and then is automatically renewed for another year and from year to year thereafter unless due notice of termination of the tenancy is given at the time and in the manner required by law for the termination of the tenancy.

While a year-to-year tenancy can be created in other ways, it most commonly is created when a lease for a year or more has expired and the tenant continues in possession paying rent, which the landlord accepts, and the parties have made no other agreement as to the character of the tenant's occupancy.

When a tenant has a lease for a year or longer, and after the lease has expired the tenant remains in possession of the premises, it is said that the tenant *holds over.* The landlord may, if he wishes, hold the tenant as a tenant from year to year. Observe that it is the landlord who may hold the tenant. The tenant cannot, by holding over, compel the landlord to extend the tenancy. The landlord may evict the tenant if he wishes to do so. But if the tenant holds over, even for one day, he becomes liable for another year's rent should the landlord wish to hold him. *Clinton Wire Cloth Co.* v. *Gardner,* 99 Ill. 151. Once the landlord accepts the rent, he also is bound to the tenancy. And once the tenancy is established neither party can terminate it in the middle of the year. And if either party wishes to end the tenancy *at the end of a yearly period,* proper notice must be served for this purpose.

This tenancy is virtually obsolete. All printed leases contain a provision stating what status the tenant will have if he remains in possession after his lease has expired. Often it states that the tenant becomes a month-to-month tenant.

45.05   Tenancy at Will

A tenancy at will may be terminated by either party whenever he wishes to do so.

> **EXAMPLE:**   A tenancy at will arises under an agreement that the tenant may occupy until the premises are sold or rented to a third person, until the landlord is ready to construct new buildings, until the land is required by the landlord for his own use, or whenever the letting is for an indefinite term.

45.06   Lease Defined

A lease is both a contract and a conveyance. It is a conveyance by the landlord to the tenant of the right to occupy the land for the term specified in the lease. It contains a contract by the tenant to pay rent to the landlord and usually contains numerous other promises and undertakings by both landlord and tenant. The legal interest of the tenant in the land is called a *leasehold estate* or *a term for years.* It is legally considered to be personal property. 51 CJS *Landlord & Tenant* § 26.

45.06(a)   Necessity of Writing

In all but a few states, a lease for less than one year may be verbal, but a lease for a period longer than one year must be in writing.

45.06(b)   Requirements of Lease—In General

Many states have laws that require a written lease to comply with requirements applicable to deeds.

45.06(c)   The Lessor

The landowner and his or her spouse should be designated as lessors. The same reasons that make it necessary for the wife or husband of a landowner to join in a deed requires the spouse to join in a lease. *Fargo* v. *Bennett,* 35 Idaho 359, 206 P. 692; *Benson* v. *Dritch,* 244 SW2d 339 (Tex. 1951). As a matter of business practice, short leases such as one-year apartment leases are often made by the owner without his wife's signature, for in such situations, trouble is extremely improbable. A lessor should be of age and of sound mind. When the lease is executed by an executor or trustee, the will or other trust instrument must be examined to determine if he has power to make the lease in question. If the lessor is a corporation, the lease must be authorized by the directors or stockholders, as required by the local law.

45.06(d)   The Lessee

The lessee should be of age and of sound mind. If the lessee is a trustee or executor, the will or other trust instrument must authorize him to enter into leases such as the one in question.

45.06(e)   Description of the Premises

The lease must describe the leased premises with certainty. There is a tendency in short-term leases to designate the leased premises inadequately. Of course, if it is an entire building that is being rented, it is sufficient to describe it by street number, city, and state.

45.06(f)   Duration or Term Lease

Leases are sometimes classified as *short-term* or *long-term* leases. This has no great legal significance. With the exception of the rule that leases for more than one year must be in writing, the rules governing short-term and long-term leases are generally the same. Long-term leases often run for ninety-nine years. In some states laws have been passed limiting the duration of leases. The lease should fix the date on which the term of the lease begins and the duration of the lease. In fixing the term of the lease, it is better to avoid a description of the term as running *from* a particular day *to* another day, since a question may arise as to whether or not a lease from or to a particular day includes or excludes such day. It is better to describe the term as *commencing on* a certain day and *ending on* a certain other day.

45.06(f)(1)   Condominium Statutes and Ordinances

Various laws and ordinances extend the duration of a residential lease when the building is converted to a condominium.

45.06(g)   Signature of Lessor and Lessee

The signature of the lessor is necessary to give effect to a lease. It is the universal practice to obtain the lessee's signature also, though it is not essential that the lease be signed by the lessee if the lessee accepts the lease and takes possession of the leased premises. *Bakker* v. *Fellows,* 153 Mich. 428, 117 NW 52 (1908). It is customary to execute leases in duplicate. If the lessor signs one duplicate and hands this to the lessee, and the lessee signs the other duplicate and hands this to the lessor, the effect is the same as if both signatures had been placed on each duplicate. *Fields* v. *Brown,* 188 Ill. 111, 64 NE 1033.

45.06(h)   Seal

In a number of states written leases must be executed with the same formality as deeds. In these states a lease should be under seal.

45.06(i)   Witnesses

A few states require a lease that exceeds a certain specified duration to be witnessed.

45.06(j)   Acknowledgment

Some states require leases that exceed a specified term to be acknowledged. In any case, if the lease is to be recorded, it should be acknowledged.

45.06(k)   Recording

Even though a lease is not recorded, the tenant's possession will normally give the whole world constructive notice of his rights. However, this rule has been abolished in a number of states as to leases exceeding a specified duration— namely, one year in California, Florida, Georgia, Hawaii, Idaho, Mississippi, Montana, Oklahoma, Rhode Island and three years in Indiana, Minnesota, New Mexico, North Carolina, Ohio, Tennessee, Wisconsin, Wyoming. A few states specify longer durations.

   In some states (New York, Pennsylvania, and Ohio, for example) the law permits the recording of a brief *memorandum of lease* instead of the original lease. This enables the parties to keep secret the rent specified in the lease.

45.07   Rent

Unless there is an agreement providing otherwise, rent is not due until the end of the rental period.

EXAMPLE: *A* agreed to rent certain premises to *B* as a tenant from month to month. Rent was fixed at $380 per month, but nothing was said as time for payment of rent. The rent is not due until the end of each month.

Most leases, however, provide that rental is payable in advance on the first of each month.

Because of the embarrassment caused a landlord by his inability to put a new tenant in possession, and because of the difficulty attendant upon renting premises out of the normal season, a number of states require a tenant who remains in possession after the termination of his lease to pay double rent for the period intervening between the expiration of the lease and his eviction. And many leases provide that a holdover tenant shall pay double rent if he remains in possession after the lease has expired. The lease may provide for additional amounts other than double rent.

45.07(a)   Rent—Net Lease and Gross Lease

There are various types of *net leases,* but, in general, such a lease requires the tenant to pay real estate taxes, special assessments, insurance premiums, and other charges normally borne by the landowner. The tenant assumes the risk that taxes may increase, special assessments may be levied, and that the building may be destroyed by fire. In a fully net lease the tenant must rebuild a destroyed building, paying rent meanwhile. In a gross lease the tenant pays only his rent, and the landlord bears taxes and other burdens normally borne by a landowner.

45.07(b)   Rent—Percentage Leases

Leases of retail locations often provide for a *percentage rent.* Such a lease usually provides a minimum fixed rent. Over and above this minimum, the rental is fixed at a percentage of the tenant's gross sales. The percentage of gross income that is to be charged usually presents no great problem, for commonly accepted percentages for each type of retail establishment are published periodically by the National Association of Realtors. However, it is obvious that if such a lease is prepared for a department store in a shopping center, it will be necessary to fix different percentages for different departments within the single store. Deductions from gross sales are usually allowed for sales and luxury taxes and merchandise returned by the shopper. Care should be exercised to include in gross sales all income from vending machines, telephone booths, pay toilets, lockers, weighing machines, stamp machines, and so on; and also services rendered on the premises, hairdressing and the like. Services rendered at cost, clothing alterations and employees' cafeteria, for example, are usually excluded. Income from subtenants and concessionaires is included. The lease should state whether *gross income* includes sales made by mail and sales to employees. The lease should require the tenant to conduct business throughout the year, for obviously, if the store is closed, the percentage rent stops or drops. Further, the lease should fix the hours and days on which the store is to be open. A provision should also be included forbidding the establishment of a competing store within a specified radius. Since the landlord is depending on the particular tenant's ability to run a profitable business, the lease should forbid any assignment or sublease or even the occupancy of the premises by anyone other than the tenant, unless the landlord consents. The lease should require "continuous operation" by the tenant and define what hours and days are meant by this phrase.

45.07(c)   Rent—Office Leases

In office leases, rent is often charged by the square foot. Hence it is important to know how many *usable* square feet the tenant is getting. The lease may define the square footage as including space occupied by pillars and so forth, which may be useless to the tenant.

45.07(d)   Rent—Escalation

Because of the push of inflation, most commercial or industrial leases today contain a rent escalation clause. It must be carefully drafted. Of course, increase in taxes is a sound basis for escalation. 48 ALR3d 287. The trick in a new building is to find some three- or four-year period that will average out as the basis on which the step-up in rent will be predicated. This is necesssary because the tax assessor sometimes gives the building assessment a "tax break" in the early years. *Rodolitz* v. *Neptune Paper Products Co.*, 22 NY2d 383, 283 NE2d 682 (1976). Increases in building maintenance wages are one valid source of escalation. *Simons* v. *Federal Bar Bldg. Corp.*, 275 A2d 545 (D.C. 1971). Energy costs are sometimes included as a separate escalator. The newer leases permit the landlord to estimate the escalation and charge each month or quarter the amount of his estimated escalation. Thus, he is using the tenant's money to meet escalations. At the end of the year he settles up.

Another type of escalator ties the increase to increased real estate taxes and *operating costs*. This last poses some problems. Obviously, it requires the landlord to furnish audited statements of increased operating costs and taxes. Also, some language is needed to limit the landlord's right to polish the brass doorknobs twice a week, so to speak, or to hire his brother at a fancy salary.

Leases that step up rent to compensate for increased operating costs leave another problem in the landlord's lap, namely, the declining value of the dollar collected as rent. The landlord copes with this by selecting an appropriate Consumer Price Index and providing that base rent shall step up quarterly or annually as the Consumer Price Index registers increases in inflation. If the landlord has a mortgage with a variable interest rate, he should try to insert an interest rate escalator provision into the lease so interest adjustments can be matched by rental adjustments.

45.07(e)   Rent—Abatement

Under various circumstances state laws allow an abatement, or reduction, of rent. A typical illustration would be an apartment landlord's failure to furnish hot water, gas, or electricity or failure to make repairs. Sec. 4.104 Unif. Resid. L. & T. Act; Ch. 5 Rest. (Second) Property.

45.08   Ground Leases and Commercial Leases Distinguished—Legal and Financial Aspects—Mortgages of the Leasehold

There is no legal distinction between commercial leases and ground leases. Nevertheless, there are economic differences between them that have legal implications. A *commercial lease* is a lease of a building or part of a building such as a store to a tenant. If the tenant agrees in his lease to make improvements, as a rule they are limited in scope. In a *ground lease,* the landowner leases the vacant ground to a tenant who covenants in the lease to erect a building on the premises. The true ground lease is a *net lease* under which the tenant pays all expenses including taxes, insurance, and repairs. The landlord in a commercial lease and his mortgagee are concerned with the tenant's credit standing, since this is their assurance that the rent will be paid. This is the reason, for example, why you will find a shopping center promoter looking for national chain stores as tenants. And because the landlord and his mortgagee depend on the cash flow from triple-A tenants, the lease will forbid any assignment or sublease without the landlord's consent. In a ground lease, on the other hand, (1) the landlord looks for his security to the fact that the tenant will erect a valuable building on the property and will have to keep up his rent in order to prevent loss of his investment in the building by the landlord's forfeiting the lease for nonpayment of rent; and (2) the tenant expects to borrow money to erect the building. This makes it necessary to draft the lease in such a fashion that the lessee's rights under the lease (the "leasehold estate") can be mortgaged without the landlord's permission and the lease should so state. And since the mortgagee who forecloses will want the unhampered right to sell to anyone, the ground lease should not limit the lessee's right to assign without the landlord's consent. Also, the term of the lease should be long enough to make the mortgage on the leasehold a legal investment for banks, insurance companies, and other institutional investors. For example, a state law may provide that a mortgage on a leasehold is not a legal investment for banks or insurance companies unless the unexpired term of the lease exceeds twenty-one years. Some states have a fifty-year minimum.

To better enable the lessee to borrow money for the erection of the building, a ground lease may provide that the landlord will join in the mortgage without, however, incurring any personal liability by signing the mortgage note. Or the lease may provide that the landlord's title will become subordinate to the mortgage on the leasehold. The landlord who signs such a lease must understand that this weakens his legal position, since foreclosure of the mortgage will extinguish his ownership. On the other hand, if the construction mortgage is only on the leasehold estate, foreclosure of the mortgage simply results in transfer of the leasehold to the mortgage lender, who then becomes the tenant paying rent to the landlord.

When the construction mortgage mortgages only the leasehold, provision should be included in the lease for special notice to the mortgagee of the leasehold in case of default in payment of rent, so that the mortgage lender can step in and cure the defaults, thereby preventing a forfeiture of the lease, which would cancel his mortgage.

45.09   Use of the Premises

Unless the terms of the lease prevent it, the tenant may use the premises in lawful ways that were not discussed during the lease negotiations. This use by the tenant is often a point of controversy. Many leases state that the premises are leased *for the business of selling cigars,* or *to be used as a real estate office.* Oddly enough, courts seem to feel that such language does not limit the tenant to the stated use. Unless the lease states that the property is to be used *only* for a particular purpose, he may make any use of the property he wants to, so long as such use is not materially different from that to which the rented premises were customarily put. *Lyon v. Bethlehem Engineering Corp.,* 253 N.Y. 111, 170 NE 512 (1930); 24 ALR2d 123.

> **SUGGESTION TO LANDLORD:** Include a clause under which the tenant covenants to use the property only for a specific purpose. Include at the end of the tenant's covenants a clause giving the landlord the right to terminate the lease if the tenant violates any of his covenants. Be sure you state clearly what the permitted use includes. For example, if you specify that the tenant is to operate a drugstore, does this permit a lunch counter?

When the lease definitely restricts the use that the tenant may make of the premises and the tenant branches out into some unauthorized business, the landlord need not terminate the lease, even if the lease gives him power to do so. He may, instead, procure a court order forbidding the tenant to engage in the unauthorized business. This is desirable when the tenant is a highly solvent one, such as a chain store, and the rent is favorable to the landlord. It also protects the landlord in those cases where he has agreed with other tenants not to allow competing businesses in the same building.

A lease of business property automatically gives the tenant the right to advertise his business on the leased property if the lease does not forbid this use.

> **EXAMPLE:** In the case of a lease of an entire building, it would give the tenant the exclusive right to place advertising signs on the walls and roofs of the building, for example, to maintain window signs and to have his name on a lobby directory board. In the case of a lease of a portion of a building, the lessee, not the landlord, would have the right to place advertising signs on the exterior walls of the portion leased to the tenant. 20 ALR2d 941.

Usually, however, where various floors are leased to different tenants, the landlord is considered as retaining exclusive possession of the roof. And obviously, if *L* leases the second floor to *A* and the third floor to *B*, *A's* signs must not extend above the dividing line between the second and third floors.

45.10   Possession—Landlord's Duty to Put Tenant in Possession

Often a landlord leases an apartment or store to a new tenant while the old tenant still occupies the premises under an unexpired lease, the idea being that when the old lease expires the old tenant will move out. At times he fails to do so. The question then arises as to whose duty it is to put the old tenant out. The court decisions are conflicting. 45 U. of Cincinnati L. Rev. 937. The Uniform Residential Landlord and Tenant Act requires the landlord to put the tenant in possession (§2.102). Many printed residential leases contain a clause to this effect.

If the landlord fails to deliver possession on time, rent abates (is reduced) for the period the new tenant is kept out of possession. Sec. 4.102 Unif. Resid. L. & T. Act.

45.11   Incidental Rights of Lessee or Tenant—Services and Easements

Among the incidental rights a tenant enjoys, though not mentioned in his lease, are:

1. The right of tenant, his guests, business visitors, deliverymen, and so on, to use the means of access the building provides, namely, front and rear entrances, arcade entrances, lobbies, corridors, stairs, escalators, and elevators, suite entrances from reception rooms or private offices (though the landlord, through reasonable regulations, may require delivery to be made at a service entrance, require freight to use freight elevators, etc.), also the right to use common toilets, common laundry facilities, and so on, and the right to have electric wires and conduits, also water and steam and gas pipes, cross the landlord's part of the property to service tenant's quarters. This is an aspect of the law of implied easements, 24 ALR2d 123.

The landlord should try to get a provision giving him the right to make reasonable changes in these facilities. To accommodate a new tenant, for example, the landlord may wish to move the washroom to another floor.

2. The right to have heat, hot water, and so forth furnished where the only means of obtaining them consists of facilities controlled by the landlord for the benefit of all tenants.

45.12   Liability of Landlord

Until recent times the rule of *caveat emptor* (let the buyer beware) applied to the landlord and tenant relationship. Unless the lease provided otherwise, the landlord had no duty to the tenant to put the rented premises in a habitable condition or to make any repairs whatever. Even if the building at the time it was rented was in a dangerous or ruinous condition or even wholly unfit for occupancy or use, or if it became so after it had been rented, the tenant had to pay the stipulated rent for the entire term of the lease. This, of course, placed the burden on a prospective tenant of making a careful inspection of the premises before signing a lease and of insisting that the lease contain covenants to keep the premises in repair if that was the tenant's wish and the landlord was willing to agree.

Since the landlord had no duty as to the condition of the premises, he was not liable to the tenant or his family for injuries or property damage suffered because of defects in the premises at the time of renting or occurring thereafter.

EXAMPLE: Landlord rented an apartment to Tenant. The flooring was obviously decayed and dangerous. It collapsed and Tenant was injured. He had no right to sue Landlord.

There were and are some exceptions to these rules:

1. When the landlord lets for a short term of a few days, weeks, or months a fully furnished house supposedly equipped for immediate occupancy as a dwelling, the landlord implicitly represents, in many states, that the premises are safe and habitable. If the premises are not habitable, as when they are infested with vermin, the tenant has the right to move out, and his liability for rent ceases. *Young* v. *Povich,* 121 Maine 141, 116 Atl. 26 (1922); 28 ALR 48. Also, the landlord is liable to the tenant and his family for injuries sustained from defects in the rented premises or the furnishings thereof. *Hacker* v. *Netschke,* 310 Mass. 754, 39 NE2d 644 (1942); *Mease* v. *Fox,* 200 NW2d 791 (Iowa 1972).

2. Where there are concealed defects that would make the premises dangerous to a tenant and that the tenant not discover on an inspection of the premises, but that are known to the landlord, the landlord must inform the tenant of the existence of such defects. If he fails to do so, and as a consequence an injury is suffered by the tenant, his family, or his customers or guests, the landlord is liable for such injuries. *Mease* v. *Fox,* 200 NW2d 791 (Iowa 1972). Lawyers call this *fraud* liability.

EXAMPLE: Premises were leased as a barber shop and residence. Sewer gas often escaped into the premises, which fact was known to the landlord. He did not disclose this fact to the tenant, and the tenant and his family became seriously ill from sewer gas. The landlord was liable for the injuries.

3. The landlord normally retains control over parts of the building used in common by the tenants, such as halls, stairs, elevators, and sidewalks leading from the building to the public street or sidewalk. With respect to such common facilities, the landlord must exercise due care to correct any dangerous conditions that develop. If he fails to do so, he is liable for injuries suffered by the tenant, his family, his customers, or other persons lawfully on the premises, such as delivery men. 67 ALR3d 587, 490; 66 *id.* 202.

EXAMPLE: Landlord leased a flat in his apartment building to Tenant. The stairways were used in common by the tenants. A stair became defective, and this condition was brought to the attention of Landlord, but he failed to correct it. Tenant slipped on the stair and was injured. Landlord was liable.

The duty of the landlord to use care to keep facilities used in common by the tenants in repair extends to appliances furnished by the landlord for the tenants' common use, such as laundry appliances, common toilets, playground equipment, and dumbwaiters. It also extends to the roof, chimneys, eaves, flues, outside walls, and swimming pools. 39 ALR3d 824. This duty extends also to the malls, walks, parking areas, etc., of a shopping center. 95 ALR2d 1344.

This liability of the landlord rests upon the fact that he is in exclusive control of these common areas. With control goes liability. This is a form of *occupier liability.*

4. Where the landlord, even though not legally obligated to do so, makes repairs, but is negligent in so doing, he is liable for any resulting injuries.

EXAMPLE: Landlord, though not obligated to do so, repaired a floor in an apartment that he rented to Tenant. The work was carelessly done, and Tenant was injured. Landlord is liable. 78 ALR2d 1258.

RECENT DEVELOPMENTS: In California the courts have decided to hold the landlord liable for injuries received by a residential tenant without regard to the presence or absence of negligence on the landlord's part.

EXAMPLE: Tenant in an apartment building owned by Landlord was injured when he slipped and fell through an untempered glass shower door. Landlord was liable. *Becker* v. *IRM Corp.,* 38 Cal.3d 424, 213 Cal. Reptr. 213, 698 F2d 116, cited in *Muro* v. *Superior Court,* 229 Cal. Reptr. 383 (Cal. App. 1986). This accords with recent decisions extending strict liability to builders of mass-produced homes, which discussions are cited in the Muro case.

REFERENCE: Prosser & Keeton, *Torts* (5th ed. 1984) § 63 *et seq.*

45.12(a)   Liability of Landlord for Injuries to Third Person

As a rule, whenever a landlord would be liable to a tenant, as, for example, when the landlord is careless with respect to care of common stairways, he will be liable to others who stand in the tenant's shoes, such as members of his family, guests, employees, and business visitors, and delivery personnel.

There are other situations where a landlord is liable to a third person.

1. When the landlord rents the premises for a purpose that involves the admission of the public as patrons of the tenant (amusement park, theater, etc.) and at the time the lease, or any renewal lease, is signed, the premises are in a dangerous condition (dangerous doorways, steps, floors), the landlord is liable to the tenant's patrons for any injuries that they may suffer. *Webel* v. *Yale University,* 125 Conn. 515, 7 A2d 215 (1939); 17 ALR3rd 422, 873.

2. With respect to pedestrians on public walks or streets adjoining the rented premises, there is an additional rule imposing liability on the landlord, namely: When the premises at the time of the renting are in a dangerous and defective condition, the landlord is liable to strangers for injuries resulting therefrom. 52 CJS 105; 31 ALR2d 1334.

EXAMPLE: At the time the premises were leased to the tenant, a hole in the sidewalk leading to a coal bin was in a defective condition, and a pedestrian was thereafter injured as a result. The landlord was held liable. *Great Atlantic & Pacific Tea Co.* v. *Traylor,* 239 Ala. 497, 195 So 724 (1940). The reason for this rule is that a dangerous condition of premises constitutes a *nuisance,* and the liability of the landlord results from his leasing premises on which a *nuisance* exists. *Morgan* v. *Sheppard,* 156 Ala. 403, 47 So 147. The liability exists even though the defect is not concealed. And if the premises were safe when originally leased but are defective when the lease is renewed, the landlord is liable for injuries sustained by strangers after the date of the renewal. Of course, the tenant would also be liable for such injuries.

NEW LAWS: There are a number of state laws making landowners liable for deaths or injuries in private swimming pools. *Raponotti* v. *Burnt-Mil Arms, Inc.,* 273 A2d 372 (N.J. 1971).

3. Where the lease involves a use of the premises that is inherently dangerous, the landlord will be liable to third persons injured by the tenant's negligence if the landlord failed to exercise due care in selecting a responsible tenant.

EXAMPLE: The landlord leased a filling station to a tenant who had no experience in this line of work. An explosion occurred and the plaintiff was injured. The landlord was held liable. *Benlehr* v. *Shell Oil Co.,* 402 NE2d 1203 (Ohio 1978).

If you are curious as to why early landlord and tenant law so heavily favored the landlord, remember the American courts tended to follow the rules laid down in England. And the English judges were wealthy landlords. It was not until the era of consumerism, that the common people received real protections.

45.12(b)   Lease Obligating Landlord to Repair

If the lease requires the landlord to make repairs, and the landlord violates this obligation, the tenant may pursue one of the following courses:

1. He may abandon the premises if they become untenantable.
2. He may make the repairs himself and deduct the reasonable expense or cost thereof from the rent.
3. He may occupy the premises without repair and deduct from the rent the decrease in rental value occasioned by the landlord's failure to repair. Here, however, the tenant runs the risk of having his lease forfeited for nonpayment of rent if he appraises the situation incorrectly.
4. He may pay full rent and sue the landlord for the decrease in rental value occasioned by the landlord's failure to repair.

When the lease obligates the landlord to repair, and he fails to do so, and the tenant suffers an injury as a result, some courts hold the landlord liable; others do not. The view that the landlord should be held liable is growing in favor. 78 ALR2d 1252. Accompanying every contract is an unspoken duty to perform with skill and care and to be liable for negligent performance. 17A CJS *Contracts* § 494(1). In any event, the landlord has no duty to inspect the rented premises he has agreed to keep in repair, for normally the landlord has no right to enter on the rented premises without the tenant's consent. It is the tenant's duty to notify the landlord of any condition requiring repair, and no liability on the landlord's part arises until this has been done and the landlord has failed to make repairs as agreed. 163 ALR 314.

45.12(c)   Ordinances and Statutes Imposing Duty to Repair

The old rules relieving the landlord of the duty to keep rented premises in repair were evolved before the emergence of large cities, with the attendant problems of urban life. Obviously, workers of low income living in tenements in large urban centers cannot afford to keep their premises in repair. If the landlord fails to make needed repairs, they simply are not made. In many states laws and ordinances have been passed imposing on landlords the duty to keep rented housing accommodations in repair. 45 Ill. L. Rev. 205; 93 ALR 778; 17 ALR2d 704. In California, Montana, North Dakota, and Oklahoma, the tenant is given the right to move out if needed repairs are not made, but if the tenant is injured because of the landlord's failure to make repairs, the landlord is not liable. In some states, Michigan, New Jersey, and New York, for example, the landlord is liable if the tenant suffers injuries as a result of the landlord's negligent failure to make repairs. *Altz* v. *Lieberson,* 233 N.Y. 16, 134 NE 703 (1922); 17 ALR2d 708.

> **EXAMPLES:**   In states following the New York rule, landlords were held liable for the following injuries: tenant injured by fall of ceiling; tenant injured as result of landlord's failure to repair hole in bathroom floor; and tenant's child injured when defective radiator valves blew off.

Many of the statutes and ordinances do not even mention the tenant. The ordinance may simply impose a fine of $100 on the landlord if, for example, he fails to keep a light burning in a stairway for twenty-four hours a day. However, in some states resourceful lawyers for tenants have persuaded the courts that such ordinances create an implied right in a tenant to sue the landlord for personal injuries sustained from an accident that would not have occurred but for the landlord's failure to comply with the ordinance. Prosser, *Torts,* 191.

In many cities, especially home-rule cities, ordinances exist making the landlord liable for failure to repair or for violation of building codes. *Bell* v. *Willoughby Tower,* 46 Ill. App.2d 45, 196 NE2d 487 (1965).

45.13(a)   Repairs—State Laws Permitting Tenant to Make Repairs

A few states have laws permitting the tenant to make minor repairs where the landlord refuses to do so, typically limited to an amount not exceeding one month's rent, and to deduct this amount from the rent. Restatement (Second) Property § 112.

45.13(b)   Repairs—Office Leases

Most office leases require the tenant to surrender the premises at the end of the lease in their original condition, *ordinary wear and tear excepted.* This last clause is given its normal meaning.

EXAMPLE: When Tenant surrendered the premises there were patches in the carpeting, a damaged air conditioner that ran all night because Landlord had installed no thermostat, and scratches in office panels. This is ordinary wear and tear. *Urban Management Corp.* v. *Ford Motor Credit Co.,* 263 So2d 404 (La. App. 1972).

45.13(c)   Repairs—Recapitulation

The problem of repairs is one of great complexity. Among the numerous problems are the following:

1. Effect of laws or ordinances authorizing Tenant to pay rent into an escrow of some sort while Landlord is in breach of his obligation to repair. 40 ALR3d 821.

2. Right of Tenant to make deductions as a setoff from rent payments because of Landlord's failure to repair. 40 ALR3d 1369.

3. Landlord's failure to repair as amounting to a constructive eviction, permitting Tenant to move without liability for further rent. 86 ALR3d 351.

4. Landlord's breach of covenant to repair as giving rise to Tenant's action for damages for mental anguish. *Cherberg* v. *Peoples Nat. Bank,* 544 P2d 1137 (Wash. 1955). (Landlord was using situation to pressure Tenant to move.)

5. Landlord may be liable for lost profits of Tenant if lease permits Landlord to terminate lease in case of fire damage and he unduly delays repairs. *Flame* v. *Oak Lane Shopping Center,* 369 A2d 1220 (Pa. 1977).

6. In an ordinary office lease situation, Landlord must make repairs at his expense where ordered by public authority. *Buckley* v. *Ligget,* 218 A2d 515 (D.C. 1966); 22 ALR3d 521.

7. If lease requires Tenant to carry insurance, Tenant is liable for repairs up to amount of any deductible in the insurance policy. *Burger Chef. Systems, Inc.* v. *Melford Co.,* 547 F2d 786 (4th Cir. 1976).

8. Where Landlord covenants to repair and carry insurance, Tenant may maintain specific performance to compel Landlord to repair. *Evco Corp.* v. *Ross,* 528 SW2d 20 (Tenn. 1975).

9. General covenant by Tenant to *repair* may compel Tenant to *rebuild* in case of destruction of building. 38 ALR2d 782, 703 (older cases). This rule may well disappear as the doctrine of unconscionability develops further.

10. Measure of damages where Landlord breaches his covenant to repair. 80 ALR2d 983.

11. Landlord's duties under covenant to repair and rebuild where building is damaged or destroyed by fire. ALR2d 682.

12. Rights and remedies of Tenant on breach of Landlord's covenant to repair. 28 ALR2d 446.

45.14   Liability of Tenant for Injuries to Third Person

When a stranger is injured by reason of a defective condition of the premises, it is often difficult to determine whether the landlord or tenant is liable. If the landlord has made no agreement to repair and the premises were in a safe condition when rented, and if the defective portion is in the exclusive possession of the tenant, the tenant is liable but the landlord is not, since the landlord has no control over such premises and is in no position to prevent the dangerous condition.

> **EXAMPLE:**   A stranger slipped and fell into a coal hole that was defectively covered but was in a safe condition when the premises were rented. The basement into which the hole opened was used by the first-floor tenant. He alone had a key to this basement, and the landlord had no access thereto. The tenant alone was liable. *West Chicago Masonic Assn.* v. *Cohn,* 192 Ill. 210, 61 NE 439 (1901).

Or suppose the tenant of an upper floor goes out leaving the water running, and the water runs over and drips through the ceiling and ruins plaster and rugs in the apartment beneath. The landlord is not liable since the tenant is in exclusive possession of his apartment, but the tenant is liable both to his landlord and to the tenant below, because the damage resulted from his carelessness.

45.14(a)   Insurance

The prudent property owner should protect himself against liability claims by taking out owners', landlords', and tenants' public liability insurance, commonly referred to as O.L.&T. insurance, which provides coverage against legal liability for accidents resulting in bodily injuries or death arising out of ownership, occupation, or use of the premises. Liability for injuries sustained by employees is not covered by this policy, but they should be covered by workmen's compensation or employer's liability insurance. Insurance should be obtained protecting the landlord against liability for property damage. If there is an elevator on the premises, insurance will be needed to protect against injuries arising through operation of the elevator. Special "dram shop" insurance should be purchased if alcoholic beverages are sold on the premises.

45.15   Repairs and Alterations by Tenants—Liability of Tenant to Landlord

When the lease does not provide otherwise, the tenant has no duty to the landlord to make any substantial, extraordinary, or general repairs, such as the replacing of a worn-out furnace or water heater. But it is the tenant's duty to repair broken windows or leaking roofs and to take such other steps as needed to prevent damage from the elements. If he fails to do so, he is liable to landlord for any resulting damage. *Suydam* v. *Jackson,* 54 N.Y. 450.

The tenant must not make any material changes in the nature and character of the building leased, as by removing walls, cutting new doorways, and the like, even though such alterations increase the value of the property. The theory is that when the tenant vacates the building, the landlord should find it in much the same condition as it was when the tenant took possession. *F. W. Woolworth Co. v. Nelson*, 204 Ala. 172, 85 So 449 (1920).

A lease provision for repairs may require the tenant to replace rotten floors, a worn-out furnace, and the like. The tenant is liable to his landlord for damage occasioned by carelessness, as where damage results from the tenant's negligence in permitting a bathtub to overflow. 10 ALR2d 1012.

45.16   Damage to or Destruction of the Leased Premises

Unless the lease provides otherwise, the rule is that when *land and building* are rented, the tenant is not excused from paying rent if *building* is destroyed by fire, flood, or wind.

> **EXAMPLE:**   A lease was made of the premises at 143 and 145 Lake Street, Chicago, Illinois. The buildings were destroyed by fire, but the liability for rent continued. A lease containing a description by street number leases the land as well as the building.

Quite a number of states—Alaska, Arizona, California, Connecticut, Kentucky, Maryland, Michigan, Minnesota, Mississippi, Montana, New Jersey, New York, North Carolina, North Dakota, Ohio, South Carolina, West Virginia, and Wisconsin, for example —have abolished this harsh rule. In these states, it is the rule that if a building is destroyed or rendered untenantable, the tenant is relieved of further liability for rent. 35 B. Y. U.L. Rev. 1284. Many lease forms provide that if the building is destroyed by fire, the lease ends automatically. Predictably, many more modern courts will take this approach even where the lease is silent.

The rule that liability for rent continues when the building is destroyed does not apply to a lease of an apartment, flat, office, or floor of a building. Such a lease is not a lease of land. 99 ALR3d 738.

When the building is not destroyed, but the apartment is rendered *untenantable* by fire, leases usually provide that the landlord has a certain time in which to make the necessary repairs, and in the meantime, the tenant is not liable for rent. Under this clause, if the landlord fails to make repairs during the specified period, the lease ends automatically.

If the lease requires the landlord to *repair* the building, this may be interpreted as requiring him to *rebuild* it if it is destroyed by fire or other casualty. 38 ALR2d 685.

> **NEW DIRECTIONS:**   The Restatement of Property 2d §5.4 takes the position that when the building is destroyed (by fire, windstorm, etc.) without fault on the tenant's part, the tenant may terminate the lease and end his liability for rent. This is a sound rule. No doubt most courts will follow this view.

REFERENCES: *Teodori* v. *Werner,* 415 Ad 31 (Pa. 1981) (tenant's liability for rent ends when building destroyed); 99 ALR3d 738; 34 Mo. L. Rev. 132; 7 Real Est. L. Rev. 187.

45.16(a)   Damage or Destruction of the Leased Premises *before* Tenant Takes Possession

If the rented premises are damaged by fire or other cause or otherwise rendered unsuitable for the use contemplated by the parties and this occurs *before* Tenant takes possession, Tenant may terminate the lease without liability to Landlord.

> **EXAMPLE:**   The building was destroyed by fire before Tenant took possession. He could cancel the lease. Restatement, Property 2d §5.2. The theory is that Tenant has no way of protecting the property before the possession date.

45.17   Repairs and Services by Landlord

Many state laws place on the landlord the burden of repairing residential premises where defects are discovered during the lease term. Restatement of Property 2d Ch. 5, statutory note 3(a). And some of these laws give the tenant the right to sue for damages if the landlord fails to repair. Some of these statutes permit the tenant to pay less than the stipulated rent. This is called an abatement of rent. Some of these statutes deal with the landlord's failure to provide services such as water, gas, and electricity. Some of these laws allow the tenant to suspend payment of rent.

Because courts today are beginning to build their local law on the basis of statutes widely enacted in other states, it seems quite likely that rules embodied in statutes of this sort will find wide expression in court decisions everywhere.

45.18   Taxes

In the absence of a provision in the lease to that effect, the tenant is not obliged to pay real estate taxes on the leased land.

45.19   Fixtures

The respective rights of landlord and tenant in and to fixtures installed by the tenant are discussed in Chapter 3.

Trade fixtures not removed by the tenant before he moves out become the property of the landlord. The fact that such items are attached to the landlord's building seems to make this result natural and acceptable to the courts. However, as to the tenant's ordinary personal property that is not in any way attached to the building, for example, furniture or stock in trade, this does not become the landlord's property simply because the tenant has moved out or been evicted. The landlord must keep or store these articles for the tenant. Some state laws cover this point.

45.20   Cancellation Clause

Leases may contain a clause conferring on the landlord the privilege of canceling the lease in the event of a sale of the property and upon giving a certain specified notice to the tenant. This clause is of value when the landlord sells the premises to a buyer who desires more or less immediate occupancy. Great care must be exercised in serving the notice of cancellation. For example, if the lease says that the *landlord* may cancel the lease in case of a sale, a notice served by his *purchaser* may be void. 163 ALR 1019. Notice of cancellation should be served personally unless the lease specifically allows notice by mail. Each tenant is entitled to his own copy of the notice.

45.21   Assignments and Subleases

Unless the lease provides otherwise, a lessee may assign his lease or sublet the premises. Whether a particular instrument is an assignment or sublease does not depend upon the name given the instrument by the parties. An assignment simply transfers the leasehold estate to a new owner, the assignee. A sublease creates a new and distinct leasehold estate in the sublessee. If the lessee transfers the *entire unexpired remainder* of the term created by the lease, the instrument is an assignment. If the lessee retains *part of the term, however small the part may be,* or transfers only part of the leased premises, the instrument is a sublease.

> **EXAMPLE:**   Landlord leases certain premises to Tenant for a term beginning on May 1, 1986, and expiring on April 30, 1988, at a rent of $1,000 per month. On July 1, 1986, Tenant executes to X a "sublease" for a term beginning on July 1, 1986, and expiring April 30, 1988, at a rent of $1,500 per month. The instrument is an assignment.

> **EXAMPLE:**   Landlord leases to Tenant certain premises for a term beginning on May 1, 1986, and expiring on April 30, 1988. On July 1, 1986, Tenant executes to X an "assignment" of said lease except the last day of the term. The instrument is a sublease.

The difference between assignment and sublease is important, since an assignee becomes liable to the original lessor for rent, whereas a sublessee is liable only to the sublessor, who, of course, is the lessee under the original lease. Of course, the lessee in the original lease continues liable for rent to the original lessor, notwithstanding the assignment or sublease.

If the lease forbids an assignment without the lessor's consent, it does not necessarily prevent a sublease. If the lease forbids a sublease, it does not necessarily prohibit an assignment. As a rule, a commercial lease prohibits both assignments and subleases without the lessor's consent.

Suppose Landlord makes a lease to Tenant Corp. and Shareholder, the holder of all the stock in Tenant Corp., sells all his stock to Buyer. This is not a violation of covenant not to make an assignment or sublease without the landlord's consent. The lease remains in Tenant Corp. Only the stock has been transferred. *Alabama Vermiculite Corp.* v. *Patterson,* 124 F.Supp. 441. Many leases forbid such a transfer of stock.

An assignment or sublease made without the lessor's consent, in defiance of the provisions of the lease, is not wholly void. If, after learning of the assignment or sublease, the lessor accepts rent from the assignee or sublessee, he waives his right to object to that particular assignment or sublease.

The spouse of the assignor need not join in assignment of the lease. A leasehold estate is personal property and there are no dower rights in personal property.

Today there is a huge volume of litigation over the assignment of commercial leases. The landlord refuses his consent (because he wants to raise the rent) and the tenant claims his refusal is unreasonable. *Warmack* v. *Merchants Nat. Bank,* 612 SW2d 733 (Ark. 1981); *Funk* v. *Frink,* 633 P2d 586 (Ida. 1981); 54 ALR3d 679. Most recent decisions are holding against the landlord. A lease is regarded as a contract and each party to a contract is under a duty to act in good faith and with commercial reasonabless. *Bass Barbara Inc.* v. *Newbill,* 93 N.M. 239, 638 P2d 1084 (1982).

45.22 Mortgages of the Leasehold

If the lease contains no provision that would prohibit a mortgage of the leasehold, the tenant may place a mortgage on the leasehold estate created by the lease. In such a mortgage, the description of the mortgaged premises should read somewhat as follows:

> Leasehold estate created by lease dated May 1, 19__ and recorded in the Recorder's Office of _____ County, _____, on May 2, 19__, as Document 1,000,000 from John Smith, as Lessor, to Henry Brown, as Lessee, demising for a term of years commencing on May 1, 19__, and ending on April 30, 19__,the premises described as follows, to wit: (here insert description of leased premises).

One difficulty with such a mortgage is the fact that the tenant may default in his rent payments, and if he does, the landlord may declare the lease forfeited. Of course, if default and forfeiture occur, the mortgage is thereby extinguished. A side agreement between the landlord and mortgagee may provide that before forfeiting the lease the landlord will give notice of the default to the mortgagee and a stated time to make good the defaults. It may also provide that if the lease is terminated, the mortgagee will be entitled to receive a new lease for the balance of the term on the same rent and terms as the old lease.

Another question that arises is with respect to the liability of the mortgagee for payment of rent. In title and intermediate states, which regard a leasehold mortgage as an assignment of the leasehold, the mortgagee becomes personally liable to the landlord for rent, under the rule stated in the preceding section that an assignee becomes liable to the original lessor for rent. *Williams* v. *Safe Deposit Co.,* 167 Md. 499, 175 Atl. 331 (1934). For this reason, it is a common practice in leasehold mortgages to omit the last day of the term, so that the mortgage mortgages the leasehold *except the last day thereof.* By excepting the last day of the term, the mortgage becomes a sublease rather than an assignment, and the mortgagee does not become personally liable to the landlord for rent due under the lease. Mortgages are treated as assignments or subleases depending on whether they cover all or less than all the unexpired term of the lease. In states that follow the lien theory of mortgages, a mere mortgage of the leasehold does not make the mortgagee liable for rent. Kratovil and Werner, *Modern Mortgage Law and Practice,* §22.09 (1981).

45.23   Deed of Rented Premises

A landlord may, of course, sell his real estate, and the buyer will take it subject to existing leases and periodic tenancies. The deed alone confers on the buyer the right to collect rent falling due after the sale and the right to declare leases forfeited for nonpayment of rent if that right is reserved in the lease. *Lipschultz* v. *Robertson,* 407 Ill. 470, 95 NE2d 357 (1950). So far as the collection of future rent is concerned, it is unnecessary that the lessor execute to his purchaser an assignment of his rights under existing leases.

A tenant has the right to continue making rent payments to his original landlord until he is notified of a sale of the property. Therefore, one who buys rented property should promptly notify all tenants that all future rent must be paid to him.

A serious question arises when the tenant prepays the rent called for by the lease and the property is thereafter sold. The buyer of the property no doubt assumes that he will be entitled to collect the future rents called for by the lease and is then confronted by a tenant armed with rent receipts for such rent. In some states, the tenant must pay such rent over again to his new landlord, whereas in other states, the rent payments are good as against the new landlord. 49 Am.Jur.2d §554.

45.24   Abandonment of the Premises

Leases usually provide that if the lessee abandons the premises before the expiration of the lease, he shall nevertheless continue liable for rent until the expiration of the lease, and any reletting by the landlord shall not relieve the tenant of further liability.

However, upon abandonment of the premises by the lessee, it is the duty of the landlord in most states to mitigate damages, that is, to take charge of the property, and, if possible, relet or rerent it and thus reduce the amount for which the lessee remains liable. 40 ALR 190, 126 ALR 1219. The lessor may deduct the expenses of such reletting, including commissions and decorating, from the rent collected on such reletting, and he may apply the balance on the original tenant's liability.

> **EXAMPLE:**   Landlord leased premises to Tenant #1 for one year at $500 per month. After six months, Tenant #1 abandoned the premises. The premises were vacant one month and were then relet to Tenant #2 for $400 per month, the expenses of reletting, including commissions and decorating, being $50. The landlord thus realized on the reletting $2,000 minus $500, or $1,500. Tenant #1's liability is $3,000 minus $1,500, or $1,500.

The courts are not in agreement as to the extent of the landlord's duty where the tenant abandons the premises. Some courts put the landlord under an obligation to seek another tenant so that the damages caused by the tenant's abandonment can be reduced. *Scheinfeld* v. *Muntz TV, Inc.,* 67 Ill. App.2d 28, 214 NE2d 506 (1966). Other courts require no affirmative action by the landlord. But they do compel him to accept a suitable subtenant found by the abandoning tenant. *Reget* v. *Dempsey-Tegeler Co.,* 96 Ill. App.2d 278, 238 NE2d 418 (1968). 48 Ill. B. J. 546. Often the lease spells out the landlord's duties.

It is usual to insert a provision in the lease to the effect that the lessor shall not be under any obligation to relet and that he may permit the premises to remain vacant and sue the lessee for the full amount of the rent. This was the law in most states even in the absence of such a provision in the lease. 40 ALR 190, 126 ALR 1219. Under today's law it is probable that the courts will compel the landlord to relet no matter what the lease says. Ordinarily the landlord will relet the premises rather than permit them to remain vacant, for rent collections from an existing tenant are money in the landlord's hands, whereas the liability of the previous tenant is at best a doubtful asset.

If the landlord relets after abandonment of the premises by the tenant, there is danger that this may amount to a surrender or termination of the lease, thus releasing the tenant from further liability for rent. In some states, a reletting automatically releases the liability of the tenant who has abandoned the premises, whereas in other states, the tenant is released *unless* the landlord gives him notice of his intention to hold him liable despite the reletting. 110 ALR 368. In the great majority of states, the question is regarded as one of intention. If the landlord's acts indicate an acceptance of the tenant's abandonment and an intention to regard the lease as terminated, the tenant's liability for future rent is terminated. 110 ALR 368. In effect, there is a *surrender.* As above suggested, the notice given by the landlord is employed to show that he does not intend to treat the lease as terminated by the abandonment. Suppose, however, that the landlord relets to a new tenant for a new term longer than the term of the original lease. In some states, this is viewed as being inconsistent with the continued existence of the earlier lease, and the earlier lease is thereby terminated. *Ralph* v. *Deiley,* 293 Pa. 90, 141 Atl. 640 (1928); 61 ALR 773. Therefore, the lease provisions covering this point *(the abandonment clause)* should include clauses giving the landlord the right to relet for a term longer than the original lease without in any way releasing the tenant's liability.

In a number of states (Alaska, Arizona, California, Connecticut, Delaware, Hawaii, Illinois, Iowa, Kansas, Kentucky, Maryland, Montana, Nebraska, Nevada,

North Dakota, Oklahoma, Oregon, Tennessee, Virginia, Washington and Wisconsin) there are laws imposing on the landlord the duty to attempt to relet the premises, thereby "mitigating the damages."

45.25   Surrender

A *surrender* is an agreement by landlord and tenant to terminate the tenant's lease or tenancy, followed by a delivery of possession of the premises to the landlord. A surrender releases the tenant from liability for rent thereafter accruing.

> **EXAMPLE:**   Premises were leased by Landlord to Tenant for the term from April 1, 1903, to April 1, 1906. On March 31, 1904, Tenant #1 told Landlord that he wished to give up his lease, and Landlord accepted this offer, telling Tenant #1 to allow a new tenant, Tenant #2 to move in and to turn the keys over to him, Tenant #2. This procedure was a surrender, and Tenant #1 was not liable for rent accruing thereafter.

Observe that it is the agreement between landlord and tenant that distinguishes a surrender from an abandonment by the tenant.

If the landlord, with the tenant's consent, gives a new lease to a stranger during the existence of the tenant's lease, this is a surrender.

> **EXAMPLE:**   Landlord leased a store to Tenant, who sold the business to Buyer. Landlord then gave Buyer a new lease. This is a surrender of the old lease.

The making of a new lease between landlord and tenant operates as a surrender of a prior inconsistent lease. If the tenant merely abandons the premises, the fact that the landlord accepts the keys does not constitute a surrender.

45.26   Home-rule Ordinances

In this period of an acute shortage of housing many local governments, especially those having home-rule powers, have enacted ordinances for the protection of tenants.

> **EXAMPLE:**   The city of Evanston, Illinois, enacted a comprehensive ordinance protecting tenants. Among its provisions is one requiring the landlord to attempt to relet the apartment where the tenant abandons it. *City of Evanston* v. *Create Inc.,* 85 Ill.2d 101, 421 NE2d 196 (1981).

45.27   Termination of Tenancy for Nonpayment of Rent

Virtually all leases provide that the lease may be forfeited and the tenant evicted for nonpayment of rent or for violation of the terms of the lease.

Although the lease contains a clause permitting the landlord to declare the lease forfeited for nonpayment of rent, the landlord must not suddenly declare a forfeiture if he has been in the habit of accepting tardy rent payments. He must

first notify the tenant to pay his rent by a specified reasonable time, and if the tenant fails to pay within the time specified, then and only then may the landlord declare a forfeiture. *Cottrell* v. *Gerson,* 371 Ill. 174, 20 NE2d 74 (1939).

Year-to-year and month-to-month tenancies likewise may be terminated on the giving of a short notice specified by law if the tenant defaults in his rent payments.

When the landlord evicts the tenant because of the tenant's defaults, the tenant's liability for future rent is ended unless the lease contains a clause, called the *survival clause,* to the effect that the tenant's liability shall survive such eviction. Such lease clauses are now commonplace.

45.28   Warranty of Habitability

Perhaps the most meaningful new rule that has gained the widest acceptance is the rule that rented residential multifamily premises must be habitable and kept this way during the rental period. *Old Town Development Co.* v. *Langford,* 349 NE2d 744 (Ind. App. 1976), citing many cases and articles. This is an "implied warranty."

What, precisely, is included in this warranty is something that the courts have not yet decided. At a minimum, the landlord warrants that the premises are free from substantial building code violations and will remain so during the rental period. Other courts go further, and it seems probable that most courts will expand the warranty beyond freedom from building code violations. Most courts, it is plain, will hold the landlord liable if the premises become unsafe or unsanitary, and thus unfit to live in. *Glasoe* v. *Trinkle,* 107 Ill.2d 1, 479 NE2d 915 (1985). *Kline* v. *Burns,* 276 A2d 248 (N.H. 1971); *Boston Housing Authy.* v. *Hemingway,* 293 NE2d 831 (Mass. 1973); 40 ALR3d 73.

Many reasons have been marshalled for finding that the landlord warrants the habitability of rented apartments. Tenants do not have the skills to keep apartments in repair and do not even have access to many plumbing, heating, and electrical facilities that fall into disrepair. *Javins* v. *First Nat. Realty Corp.,* 428 F2d 1071; *DePaul* v. *Kauffman,* 272 A2d 500 (Pa. 1971); *Mease* v. *Fox,* 200 NW2d 791 (Iowa 1972); 40 ALR3d 646.

REFERENCES: 56 B.U.L Rev. 1; 62 Cal. L. Rev. 1444; 25 Case Western L. Rev. 371; 56 Cornell L. Rev. 489; 77 Dick. L. Rev. 77; 1975 Duke L. J. 999; 40 Fordham L. Rev. 123; 58 Iowa L. Rev. 656; 39 Mo. L. Rev. 56; 16 Vill. L. Rev. 395; 22 Case Western Reserve L. Rev. 739; 46 Chicago–Kent L. Rev. 1; 20 Cleve. St. L. Rev. 169; 2 Conn. L. J. 61; 56 Cornell L. Rev. 489; 20 DePaul L. Rev. 955; 1970 Duke L. J. 1040; 40 Fordham L. Rev. 123; 2 Rurgers–Camden L. J. 120; 23 U. Fla. L. Rev. 785; 31 U. Pitt. L. Rev. 138; 6 U. of San Francisco L. Rev. 147; 16 Vill. L. Rev. 383, 395.

45.28(a)   Two Flats

The warranties rule applies to two flats. *South Austin Realty Assn.* v. *Sombright,* 361 NE2d 795 (1977).

45.28(b)   Business Properties

The courts have not applied the warranty of habitability to business properties. *Yuan Kane, Inc.* v. *Wm. Levy*, 26 Ill. App.3d 889, 326 NE2d 51 (1975); *Firemens Fund Ins. Co.* v. *BPS Co.*, 491 NE2d 365 (Ohio, 1985).

45.28(c)   Homes

It has been held that the warranty applies to rental of a home. *Pole Realty Co.*, v. *Sorrells*, 84 Ill.2d 178, 417 NE2d 1297 (1981); *Fair* v. *Negley*, 390 A2d 240 (Pa. 1978); *Lemle* v. *Breiden*, 462 P2d 470 (Hawaii 1969).

45.28(d)   Disclaimer of Warranty

It has been held that a clause in the lease whereby the tenant waives or disclaims the benefit of any warranty of habitability is against public policy and void. *Teller* v. *McCoy*, 153 SE2d 114 (W. Va. 1979); *Boston Housing Authy.* v. *Hemingway*, 293 NE2d 831 (Mass. 1973).

45.29   Reduction of Rent

Some courts have awarded the tenant a reduction in rent proportionate to the loss of habitability. *McKenna* v. *Begin*, 325 NE2d 587 (Mass. 1975); *Javins* v. *First Nat. Realty Corp.*, 428 F2d 1071 (1970); *Hinson* v. *Deli*, 26 Cal. App.3d 62; 102 Cal. Reptr. 66 (1972); *Academy Spires, Inc.* v. *Brown*, 111 N.J.S. 477, 268 A2d 556 (1970). They have even extended this remedy to public housing. *Housing Authority of City of Newark* v. *Scott*, 348 A2d 195 (N.J. 1976).

> **NEW LAWS:**   Some states (Hawaii, Louisiana, Maine, Massachusetts, Virginia, Washington, West Virginia, and Wisconsin) have passed laws providing for rent reduction.

> **NEW DIRECTIONS:**   Where the building is in violation of the implied warranty of habitability but the tenant pays full rent, the new decisions say that the landlord is liable to repay the excess rent to the tenant. It has been held that he can sue the landlord to get back part of the rent paid. *Berzito* v. *Gambino*, 114 N.J.S. 124, 274 A2d 865 (1970). He can also sue the landlord for damages. *Marini* v. *Ireland*, 56 N.J. 130, 265 A2d 526 (1970); *Winn* v. *Sampson Co.*, 398 P2d 272 (1965).

> **NEW LAWS:**   Maine has a new law to this effect.

45.30   Building Code Violations

If the building contains substantial building code violations, this may have one of a number of consequences: (1) It may constitute a breach of the implied cove-

nant of habitability and this in turn may entitle the tenant to a reduction in rent. (2) It may give the tenant the right to withhold payment of rent and to pay the rent into a court or into some escrow provided by law. (3) It may give the tenant the right to pay full rent but to sue the landlord for damages. (4) It may invalidate the lease, depriving the landlord of the benefit of lease provisions favorable to the landlord. (5) It may render the landlord liable for personal injury sustained as a result of the code violation.

> **NOTE FOR LAWYERS:** The subject of building and housing code violations has attracted much attention. 21 Baylor L. Rev. 372 (1969); 56 B.U.L. Rev. 1 (1976); 53 Cal. L. Rev. 304; 5 Duquesne L. Rev. 413; 56 Iowa L. Rev. 460; 56 Geo. L. J. 920; 39 Geo. Wash. L. Rev. 152; 55 Minn. L. Rev. 82; 66 Mich. L. Rev. 1753; 12 Villanova L. Rev. 631; 32 U. Pitt. L. Rev. 626; 30 *id.* 148; 39 U. Cinn. L. Rev. 600; 25 Wash. & Lee L. Rev. 335.

45.31 Void Lease because of Building Code Violations

The presence of building code violations when the lease is signed may affect the validity of the lease.

> **NEW DIRECTIONS:** Courts have held that the presence of building code violations when a lease of the apartment was signed rendered the lease void. *Glyco* v. *Schultz,* 289 NE2d 919 (Ohio 1972); *King* v. *Moorhead,* 495 SW2d 65 (Mo. 1973); 66 Mich. L. Rev. 1953. This rule deprives the landlord of the benefit of all "fine print" in the lease. *Saunders* v. *First Nat. Realty Corp.,* 245 A2d 836 (1968); *Longnecker* v. *Hardin,* 130 Ill. App.2d 468, 264 NE2d 878 (1970); 21 Vand. L. Rev. 1117; *Robinson* v. *Diamond Housing Corp.,* 463 F2d 853 (1972). Or the tenant may choose to declare the lease void. *Mease* v. *Fox,* 200 NW2d 791 (Iowa 1972). If the code violations were not in existence when the lease was made it is not void. *Hinson* v. *Deli,* 2 Cal. Reptr. 661.

45.32 Rent Withholding

Up to present time, if a tenant failed to pay rent, the landlord could have him evicted. Today the courts that recognize an implied warranty of habitability and freedom from building code violations have begun to devise additional remedies for the tenant if the premises are in disrepair. One of these is rent withholding, under which the tenant pays the rent to the eviction court. Some cities and states have enacted laws along this line. *Clore* v. *Fredman,* 59 Ill.2d 20, 319 NE2d 18 (1975); *Mease* v. *Fox,* 200 NW2d 791 (Ia. 1972), 40 ALR3d 821. As a rule, when the building code violations have been corrected, the rent deposited in the escrow (or a part thereof) is released to the landlord. *Klein* v. *Allegheny County,* 269 A2d 647 (1972); *Bell* v. *Tsintolas Realty Co.,* 430 F2d 474 (1970); 29 Md. L. Rev. 202; 40 ALR3d 821; 46 L.A.B. Bull. 161. Of course, eviction is postponed as long as the rent is being paid into the escrow. *Kipsborough Realty Corp.* v. *Goldbetter,* 367 NYS2d 916 (1975); *Sabul* v. *Lipscomb,* 310 A2d 890 (Del.1973).

> **NEW DIRECTIONS:** Courts have begun to evolve additional new remedies for tenants where building code violations exist. First, the court finds that there

is an implied covenant or obligation on the landlord's part to keep the premises free from major building code violations. Then, if the landlord fails to perform this duty, the court finds the tenant is entitled to a rent reduction. *Jack Spring Inc.* v. *Little,* 50 Ill.2d 351, 266 NE2d 338 (1972). Or the tenant can make the repairs and deduct the cost from future rents. *Marini* v. *Ireland,* 56 N.J. 130, 265 A2d 526 (1970); *Mease* v. *Fox,* 200 NW2d 791 (Iowa 1972).

REFERENCES *on rent withholding because of implied warranty of habitability or presence of building code violations:* 21 Baylor L. Rev. 372; 53 Cal. L. Rev. 304; 5 Duquesne L. Rev. 413; 56 Geo. L. J. 920; 39 Geo. Wash. L. Rev. 152; 57 Ill. B. J. 920; 2 Loyola U. L. Rev. (La.) 105; 55 Minn. L. Rev. 82; 66 Mich. L. Rev. 1753; 30 U. Pitt. L. Rev. 148; 66 N.W.U. L. Rev. 790.

45.33   Retaliatory Evictions

As the renters have grown more militant in reporting building code violations to the city authorities, landlords have retaliated by refusing to renew the leases of the militants. Up to recent times, the landlord would have been within his rights.

NEW DIRECTIONS: Today many courts would not permit the landlord to evict a tenant where his sole reason for doing so is a desire to retaliate for the reporting of building code violations. *Clore* v. *Fredman,* 59 Ill.2d 20, 319 NE2d 18 (1974); 40 ALR3d 753; 18 Will. L. Rev. 1119 (1973).

EXAMPLE: *T,* a tenant in an apartment, complained repeatedly to the land-lord, *L,* about building code violations. Receiving no satisfaction, *T* complained to the building department, which ordered *L* to cure the defects. When *T's* lease expired, *L* filed an eviction suit. The court refused to evict *T,* because *L* was retaliating against *T.* The court allowed *T* to remain in possession until the code violations were eliminated and *T* could find another place to live. *Markese* v. *Cooper,* 333 NYS2d 63.

There are a number of cases holding that the entire doctrine of retaliatory eviction is inapplicable where the landlord simply seeks to oust the tenant so that he can remove a crumbling building from the housing market altogether. *Robinson* v. *Diamond Housing Corp.,* 463 F2d 853 (1972). This appears to make sense. If the landlord simply cannot keep the building in good shape, he should be permitted to demolish it. 51 N.C.L. Rev. 162 (1972).

But if the landlord raises the rent outrageously to get rid of a tenant who complains about building code violations, the tenant can move out and sue the landlord for damages, including damages for mental distress and punitive damages, that is, damages in an amount sufficient to constitute a punishment for the landlord's wrongdoing. *Aweeka* v. *Bonds,* 97 Cal. Reptr. 650 (1971).

So far the doctrine of retaliatory evictions has been applied only to residential properties. *Commercial Area Development* v. *Goodie Brand Packing,* 372 NYS2d 324 (1975).

NEW LAWS: Many states have enacted laws forbidding retaliatory eviction. However, most of the law is judge-made law.

45.33(a)   Retaliatory Eviction—Motive

To retaliate is to "get even" with someone for something he has done. This requires an *intention* to get even. As to landlord's motives, see Player, *Motive and Retaliatory Eviction of Tenants,* 1974 U. of Ill. L. F. 610.

> **EXAMPLE (1):**   Tenant complains to the city about building code violations in the building. Immediately, Landlord serves notice on Tenant that his month-to-month tenancy is terminated. There is an intention to retaliate.

> **EXAMPLE (2):**   Facts as in the example given above, but Landlord does not act until three years after Tenant's complaint.

Establishing intention to get even is simple in Example (1). It is next to impossible in Example (2).

45.33(b)   Retaliatory Eviction—The Time Factor

Many states have passed laws that fix a time that determines motivation.

> **EXAMPLE:**   In California, if Landlord acts against Tenant within sixty days after Tenant has complained, it is assumed he is trying to "get even." Other states have other limits. Player, *supra,* p. 615.

45.33(c)   Retaliatory Eviction—Landlord's Protected Activities

Landlord is not trying to "get even" if Tenant complains, and Landlord raises rents generally and evenly so that he can pay for repairs. Landlord must spread the cost over the anticipated life of the repairs. Player, *supra,* p. 623.

A landlord may take the entire building off the rental market if he feels the cost of needed repairs would be beyond his means, but he must not single out the tenant who complained and evict only him.

45.33(d)   Retaliatory Eviction—The Philosophy Underpinning the New Rule

The philosophy that sustains and supports the new rule was expounded in *Edwards* v. *Habib,* 397 F2d 687 (D.C. Cir. 1968). The court reasoned: (1) building codes cannot be enforced unless tenants can report violations without fear of Landlord's vengeance; (2) use of the state courts to evict complaining tenants would be action by the state taken to punish Tenant for exercising his constitutional right of *free speech.* Player, *Motive and Retaliatory Eviction,* 1974 U. of Ill. Law Forum 610 (excellent reference).

45.33(e)   Retaliatory Eviction—Protected Activities

Tenant activities against which Landlord must not retaliate include: (1) tenants' meetings; (2) complaints to the building code department; (3) forming a tenants' union; and (4) lawful rent withholding. Player, *supra*, p. 614.

45.33(f)   Laws and Ordinances

Various laws and ordinances give specific protection to the residential tenant against unfair conduct of the landlord.

> **EXAMPLE:**   Illinois has a statute and Illinois cities have ordinances on the subject of retaliatory eviction and rent withholding. *Clore* v. *Fredman*, 59 Ill.2d 20, 319 NE2d 18 (1974).

45.34   Limitations on the Landlord's Right to Select Tenants, Renew Leases and Tenancies, and to Evict Tenants

Under the old law, which is still true except regarding residential units, the landlord could rent to whomever he pleased, refuse to rent, refuse to renew leases, and evict any tenant whose lease or tenancy has been terminated. Now the court decisions and statutes are beginning to impose limits in all these regards:

> **NEW DIRECTIONS:**   Public housing. Where a public body is the landlord, the tenant's tenancy cannot be terminated without a hearing and inquiry into the reasonableness of the termination. *Thorpe* v. *Housing Authority*, 393 U.S. 268 (1968). Thus in the case of such a landlord there are strict limits on the landlord's right to evict. *CHA* v. *Harris*, 275 NE2d 353 (Ill. 1976).

45.35   The Quasi-public Landlord

It certainly seems logical to hold that where a public body, such as a city or a housing authority, is the landlord, the tenant will have constitutional rights that tenants of private landlord do not have. But in recent times the notion has gained currency that private landlords who receive government assistance in some form are *quasi-public landlords,* and their tenants have at least some of the rights of tenants in public projects.

> **EXAMPLE:**   *L,* a landlord whose building was erected by FHA financing and who received a real estate tax exemption, could not refuse to accept *T* as a tenant because *T* was a welfare recipient. *Colon* v. *Tompkins Square Neighbors,* 294 F. Supp. 134 (1968). *L* cannot accept benefits from the government and turn his back on the wards of the government.

> **EXAMPLE:**   *L,* a landlord, in the identical situation of the landlord in the preceding example, refused to renew *T's* lease. *T* had been an outspoken advocate

of tenants' rights and had organized demonstrations against *L*. The court held that *L* could not evict *T* without giving him notice and a hearing to show that *L* was acting with good cause. *McQueen v. Drucker,* 317 F.Supp. 1122 (1970). *T* had the right to free speech.

EXAMPLE: Some courts require such landlords to give the tenants notice and to hold a hearing when the landlord wants to increase rents. 28 ALR Fed. 839.

This court-made law has now been formalized in HUD rules. 8 Urb. Law. 605 (1976).

45.36   Deposits in Court

Where a dispute exists between landlord and tenant, the eviction court has power to order the rent deposited in court until the dispute is resolved. *McNeal* v. *Habib,* 346 A2d 508 (D.C. 1975).

45.37   Landlord's Duty to Protect against Criminal Acts

Traditionally, the landlord has been regarded as having no duty to protect his tenants against criminal acts of third parties. 59 Georgetown L.J. 1163.

NEW DIRECTIONS: However, under the new notion that the lease is a contract for services, the courts are beginning to place upon the landlord the duty to protect the tenant against criminal acts of third persons which he should have foreseen might occur. *Kline* v. *1500 Mass. Ave. Apt. Corp.,* 439 F2d 477. This would be especially true if the landlord's advertisements make mention of security protection or where the building is in a high-crime area or where the building has a record of criminal activity. 59 Georgetown L. J. 1185. There will be a tendency toward the application of a ''higher-the-amount-of-rent, the-greater-the-duty-of-care'' principle applied in the case of hotel guests. 59 Georgetown L. J. 1189; 48 ALR3d 331.

EXAMPLE: *T,* an elderly tenant, was assaulted and robbed as he entered his apartment. The apartment was in a high-crime area. *T* sued his landlord, *L,* contending *L* was negligent in failing to provide adequate lighting and door locks. The Michigan Supreme Court held *L* was liable. *Johnston* v. *Harris,* 198 NW2d 409 (Mich. 1972); 43 ALR3d 331.

EXAMPLE: *L* held liable to *T* because *L* failed to furnish adequate locks. *Braitman* v. *Erie Inv. Co.,* 350 A2d 268 (N.J. 1976).

EXAMPLE: *L* held liable where an intruder set fire to the building, causing damage to *T*'s property. *Warner* v. *Arnold,* 210 SE2d 350 (1974).

EXAMPLE: If a second burglary occurs, *L* is clearly liable. The facts show that burglary was foreseeable. *Stribling* v. *CHA.* 34 Ill. App.3d 551; 346 NE2d 47 (1975).

REFERENCES: *Pippin* v. *CHA,* 78 Ill.2d 204, 399 NE2d 596 (1979). *Loesser* v. *Nathan Hale Gardens,* 425 NYS2d 104 (1980); *Secretary of Housing* v. *Layfeld,* 152 Cal. Reptr. 342 (1978); *Smith* v. *General Apartment Co.,* 312 SE2d 74 (Ga. 1977); *Bratman* v. *Overlook Terrace,* 68 N.J. 368, 346 A2d 76 (1975); *Knapp* v. *Wilson,* 535 SW2d 371 (Tex. 1976); 1970 Duke L. J. 543; 74 Dick. L. Rev. 543; 5 U. of San Francisco L. Rev. 378; 62 Va. L. Rev. 383 (1976); 9 R.E.L.J. 311 (1980); 43 ALR3d 331; 44 U. Conn. L. Rev. 405 (1975); 70 Dick. L. Rev. 236 (1966); 63 Mass. L. Rev. 61 (1978); 8 R.E.L.J. 61 (1978); 9 Urb. L. Ann. 259 (1975); 30 Stanf. L. Rev. 725 (1978); 8 Suffolk L. Rev. 1305; 5 U. of Richmond L. Rev. 148; 1975 Wis. L. Rev. 160; 67 ALR3d 490, 587; 66 *id.* 202.

45.38   Tenant Unions

Because one tenant has little bargaining power as against a landlord, tenant unions have been formed. 59 Ill. B. J. 732; 23 U. Fla. L. Rev. 79. These unions engage in collective bargaining with landlords. Tenant organizations have recognized the need for more tenant control and have developed a variety of goals. The most frequently sought goals include: (1) negotiation of a new lease for use between individual tenants and the landlord; (2) development of a grievance procedure and/or plan for arbitration of disputes; (3) recognition of the tenant organization as the exclusive representative of the landlord's tenants; (4) formulation of a satisfactory way to handle tenant needs and to bring the buildings into compliance with the building code; (5) participation of the tenant organization in decisions about rent increases; and (6) provision of adequate security for the dwelling units. 46 L.A.B. Bull. 163. Some tenant unions have engaged in rent strikes. 3 Columbia J. Law & Social Problems 1 (1967). By legal maneuvers some unions have been able to stall evictions for as long as nine months. 46 L.A.B. Bull. 162.

A landlord must not refuse to renew a tenant's lease simply because the tenant has been active in a tenants' union. *Engler* v. *Capital Management Corp.,* 271 A2d 615 (N.J. 1970).

45.39   Rent Control

A number of local governments have adopted residential rent control ordinances. Such ordinances have been held valid. *Inganamort* v. *Borough of Ft. Lee,* 62 N.J. 521, 303 A2d 298 (1973); *Birkenfeld* v. *City of Berkeley,* 550 P2d 1001 (Cal. 1976); *Marshall House* v. *Rent Control Bd.,* 266 NE2d 876 (Mass. 1971); 30 Rutgers L. Rev. 1025.

45.40   Eviction—Partial Eviction—Constructive Eviction—Partial Constructive Eviction

A landlord who evicts his tenant wrongfully obviously can no longer collect rent. Indeed, even if the eviction is only from part of the premises, the same result follows.

EXAMPLE: Landlord leased Lot 1 to Tenant. The lot was improved with a house and garage. Landlord wrongfully took possession of the garage. Tenant is not liable for rent, even though he continues to occupy the house. *Tuchin* v. *Chambers,* 439 SW2d 849 (Tex. 1969).

If the landlord's conduct makes the premises untenantable, or if the stairways, walks, or elevators become unusable, a *constructive eviction* occurs, and if the tenant moves out as a result, he is no longer liable for rent. *Mease* v. *Fox,* 200 NW2d 791 (Iowa 1972).

EXAMPLE: Landlord fails to supply heat in the wintertime to an apartment rented to Tenant. Tenant moves out. He is no longer liable for rent.

EXAMPLE: Infestation of a house presents a harder problem because the tenant has some measure of control here. Nevertheless, infestation of a house with rats is a constructive eviction, since this may be beyond tenant's control. *Lemle* v. *Breeden,* 51 Hawaii 426, 462 P2d 470 (1969). Of course, this would be a constructive eviction in an apartment.

EXAMPLE: Water leaking through a roof or into a basement is a constructive eviction. 33 ALR3d 1356.

Matters wholly beyond the control of the landlord are not a constructive eviction.

EXAMPLE: An adjoining tenant had noisy machinery that prevented tenant from holding seminars. There is no constructive eviction. *Finkelstien* v. *Levinson,* 343 NYS2d 849 (1973).

NEW DIRECTIONS: Changes are taking place in the old law of constructive eviction. The right to move out is worthless when there is an acute shortage of rental apartments. Thus, the line between actual eviction and constructive eviction has become blurred, and the courts are introducing new ideas that are designed to achieve justice and to place little emphasis on labels.

EXAMPLE: Landlord leased a restaurant to Tenant who took possession, not knowing that part of the leased premises was not available for occupancy. The court held this was "actual partial eviction" and that Tenant could occupy the occupiable part without paying rent. *Metzenbaum* v. *Crepes D'Asic,* 367 NYS2d 645.

EXAMPLE: Landlord leased Tenant an apartment. Tenant was forced to discontinue use of the terrace because of water dripping from the building's air conditioner. The court permitted Tenant to remain in occupancy and to discontinue paying rent. The court held this was "partial constructive eviction." *East Haven Assoc., Inc.,* v. *Gurian,* 313 NYS2d 927 (1970); 1 ALR4th 849.

EXAMPLE: Tenant, an orthodontist, resisted eviction because Landlord was not furnishing proper heating and air conditioning. The court held that because of this breach on Landlord's part, Tenant was not required to pay the rent and could not be evicted. *Demirci* v. *Burns,* 124 N.J.S. 274, 306 A2d 468 (1973).

EXAMPLE: Landlord leased a store building to Tenant, with a covenant to repair. Part of the building was destroyed by fire. The court allowed Tenant to occupy the remainder of the building with a reduction of rent. *Coppola* v. *Tidewater Oil Co.,* 244 NYS2d 898 (1963).

NEW LAWS: Statutes are being enacted on the subject of rent withholding and the other new rules. *De Paul* v. *Kauffman,* 441 Pa. 386, 272 A2d 500 (1971). The New Jersey statute even includes mobile homes in its retaliatory eviction statute. In Maryland tenants may repudiate the lease within thirty days of occupancy if the warranty of habitability has been breached.

45.40(a)   Prior Law

Up to the present time the law has been that a tenant who claims that his landlord's conduct amounts to a constructive eviction must vacate the premises within a reasonable time after the landlord has failed to correct the condition. 75 ALR 1114. Some courts will continue to adhere to this view. However, the newer view recognizes the dilemma that confronts the tenant and permits him to use this defense while retaining occupancy of the rented premises. 1 ALR4th 849.

REFERENCE: Restatement of Property 2d §6.1, Comment h, adopts the view of the recent decisions that the tenant need not abandon the premises where the landlord is guilty of conduct amounting to a constructive eviction. Instead, he may sue for damages or claim an abatement of rent.

45.41   Unconscionability

The notion that the court can strike down an unconscionable lease or any unconscionable provision thereof has become part of the law of landlord and tenant. Restatement of Property 2d §5.5; Sec. 1.303 Unif. Resid. L. & T. Act.

EXAMPLE: An apartment lease obligated Tenant to pay Landlord an additional rent in attorneys' fees upon commencement of any proceeding by Landlord as a result of Tenant's default. The clause was held void. *Weidmen* v. *Tomaselli,* 365 NYS2d 681.

EXAMPLE: Landlord, an oil company, leased a filling station to Tenant under a lease with a clause stating that Landlord would not be liable for loss or damage resulting from the negligence of Landlord's employees and that Tenant would pay for any such loss. One of Landlord's employees sprayed gasoline over Tenant, and severe burns resulted. The court held the clause void and awarded damages to Tenant. *Weaver* v. *American Oil Co.,* 276 NE2d 144 (Ind. 1971).

The courts have even held that Landlord must renew a lease if refusal to do so would be unconscionable.

EXAMPLE: Landlord, an oil company, had leased the filling station to Tenant for many years. Tenant had spent a great deal of money in improving the station and building up a business. The court compelled Landlord to renew the lease. *Shell Oil Co. v. Marinello,* 294 A2d 253 (N.J.)

45.42 Fair Dealing

Some courts will strike down any provision of a lease if enforcement would not be considered "fair dealing." Berger, *Hard Leases Make Bad Law,* 74 Columb. L. Rev. 791, 805.

> **EXAMPLE:**   Landlord leased commercial premises to Tenant with an option to renew. Tenant failed to exercise the option within the time allowed, but Landlord, after such expiration, notified Tenant that his lease would soon end. Tenant then tendered to Landlord the money needed to renew the lease, but Landlord refused. The court held that Landlord was not injured by the technical defect and compelled Landlord to renew the lease. *George W. Miller & Co. v. Wolf Sales & Service Co.,* 318 NYS2d 24 (1971); 74 Columb. L. Rev. 791, 805.

CHAPTER 46

Racial Discrimination in Real Estate

46.01 History

The history of slavery and race relations up to the time of World War I is thoroughly documented. The modern history begins with World War I and much of it occurred in Chicago.

During World War I the Chicago meat packers recruited black workers in the southern states. Up to that time the black areas of Chicago had been relatively stable. But with the vast demand for meat for our allies and ourselves created by the war and the dwindling pool of white manpower, the meat packers saw fit to bring blacks into Chicago, and the black areas began to expand into adjoining white areas. Tension resulted. Rioting broke out and many deaths occurred.

This was followed by another period of violence, during which new black churches were bombed.

Finally, the police brought the situation under control.

In lieu of violence, white neighborhoods created the restrictive covenant. This document was an agreement designed to cover an entire neighborhood. The property owners in the areas bordering black areas agreed that their properties would never be occupied by blacks. The theory was that agreements not to *sell* to blacks were invalid under the old English rules forbidding restraints on sales of land. But a restriction dealing only with *occupancy* was thought to be valid. *Doherty* v. *Rice,* 240 Wis. 389, 3 NW2d 734 (1942).

However, in time these covenants were attacked on the ground that they could be enforced only by court proceedings. Court proceedings are *state action.* State action that produces racial discrimination is forbidden by the Constitution. The Supreme Court ultimately so held. *Shelley* v. *Kraemer,* 334 U.S. 1, 3 ALR2d 441 (1948). *Shelley* v. *Kraemer* has been the subject of much learned comment, for example, 110 U. Pa. L. Rev. 473; 108 *id.* 1; 60 Columb. L. Rev. 1083; 84 Harv. L. Rev. 59.

46.02   Racial Discrimination—Federal Laws—History

The Thirteenth Amendment to the federal Constitution abolished slavery. It took effect on December 18, 1865. Many southern legislatures adopted the "Black Codes," which, in effect, placed severe restrictions on the newly won rights of Negroes. Congress therefore passed a civil rights bill effective on April 9, 1866. Thereafter the Fourteenth Amendment was ratified on July 28, 1868, and the Fifteenth Amendment on March 30, 1870. On May 31, 1870, a new civil rights act was passed. And on April 20, 1871, Congress enacted another statute, and still another statute on March 1, 1875. 42 USCA § 1981 *et seq.* These laws are hereafter referred to as the Civil War laws. The history is set forth in detail in 50 Mich. L. Rev. 1323 (1952). Paralleling the new laws creating new rights were new laws giving the federal courts power to enforce these rights. 90 Harv. L. Rev. 1133, 1147 (1977).

The Civil War laws were neglected for a long period of time. When they were revived in 1961, there was still no inkling that they would be used by Negroes to enforce their rights in real estate. 90 Harv. L. Rev. 1133.

Then came the decision in *Jones* v. *Alfred H. Mayer Co.*, 392 U.S. 409, 20 L.Ed.2d 1189 (1968), decided under the Civil War laws. Please note that this case was pending in the lower courts while Congress was deliberating on the Open Occupancy Law of 1968.

In the *Jones* case, a black person sought to purchase a home from a builder. The builder refused to sell on racially motivated grounds. A suit was filed seeking to enjoin the builder from so discriminating. The court ordered the builder to sell the home to the black person at the price that was prevailing at the time of the wrongful refusal, a price that was substantially less than the then prevailing price. The court held that the Civil War laws were still alive.

46.03   Federal Legislation—The 1968 Law

A federal "open occupancy" law was enacted in 1968. 42 USCA § 3601 (Title VIII). The law covers dwellings, including homes and multifamily residences (two-flats, duplexes, apartments), and also vacant land acquired for construction for such purposes. No doubt acquisition of vacant land zoned for residential purposes will be regarded as subject to the law. Condominiums and cooperatives also come under the law. The law applies to sales, leases, and all types of rental agreements. It does not include properties used *exclusively* for commercial or industrial purposes. But if *part* of the building is used for residential purposes, the building is subject to the law.

The law creates new and important rights. Some are spelled out fairly clearly. Others will come into sharper focus only after the Supreme Court has interpreted the law. Some observations can be made. Where *bias* against a person is based on race, color, religion, or national origin, the following are unlawful:

> 1. To refuse to sell or lease or negotiate for sale or lease because of such bias, or to discriminate in the furnishing of services or facilities.

EXAMPLE: A landlord cannot furnish maid service to white tenants and refuse this service to blacks.

2. To discriminate in exacting terms of the sale or lease, for example, by asking a higher price because of the race of the buyer.

3. To advertise in the newspapers or post notices on the building that particular races will not be welcomed as buyers or tenants.

4. To state that a dwelling is not available, where such statement is made because of the race of the party seeking to buy or rent.

5. For a lender to refuse a party a loan or to insist on higher interest rates or harsher loan terms because of racial reasons.

6. For real estate brokers to refuse membership in their organizations or multiple-listing services because of racial reasons.

7. To induce a person to sell by creating fears of racial change in the neighborhood.

Enforcement of the law is complex. In general, the Secretary of the Department of Housing and Urban Development (HUD) is entrusted with some of the machinery of enforcement. The following procedures are available:

1. If there is a substantially equivalent remedy under a state law or ordinance, HUD notifies the appropriate state officials to enforce the law.

2. The party discriminated against may file a suit for damages. *U.S.* v. *Peltzer,* 377 F.Supp. 121 (N.D. Ala. 1974).

3. The court may issue injunctions restraining violation of the law, and set aside deeds or leases, except that no deed or lease shall be set aside if entered into before a court order has issued and the grantee or lessee had no actual knowledge of the proceedings. One is left with the inference that a court that sets aside a deed to a white person can order a sale thereof to a black who made an earlier comparable offer and was rejected because of racial bias.

4. The United States Attorney General may obtain injunctions restraining violations of the law if a ''pattern or practice'' is evident. *U.S.* v. *Mintzes,* 304 F.Supp. 1305 (D.Md 1969).

5. In certain instances the law provides for fines against, or imprisonment of, persons using force or threat of force to bring about racial discrimination in housing.

46.04   Federal Legislation—The Civil War Laws

In the Civil War laws it is provided that American citizens of every race and color shall have the *same right* throughout the country to purchase, lease, sell, hold, and convey real and personal property as is enjoyed by white persons. Laying stress on the phrase "the same right," the Supreme Court has held that this law prohibits all racial discrimination, *private and public,* in the sale and rental of property. Thus every "racially motivated refusal to sell or rent" is prohibited. *Jones* v. *Alfred H. Mayer Co.,* 392 U.S. 409 (1968). This law to some extent overlaps the Open Housing Act of 1968, to some extent goes beyond it, and to some extent omits protection afforded by the 1968 law. 42 USCA § 1981 *et seq.*

EXAMPLE: *W,* a white, owns his home which he occupies with his family. This is the only land he owns. He offers it for sale without employing a broker, but declines to sell to *B,* a black. His refusal is motivated by *B's* race. This refusal is wrongful under the Civil War law. Such a situation is expressly omitted from the coverage of the 1968 law under which a person owning only one home and selling it without a broker is not forbidden to discriminate.

EXAMPLE: *W* refuses to sell his store to *B,* a black, his refusal being racially motivated. This refusal is prohibited by the Civil War law, but does not come under the 1968 law.

EXAMPLE: *W* owns a large apartment building. For racial reasons he refuses to rent an apartment to *B,* a black. Both laws forbid this type of discrimination.

As the Supreme Court has pointed out, the Civil War law does *not* do the following:

1. It does not forbid discrimination on grounds of religion or national origin:

EXAMPLE: *A,* a member of *XYZ Church,* owns only one home. He offers his home for sale without the aid of a real estate broker. As purchasers appear, he states verbally that he will sell only to members of *XYZ Church.* The 1866 law does not forbid such action.

2. It does not deal specifically with discrimination in the provision of services or facilities in connection with the sale or rental of a dwelling, for example, furnishing maid service to apartment tenants.
3. It does not prohibit advertising or other representations that indicate discriminatory preferences.
4. It does not refer explicitly to discrimination in financing arrangements or in the provision of real estate brokerage services.
5. It does not enable a rejected purchaser or tenant to call upon the Attorney General or any other federal officer for aid.
6. It makes no express provision for the bringing of damage suits by rejected purchasers or tenants, but the court has indicated it has kept an open mind on the question of whether a right to damages could be implied or inferred from the language and purpose of the law.

Racial covenants are totally invalid now.

46.05   Remedies for Racial Discrimination

In considering the remedies available for racial discrimination, one must remember that today's courts do not hesitate to improvise remedies where the statute is silent. These are called *implied remedies.* 61 L.Ed.2d 910. Damages have been allowed. 85 ALR3d 351.

EXAMPLE: Landlord refused to rent to Tenant because she was black. She recovered damages of $10,000 for emotional distress and $10,000 punitive damages (to punish Landlord). *Parker* v. *Shonfeld,* 409 F.Supp. 876 (1976).

EXAMPLE: A white plaintiff can sue a landlord who refuses to rent to her because she has a black husband. *Hodge* v. *Sieler,* 558 F2d 284 (Cal. 5th 1977).

And, as has been mentioned, there are laws giving the federal courts power to entertain suits charging racial bias. 90 Harv. L. Rev. 1133.

REFERENCES: 7 Boston Coll. Ind. & Comm. L. Rev 495 (1966); 5 Columb. Human Rts. Rev. 335 (1973); 1970 Duke L. J. 819; 82 Harv. L. Rev. 834 (1969); 18 West. Res. L. Rev. 278 (1966).

46.06   Fair Housing Developments—Zoning

In the area of racial litigation, some aspects are beginning to crystallize: (1) In instances of isolated individual discrimination, the court decisions appear to give adequate implementation to state and federal legislation. The damage awards for *individual* acts of racial discrimination are growing in size. They are calculated to offer deterrence to individuals and to groups, such as real estate boards, that might otherwise be tempted to perpetuate discriminatory practices. (2) With respect to *villages* that seek to perpetuate geographic racial discrimination, the litigation has been largely ineffective.

The litigation has been protracted and indescribably expensive. Case after case has gone up and down from trial courts to reviewing courts like a yo-yo, running up astronomic attorneys' fees and court costs.

The Department of Justice, in consequence, has made a frontal attack on suburban segregation policies, hoping to open up white villages to minorities. The philosophy here, in addition to the strictly legal notion of achieving the racial equality mandated by the Constitution, is that of providing homes for minorities close to the places of employment offered by prospering suburbs.

EXAMPLE: Black Jack was an unincorporated area in St. Louis County. Developers announced a plan for low-income, multiracial housing. The community incorporated as a city and passed a zoning ordinance that excluded multifamily dwellings. A federal court struck down the ordinance as palpably discriminatory. The plaintiff developers then sought a court order compelling the village to admit multiracial housing. The court of appeals ordered the city to come up with a plan that would provide low-income housing. *Park View Heights Corp.* v. *City of Black Jack,* 605 F2d 1033 (8th Cir. 1979).

These decisions are indicative of the assumption by the Justice Department of an activist role in this area.

In general, where the public authorities are taking action that will concentrate location of low-income housing in racially segregated areas, most courts will endeavor to block this move. 52 J. of Urb. L. 897.

EXAMPLE: A developer wanted to build a multifamily residential housing project and sought rezoning for that purpose. It was refused. However, the courts found that the refusal to rezone was due to the opposition of the white residents. The court ordered rezoning. *Dailey* v. *City of Lawton,* 425 F2d 1037 (1970), 5 J. of Law Reform 357 (1972).

46.07   Permitted Discriminations

The federal law does not prohibit an owner from considering any factors other than race which he feels are relevant in determining whether to rent to one individual or another. Such factors, which an owner might consider, include the credit standing of the applicant, his assets, his financial stability, his reputation in the community, his age, the size of his family, the ages of his children, his past experience as a lessee or tenant, the length of time he plans to occupy the premises, and whether he is or is not a transient.

The owner may also consider more subjective factors in determining whether he will rent to one individual or another. Thus, he may consider the applicant's appearance, his demeanor, the owner's estimate of his trustworthiness or truthfulness, or other subjective factors. Indeed, businessmen utilize such conclusions and opinions in their daily affairs.

Nonetheless, the owner may later be called upon to demonstrate in court that these and not racial motivations were responsible for his decision in refusing to rent or sell to a black. Subjective factors are by their nature difficult to prove and often have little more than the credibility of the individual witness behind them.

An owner may even refuse to rent to an individual simply because he does not like him. No one is required to rent or sell to an individual he doesn't like. As in other cases, however, the owner may later be called upon to demonstrate in court that his personal dislike of an individual, rather than the individual's race, was responsible for his decision to refuse him as a tenant.

Any factor, other than race, which is relevant to a decision whether to rent or sell to an individual may be considered, and the list of factors set forth above is not intended to be, and could not constitute, an exclusive list.

EXAMPLE: *L* refused to rent to *B,* a black, because *B* did not meet *L*'s requirement that a tenant have an income equal to 90 percent of the rent. This was not discriminatory. *Boyd* v. *Lefrak Org.,* 509 F2d 1110 (1975); 89 Harv. L. Rev. 1631; 7 Seton Hall L. Rev. 168 (1975).

46.08   State Constitutions, State Laws, Court Decisions, Ordinances, Commission Rulings and Orders

An increasing number of states and cities have enacted laws and ordinances forbidding racial discrimination in housing. Such laws set up commissions to hear complaints of racial discrimination. The following are illustrations of state commission orders and court decisions enforcing local open housing laws.

EXAMPLE: A white apartment owner discriminated against a black prospective tenant by refusing to rent him an apartment. The black filed a complaint with the state commission. An order was entered requiring the owner to rent an apartment to the black at the regular prevailing rental and to desist from acts of discrimination in rental practices against the black or any other persons because of race, religion, or national origin. *In re Ruth,* 12 Race Relations Rep. 1703. (Cal).

EXAMPLE: A commission ordered the landlord to rent to a black who had been refused occupancy for racial reasons. White tenants who later moved in with knowledge of the problem were required to vacate. *City of N.Y.* v. *Camp Const. Co.,* 11 Race Relations Rep. 1949 (N.Y.).

EXAMPLE: The court sustained a commission order ousting a white tenant because he was not a bona fide tenant ignorant of the landlord's earlier attempt to discriminate against a black seeking to rent the same apartment. *Feigenblum* v. *Comm.,* 278 NYS2d 652.

EXAMPLE: A white subdivision was subject to a recorded declaration giving the homeowners' association a preemptive option, that is, the right to buy any homesite at the same price another party would offer. A homeowner entered into a contract to sell to a black. The contract was specifically made subject to the recorded declaration. The association then gave notice of exercise of its preemptive privilege. The court held that exercise of such a privilege would be illegal under the state fair housing law if done solely because of racial bias. *Vaught* v. *Village Creek,* 7 Race Relations Rep. 849.

46.09 Landlord and Tenant

Quite a number of cases arising either under federal or state law have held the landlord guilty of racial discrimination. See 11 U. of Fla. L. Rev. 344.

EXAMPLE: The landlord accepted a black tenant and then resorted to incredibly evasive tactics to discourage the tenant. He was held liable for damages. *Jackson* v. *Concord Co.,* 253 A2d 793.

EXAMPLE: The landlord refused to rent a house to a black, and a relative of the landlord agreed to cover up for the landlord by buying the house. Both were held liable. *Rody* v. *Hollis,* 599 P2d 97 (Wash. 1972). The damages awarded can be great ($20,000). *Parker* v. *Shonfeld,* 409 F.Supp. 896 (1976).

EXAMPLE: The owner of an apartment complex restricted blacks to buildings 65 and 66, and there were only two black families in the remainder of the complex. Racial discrimination was established. *Midland Homes* v. *Penn. Hum. Rel. Comm.,* 333 A2d 516 (Pa. 1975).

EXAMPLE: The commission found the landlord guilty of discrimination in rejecting a black tenant but refused to oust a white tenant to whom the landlord later rented the apartment. The white tenant was an innocent party unaware of the discrimination. The court sustained this ruling. *Comm.* v. *City Builders, Inc.,* 277 NYS2d 434.

EXAMPLE: Evicting black tenants to create an "all adult" building is discriminatory and damages must be paid. *Betsey* v. *Turtle Creek Associates,* 736 F2d 983 (Cal. 4th 1984).

EXAMPLE: Exclusive rental agents found to have refused to rent to plaintiffs on the basis of their race are liable under the law for their unlawful conduct even where the management agreement stated that leases and tenants shall be approved by owner and where their actions are at behest of their principal. *Jeanty* v. *McKey & Pogue, Inc.,* 496 F2d 1119 (7th Cir. 1974).

EXAMPLE: A landlord had no right to evict a white tenant because the tenant married a black. *Prendergast* v. *Synder,* 50 Cal. Reptr. 903, 413 P2d 847.

But at times the court finds that discrimination is not present.

EXAMPLE: *L* refused to rent to a black lawyer, claiming that *L* disliked all lawyers and regarded them as troublemakers. No discrimination was shown. *Kramarsky* v. *Stahl Management,* N.Y. S.Ct. 11/3/77.

46.10   Brokers

A broker may lose his license under state law if he is guilty of racial discrimination.

EXAMPLE: *B,* a broker, represented to a black person that a home was not available for sale. In fact, it was so available. *B* was suspended. *Strickland* v. *Dept. of Registration,* 376 NE2d 255 (Ill. 1978).

EXAMPLE: *B,* a broker, engaged in blockbusting, that is, he represented that the area was changing, values were declining, and women were not safe. *B* was disciplined. *In the Matter of Butterfly & Green Inc.* v. *Lorenzo,* 30 NYS2d 250, 326 NE2d 799 (1975).

Quite a number of city ordinances forbidding discrimination—for example, by real estate brokers—have been upheld as valid. *Chicago Real Estate Board* v. *Chicago,* 36 Ill.2d 530, 224 NE2d 793.

Federal and state legislation forbidding "blockbusting" by real estate brokers is valid. 34 ALR3d 1432; *U.S.* v. *Hunter,* 459 F2d 205 (4th Cir. 1972).

EXAMPLE: A broker is forbidden to tell property owners that the neighborhood is "going colored." This is true even if the prospective buyer asks this question. *Brown* v. *State Realty Co.,* 304 F.Supp. 1236.

EXAMPLE: The rule against blockbusting applies even to statements such as "This is a changing neighborhood." *U.S.* v. *Mintzes,* 304 F.Supp. 1305.

Of course, a broker who violates either law is liable for damages.

46.11   Seller and Buyer

Racial discrimination by a seller is illegal.

> **EXAMPLE:**   A black bought a vacant lot adjoining the white seller's home, using a white nominee to accomplish the purchase. When the seller discovered the identity of the real purchaser he brought suit. The court refused to set aside the transaction. *Hirsch* v. *Silberstein,* 227 A2d 638 (Pa.).

46.12   Mortgages—Redlining

It is illegal for mortgage lenders to "redline" black areas. The word "redlining" comes from the practice of marking black areas in red on a map, thus indicating the areas where loans will not be made. 8 Pac. L.J. 719.

46.13   Mortgages—Foreclosure

A mortgage lender must not discriminate against black persons in its foreclosure practices. *Harper* v. *Union Sav. Assn.,* 459 F.Supp. 1254 (1977).

> **EXAMPLE:**   If a mortgagee routinely grants a sixty-day grace period to whites, it must do likewise regarding blacks.

46.14   Builder-seller Discrimination

A builder–seller must not discriminate among his customers.

> **EXAMPLE:**   A Corp. had *X, Y, and Z* as its shareholders. It engaged in the building and selling of homes in a black area of Chicago. *X, Y, and Z* also had other corporations engaged in building identical homes in white areas of the Chicago metropolitan area. In the black area, *A Corp.* sold only on installment contracts, even where the buyers could make large cash payments and obtain mortgages. It sold at prices higher than it charged for identical homes in white areas. The corporation and *X, Y, and Z* were held guilty of racial discrimination. *Clark* v. *Universal Builders,* 501 F2d 324 (Cal. 7th 1973), 88 Harv. L. Rev. 1610, 1975 Duke L. J. 781, 12 Houston L. Rev. 476, 28 Rutgers L. Rev. 1009.

46.15   Housing Projects

Many local housing authorities and HUD have been instructed by the courts to develop housing projects in predominantly white areas. They must not be confined to the ghetto areas of the inner city. *Hills* v. *Grautreaux,* 425 U.S. 284, 96 S.Ct. 1538, 47 L.Ed.2d 792 (1976).

46.16   City Services

The city must not discriminate racially in its provisions of municipal services.

> **EXAMPLE:**   In one town in question, 97 percent of the homes that fronted on unpaved streets and were not served by sewers were occupied by blacks; all street lights were installed in white sections; surface water drainage, traffic control signs, and so forth were all in white sections. This was invalid. *Hawkins* v. *Town of Shaw,* 437 F2d 1286 (5th Cir. 1971).

46.17   Proof of Discrimination

Basically, what current legislation forbids is discrimination. *Discrimination* is not merely a state of mind. *Prejudice* is a state of mind, but *discrimination* is prejudice coupled with action or inaction motivated by that prejudice.

Discrimination can be shown by *express* proof of *intention. Hawkins* v. *Town of Shaw,* 461 F2d 1171 (5th Cir. 1972).

> **EXAMPLE:**   A builder stated that "no one is going to force me to sell a house in this development to a black." This proves discrimination if followed by sales only to white persons. *Jones* v. *The Haridor Realty Corp.,* 37 N.J. 384, 181 A2d 481.

Or it may be established by circumstantial evidence.

> **EXAMPLE:**   A offered a house for sale for $75,000 on terms set forth in a broker's listing. Promptly B, a black, tendered an offer at the price and terms stated. A's refusal of B's offer would be evidence of discrimination, especially if A sold later to a white person at the same price, thereby showing that his refusal of B was not motivated by a desire to withdraw the house from sale.

> **EXAMPLE:**   The fact that there are no black tenants in an apartment building will weigh against the owner, and the refusal of even one financially qualified black applicant for an apartment may be sufficient proof of discrimination. *U.S.* v. *Real Estate Development Corp.,* 347 F.Supp. 776.

46.18   Impact or Intent

A deeply troubling question relates to the necessity of establishing the presence of discriminatory intent where racial discrimination is charged.

If the lawsuit charges a violation of the federal Constitution, one frequently cited decision holds that it is necessary to prove an intention to discriminate.

EXAMPLE: The village of Arlington Heights (a suburb of Chicago) had a traditional zoning ordinance, establishing some single-family zones. A developer sought a rezoning of land in such a zone so that he could construct low-income housing, which, of course, would accommodate black persons. The village population was white. The village refused the rezoning. The Supreme Court held that no violation of the federal *Constitution* was shown. There was no *intention* to discriminate, *Village of Arlington Heights* v. *Metrop. Housing Develop. Corp.*, 429 U.S. 252, 50 L.Ed.2d 450 (1971), 91 Harv L. Rev. 1427.

In a later phase of this case, the issue was whether the Open Housing Act of 1968 had been violated.

EXAMPLE: In this lawsuit the court pointed out that the construction of the apartments would give the village its first subsidized low-cost housing. This would enable blacks to move into a village that had theretofore been exclusively white. Thus the village's refusal to rezone had a discriminatory *impact* in that it perpetuated segregation in Arlington Heights. A violation of the statute had been established. *Metrop. Housing Develop. Corp.* v. *Village of Arlington Heights*, 558 F2d 1283 (Cal. 7th 1977).

46.19   Testers and Steering

A group of blacks visited real estate brokers in the village of Bellwood, Illinois, asking to be shown homes. In point of fact, they were not genuine purchasers. They were "testing" the brokers. The brokers attempted to "steer" these "purchasers" to black areas of the village. The court held that *steering* was illegal and that *testers* could sue to have a court prohibit this steering. *Gladstone Realtors* v. *Village of Bellwood*, 99 S.Ct. 1601 (1979).

46.20   Miscellaneous Rulings

The Department of Justice has made some strong rulings in this area.

EXAMPLE: The department has ruled that an appraisal report must not refer to population changes as affecting the value of the property.

CHAPTER 47

Discrimination Against Children in Real Estate Transactions

47.01 In General

Landowners have always sought to limit the nature of the occupancy of land. Such restraints, embodied in deeds, mortgages, leases, and declarations of restrictions, have encountered legal obstacles and have often been invalidated. All states have some form of the so-called rule against unreasonable restraints on alienation (sale).

> **EXAMPLE:** Father makes a deed to Son with clauses that the real estate shall never be sold. This restriction is invalid.

This rule, for technical reasons too complex to explain here, does not apply to restrictions on *occupancy. Doherty* v *Rice,* 240 Wis. 389, 3 NW2d 734 (1942). Hence, lawyers tend to prefer to create restrictions on occupancy rather than restrictions on sale.

Today we have statutes and court decisions that invalidate restraints of various kinds. There is a public clamor for the invalidation of some existing restraints, such as those forbidding occupancy by children. The law is complex and chaotic.

47.02 Retirement Communities

There are many retirement communities in this country. The general plan of restrictions and declarations recorded by the land developer usually forbids occupancy by children under 21 years or some similar age. Since public schools are not needed, real estate taxes are lower. Playground facilities are not needed. Moreover, public opinion polls show that older people prefer the quiet of an environment without children. It seems likely that the courts will sustain as valid restrictions of this nature. *Riley* v. *Stoves,* 526 P2d 474 (Ariz. 1974), *Preston Tower Condo Assn.* v. *S. B. Realty,* 685 SW2d 98 (Tex. Civ. App. 1985); 100 ALR3d 231.

47.03   Zoning

The zoning problem also presents a dual set of issues. Some courts have ruled that zoning ordinances restricting units that would be suitable for families are invalid. *Duggan* v. *County of Cook,* 324 NE2d 406 (Ill. App. 1975); *Malino* v. *Mayor of Glassboro,* 281 A2d 401 (N.J. App. 1971); 24 DePaul L. Rev. 784 (1975). Other courts have held that a municipality may limit a particular residential zone to senior citizens. Their needs (curb ramps for wheelchairs, for example) are largely peculiar to the elderly, and they need a zone that caters to these needs. *Hinman* v. *Planning and Zoning Comm.,* 214 A2d 131 (Conn. 1965); *Taxpayers' Assn.* v. *Weymouth Township,* 364 A2d 1016 (N.J. 1976).

As can be seen, satisfying the needs of one age group may be adverse to the needs of the other age group. If the zoning ordinance limits occupancy of an area to senior citizens, it zones out children. If the zoning decisions prohibit the barring of children from residential areas, the establishment of retirement communities is made more difficult. These authors believe that public policy decisions must be made, and that those decisions must relate to both public and private land use control devices in a way that accommodates the needs of both age groups.

REFERENCES: 31 Ark. L. Rev. 707 (1978); 5 Fla. St. U. L. Rev. 423 (1977); 76 Mich. L. Rev. 64 (1977); 6 Urb. Law. 685; 83 ALR3d 1084, 1103.

47.04   Condominiums

Condominium documents that forbid occupancy by children have been sustained. *Starlake North Commodore Assn. Inc.* v. *Parker,* 423 So2d 509 (Fla. App. 1982); *Constellation Condo Assn. Inc.* v. *Harrington,* 467 So2d 378 (Fla. 1985); *Covered Bridge Condo Assn.* v. *Chambliss,* 705 SW2d 211 (Tex. App. 1985). Retirement is a major industry in Florida, and many retirees live in condominiums. These court decisions are sensitive to that fact.

47.05   Mobile Home Parks

Limiting occupancy to adults in mobile home parks has been sustained. *Dubrevil* v. *West Winds Mobile Lodge,* 213 Cal. Reptr. 12 (1985).

47.06   Statutes and Ordinances

A number of states (for example, Arizona, California, Connecticut, Delaware, Illinois, Maine, Massachusetts, New Jersey, New York, and Oregon) have laws or ordinances prohibiting housing discrimination against children. 36 Okla. L. Rev. 361. In some states these laws forbid landlords to bar children. *Marina Point Ltd.* v. *Wolfson,* 30 Cal. 2d 721, 180 Cal. Reptr. 496, 640 P2d 115 (1982). In other states landlords are not affected. *Dept. of Civil Rights* v. *Beznos Corp.,* 336 NW2d 494 (Mich. App. 1983). In California and Oregon the law applies to condominiums. *O'Connor* v. *Village Green Owners Assn.,* 662 P2d 427 (Cal. 1983). The law must be carefully checked in each state. Ordinances as well as statutes must be checked. State laws forbidding all types of discrimination are being widely enacted. A social problem of major proportions is developing. Landlords are barring children. The question is being asked, Where will children live? 25 DePaul L. Rev. 64; 16 J. of Fam. L. 559; 67 Ky. L. J. 967; 40 Ohio St. L. J. 195; 19 Santa Clara L. Rev., 21.

The issue of discrimination against children remains unresolved.

CHAPTER 48

Real Estate Taxes
and Special Assessments

48.01   In General

General taxes are levied by various taxing bodies, such as states, cities, villages, counties, or school districts, to raise revenue needed for the performance of various public functions, such as maintaining roads, schools, parks, police departments, fire departments, county hospitals, and mental institutions. One of the most important sources of revenue is the tax on real estate. Although this tax is encountered in most, if not all, states, laws regarding levy, assessment, and collection of the tax vary considerably, so that few general statements can be made that will be universally true.

48.02   Steps in Taxation

The nine principal steps in real estate taxation are: budgeting, appropriation, levy, assessment, review of the assessment, equalization, computation, collection of the tax through voluntary payment by the taxpayer, and collection of the tax through compulsory methods, such as tax sale.

48.02(a)   Budgeting

Budgeting involves an annual determination of how much money is to be spent by each taxing body and for what purposes. Keep in mind that in each state there are numerous bodies—cities, villages, counties, school boards, and sanitary districts—that have the power to levy taxes, and each body must prepare its annual budget and make its annual appropriation and tax levy.

48.02(b)   Appropriation

Appropriation is the step where the taxing body formally enacts into law its decision to spend the money, with a specification of the particular purpose for which the money is to be spent, the amount to be spent for each purpose, and the source from which the funds are to be derived.

48.02(c)   Levy

The appropriation usually provides that part of the money to be spent is to be raised by property taxation. It thereupon becomes necessary to levy a tax for this purpose. When the legislative body of some taxing unit, such as the village board of a village or the school board of a school district, votes to impose a tax of a specified amount on persons or property, this action is known as the levy of a tax. The levy is an indispensable step in arriving at a valid tax.

It is the levy that provides a field day for tax lawyers. Various technical defects will invalidate part or all of the tax levy, and attorneys for railroads and other big taxpayers are most astute in discovering these technical defects. As a rule, only those taxpayers who file proper objections may take advantage of these technical defects. Taxpayers who pay their money without formal objection cannot get their money back if the tax is later held invalid.

48.02(d)   Tax Rate Limitations

In levying taxes, taxing bodies must see to it that they do not spend more than the law allows. Tax rate limitations will be found in both state constitutions and state laws.

48.02(e)   Assessment

Assessment of real estate for taxation involves determining the value of each parcel of land to be taxed. In assessing real estate, a book or list is first prepared by the proper officer, containing a description of all the taxable real estate in the town, county, or district and the names of the owners thereof. This book is turned over to the tax assessor, who proceeds to place a valuation on each parcel of land and enters such valuation in the book. This book is called the *tax list* or *assessment roll*.

In assessing land the assessor should consider various factors, such as market price of similar land, income, depreciation, obsolescence, and reproduction cost of buildings. Actual methods vary widely. Farmland is still usually taxed at its market value, but urban land is often assessed differently. In assessing urban land, assessors often place a value on the land as though it were vacant and then value the building at what it would cost to build today, deducting from this figure an allowance for depreciation. The two valuations are then added together to fix the total assessment. Assessors may employ experts and use scientific procedures as a basis for their valuations. But any wholesale turning over of valuation to experts would be illegal, for it is the assessor's judgment, based perhaps on expert advice, that the law requires.

In some states it is the practice to assess property at a certain percentage of its true value. This is not objectionable as long as the assessor assesses all property at the same proportion of its true value. Likewise, if all the property is uniformly overvalued, the courts will not intervene. The main thing is uniformity. If a taxpayer can show that his property is assessed at its full value, whereas the rest of the property in the district is uniformly assessed at less than its full value, the court will lower the assessment complained of to the general level.

48.02(e)(1)   Uniformity

Under various constitutional provisions it is required that the taxation of property be equal and uniform, so that taxpayers owning tracts of substantially equal value will pay substantially the same amount of taxes. This is an ideal difficult, if not impossible, to attain, and courts are aware of that fact. Hence if the assessor has made an honest mistake in assessing a particular tract of land, the courts as a rule will not intervene. Courts do not sit to correct mere errors in an assessment. The error can be corrected only by an appeal to the board of review or other body designated to review and correct the assessor's valuations.

48.02(e)(2)   Exemptions

Each state grants various exemptions from taxation. The nature and form of these exemptions vary from state to state. Common exemptions are those extended to public property, charitable organizations, schools, religious institutions, and cemeteries. There are also some states that extend partial exemptions to senior citizens.

48.02(e)(3)   Review of Assessment

All states provide some method by which the taxpayer can have the assessor's valuation reviewed and corrected by some higher authority. The procedures vary widely. In New England the reviewing board is often a town tribunal, such as the selectmen. In other areas the reviewing officials may be called a *board of equalization* or a *board of review.* In some states a further appeal is provided to a higher board of review. In other states the decision of the first board of review can be appealed directly to some court. Culp, *Administrative Remedies in the Assessment and Enforcement of State Taxes* 17 N.C. L. Rev. 118 (1939). As a rule, the taxpayer cannot appeal to the courts unless he has first appeared before the board of review or other initial reviewing body. *First Nat. Bank* v. *Weld County,* 264 U.S. 450 (1924).

48.02(e)(4)   Equalization

Equalization is the raising or lowering of assessed values in a particular county or taxing district in order to equalize them with the total assessments in other counties or taxing districts.

> **EXAMPLE:**   The board of equalization deducts a certain percentage from all assessments made in a certain township because the township assessor valued the property on a higher level than did the assessors of other townships.

This function is usually performed by a board known as the *board of equalization.* The board of equalization does not handle complaints of individual taxpayers, but raises or lowers the assessment of each county or taxing district as a whole in order to bring the assessment into line with assessments in other counties or taxing districts.

48.02(f)   Computation of Tax

The amount of the tax that a particular tract of land must pay is computed by multiplying the assessed value of the tract by the tax rate applicable to the land in that particular taxing district. The tax is then entered on the tax books.

48.02(g)   Lien

Tax laws usually provide that real estate taxes are a lien on the land. Often it is provided that such a lien is prior and superior to all other liens, both those that antedate and those that come after the date on which the tax lien attaches to the land.

48.02(h)   Payment

Payment to the proper official at the proper time discharges the lien of the tax.
When the *tax records* show a tax is paid, a purchaser or mortgagee who relies on such records is protected against enforcement of the tax should it later develop that the tax actually remains unpaid. *Jackson Park Hospital* v. *Courtney,* 4 NE2d 846 (Ill. 1936). A number of states make provision for the issuance of a certificate by some tax official showing all unpaid taxes on the property. Purchasers who rely on such certificates are generally protected against errors in the certificate. *Burton* v. *City of Denver,* 61 P2d 856 (Colo. 1936); *Amerada Petroleum Corp.* v. *1010.61 Acres of Land,* 146 F2d 99 (1944); 21 ALR2d 1273. When a landowner redeems from a tax sale and the certificate of redemption shows that all delinquent taxes have been thereby redeemed, a purchaser or mortgagee who relies on such a certificate will be protected if it later develops that some delinquent taxes in fact remain. *Jones* v. *Sturzenberg,* 210 P. 835 (Cal. 1922).

A purchaser or mortgagee is not ordinarily protected in relying on a *tax receipt* showing full payment of the taxes. Despite issuance of the receipt, the tax collector is allowed to show that a part of the tax remains unpaid. However, South Dakota has a law making a tax receipt conclusive evidence that all prior taxes have been paid.

48.02(i)   Proceedings to Enforce Payment of Taxes

Various special remedies are provided by local law for the collection of unpaid real estate taxes.

Tax sale is a common method. It is usually preceded by the giving of notice, often by publication, to the delinquent taxpayer. Unless the taxpayer appears and defends, which he may do if the tax is illegal or if he has some other defense, a judgment will be rendered for the amount of the tax and penalty due. This judgment orders the land to be sold. Thereafter, notice of the coming sale is published, and on the date fixed for sale the land is sold at public sale. Usually a certificate of sale is issued to the purchaser, stating that he will be entitled to a deed at the expiration of the redemption period if no redemption is made. In some states, the state, county, or city is permitted to bid at the tax sale.

The landowner or other persons interested, such as mortagees, may redeem the land from the tax within the period specified by the local law. If redemption is not made, a tax deed is issued to the purchaser.

Although state laws vary as to the validity of tax titles, a tax title acquired through normal tax sale usually constitutes the flimsiest sort of title, since deviation from the technical requirements of the law will invalidate the title. In some states, however, a tax deed is regarded as a conveyance of good title to the land. *Thomas* v. *Kolker,* 73 A2d 886 (Md. 1950); *Shapiro* v. *Hruby,* 172 NE2d 775 (Ill. 1961).

An alternative method of enforcement of the tax lien is by foreclosure, the procedure being similar to that employed in mortgage foreclosure. In some states a good title can be acquired through tax foreclosure.

48.02(j)   Validity of Tax Sale—Notice Requirements—Mortgages

The Supreme Court has held that a tax sale is ineffective to extinguish a mortgage unless at least a mailed notice has been given the mortgagee by the tax collector. *Mennonite Board of Missions* v. *Adams,* 103 S. Ct. 2706, 77 L.Ed.2d 180 (1982). In Illinois the courts get around this decision by requiring the tax sale purchaser to notify the mortgagee before the tax deed issues. *Rosewell* v. *C. T. & T. Co.,* 99 Ill.2d 407, 76 Ill. Dec. 831, 459 NE2d 966 (1984). Of course, each state has its procedure, which should comply with the notice standard, set by the *Mennonite* decision.

48.02(j)(1)   Effect of Tax Sale on Junior Interests

When real estate taxes obtain priority over junior interests either because they become a lien prior to the creation of the junior interests or by force of law, the law of many states results in a purchaser at a tax sale taking a title that is free of encumbrances such as mortgages, liens, and so forth.

48.02(j)(2)   Termination of Easement by Tax Sale

An almost insoluble problem exists with respect to the effect of a tax sale of the servient tenement. The owner of the easement, of course, receives his tax bill on the dominant tenement. He does not even receive the tax bill on the servient tenement.

> **EXAMPLE:**   A owns Lot 1 and B owns Lot 2. A grants to B an easement for ingress and egress for driveway purposes over the southern twenty feet of Lot 1. A fails to pay his taxes and all of Lot 1 is sold to X at a tax sale. Under the law in this state, a tax sale wipes out all prior easements. Obviously B must arrange to keep a check on the taxes on A's Lot 1 and pay them, if necessary, to prevent loss of his easement. He can include a provision in the easement grant requiring A annually to furnish B a paid tax bill, and also a provision that any taxes advanced by B, or his successors, will be a foreclosable lien on Lot 1.

The law on this subject has been in some confusion. In some states a tax sale does *not* destroy easements. *Northwestern Imp. Co.* v. *Lowry,* 66 P2d 792 (Mont. 1937); *Ariz. R.C.I.A. Lands, Inc.* v. *Ainsworth,* 515 P2d 335 (Ariz. 1973); *Clippinger* v. *Birge,* 547 P2d 871 (Wash. 1975); Restatement, Property § 509(2)(e). One basis of this rule is the thought that the land was assessed based upon its *value.* That value was determined by taking the easement into consideration.

> **EXAMPLE:**   Tract A is valued at $10,000 without being encumbered by an easement. Assessment is based upon this value. If the property were encumbered by an easement, its value would be $9,000. The assessment in the later case would be based upon $9,000.

By this same theory, the holder of the dominant estate is protected in that the easement will continue for the benefit of his land irrespective of the failure of the owner of the servient estate to pay taxes. The result is justified by the theory that the easement enhances the value of the dominant estate, and assessment is based upon this enhanced value. 20 U. Chi. L. Rev. 262, 264 (1953). In almost all states laws have been passed to conform to the above. Ill. Rev. Stat. Ch. 120 § 7476. The minority view is discussed elsewhere. Note, 51 Harv. L. Rev. 361 (1937); see *Powell on Real Property,* par. 686.

In a similar view, a tax sale will generally not extinguish a restrictive covenant to which the land is subject. 168 ALR 529, 536.

> REFERENCE: Kratovil, *Tax Sales: Extinguishment of Easements, Building Restrictions, and Covenants,* 19 Houst. L. Rev. 55 (1982).

48.03   Special Assessments

There is a distinction between public improvements, which benefit the entire community, and local improvements, which benefit particular real estate or limited areas of land. The latter improvements are usually financed by means of special, or local, assessments. These assessments are, in a certain sense, taxes. But an assessment differs from a general tax in that an assessment is levied only on property in the immediate vicinity of some local public improvement and is valid only where the property assessed receives some special benefit differing from the benefit that the general public enjoys. *Production Tool Supply Co.* v. *City of Roseville,* 253 NW2d 350 (Mich. 1977). In fact if the primary purpose of an improvement is to benefit the public generally, as with, for example, the erection of a county courthouse, it cannot be financed by special assessments even though it may incidentally benefit property in the particular locality.

Special assessments are often imposed for opening, paving, grading, and guttering streets, construction of sidewalks and sewers, installation of street lighting, and so on.

Index*

*References are to section numbers.